에듀윌이
너를
지지할게

ENERGY

KB208049

처음에는 당신이 원하는 곳으로
갈 수는 없겠지만,
당신이 지금 있는 곳에서
출발할 수는 있을 것이다.

– 작자 미상

2025

에듀윌 9급공무원
7개년 기출문제집

영어

공무원 영어 시험, 어떻게 바뀌나요?

☑ 인사혁신처 예시문제 분석

2024 국가직 9급
어휘 5
문법 3
생활영어 3
독해 9

인사혁신처 1차 예시문제
어휘 2
문법 3
생활영어 2
독해 13

인사혁신처 2차 예시문제
어휘 2
문법 3
생활영어 2
독해 13

☑ 공무원 영어 시험, 이렇게 바뀝니다.

1 문법, 어휘 문제는 쉬워진다!

문법 문제에서는 영작형, 문장형 문법 문항이 사라져 난이도가 쉬워졌습니다. 어휘 문제는 유의어를 묻는 암기형 문제에서 탈피하고 문맥상 추론을 통한 정답 선택형 문제가 제시되었습니다.

2 실용문 독해, 생활영어가 쉽게 출제된다!

업무현장에서 접할 수 있는 소재를 활용한 실용문 독해, 생활영어 문제가 새롭게 출제됩니다. 해당 문제의 난이도는 기존 독해 문제보다 쉽게 출제될 것으로 예상됩니다.

3 시험의 변별력은 기존 독해 유형의 문제에 주어진다!

새로운 유형은 지문의 길이가 길지만, 빠르고 명확하게 답을 찾을 수 있는 문제가 출제될 것으로 예상됩니다. 대의 파악, 내용 불일치, 글의 일관성, 빈칸 추론 등 기존 독해 유형 문제도 높은 비중으로 출제되며, 이 문항에 변별력이 주어질 가능성이 높습니다.

에듀윌과 함께 시작하면,
당신도 합격할 수 있습니다!

대학 진학 후 진로를 고민하다 1년 만에
서울시 행정직 9급, 7급에 모두 합격한 대학생

직장생활과 병행하며 7개월간 공부해
국가공무원 세무직에 당당히 합격한 51세 직장인까지

누구나 합격할 수 있습니다.
시작하겠다는 '다짐' 하나면 충분합니다.

마지막 페이지를 덮으면,

에듀윌과 함께
공무원 합격이 시작됩니다.

70개월 베스트셀러 1위
에듀윌 공무원 교재

기초부터 확실하게 기본 이론

기본서
국어 독해

기본서
국어 문법

기본서
영어 독해

기본서
영어 문법

기본서
한국사

기본서
행정학

기본서
행정법총론

다양한 출제 유형 대비 문제집

단원별 기출&예상 문제집
국어

단원별 기출&예상 문제집
한국사

단원별 기출&예상 문제집
행정학

단원별 기출&예상 문제집
행정법총론

출제경향 파악 기출문제집

9급공무원 기출문제집
영어

9급공무원 기출문제집
한국사

9급공무원 기출문제집
행정학

9급공무원 기출문제집
행정법총론

7급공무원 시험 대비 PSAT 교재

민간경력자
PSAT 기출문제집

7급공무원
PSAT 기출문제집

영어 집중 영단어 교재

영어 빈출 VOCA

더 많은
공무원 교재

1초 합격예측
모바일 성적분석표

1초 안에 '클릭' 한 번으로 성적을 확인하실 수 있습니다!

활용
GUIDE

실시간 성적분석 방법!

STEP 1
QR 코드
스캔

▶

STEP 2
모바일
OMR 입력

▶

STEP 3
자동채점 &
성적분석표 확인

STEP 1

QR 코드 스캔

- 교재의 QR 코드를 모바일로 스캔 후 에듀윌 회원 로그인
- QR 코드 하단의 바로가기 주소로도 접속 가능

STEP 2

모바일 OMR 입력

- 회차 확인 후 '응시하기' 클릭
- 모바일 OMR에 답안 입력
- 문제풀이 시간까지 측정 가능

STEP 3

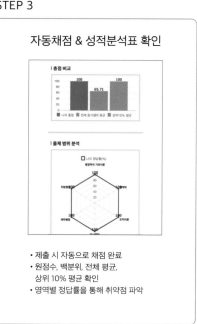

자동채점 & 성적분석표 확인

- 제출 시 자동으로 채점 완료
- 원점수, 백분위, 전체 평균, 상위 10% 평균 확인
- 영역별 정답률을 통해 취약점 파악

※ 본 서비스는 에듀윌 공무원 교재(연도별, 회차별 문항이 수록된 교재)를 구입하는 분에게 제공됨.

공무원,
에듀윌을 선택해야 하는 이유

합격자 수 수직 상승
2,100%

2017년

2022년

명품 강의 만족도
99%

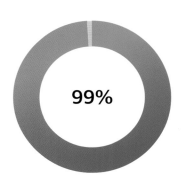

99%

공무원

베스트셀러 1위
70개월(5년 10개월)

5년 연속 공무원 교육
1위

* 2017/2022 에듀윌 공무원 과정 최종 환급자 수 기준   * 9급공무원 대표 교수진 2023년 7월 ~ 2024년 4월 강의 만족도 평균(배영표, 헤더진, 한유진, 이광호, 김용철)
* YES24 수험서 자격증 공무원 베스트셀러 1위 (2017년 3월, 2018년 4월~6월, 8월, 2019년 4월, 6월~12월, 2020년 1월~12월, 2021년 1월~12월, 2022년 1월~12월,
  2023년 1월~12월, 2024년 1월~7월, 9월~10월 월별 베스트, 매월 1위 교재는 다름)
* 2023, 2022, 2021 대한민국 브랜드만족도 7·9급공무원 교육 1위 (한경비즈니스) / 2020, 2019 한국브랜드만족지수 7·9급공무원 교육 1위 (주간동아, G밸리뉴스)

1위 에듀윌만의
체계적인 합격 커리큘럼

원하는 시간과 장소에서
온라인 강의

① 업계 최초! 기억 강화 시스템 적용
② 과목별 테마특강, 기출문제 해설강의 무료 제공
③ 초보 수험생 필수 기초강의와 합격필독서 무료 제공

쉽고 빠른 합격의 첫걸음 합격필독서 무료 신청

최고의 학습 환경과 빈틈 없는 학습 관리
직영 학원

① 현장 강의와 온라인 강의를 한번에
② 확실한 합격관리 시스템, 아케르
③ 완벽 몰입이 가능한 프리미엄 학습 공간

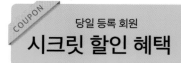

COUPON
당일 등록 회원
시크릿 할인 혜택

합격전략 설명회 신청 시 당일 등록 수강 할인권 제공

친구 추천 이벤트

" **친구 추천**하고 한 달 만에
920만원 받았어요 "

친구 1명 추천할 때마다 현금 10만원 제공
추천 참여 횟수 무제한 반복 가능

※ *a*o*h**** 회원의 2021년 2월 실제 리워드 금액 기준
※ 해당 이벤트는 예고 없이 변경되거나 종료될 수 있습니다.

친구 추천 이벤트
바로가기

2025년 시험 대비
기출문제를 풀어야 하는 이유

Reason 1 기존 독해 유형 문제가 시험의 당락을 좌우한다.

문법과 어휘 문제가 쉬워지고, 신유형 독해 문제도 어렵지 않은 난이도로 출제됨에 따라 기존 독해 유형 문제에 변별력이 주어질 가능성이 높습니다. 기존 독해 유형 문제는 6~7문항 정도로 높은 비중으로 출제될 것으로 보입니다.

인사혁신처 1차 예시문제   인사혁신처 2차 예시문제

Reason 2 기출된 어휘만 학습해도 충분하다.

어휘 문제는 암기를 덜 요구하는 기본 어휘 위주로 출제될 예정입니다. 따라서 지엽적인 어휘를 학습할 필요가 없습니다.

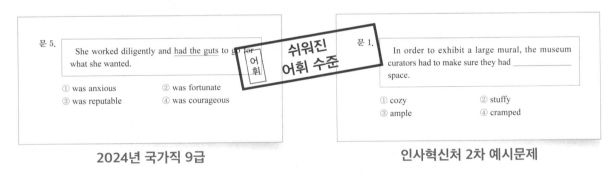

2024년 국가직 9급   인사혁신처 2차 예시문제

Reason 3 기출문제로 문법 영역을 완벽히 대비할 수 있다.

문법 문제는 기존 시험에서 물어보던 포인트를 더 쉬운 형태로 물어보는 문제로 바뀔 것입니다. 따라서 기출문제를 완벽히 풀어 낸다면, 문법 영역에 완벽히 대비할 수 있을 것입니다.

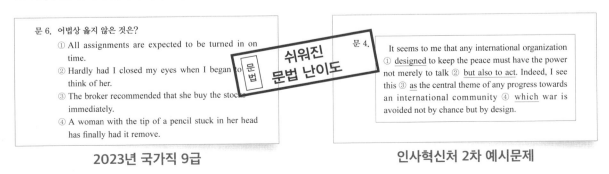

2023년 국가직 9급   인사혁신처 2차 예시문제

당신의 미래를 응원합니다

수험생 여러분 안녕하세요,
유난히 지독하게 무더웠던 여름, 그리고 가을을 지나 지금, 이 순간에도 학습에 여념이 없을 여러분들을 생각하며,
탈고와 함께 머리글을 씁니다.

2025년도 9급공무원 공채 시험은 어느 때보다 특별한 의미로 다가오는데요, 영어 과목의 출제 경향에서 대폭 변
화가 이루어지기 때문입니다. 인사혁신처에서 공개한 문제를 통해 영어 과목의 변화를 꼽자면, '실무 중심'과 '추론'
으로 요약할 수 있을 듯합니다. 영역별 문항 개수와 출제 유형에서도 작은 변화가 있지만, 공개 문제 분석 결과 수
험생들이 크게 우려할 만한 부분은 없어 보입니다. 오히려 기출 범위 내의 요소요소들이 반영된 부분을 확인할 수
있었으며, 이를 통해 기출문제 풀이는 여전히 중요하다는 결론을 내리게 되었습니다.

공무원 수험에 있어서 기출문제가 갖는 의미는 시기에 따라 작은 변화는 있었지만, 본질적으로 수험생들에게 과거
를 통해 미래를 예측하고 대비할 수 있게 하는 최고의 무기가 아닐까 합니다. 혹자는 매년 문제가 다르게 출제된
다며 기출문제 풀이의 무용론을 펼치기도 하지만 문법과 어휘 영역은 출제 빈도가 높았던 부분에서 매년 응용되
어 출제되고 있고, 동일한 패턴의 문제 역시 반복적으로 나오고 있습니다. 꼭 이런 면이 아니더라도 문제의 경향을
파악하고, 이미 출제된 문제를 접해봄으로써 실전에 앞선 예행연습으로 본다면 기출문제 풀이의 가치는 더 이상의
설명이 필요 없으리라 봅니다.

〈에듀윌 9급공무원 7개년 기출문제집 영어〉는 단순한 문제 해설에 그치는 것이 아니라 **기출분석 리포트, 합격예상
및 취약영역 체크** 등 함께 활용하면 더욱 좋은 자료들을 함께 수록하였고, **2025 출제예상문제와 인사혁신처 예시
문제 1, 2차**가 수록되어 있어 실력 점검과 향상을 위한 도구로 활용할 수 있습니다.

부디 이 교재를 통해 인연을 맺은 모든 수험생이 건강하게 수험생활을 마무리하고, 원하는 바를 꼭 이룰 수 있기를
간절히 바라봅니다.
수험생 여러분, 응원합니다!

헤더진

이 책의 구성

2024~2018년도 7개년 기출문제 + SPECIAL TEST

문제편

❶ 1초 합격예측 서비스
회차별 QR 코드 스캔 후, 모바일 OMR을 이용
하여 기출문제를 실전처럼 풀이할 수 있습니다.

❶ SPECIAL TEST 2025 출제예상문제
변경된 출제기조가 적용된 2025년 시험에서
출제가 예상되는 문제를 특별제공합니다.

직렬별 기출분석 REPORT

수준&약점 체크 가능한 해설

해설편

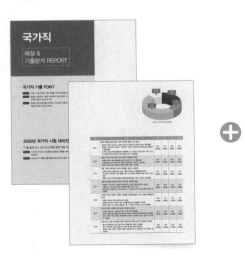

❶ 출제 POINT & 대비전략
과년도 기출의 핵심 내용과 2025년도
시험 대비 전략을 한눈에 파악할 수 있습니다.

❷ 최근 7개년 출제경향 & 출제비중
회차별 출제경향과 영역별 출제비중을 확인할
수 있습니다.

❶ 합격예상 체크 + 취약영역 체크
채점 후 나의 수준을 파악하고 취약영역을
체계적으로 분석할 수 있습니다.

❷ 자세하고 풍부한 해설
선택지 하나하나를 꼼꼼히 분석한 해설과 해석,
어휘까지 정리하여 충분한 학습이 가능합니다.

❸ 문항별 오답률 + 선택지 선택률
함정 선택지와 오답률 높은 문항을 확인하여
문제풀이 정확성을 높일 수 있습니다.

에듀윌 기출문제집의 자신감

완벽한 학습을 도와줄 무료 합격팩

1

최신기출
해설특강

최신 3개년 주요 직렬 해설강의 무료제공

에듀윌 도서몰(book.eduwill.net) 접속 → 동영상강의실 → 공무원
→ '[최신기출 해설특강] 9급공무원 영어(국가직/지방직) + 인혁처 예시문제'
→ 수강
(또는 좌측 QR코드를 통해 바로 접속)

2

1초
합격예측
서비스

1초 합격예측! 모바일 성적분석표 발급 서비스

· 회차별 QR 스캔 후 모바일 OMR 자동채점으로 점수 확인
· 모바일 성적분석표 즉시 발급(전체&상위 10% 평균, 백분위, 영역별
  정답률 등)
  ※ 자세한 내용은 앞광고 4페이지를 확인하세요!

3

OMR 카드
+
빠른 정답표

실전 연습을 위한 OMR 카드 + 빠른 정답표

· 여러 번 사용할 수 있는 특수 OMR 카드로 실전처럼 마킹하며
  문제풀이와 회독 가능
· 한 장으로 제공되는 정답표를 활용하여 빠른 채점 가능

※ 1~2 서비스는 에듀윌 회원가입 후 이용하실 수 있습니다.

이 책의 차례

SPECIAL TEST

9 급
공 무 원
기 출

영어

2025 출제예상문제

| 풀이 시간: ____:____ ~ ____:____ / 점수: ____점

※ 밑줄 친 부분에 들어갈 말로 가장 적절한 것을 고르시오.

[문 1 ~ 문 3]

문 1.

> Some of the relics may take longer to move because they are very _____.

① fragile
② virtual
③ imaginary
④ attractive

문 2.

> Under the law on government officials' ethics, the president, cabinet members and other top-ranking government officials are subject to _____ their own and their families' assets and properties.

① amend
② insist
③ disclose
④ restrict

문 3.

> In the 20th century, there was some hope that was generated through the development of pharmaceuticals for treating brain disorders, and while many drugs that can alleviate symptoms of brain disorders _____, practically none of them can be considered to be cured.

① to have developed
② have developed
③ having been developed
④ have been developed

※ 밑줄 친 부분 중 어법상 옳지 않은 것을 고르시오.

[문 4 ~ 문 5]

문 4.

> The vast majority of companies, schools, and organizations ① measure and reward "high performance" in terms of individual metrics such as sales numbers, résumé accolades, and test scores. The problem with this approach is ② what it is based on a belief we thought science had fully confirmed: that we live in a world of "survival of the fittest." But this belief is inaccurate. Thanks to new research, we now know ③ that achieving our highest potential is not about survival of the fittest ④ but survival of the best fit.

문 5.

> Cultural globalization has multiple centers in Asia like Bollywood movies ① made in India and Kung Fu movies made in Hong Kong. They are subtitled in as many as 17 languages and distributed to specific diasporas. These cultural spaces, which are dominated by languages like Hindi and Mandarin, ② ignore and challenge the spread of English. Thus some researchers challenges the idea ③ which Asian youth are passive victims of cultural globalization, or "world culture" that ④ comes out of the West.
>
> *diaspora: 디아스포라
> (이주하여 해외에 사는 사람들 또는 그 집단)

※ 밑줄 친 부분에 들어갈 말로 가장 적절한 것을 고르시오.

[문 6 ~ 문 7]

문 6.

Sue Ferguson

You know what? Kyobo book Centre is having a grand sale next week.

10:42

Mike Owen

Wow, it would be a great opportunity to buy books at a bargain.

10:42

Sue Ferguson

Yeah, the sale will go on for five days.

10:43

Mike Owen

I need to buy a few novels. Why don't we go together?

10:44

Sue Ferguson

Okay. Then, my schedule is pretty flexible next week.

10:45

Mike Owen

How about meeting on Wednesday? Is that okay with you?

10:45

Sue Ferguson

_____

10:46

① Yes. It's open from Tuesday to Sunday.
② Sure. I hope they have all the books you need.
③ That's right. That book will be released soon.
④ Don't worry. I'll look for a good book for you.

문 7.

A: Jordan! Would you please keep it down?
B: Mom! I'm not doing anything! Why do you say that? I'm not the only child in this house.
A: You were running, weren't you? It's too noisy. I need some peace.
B: _____

① You're right. This area is very noisy at night.
② Now, listen to me. Don't run in the hallway.
③ Watch out! A child is running into the street.
④ It's not me. John is the one who's making the noise.

※ 다음 글을 읽고 물음에 답하시오.   [문 8 ~ 문 9]

Mr. Clarence Foster
Suite 450, Waterfront Plaza, North California Blvd.
Walnut Creek, CA 94596

Dear Mr. Foster:

  On November 10, 2024, two days after my husband and I moved to Waterfront Plaza, I called you about the following problems in our unit:
• pest infestation of the kitchen cabinets and gas stove
• peeling paint on the front door
• broken bedroom door

  You assured me that you would send maintenance personnel to conduct pest control, repaint the front door, and fix the bedroom door by November 17th. It is now one week past that date and no <u>remedy</u> has been made.

  In an attempt to address this situation, I have compiled and attached certified copies of three estimates for the repairs. Unless you complete the agreed upon repairs by December 3, I will make my own arrangements for the work and propose that the costs be deducted from next month's rent.

  I would appreciate a prompt response to this proposal.

Sincerely,
Samantha Bailey

문 8. 윗글에서 Bailey에 관한 내용과 일치하지 않는 것은?

① She is fairly new to Waterfront Plaza.
② She will not pay her next month's rent.
③ She cannot wait for the repairs any longer.
④ She cares about hygiene in her place.

문 9. 밑줄 친 remedy의 의미와 가장 가까운 것은?

① solution   ② damage
③ therapy   ④ help

※ 다음 글을 읽고 물음에 답하시오.   [문 10 ~ 문 11]

              (A)   at the place with lots of amazing animals? Camperdown Zoo is open all year round, and we have lots of happy animals that are looking forward to your visit.

  You will find us within the beautiful Camperdown Country Park, which is about a 15-minute drive away from Dundee.

Opening Times
■ **March to September**
  10:00 a.m.−4:30 p.m. daily (last admission 3:45 p.m.)
■ **October to February**
  10:00 a.m.−3:30 p.m. daily (last admission 2:45 p.m.)

Admission Fee
■ Adults (18 and older): $5.50
■ Children 3−17 years: $4.50
■ Children up to 3 years: $2.00

  Children under 14 years of age MUST be accompanied by an adult.

  Eduactional tours, group rates, and lessons are also available: just give our Education Coordinator a call on 361-243-4328 for more information.

문 10. (A)에 들어갈 내용으로 가장 적절한 것은?

① Want to enjoy hunting
② Dram of building a villa
③ Fancy a fun family outing
④ Carry out an environmental campaign

문 11. 위 안내문의 내용과 일치하지 않는 것은?

① 연중 내내 개장하는 동물원이다.
② 10월의 마지막 입장 시간은 오후 3시 30분이다.
③ 18세 이상의 성인 요금은 5달러 50센트이다.
④ 14살 미만의 어린이들은 어른과 반드시 동행해야 한다.

문 12. 다음 글의 목적으로 가장 적절한 것은?

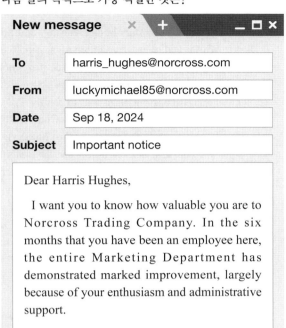

New message

To	harris_hughes@norcross.com
From	luckymichael85@norcross.com
Date	Sep 18, 2024
Subject	Important notice

Dear Harris Hughes,

I want you to know how valuable you are to Norcross Trading Company. In the six months that you have been an employee here, the entire Marketing Department has demonstrated marked improvement, largely because of your enthusiasm and administrative support.

However, it is our policy at Norcross to assess employee performance and increase salary annually. Since you have not yet reached your first anniversary as an employee with us, I cannot accept your request.

In December of this year, I will be happy to meet with you and review your salary. At that time, it will be appropriate for me to consider raising your current salary.

Thank you again for your excellent service to the company.

Sincerely,
Michael Sanderson
Director
Human Resources Division

① To protest the decision to freeze one's salary
② To turn down a request for a raise
③ To try to explain for not being promoted
④ To inform about wage negotiation

문 13. 다음 글의 주제로 가장 적절한 것은?

Behavioral psychology is characterized by its central stimulus-response theory, which Pavlov confirmed when he got dogs to salivate at the sound of a bell. S-R theory regards a person as a kind of machine that can be conditioned or programmed for any desired result — you just need to find and use the right stimulus. But much is elided by that hyphen between S and R. All the rich, important parts of psychology — and of humanity — are disregarded in the simple cause-and-effect logic. Thinking of a human as no more than a creature responding in controllable ways to specific stimuli diminishes our humanness. It disregards the psyche — the very subject of study in psychology. We are much more than just our conditioning; there is more to our lives than a series of set responses. Unfortunately, much of modern psychology — psychology as a science — is descended from or influenced by behavioral psychology and its attendant impoverishment of human experience.

*elide: 생략하다

① problems and limits of behavioral psychology
② the way a stimulus leads to the same response
③ reasons psychology belongs to behavioral science
④ danger of manipulation of emotions in experiments

문 14. Plogging Event에 관한 다음 안내문의 내용과 일치하는 것은?

Plogging Event

Have you heard of Plogging? It comes from the Swedish word for pick up, "plocka upp" and is a combination of jogging and picking up litter. In 2016, it started in Sweden and has recently come to the UK, becoming a new movement for saving nature.

When & Where
• 9 a.m. on the first Monday of each month
• Outside the ETNA Centre, East Twickenham

What to Prepare
• Just bring your running shoes, and we will provide all the other equipment.
• There is no fee to participate, but you are welcome to donate toward our conservation work.

※ No reservations are necessary to participate.
For more information, visit www.environmenttrust.org.

① 스웨덴에서 시작된 새로운 운동 종목이다.
② 걸으면서 쓰레기를 줍는 자연 보호 운동이다.
③ 운동화를 포함한 모든 장비들이 지급된다.
④ 참가비는 무료이지만 기부는 가능하다.

문 15. 다음 글의 제목으로 가장 적절한 것은?

Consider what occurs before, during, and after a trip with loved ones. If you plan a vacation well in advance, you experience several exciting months of anticipation. Then you have the actual experience of a trip with friends or family, followed by many years of fond memories. Compare all of this happiness with the cheap thrill of buying a new shirt for yourself, or even a new car. You might get a small spike in happiness immediately after the purchase, but the excitement of buying that new car fades quickly when you're sitting in traffic the following Monday morning. Even brief interpersonal experiences, such as going out to dinner with your spouse or taking your kids to a sporting event, are a much better use of your financial resources.

*spike 급증

① Don't Depend on Others for Your Happiness
② Lowering Expectations Is the Key to Happiness
③ Travel Alone or with Someone: Which Is Better?
④ Spend Financial Resources on Experiences with Others

문 16. 다음 글의 흐름상 어색한 문장은?

Countershading is the process of optical flattening that provides camouflage to animals. When sunlight illuminates an object from above, the object will be brightest on top. ① The color of the object will gradually shade darker toward the bottom. This shading gives the object depth and allows the viewer to distinguish its shape. ② Thus even if an animal is exactly, but uniformly, the same color as the substrate, it will be easily visible when illuminated. Most animals, however, are darker above than they are below. ③ When they are illuminated from above, the darker back is lightened and the lighter belly is shaded. The animal thus appears to be a single color and easily blends in with the substrate. ④ For this reason, countersading can be lost in lightless environments. This pattern of coloration, or countershading, destroys the visual impression of shape in the organism. It allows the animal to blend in with its background.

문 17. 주어진 문장이 들어갈 위치로 가장 적절한 것은?

The story plays out backwards to create a similar feeling in the audience.

Neuroscientist David Eagleman has written a book called *Sum*, in which each chapter describes a fanciful version of what happens after we die. In the particularly provocative final chapter, he describes a scenario in which we finally see our entire life clearly — or so we think — when we get to the end of our lives. Then, after we die, we see our life again in reverse. (①) When we see our journey from a different perspective, from the end to the beginning, each episode looks completely different. (②) This time we realize that everything we believed was in fact incorrect. (③) This is similar to the Christopher Nolan film *Memento* in which one of the characters has no long-term memory. (④) As earlier scenes are revealed, the audience realizes that their interpretations of what happened before are all wrong.

문 18. 주어진 글 다음에 이어질 글의 순서로 가장 적절한 것은?

> Many people are familiar with the Mayans' interest in calendars and astronomy, but they were also fascinated by the weather.

(A) In addition, at the top of this lighthouse, the clever Mayans strategically placed a variety of seashells. Depending on wind speed and direction, the shells would whistle at different pitches.

(B) Sometime between 1200 and 1400 AD, they constructed a lighthouse in what is now Cozumel, Mexico, called the "Tumba del Caracol." The Mayans put candles in the lighthouse, which served the traditional function of warning ships that they were close to land.

(C) Depending on which shells were whistling and at what pitch — and their knowledge of what conditions produced storms — the Mayans are said to have been able to predict storms approaching from the Caribbean.

① (A) − (C) − (B)　　② (B) − (A) − (C)
③ (B) − (C) − (A)　　④ (C) − (A) − (B)

※ 밑줄 친 부분에 들어갈 말로 가장 적절한 것을 고르시오.
[문 19 ~ 문 20]

문 19.

> As a driver, we are all under the same rules of the road. The rich man in his shiny new sports car pays the same price for speeding as the poor one in his old car. Regardless of our social positions, we all stand on the same line waiting to register our car or renew our license. While driving, a 110-pound disabled person has the same mobility as a 230-pound bodybuilder. In fact, the automobile has provided the same mobility for some groups who were once left behind in their homes, including women, residents of rural areas, and the disabled. From this point of view, the car looks like _____.

① a luxury item
② a great equalizer
③ a local symbol
④ a measurement of success

문 20.

> The intangible nature of services forces consumers to rely heavily on _____. Therefore, a high risk remains associated with the purchase of services. For example, consumers who want to purchase an automobile will test-drive the car and review and consult the consumer performance data that are available on that model. Conversely, consumers who rent cars cannot evaluate their purchases until after they have committed their payment. Consumers can't test-drive potential rental cars prior to making a decision at the time of rental. Similarly, consumers are taking a risk when they choose a restaurant because they cannot sample meals before they are purchased.

① word of mouth more than on mass media
② local businesses rather than national chains
③ highly priced products to guide purchase decisions
④ experience qualities in the final evaluation of services

해설편 ▶ P.6

2025년도 9급 출제기조 전환대비 예시문제

응시번호	
성 명	

문제책형

응시자 주의사항

1. **시험 시작 전**에 시험문제를 열람하는 행위나 **시험 종료 후** 답안을 작성하는 행위를 한 사람은 「지방공무원 임용령」 제65조 등 관련 법령에 의거 **부정행위자**로 처리됩니다.

2. 시험 시작 즉시 **과목편철 순서, 문제누락 여부, 인쇄상태 이상 유무 및 표지와 개별과목의 문제책형 일치 여부 등을 확인**한 후 문제책 표지에 응시번호, 성명을 기재합니다.

3. 반드시 본인의 **응시표에 인쇄된 시험과목 순서에 따라** 제4과목과 제5과목의 **답안을 표기**하여야 합니다. 과목 순서를 바꾸어 표기한 경우에도 **본인의 응시표에 기재된 과목 순서대로 채점**되므로 반드시 유의하시기 바랍니다.

4. 시험이 시작되면 문제를 주의 깊게 읽은 후, **문항의 취지에 가장 적합한 하나의 정답만을 고르며**, 문제 내용에 관한 질문은 받지 않습니다.

5. **시험시간 관리의 책임**은 전적으로 응시자 본인에게 있습니다.

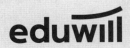

1차 인사혁신처 예시문제

| 풀이 시간: ____:____ ~ ____:____ / 점수: ____점

※ 밑줄 친 부분에 들어갈 말로 가장 적절한 것을 고르시오.

[문 1 ～ 문 3]

문 1.

Recently, increasingly _____ weather patterns, often referred to as "abnormal climate," have been observed around the world.

① irregular
② consistent
③ predictable
④ ineffective

문 2.

Most economic theories assume that people act on a _____ basis; however, this doesn't account for the fact that they often rely on their emotions instead.

① temporary
② rational
③ voluntary
④ commercial

문 3.

By the time she _____ her degree, she will have acquired valuable knowledge on her field of study.

① will have finished
② is finishing
③ will finish
④ finishes

※ 밑줄 친 부분 중 어법상 옳지 않은 것을 고르시오.

[문 4 ～ 문 5]

문 4.

You may conclude that knowledge of the sound systems, word patterns, and sentence structures ① are sufficient to help a student ② become competent in a language. Yet we have ③ all worked with language learners who understand English structurally but still have difficulty ④ communicating.

문 5.

Beyond the cars and traffic jams, she said it took a while to ① get used to have so many people in one place, ② all of whom were moving so fast. "There are only 18 million people in Australia ③ spread out over an entire country," she said, "compared to more than six million people in ④ the state of Massachusetts alone."

※ 밑줄 친 부분에 들어갈 말로 가장 적절한 것을 고르시오.

[문 6 ～ 문 7]

문 6.

A: Hello. I'd like to book a flight from Seoul to Oakland.
B: Okay. Do you have any specific dates in mind?
A: Yes. I am planning to leave on May 2nd and return on May 14th.
B: Okay, I found one that fits your schedule. What class would you like to book?
A: Economy class is good enough for me.
B: Any preference on your seating?
A: _____
B: Great. Your flight is now booked.

① Yes. I'd like to upgrade to business class.
② No. I'd like to buy a one-way ticket.
③ No. I don't have any luggage.
④ Yes. I want an aisle seat.

문 7.

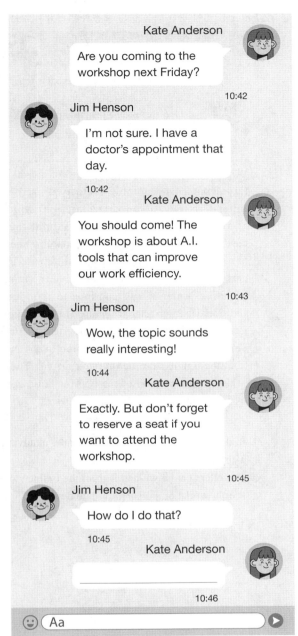

① You need to bring your own laptop.

② I already have a reservation.

③ Follow the instructions on the bulletin board.

④ You should call the doctor's office for an appointment.

※ 다음 글을 읽고 물음에 답하시오. [문 8 ~ 문 9]

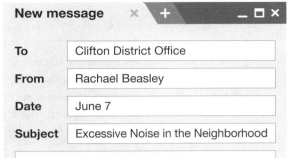

To whom it may concern,

I hope this email finds you well. I am writing to express my concern and frustration regarding the excessive noise levels in our neighborhood, specifically coming from the new sports field.

As a resident of Clifton district, I have always appreciated the peace of our community. However, the ongoing noise disturbances have significantly impacted my family's well-being and our overall quality of life. The sources of the noise include crowds cheering, players shouting, whistles, and ball impacts.

I kindly request that you look into this matter and take appropriate steps to address the noise disturbances. Thank you for your attention to this matter, and I appreciate your prompt response to help restore the tranquility in our neighborhood.

Sincerely,
Rachael Beasley

문 8. 윗글의 목적으로 가장 적절한 것은?

① 체육대회 소음에 대해 주민들의 양해를 구하려고

② 새로 이사 온 이웃 주민의 소음에 대해 항의하려고

③ 인근 스포츠 시설의 소음에 대한 조치를 요청하려고

④ 밤시간 악기 연주와 같은 소음의 차단을 부탁하려고

문 9. 밑줄 친 "steps"의 의미와 가장 가까운 것은?

① movements　　② actions

③ levels　　④ stairs

※ 다음 글을 읽고 물음에 답하시오. [문 10 ~ 문 11]

(A)

We're pleased to announce the upcoming City Harbour Festival, an annual event that brings our diverse community together to celebrate our shared heritage, culture, and local talent. Mark your calendars and join us for an exciting weekend!

Details
- **Dates**: Friday, June 16 – Sunday, June 18
- **Times**: 10 : 00 a.m. – 8 : 00 p.m. (Friday & Saturday)
  10 : 00 a.m. – 6 : 00 p.m. (Sunday)
- **Location**: City Harbour Park, Main Street, and surrounding areas

Highlights
- **Live Performances**
  Enjoy a variety of live music, dance, and theatrical performances on multiple stages throughout the festival grounds.

- **Food Trucks**
  Have a feast with a wide selection of food trucks offering diverse and delicious cuisines, as well as free sample tastings.

For the full schedule of events and activities, please visit our website at www.cityharbourfestival.org or contact the Festival Office at (552) 234-5678.

문 10. (A)에 들어갈 윗글의 제목으로 가장 적절한 것은?
① Make Safety Regulations for Your Community
② Celebrate Our Vibrant Community Events
③ Plan Your Exciting Maritime Experience
④ Recreate Our City's Heritage

문 11. City Harbour Festival에 관한 윗글의 내용과 일치하지 않는 것은?
① 일 년에 한 번 개최된다.
② 일요일에는 오후 6시까지 열린다.
③ 주요 행사로 무료 요리 강습이 진행된다.
④ 웹사이트나 전화 문의를 통해 행사 일정을 알 수 있다.

문 12. Enter-K 앱에 관한 다음 글의 내용과 일치하지 않는 것은?

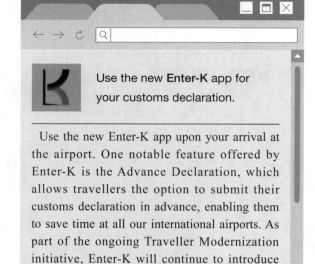

Use the new **Enter-K** app for your customs declaration.

Use the new Enter-K app upon your arrival at the airport. One notable feature offered by Enter-K is the Advance Declaration, which allows travellers the option to submit their customs declaration in advance, enabling them to save time at all our international airports. As part of the ongoing Traveller Modernization initiative, Enter-K will continue to introduce additional border-related features in the future, further improving the overall border experience. Simply download the latest version of the app from the online store before your arrival. There is also a web version of the app for those who are not comfortable using mobile devices.

① It allows travellers to declare customs in advance.
② More features will be added later.
③ Travellers can download it from the online store.
④ It only works on personal mobile devices.

문 13. Office of the Labor Commissioner에 관한 다음 글의 내용과 일치하는 것은?

Office of the Labor Commissioner (OLC)
Responsibilities

The OLC is the principal labor regulatory agency for the state. The OLC is responsible for ensuring that minimum wage, prevailing wage, and overtime are paid to employees, and that employee break and lunch periods are provided. In addition, the OLC has authority over the employment of minors. It is the vision and mission of this office to resolve labor-related problems in an efficient, professional, and effective manner. This includes educating employers and employees regarding their rights and responsibilities under the law. The OLC takes enforcement action when necessary to ensure that workers are treated fairly and compensated for all time worked.

① It ensures that employees pay taxes properly.
② It has authority over employment of adult workers only.
③ It promotes employers' business opportunities.
④ It takes action when employees are unfairly treated.

문 14. 다음 글의 주제로 가장 적절한 것은?

The Ministry of Food and Drug Safety warned that cases of food poisoning have occurred as a result of cross-contamination, where people touch eggs and neglect to wash their hands before preparing food or using utensils. To mitigate such risks, the ministry advised refrigerating eggs and ensuring they are thoroughly cooked until both the yolk and white are firm. Over the past five years, a staggering 7,400 people experienced food poisoning caused by Salmonella bacteria. Salmonella thrives in warm temperatures, with approximately 37 degrees Celsius being the optimal growth condition. Consuming raw or undercooked eggs and failing to separate raw and cooked foods were identified as the most common causes of Salmonella infection. It is crucial to prioritize food safety measures and adhere to proper cooking practices to minimize the risk of Salmonella-related illnesses.

① Benefits of consuming eggs to the immune system
② Different types of treatments for Salmonella infection
③ Life span of Salmonella bacteria in warm temperatures
④ Safe handling of eggs for the prevention of Salmonella infection

문 15. 다음 글의 요지로 가장 적절한 것은?

Despite ongoing efforts to address educational disparities, the persistent achievement gap among students continues to highlight significant inequities in the education system. Recent data reveal that marginalized students, including those from low-income back grounds and vulnerable groups, continue to lag behind their peers in academic performance. The gap poses a challenge to achieving educational equity and social mobility. Experts emphasize the need for targeted interventions, equitable resource allocation, and inclusive policies to bridge this gap and ensure equal opportunities for all students, irrespective of their socioeconomic status or background. The issue of continued educational divide should be addressed at all levels of education system in an effort to find a solution.

① We should deal with persistent educational inequities.
② Educational experts need to focus on new school policies.
③ New teaching methods are necessary to bridge the achievement gap.
④ Family income should not be considered in the discussion of education.

문 16. 다음 글의 흐름상 어색한 문장은?

Every parent or guardian of small children will have experienced the desperate urge to get out of the house and the magical restorative effect of even a short trip to the local park. ① There is probably more going on here than just letting off steam. ② The benefits for kids of getting into nature are huge, ranging from better academic performance to improved mood and focus. ③ Outdoor activities make it difficult for them to spend quality time with their family. ④ Childhood experiences of nature can also boost environmentalism in adulthood. Having access to urban green spaces can play a role in children's social networks and friendships.

문 17. 주어진 문장이 들어갈 위치로 가장 적절한 것은?

In particular, in many urban counties, air pollution, as measured by the amount of total suspended particles, had reached dangerous levels.

Economists Chay and Greenstone evaluated the value of cleaning up of air pollution after the Clean Air Act of 1970. (①) Before 1970, there was little federal regulation of air pollution, and the issue was not high on the agenda of state legislators. (②) As a result, many counties allowed factories to operate without any regulation on their pollution, and in several heavily industrialized counties, pollution had reached very high levels. (③) The Clean Air Act established guidelines for what constituted excessively high levels of five particularly dangerous pollutants. (④) Following the Act in 1970 and the 1977 amendment, there were improvements in air quality.

문 18. 주어진 글 다음에 이어질 글의 순서로 가장 적절한 것은?

> Before anyone could witness what had happened, I shoved the loaves of bread up under my shirt, wrapped the hunting jacket tightly about me, and walked swiftly away.

> (A) When I dropped them on the table, my sister's hands reached to tear off a chunk, but I made her sit, forced my mother to join us at the table, and poured warm tea.
> (B) The heat of the bread burned into my skin, but I clutched it tighter, clinging to life. By the time I reached home, the loaves had cooled somewhat, but the insides were still warm.
> (C) I sliced the bread. We ate an entire loaf, slice by slice. It was good hearty bread, filled with raisins and nuts.

① (A) − (B) − (C)　　② (B) − (A) − (C)
③ (B) − (C) − (A)　　④ (C) − (A) − (B)

※ 밑줄 친 부분에 들어갈 말로 가장 적절한 것을 고르시오.
[문 19 ~ 문 20]

문 19.

> Falling fertility rates are projected to result in shrinking populations for nearly every country by the end of the century. The global fertility rate was 4.7 in 1950, but it dropped by nearly half to 2.4 in 2017. It is expected to fall below 1.7 by 2100. As a result, some researchers predict that the number of people on the planet would peak at 9.7 billion around 2064 before falling down to 8.8 billion by the century's end. This transition will also lead to a significant aging of populations, with as many people reaching 80 years old as there are being born. Such a demographic shift _____, including taxation, healthcare for the elderly, caregiving responsibilities, and retirement. To ensure a "soft landing" into a new demographic landscape, researchers emphasize the need for careful management of the transition.

① raises concerns about future challenges
② mitigates the inverted age structure phenomenon
③ compensates for the reduced marriage rate issue
④ provides immediate solutions to resolve the problems

문 20.

> Many listeners blame a speaker for their inattention by thinking to themselves: "Who could listen to such a character? Will he ever stop reading from his notes?" The good listener reacts differently. He may well look at the speaker and think, "This man is incompetent. Seems like almost anyone would be able to talk better than that." But from this initial similarity he moves on to a different conclusion, thinking "But wait a minute. I'm not interested in his personality or delivery. I want to find out what he knows. Does this man know some things that I need to know?" Essentially, we "listen with our own experience." Is the speaker to be held responsible because we are poorly equipped to comprehend his message? We cannot understand everything we hear, but one sure way to raise the level of our understanding is to _____.

① ignore what the speaker knows
② analyze the character of a speaker
③ assume the responsibility which is inherently ours
④ focus on the speaker's competency of speech delivery

해설편 ▶ P.14

2차 인사혁신처 예시문제

| 풀이 시간: _____:_____ ~ _____:_____ / 점수: _____점

※ 밑줄 친 부분에 들어갈 말로 가장 적절한 것을 고르시오.

[문 1~문 3]

문 1.

In order to exhibit a large mural, the museum curators had to make sure they had _____ space.

① cozy
② stuffy
③ ample
④ cramped

문 2.

Even though there are many problems that have to be solved, I want to emphasize that the safety of our citizens is our top _____.

① secret
② priority
③ solution
④ opportunity

문 3.

Overpopulation may have played a key role: too much exploitation of the rain-forest ecosystem, on which the Maya depended for food, as well as water shortages, seems to _____ the collapse.

① contribute to
② be contributed to
③ have contributed to
④ have been contributed to

※ 밑줄 친 부분 중 어법상 옳지 않은 것을 고르시오.

[문 4 ~문 5]

문 4.

It seems to me that any international organization ① designed to keep the peace must have the power not merely to talk ② but also to act. Indeed, I see this ③ as the central theme of any progress towards an international community ④ which war is avoided not by chance but by design.

문 5.

We have already ① arrived in a digitized world. Digitization affects not only traditional IT companies, but companies across the board, in all sectors. New and changed business models ② are emerged: cars ③ are being shared via apps, languages learned online, and music streamed. But industry is changing too: 3D printers make parts for machines, robots assemble them, and entire factories are intelligently ④ connected with one another.

※ 밑줄 친 부분에 들어갈 말로 가장 적절한 것을 고르시오.

[문 6 ~문 7]

문 6.

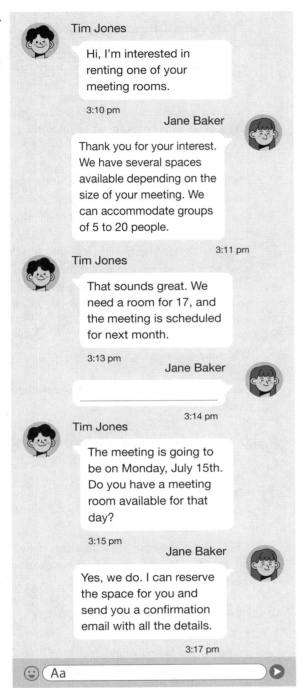

Tim Jones

Hi, I'm interested in renting one of your meeting rooms.

3:10 pm

Jane Baker

Thank you for your interest. We have several spaces available depending on the size of your meeting. We can accommodate groups of 5 to 20 people.

3:11 pm

Tim Jones

That sounds great. We need a room for 17, and the meeting is scheduled for next month.

3:13 pm

Jane Baker

_____

3:14 pm

Tim Jones

The meeting is going to be on Monday, July 15th. Do you have a meeting room available for that day?

3:15 pm

Jane Baker

Yes, we do. I can reserve the space for you and send you a confirmation email with all the details.

3:17 pm

Aa

① Could I have your contact information?
② Can you tell me the exact date of your meeting?
③ Do you need a beam projector or a copy machine?
④ How many people are going to attend the meeting?

문 7.

A: What do you think of this bicycle?
B: Wow, it looks very nice! Did you just get it?
A: No, this is a shared bike. The city launched a bike sharing service.
B: Really? How does it work? I mean, how do I use that service?
A: It's easy. _____.
B: It doesn't sound complicated. Maybe I'll try it this weekend.
A: By the way, it's an electric bicycle.
B: Yes, I can tell. It looks cool.

① You can save energy because it's electric
② Just apply for a permit to park your own bike
③ Just download the bike sharing app and pay online
④ You must wear a helmet at all times for your safety

※ 다음 글을 읽고 물음에 답하시오. [문 8 ~문 9]

Agricultural Marketing Office

Mission

We administer programs that create domestic and international marketing opportunities for national producers of food, fiber, and specialty crops. We also provide the agriculture industry with valuable services to ensure the quality and availability of wholesome food for consumers across the country and around the world.

Vision

We facilitate the strategic marketing of national agricultural products in domestic and international markets while ensuring <u>fair</u> trading practices and promoting a competitive and efficient marketplace to the benefit of producers, traders, and consumers of national food, fiber, and specialty crops.

Core Values
• Honesty & Integrity: We expect and require complete honesty and integrity in all we do.
• Independence & Objectivity: We act independently and objectively to create trust in our programs and services.

문 8. 윗글에서 Agricultural Marketing Office에 관한 내용과 일치하는 것은?

① It creates marketing opportunities for domestic producers.
② It limits wholesome food consumption around the world.
③ It is committed to benefiting consumers over producers.
④ It receives mandates from other agencies before making decisions.

문 9. 밑줄 친 fair의 의미와 가장 가까운 것은?

① free ② mutual
③ profitable ④ impartial

※ 다음 글을 읽고 물음에 답하시오. [문 10~문 11]

(A)

As a close neighbor, you will want to learn how to save your lake.

While it isn't dead yet, Lake Dimmesdale is heading toward this end. So pay your respects to this beautiful body of water while it is still alive.

Some dedicated people are working to save it now. They are having a special meeting to tell you about it. Come learn what is being done and how you can help. This affects your property value as well.

Who wants to live near a dead lake?

Sponsored by Central State Regional Planning Council

• Location: Green City Park Opposite Southern State College(in case of rain: College Library Room 203)
• Date: Saturday, July 6, 2024
• Time: 2:00 p.m.

For any questions about the meeting, please visit our website at www.planningcouncilsavelake.org or contact our office at (432) 345-6789.

문 10. (A)에 들어갈 윗글의 제목으로 가장 적절한 것은?

① Lake Dimmesdale Is Dying
② Praise to the Lake's Beauty
③ Cultural Value of Lake Dimmesdale
④ Significance of the Lake to the College

문 11. 위 안내문의 내용과 일치하지 않는 것은?

① 호수를 살리기 위해 노력하는 사람들이 있다.
② 호수를 위한 활동이 주민들의 재산에 영향을 미친다.
③ 우천 시에는 대학의 구내식당에서 회의가 열린다.
④ 웹사이트 방문이나 전화로 회의에 관해 질문할 수 있다.

문 12. 다음 글의 목적으로 가장 적절한 것은?

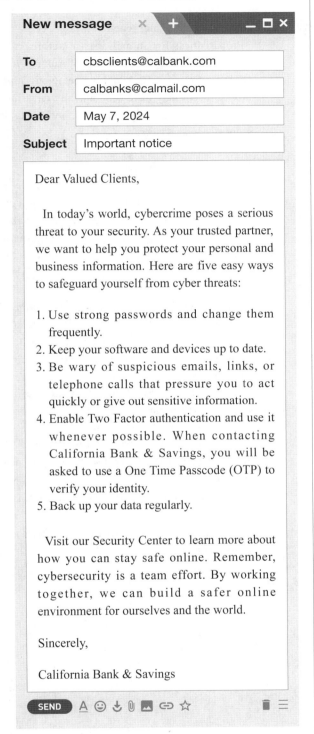

New message

To	cbsclients@calbank.com
From	calbanks@calmail.com
Date	May 7, 2024
Subject	Important notice

Dear Valued Clients,

In today's world, cybercrime poses a serious threat to your security. As your trusted partner, we want to help you protect your personal and business information. Here are five easy ways to safeguard yourself from cyber threats:

1. Use strong passwords and change them frequently.
2. Keep your software and devices up to date.
3. Be wary of suspicious emails, links, or telephone calls that pressure you to act quickly or give out sensitive information.
4. Enable Two Factor authentication and use it whenever possible. When contacting California Bank & Savings, you will be asked to use a One Time Passcode (OTP) to verify your identity.
5. Back up your data regularly.

Visit our Security Center to learn more about how you can stay safe online. Remember, cybersecurity is a team effort. By working together, we can build a safer online environment for ourselves and the world.

Sincerely,

California Bank & Savings

SEND

① to inform clients of how to keep themselves safe from cyber threats
② to inform clients of how to update their software and devices
③ to inform clients of how to make their passwords stronger
④ to inform clients of how to safeguard their OTPs

문 13. 다음 글의 주제로 가장 적절한 것은?

The International Space Station, orbiting some 240 miles above the planet, is about to join the effort to monitor the world's wildlife — and to revolutionize the science of animal tracking. A large antenna and other equipment aboard the orbiting outpost, installed by spacewalking Russian astronauts in 2018, are being tested and will become fully operational this summer. The system will relay a much wider range of data than previous tracking technologies, logging not just an animal's location but also its physiology and environment. This will assist scientists, conservationists and others whose work requires close monitoring of wildlife on the move and provide much more detailed information on the health of the world's ecosystems.

① evaluation of sustainability of global ecosystems
② successful training projects of Russian astronauts
③ animal experiments conducted in the orbiting outpost
④ innovative wildlife monitoring from the space station

문 14. 다음 글의 내용과 일치하지 않는 것은?

The David Williams Library and Museum is open 7 days a week, from 9:00 a.m. to 5:00 p.m. (NOV − MAR) and 9:00 a.m. to 6:00 p.m. (APR − OCT). Online tickets may be purchased at the link below. You will receive an email confirmation after making a purchase (be sure to check your SPAM folder). Bring this confirmation — printed or on smart device — as proof of purchase.

• **Online tickets**: buy.davidwilliams.com/events

The David Williams Library and Museum and the Home of David Williams (operated by the National Heritage Service) offer separate $10.00 adult admission tickets. Tickets for tours of the Home may be purchased on-site during normal business hours.

• **CLOSED**: Thanksgiving, Christmas and New Year's Day

There is no charge for conducting research in the David Williams Library research room.

For additional information, call 1 (800) 333-7777.

① The Library and Museum closes at 5:00 p.m. in December.
② Visitors can buy tour tickets for the Home on-site.
③ The Home of David Williams is open all year round.
④ One can do research in the Library research room for free.

문 15. 다음 글의 요지로 가장 적절한 것은?

Animal Health Emergencies
   Preparedness for animal disease outbreaks has been a top priority for the Board of Animal Health (BOAH) for decades. A highly contagious animal disease event may have economically devastating effects as well as public health or food safety and security consequences.

Foreign Animal Diseases
   A foreign animal disease (FAD) is a disease that is not currently found in the country, and could cause significant illness or death in animals or cause extensive economic harm by eliminating trading opportunities with other countries and states.

   Several BOAH veterinarians who are trained in diagnosing FADs are available 24 hours a day to investigate suspected cases of a FAD. An investigation is triggered when report of animals with clinical signs indicative of a FAD is received or when diagnostic laboratory identifies a suspicious test result.

① BOAH focuses on training veterinarians for FADs.
② BOAH's main goal is to repsond to animal disease epidemic.
③ BOAH actively promotes international trade opportunities.
④ BOAH aims to lead laboratory research on the causes of FADs.

문 16. 다음 글의 흐름상 어색한 문장은?

> A very common type of writing task — one that appears in every academic discipline — is a reaction or response. ① In a reaction essay, the writer is usually given a "prompt" — a visual or written stimulus — to think about and then respond to. ② It is very important to gather reliable facts so that you can defend your argument effectively. ③ Common prompts or stimuli for this type of writing include quotes, pieces of literature, photos, paintings, multimedia presentations, and news events. ④ A reaction focuses on the writer's feelings, opinions, and personal observations about the particular prompt. Your task in writing a reaction essay is twofold: to briefly summarize the prompt and to give your personal reaction to it.

문 17. 주어진 문장이 들어갈 위치로 가장 적절한 것은?

> For others, activism is controversial and disruptive; after all, it often manifests as confrontational activity that directly challenges the order of things.

> Activism is frequently defined as intentional, vigorous or energetic action that individuals and groups practice to bring about a desired goal. (①) For some, activism is a theoretically or ideologically focused project intended to effect a perceived need for political or social change. (②) Activism is uncomfortable, sometimes messy, and almost always strenuous. (③) In addition, it does not occur without the presence and commitment of activists, that is, folks who develop workable strategies, focus a collective spotlight onto particular issues, and ultimately move people into action. (④) As a noted scholar suggests, effective activists also make noise, sometimes loudly.

문 18. 주어진 글 다음에 이어질 글의 순서로 가장 적절한 것은?

> Nick started a fire with some chunks of pine he got with the ax from a stump. Over the fire he stuck a wire grill, pushing the four legs down into the ground with his boot.

> (A) They began to bubble, making little bubbles that rose with difficulty to the surface. There was a good smell. Nick got out a bottle of tomato ketchup and cut four slices of bread.
> (B) The little bubbles were coming faster now. Nick sat down beside the fire and lifted the frying pan off.
> (C) Nick put the frying pan on the grill over the flames. He was hungrier. The beans and spaghetti warmed. He stirred them and mixed them together.

① (B) − (A) − (C)   ② (B) − (C) − (A)

③ (C) − (A) − (B)   ④ (C) − (B) − (A)

※ 밑줄 친 부분에 들어갈 말로 가장 적절한 것을 고르시오.
[문 19~문 20]

문 19.

Technological progress can destroy jobs in a single industry such as textiles. However, historical evidence shows that technological progress does not produce unemployment in a country as a whole. Technological progress increases productivity and incomes in the overall economy, and higher incomes lead to higher demand for goods and thus ＿＿＿＿＿＿＿＿＿＿＿＿＿＿＿. As a result, workers who lose jobs in one industry will be able to find jobs in others, although for many of them this might take time and some of them, like the Luddites, will end up with lower wages in their new jobs.

① increased job losses
② delayed promotion at work
③ greater work satisfaction
④ higher demand for labor

문 20.

There is no substitute for oil, which is one reason ＿＿＿＿＿＿＿＿＿＿＿＿＿＿＿, taking the global economy along with it. While we can generate electricity through coal or natural gas, nuclear or renewables — switching from source to source, according to price — oil remains by far the predominant fuel for transportation. When the global economy heats up, demand for oil rises, boosting the price and encouraging producers to pump more. Inevitably, those high prices eat into economic growth and reduce demand just as suppliers are overproducing. Prices crash, and the cycle starts all over again. That's bad for producers, who can be left holding the bag when prices plummet, and it hurts consumers and industries uncertain about future energy prices. Low oil prices in the 1990s lulled U.S. auto companies into disastrous complacency; they had few efficient models available when oil turned expensive.

① the automobile industry thrives
② it creates disruptions between borders
③ it is prone to big booms and deep busts
④ the research on renewable energy is limited

해설편 ▶ P.19

국가직 9급 공개경쟁채용 필기시험

응 시 번 호		문 제 책 형	
성 명			

【시 험 과 목】

제1과목	국 어	제2과목	영 어	제3과목	한 국 사
제4·5과목	행정법총론, 행정학개론				

응시자 주의사항

1. **시험 시작 전**에 시험문제를 열람하는 행위나 **시험 종료 후** 답안을 작성하는 행위를 한 사람은 「지방공무원 임용령」 제65조 등 관련 법령에 의거 **부정행위자**로 처리됩니다.

2. 시험 시작 즉시 **과목편철 순서, 문제누락 여부, 인쇄상태 이상 유무 및 표지와 개별과목의 문제책형 일치 여부 등을 확인**한 후 문제책 표지에 응시번호, 성명을 기재합니다.

3. 반드시 본인의 **응시표에 인쇄된 시험과목 순서에 따라** 제4과목과 제5과목의 **답안을 표기**하여야 합니다. 과목 순서를 바꾸어 표기한 경우에도 **본인의 응시표에 기재된 과목 순서대로 채점**되므로 반드시 유의하시기 바랍니다.

4. 시험이 시작되면 문제를 주의 깊게 읽은 후, **문항의 취지에 가장 적합한 하나의 정답만을 고르며**, 문제 내용에 관한 질문은 받지 않습니다.

5. **시험시간 관리의 책임**은 전적으로 응시자 본인에게 있습니다.

2024

3월 23일 시행
국가직 9급

| 풀이 시간: ___:___ ~ ___:___ / 점수: ___점

문 1. 밑줄 친 부분에 들어갈 말로 적절한 것은?

> Obviously, no aspect of the language arts stands alone either in learning or in teaching. Listening, speaking, reading, writing, viewing, and visually representing are _____.

① distinct
② distorted
③ interrelated
④ independent

※ 밑줄 친 부분의 의미와 가장 가까운 것을 고르시오.

[문 2 ~ 문 5]

문 2.

> The money was so cleverly concealed that we were forced to abandon our search for it.

① spent
② hidden
③ invested
④ delivered

문 3.

> To appease critics, the wireless industry has launched a $12 million public-education campaign on the drive-time radio.

① soothe
② counter
③ enlighten
④ assimilate

문 4.

> Center officials play down the troubles, saying they are typical of any start-up operation.

① discern
② dissatisfy
③ underline
④ underestimate

문 5.

> She worked diligently and had the guts to go for what she wanted.

① was anxious
② was fortunate
③ was reputable
④ was courageous

문 6. 밑줄 친 부분 중 어법상 옳지 않은 것은?

> ① Despite the belief that the quality of older houses is superior to ② those of modern houses, the foundations of most pre-20th-century houses are dramatically shallow ③ compared to today's, and have only stood the test of time due to the flexibility of ④ their timber framework or the lime mortar between bricks and stones.

문 7. 밑줄 친 부분이 어법상 옳지 않은 것은?

① They are not interested in reading poetry, still more in writing.
② Once confirmed, the order will be sent for delivery to your address.
③ Provided that the ferry leaves on time, we should arrive at the harbor by morning.
④ Foreign journalists hope to cover as much news as possible during their short stay in the capital.

문 8. 우리말을 영어로 바르게 옮긴 것은?

① 지원자 수가 증가하고 있어서 우리는 기쁘다.
  → We are glad that the number of applicants is increasing.
② 나는 2년 전에 그에게서 마지막 이메일을 받았다.
  → I've received the last e-mail from him two years ago.
③ 어젯밤에 그가 잔 침대는 꽤 편안했다.
  → The bed which he slept last night was quite comfortable.
④ 그들은 영상으로 새해 인사를 교환했다.
  → They exchanged New Year's greetings each other on screen.

※ 밑줄 친 부분에 들어갈 말로 적절한 것을 고르시오.

[문 9 ~ 문 11]

문 9.

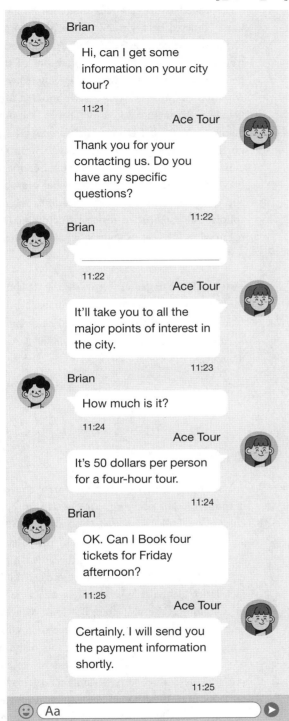

Brian
Hi, can I get some information on your city tour?
11:21

Ace Tour
Thank you for your contacting us. Do you have any specific questions?
11:22

Brian
_____
11:22

Ace Tour
It'll take you to all the major points of interest in the city.
11:23

Brian
How much is it?
11:24

Ace Tour
It's 50 dollars per person for a four-hour tour.
11:24

Brian
OK. Can I Book four tickets for Friday afternoon?
11:25

Ace Tour
Certainly. I will send you the payment information shortly.
11:25

① How long is the tour?
② What does the city tour include?
③ Do you have a list of tour packages?
④ Can you recommend a good tour guide book?

문 10.

A: Thank you. We appreciate your order.
B: You are welcome. Could you send the goods by air freight? We need them fast.
A: Sure. We'll send them to your department right away.
B: Okay. I hope we can get the goods early next week.
A: If everything goes as planned, you'll get them by Monday.
B: Monday sounds good.
A: Please pay within 2 weeks. Air freight costs will be added on the invoice.
B: _____
A: I am afraid the free delivery service is no longer available.

① I see. When will we be getting the invoice from you?
② Our department may not be able to pay within two weeks.
③ Can we send the payment to your business account on Monday?
④ Wait a minute. I thought the delivery costs were at your expense.

문 11.

A: Have you found your phone?
B: Unfortunately, no. I'm still looking for it.
A: Have you contacted the subway's lost and found office?
B: _____.
A: If I were you, I would do that first.
B: Yeah, you are right. I'll check with the lost and found before buying a new phone.

① I went there to ask about the phone
② I stopped by the office this morning
③ I haven't done that yet, actually
④ I tried searching everywhere

문 12. Northeastern Wildlife Exposition에 관한 다음 글의 내용과 일치하는 것은?

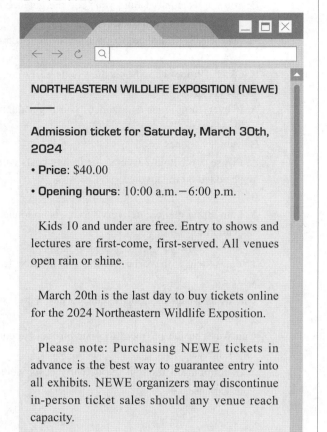

NORTHEASTERN WILDLIFE EXPOSITION (NEWE)
——

Admission ticket for Saturday, March 30th, 2024
• **Price**: $40.00
• **Opening hours**: 10:00 a.m.−6:00 p.m.

　Kids 10 and under are free. Entry to shows and lectures are first-come, first-served. All venues open rain or shine.

　March 20th is the last day to buy tickets online for the 2024 Northeastern Wildlife Exposition.

　Please note: Purchasing NEWE tickets in advance is the best way to guarantee entry into all exhibits. NEWE organizers may discontinue in-person ticket sales should any venue reach capacity.

① 10세 어린이는 입장료 40불을 지불해야 한다.
② 공연과 강연의 입장은 선착순이다.
③ 비가 올 경우에는 행사장을 닫는다.
④ 입장권은 온라인으로만 구매할 수 있다.

문 13. 다음 글의 내용과 일치하지 않는 것은?

　The tragedies of the Greek dramatist Sophocles have come to be regarded as the high point of classical Greek drama. Sadly, only seven of the 123 tragedies he wrote have survived, but of these perhaps the finest is *Oedipus the King*. The play was one of three written by Sophocles about Oedipus, the mythical king of Thebes (the others being *Antigone* and *Oedipus at Colonus*), known collectively as the Theban plays. Sophocles conceived each of these as a separate entity, and they were written and produced several years apart and out of chronological order. *Oedipus the King* follows the established formal structure and it is regarded as the best example of classical Athenian tragedy.

① A total of 123 tragedies were written by Sophocles.
② *Antigone* is also about the king Oedipus.
③ The Theban plays were created in time order.
④ *Oedipus the King* represents the classical Athenian tragedy.

문 14. 다음 글의 주제로 적절한 것은?

　It seems incredible that one man could be responsible for opening our eyes to an entire culture, but until British archaeologist Arthur Evans successfully excavated the ruins of the palace of Knossos on the island of Crete, the great Minoan culture of the Mediterranean was more legend than fact. Indeed its most famed resident was a creature of mythology: the half-man, half-bull Minotaur, said to have lived under the palace of mythical King Minos. But as Evans proved, this realm was no myth. In a series of excavations in the early years of the 20th century, Evans found a trove of artifacts from the Minoan age, which reached its height from 1900 to 1450 B.C.: jewelry, carvings, pottery, altars shaped like bull's horns, and wall paintings showing Minoan life.

① King Minos' successful excavations
② Appreciating artifacts from the Minoan age
③ Magnificence of the palace on the island of Crete
④ Bringing the Minoan culture to the realm of reality

문 15. 다음 글의 제목으로 적절한 것은?

Currency debasement of a good money by a bad money version occurred via coins of a high percentage of precious metal, reissued at lower percentages of gold or silver diluted with a lower value metal. This adulteration drove out the good coin for the bad coin. No one spent the good coin, they kept it, hence the good coin was driven out of circulation and into a hoard. Meanwhile the issuer, normally a king who had lost his treasure on interminable warfare and other such dissolute living, was behind the move. They collected all the good old coins they could, melted them down and reissued them at lower purity and pocketed the balance. It was often illegal to keep the old stuff back but people did, while the king replenished his treasury, at least for a time.

① How Bad Money Replaces Good
② Elements of Good Coins
③ Why Not Melt Coins?
④ What Is Bad Money?

문 16. 다음 글의 흐름상 어색한 문장은?

In spite of all evidence to the contrary, there are people who seriously believe that NASA's Apollo space program never really landed men on the moon. These people claim that the moon landings were nothing more than a huge conspiracy, perpetuated by a government desperately in competition with the Russians and fearful of losing face. ① These conspiracy theorists claim that the United States knew it couldn't compete with the Russians in the space race and was therefore forced to fake a series of successful moon landings. ② Advocates of a conspiracy cite several pieces of what they consider evidence. ③ Crucial to their case is the claim that astronauts never could have safely passed through the Van Allen belt, a region of radiation trapped in Earth's magnetic field. ④ They also point to the fact that the metal coverings of the spaceship were designed to block radiation. If the astronauts had truly gone through the belt, say conspiracy theorists, they would have died.

문 17. 주어진 문장이 들어갈 위치로 적절한 것은?

Tribal oral history and archaeological evidence suggest that sometime between 1500 and 1700 a mudslide destroyed part of the village, covering several longhouses and sealing in their contents.

From the village of Ozette on the westernmost point of Washington's Olympic Peninsula, members of the Makah tribe hunted whales. (①) They smoked their catch on racks and in smokehouses and traded with neighboring groups from around the Puget Sound and nearby Vancouver Island. (②) Ozette was one of five main villages inhabited by the Makah, an Indigenous people who have been based in the region for millennia. (③) Thousands of artifacts that would not otherwise have survived, including baskets, clothing, sleeping mats, and whaling tools, were preserved under the mud. (④) In 1970, a storm caused coastal erosion that revealed the remains of these longhouses and artifacts.

문 18. 주어진 글 다음에 이어질 글의 순서로 적절한 것은?

Interest in movie and sports stars goes beyond their performances on the screen and in the arena.

(A) The doings of skilled baseball, football, and basketball players out of uniform similarly attract public attention.
(B) Newspaper columns, specialized magazines, television programs, and Web sites record the personal lives of celebrated Hollywood actors, sometimes accurately.
(C) Both industries actively promote such attention, which expands audiences and thus increases revenues. But a fundamental difference divides them: What sports stars do for a living is authentic in a way that what movie stars do is not.

① (A) − (C) − (B)   ② (B) − (A) − (C)
③ (B) − (C) − (A)   ④ (C) − (A) − (B)

※ 밑줄 친 부분에 들어갈 말로 적절한 것을 고르시오.
[문 19 ~ 문 20]

문 19.

_____.

Nearly every major politician hires media consultants and political experts to provide advice on how to appeal to the public. Virtually every major business and special-interest group has hired a lobbyist to take its concerns to Congress or to state and local governments. In nearly every community, activists try to persuade their fellow citizens on important policy issues. The workplace, too, has always been fertile ground for office politics and persuasion. One study estimates that general managers spend upwards of 80% of their time in verbal communication — most of it with the intent of persuading their fellow employees. With the advent of the photocopying machine, a whole new medium for office persuasion was invented — the photocopied memo. The Pentagon alone copies an average of 350,000 pages a day, the equivalent of 1,000 novels.

① Business people should have good persuasion skills
② Persuasion shows up in almost every walk of life
③ You will encounter countless billboards and posters
④ Mass media campaigns are useful for the government

문 20.

It is important to note that for adults, social interaction mainly occurs through the medium of language. Few native-speaker adults are willing to devote time to interacting with someone who does not speak the language, with the result that the adult foreigner will have little opportunity to engage in meaningful and extended language exchanges. In contrast, the young child is often readily accepted by other children, and even adults. For young children, language is not as essential to social interaction. So-called 'parallel play', for example, is common among young children. They can be content just to sit in each other's company speaking only occasionally and playing on their own. Adults rarely find themselves in situations where _____.

① language does not play a crucial role in social interaction
② their opinions are readily accepted by their colleagues
③ they are asked to speak another language
④ communication skills are highly required

해설편 ▶ P.28

2023

| 풀이 시간: ＿＿:＿＿ ~ ＿＿:＿＿ / 점수: ＿＿점

1초 합격예측! 모바일 성적분석표

QR 코드로 접속하여 문제 풀이시간을 측정하고,
〈1초 합격예측 & 모바일 성적분석표〉 서비스를 통해
지금 바로! 실력을 점검해 보세요.
https://eduwill.kr/p4Of

※ 밑줄 친 부분의 의미와 가장 가까운 것을 고르시오.

[문 1 ~ 문 4]

문 1.

> Jane wanted to have a small wedding rather than a fancy one. Thus, she planned to invite her family and a few of her intimate friends to eat delicious food and have some pleasant moments.

① nosy　　　　　　　② close
③ outgoing　　　　　④ considerate

문 2.

> The incessant public curiosity and consumer demand due to the health benefits with lesser cost has increased the interest in functional foods.

① rapid　　　　　　② constant
③ significant　　　　④ intermittent

문 3.

> Because of the pandemic, the company had to hold off the plan to provide the workers with various training programs.

① elaborate　　　　② release
③ modify　　　　　④ suspend

문 4.

> The new Regional Governor said he would abide by the decision of the High Court to release the prisoner.

① accept　　　　　② report
③ postpone　　　　④ announce

문 5. 밑줄 친 부분 중 어법상 옳지 않은 것은?

> While advances in transplant technology have made ① it possible to extend the life of individuals with end-stage organ disease, it is argued ② that the biomedical view of organ transplantation as a bounded event, which ends once a heart or kidney is successfully replaced, ③ conceal the complex and dynamic process that more ④ accurately represents the experience of receiving an organ.

문 6. 어법상 옳지 않은 것은?

① All assignments are expected to be turned in on time.
② Hardly had I closed my eyes when I began to think of her.
③ The broker recommended that she buy the stocks immediately.
④ A woman with the tip of a pencil stuck in her head has finally had it remove.

문 7. 우리말을 영어로 잘못 옮긴 것은?

① 내 고양이 나이는 그의 고양이 나이의 세 배이다.
　→ My cat is three times as old as his.
② 우리는 그 일을 이번 달 말까지 끝내야 한다.
　→ We have to finish the work until the end of this month.
③ 그녀는 이틀에 한 번 머리를 감는다.
　→ She washes her hair every other day.
④ 너는 비가 올 경우에 대비하여 우산을 갖고 가는 게 낫겠다.
　→ You had better take an umbrella in case it rains.

문 8. 다음 글의 내용과 일치하지 않는 것은?

　　Are you getting enough choline? Chances are, this nutrient isn't even on your radar. It's time choline gets the attention it deserves. A shocking 90 percent of Americans aren't getting enough choline, according to a recent study. Choline is essential to health at all ages and stages, and is especially critical for brain development. Why aren't we getting enough? Choline is found in many different foods but in small amounts. Plus, the foods that are rich in choline aren't the most popular: think liver, egg yolks and lima beans. Taylor Wallace, who worked on a recent analysis of choline intake in the United States, says, "There isn't enough awareness about choline even among health-care professionals because our government hasn't reviewed the data or set policies around choline since the late '90s."

① A majority of Americans are not getting enough choline.
② Choline is an essential nutrient required for brain development.
③ Foods such as liver and lima beans are good sources of choline.
④ The importance of choline has been stressed since the late '90s in the U.S.

문 9. 다음 글의 내용과 일치하는 것은?

　　Around 1700 there were, by some accounts, more than 2,000 London coffeehouses, occupying more premises and paying more rent than any other trade. They came to be known as penny universities, because for that price one could purchase a cup of coffee and sit for hours listening to extraordinary conversations. Each coffeehouse specialized in a different type of clientele. In one, physicians could be consulted. Others served Protestants, Puritans, Catholics, Jews, literati, merchants, traders, Whigs, Tories, army officers, actors, lawyers, or clergy. The coffeehouses provided England's first egalitarian meeting place, where a man chatted with his tablemates whether he knew them or not.

① The number of coffeehouses was smaller than that of any other business.
② Customers were not allowed to stay for more than an hour in a coffeehouse.
③ Religious people didn't get together in a coffeehouse to chat.
④ One could converse even with unknown tablemates in a coffeehouse.

※ 밑줄 친 부분에 들어갈 말로 알맞은 것을 고르시오.

[문 10 ～ 문 11]

문 10.

> A: I got this new skin cream from a drugstore yesterday. It is supposed to remove all wrinkles and make your skin look much younger.
> B: _____
> A: Why don't you believe it? I've read in a few blogs that the cream really works.
> B: I assume that the cream is good for your skin, but I don't think that it is possible to get rid of wrinkles or magically look younger by using a cream.
> A: You are so pessimistic.
> B: No, I'm just being realistic. I think you are being gullible.

① I don't buy it.
② It's too pricey.
③ I can't help you out.
④ Believe it or not, it's true.

문 11.

> A: I'd like to go sightseeing downtown. Where do you think I should go?
> B: I strongly suggest you visit the national art gallery.
> A: Oh, that's a great idea. What else should I check out?
> B: _____
> A: I don't have time for that. I need to meet a client at three.
> B: Oh, I see. Why don't you visit the national park, then?
> A: That sounds good. Thank you!

① This is the map that your client needs. Here you go.
② A guided tour to the river park. It takes all afternoon.
③ You should check it out as soon as possible.
④ The checkout time is three o'clock.

문 12. 두 사람의 대화 중 자연스럽지 않은 것은?

① A: He's finally in a hit movie!
　 B: Well, he's got it made.
② A: I'm getting a little tired now.
　 B: Let's call it a day.
③ A: The kids are going to a birthday party.
　 B: So, it was a piece of cake.
④ A: I wonder why he went home early yesterday.
　 B: I think he was under the weather.

문 13. 다음 글의 제목으로 알맞은 것은?

> The feeling of being loved and the biological response it stimulates is triggered by nonverbal cues: the tone in a voice, the expression on a face, or the touch that feels just right. Nonverbal cues — rather than spoken words — make us feel that the person we are with is interested in, understands, and values us. When we're with them, we feel safe. We even see the power of nonverbal cues in the wild. After evading the chase of predators, animals often nuzzle each other as a means of stress relief. This bodily contact provides reassurance of safety and relieves stress.

① How Do Wild Animals Think and Feel?
② Communicating Effectively Is the Secret to Success
③ Nonverbal Communication Speaks Louder than Words
④ Verbal Cues: The Primary Tools for Expressing Feelings

문 14. 다음 글의 주제로 알맞은 것은?

There are times, like holidays and birthdays, when toys and gifts accumulate in a child's life. You can use these times to teach a healthy nondependency on things. Don't surround your child with toys. Instead, arrange them in baskets, have one basket out at a time, and rotate baskets occasionally. If a cherished object is put away for a time, bringing it out creates a delightful remembering and freshness of outlook. Suppose your child asks for a toy that has been put away for a while. You can direct attention toward an object or experience that is already in the environment. If you lose or break a possession, try to model a good attitude ("I appreciated it while I had it!") so that your child can begin to develop an attitude of nonattachment. If a toy of hers is broken or lost, help her to say, "I had fun with that."

① building a healthy attitude toward possessions
② learning the value of sharing toys with others
③ teaching how to arrange toys in an orderly manner
④ accepting responsibility for behaving in undesirable ways

문 15. 다음 글의 요지로 알맞은 것은?

Many parents have been misguided by the "self-esteem movement," which has told them that the way to build their children's self-esteem is to tell them how good they are at things. Unfortunately, trying to convince your children of their competence will likely fail because life has a way of telling them unequivocally how capable or incapable they really are through success and failure. Research has shown that how you praise your children has a powerful influence on their development. Some researchers found that children who were praised for their intelligence, as compared to their effort, became overly focused on results. Following a failure, these same children persisted less, showed less enjoyment, attributed their failure to a lack of ability, and performed poorly in future achievement efforts. Praising children for intelligence made them fear difficulty because they began to equate failure with stupidity.

① Frequent praises increase self-esteem of children.
② Compliments on intelligence bring about negative effect.
③ A child should overcome fear of failure through success.
④ Parents should focus on the outcome rather than the process.

문 16. 밑줄 친 부분에 들어갈 말로 알맞은 것은?

In recent years, the increased popularity of online marketing and social media sharing has boosted the need for advertising standardization for global brands. Most big marketing and advertising campaigns include a large online presence. Connected consumers can now zip easily across borders via the internet and social media, making it difficult for advertisers to roll out adapted campaigns in a controlled, orderly fashion. As a result, most global consumer brands coordinate their digital sites internationally. For example, Coca-Cola web and social media sites around the world, from Australia and Argentina to France, Romania, and Russia, are surprisingly _____. All feature splashes of familiar Coke red, iconic Coke bottle shapes, and Coca-Cola's music and "Taste the Feeling" themes.

① experimental
② uniform
③ localized
④ diverse

문 17. 다음 글의 흐름상 어색한 문장은?

In our monthly surveys of 5,000 American workers and 500 U.S. employers, a huge shift to hybrid work is abundantly clear for office and knowledge workers. ① An emerging norm is three days a week in the office and two at home, cutting days on site by 30 % or more. You might think this cutback would bring a huge drop in the demand for office space. ② But our survey data suggests cuts in office space of 1 % to 2 % on average, implying big reductions in density not space. We can understand why. High density at the office is uncomfortable and many workers dislike crowds around their desks. ③ Most employees want to work from home on Mondays and Fridays. Discomfort with density extends to lobbies, kitchens, and especially elevators. ④ The only sure-fire way to reduce density is to cut days on site without cutting square footage as much. Discomfort with density is here to stay according to our survey evidence.

문 18. 주어진 문장이 들어갈 위치로 가장 알맞은 곳은?

They installed video cameras at places known for illegal crossings, and put live video feeds from the cameras on a Web site.

Immigration reform is a political minefield. (①) About the only aspect of immigration policy that commands broad political support is the resolve to secure the U.S. border with Mexico to limit the flow of illegal immigrants. (②) Texas sheriffs recently developed a novel use of the Internet to help them keep watch on the border. (③) Citizens who want to help monitor the border can go online and serve as "virtual Texas deputies." (④) If they see anyone trying to cross the border, they send a report to the sheriff's office, which follows up, sometimes with the help of the U.S. Border Patrol.

문 19. 주어진 글 다음에 이어질 글의 순서로 알맞은 것은?

> All civilizations rely on government administration. Perhaps no civilization better exemplifies this than ancient Rome.

> (A) To rule an area that large, the Romans, based in what is now central Italy, needed an effective system of government administration.
> (B) Actually, the word "civilization" itself comes from the Latin word civis, meaning "citizen."
> (C) Latin was the language of ancient Rome, whose territory stretched from the Mediterranean basin all the way to parts of Great Britain in the north and the Black Sea to the east.

① (A) − (B) − (C)
② (B) − (A) − (C)
③ (B) − (C) − (A)
④ (C) − (A) − (B)

문 20. 밑줄 친 부분에 들어갈 말로 알맞은 것은?

> Over the last fifty years, all major subdisciplines in psychology have become more and more isolated from each other as training becomes increasingly specialized and narrow in focus. As some psychologists have long argued, if the field of psychology is to mature and advance scientifically, its disparate parts (for example, neuroscience, developmental, cognitive, personality, and social) must become whole and integrated again. Science advances when distinct topics become theoretically and empirically integrated under simplifying theoretical frameworks. Psychology of science will encourage collaboration among psychologists from various sub-areas, helping the field achieve coherence rather than continued fragmentation. In this way, psychology of science might act as a template for psychology as a whole by integrating under one discipline all of the major fractions/factions within the field. It would be no small feat and of no small import if the psychology of science could become a model for the parent discipline on how to combine resources and study science _____.

① from a unified perspective
② in dynamic aspects
③ throughout history
④ with accurate evidence

해설편 ▶ P.34

| 풀이 시간: ____:____ ~ ____:____ / 점수: ____점

※ 밑줄 친 부분의 의미와 가장 가까운 것을 고르시오.
[문 1 ~ 문 3]

문 1.

> For years, detectives have been trying to <u>unravel</u> the mystery of the sudden disappearance of the twin brothers.

① solve
② create
③ imitate
④ publicize

문 2.

> Before the couple experienced parenthood, their four-bedroom house seemed unnecessarily <u>opulent</u>.

① hidden
② luxurious
③ empty
④ solid

문 3.

> The boss <u>hit the roof</u> when he saw that we had already spent the entire budget in such a short period of time.

① was very satisfied
② was very surprised
③ became extremely calm
④ became extremely angry

※ 밑줄 친 부분에 들어갈 말로 가장 적절한 것을 고르시오.
[문 4 ~ 문 5]

문 4.

> A mouse potato is the computer _____ of television's couch potato: someone who tends to spend a great deal of leisure time in front of the computer in much the same way the couch potato does in front of the television.

① technician
② equivalent
③ network
④ simulation

문 5.

> Mary decided to _____ her Spanish before going to South America.

① brush up on
② hear out
③ stick up for
④ lay off

문 6. 어법상 옳은 것은?

① A horse should be fed according to its individual needs and the nature of its work.
② My hat was blown off by the wind while walking down a narrow street.
③ She has known primarily as a political cartoonist throughout her career.
④ Even young children like to be complimented for a job done good.

문 7. 다음 글의 내용과 일치하지 않는 것은?

Umberto Eco was an Italian novelist, cultural critic and philosopher. He is widely known for his 1980 novel *The Name of the Rose*, a historical mystery combining semiotics in fiction with biblical analysis, medieval studies and literary theory. He later wrote other novels, including *Foucault's Pendulum* and *The Island of the Day Before*. Eco was also a translator: he translated Raymond Queneau's book *Exercices de style* into Italian. He was the founder of the Department of Media Studies at the University of the Republic of San Marino. He died at his Milanese home of pancreatic cancer, from which he had been suffering for two years, on the night of February 19, 2016.

① *The Name of the Rose* is a historical novel.
② Eco translated a book into Italian.
③ Eco founded a university department.
④ Eco died in a hospital of cancer.

문 8. 밑줄 친 부분 중 어법상 옳지 않은 것은?

To find a good starting point, one must return to the year 1800 during ① which the first modern electric battery was developed. Italian Alessandro Volta found that a combination of silver, copper, and zinc ② were ideal for producing an electrical current. The enhanced design, ③ called a Voltaic pile, was made by stacking some discs made from these metals between discs made of cardboard soaked in sea water. There was ④ such talk about Volta's work that he was requested to conduct a demonstration before the Emperor Napoleon himself.

문 9. 다음 글의 제목으로 가장 적절한 것은?

Lasers are possible because of the way light interacts with electrons. Electrons exist at specific energy levels or states characteristic of that particular atom or molecule. The energy levels can be imagined as rings or orbits around a nucleus. Electrons in outer rings are at higher energy levels than those in inner rings. Electrons can be bumped up to higher energy levels by the injection of energy — for example, by a flash of light. When an electron drops from an outer to an inner level, "excess" energy is given off as light. The wavelength or color of the emitted light is precisely related to the amount of energy released. Depending on the particular lasing material being used, specific wavelengths of light are absorbed (to energize or excite the electrons) and specific wavelengths are emitted (when the electrons fall back to their initial level).

① How Is Laser Produced?
② When Was Laser Invented?
③ What Electrons Does Laser Emit?
④ Why Do Electrons Reflect Light?

문 10. 다음 글의 흐름상 가장 어색한 문장은?

Markets in water rights are likely to evolve as a rising population leads to shortages and climate change causes drought and famine. ① But they will be based on regional and ethical trading practices and will differ from the bulk of commodity trade. ② Detractors argue trading water is unethical or even a breach of human rights, but already water rights are bought and sold in arid areas of the globe from Oman to Australia. ③ Drinking distilled water can be beneficial, but may not be the best choice for everyone, especially if the minerals are not supplemented by another source. ④ "We strongly believe that water is in fact turning into the new gold for this decade and beyond," said Ziad Abdelnour. "No wonder smart money is aggressively moving in this direction."

※ 밑줄 친 부분에 들어갈 말로 가장 적절한 것을 고르시오.
[문 11 ~ 문 12]

문 11.

A: I heard that the university cafeteria changed their menu.
B: Yeah, I just checked it out.
A: And they got a new caterer.
B: Yes. Sam's Catering.
A: _____?
B: There are more dessert choices. Also, some sandwich choices were removed.

① What is your favorite dessert
② Do you know where their office is
③ Do you need my help with the menu
④ What's the difference from the last menu

문 12.

A: Hi there. May I help you?
B: Yes, I'm looking for a sweater.
A: Well, this one is the latest style from the fall collection. What do you think?
B: It's gorgeous. How much is it?
A: Let me check the price for you. It's $120.
B: _____.
A: Then how about this sweater? It's from the last season, but it's on sale for $50.
B: Perfect! Let me try it on.

① I also need a pair of pants to go with it
② That jacket is the perfect gift for me
③ It's a little out of my price range
④ We are open until 7 p.m. on Saturdays

※ 우리말을 영어로 잘못 옮긴 것을 고르시오.   [문 13 ~ 문 14]

문 13. ① 우리가 영어를 단시간에 배우는 것은 결코 쉬운 일이 아니다.
   → It is by no means easy for us to learn English in a short time.
② 우리 인생에서 시간보다 더 소중한 것은 없다.
   → Nothing is more precious as time in our life.
③ 아이들은 길을 건널 때 아무리 조심해도 지나치지 않다.
   → Children cannot be too careful when crossing the street.
④ 그녀는 남들이 말하는 것을 쉽게 믿는다.
   → She easily believes what others say.

문 14.① 커피 세 잔을 마셨기 때문에, 그녀는 잠을 이룰 수 없다.
→ Having drunk three cups of coffee, she can't fall asleep.
② 친절한 사람이어서, 그녀는 모든 이에게 사랑받는다.
→ Being a kind person, she is loved by everyone.
③ 모든 점이 고려된다면, 그녀가 그 직위에 가장 적임인 사람이다.
→ All things considered, she is the best-qualified person for the position.
④ 다리를 꼰 채로 오랫동안 앉아 있는 것은 혈압을 상승시킬 수 있다.
→ Sitting with the legs crossing for a long period can raise blood pressure.

문 15. 밑줄 친 (A), (B)에 들어갈 말로 가장 적절한 것은?

Beliefs about maintaining ties with those who have died vary from culture to culture. For example, maintaining ties with the deceased is accepted and sustained in the religious rituals of Japan. Yet among the Hopi Indians of Arizona, the deceased are forgotten as quickly as possible and life goes on as usual. _____(A)_____, the Hopi funeral ritual concludes with a break-off between mortals and spirits. The diversity of grieving is nowhere clearer than in two Muslim societies — one in Egypt, the other in Bali. Among Muslims in Egypt, the bereaved are encouraged to dwell at length on their grief, surrounded by others who relate to similarly tragic accounts and express their sorrow. _____(B)_____, in Bali, bereaved Muslims are encouraged to laugh and be joyful rather than be sad.

	(A)	(B)
①	However	Similarly
②	In fact	By contrast
③	Therefore	For example
④	Likewise	Consequently

문 16. 밑줄 친 부분에 들어갈 말로 가장 적절한 것은?

Scientists have long known that higher air temperatures are contributing to the surface melting on Greenland's ice sheet. But a new study has found another threat that has begun attacking the ice from below: Warm ocean water moving underneath the vast glaciers is causing them to melt even more quickly. The findings were published in the journal *Nature Geoscience* by researchers who studied one of the many "ice tongues" of the Nioghalvfjerdsfjorden Glacier in northeast Greenland. An ice tongue is a strip of ice that floats on the water without breaking off from the ice on land. The massive one these scientists studied is nearly 50 miles long. The survey revealed an underwater current more than a mile wide where warm water from the Atlantic Ocean is able to flow directly towards the glacier, bringing large amounts of heat into contact with the ice and _____ the glacier's melting.

① separating
② delaying
③ preventing
④ accelerating

문 17. 다음 글의 제목으로 가장 적절한 것은?

Do people from different cultures view the world differently? A psychologist presented realistic animated scenes of fish and other underwater objects to Japanese and American students and asked them to report what they had seen. Americans and Japanese made about an equal number of references to the focal fish, but the Japanese made more than 60 percent more references to background elements, including the water, rocks, bubbles, and inert plants and animals. In addition, whereas Japanese and American participants made about equal numbers of references to movement involving active animals, the Japanese participants made almost twice as many references to relationships involving inert, background objects. Perhaps most tellingly, the very first sentence from the Japanese participants was likely to be one referring to the environment, whereas the first sentence from Americans was three times as likely to be one referring to the focal fish.

① Language Barrier Between Japanese and Americans
② Associations of Objects and Backgrounds in the Brain
③ Cultural Differences in Perception
④ Superiority of Detail-oriented People

문 18. 주어진 문장이 들어갈 위치로 가장 적절한 곳은?

Thus, blood, and life-giving oxygen, are easier for the heart to circulate to the brain.

People can be exposed to gravitational force, or g-force, in different ways. It can be localized, affecting only a portion of the body, as in getting slapped on the back. It can also be momentary, such as hard forces endured in a car crash. A third type of g-force is sustained, or lasting for at least several seconds. (①) Sustained, body wide g-forces are the most dangerous to people. (②) The body usually withstands localized or momentary g-force better than sustained g-force, which can be deadly because blood is forced into the legs, depriving the rest of the body of oxygen. (③) Sustained g-force applied while the body is horizontal, or lying down, instead of sitting or standing tends to be more tolerable to people, because blood pools in the back and not the legs. (④) Some people, such as astronauts and fighter jet pilots, undergo special training exercises to increase their bodies' resistance to g-force.

문 19. 다음 글의 요지로 가장 적절한 것은?

　　If someone makes you an offer and you're legitimately concerned about parts of it, you're usually better off proposing all your changes at once. Don't say, "The salary is a bit low. Could you do something about it?" and then, once she's worked on it, come back with "Thanks. Now here are two other things I'd like..." If you ask for only one thing initially, she may assume that getting it will make you ready to accept the offer (or at least to make a decision). If you keep saying "and one more thing...," she is unlikely to remain in a generous or understanding mood. Furthermore, if you have more than one request, don't simply mention all the things you want A, B, C, and D; also signal the relative importance of each to you. Otherwise, she may pick the two things you value least, because they're pretty easy to give you, and feel she's met you halfway.

① Negotiate multiple issues simultaneously, not serially.
② Avoid sensitive topics for a successful negotiation.
③ Choose the right time for your negotiation.
④ Don't be too direct when negotiating salary.

문 20. 주어진 글 다음에 이어질 글의 순서로 가장 적절한 것은?

　　Today, Lamarck is unfairly remembered in large part for his mistaken explanation of how adaptations evolve. He proposed that by using or not using certain body parts, an organism develops certain characteristics.

(A) There is no evidence that this happens. Still, it is important to note that Lamarck proposed that evolution occurs when organisms adapt to their environments. This idea helped set the stage for Darwin.

(B) Lamarck thought that these characteristics would be passed on to the offspring. Lamarck called this idea *inheritance of acquired characteristics*.

(C) For example, Lamarck might explain that a kangaroo's powerful hind legs were the result of ancestors strengthening their legs by jumping and then passing that acquired leg strength on to the offspring. However, an acquired characteristic would have to somehow modify the DNA of specific genes in order to be inherited.

① (A) − (C) − (B)
② (B) − (A) − (C)
③ (B) − (C) − (A)
④ (C) − (A) − (B)

해설편 ▶ P.40

2021

4월 17일 시행
국가직 9급

| 풀이 시간: ___:___ ~ ___:___ / 점수: ___점

※ 밑줄 친 부분의 의미와 가장 가까운 것을 고르시오.
[문 1 ~ 문 3]

문 1.

Privacy as a social practice shapes individual behavior in conjunction with other social practices and is therefore central to social life.

① in combination with ② in comparison with
③ in place of ④ in case of

문 2.

The influence of Jazz has been so pervasive that most popular music owes its stylistic roots to jazz.

① deceptive ② ubiquitous
③ persuasive ④ disastrous

문 3.

This novel is about the vexed parents of an unruly teenager who quits school to start a business.

① callous ② annoyed
③ reputable ④ confident

문 4. 밑줄 친 부분에 들어갈 말로 가장 적절한 것은?

A group of young demonstrators attempted to _____ the police station.

① line up ② give out
③ carry on ④ break into

문 5. 다음 글의 내용과 일치하는 것은?

The most notorious case of imported labor is of course the Atlantic slave trade, which brought as many as ten million enslaved Africans to the New World to work the plantations. But although the Europeans may have practiced slavery on the largest scale, they were by no means the only people to bring slaves into their communities: earlier, the ancient Egyptians used slave labor to build their pyramids, early Arab explorers were often also slave traders, and Arabic slavery continued into the twentieth century and indeed still continues in a few places. In the Americas some native tribes enslaved members of other tribes, and slavery was also an institution in many African nations, especially before the colonial period.

① African laborers voluntarily moved to the New World.
② Europeans were the first people to use slave labor.
③ Arabic slavery no longer exists in any form.
④ Slavery existed even in African countries.

문 6. 어법상 옳은 것은?

① This guide book tells you where should you visit in Hong Kong.
② I was born in Taiwan, but I have lived in Korea since I started work.
③ The novel was so excited that I lost track of time and missed the bus.
④ It's not surprising that book stores don't carry newspapers any more, doesn't it?

문 7. 다음 글의 제목으로 가장 적절한 것은?

Warming temperatures and loss of oxygen in the sea will shrink hundreds of fish species — from tunas and groupers to salmon, thresher sharks, haddock and cod — even more than previously thought, a new study concludes. Because warmer seas speed up their metabolisms, fish, squid and other water-breathing creatures will need to draw more oxygen from the ocean. At the same time, warming seas are already reducing the availability of oxygen in many parts of the sea. A pair of University of British Columbia scientists argue that since the bodies of fish grow faster than their gills, these animals eventually will reach a point where they can't get enough oxygen to sustain normal growth. "What we found was that the body size of fish decreases by 20 to 30 percent for every 1 degree Celsius increase in water temperature," says author William Cheung.

① Fish Now Grow Faster than Ever
② Oxygen's Impact on Ocean Temperatures
③ Climate Change May Shrink the World's Fish
④ How Sea Creatures Survive with Low Metabolism

문 8. 밑줄 친 부분 중 어법상 옳지 않은 것은?

Urban agriculture (UA) has long been dismissed as a fringe activity that has no place in cities; however, its potential is beginning to ① be realized. In fact, UA is about food self-reliance: it involves ② creating work and is a reaction to food insecurity, particularly for the poor. Contrary to ③ which many believe, UA is found in every city, where it is sometimes hidden, sometimes obvious. If one looks carefully, few spaces in a major city are unused. Valuable vacant land rarely sits idle and is often taken over — either formally, or informally — and made ④ productive.

문 9. 주어진 문장이 들어갈 위치로 가장 적절한 것은?

For example, the state archives of New Jersey hold more than 30,000 cubic feet of paper and 25,000 reels of microfilm.

Archives are a treasure trove of material: from audio to video to newspapers, magazines and printed material — which makes them indispensable to any History Detective investigation. While libraries and archives may appear the same, the differences are important. (①) An archive collection is almost always made up of primary sources, while a library contains secondary sources. (②) To learn more about the Korean War, you'd go to a library for a history book. If you wanted to read the government papers, or letters written by Korean War soldiers, you'd go to an archive. (③) If you're searching for information, chances are there's an archive out there for you. Many state and local archives store public records — which are an amazing, diverse resource. (④) An online search of your state's archives will quickly show you they contain much more than just the minutes of the legislature — there are detailed land grant information to be found, old town maps, criminal records and oddities such as peddler license applications.

*treasure trove 귀중한 발굴물(수집물)

**land grant (대학 · 철도 등을 위해) 정부가 주는 땅문 10. 다음 글의 흐름상 가장 어색한 문장은?

The term burnout refers to a "wearing out" from the pressures of work. Burnout is a chronic condition that results as daily work stressors take their toll on employees. ① The most widely adopted conceptualization of burnout has been developed by Maslach and her colleagues in their studies of human service workers. Maslach sees burnout as consisting of three interrelated dimensions. The first dimension — emotional exhaustion — is really the core of the burnout phenomenon. ② Workers suffer from emotional exhaustion when they feel fatigued, frustrated, used up, or unable to face another day on the job. The second dimension of burnout is a lack of personal accomplishment. ③ This aspect of the burnout phenomenon refers to workers who see themselves as failures, incapable of effectively accomplishing job requirements. ④ Emotional labor workers enter their occupation highly motivated although they are physically exhausted. The third dimension of burnout is depersonalization. This dimension is relevant only to workers who must communicate interpersonally with others (e.g. clients, patients, students) as part of the job.

※ 밑줄 친 부분에 들어갈 말로 가장 적절한 것을 고르시오.
[문 11 ~ 문 12]

문 11.

A: Were you here last night?
B: Yes. I worked the closing shift. Why?
A: The kitchen was a mess this morning. There was food spattered on the stove, and the ice trays were not in the freezer.
B: I guess I forgot to go over the cleaning checklist.
A: You know how important a clean kitchen is.
B: I'm sorry. _____

① I won't let it happen again.
② Would you like your bill now?
③ That's why I forgot it yesterday.
④ I'll make sure you get the right order.

문 12.

A: Have you taken anything for your cold?
B: No, I just blow my nose a lot.
A: Have you tried nose spray?
B: _____
A: It works great.
B: No, thanks. I don't like to put anything in my nose, so I've never used it.

① Yes, but it didn't help.
② No, I don't like nose spray.
③ No, the pharmacy was closed.
④ Yeah, how much should I use?

문 13. 다음 글의 내용과 일치하지 않는 것은?

Deserts cover more than one-fifth of the Earth's land area, and they are found on every continent. A place that receives less than 25 centimeters (10 inches) of rain per year is considered a desert. Deserts are part of a wider class of regions called drylands. These areas exist under a "moisture deficit," which means they can frequently lose more moisture through evaporation than they receive from annual precipitation. Despite the common conceptions of deserts as hot, there are cold deserts as well. The largest hot desert in the world, northern Africa's Sahara, reaches temperatures of up to 50 degrees Celsius (122 degrees Fahrenheit) during the day. But some deserts are always cold, like the Gobi Desert in Asia and the polar deserts of the Antarctic and Arctic, which are the world's largest. Others are mountainous. Only about 20 percent of deserts are covered by sand. The driest deserts, such as Chile's Atacama Desert, have parts that receive less than two millimeters (0.08 inches) of precipitation a year. Such environments are so harsh and otherworldly that scientists have even studied them for clues about life on Mars. On the other hand, every few years, an unusually rainy period can produce "super blooms," where even the Atacama becomes blanketed in wildflowers.

① There is at least one desert on each continent.
② The Sahara is the world's largest hot desert.
③ The Gobi Desert is categorized as a cold desert.
④ The Atacama Desert is one of the rainiest deserts.

※ 우리말을 영어로 가장 잘 옮긴 것을 고르시오.

[문 14 ~ 문 15]

문 14. ① 나는 너의 답장을 가능한 한 빨리 받기를 고대한다.

→ I look forward to receive your reply as soon as possible.

② 그는 내가 일을 열심히 했기 때문에 월급을 올려 주겠다고 말했다.

→ He said he would rise my salary because I worked hard.

③ 그의 스마트 도시 계획은 고려할 만했다.

→ His plan for the smart city was worth considered.

④ Cindy는 피아노 치는 것을 매우 좋아했고 그녀의 아들도 그랬다.

→ Cindy loved playing the piano, and so did her son.

문 15. ① 당신이 부자일지라도 당신은 진실한 친구들을 살 수는 없다.

→ Rich as if you may be, you can't buy sincere friends.

② 그것은 너무나 아름다운 유성 폭풍이어서 우리는 밤새 그것을 보았다.

→ It was such a beautiful meteor storm that we watched it all night.

③ 학위가 없는 것이 그녀의 성공을 방해했다.

→ Her lack of a degree kept her advancing.

④ 그는 사형이 폐지되어야 하는지 아닌지에 대한 에세이를 써야 한다.

→ He has to write an essay on if or not the death penalty should be abolished.

※ 밑줄 친 부분에 들어갈 말로 가장 적절한 것을 고르시오.

[문 16 ~ 문 17]

문 16.

Social media, magazines and shop windows bombard people daily with things to buy, and British consumers are buying more clothes and shoes than ever before. Online shopping means it is easy for customers to buy without thinking, while major brands offer such cheap clothes that they can be treated like disposable items — worn two or three times and then thrown away. In Britain, the average person spends more than £1,000 on new clothes a year, which is around four percent of their income.

That might not sound like much, but that figure hides two far more worrying trends for society and for the environment. First, a lot of that consumer spending is via credit cards. British people currently owe approximately £670 per adult to credit card companies. That's 66 percent of the average wardrobe budget. Also, not only are people spending money they don't have, they're using it to buy things _____. Britain throws away 300,000 tons of clothing a year, most of which goes into landfill sites.

① they don't need
② that are daily necessities
③ that will be soon recycled
④ they can hand down to others

문 17.

Excellence is the absolute prerequisite in fine dining because the prices charged are necessarily high. An operator may do everything possible to make the restaurant efficient, but the guests still expect careful, personal service: food prepared to order by highly skilled chefs and delivered by expert servers. Because this service is, quite literally, manual labor, only marginal improvements in productivity are possible. For example, a cook, server, or bartender can move only so much faster before she or he reaches the limits of human performance. Thus, only moderate savings are possible through improved efficiency, which makes an escalation of prices _____. (It is an axiom of economics that as prices rise, consumers become more discriminating.) Thus, the clientele of the fine-dining restaurant expects, demands, and is willing to pay for excellence.

① ludicrous   ② inevitable
③ preposterous   ④ inconceivable

문 18. 주어진 글 다음에 이어질 글의 순서로 가장 적절한 것은?

> To be sure, human language stands out from the decidedly restricted vocalizations of monkeys and apes. Moreover, it exhibits a degree of sophistication that far exceeds any other form of animal communication.

> (A) That said, many species, while falling far short of human language, do nevertheless exhibit impressively complex communication systems in natural settings.
> (B) And they can be taught far more complex systems in artificial contexts, as when raised alongside humans.
> (C) Even our closest primate cousins seem incapable of acquiring anything more than a rudimentary communicative system, even after intensive training over several years. The complexity that is language is surely a species-specific trait.

① (A) − (B) − (C)
② (B) − (C) − (A)
③ (C) − (A) − (B)
④ (C) − (B) − (A)

문 19. 다음 글의 주제로 가장 적절한 것은?

> During the late twentieth century socialism was on the retreat both in the West and in large areas of the developing world. During this new phase in the evolution of market capitalism, global trading patterns became increasingly interlinked, and advances in information technology meant that deregulated financial markets could shift massive flows of capital across national boundaries within seconds. 'Globalization' boosted trade, encouraged productivity gains and lowered prices, but critics alleged that it exploited the low-paid, was indifferent to environmental concerns and subjected the Third World to a monopolistic form of capitalism. Many radicals within Western societies who wished to protest against this process joined voluntary bodies, charities and other non-governmental organizations, rather than the marginalized political parties of the left. The environmental movement itself grew out of the recognition that the world was interconnected, and an angry, if diffuse, international coalition of interests emerged.

① The affirmative phenomena of globalization in the developing world in the past
② The decline of socialism and the emergence of capitalism in the twentieth century
③ The conflict between the global capital market and the political organizations of the left
④ The exploitative characteristics of global capitalism and diverse social reactions against it

문 20. 다음 글에 나타난 Johnbull의 심경으로 가장 적절한 것은?

> In the blazing midday sun, the yellow egg-shaped rock stood out from a pile of recently unearthed gravel. Out of curiosity, sixteen-year-old miner Komba Johnbull picked it up and fingered its flat, pyramidal planes. Johnbull had never seen a diamond before, but he knew enough to understand that even a big find would be no larger than his thumbnail. Still, the rock was unusual enough to merit a second opinion. Sheepishly, he brought it over to one of the more experienced miners working the muddy gash deep in the jungle. The pit boss's eyes widened when he saw the stone. "Put it in your pocket," he whispered. "Keep digging." The older miner warned that it could be dangerous if anyone thought they had found something big. So Johnbull kept shoveling gravel until nightfall, pausing occasionally to grip the heavy stone in his fist. Could it be?

① thrilled and excited
② painful and distressed
③ arrogant and convinced
④ detached and indifferent

해설편 ▶ P.46

2020

7월 11일 시행
국가직 9급

| 풀이 시간: ___ : ___ ~ ___ : ___ / 점수: ___ 점

※ 밑줄 친 부분의 의미와 가장 가까운 것을 고르시오.

[문 1 ~ 문 4]

문 1.

Extensive lists of microwave oven models and styles along with <u>candid</u> customer reviews and price ranges are available at appliance comparison websites.

① frank
② logical
③ implicit
④ passionate

문 2.

It had been known for a long time that Yellowstone was volcanic in nature and the one thing about volcanoes is that they are generally <u>conspicuous</u>.

① passive
② vaporous
③ dangerous
④ noticeable

문 3.

He's the best person to tell you how to get there because he knows the city <u>inside out</u>.

① eventually
② culturally
③ thoroughly
④ tentatively

문 4.

All along the route were thousands of homespun attempts to <u>pay tribute to</u> the team, including messages etched in cardboard, snow and construction paper.

① honor
② compose
③ publicize
④ join

문 5. 어법상 옳은 것은?

① The traffic of a big city is busier than those of a small city.
② I'll think of you when I'll be lying on the beach next week.
③ Raisins were once an expensive food, and only the wealth ate them.
④ The intensity of a color is related to how much gray the color contains.

문 6. 우리말을 영어로 가장 잘 옮긴 것은?

① 몇 가지 문제가 새로운 회원들 때문에 생겼다.
→ Several problems have raised due to the new members.
② 그 위원회는 그 건물의 건설을 중단하라고 명했다.
→ The committee commanded that construction of the building cease.
③ 그들은 한 시간에 40마일이 넘는 바람과 싸워야 했다.
→ They had to fight against winds that will blow over 40 miles an hour.
④ 거의 모든 식물의 씨앗은 혹독한 날씨에도 살아남는다.
→ The seeds of most plants are survived by harsh weather.

문 7. 우리말을 영어로 잘못 옮긴 것은?

① 인간은 환경에 자신을 빨리 적응시킨다.
→ Human beings quickly adapt themselves to the environment.
② 그녀는 그 사고 때문에 그녀의 목표를 포기할 수밖에 없었다.
→ She had no choice but to give up her goal because of the accident.
③ 그 회사는 그가 부회장으로 승진하는 것을 금했다.
→ The company prohibited him from promoting to vice-president.
④ 그 장난감 자동차를 조립하고 분리하는 것은 쉽다.
→ It is easy to assemble and take apart the toy car.

문 8. 다음 글의 요지로 가장 적절한 것은?

Listening to somebody else's ideas is the one way to know whether the story you believe about the world — as well as about yourself and your place in it — remains intact. We all need to examine our beliefs, air them out and let them breathe. Hearing what other people have to say, especially about concepts we regard as foundational, is like opening a window in our minds and in our hearts. Speaking up is important. Yet to speak up without listening is like banging pots and pans together: even if it gets you attention, it's not going to get you respect. There are three prerequisites for conversation to be meaningful: 1. You have to know what you're talking about, meaning that you have an original point and are not echoing a worn-out, hand-me-down or pre-fab argument; 2. You respect the people with whom you're speaking and are authentically willing to treat them courteously even if you disagree with their positions; 3. You have to be both smart and informed enough to listen to what the opposition says while handling your own perspective on the topic with uninterrupted good humor and discernment.

① We should be more determined to persuade others.
② We need to listen and speak up in order to communicate well.
③ We are reluctant to change our beliefs about the world we see.
④ We hear only what we choose and attempt to ignore different opinions.

문 9. 다음 글의 제목으로 가장 적절한 것은?

The future may be uncertain, but some things are undeniable: climate change, shifting demographics, geopolitics. The only guarantee is that there will be changes, both wonderful and terrible. It's worth considering how artists will respond to these changes, as well as what purpose art serves, now and in the future. Reports suggest that by 2040 the impacts of human-caused climate change will be inescapable, making it the big issue at the centre of art and life in 20 years' time. Artists in the future

will wrestle with the possibilities of the post-human and post-Anthropocene — artificial intelligence, human colonies in outer space and potential doom. The identity politics seen in art around the #MeToo and Black Lives Matter movements will grow as environmentalism, border politics and migration come even more sharply into focus. Art will become increasingly diverse and might not 'look like art' as we expect. In the future, once we've become weary of our lives being visible online for all to see and our privacy has been all but lost, anonymity may be more desirable than fame. Instead of thousands, or millions, of likes and followers, we will be starved for authenticity and connection. Art could, in turn, become more collective and experiential, rather than individual.

① What will art look like in the future?
② How will global warming affect our lives?
③ How will artificial intelligence influence the environment?
④ What changes will be made because of political movements?

문 10. 다음 글의 내용과 일치하지 않는 것은?

The Second Amendment of the U.S. Constitution states: "A well-regulated Militia, being necessary to the security of a free State, the right of the people to keep and bear Arms, shall not be infringed." Supreme Court rulings, citing this amendment, have upheld the right of states to regulate firearms. However, in a 2008 decision confirming an individual right to keep and bear arms, the court struck down Washington, D.C. laws that banned handguns and required those in the home to be locked or disassembled. A number of gun advocates consider ownership a birthright and an essential part of the nation's heritage. The United States, with less than 5 percent of the world's population, has about 35~50 percent of the world's civilian-owned guns, according to a 2007 report by the Switzerland-based Small Arms Survey. It ranks number one in firearms per capita. The United States also has the highest homicide-by-firearm rate among the world's most developed nations. But many gun-rights proponents say these statistics do not indicate a cause-and-effect relationship and note that the rates of gun homicide and other gun crimes in the United States have dropped since highs in the early 1990's.

① In 2008, the U.S. Supreme Court overturned Washington, D.C. laws banning handguns.
② Many gun advocates claim that owning guns is a natural-born right.
③ Among the most developed nations, the U.S. has the highest rate of gun homicides.
④ Gun crimes in the U.S. have steadily increased over the last three decades.

문 11. 두 사람의 대화 중 가장 어색한 것은?

① A: When is the payment due?
  B: You have to pay by next week.
② A: Should I check this baggage in?
  B: No, it's small enough to take on the plane.
③ A: When and where shall we meet?
  B: I'll pick you up at your office at 8:30.
④ A: I won the prize in a cooking contest.
  B: I couldn't have done it without you.

문 12. 밑줄 친 부분에 들어갈 말로 가장 적절한 것은?

A: Thank you for calling the Royal Point Hotel Reservations Department. My name is Sam. How may I help you?
B: Hello, I'd like to book a room.
A: We offer two room types: the deluxe room and the luxury suite.
B: _____?
A: For one, the suite is very large. In addition to a bedroom, it has a kitchen, living room and dining room.
B: It sounds expensive.
A: Well, it's $200 more per night.
B: In that case, I'll go with the deluxe room.

① Do you need anything else
② May I have the room number
③ What's the difference between them
④ Are pets allowed in the rooms

문 13. 밑줄 친 (A), (B)에 들어갈 말로 가장 적절한 것은?

Advocates of homeschooling believe that children learn better when they are in a secure, loving environment. Many psychologists see the home as the most natural learning environment, and originally the home was the classroom, long before schools were established. Parents who homeschool argue that they can monitor their children's education and give them the attention that is lacking in a traditional school setting. Students can also pick and choose what to study and when to study, thus enabling them to learn at their own pace. ____(A)____, critics of homeschooling say that children who are not in the classroom miss out on learning important social skills because they have little interaction with their peers. Several studies, though, have shown that the home-educated children appear to do just as well in terms of social and emotional development as other students, having spent more time in the comfort and security of their home, with guidance from parents who care about their welfare. ____(B)____, many critics of homeschooling have raised concerns about the ability of parents to teach their kids effectively.

	(A)	(B)
①	Therefore	Nevertheless
②	In contrast	In spite of this
③	Therefore	Contrary to that
④	In contrast	Furthermore

문 14. 다음 글의 주제로 가장 적절한 것은?

For many people, work has become an obsession. It has caused burnout, unhappiness and gender inequity, as people struggle to find time for children or passions or pets or any sort of life besides what they do for a paycheck. But increasingly, younger workers are pushing back. More of them expect and demand flexibility — paid leave for a new baby, say, and generous vacation time, along with daily things, like the ability to work remotely, come in late or leave early, or make time for exercise or meditation. The rest of their lives happens on their phones, not tied to a certain place or time — why should work be any different?

① ways to increase your paycheck
② obsession for reducing inequity
③ increasing call for flexibility at work
④ advantages of a life with long vacations

문 15. 주어진 글 다음에 이어질 글의 순서로 가장 적절한 것은?

Past research has shown that experiencing frequent psychological stress can be a significant risk factor for cardiovascular disease, a condition that affects almost half of those aged 20 years and older in the United States.

(A) Does this mean, though, that people who drive on a daily basis are set to develop heart problems, or is there a simple way of easing the stress of driving?

(B) According to a new study, there is. The researchers noted that listening to music while driving helps relieve the stress that affects heart health.

(C) One source of frequent stress is driving, either due to the stressors associated with heavy traffic or the anxiety that often accompanies inexperienced drivers.

① (A) − (C) − (B)
② (B) − (A) − (C)
③ (C) − (A) − (B)
④ (C) − (B) − (A)

문 16. 다음 글의 흐름상 가장 어색한 문장은?

When the brain perceives a threat in the immediate surroundings, it initiates a complex string of events in the body. It sends electrical messages to various glands, organs that release chemical hormones into the bloodstream. Blood quickly carries these hormones to other organs that are then prompted to do various things. ① The adrenal glands above the kidneys, for example, pump out adrenaline, the body's stress hormone. ② Adrenaline travels all over the body doing things such as widening the eyes to be on the lookout for signs of danger, pumping the heart faster to keep blood and extra hormones flowing, and tensing the skeletal muscles so they are ready to lash out at or run from the threat. ③ The whole process is called the fight-or-flight response, because it prepares the body to either battle or run for its life. ④ Humans consciously control their glands to regulate the release of various hormones. Once the response is initiated, ignoring it is impossible, because hormones cannot be reasoned with.

문 17. 주어진 문장이 들어갈 위치로 가장 적절한 것은?

It was then he remembered his experience with the glass flask, and just as quickly, he imagined that a special coating might be applied to a glass windshield to keep it from shattering.

In 1903 the French chemist, Edouard Benedictus, dropped a glass flask one day on a hard floor and broke it. (①) However, to the astonishment of the chemist, the flask did not shatter, but still retained most of its original shape. (②) When he examined the flask he found that it contained a film coating inside, a residue remaining from a solution of collodion that the flask had contained. (③) He made a note of this unusual phenomenon, but thought no more of it until several weeks later when he read stories in the newspapers about people in automobile accidents who were badly hurt by flying windshield glass. (④) Not long thereafter, he succeeded in producing the world's first sheet of safety glass.

문 18. 다음 글의 내용과 일치하지 않는 것은?

Dubrovnik, Croatia, is a mess. Because its main attraction is its seaside Old Town surrounded by 80-foot medieval walls, this Dalmatian Coast town does not absorb visitors very well. And when cruise ships are docked here, a legion of tourists turn Old Town into a miasma of tank-top-clad tourists marching down the town's limestone-blanketed streets. Yes, the city of Dubrovnik has been proactive in trying to curb cruise ship tourism, but nothing will save Old Town from the perpetual swarm of tourists. To make matters worse, the lure of making extra money has inspired many homeowners in Old Town to turn over their places to Airbnb, making the walled portion of town one giant hotel. You want an "authentic" Dubrovnik experience in Old Town, just like a local? You're not going to find it here. Ever.

① Old Town은 80피트 중세 시대 벽으로 둘러싸여 있다.
② 크루즈 배가 정박할 때면 많은 여행객이 Old Town 거리를 활보한다.
③ Dubrovnik 시는 크루즈 여행을 확대하려고 노력해 왔다.
④ Old Town에서는 많은 집이 여행객 숙소로 바뀌었다.

문 19. 밑줄 친 (A), (B)에 들어갈 말로 가장 적절한 것은?

When an organism is alive, it takes in carbon dioxide from the air around it. Most of that carbon dioxide is made of carbon-12, but a tiny portion consists of carbon-14. So the living organism always contains a very small amount of radioactive carbon, carbon-14. A detector next to the living organism would record radiation given off by the carbon-14 in the organism. When the organism dies, it no longer takes in carbon dioxide. No new carbon-14 is added, and the old carbon-14 slowly decays into nitrogen. The amount of carbon-14 slowly _____(A)_____ as time goes on. Over time, less and less radiation from carbon-14 is produced. The amount of carbon-14 radiation detected for an organism is a measure, therefore, of how long the organism has been _____(B)_____. This method of determining the age of an organism is called carbon-14 dating. The decay of carbon-14 allows archaeologists to find the age of once-living materials. Measuring the amount of radiation remaining indicates the approximate age.

	(A)	(B)
①	decreases	dead
②	increases	alive
③	decreases	productive
④	increases	inactive

문 20. 밑줄 친 부분에 들어갈 말로 가장 적절한 것은?

All creatures, past and present, either have gone or will go extinct. Yet, as each species vanished over the past 3.8-billion-year history of life on Earth, new ones inevitably appeared to replace them or to exploit newly emerging resources. From only a few very simple organisms, a great number of complex, multicellular forms evolved over this immense period. The origin of new species, which the nineteenth-century English naturalist Charles Darwin once referred to as "the mystery of mysteries," is the natural process of speciation responsible for generating this remarkable _____ with whom humans share the planet. Although taxonomists presently recognize some 1.5 million living species, the actual number is possibly closer to 10 million. Recognizing the biological status of this multitude requires a clear understanding of what constitutes a species, which is no easy task given that evolutionary biologists have yet to agree on a universally acceptable definition.

① technique of biologists
② diversity of living creatures
③ inventory of extinct organisms
④ collection of endangered species

해설편 ▶ P.52

| 풀이 시간: _____:_____ ~ _____:_____ / 점수: _____점

※ 밑줄 친 부분의 의미와 가장 가까운 것을 고르시오.

[문 1 ~ 문 2]

문 1.

Natural Gas World subscribers will receive accurate and reliable key facts and figures about what is going on in the industry, so they are fully able to <u>discern</u> what concerns their business.

① distinguish
② strengthen
③ undermine
④ abandon

문 2.

Ms. West, the winner of the silver in the women's 1,500m event, <u>stood out</u> through the race.

① was overwhelmed
② was impressive
③ was depressed
④ was optimistic

문 3. 두 사람의 대화 중 가장 어색한 것은?

① A: I'm traveling abroad, but I'm not used to staying in another country.
　 B: Don't worry. You'll get accustomed to it in no time.
② A: I want to get a prize in the photo contest.
　 B: I'm sure you will. I'll keep my fingers crossed!
③ A: My best friend moved to Sejong City. I miss her so much.
　 B: Yeah. I know how you feel.
④ A: Do you mind if I talk to you for a moment?
　 B: Never mind. I'm very busy right now.

문 4. 밑줄 친 부분에 들어갈 말로 가장 적절한 것은?

A: Would you like to try some dim sum?
B: Yes, thank you. They look delicious. What's inside?
A: These have pork and chopped vegetables, and those have shrimps.
B: And, um, _____?
A: You pick one up with your chopsticks like this and dip it into the sauce. It's easy.
B: Okay. I'll give it a try.

① how much are they
② how do I eat them
③ how spicy are they
④ how do you cook them

※ 우리말을 영어로 잘못 옮긴 것을 고르시오. [문 5 ~ 문 6]

문 5. ① 제가 당신께 말씀드렸던 새로운 선생님은 원래 페루 출신입니다.
　　 → The new teacher I told you about is originally from Peru.
② 나는 긴급한 일로 자정이 5분이나 지난 후 그에게 전화했다.
　　 → I called him five minutes shy of midnight on an urgent matter.
③ 상어로 보이는 것이 산호 뒤에 숨어 있었다.
　　 → What appeared to be a shark was lurking behind the coral reef.
④ 그녀는 일요일에 16세의 친구와 함께 산 정상에 올랐다.
　　 → She reached the mountain summit with her 16-year-old friend on Sunday.

문 6. ① 개인용 컴퓨터를 가장 많이 가지고 있는 나라는 종종 바뀐다.
　　 → The country with the most computers per person changes from time to time.
② 지난 여름 나의 사랑스러운 손자에게 일어난 일은 놀라웠다.
　　 → What happened to my lovely grandson last summer was amazing.
③ 나무 숟가락은 아이들에게 매우 좋은 장난감이고 플라스틱 병 또한 그렇다.
　　 → Wooden spoons are excellent toys for children, and so are plastic bottles.
④ 나는 은퇴 후부터 내내 이 일을 해 오고 있다.
　　 → I have been doing this work ever since I retired.

※ 밑줄 친 부분 중 어법상 옳지 않은 것을 고르시오.

[문 7 ~ 문 8]

문 7.

Domesticated animals are the earliest and most effective 'machines' ① available to humans. They take the strain off the human back and arms. ② Utilizing with other techniques, animals can raise human living standards very considerably, both as supplementary foodstuffs (protein in meat and milk) and as machines ③ to carry burdens, lift water, and grind grain. Since they are so obviously ④ of great benefit, we might expect to find that over the centuries humans would increase the number and quality of the animals they kept. Surprisingly, this has not usually been the case.

문 8.

A myth is a narrative that embodies — and in some cases ① helps to explain — the religious, philosophical, moral, and political values of a culture. Through tales of gods and supernatural beings, myths ② try to make sense of occurrences in the natural world. Contrary to popular usage, myth does not mean "falsehood." In the broadest sense, myths are stories — usually whole groups of stories — ③ that can be true or partly true as well as false; regardless of their degree of accuracy, however, myths frequently express the deepest beliefs of a culture. According to this definition, the *Iliad* and the *Odyssey*, the Koran, and the Old and New Testaments can all ④ refer to as myths.

문 9. 다음 글의 제목으로 가장 적절한 것은?

Mapping technologies are being used in many new applications. Biological researchers are exploring the molecular structure of DNA ("mapping the genome"), geophysicists are mapping the structure of the Earth's core, and oceanographers are mapping the ocean floor. Computer games have various imaginary "lands" or levels where rules, hazards, and rewards change. Computerization now challenges reality with "virtual reality," artificial environments that simulate special situations, which may be useful in training and entertainment. Mapping techniques are being used also in the realm of ideas. For example, relationships between ideas can be shown using what are called concept maps. Starting from a general or "central" idea, related ideas can be connected, building a web around the main concept. This is not a map by any traditional definition, but the tools and techniques of cartography are employed to produce it, and in some ways it resembles a map.

① Computerized Maps vs. Traditional Maps
② Where Does Cartography Begin?
③ Finding Ways to DNA Secrets
④ Mapping New Frontiers

문 10. 다음 글의 요지로 가장 적절한 것은?

When giving performance feedback, you should consider the recipient's past performance and your estimate of his or her future potential in designing its frequency, amount, and content. For high performers with potential for growth, feedback should be frequent enough to prod them into taking corrective action, but not so frequent that it is experienced as controlling and saps their initiative. For adequate performers who have settled into their jobs and have limited potential for advancement, very little feedback is needed because they have displayed reliable and steady behavior in the past, knowing their tasks and realizing what needs to be done. For poor performers — that is, people who will need to be removed from their jobs if their performance doesn't improve — feedback should be frequent and very specific, and the connection between acting on the feedback and negative sanctions such as being laid off or fired should be made explicit.

① Time your feedback well.
② Customize negative feedback.
③ Tailor feedback to the person.
④ Avoid goal-oriented feedback.

문 11. 다음 글의 내용과 일치하지 않는 것은?

> Langston Hughes was born in Joplin, Missouri, and graduated from Lincoln University, in which many African-American students have pursued their academic disciplines. At the age of eighteen, Hughes published one of his most well-known poems, "Negro Speaks of Rivers." Creative and experimental, Hughes incorporated authentic dialect in his work, adapted traditional poetic forms to embrace the cadences and moods of blues and jazz, and created characters and themes that reflected elements of lower-class black culture. With his ability to fuse serious content with humorous style, Hughes attacked racial prejudice in a way that was natural and witty.

① Hughes는 많은 미국 흑인들이 다녔던 대학교를 졸업하였다.
② Hughes는 실제 사투리를 그의 작품에 반영하였다.
③ Hughes는 하층 계급 흑인들의 문화적 요소를 반영한 인물을 만들었다.
④ Hughes는 인종편견을 엄숙한 문체로 공격하였다.

문 12. 밑줄 친 부분 중 글의 흐름상 가장 어색한 것은?

> In 2007, our biggest concern was "too big to fail." Wall Street banks had grown to such staggering sizes, and had become so central to the health of the financial system, that no rational government could ever let them fail. ① Aware of their protected status, banks made excessively risky bets on housing markets and invented ever more complicated derivatives. ② New virtual currencies such as bitcoin and ethereum have radically changed our understanding of how money can and should work. ③ The result was the worst financial crisis since the breakdown of our economy in 1929. ④ In the years since 2007, we have made great progress in addressing the too-big-to-fail dilemma. Our banks are better capitalized than ever. Our regulators conduct regular stress tests of large institutions.

문 13. 다음 글의 주제로 가장 적절한 것은?

> Imagine that two people are starting work at a law firm on the same day. One person has a very simple name. The other person has a very complex name. We've got pretty good evidence that over the course of their next 16 plus years of their career, the person with the simpler name will rise up the legal hierarchy more quickly. They will attain partnership more quickly in the middle parts of their career. And by about the eighth or ninth year after graduating from law school the people with simpler names are about seven to ten percent more likely to be partners — which is a striking effect. We try to eliminate all sorts of other alternative explanations. For example, we try to show that it's not about foreignness because foreign names tend to be harder to pronounce. But even if you look at just white males with Anglo-American names — so really the true in-group, you find that among those white males with Anglo names they are more likely to rise up if their names happen to be simpler. So simplicity is one key feature in names that determines various outcomes.

① the development of legal names
② the concept of attractive names
③ the benefit of simple names
④ the roots of foreign names

※ 밑줄 친 부분의 의미와 가장 가까운 것을 고르시오.
[문 14 ~ 문 15]

문 14.
> Schooling is compulsory for all children in the United States, but the age range for which school attendance is required varies from state to state.

① complementary   ② systematic
③ mandatory   ④ innovative

문 15.
> Although the actress experienced much turmoil in her career, she never disclosed to anyone that she was unhappy.

① let on   ② let off
③ let up   ④ let down

문 16. 밑줄 친 (A), (B)에 들어갈 말로 가장 적절한 것은?

Visionaries are the first people in their industry segment to see the potential of new technologies. Fundamentally, they see themselves as smarter than their opposite numbers in competitive companies — and, quite often, they are. Indeed, it is their ability to see things first that they want to leverage into a competitive advantage. That advantage can only come about if no one else has discovered it. They do not expect, _____(A)_____, to be buying a well-tested product with an extensive list of industry references. Indeed, if such a reference base exists, it may actually turn them off, indicating that for this technology, at any rate, they are already too late. Pragmatists, _____(B)_____, deeply value the experience of their colleagues in other companies. When they buy, they expect extensive references, and they want a good number to come from companies in their own industry segment.

	(A)	(B)
①	therefore	on the other hand
②	however	in addition
③	nonetheless	at the same time
④	furthermore	in conclusion

문 17. 주어진 문장이 들어갈 위치로 가장 적절한 것은?

Some of these ailments are short-lived; others may be long-lasting.

For centuries, humans have looked up at the sky and wondered what exists beyond the realm of our planet. (①) Ancient astronomers examined the night sky hoping to learn more about the universe. More recently, some movies explored the possibility of sustaining human life in outer space, while other films have questioned whether extraterrestrial life forms may have visited our planet. (②) Since astronaut Yuri Gagarin became the first man to travel in space in 1961, scientists have researched what conditions are like beyond the Earth's atmosphere, and what effects space travel has on the human body. (③) Although most astronauts do not spend more than a few months in space, many experience physiological and psychological problems when they return to the Earth. (④) More than two-thirds of all astronauts suffer from motion sickness while traveling in space. In the gravity-free environment, the body cannot differentiate up from down. The body's internal balance system sends confusing signals to the brain, which can result in nausea lasting as long as a few days.

문 18. 밑줄 친 부분에 들어갈 말로 가장 적절한 것은?

Why bother with the history of everything? _____. In literature classes you don't learn about genes; in physics classes you don't learn about human evolution. So you get a partial view of the world. That makes it hard to find *meaning* in education. The French sociologist Emile Durkheim called this sense of disorientation and meaninglessness *anomie*, and he argued that it could lead to despair and even suicide. The German sociologist Max Weber talked of the "disenchantment" of the world. In the past, people had a unified vision of their world, a vision usually provided by the origin stories of their own religious traditions. That unified vision gave a sense of purpose, of meaning, even of enchantment to the world and to life. Today, though, many writers have argued that a sense of meaninglessness is inevitable in a world of science and rationality. Modernity, it seems, means meaninglessness.

① In the past, the study of history required disenchantment from science
② Recently, science has given us lots of clever tricks and meanings
③ Today, we teach and learn about our world in fragments
④ Lately, history has been divided into several categories

문 19. 다음 글의 내용과 일치하지 않는 것은?

The earliest government food service programs began around 1900 in Europe. Programs in the United States date from the Great Depression, when the need to use surplus agricultural commodities was joined to concern for feeding the children of poor families. During and after World War II, the explosion in the number of working women fueled the need for a broader program. What was once a function of the family — providing lunch — was shifted to the school food service system. The National School Lunch Program is the result of these efforts. The program is designed to provide federally assisted meals to children of school age. From the end of World War II to the early 1980s, funding for school food service expanded steadily. Today it helps to feed children in almost 100,000 schools across the United States. Its first function is to provide a nutritious lunch to all students; the second is to provide nutritious food at both breakfast and lunch to underprivileged children. If anything, the role of school food service as a replacement for what was once a family function has been expanded.

① The increase in the number of working women boosted the expansion of food service programs.
② The US government began to feed poor children during the Great Depression despite the food shortage.
③ The US school food service system presently helps to feed children of poor families.
④ The function of providing lunch has been shifted from the family to schools.

문 20. 주어진 문장 다음에 이어질 글의 순서로 가장 적절한 것은?

South Korea boasts of being the most wired nation on earth.

(A) This addiction has become a national issue in Korea in recent years, as users started dropping dead from exhaustion after playing online games for days on end. A growing number of students have skipped school to stay online, shockingly self-destructive behavior in this intensely competitive society.
(B) In fact, perhaps no other country has so fully embraced the Internet.
(C) But such ready access to the Web has come at a price as legions of obsessed users find that they cannot tear themselves away from their computer screens.

① (A) − (B) − (C)   ② (A) − (C) − (B)
③ (B) − (A) − (C)   ④ (B) − (C) − (A)

해설편 ▶ P.58

2018

4월 7일 시행
국가직 9급

| 풀이 시간: ____:____ ~ ____:____ / 점수: ____점

※ 밑줄 친 부분에 들어갈 말로 가장 적절한 것을 고르시오.
[문 1 ~ 문 2]

문 1.

A: Can I ask you for a favor?
B: Yes, what is it?
A: I need to get to the airport for my business trip, but my car won't start. Can you give me a lift?
B: Sure. When do you need to be there by?
A: I have to be there no later than 6 : 00.
B: It's 4 : 30 now. _____.
   We'll have to leave right away.

① That's cutting it close
② I took my eye off the ball
③ All that glitters is not gold
④ It's water under the bridge

문 2.

Fear of loss is a basic part of being human. To the brain, loss is a threat and we naturally take measures to avoid it. We cannot, however, avoid it indefinitely. One way to face loss is with the perspective of a stock trader. Traders accept the possibility of loss as part of the game, not the end of the game. What guides this thinking is a portfolio approach; wins and losses will both happen, but it's the overall portfolio of outcomes that matters most. When you embrace a portfolio approach, you will be _____ because you know that they are small parts of a much bigger picture.

① less inclined to dwell on individual losses
② less interested in your investments
③ more averse to the losses
④ more sensitive to fluctuations in the stock market

문 3. 다음 글의 제목으로 가장 적절한 것은?

Over the last years of traveling, I've observed how much we humans live in the past. The past is around us constantly, considering that, the minute something is manifested, it is the past. Our surroundings, our homes, our environments, our architecture, our products are all past constructs. We should live with what is part of our time, part of our collective consciousness, those things that were produced during our lives. Of course, we do not have the choice or control to have everything around us relevant or conceived during our time, but what we do have control of should be a reflection of the time in which we exist and communicate the present. The present is all we have, and the more we are surrounded by it, the more we are aware of our own presence and participation.

① Travel: Tracing the Legacies of the Past
② Reflect on the Time That Surrounds You Now
③ Manifestation of a Hidden Life
④ Architecture of a Futuristic Life

문 4. 밑줄 친 부분 중 어법상 옳지 않은 것은?

It would be difficult ① to imagine life without the beauty and richness of forests. But scientists warn we cannot take our forest for ② granted. By some estimates, deforestation ③ has been resulted in the loss of as much as eighty percent of the natural forests of the world. Currently, deforestation is a global problem, ④ affecting wilderness regions such as the temperate rainforests of the Pacific.

문 5. 밑줄 친 부분의 의미와 가장 가까운 것은?

Robert J. Flaherty, a legendary documentary filmmaker, tried to show how indigenous people gathered food.

① native   ② ravenous
③ impoverished   ④ itinerant

문 6. 밑줄 친 부분에 들어갈 말로 가장 적절한 것은?

> Listening to music is _____ being a rock star. Anyone can listen to music, but it takes talent to become a musician.

① on a par with　　　　② a far cry from
③ contingent upon　　　④ a prelude to

문 7. 다음 글의 흐름상 가장 어색한 문장은?

> Biologists have identified a gene that will allow rice plants to survive being submerged in water for up to two weeks — over a week longer than at present. Plants under water for longer than a week are deprived of oxygen and wither and perish. ① The scientists hope their discovery will prolong the harvests of crops in regions that are susceptible to flooding. ② Rice growers in these flood-prone areas of Asia lose an estimated one billion dollars annually to excessively waterlogged rice paddies. ③ They hope the new gene will lead to a hardier rice strain that will reduce the financial damage incurred in typhoon and monsoon seasons and lead to bumper harvests. ④ This is dreadful news for people in these vulnerable regions, who are victims of urbanization and have a shortage of crops. Rice yields must increase by 30 percent over the next 20 years to ensure a billion people can receive their staple diet.

문 8. 밑줄 친 부분에 들어갈 말로 가장 적절한 것은?

> A: Do you know how to drive?
> B: Of course. I'm a great driver.
> A: Could you teach me how to drive?
> B: Do you have a learner's permit?
> A: Yes, I got it just last week.
> B: Have you been behind the steering wheel yet?
> A: No, but I can't wait to _____.

① take a rain check　　　② get my feet wet
③ get an oil change　　　④ change a flat tire

문 9. 다음 글의 내용과 일치하는 것은?

> Sharks are covered in scales made from the same material as teeth. These flexible scales protect the shark and help it swim quickly in water. A shark can move the scales as it swims. This movement helps reduce the water's drag. Amy Lang, an aerospace engineer at the University of Alabama, studies the scales on the shortfin mako, a relative of the great white shark. Lang and her team discovered that the mako shark's scales differ in size and in flexibility in different parts of its body. For instance, the scales on the sides of the body are tapered — wide at one end and narrow at the other end. Because they are tapered, these scales move very easily. They can turn up or flatten to adjust to the flow of water around the shark and to reduce drag. Lang feels that shark scales can inspire designs for machines that experience drag, such as airplanes.

① A shark has scales that always remain immobile to protect itself as it swims.
② Lang revealed that the scales of a mako shark are utilized to lessen drag in water.
③ A mako shark has scales of identical size all over its body.
④ The scientific designs of airplanes were inspired by shark scales.

문 10. 밑줄 친 부분 중 어법상 옳지 않은 것은?

> Focus means ① getting stuff done. A lot of people have great ideas but don't act on them. For me, the definition of an entrepreneur, for instance, is someone who can combine innovation and ingenuity with the ability to execute that new idea. Some people think that the central dichotomy in life is whether you're positive or negative about the issues ② that interest or concern you. There's a lot of attention ③ paying to this question of whether it's better to have an optimistic or pessimistic lens. I think the better question to ask is whether you are going to do something about it or just ④ let life pass you by.

문 11. 밑줄 친 부분 중 글의 흐름상 가장 어색한 것은?

> Most people like to talk, but few people like to listen, yet listening well is a ① <u>rare</u> talent that everyone should treasure. Because they hear more, good listeners tend to know more and to be more sensitive to what is going on around them than most people. In addition, good listeners are inclined to accept or tolerate rather than to judge and criticize. Therefore, they have ② <u>fewer</u> enemies than most people. In fact, they are probably the most beloved of people. However, there are ③ <u>exceptions</u> to that generality. For example, John Steinbeck is said to have been an excellent listener, yet he was hated by some of the people he wrote about. No doubt his ability to listen contributed to his capacity to write. Nevertheless, the result of his listening didn't make him ④ <u>unpopular</u>.

문 12. 다음 글의 주제로 가장 적절한 것은?

> Worry is like a rocking horse. No matter how fast you go, you never move anywhere. Worry is a complete waste of time and creates so much clutter in your mind that you cannot think clearly about anything. The way to learn to stop worrying is by first understanding that you energize whatever you focus your attention on. Therefore, the more you allow yourself to worry, the more likely things are to go wrong! Worrying becomes such an ingrained habit that to avoid it you consciously have to train yourself to do otherwise. Whenever you catch yourself having a fit of worry, stop and change your thoughts. Focus your mind more productively on what you do want to happen and dwell on what's already wonderful in your life so more wonderful stuff will come your way.

① What effects does worry have on life?
② Where does worry originate from?
③ When should we worry?
④ How do we cope with worrying?

문 13. 다음 글의 내용과 일치하지 않는 것은?

> Students at Macaulay Honors College (MHC) don't stress about the high price of tuition. That's because theirs is free. At Macaulay and a handful of other service academies, work colleges, single-subject schools and conservatories, 100 percent of the student body receive a full tuition scholarship for all four years. Macaulay students also receive a laptop and $7,500 in "opportunities funds" to pursue research, service experiences, study abroad programs and internships. "The most important thing is not the free tuition, but the freedom of studying without the burden of debt on your back," says Ann Kirschner, university dean of Macaulay Honors College. The debt burden, she says, "really compromises decisions students make in college, and we are giving them the opportunity to be free of that." Schools that grant free tuition to all students are rare, but a greater number of institutions provide scholarships to enrollees with high grades. Institutions such as Indiana University Bloomington offer automatic awards to high-performing students with stellar GPAs and class ranks.

① MHC에서는 모든 학생이 4년간 수업료를 내지 않는다.
② MHC에서는 학생들에게 컴퓨터 구입 비용과 교외활동 비용을 합하여 $7,500를 지급한다.
③ 수업료로 인한 빚 부담이 있으면 학생들이 자유롭게 공부할 수 없다고 Kirschner 학장은 말한다.
④ MHC와 달리 학업 우수자에게만 장학금을 주는 대학도 있다.

※ 밑줄 친 부분의 의미와 가장 가까운 것을 고르시오.

[문 14 ~ 문 15]

문 14.

The police spent seven months working on the crime case but were never able to determine the identity of the malefactor.

① culprit　　　　　② dilettante
③ pariah　　　　　④ demagogue

문 15.

While at first glance it seems that his friends are just leeches, they prove to be the ones he can depend on through thick and thin.

① in no time
② from time to time
③ in pleasant times
④ in good times and bad times

문 16. 주어진 문장이 들어갈 위치로 가장 적절한 것은?

Some remain intensely proud of their original accent and dialect words, phrases and gestures, while others accommodate rapidly to a new environment by changing their speech habits, so that they no longer "stand out in the crowd."

Our perceptions and production of speech change with time. (①) If we were to leave our native place for an extended period, our perception that the new accents around us were strange would only be temporary. (②) Gradually, we will lose the sense that others have an accent and we will begin to fit in — to accommodate our speech patterns to the new norm. (③) Not all people do this to the same degree. (④) Whether they do this consciously or not is open to debate and may differ from individual to individual, but like most processes that have to do with language, the change probably happens before we are aware of it and probably couldn't happen if we were.

문 17. 다음 글의 내용과 일치하지 않는 것은?

Insomnia can be classified as transient, acute, or chronic. Transient insomnia lasts for less than a week. It can be caused by another disorder, by changes in the sleep environment, by the timing of sleep, severe depression, or by stress. Its consequences such as sleepiness and impaired psychomotor performance are similar to those of sleep deprivation. Acute insomnia is the inability to consistently sleep well for a period of less than a month. Acute insomnia is present when there is difficulty initiating or maintaining sleep or when the sleep that is obtained is not refreshing. These problems occur despite adequate opportunity and circumstances for sleep and they can impair daytime functioning. Acute insomnia is also known as short term insomnia or stress related insomnia. Chronic insomnia lasts for longer than a month. It can be caused by another disorder, or it can be a primary disorder. People with high levels of stress hormones or shifts in the levels of cytokines are more likely than others to have chronic insomnia. Its effects can vary according to its causes. They might include muscular weariness, hallucinations, and/or mental fatigue. Chronic insomnia can also cause double vision.

*cytokines: groups of molecules released by certain cells of the immune system

① Insomnia can be classified according to its duration.
② Transient insomnia occurs solely due to an inadequate sleep environment.
③ Acute insomnia is generally known to be related to stress.
④ Chronic insomnia patients may suffer from hallucinations.

문 18. 밑줄 친 부분에 들어갈 말로 가장 적절한 것은?

> Kisha Padbhan, founder of Everonn Education, in Mumbai, looks at his business as nation-building. India's student-age population of 230million (kindergarten to college) is one of the largest in the world. The government spends $83 billion on instruction, but there are serious gaps. "There aren't enough teachers and enough teacher-training institutes," says Kisha. "What children in remote parts of India lack is access to good teachers and exposure to good-quality content." Everonn's solution? The company uses a satellite network, with two-way video and audio _____. It reaches 1,800 colleges and 7,800 schools across 24 of India's 28 states. It offers everything from digitized school lessons to entrance exam prep for aspiring engineers and has training for job-seekers, too.

① to improve the quality of teacher training facilities
② to bridge the gap through virtual classrooms
③ to get students familiarized with digital technology
④ to locate qualified instructors across the nation

문 19. 주어진 문장 다음에 이어질 글의 순서로 가장 적절한 것은?

> A technique that enables an individual to gain some voluntary control over autonomic, or involuntary, body functions by observing electronic measurements of those functions is known as biofeedback.

(A) When such a variable moves in the desired direction (for example, blood pressure down), it triggers visual or audible displays — feedback on equipment such as television sets, gauges, or lights.

(B) Electronic sensors are attached to various parts of the body to measure such variables as heart rate, blood pressure, and skin temperature.

(C) Biofeedback training teaches one to produce a desired response by reproducing thought patterns or actions that triggered the displays.

① (A) − (B) − (C)
② (B) − (C) − (A)
③ (B) − (A) − (C)
④ (C) − (A) − (B)

문 20. 우리말을 영어로 잘못 옮긴 것은?

① 그 연사는 자기 생각을 청중에게 전달하는 데 능숙하지 않았다.
   → The speaker was not good at getting his ideas across to the audience.
② 서울의 교통 체증은 세계 어느 도시보다 심각하다.
   → The traffic jams in Seoul are more serious than those in any other city in the world.
③ 네가 말하고 있는 사람과 시선을 마주치는 것은 서양 국가에서 중요하다.
   → Making eye contact with the person you are speaking to is important in western countries.
④ 그는 사람들이 생각했던 만큼 인색하지 않았다는 것이 드러났다.
   → It turns out that he was not so stingier as he was thought to be.

오랫동안 꿈을 그리는 사람은
마침내 그 꿈을 닮아간다.

– 앙드레 말로(Andre Malraux)

지방직 9급 공개경쟁채용 필기시험

응 시 번 호		문 제 책 형
성 명		

【시 험 과 목】

제1과목	국 어	제2과목	영 어	제3과목	한 국 사
제4·5과목	행정법총론, 행정학개론				

응시자 주의사항

1. **시험 시작 전**에 시험문제를 열람하는 행위나 **시험 종료 후** 답안을 작성하는 행위를 한 사람은 「지방공무원 임용령」제65조 등 관련 법령에 의거 **부정행위자**로 처리됩니다.

2. 시험 시작 즉시 **과목편철 순서, 문제누락 여부, 인쇄상태 이상 유무 및 표지와 개별과목의 문제책형 일치 여부 등을 확인**한 후 문제책 표지에 응시번호, 성명을 기재합니다.

3. 반드시 본인의 **응시표에 인쇄된 시험과목 순서에 따라** 제4과목과 제5과목의 **답안을 표기**하여야 합니다. 과목 순서를 바꾸어 표기한 경우에도 **본인의 응시표에 기재된 과목 순서대로 채점**되므로 반드시 유의하시기 바랍니다.

4. 시험이 시작되면 문제를 주의 깊게 읽은 후, **문항의 취지에 가장 적합한 하나의 정답만을 고르며**, 문제 내용에 관한 질문은 받지 않습니다.

5. **시험시간 관리의 책임**은 전적으로 응시자 본인에게 있습니다.

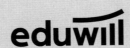

2024

| 풀이 시간: ___:___ ~ ___:___ / 점수: ___점

※ 밑줄 친 부분의 의미와 가장 가까운 것을 고르시오.

[문 1~문 4]

문 1.

> While Shakespeare's comedies share many similarities, they also differ underlined markedly from one another.

① softly
② obviously
③ marginally
④ indiscernibly

문 2.

> Jane poured out the strong, dark tea and diluted it with milk.

① washed
② weakened
③ connected
④ fermented

문 3.

> The Prime Minister is believed to have ruled out cuts in child benefit or pensions.

① excluded
② supported
③ submitted
④ authorized

문 4.

> If you let on that we are planning a surprise party, Dad will never stop asking you questions.

① reveal
② observe
③ believe
④ possess

문 5. 밑줄 친 부분에 들어갈 말로 가장 적절한 것은?

> Automatic doors in supermarkets _____ the entry and exit of customers with bags or shopping carts.

① ignore
② forgive
③ facilitate
④ exaggerate

문 6. 밑줄 친 부분 중 어법상 옳지 않은 것은?

> One of the many ① virtues of the book you are reading ② is that it provides an entry point into *Maps of Meaning*, ③ which is a highly complex work ④ because of the author was working out his approach to psychology as he wrote it.

문 7. 밑줄 친 부분이 어법상 옳지 않은 것은?

① You must plan not to spend too much on the project.
② My dog disappeared last month and hasn't been seen since.
③ I'm sad that the people who daughter I look after are moving away.
④ I bought a book on my trip, and it was twice as expensive as it was at home.

문 8. 우리말을 영어로 잘못 옮긴 것은?

① 그는 이곳에서 일하는 것이 흥미롭다는 것을 알았다.
→ He found it exciting to work here.
② 그녀는 나에게 일찍 떠날 것이라고 언급했다.
→ She mentioned me that she would be leaving early.
③ 나는 그가 오는 것을 원하지 않았다.
→ I didn't want him to come.
④ 좀 더 능숙하고 경험 많은 선생님이었다면 그를 달리 대했을 것이다.
→ A more skillful and experienced teacher would have treated him otherwise.

※ 밑줄 친 부분에 들어갈 말로 가장 적절한 것을 고르시오.
[문 9~문 11]

문 9.

> A: Charles, I think we need more chairs for our upcoming event.
> B: Really? I thought we already had enough chairs.
> A: My manager told me that more than 350 people are coming.
> B: _____
> A: I agree. I am also a bit surprised.
> B: Looks like I'll have to order more then. Thanks.

① I wonder if the manager is going to attend the event.
② I thought more than 350 people would be coming.
③ That's actually not a large number.
④ That's a lot more than I expected.

문 10.

> A: Can I get the document you referred to at the meeting yesterday?
> B: Sure. What's the title of the document?
> A: I can't remember its title, but it was about the community festival.
> B: Oh, I know what you're talking about.
> A: Great. Can you send it to me via email?
> B: I don't have it with me. Mr. Park is in charge of the project, so he should have it.
> A: _____
> B: Good luck. Hope you get the document you want.

① Can you check if he is in the office?
② Mr. Park has sent the email to you again.
③ Are you coming to the community festival?
④ Thank you for letting me know. I'll contact him.

문 11.

> A: Hello, can I ask you a question about the presentation next Tuesday?
> B: Do you mean the presentation about promoting the volunteer program?
> A: Yes. Where is the presentation going to be?
> B: Let me check. It is room 201.
> A: I see. Can I use my laptop in the room?
> B: Sure. We have a PC in the room, but you can use yours if you want.
> A: _____
> B: We can meet in the room two hours before the presentation. Would that work for you?
> A: Yes. Thank you very much!

① A computer technician was here an hour ago.
② When can I have a rehearsal for my presentation?
③ Should we recruit more volunteers for our program?
④ I don't feel comfortable leaving my laptop in the room.

문 12. 다음 이메일의 내용과 일치하지 않는 것은?

문 13. 다음 글의 내용과 일치하지 않는 것은?

According to the historians, neckties date back to 1660. In that year, a group of soldiers from Croatia visited Paris. These soldiers were war heroes whom King Louis XIV admired very much. Impressed with the colored scarves that they wore around their necks, the king decided to honor the Croats by creating a military regiment called the Royal Cravattes. The word *cravat* comes from the word *Croat*. All the soldiers in this regiment wore colorful scarves or cravats around their necks. This new style of neckwear traveled to England. Soon all upper class men were wearing cravats. Some cravats were quite extreme. At times, they were so high that a man could not move his head without turning his whole body. The cravats were made of many different materials from plaid to lace, which made them suitable for any occasion.

① A group of Croatian soldiers visited Paris in 1660.
② The Royal Cravattes was created in honor of the Croatian soldiers wearing scarves.
③ Some cravats were too uncomfortable for a man to move his head freely.
④ The materials used to make the cravats were limited.

① 주 회의실은 200명 이상의 대표자를 수용할 수 있어야 한다.
② wi-fi가 있는 작은 회의실 3개가 필요하다.
③ 3일간의 저녁 식사를 위한 식당 예약이 필요하다.
④ 매일 밤 100명 이상의 대표자를 위한 숙박시설이 필요하다.

문 14. 다음 글의 주제로 적절한 것은?

In recent years Latin America has made huge strides in exploiting its incredible wind, solar, geothermal and biofuel energy resources. Latin America's electricity sector has already begun to gradually decrease its dependence on oil. Latin America is expected to almost double its electricity output between 2015 and 2040. Practically none of Latin America's new large-scale power plants will be oil-fueled, which opens up the field for different technologies. Countries in Central America and the Caribbean, which traditionally imported oil, were the first to move away from oil-based power plants, after suffering a decade of high and volatile prices at the start of the century.

① booming oil industry in Latin America
② declining electricity business in Latin America
③ advancement of renewable energy in Latin America
④ aggressive exploitation of oil-based resources in Latin America

문 15. 다음 글의 제목으로 적절한 것은?

Every organization has resources that it can use to perform its mission. How well your organization does its job is partly a function of how many of those resources you have, but mostly it is a function of how well you use the resources you have, such as people and money. You as the organization's leader can always make the use of those resources more efficient and effective, provided that you have control of the organization's personnel and agenda, a condition that does not occur automatically. By managing your people and your money carefully, by treating the most important things as the most important, by making good decisions, and by solving the problems that you encounter, you can get the most out of what you have available to you.

① Exchanging Resources in an Organization
② Leaders' Ability to Set up External Control
③ Making the Most of the Resources: A Leader's Way
④ Technical Capacity of an Organization: A Barrier to Its Success

문 16. 다음 글의 흐름상 어색한 문장은?

Critical thinking sounds like an unemotional process but it can engage emotions and even passionate responses. In particular, we may not like evidence that contradicts our own opinions or beliefs. ① If the evidence points in a direction that is challenging, that can rouse unexpected feelings of anger, frustration or anxiety. ② The academic world traditionally likes to consider itself as logical and free of emotions, so if feelings do emerge, this can be especially difficult. ③ For example, looking at the same information from several points of view is not important. ④ Being able to manage your emotions under such circumstances is a useful skill. If you can remain calm, and present your reasons logically, you will be better able to argue your point of view in a convincing way.

문 17. 주어진 글 다음에 이어질 글의 순서로 적절한 것은?

Computer assisted language learning(CALL) is both exciting and frustrating as a field of research and practice.

(A) Yet the technology changes so rapidly that CALL knowledge and skills must be constantly renewed to stay apace of the field.
(B) It is exciting because it is complex, dynamic and quickly changing — and it is frustrating for the same reasons.
(C) Technology adds dimensions to the domain of language learning, requiring new knowledge and skills for those who wish to apply it into their professional practice.

① (A) − (C) − (B) ② (B) − (A) − (C)
③ (B) − (C) − (A) ④ (C) − (B) − (A)

문 18. 주어진 문장이 들어갈 위치로 적절한 것은?

But she quickly popped her head out again.

The little mermaid swam right up to the small window of the cabin, and every time a wave lifted her up, she could see a crowd of well-dressed people through the clear glass. Among them was a young prince, the handsomest person there, with large dark eyes. (①) It was his birthday, and that's why there was so much excitement. (②) When the young prince came out on the deck, where the sailors were dancing, more than a hundred rockets went up into the sky and broke into a glitter, making the sky as bright as day. (③) The little mermaid was so startled that she dove down under the water. (④) And look! It was just as if all the stars up in heaven were falling down on her. Never had she seen such fireworks.

※ 밑줄 친 부분에 들어갈 말로 적절한 것을 고르시오.
[문 19 ~ 문 20]

문 19.

Javelin Research noticed that not all Millennials are currently in the same stage of life. While all Millennials were born around the turn of the century, some of them are still in early adulthood, wrestling with new careers and settling down. On the other hand, the older Millennials have a home and are building a family. You can imagine how having a child might change your interests and priorities, so for marketing purposes, it's useful to split this generation into Gen Y.1 and Gen Y.2. Not only are the two groups culturally different, but they're in vastly different phases of their financial life. The younger group is financial beginners, just starting to show their buying power. The latter group has a credit history, may have their first mortgage and is raising young children. The _____ in priorities and needs between Gen Y.1 and Gen Y.2 is vast.

① contrast　　　　② reduction
③ repetition　　　④ ability

문 20.

Cost pressures in liberalized markets have different effects on existing and future hydropower schemes. Because of the cost structure, existing hydropower plants will always be able to earn a profit. Because the planning and construction of future hydropower schemes is not a short-term process, it is not a popular investment, in spite of low electricity generation costs. Most private investors would prefer to finance _____, leading to the paradoxical situation that although an existing hydropower plant seems to be a cash cow, nobody wants to invest in a new one. Where public shareholders/owners (states, cities, municipalities) are involved, the situation looks very different because they can see the importance of the security of supply and also appreciate long-term investments.

① more short-term technologies
② all high technology industries
③ the promotion of the public interest
④ the enhancement of electricity supply

해설편 ▶ P.72

2023

6월 10일 시행
지방직(= 서울시) 9급

| 풀이 시간: ____:____ ~ ____:____ / 점수: ____점

1초 합격예측! 모바일 성적분석표

QR 코드로 접속하여 문제 풀이시간을 측정하고, 〈1초 합격예측 & 모바일 성적분석표〉 서비스를 통해 지금 바로! 실력을 점검해 보세요.
https://eduwill.kr/q4Of

※ 밑줄 친 부분의 의미와 가장 가까운 것을 고르시오.
[문 1 ~ 문 4]

문 1.

Further explanations on our project will be given in subsequent presentations.

① required
② following
③ advanced
④ supplementary

문 2.

Folkways are customs that members of a group are expected to follow to show courtesy to others. For example, saying "excuse me" when you sneeze is an American folkway.

① charity
② humility
③ boldness
④ politeness

문 3.

These children have been brought up on a diet of healthy food.

① raised
② advised
③ observed
④ controlled

문 4.

Slavery was not done away with until the nineteenth century in the U.S.

① abolished
② consented
③ criticized
④ justified

문 5. 밑줄 친 부분에 들어갈 말로 가장 적절한 것은?

Voters demanded that there should be greater _____ in the election process so that they could see and understand it clearly.

① deception
② flexibility
③ competition
④ transparency

문 6. 밑줄 친 부분 중 어법상 옳지 않은 것은?

One reason for upsets in sports — ① in which the team ② predicted to win and supposedly superior to their opponents surprisingly loses the contest — is ③ what the superior team may not have perceived their opponents as ④ threatening to their continued success.

문 7. 밑줄 친 부분이 어법상 옳지 않은 것은?

① I should have gone this morning, but I was feeling a bit ill.
② These days we do not save as much money as we used to.
③ The rescue squad was happy to discover an alive man.
④ The picture was looked at carefully by the art critic.

문 8. 우리말을 영어로 잘못 옮긴 것은?

① 우리는 그의 연설에 감동하게 되었다.
→ We were made touching with his speech.

② 비용은 차치하고 그 계획은 훌륭한 것이었다.
→ Apart from its cost, the plan was a good one.

③ 그들은 뜨거운 차를 마시는 동안에 일몰을 보았다.
→ They watched the sunset while drinking hot tea.

④ 과거 경력 덕분에 그는 그 프로젝트에 적합하였다.
→ His past experience made him suited for the project.

※ 밑줄 친 부분에 들어갈 말로 가장 적절한 것을 고르시오.
[문 9 ~ 문 10]

문 9.

A: Pardon me, but could you give me a hand, please?
B: _____
A: I'm trying to find the Personnel Department. I have an appointment at 10.
B: It's on the third floor.
A: How can I get up there?
B: Take the elevator around the corner.

① We have no idea how to handle this situation.
② Would you mind telling us who is in charge?
③ Yes. I could use some help around here.
④ Sure. Can I help you with anything?

문 10.

A: You were the last one who left the office, weren't you?
B: Yes. Is there any problem?
A: I found the office lights and air conditioners on this morning.
B: Really? Oh, no. Maybe I forgot to turn them off last night.
A: Probably they were on all night.
B: _____

① Don't worry. This machine is working fine.
② That's right. Everyone likes to work with you.
③ I'm sorry. I promise I'll be more careful from now on.
④ Too bad. You must be tired because you get off work too late.

문 11. 두 사람의 대화 중 자연스럽지 않은 것은?

① A: How would you like your hair done?
B: I'm a little tired of my hair color. I'd like to dye it.

② A: What can we do to slow down global warming?
B: First of all, we can use more public transportation.

③ A: Anna, is that you? Long time no see! How long has it been?
B: It took me about an hour and a half by car.

④ A: I'm worried about Paul. He looks unhappy. What should I do?
B: If I were you, I'd wait until he talks about his troubles.

문 12. 다음 글의 제목으로 가장 적절한 것은?

Well-known author Daniel Goleman has dedicated his life to the science of human relationships. In his book *Social Intelligence* he discusses results from neuro-sociology to explain how sociable our brains are. According to Goleman, we are drawn to other people's brains whenever we engage with another person. The human need for meaningful connectivity with others, in order to deepen our relationships, is what we all crave, and yet there are countless articles and studies suggesting that we are lonelier than we ever have been and loneliness is now a world health epidemic. Specifically, in Australia, according to a national Lifeline survey, more than 80% of those surveyed believe our society is becoming a lonelier place. Yet, our brains crave human interaction.

① Lonely People
② Sociable Brains
③ Need for Mental Health Survey
④ Dangers of Human Connectivity

문 13. 다음 글의 주제로 가장 적절한 것은?

Certainly some people are born with advantages (e.g., physical size for jockeys, height for basketball players, an "ear" for music for musicians). Yet only dedication to mindful, deliberate practice over many years can turn those advantages into talents and those talents into successes. Through the same kind of dedicated practice, people who are not born with such advantages can develop talents that nature put a little farther from their reach. For example, even though you may feel that you weren't born with a talent for math, you can significantly increase your mathematical abilities through mindful, deliberate practice. Or, if you consider yourself "naturally" shy, putting in the time and effort to develop your social skills can enable you to interact with people at social occasions with energy, grace, and ease.

① advantages some people have over others
② importance of constant efforts to cultivate talents
③ difficulties shy people have in social interactions
④ need to understand one's own strengths and weaknesses

문 14. 다음 글의 요지로 가장 적절한 것은?

Dr. Roossinck and her colleagues found by chance that a virus increased resistance to drought on a plant that is widely used in botanical experiments. Their further experiments with a related virus showed that was true of 15 other plant species, too. Dr. Roossinck is now doing experiments to study another type of virus that increases heat tolerance in a range of plants. She hopes to extend her research to have a deeper understanding of the advantages that different sorts of viruses give to their hosts. That would help to support a view which is held by an increasing number of biologists, that many creatures rely on symbiosis, rather than being self-sufficient.

① Viruses demonstrate self-sufficiency of biological beings.
② Biologists should do everything to keep plants virus-free.
③ The principle of symbiosis cannot be applied to infected plants.
④ Viruses sometimes do their hosts good, rather than harming them.

문 15. 다음 글의 내용과 일치하지 않는 것은?

> The traditional way of making maple syrup is interesting. A sugar maple tree produces a watery sap each spring, when there is still lots of snow on the ground. To take the sap out of the sugar maple tree, a farmer makes a slit in the bark with a special knife, and puts a "tap" on the tree. Then the farmer hangs a bucket from the tap, and the sap drips into it. That sap is collected and boiled until a sweet syrup remains—forty gallons of sugar maple tree "water" make one gallon of syrup. That's a lot of buckets, a lot of steam, and a lot of work. Even so, most of maple syrup producers are family farmers who collect the buckets by hand and boil the sap into syrup themselves.

① 사탕단풍나무에서는 매년 봄에 수액이 생긴다.
② 사탕단풍나무의 수액을 얻기 위해 나무껍질에 틈새를 만든다.
③ 단풍나무시럽 1갤론을 만들려면 수액 40갤론이 필요하다.
④ 단풍나무시럽을 만들기 위해 기계로 수액 통을 수거한다.

문 16. 다음 글의 흐름상 어색한 문장은?

> I once took a course in short-story writing and during that course a renowned editor of a leading magazine talked to our class. ① He said he could pick up any one of the dozens of stories that came to his desk every day and after reading a few paragraphs he could feel whether or not the author liked people. ② "If the author doesn't like people," he said, "people won't like his or her stories." ③ The editor kept stressing the importance of being interested in people during his talk on fiction writing. ④ Thurston, a great magician, said that every time he went on stage he said to himself, "I am grateful because I'm successful." At the end of the talk, he concluded, "Let me tell you again. You have to be interested in people if you want to be a successful writer of stories."

문 17. 주어진 글 다음에 이어질 글의 순서로 가장 적절한 것은?

> Just a few years ago, every conversation about artificial intelligence (AI) seemed to end with an apocalyptic prediction.

> (A) More recently, however, things have begun to change. AI has gone from being a scary black box to something people can use for a variety of use cases.
> (B) In 2014, an expert in the field said that, with AI, we are summoning the demon, while a Nobel Prize winning physicist said that AI could spell the end of the human race.
> (C) This shift is because these technologies are finally being explored at scale in the industry, particularly for market opportunities.

① (A) − (B) − (C)
② (B) − (A) − (C)
③ (B) − (C) − (A)
④ (C) − (A) − (B)

문 18. 주어진 문장이 들어갈 위치로 가장 적절한 것은?

> Yet, requests for such self-assessments are pervasive throughout one's career.

> The fiscal quarter just ended. Your boss comes by to ask you how well you performed in terms of sales this quarter. How do you describe your performance? As excellent? Good? Terrible? (①) Unlike when someone asks you about an objective performance metric (e.g., how many dollars in sales you brought in this quarter), how to subjectively describe your performance is often unclear. There is no right answer. (②) You are asked to subjectively describe your own performance in school applications, in job applications, in interviews, in performance reviews, in meetings—the list goes on. (③) How you describe your performance is what we call your level of self-promotion. (④) Since self-promotion is a pervasive part of work, people who do more self-promotion may have better chances of being hired, being promoted, and getting a raise or a bonus.

※ 밑줄 친 부분에 들어갈 말로 가장 적절한 것을 고르시오.
[문 19 ~ 문 20]

문 19.

We live in the age of anxiety. Because being anxious can be an uncomfortable and scary experience, we resort to conscious or unconscious strategies that help reduce anxiety in the moment— watching a movie or TV show, eating, video-game playing, and overworking. In addition, smartphones also provide a distraction any time of the day or night. Psychological research has shown that distractions serve as a common anxiety avoidance strategy. _____, however, these avoidance strategies make anxiety worse in the long run. Being anxious is like getting into quicksand — the more you fight it, the deeper you sink. Indeed, research strongly supports a well-known phrase that "What you resist, persists."

① Paradoxically
② Fortunately
③ Neutrally
④ Creatively

문 20.

How many different ways do you get information? Some people might have six different kinds of communications to answer — text messages, voice mails, paper documents, regular mail, blog posts, messages on different online services. Each of these is a type of in-box, and each must be processed on a continuous basis. It's an endless process, but it doesn't have to be exhausting or stressful. Getting your information management down to a more manageable level and into a productive zone starts by _____. Every place you have to go to check your messages or to read your incoming information is an in-box, and the more you have, the harder it is to manage everything. Cut the number of in-boxes you have down to the smallest number possible for you still to function in the ways you need to.

① setting several goals at once
② immersing yourself in incoming information
③ minimizing the number of in-boxes you have
④ choosing information you are passionate about

해설편 ▶ P.77

2022

6월 18일 시행
지방직(= 서울시) 9급

| 풀이 시간: ____:____ ~ ____:____ / 점수: ____ 점

1초 합격예측! 모바일 성적분석표

QR 코드로 접속하여 문제 풀이시간을 측정하고, 〈1초 합격예측 & 모바일 성적분석표〉 서비스를 통해 지금 바로! 실력을 점검해 보세요.

http://eduwill.kr/nH6j

※ 밑줄 친 부분의 의미와 가장 가까운 것을 고르시오.

[문 1 ~ 문 3]

문 1.
School teachers have to be flexible to cope with different ability levels of the students.

① strong   ② adaptable
③ honest   ④ passionate

문 2.
Crop yields vary, improving in some areas and falling in others.

① change   ② decline
③ expand   ④ include

문 3.
I don't feel inferior to anyone with respect to my education.

① in danger of   ② in spite of
③ in favor of   ④ in terms of

문 4. 밑줄 친 부분에 들어갈 말로 가장 적절한 것은?

Sometimes we _____ money long before the next payday.

① turn into   ② start over
③ put up with   ④ run out of

※ 어법상 옳지 않은 것을 고르시오. [문 5 ~ 문 6]

문 5. ① He asked me why I kept coming back day after day.
② Toys children wanted all year long has recently discarded.
③ She is someone who is always ready to lend a helping hand.
④ Insects are often attracted by scents that aren't obvious to us.

문 6. ① You can write on both sides of the paper.
② My home offers me a feeling of security, warm, and love.
③ The number of car accidents is on the rise.
④ Had I realized what you were intending to do, I would have stopped you.

※ 우리말을 영어로 잘못 옮긴 것을 고르시오. [문 7 ~ 문 8]

문 7. ① 나는 단 한 푼의 돈도 낭비할 수 없다.
→ I can afford to waste even one cent.
② 그녀의 얼굴에서 미소가 곧 사라졌다.
→ The smile soon faded from her face.
③ 그녀는 사임하는 것 외에는 대안이 없었다.
→ She had no alternative but to resign.
④ 나는 5년 후에 내 사업을 시작할 작정이다.
→ I'm aiming to start my own business in five years.

문 8. ① 식사를 마치자마자 나는 다시 배고프기 시작했다.
   → No sooner I have finishing the meal than I started feeling hungry again.
② 그녀는 조만간 요금을 내야만 할 것이다.
   → She will have to pay the bill sooner or later.
③ 독서와 정신의 관계는 운동과 신체의 관계와 같다.
   → Reading is to the mind what exercise is to the body.
④ 그는 대학에서 의학을 공부했으나 결국 회계 회사에서 일하게 되었다.
   → He studied medicine at university but ended up working for an accounting firm.

문 9. 두 사람의 대화 중 가장 어색한 것은?
① A: I like this newspaper because it's not opinionated.
   B: That's why it has the largest circulation.
② A: Do you have a good reason for being all dressed up?
   B: Yeah, I have an important job interview today.
③ A: I can hit the ball straight during the practice but not during the game.
   B: That happens to me all the time, too.
④ A: Is there any particular subject you want to paint on canvas?
   B: I didn't do good in history when I was in high school.

문 10. 밑줄 친 부분에 들어갈 말로 가장 적절한 것은?

A: Hey! How did your geography test go?
B: Not bad, thanks. I'm just glad that it's over! How about you? How did your science exam go?
A: Oh, it went really well. _____. I owe you a treat for that.
B: It's my pleasure. So, do you feel like preparing for the math exam scheduled for next week?
A: Sure. Let's study together.
B: It sounds good. See you later.

① There's no sense in beating yourself up over this
② I never thought I would see you here
③ Actually, we were very disappointed
④ I can't thank you enough for helping me with it

문 11. 주어진 글 다음에 이어질 글의 순서로 가장 적절한 것은?

For people who are blind, everyday tasks such as sorting through the mail or doing a load of laundry present a challenge.

(A) That's the thinking behind Aira, a new service that enables its thousands of users to stream live video of their surroundings to an on-demand agent, using either a smartphone or Aira's proprietary glasses.
(B) But what if they could "borrow" the eyes of someone who could see?
(C) The Aira agents, who are available 24/7, can then answer questions, describe objects or guide users through a location.

① (A) – (B) – (C)   ② (A) – (C) – (B)
③ (B) – (A) – (C)   ④ (C) – (A) – (B)

문 12. 주어진 문장이 들어갈 위치로 가장 적절한 곳은?

> The comparison of the heart to a pump, however, is a genuine analogy.

An analogy is a figure of speech in which two things are asserted to be alike in many respects that are quite fundamental. Their structure, the relationships of their parts, or the essential purposes they serve are similar, although the two things are also greatly dissimilar. Roses and carnations are not analogous. (①) They both have stems and leaves and may both be red in color. (②) But they exhibit these qualities in the same way; they are of the same genus. (③) These are disparate things, but they share important qualities: mechanical apparatus, possession of valves, ability to increase and decrease pressures, and capacity to move fluids. (④) And the heart and the pump exhibit these qualities in different ways and in different contexts.

문 13. 다음 글의 제목으로 가장 적절한 것은?

One of the areas where efficiency can be optimized is the work force, through increasing individual productivity — defined as the amount of work (products produced, customers served) an employee handles in a given time. In addition to making sure you have invested in the right equipment, environment, and training to ensure optimal performance, you can increase productivity by encouraging staffers to put an end to a modern-day energy drain: multitasking. Studies show it takes 25 to 40 percent longer to get a job done when you're simultaneously trying to work on other projects. To be more productive, says Andrew Deutscher, vice president of business development at consulting firm The Energy Project, "do one thing, uninterrupted, for a sustained period of time."

① How to Create More Options in Life
② How to Enhance Daily Physical Performance
③ Multitasking is the Answer for Better Efficiency
④ Do One Thing at a Time for Greater Efficiency

문 14. 글의 흐름상 가장 어색한 문장은?

The skill to have a good argument is critical in life. But it's one that few parents teach to their children. ① We want to give kids a stable home, so we stop siblings from quarreling and we have our own arguments behind closed doors. ② Yet if kids never get exposed to disagreement, we may eventually limit their creativity. ③ Children are most creative when they are free to brainstorm with lots of praise and encouragement in a peaceful environment. ④ It turns out that highly creative people often grow up in families full of tension. They are not surrounded by fistfights or personal insults, but real disagreements. When adults in their early 30s were asked to write imaginative stories, the most creative ones came from those whose parents had the most conflict a quarter-century earlier.

※ 다음 글의 내용과 일치하지 않는 것을 고르시오.
[문 15 ~ 문 16]

문 15.

Christopher Nolan is an Irish writer of some renown in the English language. Brain damaged since birth, Nolan has had little control over the muscles of his body, even to the extent of having difficulty in swallowing food. He must be strapped to his wheelchair because he cannot sit up by himself. Nolan cannot utter recognizable speech sounds. Fortunately, though, his brain damage was such that Nolan's intelligence was undamaged and his hearing was normal; as a result, he learned to understand speech as a young child. It was only many years later, though, after he had reached 10 years, and after he had learned to read, that he was given a means to express his first words. He did this by using a stick which was attached to his head to point to letters. It was in this 'unicorn' manner, letter-by-letter, that he produced an entire book of poems and short stories, *Dam-Burst of Dreams*, while still a teenager.

① Christopher Nolan은 뇌 손상을 갖고 태어났다.
② Christopher Nolan은 음식을 삼키는 것도 어려웠다.
③ Christopher Nolan은 청각 장애로 인해 들을 수 없었다.
④ Christopher Nolan은 10대일 때 책을 썼다.

문 16.

In many Catholic countries, children are often named after saints; in fact, some priests will not allow parents to name their children after soap opera stars or football players. Protestant countries tend to be more free about this; however, in Norway, certain names such as Adolf are banned completely. In countries where infant mortality is very high, such as in Africa, tribes only name their children when they reach five years old, the age in which their chances of survival begin to increase. Until that time, they are referred to by the number of years they are. Many nations in the Far East give their children a unique name which in some way describes the circumstances of the child's birth or the parents' expectations and hopes for the child. Some Australian aborigines can keep changing their name throughout their life as the result of some important experience which has in some way proved their wisdom, creativity or determination. For example, if one day, one of them dances extremely well, he or she may decide to re-name him/herself 'supreme dancer' or 'light feet'.

① Children are frequently named after saints in many Catholic countries.

② Some African children are not named until they turn five years old.

③ Changing one's name is totally unacceptable in the culture of Australian aborigines.

④ Various cultures name their children in different ways.

문 17. 다음 글의 요지로 가장 적절한 것은?

In one study, done in the early 1970s when young people tended to dress in either "hippie" or "straight" fashion, experimenters donned hippie or straight attire and asked college students on campus for a dime to make a phone call. When the experimenter was dressed in the same way as the student, the request was granted in more than two-thirds of the instances; when the student and requester were dissimilarly dressed, the dime was provided less than half the time. Another experiment showed how automatic our positive response to similar others can be. Marchers in an antiwar demonstration were found to be more likely to sign the petition of a similarly dressed requester and to do so without bothering to read it first.

① People are more likely to help those who dress like themselves.

② Dressing up formally increases the chance of signing the petition.

③ Making a phone call is an efficient way to socialize with other students.

④ Some college students in the early 1970s were admired for their unique fashion.

문 18. (A)와 (B)에 들어갈 말로 가장 적절한 것은?

Duration shares an inverse relationship with frequency. If you see a friend frequently, then the duration of the encounter will be shorter. Conversely, if you don't see your friend very often, the duration of your visit will typically increase significantly. _____(A)_____, if you see a friend every day, the duration of your visits can be low because you can keep up with what's going on as events unfold. If, however, you only see your friend twice a year, the duration of your visits will be greater. Think back to a time when you had dinner in a restaurant with a friend you hadn't seen for a long period of time. You probably spent several hours catching up on each other's lives. The duration of the same dinner would be considerably shorter if you saw the person on a regular basis. _____(B)_____, in romantic relationships the frequency and duration are very high because couples, especially newly minted ones, want to spend as much time with each other as possible. The intensity of the relationship will also be very high.

	(A)	(B)
①	For example	Conversely
②	Nonetheless	Furthermore
③	Therefore	As a result
④	In the same way	Thus

※ 밑줄 친 부분에 들어갈 말로 가장 적절한 것을 고르시오.
[문 19 ~ 문 20]

문 19.

One of the most frequently used propaganda techniques is to convince the public that the propagandist's views reflect those of the common person and that he or she is working in their best interests. A politician speaking to a blue-collar audience may roll up his sleeves, undo his tie, and attempt to use the specific idioms of the crowd. He may even use language incorrectly on purpose to give the impression that he is "just one of the folks." This technique usually also employs the use of glittering generalities to give the impression that the politician's views are the same as those of the crowd being addressed. Labor leaders, businesspeople, ministers, educators, and advertisers have used this technique to win our confidence by appearing to be _____.

① beyond glittering generalities
② just plain folks like ourselves
③ something different from others
④ better educated than the crowd

문 20.

As a roller coaster climbs the first lift hill of its track, it is building potential energy — the higher it gets above the earth, the stronger the pull of gravity will be. When the coaster crests the lift hill and begins its descent, its potential energy becomes kinetic energy, or the energy of movement. A common misperception is that a coaster loses energy along the track. An important law of physics, however, called the law of conservation of energy, is that energy can never be created nor destroyed. It simply changes from one form to another. Whenever a track rises back uphill, the cars' momentum — their kinetic energy — will carry them upward, which builds potential energy, and roller coasters repeatedly convert potential energy to kinetic energy and back again. At the end of a ride, coaster cars are slowed down by brake mechanisms that create _____ between two surfaces. This motion makes them hot, meaning kinetic energy is changed to heat energy during braking. Riders may mistakenly think coasters lose energy at the end of the track, but the energy just changes to and from different forms.

① gravity ② friction
③ vaccum ④ acceleration

ㅣ풀이 시간: _____:_____ ~ _____:_____ / 점수: _____점

문 1. 밑줄 친 부분의 의미와 가장 가까운 것은?

> For many compulsive buyers, the act of purchasing, rather than what they buy, is what leads to gratification.

① liveliness   ② confidence
③ tranquility   ④ satisfaction

※ 밑줄 친 부분에 들어갈 말로 가장 적절한 것을 고르시오.

[문 2 ~ 문 4]

문 2.

> Globalization leads more countries to open their markets, allowing them to trade goods and services freely at a lower cost with greater _____.

① extinction   ② depression
③ efficiency   ④ caution

문 3.

> We're familiar with the costs of burnout: Energy, motivation, productivity, engagement, and commitment can all take a hit, at work and at home. And many of the _____ are fairly intuitive: Regularly unplug. Reduce unnecessary meetings. Exercise. Schedule small breaks during the day. Take vacations even if you think you can't afford to be away from work, because you can't afford not to be away now and then.

① fixes   ② damages
③ prizes   ④ complications

문 4.

> The government is seeking ways to soothe salaried workers over their increased tax burdens arising from a new tax settlement system. During his meeting with the presidential aides last Monday, the President _____ those present to open up more communication channels with the public.

① fell on   ② called for
③ picked up   ④ turned down

문 5. 밑줄 친 부분의 의미와 가장 가까운 것은?

> In studying Chinese calligraphy, one must learn something of the origins of Chinese language and of how they were originally written. However, except for those brought up in the artistic traditions of the country, its aesthetic significance seems to be very difficult to apprehend.

① encompass   ② intrude
③ inspect   ④ grasp

※ 우리말을 영어로 잘못 옮긴 것을 고르시오.   [문 6 ~ 문 7]

문 6. ① 그의 소설들은 읽기가 어렵다.
  → His novels are hard to read.
② 학생들을 설득하려고 해 봐야 소용없다.
  → It is no use trying to persuade the students.
③ 나의 집은 5년마다 페인트칠된다.
  → My house is painted every five years.
④ 내가 출근할 때 한 가족이 위층에 이사 오는 것을 보았다.
  → As I went out for work, I saw a family moved in upstairs.

문 7. ① 경찰 당국은 자신의 이웃을 공격했기 때문에 그 여성을 체포하도록 했다.
  → The police authorities had the woman arrested for attacking her neighbor.
② 네가 내는 소음 때문에 내 집중력을 잃게 하지 말아라.
  → Don't let me distracted by the noise you make.
③ 가능한 한 빨리 제가 결과를 알도록 해 주세요.
  → Please let me know the result as soon as possible.
④ 그는 학생들에게 모르는 사람들에게 전화를 걸어 성금을 기부할 것을 부탁하도록 시켰다.
  → He had the students phone strangers and ask them to donate money.

문 8. 어법상 옳은 것은?

① My sweet-natured daughter suddenly became unpredictably.

② She attempted a new method, and needless to say had different results.

③ Upon arrived, he took full advantage of the new environment.

④ He felt enough comfortable to tell me about something he wanted to do.

문 9. 다음 글의 제목으로 가장 적절한 것은?

　The definition of 'turn' casts the digital turn as an analytical strategy which enables us to focus on the role of digitalization within social reality. As an analytical perspective, the digital turn makes it possible to analyze and discuss the societal meaning of digitalization. The term 'digital turn' thus signifies an analytical approach which centers on the role of digitalization within a society. If the linguistic turn is defined by the epistemological assumption that reality is constructed through language, the digital turn is based on the assumption that social reality is increasingly defined by digitalization. Social media symbolize the digitalization of social relations. Individuals increasingly engage in identity management on social networking sites(SNS). SNS are polydirectional, meaning that users can connect to each other and share information.

*epistemological 인식론의

① Remaking Identities on SNS

② Linguistic Turn Versus Digital Turn

③ How to Share Information in the Digital Age

④ Digitalization Within the Context of Social Reality

문 10. 주어진 글 다음에 이어질 글의 순서로 가장 적절한 것은?

　Growing concern about global climate change has motivated activists to organize not only campaigns against fossil fuel extraction consumption, but also campaigns to support renewable energy.

(A) This solar cooperative produces enough energy to power 1,400 homes, making it the first large-scale solar farm cooperative in the country and, in the words of its members, a visible reminder that solar power represents "a new era of sustainable and 'democratic' energy supply that enables ordinary people to produce clean power, not only on their rooftops, but also at utility scale."

(B) Similarly, renewable energy enthusiasts from the United States have founded the Clean Energy Collective, a company that has pioneered "the model of delivering clean power-generation through medium-scale facilities that are collectively owned by participating utility customers."

(C) Environmental activists frustrated with the UK government's inability to rapidly accelerate the growth of renewable energy industries have formed the Westmill Wind Farm Co-operative, a community-owned organization with more than 2,000 members who own an onshore wind farm estimated to produce as much electricity in a year as that used by 2,500 homes. The Westmill Wind Farm Co-operative has inspired local citizens to form the Westmill Solar Co-operative.

① (C) − (A) − (B)　　② (A) − (C) − (B)

③ (B) − (C) − (A)　　④ (C) − (B) − (A)

문 11. 밑줄 친 부분에 들어갈 말로 가장 적절한 것은?

A: Did you have a nice weekend?

B: Yes, it was pretty good. We went to the movies.

A: Oh! What did you see?

B: *Interstellar*. It was really good.

A: Really? _____

B: The special effects. They were fantastic. I wouldn't mind seeing it again.

① What did you like the most about it?

② What's your favorite movie genre?

③ Was the film promoted internationally?

④ Was the movie very costly?

문 12. 두 사람의 대화 중 가장 어색한 것은?

① A: I'm so nervous about this speech that I must give today.

B: The most important thing is to stay cool.

② A: You know what? Minsu and Yujin are tying the knot!

B: Good for them! When are they getting married?

③ A: A two-month vacation just passed like one week. A new semester is around the corner.

B: That's the word. Vacation has dragged on for weeks.

④ A: How do you say 'water' in French?

B: It is right on the tip of my tongue, but I can't remember it.

문 13. 다음 글의 내용과 일치하지 않는 것은?

Women are experts at gossiping, and they always talk about trivial things, or at least that's what men have always thought. However, some new research suggests that when women talk to women, their conversations are far from frivolous, and cover many more topics (up to 40 subjects) than when men talk to other men. Women's conversations range from health to their houses, from politics to fashion, from movies to family, from education to relationship problems, but sports are notably absent. Men tend to have a more limited range of subjects, the most popular being work, sports, jokes, cars, and women. According to Professor Petra Boynton, a psychologist who interviewed over 1,000 women, women also tend to move quickly from one subject to another in conversation, while men usually stick to one subject for longer periods of time. At work, this difference can be an advantage for men, as they can put other matters aside and concentrate fully on the topic being discussed. On the other hand, it also means that they sometimes find it hard to concentrate when several things have to be discussed at the same time in a meeting.

① 남성들은 여성들의 대화 주제가 항상 사소한 것들이라고 생각해 왔다.

② 여성들의 대화 주제는 건강에서 스포츠에 이르기까지 매우 다양하다.

③ 여성들은 대화하는 중에 주제의 변환을 빨리한다.

④ 남성들은 회의 중 여러 주제가 논의될 때 집중하기 어렵다.

문 14. 다음 글의 흐름상 적절하지 않은 문장은?

There was no divide between science, philosophy, and magic in the 15th century. All three came under the general heading of 'natural philosophy'. ① Central to the development of natural philosophy was the recovery of classical authors, most importantly the work of Aristotle. ② Humanists quickly realized the power of the printing press for spreading their knowledge. ③ At the beginning of the 15th century Aristotle remained the basis for all scholastic speculation on philosophy and science. ④ Kept alive in the Arabic translations and commentaries of Averroes and Avicenna, Aristotle provided a systematic perspective on mankind's relationship with the natural world. Surviving texts like his *Physics*, *Metaphysics*, and *Meteorology* provided scholars with the logical tools to understand the forces that created the natural world.

문 15. 어법상 옳지 않은 것은?

① Fire following an earthquake is of special interest to the insurance industry.

② Word processors were considered to be the ultimate tool for a typist in the past.

③ Elements of income in a cash forecast will be vary according to the company's circumstances.

④ The world's first digital camera was created by Steve Sasson at Eastman Kodak in 1975.

※ 밑줄 친 부분에 들어갈 말로 가장 적절한 것을 고르시오.

[문 16 ~ 문 17]

문 16.

The slowing of China's economy from historically high rates of growth has long been expected to ＿＿＿＿＿ growth elsewhere. "The China that had been growing at 10 percent for 30 years was a powerful source of fuel for much of what drove the global economy forward", said Stephen Roach at Yale. The growth rate has slowed to an official figure of around 7 percent. "That's a concrete deceleration", Mr. Roach added.

① speed up

② weigh on

③ lead to

④ result in

문 17.

As more and more leaders work remotely or with teams scattered around the nation or the globe, as well as with consultants and freelancers, you'll have to give them more _____. The more trust you bestow, the more others trust you. I am convinced that there is a direct correlation between job satisfaction and how empowered people are to fully execute their job without someone shadowing them every step of the way. Giving away responsibility to those you trust can not only make your organization run more smoothly but also free up more of your time so you can focus on larger issues.

① work
② rewards
③ restrictions
④ autonomy

문 18. 다음 글의 요지로 가장 적절한 것은?

"In Judaism, we're largely defined by our actions," says Lisa Grushcow, the senior rabbi at Temple Emanu-El-Beth Sholom in Montreal. "You can't really be an armchair do-gooder." This concept relates to the Jewish notion of tikkun olam, which translates as "to repair the world." Our job as human beings, she says, "is to mend what's been broken. It's incumbent on us to not only take care of ourselves and each other but also to build a better world around us." This philosophy conceptualizes goodness as something based in service. Instead of asking "Am I a good person?" you may want to ask "What good do I do in the world?" Grushcow's temple puts these beliefs into action inside and outside their community. For instance, they sponsored two refugee families from Vietnam to come to Canada in the 1970s.

① We should work to heal the world.
② Community should function as a shelter.
③ We should conceptualize goodness as beliefs.
④ Temples should contribute to the community.

문 19. (A)와 (B)에 들어갈 말로 가장 적절한 것은?

Ancient philosophers and spiritual teachers understood the need to balance the positive with the negative, optimism with pessimism, a striving for success and security with an openness to failure and uncertainty. The Stoics recommended "the premeditation of evils," or deliberately visualizing the worst-case scenario. This tends to reduce anxiety about the future: when you soberly picture how badly things could go in reality, you usually conclude that you could cope. _____(A)_____, they noted, imagining that you might lose the relationships and possessions you currently enjoy increases your gratitude for having them now. Positive thinking, _____(B)_____, always leans into the future, ignoring present pleasures.

	(A)	(B)
①	Nevertheless	in addition
②	Furthermore	for example
③	Besides	by contrast
④	However	in conclusion

문 20. 주어진 문장이 들어갈 위치로 가장 적절한 것은?

And working offers more than financial security.

Why do workaholics enjoy their jobs so much? Mostly because working offers some important advantages. (①) It provides people with paychecks — a way to earn a living. (②) It provides people with self-confidence; they have a feeling of satisfaction when they've produced a challenging piece of work and are able to say, "I made that". (③) Psychologists claim that work also gives people an identity; they work so that they can get a sense of self and individualism. (④) In addition, most jobs provide people with a socially acceptable way to meet others. It could be said that working is a positive addiction; maybe workaholics are compulsive about their work, but their addiction seems to be a safe — even an advantageous — one.

해설편 ▶ P.87

2020

| 풀이 시간: ____:____ ~ ____:____ / 점수: ____점

1초 합격예측! 모바일 성적분석표

QR 코드로 접속하여 문제 풀이시간을 측정하고,
〈1초 합격예측 & 모바일 성적분석표〉 서비스를 통해
지금 바로! 실력을 점검해 보세요.
http://eduwill.kr/8iy6

문 1. 밑줄 친 부분에 들어갈 말로 가장 적절한 것은?

> The issue with plastic bottles is that they're not _____, so when the temperatures begin to rise, your water will also heat up.

① sanitary
② insulated
③ recyclable
④ waterproof

※ 밑줄 친 부분의 의미와 가장 가까운 것을 고르시오.
[문 2 ~ 문 4]

문 2.

> The cruel sights touched off thoughts that otherwise wouldn't have entered her mind.

① looked after
② gave rise to
③ made up for
④ kept in contact with

문 3.

> Strategies that a writer adopts during the writing process may alleviate the difficulty of attentional overload.

① complement
② accelerate
③ calculate
④ relieve

문 4.

> The school bully did not know what it was like to be shunned by the other students in the class.

① avoided
② warned
③ punished
④ imitated

문 5. 어법상 옳은 것은?

① Of the billions of stars in the galaxy, how much are able to hatch life?
② The Christmas party was really excited and I totally lost track of time.
③ I must leave right now because I am starting work at noon today.
④ They used to loving books much more when they were younger.

문 6. 밑줄 친 부분의 의미와 가장 가까운 것은?

> After Francesca made a case for staying at home during the summer holidays, an uncomfortable silence fell on the dinner table. Robert was not sure if it was the right time for him to tell her about his grandiose plan.

① objected to
② dreamed about
③ completely excluded
④ strongly suggested

문 7. 우리말을 영어로 잘못 옮긴 것은?

① 보증이 만료되어서 수리는 무료가 아니었다.
→ Since the warranty had expired, the repairs were not free of charge.
② 설문지를 완성하는 누구에게나 선물카드가 주어질 예정이다.
→ A gift card will be given to whomever completes the questionnaire.
③ 지난달 내가 휴가를 요청했더라면 지금 하와이에 있을 텐데.
→ If I had asked for a vacation last month, I would be in Hawaii now.
④ 그의 아버지가 갑자기 작년에 돌아가셨고, 설상가상으로 그의 어머니도 병에 걸리셨다.
→ His father suddenly passed away last year, and, what was worse, his mother became sick.

문 8. 밑줄 친 부분 중 어법상 옳지 않은 것은?

> Elizabeth Taylor had an eye for beautiful jewels and over the years amassed some amazing pieces, once ① declaring "a girl can always have more diamonds." In 2011, her finest jewels were sold by Christie's at an evening auction ② that brought in $115.9 million. Among her most prized possessions sold during the evening sale ③ were a 1961 bejeweled timepiece by Bulgari. Designed as a serpent to coil around the wrist, with its head and tail ④ covered with diamonds and having two hypnotic emerald eyes, a discreet mechanism opens its fierce jaws to reveal a tiny quartz watch.

문 9. 밑줄 친 (A), (B)에 들어갈 말로 가장 적절한 것은?

> Assertive behavior involves standing up for your rights and expressing your thoughts and feelings in a direct, appropriate way that does not violate the rights of others. It is a matter of getting the other person to understand your viewpoint. People who exhibit assertive behavior skills are able to handle conflict situations with ease and assurance while maintaining good interpersonal relations. _____(A)_____, aggressive behavior involves expressing your thoughts and feelings and defending your rights in a way that openly violates the rights of others. Those exhibiting aggressive behavior seem to believe that the rights of others must be subservient to theirs. _____(B)_____, they have a difficult time maintaining good interpersonal relations. They are likely to interrupt, talk fast, ignore others, and use sarcasm or other forms of verbal abuse to maintain control.

	(A)	(B)
①	In contrast	Thus
②	Similarly	Moreover
③	However	On one hand
④	Accordingly	On the other hand

문 10. 다음 글의 주제로 가장 적절한 것은?

> The e-book applications available on tablet computers employ touchscreen technology. Some touchscreens feature a glass panel covering two electronically-charged metallic surfaces lying face-to-face. When the screen is touched, the two metallic surfaces feel the pressure and make contact. This pressure sends an electrical signal to the computer, which translates the touch into a command. This version of the touchscreen is known as a resistive screen because the screen reacts to pressure from the finger. Other tablet computers feature a single electrified metallic layer under the glass panel. When the user touches the screen, some of the current passes through the glass into the user's finger. When the charge is transferred, the computer interprets the loss in power as a command and carries out the function the user desires. This type of screen is known as a capacitive screen.

① how users learn new technology
② how e-books work on tablet computers
③ how touchscreen technology works
④ how touchscreens have evolved

문 11. 밑줄 친 부분에 들어갈 말로 가장 적절한 것은?

> A: Oh, another one! So many junk emails!
> B: I know. I receive more than ten junk emails a day.
> A: Can we stop them from coming in?
> B: I don't think it's possible to block them completely.
> A: _____?
> B: Well, you can set up a filter on the settings.
> A: A filter?
> B: Yeah. The filter can weed out some of the spam emails.

① Do you write emails often
② Isn't there anything we can do
③ How did you make this great filter
④ Can you help me set up an email account

문 12. 두 사람의 대화 중 가장 자연스러운 것은?

① A: Do you know what time it is?
   B: Sorry, I'm busy these days.
② A: Hey, where are you headed?
   B: We are off to the grocery store.
③ A: Can you give me a hand with this?
   B: OK. I'll clap for you.
④ A: Has anybody seen my purse?
   B: Long time no see.

문 13. 우리말을 영어로 잘못 옮긴 것은?

① 나는 네 열쇠를 잃어버렸다고 네게 말한 것을 후회한다.
   → I regret to tell you that I lost your key.
② 그 병원에서의 그의 경험은 그녀의 경험보다 더 나빴다.
   → His experience at the hospital was worse than hers.
③ 그것은 내게 지난 24년의 기억을 상기시켜준다.
   → It reminds me of the memories of the past 24 years.
④ 나는 대화할 때 내 눈을 보는 사람들을 좋아한다.
   → I like people who look me in the eye when I have a conversation.

문 14. 다음 글의 제목으로 가장 적절한 것은?

Louis XIV needed a palace worthy of his greatness, so he decided to build a huge new house at Versailles, where a tiny hunting lodge stood. After almost fifty years of labor, this tiny hunting lodge had been transformed into an enormous palace, a quarter of a mile long. Canals were dug to bring water from the river and to drain the marshland. Versailles was full of elaborate rooms like the famous Hall of Mirrors, where seventeen huge mirrors stood across from seventeen large windows, and the Salon of Apollo, where a solid silver throne stood. Hundreds of statues of Greek gods such as Apollo, Jupiter, and Neptune stood in the gardens; each god had Louis's face!

① True Face of Greek Gods
② The Hall of Mirrors vs. the Salon of Apollo
③ Did the Canal Bring More Than Just Water to Versailles?
④ Versailles: From a Humble Lodge to a Great Palace

문 15. 글의 흐름상 가장 어색한 문장은?

Philosophers have not been as concerned with anthropology as anthropologists have with philosophy. ① Few influential contemporary philosophers take anthropological studies into account in their work. ② Those who specialize in philosophy of social science may consider or analyze examples from anthropological research, but do this mostly to illustrate conceptual points or epistemological distinctions or to criticize epistemological or ethical implications. ③ In fact, the great philosophers of our time often drew inspiration from other fields such as anthropology and psychology. ④ Philosophy students seldom study or show serious interest in anthropology. They may learn about experimental methods in science, but rarely about anthropological fieldwork.

문 16. 밑줄 친 부분에 들어갈 말로 가장 적절한 것은?

All of us inherit something: in some cases, it may be money, property or some object — a family heirloom such as a grandmother's wedding dress or a father's set of tools. But beyond that, all of us inherit something else, something _____, something we may not even be fully aware of. It may be a way of doing a daily task, or the way we solve a particular problem or decide a moral issue for ourselves. It may be a special way of keeping a holiday or a tradition to have a picnic on a certain date. It may be something important or central to our thinking, or something minor that we have long accepted quite casually.

① quite unrelated to our everyday life
② against our moral standards
③ much less concrete and tangible
④ of great monetary value

문 17. 다음 글의 요지로 가장 적절한 것은?

Evolutionarily, any species that hopes to stay alive has to manage its resources carefully. That means that first call on food and other goodies goes to the breeders and warriors and hunters and planters and builders and, certainly, the children, with not much left over for the seniors, who may be seen as consuming more than they're contributing. But even before modern medicine extended life expectancies, ordinary families were including grandparents and even great-grandparents. That's because what old folk consume materially, they give back behaviorally — providing a leveling, reasoning center to the tumult that often swirls around them.

① Seniors have been making contributions to the family.
② Modern medicine has brought focus to the role of old folk.
③ Allocating resources well in a family determines its prosperity.
④ The extended family comes at a cost of limited resources.

문 18. 주어진 글 다음에 이어질 글의 순서로 가장 적절한 것은?

Nowadays the clock dominates our lives so much that it is hard to imagine life without it. Before industrialization, most societies used the sun or the moon to tell the time.

(A) For the growing network of railroads, the fact that there were no time standards was a disaster. Often, stations just some miles apart set their clocks at different times. There was a lot of confusion for travelers.

(B) When mechanical clocks first appeared, they were immediately popular. It was fashionable to have a clock or a watch. People invented the expression "of the clock" or "o'clock" to refer to this new way to tell the time.

(C) These clocks were decorative, but not always useful. This was because towns, provinces, and even neighboring villages had different ways to tell the time. Travelers had to reset their clocks repeatedly when they moved from one place to another. In the United States, there were about 70 different time zones in the 1860s.

① (A) − (B) − (C)
② (B) − (A) − (C)
③ (B) − (C) − (A)
④ (C) − (A) − (B)

문 19. 주어진 문장이 들어갈 위치로 가장 적절한 것은?

> But there is also clear evidence that millennials, born between 1981 and 1996, are saving more aggressively for retirement than Generation X did at the same ages, 22 ~ 37.

Millennials are often labeled the poorest, most financially burdened generation in modern times. Many of them graduated from college into one of the worst labor markets the United States has ever seen, with a staggering load of student debt to boot. (①) Not surprisingly, millennials have accumulated less wealth than Generation X did at a similar stage in life, primarily because fewer of them own homes. (②) But newly available data providing the most detailed picture to date about what Americans of different generations save complicates that assessment. (③) Yes, Gen Xers, those born between 1965 and 1980, have a higher net worth. (④) And that might put them in better financial shape than many assume.

문 20. 다음 글의 내용과 일치하지 않는 것은?

> Carbonate sands, which accumulate over thousands of years from the breakdown of coral and other reef organisms, are the building material for the frameworks of coral reefs. But these sands are sensitive to the chemical make-up of sea water. As oceans absorb carbon dioxide, they acidify — and at a certain point, carbonate sands simply start to dissolve. The world's oceans have absorbed around one-third of human-emitted carbon dioxide. The rate at which the sands dissolve was strongly related to the acidity of the overlying seawater, and was ten times more sensitive than coral growth to ocean acidification. In other words, ocean acidification will impact the dissolution of coral reef sands more than the growth of corals. This probably reflects the corals' ability to modify their environment and partially adjust to ocean acidification, whereas the dissolution of sands is a geochemical process that cannot adapt.

① The frameworks of coral reefs are made of carbonate sands.
② Corals are capable of partially adjusting to ocean acidification.
③ Human-emitted carbon dioxide has contributed to the world's ocean acidification.
④ Ocean acidification affects the growth of corals more than the dissolution of coral reef sands.

해설편 ▶ P.92

2019

6월 15일 시행

지방직 9급

| 풀이 시간: ____:____ ~ ____:____ / 점수: ____점

1초 합격예측! 모바일 성적분석표

QR 코드로 접속하여 문제 풀이시간을 측정하고,
〈1초 합격예측 & 모바일 성적분석표〉 서비스를 통해
지금 바로! 실력을 점검해 보세요.

http://eduwill.kr/6iy6

※ 밑줄 친 부분의 의미와 가장 가까운 것을 고르시오.

[문 1 ~ 문 2]

문 1.

I came to see these documents as relics of a sensibility now dead and buried, which needed to be <u>excavated</u>.

① exhumed　　　② packed
③ erased　　　　④ celebrated

문 2.

Riding a roller coaster can be a joy ride of emotions: the nervous anticipation as you're strapped into your seat, the questioning and regret that comes as you go up, up, up, and the <u>sheer</u> adrenaline rush as the car takes that first dive.

① utter　　　　② scary
③ occasional　　④ manageable

문 3. 두 사람의 대화 중 가장 어색한 것은?

① A: What time are we having lunch?
　 B: It'll be ready before noon.
② A: I called you several times. Why didn't you answer?
　 B: Oh, I think my cell phone was turned off.
③ A: Are you going to take a vacation this winter?
　 B: I might. I haven't decided yet.
④ A: Hello. Sorry I missed your call.
　 B: Would you like to leave a message?

문 4. 밑줄 친 부분에 들어갈 말로 가장 적절한 것은?

A: Hello. I need to exchange some money.
B: Okay. What currency do you need?
A: I need to convert dollars into pounds. What's the exchange rate?
B: The exchange rate is 0.73 pounds for every dollar.
A: Fine. Do you take a commission?
B: Yes, we take a small commission of 4 dollars.
A: _____?
B: We convert your currency back for free. Just bring your receipt with you.

① How much does this cost
② How should I pay for that
③ What's your buy-back policy
④ Do you take credit cards

문 5. 밑줄 친 부분 중 어법상 옳지 않은 것은?

Each year, more than 270,000 pedestrians ① <u>lose</u> their lives on the world's roads. Many leave their homes as they would on any given day never ② <u>to return</u>. Globally, pedestrians constitute 22% of all road traffic fatalities, and in some countries this proportion is ③ <u>as high as</u> two thirds of all road traffic deaths. Millions of pedestrians are non-fatally ④ <u>injuring</u> — some of whom are left with permanent disabilities. These incidents cause much suffering and grief as well as economic hardship.

문 6. 어법상 옳은 것은?

① The paper charged her with use the company's money for her own purposes.
② The investigation had to be handled with the utmost care lest suspicion be aroused.
③ Another way to speed up the process would be made the shift to a new system.
④ Burning fossil fuels is one of the lead cause of climate change.

문 7. 주어진 글 다음에 이어질 글의 순서로 가장 적절한 것은?

> There is a thought that can haunt us: since everything probably affects everything else, how can we ever make sense of the social world? If we are weighed down by that worry, though, we won't ever make progress.

> (A) Every discipline that I am familiar with draws caricatures of the world in order to make sense of it. The modern economist does this by building *models*, which are deliberately stripped down representations of the phenomena out there.
>
> (B) The economist John Maynard Keynes described our subject thus: "Economics is a science of thinking in terms of models joined to the art of choosing models which are relevant to the contemporary world."
>
> (C) When I say "stripped down," I really mean stripped down. It isn't uncommon among us economists to focus on one or two causal factors, exclude everything else, hoping that this will enable us to understand how just those aspects of reality work and interact.

① (A) − (B) − (C) ② (A) − (C) − (B)
③ (B) − (C) − (A) ④ (B) − (A) − (C)

문 8. 다음 글의 내용과 일치하는 것은?

> Prehistoric societies some half a million years ago did not distinguish sharply between mental and physical disorders. Abnormal behaviors, from simple headaches to convulsive attacks, were attributed to evil spirits that inhabited or controlled the afflicted person's body. According to historians, these ancient peoples attributed many forms of illness to demonic possession, sorcery, or the behest of an offended ancestral spirit. Within this system of belief, called *demonology*, the victim was usually held at least partly responsible for the misfortune. It has been suggested that Stone Age cave dwellers may have treated behavior disorders with a surgical method called *trephining*, in which part of the skull was chipped away to provide an opening through which the evil spirit could escape.

> People may have believed that when the evil spirit left, the person would return to his or her normal state. Surprisingly, trephined skulls have been found to have healed over, indicating that some patients survived this extremely crude operation.
>
> *convulsive 경련의
> **behest 명령

① Mental disorders were clearly differentiated from physical disorders.
② Abnormal behaviors were believed to result from evil spirits affecting a person.
③ An opening was made in the skull for an evil spirit to enter a person's body.
④ No cave dwellers survived trephining.

문 9. 다음 글의 주제로 가장 적절한 것은?

> As the digital revolution upends newsrooms across the country, here's my advice for all the reporters. I've been a reporter for more than 25 years, so I have lived through a half dozen technological life cycles. The most dramatic transformations have come in the last half dozen years. That means I am, with increasing frequency, making stuff up as I go along. Much of the time in the news business, we have no idea what we are doing. We show up in the morning and someone says, "Can you write a story about (pick one) tax policy/immigration/climate change?" When newspapers had once-a-day deadlines, we said a reporter would learn in the morning and teach at night — write a story that could inform tomorrow's readers on a topic the reporter knew nothing about 24 hours earlier. Now it is more like learning at the top of the hour and teaching at the bottom of the same hour. I'm also running a political podcast, for example, and during the presidential conventions, we should be able to use it to do real-time interviews anywhere. I am just increasingly working without a script.

① a reporter as a teacher
② a reporter and improvisation
③ technology in politics
④ fields of journalism and technology

문 10. 글의 흐름상 가장 어색한 문장은?

　　Children's playgrounds throughout history were the wilderness, fields, streams, and hills of the country and the roads, streets, and vacant places of villages, towns, and cities. ① The term *playground* refers to all those places where children gather to play their free, spontaneous games. ② Only during the past few decades have children vacated these natural playgrounds for their growing love affair with video games, texting, and social networking. ③ Even in rural America few children are still roaming in a free-ranging manner, unaccompanied by adults. ④ When out of school, they are commonly found in neighborhoods digging in sand, building forts, playing traditional games, climbing, or playing ball games. They are rapidly disappearing from the natural terrain of creeks, hills, and fields, and like their urban counterparts, are turning to their indoor, sedentary cyber toys for entertainment.

※ 밑줄 친 부분의 의미와 가장 가까운 것을 고르시오.

[문 11 ～ 문 12]

문 11.

　　Time does seem to slow to a trickle during a boring afternoon lecture and race when the brain is engrossed in something highly entertaining.

① enhanced by　　　　② apathetic to
③ stabilized by　　　　④ preoccupied with

문 12.

　　These daily updates were designed to help readers keep abreast of the markets as the government attempted to keep them under control.

① be acquainted with　　② get inspired by
③ have faith in　　　　④ keep away from

※ 밑줄 친 (A), (B)에 들어갈 말로 가장 적절한 것을 고르시오.

[문 13 ～ 문 14]

문 13.

　　In the 1840s, the island of Ireland suffered famine. Because Ireland could not produce enough food to feed its population, about a million people died of ＿＿＿(A)＿＿＿; they simply didn't have enough to eat to stay alive. The famine caused another 1.25 million people to ＿＿＿(B)＿＿＿; many left their island home for the United States; the rest went to Canada, Australia, Chile, and other countries. Before the famine, the population of Ireland was approximately 6 million. After the great food shortage, it was about 4 million.

	(A)	(B)
①	dehydration	be deported
②	trauma	immigrate
③	starvation	emigrate
④	fatigue	be detained

문 14.

　　Today the technology to create the visual component of virtual-reality (VR) experiences is well on its way to becoming widely accessible and affordable. But to work powerfully, virtual reality needs to be about more than visuals. ＿＿＿(A)＿＿＿ what you are hearing convincingly matches the visuals, the virtual experience breaks apart. Take a basketball game. If the players, the coaches, the announcers, and the crowd all sound like they're sitting midcourt, you may as well watch the game on television — you'll get just as much of a sense that you are "there." ＿＿＿(B)＿＿＿, today's audio equipment and our widely used recording and reproduction formats are simply inadequate to the task of re-creating convincingly the sound of a battlefield on a distant planet, a basketball game at courtside, or a symphony as heard from the first row of a great concert hall.

	(A)	(B)
①	If	By contrast
②	Unless	Consequently
③	If	Similarly
④	Unless	Unfortunately

문 15. 주어진 문장이 들어갈 위치로 가장 적절한 것은?

> The same thinking can be applied to any number of goals, like improving performance at work.

The happy brain tends to focus on the short term. (①) That being the case, it's a good idea to consider what short-term goals we can accomplish that will eventually lead to accomplishing long-term goals. (②) For instance, if you want to lose thirty pounds in six months, what short-term goals can you associate with losing the smaller increments of weight that will get you there? (③) Maybe it's something as simple as rewarding yourself each week that you lose two pounds. (④) By breaking the overall goal into smaller, shorter-term parts, we can focus on incremental accomplishments instead of being overwhelmed by the enormity of the goal in our profession.

문 16. 우리말을 영어로 잘못 옮긴 것은?

① 혹시 내게 전화하고 싶은 경우에 이게 내 번호야.
   → This is my number just in case you would like to call me.
② 나는 유럽 여행을 준비하느라 바쁘다.
   → I am busy preparing for a trip to Europe.
③ 그녀는 남편과 결혼한 지 20년 이상 되었다.
   → She has married to her husband for more than two decades.
④ 나는 내 아들이 읽을 책을 한 권 사야 한다.
   → I should buy a book for my son to read.

※ 다음 글의 내용과 일치하지 않는 것을 고르시오.
[문 17 ~ 문 18]

문 17.

In the nineteenth century, the most respected health and medical experts all insisted that diseases were caused by "miasma," a fancy term for bad air. Western society's system of health was based on this assumption: to prevent diseases, windows were kept open or closed, depending on whether there was more miasma inside or outside the room; it was believed that doctors could not pass along disease because gentlemen did not inhabit quarters with bad air. Then the idea of germs came along. One day, everyone believed that bad air makes you sick. Then, almost overnight, people started realizing there were invisible things called microbes and bacteria that were the real cause of diseases. This new view of disease brought sweeping changes to medicine, as surgeons adopted antiseptics and scientists invented vaccines and antibiotics. But, just as momentously, the idea of germs gave ordinary people the power to influence their own lives. Now, if you wanted to stay healthy, you could wash your hands, boil your water, cook your food thoroughly, and clean cuts and scrapes with iodine.

① In the nineteenth century, opening windows was irrelevant to the density of miasma.
② In the nineteenth century, it was believed that gentlemen did not live in places with bad air.
③ Vaccines were invented after people realized that microbes and bacteria were the real cause of diseases.
④ Cleaning cuts and scrapes could help people to stay healthy.

문 18.

　　Followers are a critical part of the leadership equation, but their role has not always been appreciated. For a long time, in fact, "the common view of leadership was that leaders actively led and subordinates, later called followers, passively and obediently followed." Over time, especially in the last century, social change shaped people's views of followers, and leadership theories gradually recognized the active and important role that followers play in the leadership process. Today it seems natural to accept the important role followers play. One aspect of leadership is particularly worth noting in this regard: Leadership is a social influence process shared among all members of a group. Leadership is not restricted to the influence exerted by someone in a particular position or role; followers are part of the leadership process, too.

① For a length of time, it was understood that leaders actively led and followers passively followed.
② People's views of subordinates were influenced by social change.
③ The important role of followers is still denied today.
④ Both leaders and followers participate in the leadership process.

※ 밑줄 친 부분에 들어갈 말로 가장 적절한 것을 고르시오.
[문 19 ~ 문 20]

문 19.

　　Language proper is itself double-layered. Single noises are only occasionally meaningful: mostly, the various speech sounds convey coherent messages only when combined into an overlapping chain, like different colors of ice-cream melting into one another. In birdsong also, ＿＿＿＿＿＿＿＿＿: the sequence is what matters. In both humans and birds, control of this specialized sound-system is exercised by one half of the brain, normally the left half, and the system is learned relatively early in life. And just as many human languages have dialects, so do some bird species: in California, the white-crowned sparrow has songs so different from area to area that Californians can supposedly tell where they are in the state by listening to these sparrows.

① individual notes are often of little value
② rhythmic sounds are important
③ dialects play a critical role
④ no sound-system exists

문 20.

　　Nobel Prize-winning psychologist Daniel Kahneman changed the way the world thinks about economics, upending the notion that human beings are rational decision-makers. Along the way, his discipline-crossing influence has altered the way physicians make medical decisions and investors evaluate risk on Wall Street. In a paper, Kahneman and his colleagues outline a process for making big strategic decisions. Their suggested approach, labeled as "Mediating Assessments Protocol," or MAP, has a simple goal: To put off gut-based decision-making until a choice can be informed by a number of separate factors. "One of the essential purposes of MAP is basically to ＿＿＿＿＿＿ intuition," Kahneman said in a recent interview with *The Post*. The structured process calls for analyzing a decision based on six to seven previously chosen attributes, discussing each of them separately and assigning them a relative percentile score, and finally, using those scores to make a holistic judgment.

① improve　　　　　② delay
③ possess　　　　　④ facilitate

해설편 ▶ P.97

| 풀이 시간: ___:___ ~ ___:___ / 점수: ___점

※ 밑줄 친 부분의 의미와 가장 가까운 것을 고르시오.

[문 1 ~ 문 2]

문 1.

> The paramount duty of the physician is to do no
> harm. Everything else — even healing — must
> take second place.

① chief   ② sworn
③ successful   ④ mysterious

문 2.

> It is not unusual that people get cold feet about
> taking a trip to the North Pole.

① become ambitious   ② become afraid
③ feel exhausted   ④ feel saddened

문 3. 밑줄 친 부분 중 어법상 옳지 않은 것은?

> I am writing in response to your request for a
> reference for Mrs. Ferrer. She has worked as my
> secretary ① for the last three years and has been an
> excellent employee. I believe that she meets all the
> requirements ② mentioned in your job description
> and indeed exceeds them in many ways. I have
> never had reason ③ to doubt her complete integrity.
> I would, therefore, recommend Mrs. Ferrer for the
> post ④ what you advertise.

문 4. 우리말을 영어로 잘못 옮긴 것은?

① 모든 정보는 거짓이었다.
   → All of the information was false.
② 토마스는 더 일찍 사과했어야 했다.
   → Thomas should have apologized earlier.
③ 우리가 도착했을 때 영화는 이미 시작했었다.
   → The movie had already started when we arrived.
④ 바깥 날씨가 추웠기 때문에 나는 차를 마시려 물을 끓였다.
   → Being cold outside, I boiled some water to have
      tea.

문 5. 밑줄 친 부분의 의미와 가장 가까운 것은?

> The student who finds the state-of-the-art approach
> intimidating learns less than he or she might have
> learned by the old methods.

① humorous   ② friendly
③ convenient   ④ frightening

문 6. 밑줄 친 부분에 들어갈 말로 가장 적절한 것은?

> Since the air-conditioners are being repaired now,
> the office workers have to _____ electric
> fans for the day.

① get rid of   ② let go of
③ make do with   ④ break up with

문 7. 어법상 옳은 것은?

① Please contact to me at the email address I gave you
   last week.
② Were it not for water, all living creatures on earth
   would be extinct.
③ The laptop allows people who is away from their
   offices to continue to work.
④ The more they attempted to explain their mistakes,
   the worst their story sounded.

문 8. 우리말을 영어로 옳게 옮긴 것은?

① 그는 며칠 전에 친구를 배웅하기 위해 역으로 갔다.
 → He went to the station a few days ago to see off his friend.

② 버릇없는 그 소년은 아버지가 부르는 것을 못 들은 체했다.
 → The spoiled boy made it believe he didn't hear his father calling.

③ 나는 버팔로에 가본 적이 없어서 그곳에 가기를 고대하고 있다.
 → I have never been to Buffalo, so I am looking forward to go there.

④ 나는 아직 오늘 신문을 못 읽었어. 뭐 재미있는 것 있니?
 → I have not read today's newspaper yet. Is there anything interested in it?

문 9. 다음 글의 흐름상 가장 어색한 문장은?

The Renaissance kitchen had a definite hierarchy of help who worked together to produce the elaborate banquets. ① At the top, as we have seen, was the *scalco*, or steward, who was in charge of not only the kitchen, but also the dining room. ② The dining room was supervised by the butler, who was in charge of the silverware and linen and also served the dishes that began and ended the banquet — the cold dishes, salads, cheeses, and fruit at the beginning and the sweets and confections at the end of the meal. ③ This elaborate decoration and serving was what in restaurants is called "the front of the house." ④ The kitchen was supervised by the head cook, who directed the undercooks, pastry cooks, and kitchen help.

문 10. 다음 글의 요지로 가장 적절한 것은?

My students often believe that if they simply meet more important people, their work will improve. But it's remarkably hard to engage with those people unless you've already put something valuable out into the world. That's what piques the curiosity of advisers and sponsors. Achievements show you have something to give, not just something to take. In life, it certainly helps to know the right people. But how hard they go to bat for you, how far they stick their necks out for you, depends on what you have to offer. Building a powerful network doesn't require you to be an expert at networking. It just requires you to be an expert at something. If you make great connections, they might advance your career. If you do great work, those connections will be easier to make. Let your insights and your outputs — not your business cards — do the talking.

① Sponsorship is necessary for a successful career.
② Building a good network starts from your accomplishments.
③ A powerful network is a prerequisite for your achievement.
④ Your insights and outputs grow as you become an expert at networking.

문 11. 밑줄 친 부분에 들어갈 말로 가장 적절한 것은?

A: My computer just shut down for no reason. I can't even turn it back on again.
B: Did you try charging it? It might just be out of battery.
A: Of course, I tried charging it.
B: _____
A: I should do that, but I'm so lazy.

① I don't know how to fix your computer.
② Try visiting the nearest service center then.
③ Well, stop thinking about your problems and go to sleep.
④ My brother will try to fix your computer because he's a technician.

문 12. 다음 글에 나타난 화자의 심경으로 가장 적절한 것은?

My face turned white as a sheet. I looked at my watch. The tests would be almost over by now. I arrived at the testing center in an absolute panic. I tried to tell my story, but my sentences and descriptive gestures got so confused that I communicated nothing more than a very convincing version of a human tornado. In an effort to curb my distracting explanation, the proctor led me to an empty seat and put a test booklet in front of me. He looked doubtfully from me to the clock, and then he walked away. I tried desperately to make up for lost time, scrambling madly through analogies and sentence completions. "Fifteen minutes remain," the voice of doom declared from the front of the classroom. Algebraic equations, arithmetic calculations, geometric diagrams swam before my eyes. "Time! Pencils down, please."

① nervous and worried
② excited and cheerful
③ calm and determined
④ safe and relaxed

문 13. 주어진 문장 다음에 이어질 글의 순서로 가장 적절한 것은?

Devices that monitor and track your health are becoming more popular among all age populations.

(A) For example, falls are a leading cause of death for adults 65 and older. Fall alerts are a popular gerotechnology that has been around for many years but have now improved.

(B) However, for seniors aging in place, especially those without a caretaker in the home, these technologies can be lifesaving.

(C) This simple technology can automatically alert 911 or a close family member the moment a senior has fallen.

*gerotechnology 노인을 위한 양로 기술

① (B) − (C) − (A)
② (B) − (A) − (C)
③ (C) − (A) − (B)
④ (C) − (B) − (A)

※ 밑줄 친 부분에 들어갈 말로 가장 적절한 것을 고르시오.
[문 14 ~ 문 15]

문 14.

A: Where do you want to go for our honeymoon?
B: Let's go to a place that neither of us has been to.
A: Then, why don't we go to Hawaii?
B: _____

① I've always wanted to go there.
② Isn't Korea a great place to live?
③ Great! My last trip there was amazing!
④ Oh, you must've been to Hawaii already.

문 15.

The secret of successful people is usually that they are able to concentrate totally on one thing. Even if they have a lot in their head, they have found a method that the many commitments don't impede each other, but instead they are brought into a good inner order. And this order is quite simple: _____. In theory, it seems to be quite clear, but in everyday life it seems rather different. You might have tried to decide on priorities, but you have failed because of everyday trivial matters and all the unforeseen distractions. Separate off disturbances, for example, by escaping into another office, and not allowing any distractions to get in the way. When you concentrate on the one task of your priorities, you will find you have energy that you didn't even know you had.

① the sooner, the better
② better late than never
③ out of sight, out of mind
④ the most important thing first

문 16. 다음 글의 제목으로 가장 적절한 것은?

With the help of the scientist, the commercial fishing industry has found out that its fishing must be done scientifically if it is to be continued. With no fishing pressure on a fish population, the number of fish will reach a predictable level of abundance and stay there. The only fluctuation would be due to natural environmental factors, such as availability of food, proper temperature, and the like. If a fishery is developed to take these fish, their population can be maintained if the fishing harvest is small. The mackerel of the North Sea is a good example. If we increase the fishery and take more fish each year, we must be careful not to reduce the population below the ideal point where it can replace all of the fish we take out each year. If we fish at this level, called the *maximum sustainable* yield, we can maintain the greatest possible yield, year after year. If we catch too many, the number of fish will decrease each year until we fish ourselves out of a job. Examples of severely overfished animals are the blue whale of the Antarctic and the halibut of the North Atlantic. Fishing just the correct amount to maintain a maximum annual yield is both a science and an art. Research is constantly being done to help us better understand the fish population and how to utilize it to the maximum without depleting the population.

① Say No to Commercial Fishing
② Sea Farming Seen As a Fishy Business
③ Why Does the Fishing Industry Need Science?
④ Overfished Animals: Cases of Illegal Fishing

문 17. 밑줄 친 (A), (B)에 들어갈 말로 가장 적절한 것은?

Does terrorism ever work? 9/11 was an enormous tactical success for al Qaeda, partly because it involved attacks that took place in the media capital of the world and the actual capital of the United States, _____(A)_____ ensuring the widest possible coverage of the event. If terrorism is a form of theater where you want a lot of people watching, no event in human history was likely ever seen by a larger global audience than the 9/11 attacks. At the time, there was much discussion about how 9/11 was like the attack on Pearl Harbor. They were indeed similar since they were both surprise attacks that drew America into significant wars. But they were also similar in another sense. Pearl Harbor was a great tactical success for Imperial Japan, but it led to a great strategic failure: Within four years of Pearl Harbor the Japanese empire lay in ruins, utterly defeated. _____(B)_____, 9/11 was a great tactical success for al Qaeda, but it also turned out to be a great strategic failure for Osama bin Laden.

	(A)	(B)
①	thereby	Similarly
②	while	Therefore
③	while	Fortunately
④	thereby	On the contrary

문 18. 다음 글의 내용과 일치하지 않는 것은?

We entered a new phase as a species when Chinese scientists altered a human embryo to remove a potentially fatal blood disorder — not only from the baby, but all of its descendants. Researchers call this process "germline modification." The media likes the phrase "designer babies." But we should call it what it is, "eugenics." And we, the human race, need to decide whether or not we want to use it. Last month, in the United States, the scientific establishment weighed in. A National Academy of Sciences and National Academy of Medicine joint committee endorsed embryo editing aimed at genes that cause serious diseases when there is "no reasonable alternative." But it was more wary of editing for "enhancement," like making already-healthy children stronger or taller. It recommended a public discussion, and said that doctors should "not proceed at this time." The committee had good reason to urge caution. The history of eugenics is full of oppression and misery.

*eugenics 우생학

① Doctors were recommended to immediately go ahead with embryo editing for enhancement.
② Recently, the scientific establishment in the U.S. joined a discussion on eugenics.
③ Chinese scientists modified a human embryo to prevent a serious blood disorder.
④ "Designer babies" is another term for the germline modification process.

문 19. 주어진 문장이 들어갈 위치로 가장 적절한 것은?

> If neither surrendered, the two exchanged blows until one was knocked out.

The ancient Olympics provided athletes an opportunity to prove their fitness and superiority, just like our modern games. (①) The ancient Olympic events were designed to eliminate the weak and glorify the strong. Winners were pushed to the brink. (②) Just as in modern times, people loved extreme sports. One of the favorite events was added in the 33rd Olympiad. This was the pankration, or an extreme mix of wrestling and boxing. The Greek word *pankration* means "total power." The men wore leather straps with metal studs, which could make a terrible mess of their opponents. (③) This dangerous form of wrestling had no time or weight limits. In this event, only two rules applied. First, wrestlers were not allowed to gouge eyes with their thumbs. Secondly, they could not bite. Anything else was considered fair play. The contest was decided in the same manner as a boxing match. Contenders continued until one of the two collapsed. (④) Only the strongest and most determined athletes attempted this event. Imagine wrestling "Mr. Fingertips," who earned his nickname by breaking his opponents' fingers!

문 20. 밑줄 친 부분에 들어갈 말로 가장 적절한 것은?

In our time it is not only the law of the market which has its own life and rules over man, but also the development of science and technique. For a number of reasons, the problems and organization of science today are such that a scientist does not choose his problems; the problems force themselves upon the scientist. He solves one problem, and the result is not that he is more secure or certain, but that ten other new problems open up in place of the single solved one. They force him to solve them; he has to go ahead at an ever-quickening pace. The same holds true for industrial techniques. The pace of science forces the pace of technique. Theoretical physics forces atomic energy on us; the successful production of the fission bomb forces upon us the manufacture of the hydrogen bomb. We do not choose our problems, we do not choose our products; we are pushed, we are forced — by what? By a system which has no purpose and goal transcending it, and which _____.

① makes man its appendix
② creates a false sense of security
③ inspires man with creative challenges
④ empowers scientists to control the market laws

해설편 ▶ P.103

법원직 9급 공개경쟁채용 필기시험

응 시 번 호	
성 명	

문 제 책 형

【시 험 과 목】

1교시	헌법, 국어, 한국사, 영어	
2교시	법원사무직렬	민법, 민사소송법, 형법, 형사소송법
	등기사무직렬	민법, 민사소송법, 상법(총론·회사편), 부동산등기법

응시자 주의사항

1. **시험 시작 전**에 시험문제를 열람하는 행위나 **시험 종료 후** 답안을 작성하는 행위를 한 사람은 「지방공무원 임용령」 제65조 등 관련 법령에 의거 **부정행위자**로 처리됩니다.

2. 시험 시작 즉시 **과목편철 순서, 문제누락 여부, 인쇄상태 이상 유무 및 표지와 개별과목의 문제책형 일치 여부 등을 확인**한 후 문제책 표지에 응시번호, 성명을 기재합니다.

3. 반드시 본인의 **응시표에 인쇄된 시험과목 순서에 따라** 제4과목과 제5과목의 **답안을 표기**하여야 합니다. 과목 순서를 바꾸어 표기한 경우에도 **본인의 응시표에 기재된 과목 순서대로 채점**되므로 반드시 유의하시기 바랍니다.

4. 시험이 시작되면 문제를 주의 깊게 읽은 후, **문항의 취지에 가장 적합한 하나의 정답만을 고르며**, 문제 내용에 관한 질문은 받지 않습니다.

5. **시험시간 관리의 책임**은 전적으로 응시자 본인에게 있습니다.

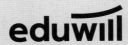

| 풀이 시간: ___ : ___ ~ ___ : ___ / 점수: ___ 점

문 1. 주어진 글 다음에 이어질 글의 순서로 가장 적절한 것은?

> Now we stand at the edge of a turning point as we face the rise of a coming wave of technology that includes both advanced AI and biotechnology. Never before have we witnessed technologies with such transformative potential, promising to reshape our world in ways that are both awe-inspiring and daunting.

(A) With AI, we could create systems that are beyond our control and find ourselves at the mercy of algorithms that we don't understand. With biotechnology, we could manipulate the very building blocks of life, potentially creating unintended consequences for both individuals and entire ecosystem.

(B) With biotechnology, we could engineer life to tackle diseases and transform agriculture, creating a world that is healthier and more sustainable. But on the other hand, the potential dangers of these technologies are equally vast and profound.

(C) On the one hand, the potential benefits of these technologies are vast and profound. With AI, we could unlock the secrets of the universe, cure diseases that have long eluded us and create new forms of art and culture that stretch the bounds of imagination.

*daunt 겁먹게(기죽게) 하다

**elude (사물이)~에게 이해되지 않다

① (B) − (A) − (C)   ② (B) − (C) − (A)

③ (C) − (A) − (B)   ④ (C) − (B) − (A)

문 2. 다음 빈칸에 들어갈 말로 가장 적절한 것은?

> Controversy over new art-making technologies is nothing new. Many painters recoiled at the invention of the camera, which they saw as a debasement of human artistry. Charles Baudelaire, the 19th-century French poet and art critic, called photography "art's most mortal enemy." In the 20th century, digital editing tools and computer-assisted design programs were similarly dismissed by purists for requiring too little skill of their human collaborators. What makes the new breed of A.I. image generating tools different is not just that they're capable of producing beautiful works of art with minimal effort. It's how they work. These tools are built by scraping millions of images from the open web, then teaching algorithms to recognize patterns and relationships in those images and generate new ones in the same style. That means that artists who upload their works to the internet may be unwittingly _____.

*unwittingly 자신도 모르게, 부지불식간에

① helping to train their algorithmic competitors

② sparking a debate over the ethics of A.I.-generated art

③ embracing digital technology as part of the creative process

④ acquiring the skills of utilizing internet to craft original creations

문 3. Duke Kahanamoku에 대한 다음 글의 내용과 가장 일치하지 않는 것은?

> Duke Kahanamoku, born August 26, 1890, near Waikiki, Hawaii, was a Hawaiian surfer and swimmer who won three Olympic gold medals for the United States and who for several years was considered the greatest freestyle swimmer in the world. He was perhaps most widely known for developing the flutter kick, which largely replaces the scissors kick. Kahanamoku set three universally recognized world records in the 100-yard freestyle between July 5, 1913, and September 5, 1917. In the 100-yard freestyle Kahanamoku was U.S. indoor champion in 1913, and outdoor titleholder in 1916-17 and 1920. At the Olympic Games in Stockholm in 1912, he won the 100-metre freestyle event, and he repeated that triumph at the 1920 Olympics in Antwerp, Belgium, where he also was a member of the victorious U.S. team in the 800-metre relay race. Kahanamoku also excelled at surfing, and he became viewed as one of the icons of the sport. Intermittently from the mid-1920s, Kahanamoku was a motion-picture actor. From 1932 to 1961 he was sheriff of the city and county of Honolulu. He served in the salaried office of official greeter of famous personages for the state of Hawaii from 1961 until his death.
>
> *intermittently 간헐적으로
>
> **sheriff 보안관

① 하와이 출신의 서퍼이자 수영 선수로 올림픽 금메달리스트이다.
② 그는 플러터 킥을 대체하는 시저스 킥을 개발한 것으로 널리 알려져 있다.
③ 벨기에 앤트워프 올림픽의 800미터 계주에서 우승한 미국 팀의 일원이었다.
④ 그는 1920년대 중반부터 간헐적으로 영화배우로도 활동했다.

문 4. 다음 빈칸에 들어갈 말로 가장 적절한 것은?

> The understandings that children bring to the classroom can already be quite powerful in the early grades. For example, some children have been found to hold onto their preconception of a flat earth by imagining a round earth to be shaped like a pancake. This construction of a new understanding is guided by a model of the earth that helps the child explain how people can stand or walk on its surface. Many young children have trouble giving up the notion that one-eighth is greater than one-fourth, because 8 is more than 4. If children were blank slates, just telling them that the earth is round or that one-fourth is greater than one-eighth would be _____. But since they already have ideas about the earth and about numbers, those ideas must be directly addressed in order to transform or expand them.

① familiar
② adequate
③ improper
④ irrelevant

문 5. Urban farming에 관한 다음 글의 내용과 가장 일치하지 않는 것은?

> Urban farming, also known as urban agriculture, involves growing food within city environments, utilizing spaces like rooftops, abandoned buildings, and community gardens. This sustainable practice is gaining traction in cities across the world, including New York, Chicago, San Francisco, London, Amsterdam, and Berlin, as well as in many African and Asian cities where it plays a crucial role in food supply and local economies. Urban farming not only helps reduce carbon footprints by minimizing transport emissions but also increases access to fresh, healthy food in urban areas. It bolsters local economies by creating jobs and keeping profits within the community. Additionally, urban farms enhance cityscapes, improve air quality, conserve water, provide educational opportunities, promote biodiversity, connect people with nature, and improve food security by producing food locally, making cities more resilient to disruptions like natural disasters.
>
> *traction 흡입력, 견인력
>
> **bolster 강화시키다

① 옥상, 버려진 건물, 그리고 공동체 정원과 같은 공간을 활용하여 도시 환경 내에서 식량을 재배하는 것이다.

② 지속 가능한 관행으로 식량 공급과 지역 경제에서 중요한 역할을 하는 많은 아프리카와 아시아를 포함한 세계의 도시들에서 인기를 얻고 있다.

③ 운송 배출을 최소화하여 탄소 발자국을 줄이는 것을 도울 뿐만 아니라 도시 지역에서 신선하고 건강한 식량에 대한 접근성을 증가시킨다.

④ 생물 다양성을 촉진하고, 지역에서 식량을 생산함으로써 식량의 안정성을 향상시키나, 자연 재해와 같은 혼란에 대한 도시의 회복력은 약화시킨다.

문 6. 밑줄 친 "unfinished animals."가 다음 글에서 의미하는 바로 가장 적절한 것은?

> Ideas or theories about human nature have a unique place in the sciences. We don't have to worry that the cosmos will be changed by our theories about the cosmos. The planets really don't care what we think or how we theorize about them. But we do have to worry that human nature will be changed by our theories of human nature. Forty years ago, the distinguished anthropologist said that human beings are "unfinished animals." What he meant is that it is human nature to have a human nature that is very much the product of the society that surrounds us. That human nature is more created than discovered. We "design" human nature, by designing the institutions within which people live. So we must ask ourselves just what kind of a human nature we want to help design.

① stuck in an incomplete stage of development

② shaped by society rather than fixed by biology

③ uniquely free from environmental context

④ born with both animalistic and spiritual aspect

문 7. 다음 글의 내용을 한 문장으로 요약하고자 한다. 빈칸 (A), (B)에 들어갈 말로 가장 적절한 것은?

Passive House is a standard and an advanced method of designing buildings using the precision of building physics to ensure comfortable conditions and to deeply reduce energy costs. It removes all guesswork from the design process. It does what national building regulations have tried to do. Passive House methods don't affect "buildability", yet they close the gap between design and performance and deliver a much higher standard of comfort and efficiency than government regulations, with all their good intentions, have managed to achieve. When we use Passive House methods, we learn how to use insulation and freely available daylight, in the most sensible way and in the right amounts for both comfort and energy efficiency. This is, I believe, fundamental to good design, and is the next step we have to make in the evolution of our dwellings and places of work. The improvements that are within our grasp are potentially transformative for mankind and the planet.

Passive House utilizes precise building physics to ensure comfort and energy efficiency, _____(A)_____ traditional regulations and offering transformative potential for _____(B)_____ design.

	(A)	(B)
①	persisting	sustainable
②	persisting	unsustainable
③	surpassing	unsustainable
④	surpassing	sustainable

문 8. 다음 글의 밑줄 친 부분 중 문맥상 낱말의 쓰임이 가장 적절하지 않은 것은?

Today, there is only one species of humans, Homo sapiens, left in the world. But that one species, despite the fact that it is over 99.9 percent genetically ① identical, has adapted itself to a wide array of disparate environments. And while some degree of human genetic variation results from each society's adaptation to its own unique environment, the cultural adaptations that each society makes in so adjusting itself will, in their turn, exact some further degree of ② variation on that society's genetic makeup. In other words, we are so entangled with our local ecologies that not only do we humans ③ transform the environment as we cull from it the various resources upon which we come to depend but also the environment, which we have so transformed, transforms us in its turn: at times exerting upon us profound biological pressures. In those regions of the world, for example, where our environmental exploitation has included the domestication of cattle — northern Europe, for instance, or East Africahuman populations have ④ reduced adult lactose tolerance: the ability to digest milk past infancy.

*lactose 유당, 젖당

문 9. 주어진 글 다음에 이어질 글의 순서로 가장 적절한 것은?

> Briefly consider a metaphor that plays a significant role in how we live our daily lives: Time Is Money.

(A) We often speak of time as if it were money — for example, in everyday expressions such as "You're wasting my time," "This device will save you hours of work," "How will you spend your weekend?" and "I've invested a lot of time in this relationship."

(B) Every metaphor brokers what is made visible or invisible; this one highlights how time is like money and obscures ways it is not. Time thus becomes something that we can waste or lose, and something that diminishes as we grow older. It is abstracted in a very linear, orderly fashion.

(C) This metaphor, however, fails to disclose important phenomenological aspects of time, such as how it may speed up or slow down, depending on our engagement with what we are doing. We may instead conceive of time as quite fluid — as a stream, for example — thought we lose sight of this to the extent that we have adopted the worldview of Time Is Money.

*obscure 모호하게 하다

① (A) − (B) − (C) ② (A) − (C) − (B)
③ (B) − (A) − (C) ④ (C) − (B) − (A)

문 10. 다음 글의 밑줄 친 부분 중, 어법상 틀린 것은?

His last thought were for his wife. "He is afraid she would ① <u>hardly</u> be able to bear it," he said to Burnet, the bishop who was allowed to be with him the last few days. Tears came into his eyes when he spoke of her. The last day came, and Lady Russell brought the three little children to say good-bye for ever to their father. "Little Fubs" was only nine, her sister Catherine seven, and the baby three years old, too young to realize his loss. He kissed them all ② <u>calmly</u>, and sent them away. His wife stayed and they ate their last meal together. Then they kissed in silence, and silently she left him. When she had gone, Lord Russel broke down completely. "Oh, what a blessing she has been to me!" he cried. "It is a great comfort to me to leave my children in such a mother's care; she has promised me to take care of ③ <u>her</u> for their sake; she will do it," he added resolutely. Lady Russell returned heavy-hearted to the sad home ④ <u>to which</u> she would never welcome him again. On July 21st, 1683, she was a widow, and her children fatherless. They left their dreary London house, and went to an old abbey in the country.

*bishop 주교(성직자)

문 11. The gig economy에 관한 다음 글의 내용과 가장 일치하지 않는 것은?

The gig economy, referring to the workforce of people engaged in freelance and side-hustle work, is growing rapidly in the United States, with 36% of employed participants in a 2022 McKinsey survey identifying as independent workers, up from 27% in 2016. This workforce includes a wide range of jobs from highly-paid professionals like lawyers to lower-earning roles like delivery drivers. Despite the flexibility and autonomy it offers, most independent workers desire more stable employment; 62% prefer permanent positions due to concerns over job security and benefits. The challenges faced by gig workers include limited access to healthcare, housing, and other basic needs, with a significant reliance on government assistance. Technological advancements have facilitated the rise in independent work, making remote and freelance jobs more accessible and appealing. The trend reflects broader economic pressures such as inflation and job market dynamics, influencing individuals to choose gig work for survival, flexibility, or enjoyment.

*side-hustle work 부업

① 조사에 참가한 사람들 중 독립 근로자의 비율이 2016년의 27%에서 36%까지 상승하였다.
② 대부분의 독립 근로자들은 안정적인 고용보다는 직업이 제공하는 유연성과 자율성을 선호하고 있다.
③ 근로자들이 직면한 어려움에는 의료, 주거 및 기타 기본 요구사항에 대한 제한된 접근성이 포함된다.
④ 기술 발전은 독립 근로의 증가를 촉진하여 원격 및 프리랜서 일자리를 접근하기 쉽고 매력적인 것으로 만들고 있다.

문 12. 주어진 글 다음에 이어질 글의 순서로 가장 적절한 것은?

We come to know and relate to the world by way of categories.

(A) The notion of an animal species, for instance, might in one setting best be thought of as described by folklore and myth, in another as a detailed legal construct, and in another as a system of scientific classification.
(B) Ordinary communication is the most immediate expression of this faculty. We refer to things through sounds and words, and we attach ideas to them that we call concepts.
(C) Some of our categories remain tacit; others are explicitly governed by custom, law, politics, or science. The application of category systems for the same things varies by context and in use.

*tacit 암묵적인, 무언의

① (B) − (A) − (C)
② (B) − (C) − (A)
③ (C) − (A) − (B)
④ (C) − (B) − (A)

문 13. 다음 글에 나타난 화자의 심경으로 가장 적절한 것은?

It's three in the morning, and we are making our way from southern to northern Utah, when the weather changes from the dry chill of the desert to the freezing gales of an alpine winter. Ice claims the road. Snowflakes flick against the windshield like tiny insects, a few at first, then so many the road disappears. We push forward into the heart of the storm. The van skids and jerks. The wind is furious, the view out the window pure white. Richard pulls over. He says we can't go any further. Dad takes the wheel, Richard moves to the passenger seat, and Mother lies next to me and Audrey on the mattress. Dad pulls onto the highway and accelerates, rapidly, as if to make a point, until he has doubled Richard's speed. "Shouldn't we drive slower?" Mother asks. Dad grins. "I'm not driving faster than our angels can fly." The van is still accelerating. To fifty, then to sixty. Richard sits tensely, his hand clutching the armrest, his knuckles bleaching each time the tires slip. Mother lies on her side, her face next to mine, taking small sips of air each time the van fishtails, then holding her breath as Dad corrects and it snakes back into the lane. She is so rigid, I think she might shatter. My body tenses with hers; together we brace a hundred times for impact.

*gale 강풍, 돌풍 **skid 미끄러지다 ***jerk 홱 움직이다
****fishtail (차량) 뒷부분이 좌우로 미끄러지다

① excited and thrilled
② anxious and fearful
③ cautious but settled
④ comfortable and relaxed

문 14. 글의 흐름으로 보아, 주어진 문장이 들어가기에 가장 적절한 곳은?

However, there are now a lot of issues with the current application of unmanned distribution.

The city lockdown policy during COVID-19 has facilitated the rapid growth of numerous takeaways, vegetable shopping, community group buying, and other businesses. (①) Last-mile delivery became an important livelihood support during the epidemic. (②) At the same time, as viruses can be transmitted through aerosols, the need for contactless delivery for last-mile delivery has gradually increased, thus accelerating the use of unmanned logistics to some extent. (③) For example, the community space is not suitable for the operation of unmanned delivery facilities due to the lack of supporting logistics infrastructure. (④) In addition, the current technology is unable to complete the delivery process and requires the collaboration of relevant space as well as personnel to help dock unmanned delivery nodes.

*last-mile delivery 최종 단계의 배송

문 15. 주어진 글 다음에 이어질 글의 순서로 가장 적절한 것은?

People are too seldom interested in having a genuine exchange of points of view where a desire to understand takes precedence over the desire to convince at any price.

(A) Yet conflict isn't just an unpopular source of pressure to act. There's also a lot of energy inherent to it, which can be harnessed to create positive change, or, in other words, improvements, with the help of a skillful approach. Basically, today's misery is the starting shot in the race towards a better future.

(B) A deviating opinion is quickly accompanied by devaluation, denigration, insults, or even physical confrontations. If you look at the "discussions" taking place on social media networks, you don't even have to look to such hot potatoes as the refugee crisis or terrorism to see a clear degradation in the way people exchange opinions.

(C) You probably know this from your own experience, too, when you have succeeded in finding a constructive solution to a conflict and, at the end of an arduous clarification process, realize that the successful outcome has been worth all the effort.

*denigration 명예훼손

**arduous 몹시 힘든, 고된

① (B) − (A) − (C) ② (B) − (C) − (A)
③ (C) − (A) − (B) ④ (C) − (B) − (A)

문 16. 다음 중 Belus Smawley에 대한 내용과 가장 일치하지 않는 것은?

Belus Smawley grew up on a farm with his parents and six siblings. In his freshman years, he was tall and able to jump higher than any other boy, trying to improve his leaping ability by touching higher and higher limbs of the oak tree on their farm. This is where his first jump shot attempt is said to have taken place. When Belus Smawley started using his shot regularly, he became the leading scorer. At the age of 18, he got accepted for a position on an AAU18 basketball team. He finished high school afterwards and got an All-American athletic scholarship for Appalachian State University (majoring in history and physical education). He became player-coach until he went to the Navy. He started playing in their basketball team and refined his jump shot. He got married and either worked as a high school teacher and basketball coach or further pursued his NBA basketball career playing fulltime for several teams. Eventually he focused on family and his teaching career, becoming the principal of a junior high school.

① 부모님과 여섯 형제와 함께 농장에서 자랐다.
② 나무의 더 높은 가지를 만지면서 점프 연습을 하였다.
③ 애팔래치아 주립대학교에서 전미 체육 장학금을 받았다.
④ 결혼 후 NBA 농구 선수로서 한 팀에서 활동했다.

문 17. 글의 흐름으로 보아, 주어진 문장이 들어가기에 가장 적절한 곳은?

> It might be understandable, then, for us to want to expect something similar from our machines: to know not only what they think they see but where, in particular, they are looking.

Humans, relative to most other species, have distinctly large and visible sclera — the whites of our eyes — and as a result we are uniquely exposed in how we direct our attention, or at the very least, our gaze. (①) Evolutionary biologists have argued, via the "cooperative eye hypothesis," that this must be a feature, not a bug: that it must point to the fact that cooperation has been uncommonly important in our survival as a species, to the point that the benefits of shared attention outweigh the loss of a certain degree of privacy or discretion. (②) This idea in machine learning goes by the name of "saliency": the idea is that if a system is looking at an image and assigning it to some category, then presumably some parts of the image were more important or more influential than others in making that determination. (③) If we could see a kind of "heat map" that highlighted these critical portions of the image, we might obtain some crucial diagnostic information that we could use as a kind of sanity check to make sure the system is behaving the way we think it should be. (④)

*sclera (눈의) 공막 **outweigh 보다 더 크다
***discretion 재량, 결정권 ****saliency 특징, 중요점

문 18. 다음 (A), (B), (C) 중, 어법상 옳은 것끼리 고른 것은?

> The climate of the irrigated plains can be glimpsed in the murals. The summer sun beats down on the hard ground, and the king himself is shaded by a large umbrella. War, often present, is also carved in vivid detail. In or about 878 BC, three men are depicted (A) (fleeing / fled) from a city which has probably been captured. Dressed in long robes, they jump into the Euphrates River (B) (which / where) one is swimming while the others hug a lifebuoy to their chests. Like a long pillow, the lifebuoy consists of the skin of an animal, inflated with air. As the hands of the refugees (C) (is / are) clutching the inflated lifebuoy, and as much of their breath is expended in blowing air into it, they can only stay afloat by swimming with their legs. Whether they reached the opposite shore will never be known.

	(A)	(B)	(C)
①	fleeing	which	is
②	fleeing	where	are
③	fled	which	is
④	fled	where	are

문 19. 다음 글의 내용과 가장 일치하지 않는 것은?

　　When the Dutch arrived in the 17th century in what's now New York City, their encounters with the indigenous peoples, known as the Lenape, were, at first, mostly amicable, according to historical records. They shared the land and traded guns, beads and wool for beaver furs. The Dutch even "purchased" Manahatta island from the Lenape in 1626. The transaction, enforced by the eventual building of wall around New Amsterdam, marked the very beginning of the Lenape's forced mass migration out of their homeland. The wall, which started showing up on maps in the 1660s, was built to keep out the Native Americans and the British. It eventually became Wall Street, and Manahatta became Manhattan, where part of the Lenape trade route, known as Wickquasgeck, became Brede weg, later Broadway. The Lenape helped shape the geography of modern-day New York City, but other traces of their legacy have all but vanished.

① 네덜란드인과 르나페 원주민들은 총과 동물의 털을 교환하는 무역을 했다.
② 이후에 월스트리트가 된 지역에 지어진 벽은 르나페 원주민이 영국인을 막기 위해 세웠다.
③ 르나페 원주민의 무역로의 일부가 나중에 브로드웨이가 되었다.
④ 르나페 원주민은 현대 뉴욕시의 지형을 형성하는 데 도움을 주었다.

문 20. 다음 글의 밑줄 친 부분 중 어법상 가장 틀린 것은?

　　Today, we take for granted that the media and the celebrity culture it sustains have created new forms of publicness, ① through which we might have intimate relationships with people we have never met. Thanks to media technologies we ② are brought ever closer to the famous, allowing us to enjoy an illusion of intimacy with them. To a greater or lesser degree, we have internalized celebrities, unconsciously made them a part of our consciousness, just ③ as if they were, in fact, friends. Celebrities take up permanent residence in our inner lives as well, ④ become central to our reveries and fantasies, guides to action, to ambition. Now, indeed, celebrity culture can be permanently insinuated into our sensibilities, as many of us carry them, their traits, and our relationships with them around as part of our mental luggage.

*reverie 몽상 **insinuate 암시하다, 일부가 되다

문 21. 다음 글의 빈칸에 들어갈 말로 가장 적절한 것은?

Festivals are significant cultural events that showcase tradition, heritage and community spirit globally. They serve as platforms to celebrate diversity, with each festival reflecting unique traditions like Brazil's Carnival or India's Diwali. Festivals also commemorate historical moments, such as Independence Day in the US or Bastille Day in France. Additionally, they preserve customs and rituals that strengthen personal and cultural identity, while fostering strong community ties through shared activities. Festivals reflect societal values, promote local crafts and arts, enhance spirituality, and attract tourism, which facilitates cultural exchange and understanding. Seasonal festivals, like Holi in India, align with natural cycles, celebrating times of renewal. Ultimately, participating in festivals reinforces community and individual identity, contributing to a global narrative that _____.

*commemorate 기념하다

① makes the participants forget their daily concerns and pains

② values diversity and encourages mutual respect and understanding

③ allows people to break the link between personal life and social life

④ keeps the festivals from determining how people think about themselves

문 22. 밑줄 친 you've been thrown a curve ball이 다음 글에서 의미하는 바로 가장 적절한 것은?

Life is full of its ups and downs. One day, you may feel like you have it all figured out. Then, in a moment's notice, you've been thrown a curve ball. You're not alone in these feelings. Everyone has to face their own set of challenges. Learning how to overcome challenges will help you stay centered and remain calm under pressure. Everyone has their own preferences for how to face a challenge in life. However, there are a few good tips and tricks to follow when the going gets tough. There's no need to feel ashamed for asking for help. Whether you choose to rely on a loved one, a stranger, a mentor, or a friend, there are people who want to help you succeed. You have to be open and willing to accept support. People who come to your aid truly do care about you. Be open to receiving help when you need it.

① 어려운 상황에 직면하다.

② 흥미로운 상황을 맞이하게 되다.

③ 대안적인 방법을 적용하게 되다.

④ 정면 승부를 피하여 에둘러 가다.

문 23. 다음 중 글에 설명된 사회적 지배력과 번식 성공 사이의 관계를 가장 잘 요약한 것은?

Social dominance refers to situations in which an individual or a group controls or dictates others' behavior primarily in competitive situations. Generally, an individual or group is said to be dominant when "a prediction is being made about the course of future interactions or the outcome of competitive situations". Criteria for assessing and assigning dominance relationships can vary from one situation to another. It is difficult to summarize available data briefly, but generally it has been found that dominant individuals, when compared to subordinate individuals, often have more freedom of movement, have priority of access to food, gain higher-quality resting spots, enjoy favorable grooming relationships, occupy more protected parts of a group, obtain higher-quality mates, command and regulate the attention of other group members, and show greater resistance to stress and disease. Despite assertions that suggest otherwise, it really is not clear how powerful the relationship is between an individual's dominance status and its lifetime reproductive success.

*dominance 지배, 우세

① 하위 개체에 비해 모든 지배적인 개체는 평생 동안 높은 번식 성공률을 보인다.
② 개체의 우세 상태와 평생 번식 성공 사이의 관계는 다면적이며 명확하게 정립되어 있다고 할 수는 없다.
③ 사회적 지배력을 갖춘 존재는 음식 및 짝과 같은 자원에 대한 접근을 통해 번식 성공에 영향을 미친다.
④ 하위 개체는 스트레스 수준이 높지 않기 때문에 평생 번식 성공률이 더 높은 경향이 있다.

문 24. 다음 글의 주제로 가장 적절한 것은?

While mindfulness meditation is generally safe, concerns arise from its side effects like panic attacks and psychosis, which are seldom reported and poorly understood in academic studies. Critics argue the rapid adoption of mindfulness by organizations and educational systems may inappropriately shift societal issues to individuals, suggesting that personal stress is due to a lack of meditation rather than addressing systemic causes like environmental pollution or workplace demands. Critics like Professor Ronald Purser suggest that mindfulness may make individuals more compliant with adverse conditions instead of empowering them to seek change. Despite these concerns, the critique isn't against mindfulness itself but against its promotion as a universal solution by entities resistant to change. For a more thorough understanding of mindfulness' benefits and risks, long-term and rigorously controlled studies are essential.

*psychosis 정신 질환

**compliant 순응하는

① the criticism regarding the safety and societal implications of the widespread adoption of mindfulness meditation
② the social and national measures which are taken to relieve personal stress and prevent social and cultural confusion
③ the basic elements of mindfulness that must precede the resolution of social problems rather than individual problems
④ the disadvantages that individuals and societies face due to the meditation performed improperly and the lack of meditation

문 25. Mike Mansfield에 관한 다음 글의 내용과 가장 일치하지 않는 것은?

A man of few words and great modesty, Mike Mansfield often said he did not want to be remembered. Yet, his fascinating life story and enormous contributions are an inspiration for all who follow. Mike Mansfield was born in New York City on March 16, 1903. Following his mother's death when Mike was 7, his father sent him and his two sisters to Great Falls, Montana, to be raised by an aunt and uncle there. At 14, he lied about his age in order to enlist in the U.S. Navy for the duration of World War I. Later, he served in the Army and the Marines, which sent him to the Philippines and China, awakening a lifelong interest in Asia. Mike Mansfield's political career was launched in 1942 when he was elected to the U.S. House of Representatives. He served five terms from Montana's 1st District. In 1952, he was elected to the U.S. Senate and re-elected in 1958, 1964 and 1970. His selection as Democratic Assistant Majority Leader was followed by election in 1961 as Senate Majority Leader. He served in that capacity until his retirement from the Senate in 1977, longer than any other Majority Leader in history.

*House of Representatives 하원 **Senate 상원

***Majority Leader 다수당 원내대표

① 말수가 적고 겸손했으며 자신이 기억되지 않기를 원했었다.
② 모친이 사망한 이후 친인척의 보살핌을 받았다.
③ 군 복무 중 아시아 파병을 계기로 아시아에 대한 관심이 커졌다.
④ 상원의원에 5번 당선되었으며 가장 긴 다수당 원내대표를 역임했다.

해설편 ▶ P.110

2023
6월 24일 시행
법원직 9급

| 풀이 시간: ___:___ ~ ___:___ / 점수: ___점

1초 합격예측! 모바일 성적분석표

QR 코드로 접속하여 문제 풀이시간을 측정하고, 〈1초 합격예측 & 모바일 성적분석표〉 서비스를 통해 지금 바로! 실력을 점검해 보세요.
https://eduwill.kr/o4Of

문 1. Henry Molaison에 대한 다음 글의 내용과 가장 일치하지 않는 것은?

Henry Molaison, a 27-year-old man, suffered from debilitating *seizures for about a decade in the 1950s. On September 1, 1953, Molaison allowed surgeons to remove a section of tissue from each side of his brain to stop the seizures. The operation worked, but Molaison was left with permanent **amnesia, unable to form new memories. This tragic outcome led to one of the most significant discoveries in 20th century brain science: the discovery that complex functions like learning and memory are linked to specific regions of the brain. Molaison became known as "H.M." in research to protect his privacy. Scientists William Scoville studied Molaison and nine other patients who had similar surgeries, finding that only those who had parts of their ***medial temporal lobes removed experienced memory problems, specifically with recent memory. He discovered that a specific structure in the brain was necessary for normal memory. Molaison's life was a series of firsts, as he couldn't remember anything he had done before. However, he was able to acquire new motor skills over time. Studies of Molaison allowed neuroscientists to further explore the brain networks involved in conscious and unconscious memories, even after his death in 2008.

*seizure 발작 **amnesia 기억 상실증
***medial temporal lobe 내측 측두엽

① 외과의사들이 발작을 멈추기 위해 그의 뇌의 양쪽에서 조직의 한 부분을 제거하게 했다.
② 수술 결과는 학습과 기억과 같은 복잡한 기능들이 뇌의 특정 영역과 연결되어 있다는 발견으로 이어졌다.
③ 살아가면서 이전에 한 일을 조금씩 기억할 수 있었지만, 시간이 지나면서 운동 능력이 약화되었다.
④ 그에 대한 연구는 의식적 기억 및 무의식적 기억과 관련된 뇌의 연결 조직을 더 탐구할 수 있게 하였다.

문 2. 다음 글의 밑줄 친 부분 중, 어법상 가장 틀린 것은?

Humans have an inborn *affinity for nature that goes beyond the tangible benefits we derive from the microbes, plants, and animals of the **biomes ① in which we live. The idea that nature in the form of landscapes, plants, and animals ② are good for our well-being is old and can be traced to Charles Darwin or earlier. This idea was called biophilia by psychologist Erich Fromm and was studied by Harvard ant biologist Edward O. Wilson and Stephen Kellert. In 1984, Wilson published Biophilia, which was followed by another book, The Biophilia Hypothesis, ③ edited by Kellert and Wilson, in 1995. Their biophilia hypothesis is ④ that humans have a universal desire to be in natural settings.

*affinity 친밀감
**biome 생물군계(生物群系)

문 3. 다음 글의 내용과 가장 일치하지 않는 것은?

Life on Earth faced an extreme test of survivability during the *Cryogenian Period, which began 720 million years ago. The planet was frozen over most of the 85 million-year period. But life somehow survived during this time called "Snowball Earth". Scientists are trying to better understand the start of this period. They believe a greatly reduced amount of the sun's warmth reached the planet's surface as its radiation bounced off the white ice sheets. Also, they said the fossils found in black shale and identified as seaweed are a sign that livable water environments were more widespread at the time than they once believed. The findings of some research support the idea that the planet was more of a "Slushball Earth" with melting snow. This enabled the earliest forms of complex life to survive in areas once thought to have been frozen solid. The researchers said the most important finding was that ice-free, open water conditions existed in place during the last part of so-called "the Ice Age". The findings demonstrate that the world's oceans were not completely frozen. It means areas of habitable refuge existed where multicellular organisms could survive.

*Cryogenian Period 크라이오제니아기(600~850만년 전 시기)

① 지구는 8천 5백만 년의 대부분의 기간 동안 얼어 있었지만 생명체는 살아남았다.
② 과학자들은 "눈덩이 지구" 기간 동안에도 지구의 표면에 다다른 태양의 온기가 크게 감소하지 않았다고 믿고 있다.
③ "슬러시볼 지구"의 기간 동안에 초기 형태의 복잡한 생명체가 생존하는 것은 가능했다.
④ 연구 결과 "빙하 시대" 후반기의 세계의 바다가 완전히 얼지 않았다는 것이 입증되었다.

문 4. 다음 빈칸에 들어갈 말로 가장 적절한 것은?

As global temperatures rise, so do sea levels, threatening coastal communities around the world. Surprisingly, even small organisms like oysters _____. Oysters are keystone species with *ripple effects on the health of their ecosystems and its inhabitants. Just one adult oyster can filter up to fifty gallons of water in a single day, making waterways cleaner. Healthy oyster reefs also provide a home for hundreds of other marine organisms, promoting biodiversity and ecosystem balance. As rising sea levels lead to pervasive flooding, oyster reefs act as walls to buffer storms and protect against further coastal erosion.

*ripple effect 파급 효과

① can come to our defense
② can be the food for emergency
③ may be contaminated by microplastics
④ can increase the income of local residents

문 5. 다음 글의 내용을 한 문장으로 요약하고자 한다. 빈칸 (A), (B)에 들어갈 말로 가장 적절한 것은?

The myth of the taste map, which claims that different sections of the tongue are responsible for specific tastes, is incorrect, according to modern science. The taste map originated from the experiments of German scientist David Hänig in the early 1900s, which found that the tongue is most sensitive to tastes along the edges and not so much at the center. However, this has been misinterpreted over the years to claim that sweet is at the front of the tongue, bitter is at the back, and salty and sour are at the sides. In reality, different tastes are sensed by *taste buds all over the tongue. Taste buds work together to make us crave or dislike certain foods, based on our long-term learning and association. For example, our ancestors needed fruit for nutrients and easy calories, so we are naturally drawn to sweet tastes, while bitterness in some plants serves as a warning of toxicity. Of course, different species in the animal kingdom also have unique taste abilities: carnivores do not eat fruit and therefore do not crave sugar like humans do.

*taste bud 미뢰

The claim that different parts of the tongue are responsible for specific tastes has been proven to be _____(A)_____ by modern science, and the taste preferences are influenced by the _____(B)_____ history.

	(A)	(B)
①	correct	evolutionary
②	false	evolutionary
③	false	psychological
④	correct	psychological

문 6. 다음 글의 밑줄 친 부분 중 어법상 가장 틀린 것은?

Language is the primary means ① by which people communicate with one another. Although most creatures communicate, human speech is more complex, more creative, and ② used more extensively than the communication systems of other animals. Language is an essential part of what it means to be human and is a basic part of all cultures. Linguistic anthropology is concerned with understanding language and its relation to culture. Language is an amazing thing ③ what we take for granted. When we speak, we use our bodies-our lungs, vocal cords, mouth, tongue, and lips-to produce noises of varying tone and pitch. And, somehow, when we and others ④ do this together, we are able to communicate with one another, but only if we speak the same language. Linguistic anthropologists want to understand the variation among languages and how language is structured, learned, and used.

문 7. 글의 흐름으로 보아, 주어진 문장이 들어가기에 가장 적절한 곳은?

Healthcare chatbots have been purposed to solve this problem and ensure proper diagnosis and advice for people from the comfort of their homes.

People have grown hesitant to approach hospitals or health centers due to the fear of contracting a disease or the heavy sum of consultation fees. (①) This leads them to self-diagnose themselves based upon unverified information sources on the Internet. (②) This often proves harmful effects on the person's mental and physical health if misdiagnosed and improper medicines are consumed. (③) Based upon the severity of the diagnosis, the chatbot prescribes over the counter treatment or escalates the diagnosis to a verified healthcare professional. (④) Interactive chatbots that have been trained on a large and wide variety of symptoms, risk factors, and treatment can handle user health queries with ease, especially in the case of COVID-19.

문 8. 주어진 글 다음에 이어질 글의 순서로 가장 적절한 것은?

> Sports fan depression is a real phenomenon that affects many *avid sports fans, especially during times of disappointment or defeat.

(A) Fans may experience a decrease in mood, appetite, and sleep quality, as well as an increase in stress levels and a heightened risk of developing anxiety or depression. There are many factors that can contribute to sports fan depression, including personal investment in a team's success, social pressures to support a particular team, and the intense media coverage and scrutiny that often accompanies high-profile sports events.

(B) For many fans, their emotional investment in their favorite teams or athletes can be so intense that losing or failing to meet expectations can lead to feelings of sadness, frustration, and even depression. Research has shown that sports fan depression can have a range of negative effects on both mental and physical health.

(C) To mitigate the negative effects of sports fan depression, it's important for fans to maintain a healthy perspective on sports and remember that they are ultimately just games. Engaging in self-care activities such as exercise, spending time with loved ones, and seeking support from a mental health professional can also be helpful.

*avid 열심인

① (A) − (C) − (B)   ② (B) − (A) − (C)
③ (B) − (C) − (A)   ④ (C) − (B) − (A)

문 9. Roald Dahl에 관한 다음 글의 내용과 가장 일치하지 않는 것은?

> Roald Dahl (1916-1990) was born in Wales of Norwegian parents. He spent his childhood in England and, at age eighteen, went to work for the Shell Oil Company in Africa. When World War II broke out, he joined the Royal Air Force and became a fighter pilot. At the age of twenty-six he moved to Washington, D.C., and it was there he began to write. His first short story, which recounted his adventures in the war, was bought by *The Saturday Evening Post*, and so began a long and illustrious career. After establishing himself as a writer for adults, Roald Dahl began writing children's stories in 1960 while living in England with his family. His first stories were written as entertainment for his own children, to whom many of his books are dedicated. Roald Dahl is now considered one of the most beloved storytellers of our time.

① 어린 시절을 영국에서 보냈고, 18세에 아프리카에서 일했다.
② 2차 세계대전이 발발했을 때는 공군에 입대하여 조종사가 되었다.
③ 전쟁에서 자신의 모험을 다룬 첫 번째 단편 소설을 썼다.
④ 성인을 위한 작가가 된 뒤 영국에서 가족과 떨어져 혼자 살면서 글을 썼다.

문 10. 다음 글에서 전체 흐름과 가장 관계 없는 문장은?

One of the most interesting discoveries in the field of new sources of sustainable energy is bio-solar energy from jellyfish. Scientists have discovered that the fluorescent protein in this animal can be used to generate solar energy in a more sustainable way than current *photovoltaic energy. How is this energy generated? ① The process involves converting the jellyfish's fluorescent protein into a solar cell that is capable of generating energy and transferring it to small devices. ② There has been constant criticism that the natural environment is being damaged by reckless solar power generation. ③ The main advantage of using these living beings as a natural energy source is that they are a clean alternative that does not use fossil fuels or require the use of limited resources. ④ Although this project is still currently in the trial phase, the expectation is that this source of energy will be able to be expanded and become a green alternative for powering the type of small electronic devices that are becoming more and more common.

*photovoltaic 광전기성의

문 11. 주어진 글 다음에 이어질 글의 순서로 가장 적절한 것은?

On the human level, a cow seems simple. You feed it grass, and it pays you back with milk. It's a trick whose secret is limited to cows and a few other mammals (most can't digest grass).

(A) A cow's complexity is even greater. In particular, a cow (plus a bull) can make a new generation of baby cows. This is a simple thing on a human level, but inexpressibly complex on a microscopic level.

(B) Seen through a microscope, though, it all gets more complicated. And the closer you look, the more complicated it gets. Milk is not a single substance, but a mixture of many. Grass is so complex that we still don't fully understand it.

(C) You don't need to understand the details to exploit the process: it's a straightforward transformation from grass into milk, more like chemistry — or *alchemy — than biology. It is, in its way, magic, but it's rational magic that works reliably. All you need is some grass, a cow and several generations of practical knowhow.

*alchemy 연금술

① (B) − (A) − (C)　　② (B) − (C) − (A)
③ (C) − (A) − (B)　　④ (C) − (B) − (A)

문 12. 글의 흐름으로 보아, 주어진 문장이 들어가기에 가장 적절한 곳은?

> But here it's worth noting that more than half the workforce has little or no opportunity for remote work.

COVID-19's spread flattened the cultural and technological barriers standing in the way of remote work. One analysis of the potential for remote work to persist showed that 20 to 25 percent of workforces in advanced economies could work from home in the range of three to five days a week. (①) This is four to five times more remote work than pre-COVID-19. (②) Moreover, not all work that can be done remotely should be; for example, negotiations, brainstorming, and providing sensitive feedback are activities that may be less effective when done remotely. (③) The outlook for remote work, then, depends on the work environment, job, and the tasks at hand, so *hybrid work setups, where some work happens on-site and some remotely, are likely to persist. (④) To unlock sustainable performance and well-being in a hybrid world, the leading driver of performance and productivity should be the sense of purpose work provides to employees, not compensation.

*hybrid 혼합체

문 13. Sigmund Freud에 관한 다음 글의 내용과 가장 일치하지 않는 것은?

Sigmund Freud was a doctor of psychology in Vienna, Austria at the end of the nineteenth century. He treated many patients with nervous problems through his "talk cure." For this type of treatment, Freud simply let his patients talk to him about anything that was bothering them. While treating his patients, he began to realize that although there were events in a patient's past that she or he might not remember consciously, these events could affect the person's actions in her or his present life. Freud called the place where past memories were hidden the unconscious mind. Images from the unconscious mind might show up in a person's dreams or through the person's actions. Freud wrote a book about his theories about the unconscious mind and dreaming in 1899. The title of the book was "The Interpretation of Dreams"

① 오스트리아의 정신과 의사였다.
② 신경 문제가 있는 환자들을 대화를 통해 치료했다.
③ 기억이 나지 않는 과거는 환자에게 영향을 미치지 못한다고 주장했다.
④ "꿈의 해석"이라는 책을 썼다.

문 14. 다음 글의 요지로 가장 적절한 것은?

All emotions tell us something about ourselves and our situation. But sometimes we find it hard to accept what we feel. We might judge ourselves for feeling a certain way, like if we feel jealous, for example. But instead of thinking we should not feel that way, it's better to notice how we actually feel. Avoiding negative feelings or pretending we don't feel the way we do can *backfire. It's harder to move past difficult feelings and allow them to fade if we don't face them and try to understand why we feel that way. You don't have to dwell on your emotions or constantly talk about how you feel. Emotional awareness simply means recognizing, respecting, and accepting your feelings as they happen.

*backfire 역효과를 내다

① 부정적인 감정은 잘 조절해서 표현해야 한다.
② 과거의 부정적 감정은 되도록 빨리 극복해야 한다.
③ 감정을 수용하기 어렵다면 전문가의 도움을 받아야 한다.
④ 우리의 감정을 인식하고 존중하며 그대로 받아들여야 한다.

문 15. 주어진 글 다음에 이어질 글의 순서로 가장 적절한 것은?

At the level of lawmaking, there is no reason why tech giants should have such an ironclad grip on technological resources and innovation.

(A) As the Daily Wire's Matt Walsh has pointed out, for example, if you don't buy your kid a smartphone, he won't have one. There is no need to put in his hand a device that enables him to indulge his every impulse without supervision.

(B) At the private and personal level, there's no reason why they should have control of your life, either. In policy, politics, and our personal lives, it should not be taken as "inevitable" that our data will be sold to the highest bidder, our children will be addicted to online games, and our lives will be lived in the metaverse.

(C) As a free people, we are entitled to exert absolute control over which kinds of digital products we consume, and in what quantities. Most especially, parents should control what tech products go to their kids.

① (B) — (A) — (C)
② (B) — (C) — (A)
③ (C) — (A) — (B)
④ (C) — (B) — (A)

문 16. 글의 흐름으로 보아, 주어진 문장이 들어가기에 가장 적절한 곳은?

> These may appear as challenges which may be impossible to address because of the uncertainty in our ability to predict future climate.

Global warming is a reality man has to live with. (①) This is a very important issue to recognize, because, of all the parameters that affect human existence, on planet earth, it is the food security that is of paramount importance to life on earth and which is most threatened by global warming. (②) Future food security will be dependent on a combination of the stresses, both biotic and *abiotic, imposed by climate change, variability of weather within the growing season, development of **cultivars more suited to different ***ambient conditions, and, the ability to develop effective adaptation strategies which allow these cultivars to express their genetic potential under the changing climate conditions. (③) However, these challenges also provide us the opportunities to enhance our understanding of soil-plant-atmosphere interaction and how one could utilize this knowledge to enable us achieve the ultimate goal of enhanced food security across all areas of the globe. (④)

*abiotic 비생물적인
**cultivar 품종
***ambient 주변의

문 17. 다음 글의 밑줄 친 부분 중, 어법상 가장 틀린 것은?

Anthropologist Paul Ekman proposed in the 1970s that humans experience six basic emotions: anger, fear, surprise, disgust, joy, and sadness. However, the exact number of emotions ① disputing, with some researchers suggesting there are only four, and others counting as many as 27. Additionally, scientists debate whether emotions are universal to all human cultures or whether we're born with them or learn them through experience. ② Despite these disagreements, emotions are clear products of activity in specific regions of the brain. The *amygdala and the **insula or insular cortex are two representative brain structures most ③ closely linked with emotions. The amygdala, a paired, almond-shaped structure deep within the brain, integrates emotions, emotional behavior, and motivation. It interprets fear, helps distinguish friends from foes, and identifies social rewards and how to attain ④ them. The insula is the source of disgust. The experience of disgust may protect you from ingesting poison or spoiled food.

*amygdala 편도체
**insula cortex 대뇌 피질

문 18. 다음 글의 주제로 가장 적절한 것은?

Do you want to be a successful anchor? If so, keep this in mind. As an anchor, the individual will be called upon to communicate news and information to viewer during newscasts, special reports and other types of news programs. This will include interpreting news events, adlibbing, and communicating breaking news effectively when scripts are not available. Anchoring duties also involve gathering and writing stories. The anchor must be able to deliver scripts clearly and effectively. Strong writing skills, solid news judgement and a strong sense of visual storytelling are essential skills. This individual must be a self-starter who cultivates sources and finds new information as a regular part of job. Live reporting skills are important, as well as the ability to adlib and describe breaking news as it takes place.

① difficulties of producing live news
② qualifications to become a news anchor
③ the importance of the social role of journalists
④ the importance of forming the right public opinion

문 19. 다음 글의 내용과 가장 일치하지 않는 것은?

Modern sculpture is generally considered to have begun with the work of French sculptor Auguste Rodin. Rodin, often considered a sculptural Impressionist, did not set out to rebel against artistic traditions, however, he incorporated novel ways of building his sculpture that defied classical categories and techniques. Specifically, Rodin modeled complex, turbulent, deeply pocketed surfaces into clay. While he never self-identified as an Impressionist, the vigorous, gestural modeling he employed in his works is often likened to the quick, gestural *brush strokes aiming to capture a fleeting moment that was typical of the Impressionists. Rodin's most original work departed from traditional themes of mythology and **allegory, in favor of modeling the human body with intense realism, and celebrating individual character and physicality.

*brush stroke 붓놀림
**allegory 우화, 풍자

① 현대 조각은 일반적으로 로댕의 작품에서 시작된 것으로 여겨진다.
② 로댕은 고전적인 기술을 거부하며 조각품을 만드는 새로운 방법을 통합했다.
③ 로댕은 자신을 인상파라고 밝히며 인상파의 전형적인 붓놀림을 보여주었다.
④ 로댕의 가장 독창적인 작품은 신화와 우화의 전통적인 주제에서 벗어나고자 했다.

문 20. 다음 글의 주제로 가장 적절한 것은?

> Cosmetics became so closely associated with portraiture that some photography handbooks included recipes for them. American photographers also, at times, used cosmetics to retouch negatives and prints, enlivening women's faces with traces of rouge. Some customers with dark skin requested photographs that would make them look lighter. A skin lightener advertisement that appeared in an African American newspaper in 1935 referenced this practice by promising that its product could achieve the same look produced by photographers: a lighter skin Cop free of *blemishes. By drawing attention to the face and encouraging cosmetics use, portrait photography heightened the aesthetic valuation of smooth and often light-colored skin.
>
> *blemish (피부 등의) 티

① side effects of excessive use of cosmetics
② overuse of cosmetics promoted by photographers
③ active use of cosmetics to make the face look better
④ decreased use of cosmetics due to advances in photography

문 21. 다음 글의 밑줄 친 부분 중 문맥상 낱말의 쓰임이 가장 적절하지 않은 것은?

> "Play is something done for its own sake." says psychiatrist Stuart Brown, author of "Play" He writes: "It's voluntary, it's pleasurable, it offers a sense of engagement, it takes you out of time. And the act itself is more important than the outcome." With this definition in mind, it's easy to recognize play's potential benefits. Play ① nurtures relationships with oneself and others. It ② relieves stress and increases happiness. It builds feelings of empathy, creativity, and collaboration. It supports the growth of *sturdiness and grit. When children are deprived of opportunities for play, their development can be significantly ③ enhanced. Play is so important that the United Nations High Commission on Human Rights declared it a ④ fundamental right of every child. Play is not **frivolous. It is not something to do after the "real work" is done. Play is the real work of childhood. Through it, children have their best chance for becoming whole, happy adults.
>
> *sturdiness 강건함
> **frivolous 경박한, 하찮은

문 22. 다음 빈칸에 들어갈 말로 가장 적절한 것은?

> Lewis Pugh is a British endurance swimmer, who is best known for his long-distance swims in cold and open waters. He swims in cold places as a way to draw attention to the urgent need to protect the world's oceans and waterways from the effects of climate change and pollution. In 2019, Pugh decided to swim in Lake Imja, which is located in the Khumbu region of Nepal, near Mount Everest. After a failed first attempt, Lewis had a *debrief to discuss the best way to swim at 5,300 meters above sea level. He is usually very aggressive when he swims because he wants to finish quickly and get out of the cold water. But this time he showed _____ and swam slowly.
>
> *debrief 평가 회의

① grief
② anger
③ humility
④ confidence

문 23. 다음 글에서 전체 흐름과 가장 관계 없는 문장은?

Fast fashion is a method of producing inexpensive clothing at a rapid pace to respond to the latest fashion trends. With shopping evolving into a form of entertainment in the age of fast fashion, customers are contributing to what sustainability experts refer to as a throwaway culture. This means customers simply discard products once they are deemed useless rather than recycling or donating them. ① The consumers are generally satisfied with the quality of fast fashion brand clothing. ② As a result, these discarded items add a huge burden to the environment. ③ To resolve the throwaway culture and fast fashion crisis, the concept of sustainability in fashion is brought to the spotlight. ④ Sustainable fashion involves apparel, footwear, and accessories that are produced, distributed, and utilized as sustainably as possible while taking into account socio-economic and environmental concerns.

문 24. 다음 글의 요지로 가장 적절한 것은?

Wrinkles are a sure sign of aging, and may also hint that bone health is on the decline. Researchers at Yale School of Medicine found that some women with deepening and worsening skin wrinkles also had lower bone density, independent of age and factors known to influence bone mass. Skin and bones share a common building-block protein, type 1 collagen, which is lost with age, says study author Dr. Lubna Pal. Wrinkles between the eyebrows — the vertical lines above the bridge of the nose — appear to be the strongest markers of *brittle bones, she says. Long-term studies are needed, but it appears the skin reflects what's happening at the level of the bone, says Pal.

*brittle 잘 부러지는

① 나이가 들면서 주름이 생기는 것은 당연한 현상이다.
② 골밀도 감소와 주름 생성의 관계에 관해서는 연구가 더 필요하다.
③ 여성이 남성보다 주름이 더 많이 생기는 이유는 골밀도 차이 때문이다.
④ 주름은 단지 피부 노화와만 연관된 것이 아니라 뼈 건강 상태와도 연관이 있다.

문 25. 다음 글의 내용과 가장 일치하지 않는 것은?

Meditation can improve your quality of life thanks to its many psychological and physical benefits. Mindfulness-based interventions, such as meditation, have been shown to improve mental health, specifically in the area of stress, according to a study in the Clinical Psychology Review. When faced with a difficult or stressful moment, our bodies create cortisol, the steroid hormone responsible for regulating stress and our natural fight-or-flight response, among many other functions. Chronic stress can cause sustained and elevated levels of cortisol, which can lead to other negative effects on your health, including *cardiovascular and immune systems and gut health. Meditation, which focuses on calming the mind and regulating emotion, can help to reduce chronic stress in the body and lower the risk of its side effects.

*cardiovascular 심혈관계의

① Meditation benefits us both mentally and physically.
② Cortisol is released in a stressful situation.
③ Stress does not usually affect our cardiovascular systems.
④ Meditation can help lower chronic stress in the body.

해설편 ▶ P.119

2022

6월 25일 시행
법원직 9급

┃ 풀이 시간: _____ : _____ ~ _____ : _____ / 점수: _____ 점

문 1. (A), (B), (C)의 각 네모 안에서 어법에 맞는 표현으로 가장 적절한 것은?

The selection of the appropriate protective clothing for any job or task (A) │is / are│ usually dictated by an analysis or assessment of the hazards presented. The expected activities of the wearer as well as the frequency and types of exposure, are typical variables that input into this determination. For example, a firefighter is exposed to a variety of burning materials. Specialized multilayer fabric systems are thus used (B) │to meet / meeting│ the *thermal challenges presented. This results in protective gear that is usually fairly heavy and essentially provides the highest levels of protection against any fire situation. In contrast, an industrial worker who has to work in areas (C) │where / which│ the possibility of a flash fire exists would have a very different set of hazards and requirements. In many cases, a flame-resistant coverall worn over cotton work clothes adequately addresses the hazard.

*thermal 열의

	(A)	(B)	(C)
①	is	to meet	where
②	is	meeting	which
③	are	meeting	where
④	are	to meet	which

문 2. 다음 글의 내용을 한 문장으로 요약하고자 한다. 빈칸 (A), (B)에 들어갈 말로 가장 적절한 것은?

In India, approximately 360 million people — one-third of the population — live in or very close to the forests. More than half of these people live below the official poverty line, and consequently they depend crucially on the resources they obtain from the forests. The Indian government now runs programs aimed at improving their lot by involving them in the commercial management of their forests, in this way allowing them to continue to obtain the food and materials they need, but at the same time to sell forest produce. If the programs succeed, forest dwellers will be more prosperous, but they will be able to preserve their traditional way of life and culture, and the forest will be managed sustainably, so the wildlife is not depleted.

⇒ The Indian government is trying to _____(A)_____ the lives of the poor who live near forests without _____(B)_____ the forests.

	(A)	(B)
①	improve	ruining
②	control	preserving
③	improve	limiting
④	control	enlarging

문 3. 다음 글의 내용을 한 문장으로 요약하고자 한다. 빈칸 (A), (B)에 들어갈 말로 가장 적절한 것은?

> In the absence of facial cues or touch during pandemic, there is a greater need to focus on other aspects of conversation, including more emphasis on tone and inflection, slowing the speed, and increasing loudness without sounding annoying. Many *nuances of the spoken word are easily missed without facial expression, so eye contact will assume an even greater importance. Some hospital workers have developed innovative ways to try to solve this problem. One of nurse specialists was deeply concerned that her chronically sick young patients could not see her face, so she printed off a variety of face stickers to get children to point towards. Some hospitals now also provide their patients with 'face-sheets' that permit easier identification of staff members, and it is always useful to reintroduce yourself and colleagues to patients when wearing masks.
>
> *nuance 미묘한 차이, 뉘앙스

> Some hospitals and workers are looking for ___(A)___ ways to ___(B)___ conversation with patients during pandemic.

	(A)	(B)
①	alternative	complement
②	bothering	analyze
③	effective	hinder
④	disturbing	improve

문 4. 주어진 글 다음에 이어질 글의 순서로 가장 적절한 것은?

> Once they leave their mother, primates have to keep on making decisions about whether new foods they encounter are safe and worth collecting.

(A) By the same token, if the sampler feels fine, it will reenter the tree in a few days, eat a little more, then wait again, building up to a large dose slowly. Finally, if the monkey remains healthy, the other members figure this is OK, and they adopt the new food.

(B) If the plant harbors a particularly strong toxin, the sampler's system will try to break it down, usually making the monkey sick in the process. "I've seen this happen," says Glander. "The other members of the troop are watching with great interest — if the animal gets sick, no other animal will go into that tree. There's a cue being given — a social cue."

(C) Using themselves as experiment tools is one option, but social primates have found a better way. Kenneth Glander calls it "sampling." When howler monkeys move into a new habitat, one member of the troop will go to a tree, eat a few leaves, then wait a day.

① (A) - (B) - (C)　　② (B) - (A) - (C)
③ (C) - (B) - (A)　　④ (C) - (A) - (B)

문 5. 다음 글의 Zainichi에 관한 내용으로 가장 일치하지 않는 것은?

Following Japan's defeat in World War II, the majority of ethnic Koreans (1-1.4 million) left Japan. By 1948, the population of ethnic Koreans settled around 600,000. These Koreans and their descendants are commonly referred to as Zainichi (literally "residing in Japan"), a term that appeared in the immediate postwar years. Ethnic Koreans who remained in Japan did so for diverse reasons. Koreans who had achieved successful careers in business, the imperial bureaucracy, and the military during the colonial period or who had taken advantage of economic opportunities that opened up immediately after the war — opted to maintain their relatively privileged status in Japanese society rather than risk returning to an impoverished and politically unstable post-liberation Korea. Some Koreans who *repatriated were so repulsed by the poor conditions they observed that they decided to return to Japan. Other Koreans living in Japan could not afford the train fare to one of the departure ports, and among them who had ethnic Japanese spouses and Japanese-born, Japanese-speaking children, it made more sense to stay in Japan rather than to navigate the cultural and linguistic challenges of a new environment.

*repatriate 본국으로 송환하다

① 주로 제2차 세계대전 이후에 일본에 남은 한국인들과 후손을 일컫는다.
② 전쟁 후에 경제적인 이득을 취한 사람들도 있었다.
③ 어떤 사람들은 한국에 갔다가 다시 일본으로 돌아왔다.
④ 한국으로 돌아갈 교통비를 마련하지 못한 사람들은 일본인과 결혼했다.

문 6. 다음 빈칸에 들어갈 말로 가장 적절한 것은?

There are a few jobs where people have had to _____. We see referees and umpires using their arms and hands to signal directions to the players — as in cricket, where a single finger upwards means that the batsman is out and has to leave the *wicket. Orchestra conductors control the musicians through their movements. People working at a distance from each other have to invent special signals if they want to communicate. So do people working in a noisy environment, such as in a factory where the machines are very loud, or lifeguards around a swimming pool full of school children.

*wicket (크리켓에서) 삼주문

① support their parents and children
② adapt to an entirely new work style
③ fight in court for basic human rights
④ develop their signing a bit more fully

문 7. 다음 글의 내용과 가장 일치하지 않는 것은?

Opponents of the use of animals in research also oppose use of animals to test the safety of drugs or other compounds. Within the pharmaceutical industry, it was noted that out of 19 chemicals known to cause cancer in humans when taken, only seven caused cancer in mice and rats using standards set by the National Cancer Instituted (Barnard and Koufman, 1997). For example, and antidepressant, nomifensin, had minimal toxicity in rats, rabbits, dogs, and monkeys yet caused liver toxicity and *anemia in humans. In these and other cases, it has been shown that some compounds have serious adverse reactions in humans that were not predicted by animal testing resulting in conditions in the treated humans that could lead to disability, or even death. And researchers who are calling for an end to animal research state that they have better methods available such as human clinical trials, observation aided by laboratory of autopsy tests.

*anemia 빈혈

① 한 기관의 실험 결과 동물과 달리 19개의 발암물질 중에 7개는 인간에게 영향을 미쳤다.
② 어떤 약물은 동물 실험 때와 달리 인간에게 간독성과 빈혈을 일으켰다.
③ 동물 실험에서 나타난 결과가 인간에게는 다르게 작용될 수 있다.
④ 동물 실험을 반대하는 연구자들은 대안적인 방법들을 제시하고 있다.

문 8. 다음 중 문맥상 낱말의 쓰임이 가장 적절하지 않은 것은?

Cold showers are any showers with a water temperature below 70°F. They may have health benefits. For people with depression, cold showers can work as a kind of gentle electroshock therapy. The cold water sends many electrical impulses to your brain. They *jolt your system to ① increase alertness, clarity, and energy levels. Endorphins, which are sometimes called happiness hormones, are also released. This effect leads to feelings of well-being and ② optimism. For people that are obese, taking a cold shower 2 or 3 times per week may contribute to increased metabolism. It may help fight obesity over time. The research about how exactly cold showers help people lose weight is ③ clear. However, it does show that cold water can even out certain hormone levels and heal the **gastrointestinal system. These effects may add to the cold shower's ability to lead to weight loss. Furthermore, when taken regularly, cold showers can make our circulatory system more efficient. Some people also report that their skin looks better as a result of cold showers, probably because of better circulation. Athletes have known this benefit for years, even if we have only ④ recently seen data that supports cold water for healing after a sport injury.

*jolt 갑자기 덜컥 움직이다
**gastrointestinal 위장의

문 9. 다음 글의 내용을 한 문장으로 요약하고자 한다. 빈칸 (A), (B)에 들어갈 말로 가장 적절한 것은?

Researchers have been interested in the habitual ways a single individual copes with conflict when it occurs. They've called this approach conflict styles. There are several apparent conflict styles, and each has its pros and cons. The collaborating style tends to solve problems in ways that maximize the chances that the best result is provided for all involved. The pluses of a collaborating style include creating trust, maintaining positive relationship, and building commitment. However, it's time consuming and it takes a lot of energy to collaborate with another during conflict. The competing style may develop hostility in the person who doesn't achieve their goals. However, the competing style tends to resolve a conflict quickly.

The collaborating style might be used for someone who put a great value in _____(A)_____, while a person who prefers _____(B)_____ may choose the competing style.

	(A)	(B)
①	financial ability	interaction
②	saving time	peacefulness
③	mutual understanding	time efficiency
④	effectiveness	consistency

문 10. 주어진 글 다음에 이어질 글의 순서로 가장 적절한 것은?

The historical evolution of Conflict Resolution gained momentum in the 1950s and 1960s, at the height of the Cold War, when the development of nuclear weapons and conflict between the superpowers seemed to threaten human survival.

(A) The combination of analysis and practice implicit in the new ideas was not easy to reconcile with traditional scholarly institutions or the traditions of practitioners such as diplomats and politicians.

(B) However, they were not taken seriously by some. The international relations profession had its own understanding of international conflict and did not see value in the new approaches as proposed.

(C) A group of pioneers from different disciplines saw the value of studying conflict as a general phenomenon, with similar properties, whether it occurs in international relations, domestic politics, industrial relations, communities, or between individuals.

① (B) − (A) − (C) ② (B) − (C) − (A)
③ (C) − (A) − (B) ④ (C) − (B) − (A)

문 11. (A), (B), (C)의 각 네모 안에서 어법에 맞는 표현으로 가장
적절한 것은?

The key to understanding economics is accepting
(A) that / what there are always unintended
consequences. Actions people take for their own good
reasons have results they don't envision or intend.
The same is true with *geopolitics. It is doubtful that
the village of Rome, when it started its expansion in
the seventh century BC, (B) had / have a master
plan for conquering the Mediterranean world five
hundred years later. But the first action its
inhabitants took against neighboring villages set in
motion a process that was both constrained by
reality and (C) filled / filling with unintended
consequences. Rome wasn't planned, and neither
did it just happen.

*geopolitics 지정학

	(A)	(B)	(C)
①	that	had	filled
②	what	had	filling
③	what	have	filled
④	that	have	filling

문 12. 다음 빈칸에 들어갈 말로 가장 적절한 것을 고르시오.

Water and civilization go hand-in-hand. The idea
of a "*hydraulic civilization" argues that water is
the unifying context and justification for many
large-scale civilizations throughout history. For
example, the various multi-century Chinese
empires survived as long as they did in part by
controlling floods along the Yellow River. One
interpretation of the hydraulic theory is that the
justification for gathering populations into large
cities is to manage water. Another interpretation
suggests that large water projects enable the rise of
big cities. The Romans understood the connections
between water and power, as the Roman Empire
built a vast network of **aqueducts throughout
land they controlled, many of which remain intact.
For example, Pont du Gard in southern France stands
today as a testament to humanity's investment in its
water infrastructure. Roman governors built roads,
bridges, and water systems as a way of _____.

*hydraulic 수력학의
**aqueduct 송수로

① focusing on educating young people
② prohibiting free trade in local markets
③ concentrating and strengthening their authority
④ giving up their properties to other countries

문 13. 주어진 글 다음에 이어질 글의 순서로 가장 적절한 것은?

> Ambiguity is so uncomfortable that it can even turn good news into bad. You go to your doctor with a persistent stomachache. Your doctor can't figure out what the reason is, so she sends you to the lab for tests.

> (A) And what happens? Your immediate relief may be replaced by a weird sense of discomfort. You still don't know what the pain was! There's got to be an explanation somewhere.
>
> (B) A week later you're called back to hear the results. When you finally get into her office, your doctor smiles and tells you the tests were all negative.
>
> (C) Maybe it is cancer and they've just missed it. Maybe it's worse. Surely they should be able to find a cause. You feel frustrated by the lack of a definitive answer.

① (B) − (A) − (C) ② (B) − (C) − (A)
③ (C) − (A) − (B) ④ (C) − (B) − (A)

문 14. 글의 흐름으로 보아, 주어진 문장이 들어가기에 가장 적절한 곳은?

> The effect, however, was just the reverse.

> How we dress for work has taken on a new element of choice, and with it, new anxieties. (①) The practice of having a "dress-down day" or "casual day," which began to emerge a decade or so ago, was intended to make life easier for employees, to enable them to save money and feel more relaxed at the office. (②) In addition to the normal workplace wardrobe, employees had to create a "workplace casual" *wardrobe. (③) It couldn't really be the sweats and T-shirts you wore around the house on the weekend. (④) It had to be a selection of clothing that sustained a certain image — relaxed, but also serious.
>
> *wardrobe 옷, 의류

문 15. 다음 글의 밑줄 친 부분 중, 어법상 가장 틀린 것은?

> You should choose the research method ① that best suits the outcome you want. You may run a survey online that enables you to question large numbers of people and ② provides full analysis in report format, or you may think asking questions one to one is a better way to get the answers you need from a smaller test selection of people. ③ Whichever way you choose, you will need to compare like for like. Ask people the same questions and compare answers. Look for both similarities and differences. Look for patterns and trends. Deciding on a way of recording and analysing the data ④ are important. A simple self created spreadsheet may well be enough to record some basic research data.

문 16. 다음 글의 요지로 가장 적절한 것은?

> Some criminal offenders may engage in illegal behavior because they love the excitement and thrills that crime can provide. In his highly influential work *Seductions of Crime*, sociologist Jack Katz argues that there are immediate benefits to criminality that "seduce" people into a life of crime. For some people, shoplifting and *vandalism are attractive because getting away with crime is a thrilling demonstration of personal competence. The need for excitement may counter fear of apprehension and punishment. In fact, some offenders will deliberately seek out especially risky situations because of the added "thrill". The need for excitement is a significant predictor of criminal choice.
>
> *vandalism 기물 파손

① 범죄를 줄이기 위해서 재소자를 상대로 한 교육이 필요하다.
② 범죄 행위에서 생기는 흥분과 쾌감이 범죄를 유발할 수 있다.
③ 엄격한 형벌 제도와 법 집행을 통해 강력 범죄를 줄일 수 있다.
④ 세밀하고 꼼꼼한 제도를 만들어 범죄 피해자를 도울 필요가 있다.

문 17. 다음 빈칸에 들어갈 말로 가장 적절한 것은?

In one classic study showing the importance of attachment, Wisconsin University psychologists Harry and Margaret Harlow investigated the responses of young monkeys. The infants were separated from their biological mothers, and two *surrogate mothers were introduced to their cages. One, the wire mother, consisted of a round wooden head, a mesh of cold metal wires, and a bottle of milk from which the baby monkey could drink. The second mother was a foam-rubber form wrapped in a heated terry-cloth blanket. The infant monkeys went to the wire mother for food, but they overwhelmingly preferred and spent significantly more time with the warm terry-cloth mother. The warm terry-cloth mother provided no food, but did provide _____.

*surrogate 대리의

① jobs
② drugs
③ comfort
④ education

문 18. 다음 글의 밑줄 친 부분 중, 어법상 가장 틀린 것은?

I was released for adoption by my biological parents and ① spend the first decade of my life in orphanages. I spent many years thinking that something was wrong with me. If my own parents didn't want me, who could? I tried to figure out ② what I had done wrong and why so many people sent me away. I don't get close to anyone now because if I do they might leave me. I had to isolate ③ myself emotionally to survive when I was a child, and I still operate on the assumptions I had as a child. I am so fearful of being deserted ④ that I won't venture out and take even minimal risks. I am 40 years old now, but I still feel like a child.

문 19. 다음 글의 밑줄 친 부분 중 어법상 가장 틀린 것은?

Music can have *psychotherapeutic effects that may transfer to everyday life. A number of scholars suggested people ① to use music as psychotherapeutic agent. Music therapy can be broadly defined as being 'the use of music as an adjunct to the treatment or rehabilitation of individuals to enhance their psychological, physical, cognitive or social ② functioning'. Positive emotional experiences from music may improve therapeutic process and thus ③ strengthen traditional cognitive/behavioral methods and their transfer to everyday goals. This may be partially because emotional experiences elicited by music and everyday behaviors ④ share overlapping neurological pathways responsible for positive emotions and motivations.

*psychotherapeutic 심리 요법의

문 20. 다음 빈칸에 들어갈 말로 가장 적절한 것은?

Cultural interpretations are usually made on the basis of _____ rather than measurable evidence. The arguments tend to be circular. People are poor because they are lazy. How do we "know" they are lazy? Because they are poor. Promoters of these interpretations rarely understand that low productivity results not from laziness and lack of effort but from lack of capital inputs to production. African farmers are not lazy, but they do lack soil nutrients, tractors, feeder roads, irrigated plots, storage facilities, and the like. Stereotypes that Africans work little and therefore are poor are put to rest immediately by spending a day in a village, where backbreaking labor by men and women is the norm.

① statistics
② prejudice
③ appearance
④ circumstances

문 21. 글의 흐름으로 보아, 주어진 문장이 들어가기에 가장 적절한 곳은?

> But the demand for food isn't *elastic; people don't eat more just because food is cheap.

The free market has never worked in agriculture and it never will. (①) The economics of a family farm are very different than a firm's: When prices fall, the firm can lay off people and idle factories. (②) Eventually the market finds a new balance between supply and demand. (③) And laying off farmers doesn't help to reduce supply. (④) You can fire me, but you can't fire my land, because some other farmer who needs more cash flow or thinks he's more efficient than I am will come in and farm it.

*elastic 탄력성 있는

문 22. 다음 글의 주제로 가장 적절한 것은?

Daily training creates special nutritional needs for an athlete, particularly the elite athlete whose training commitment is almost a fulltime job. But even recreational sport will create nutritional challenges. And whatever your level of involvement in sport, you must meet these challenges if you're to achieve the maximum return from training. Without sound eating, much of the purpose of your training might be lost. In the worst-case scenario, dietary problems and deficiencies may directly impair training performance. In other situations, you might improve, but at a rate that is below your potential or slower than your competitors. However, on the positive side, with the right everyday eating plan your commitment to training will be fully rewarded.

① how to improve body flexibility
② importance of eating well in exercise
③ health problems caused by excessive diet
④ improving skills through continuous training

문 23. 다음 글의 주제로 가장 적절한 것은?

A very well-respected art historian called Ernst Gombrich wrote about something called "the beholder's share". It was Gombrich's belief that a viewer "completed" the artwork, that part of an artwork's meaning came from the person viewing it. So you see — there really are no wrong answers as it is you, as the viewer who is completing the artwork. If you're looking at art in a gallery, read the wall text at the side of the artwork. If staff are present, ask questions. Ask your fellow visitors what they think. Asking questions is the key to understanding more — and that goes for anything in life — not just art. But above all, have confidence in front of an artwork. If you are contemplating an artwork, then you are the intended viewer and what you think matters. You are the only critic that counts.

① 미술 작품의 가치는 일정 부분 정해져 있다.
② 미술 작품을 제작할 때 대중의 요구를 반영해야 한다.
③ 미술작품은 감상하는 사람으로 인하여 비로소 완성된다.
④ 미술 감상의 출발은 작가의 숨겨진 의도를 파악하는 것이다.

문 24. Argentina에 관한 다음 글의 내용과 가장 일치하지 않는 것은?

> Argentina is the world's eighth largest country, comprising almost the entire southern half of South America. Colonization by Spain began in the early 1500s, but in 1816 Jose de San Martin led the movement for Argentine independence. The culture of Argentina has been greatly influenced by the massive European migration in the late nineteenth and early twentieth centuries, primarily from Spain and Italy. The majority of people are at least nominally Catholic, and the country has the largest Jewish population (about 300,000) in South America. From 1880 to 1930, thanks to its agricultural development, Argentina was one of the world's top ten wealthiest nations.

① Jose de San Martin이 스페인으로부터의 독립운동을 이끌었다.
② 북미 출신 이주민들이 그 문화에 많은 영향을 끼쳤다.
③ 남미지역 중에서 가장 많은 유대인들이 살고 있는 곳이다.
④ 농업의 발전으로 한때 부유한 국가였다.

문 25. Sonja Henie에 관한 다음 글의 내용과 가장 일치하지 않는 것은?

> Sonja Henie is famous for her skill into a career as one of the world's most famous figure skaters — in the rink and on the screen. Henie, winner of three Olympic gold medals and a Norwegian and European champion, invented a thrillingly theatrical and athletic style of figure skating. She introduced short skirts, white skates, and attractive moves. Her spectacular spins and jumps raised the bar for all competitors. In 1936, Twentieth-Century Fox signed her to star in One in a Million, and she soon became one of Hollywood's leading actresses. In 1941, the movie 'Sun Valley Serenade' received three Academy Award nominations which she played as an actress. Although the rest of Henie's films were less acclaimed, she triggered a popular surge in ice skating. In 1938, she launched extravagant touring shows called Hollywood Ice Revues. Her many ventures made her a fortune, but her greatest legacy was inspiring little girls to skate.

① 피겨 스케이터와 영화배우로서의 업적으로 유명하다.
② 올림픽과 다른 대회들에서 좋은 성적을 거두었다.
③ 출연한 영화가 1941년에 영화제에서 3개 부문에 수상했다.
④ 어린 여자아이들에게 스케이트에 대한 영감을 주었다.

해설편 ▶ P.127

2021

| 풀이 시간: ____:____ ~ ____:____ / 점수: ____점

문 1. 다음 글의 내용을 한 문장으로 요약하고자 한다. 빈칸 (A)와 (B)에 들어갈 말로 가장 적절한 것은?

Microorganisms are not calculating entities. They don't care what they do to you any more than you care what distress you cause when you slaughter them by the millions with a soapy shower. The only time a pathogen cares about you is when it kills you too well. If they eliminate you before they can move on, then they may well die out themselves. This in fact sometimes happens. History, Jared Diamond notes, is full of diseases that "once caused terrifying epidemics and then disappeared as mysteriously as they had come." He cites the robust but mercifully transient English sweating sickness, which raged from 1485 to 1552, killing tens of thousands as it went, before burning itself out. Too much efficiency is not a good thing for any infectious organism.

*pathogen 병원체

⬇

The more _____(A)_____ pathogens are, the faster it is likely to _____(B)_____ .

	(A)	(B)
①	weaker	disappear
②	weaker	spread
③	infectious	spread
④	infectious	disappear

문 2. 밑줄 친 "drains the mind"가 글에서 의미하는 바로 가장 적절한 것은?

If the writing is solid and good, the mood and temper of the writer will eventually be revealed and not at the expense of the work. Therefore, to achieve style, begin by affecting none — that is, draw the reader's attention to the sense and substance of the writing. A careful and honest writer does not need to worry about style. As you become proficient in the use of language, your style will emerge, because you yourself will emerge, and when this happens you will find it increasingly easy to break through the barriers that separate you from other minds and at last, make you stand in the middle of the writing. Fortunately, the act of composition, or creation, disciplines the mind; writing is one way to go about thinking, and the practice and habit of writing drains the mind.

① to heal the mind
② to help to be sensitive
③ to satisfy his/her curiosity
④ to place oneself in the background

문 3. (A), (B), (C)의 각 네모 안에서 어법에 맞는 표현으로 가장 적절한 것은?

Some of our dissatisfactions with self and with our lot in life are based on real circumstances, and some are false and simply (A) (perceive / perceived) to be real. The perceived must be sorted out and discarded. The real will either fall into the changeable or the unchangeable classification. If it's in the latter, we must strive to accept it. If it's in the former, then we have the alternative to strive instead to remove, exchange, or modify it. All of us have a unique purpose in life; and all of us are gifted, just (B) (different / differently) gifted. It's not an argument about whether it's fair or unfair to have been given one, five, or ten talents; it's about what we have done with our talents. It's about how well we have invested (C) (them / those) we have been given. If one holds on to the outlook that their life is unfair, then that's really holding an offense against God.

	(A)	(B)	(C)
①	perceive	different	them
②	perceive	differently	those
③	perceived	different	them
④	perceived	differently	those

문 4. 주어진 글 다음에 이어질 글의 순서로 가장 적절한 것은?

> People assume that, by charging a low price or one lower than their competitors, they will get more customers. This is a common fallacy.

> (A) It is, therefore, far better to have lower-volume, higher-margin products and services as you start; you can always negotiate to reduce your price if you are forced to, but it is rare that you will be able to negotiate an increase.
>
> (B) It is because when you charge reduced prices compared to your competition, you attract the lower end of the customer market. These customers want more for less and often take up more time and overhead in your business. They may also be your most difficult customers to deal with and keep happy.
>
> (C) You also, ironically, repel the better customers because they will pay a higher price for a higher level of product or service. We have seen many competitors come into the market and charge day rates that aren't sustainable. They often struggle even to fill their quota, and soon enough they give up and move on to doing something else.
>
> *repel 쫓아버리다

① (B) − (A) − (C)
② (B) − (C) − (A)
③ (C) − (A) − (B)
④ (C) − (B) − (A)

문 5. 다음 글의 밑줄 친 부분 중, 어법상 가장 틀린 것은?

> Children who enjoy writing are often interested in seeing ① their work in print. One informal approach is to type, print, and post their poetry. Or you can create a photocopied anthology of the poetry of many child writers. But for children who are truly dedicated and ambitious, ② submit a poem for publication is a worthy goal. And there are several web and print resources that print children's original poetry. Help child poets become familiar with the protocol for submitting manuscripts (style, format, and so forth). Let them choose ③ which poems they are most proud of, keep copies of everything submitted, and get parent permission. Then celebrate with them when their work is accepted and appear in print. Congratulate them, ④ publicly showcase their accomplishment, and spread the word. Success inspires success. And, of course, if their work is rejected, offer support and encouragement.
>
> *anthology 문집, 선집
> **protocol 규약, 의례

문 6. 글의 흐름으로 보아, 주어진 문장이 들어가기에 가장 적절한 곳은?

> With love and strength from the tribe, the tiny seeds mature and grow tall and crops for the people.

> In the Pueblo Indian culture, corn is to the people the very symbol of life. (①) The Corn Maiden "grandmother of the sun and the light" brought this gift, bringing the power of life to the people. (②) As the corn is given life by the sun, the Corn Maiden brings the fire of the sun into the human bodies, giving man many representations of her love and power through nature. (③) Each Maiden brings one seed of corn that is nurtured with love like that given to a child and this one seed would sustain the entire tribe forever. (④) The spirit of the Corn Maidens is forever present with the tribal people.

문 7. 다음 빈칸에 들어갈 말로 가장 적절한 것은?

Beeches, oaks, spruce and pines produce new growth all the time, and have to get rid of the old. The most obvious change happens every autumn. The leaves have served their purpose: they are now worn out and riddled with insect damage. Before the trees bid them adieu, they pump waste products into them. You could say they are taking this opportunity to relieve themselves. Then they grow a layer of weak tissue to separate each leaf from the twig it's growing on, and the leaves tumble to the ground in the next breeze. The rustling leaves that now blanket the ground — and make such a satisfying scrunching sound when you scuffle through them — are basically _____.

① tree toilet paper
② the plant kitchen
③ lungs of the tree
④ parents of insects

문 8. 글의 흐름상 가장 어색한 문장은?

Fiction has many uses and one of them is to build empathy. When you watch TV or see a film, you are looking at things happening to other people. Prose fiction is something you build up from 26 letters and a handful of punctuation marks, and you, and you alone, using your imagination, create a world and live there and look out through other eyes. ① You get to feel things, and visit places and worlds you would never otherwise know. ② Fortunately, in the last decade, many of the world's most beautiful and unknown places have been put in the spotlight. ③ You learn that everyone else out there is a me, as well. ④ You're being someone else, and when you return to your own world, you're going to be slightly changed.

문 9. 다음 빈칸에 들어갈 말로 가장 적절한 것은?

The seeds of willows and poplars are so minuscule that you can just make out two tiny dark dots in the fluffy flight hairs. One of these seeds weighs a mere 0.0001 grams. With such a meagre energy reserve, a seedling can grow only 1–2 millimetres before it runs out of steam and has to rely on food it makes for itself using its young leaves. But that only works in places where there's no competition to threaten the tiny sprouts. Other plants casting shade on it would extinguish the new life immediately. And so, if a fluffy little seed package like this falls in a spruce or beech forest, the seed's life is over before it's even begun. That's why willows and poplars _____.

*minuscule 아주 작은

① prefer settling in unoccupied territory
② have been chosen as food for herbivores
③ have evolved to avoid human intervention
④ wear their dead leaves far into the winter

문 10. 다음 글의 밑줄 친 부분 중 문맥상 낱말의 쓰임이 가장 적절하지 않은 것은?

Good walking shoes are important. Most major athletic brands offer shoes especially designed for walking. Fit and comfort are more important than style; your shoes should feel ① supportive but not tight or constricting. The uppers should be light, breathable, and flexible, the insole moisture-resistant, and the sole ② shock-absorbent. The heel wedge should be ③ lowered, so the sole at the back of the shoe is two times thicker than at the front. Finally, the toe box should be ④ spacious, even when you're wearing athletic socks.

① supportive   ② shock-absorbent
③ lowered   ④ spacious

문 11. 다음 글의 요지로 가장 알맞은 것은?

If your kids fight every time they play video games, make sure you're close enough to be able to hear them when they sit down to play. Listen for the particular words or tones of voice they are using that are aggressive, and try to intervene before it develops. Once tempers have settled, try to seat your kids down and discuss the problem without blaming or accusing. Give each kid a chance to talk, uninterrupted, and have them try to come up with solutions to the problem themselves. By the time kids are elementary-school age, they can evaluate which of those solutions are win-win solutions and which ones are most likely to work and satisfy each other over time. They should also learn to revisit problems when solutions are no longer working.

① Ask your kids to evaluate their test.
② Make your kids compete each other.
③ Help your kids learn to resolve conflict.
④ Teach your kids how to win an argument.

문 12. 다음 글의 요지로 가장 적절한 것은?

There's a current trend to avoid germs at all cost. We disinfect our bathrooms, kitchens, and the air. We sanitize our hands and gargle with mouthwash to kill germs. Some folks avoid as much human contact as possible and won't even shake your hand for fear of getting germs. I think it's safe to say that some people would purify everything but their minds. Remember the story of "the Boy in the Bubble"? He was born without an immune system and had to live in a room that was completely germ free, with no human contact. Of course, everyone should take prudent measures to maintain reasonable standards of cleanliness and personal hygiene, but in many cases, aren't we going overboard? When we come in contact with most germs, our body destroys them, which in turn strengthens our immune system and its ability to further fight off disease. Thus, these "good germs" actually make us healthier. Even if it were possible to avoid all germs and to live in a sterile environment, wouldn't we then be like "the Boy in the Bubble"?

① 세균에 감염되지 않도록 개인의 위생 환경 조성이 필요하다.
② 면역 능력이 상실된 채로 태어난 유아에 대한 치료가 시급하다.
③ 지역사회의 방역 능력 강화를 위해 국가의 재정 지원이 시급하다.
④ 과도하게 세균을 제거하려고 하는 것이 오히려 면역 능력을 해친다.

문 13. 다음 글의 밑줄 친 부분을 어법상 바르게 고친 것이 아닌 것은?

① Knowing as the Golden City, Jaisalmer, a former caravan center on the route to the Khyber Pass, rises from a sea of sand, its 30-foot-high walls and medieval sandstone fort ② shelters carved spires and palaces that soar into the sapphire sky. With its tiny winding lanes and hidden temples, Jaisalmer is straight out of The Arabian Nights, and so little has life altered here ③ which it's easy to imagine yourself back in the 13th century. It's the only fortress city in India still functioning, with one quarter of its population ④ lived within the walls, and it's just far enough off the beaten path to have been spared the worst ravages of tourism. The city's wealth originally came from the substantial tolls it placed on passing camel caravans.

① Knowing → Known   ② shelters → sheltering
③ which → that   ④ lived → lives

문 14. 다음 글에서 필자가 주장하는 바로 가장 적절한 것은?

The learned are neither apathetic nor indifferent regarding the world's problems. More books on these issues are being published than ever, though few capture the general public's attention. Likewise, new research discoveries are constantly being made at universities, and shared at conferences worldwide. Unfortunately, most of this activity is self-serving. With the exception of science — and here, too, only selectively — new insights are not trickling down to the public in ways to help improve our lives. Yet, these discoveries aren't simply the property of the elite, and should not remain in the possession of a select few professionals. Each person must make his and her own life's decisions, and make those choices in light of our current understanding of who we are and what is good for us. For that matter, we must find a way to somehow make new discoveries accessible to every person.

*apathetic 냉담한, 무관심한

**trickle 흐르다

① 학자들은 연구 논문을 작성할 때 주관성을 배제해야 한다.
② 새로운 연구 결과에 모든 사람이 접근할 수 있게 해야 한다.
③ 소수 엘리트 학자들의 폐쇄성을 극복할 계기를 마련해야 한다.
④ 학자들이 연구 과정에서 겪는 어려움을 극복하도록 도와야 한다.

문 15. 다음 글의 주제로 가장 알맞은 것은?

Language gives individual identity and a sense of belonging. When children proudly learn their language and are able to speak it at home and in their neighborhood, the children will have a high self-esteem. Moreover, children who know the true value of their mother tongue will not feel like they are achievers when they speak a foreign language. With improved self-identity and self-esteem, the classroom performance of a child also improves because such a child goes to school with less worries about linguistic marginalization.

*linguistic marginalization 언어적 소외감

① the importance of mother tongue in child development
② the effect on children's foreign language learning
③ the way to improve children's self-esteem
④ the efficiency of the linguistic analysis

문 16. 다음 글의 주제로 가장 적절한 것은?

Many animals are not loners. They discovered, or perhaps nature discovered for them, that by living and working together, they could interact with the world more effectively. For example, if an animal hunts for food by itself, it can only catch, kill, and eat animals much smaller than itself — but if animals band together in a group, they can catch and kill animals bigger than they are. A pack of wolves can kill a horse, which can feed the group very well. Thus, more food is available to the same animals in the same forest if they work together than if they work alone. Cooperation has other benefits: The animals can alert each other to danger, can find more food (if they search separately and then follow the ones who succeed in finding food), and can even provide some care to those who are sick and injured. Mating and reproduction are also easier if the animals live in a group than if they live far apart.

① benefits of being social in vanimals
② drawbacks of cooperative behaviors
③ common traits of animals and humans
④ competitions in mating and reproduction

문 17. 다음 글의 밑줄 친 부분 중, 문맥상 낱말의 쓰임이 가장 적절하지 않은 것은?

My own curiosity had been encouraged by my studies in philosophy at university. The course listed the numerous philosophers that we were supposed to study and I thought at first that our task was to learn and absorb their work as a sort of secular Bible. But I was ① delighted to discover that my tutor was not interested in me reciting their theories but only in helping me to develop my own, using the philosophers of the past as stimulants not authorities. It was the key to my intellectual ② freedom. Now I had official permission to think for myself, to question anything and everything and only agree if I thought it right. A ③ good education would have given me that permission much earlier. Some, alas, never seem to have received it and go on reciting the rules of others as if they were sacrosanct. As a result, they become the unwitting ④ opponents of other people's worlds. Philosophy, I now think, is too important to be left to professional philosophers. We should all learn to think like philosophers, starting at primary school.

*sacrosanct 신성불가침의
**unwitting 자신도 모르는

문 18. (A), (B), (C)의 괄호 안에서 어법에 맞는 표현으로 가장 적절한 것은?

Looking back, scientists have uncovered a mountain of evidence (A) [that / what] Mayan leaders were aware for many centuries of their uncertain dependence on rainfall. Water shortages were not only understood but also recorded and planned for. The Mayans enforced conservation during low rainfall years, tightly regulating the types of crops grown, the use of public water, and food rationing. During the first half of their three-thousand-year reign, the Mayans continued to build larger underground artificial lakes and containers (B) [stored / to store] rainwater for drought months. As impressive as their elaborately decorated temples (C) [did / were], their efficient systems for collecting and warehousing water were masterpieces in design and engineering.

*rationing 배급

	(A)	(B)	(C)
①	that	to store	were
②	what	stored	did
③	that	to store	did
④	what	stored	were

문 19. 주어진 글 다음에 이어질 글의 순서로 가장 적절한 것은?

Religion can certainly bring out the best in a person, but it is not the only phenomenon with that property.

(A) People who would otherwise be self-absorbed or shallow or crude or simply quitters are often ennobled by their religion, given a perspective on life that helps them make the hard decisions that we all would be proud to make.

(B) Having a child often has a wonderfully maturing effect on a person. Wartime, famously, gives people an abundance of occasions to rise to, as do natural disasters like floods and hurricanes.

(C) But for day-in, day-out lifelong bracing, there is probably nothing so effective as religion: it makes powerful and talented people more humble and patient, it makes average people rise above themselves, it provides sturdy support for many people who desperately need help staying away from drink or drugs or crime.

① (B) − (A) − (C)   ② (B) − (C) − (A)
③ (C) − (A) − (B)   ④ (C) − (B) − (A)

문 20. 주어진 글 다음에 이어질 글의 순서로 가장 적절한 것은?

> More people require more resources, which means that as the population increases, the Earth's resources deplete more rapidly.

(A) Population growth also results in increased greenhouse gases, mostly from CO2 emissions. For visualization, during that same 20th century that saw fourfold population growth, CO2 emissions increased twelvefold.

(B) The result of this depletion is deforestation and loss of biodiversity as humans strip the Earth of resources to accommodate rising population numbers.

(C) As greenhouse gases increase, so do climate patterns, ultimately resulting in the long-term pattern called climate change.

*deplete 고갈시키다, 대폭 감소시키다

① (A) – (B) – (C) ② (B) – (A) – (C)
③ (B) – (C) – (A) ④ (C) – (A) – (B)

문 21. 다음 글에서 전체 흐름과 관계 없는 문장은?

> Medical anthropologists with extensive training in human biology and physiology study disease transmission patterns and how particular groups adapt to the presence of diseases like malaria and sleeping sickness. ① Because the transmission of viruses and bacteria is strongly influenced by people's diets, sanitation, and other behaviors, many medical anthropologists work as a team with epidemiologists to identify cultural practices that affect the spread of disease. ② Though it may be a commonly held belief that most students enter medicine for humanitarian reasons rather than for the financial rewards of a successful medical career, in developed nations the prospect of status and rewards is probably one incentive. ③ Different cultures have different ideas about the causes and symptoms of disease, how best to treat illnesses, the abilities of traditional healers and doctors, and

the importance of community involvement in the healing process. ④ By studying how a human community perceives such things, medical anthropologists help hospitals and other agencies deliver health care services more effectively.

*epidemiologist 유행[전염]병학자

문 22. 주어진 글 다음에 이어질 글의 순서로 가장 적절한 것은?

> Sequoya (1760?-1843) was born in eastern Tennessee, into a prestigious family that was highly regarded for its knowledge of Cherokee tribal traditions and religion.

(A) Recognizing the possibilities writing had for his people, Sequoya invented a Cherokee alphabet in 1821. With this system of writing, Sequoya was able to record ancient tribal customs.

(B) More importantly, his alphabet helped the Cherokee nation develop a publishing industry so that newspapers and books could be printed. School-age children were thus able to learn about Cherokee culture and traditions in their own language.

(C) As a child, Sequoya learned the Cherokee oral tradition; then, as an adult, he was introduced to Euro-American culture. In his letters, Sequoya mentions how he became fascinated with the writing methods European Americans used to communicate.

① (B) – (A) – (C) ② (B) – (C) – (A)
③ (C) – (A) – (B) ④ (C) – (B) – (A)

문 23. Peanut Butter Drive에 관한 다음 안내문의 내용과 가장 일치하지 않는 것은?

SPREAD THE LOVE
Fight Hunger During the Peanut Butter Drive

Make a contribution to our community by helping local families who need a little assistance. We are kicking off our 4th annual area-wide peanut butter drive to benefit children, families and seniors who face hunger in Northeast Louisiana.

Peanut butter is a much needed staple at Food Banks as it is a protein-packed food that kids and adults love. Please donate peanut butter in plastic jars or funds to the Monroe Food Bank by Friday, March 29th at 4:00 pm. Donations of peanut butter can be dropped off at the food bank's distribution center located at 4600 Central Avenue in Monroe on Monday through Friday, 8:00 am to 4:00 pm. Monetary donations can be made here or by calling 427-418-4581.

For other drop-off locations, visit our website at https://www.foodbanknela.org

---

① 배고픈 사람들에게 도움을 주려는 행사이다.
② 토요일과 일요일에도 땅콩버터를 기부할 수 있다.
③ 전화를 걸어 금전 기부를 할 수도 있다.
④ 땅콩버터를 기부하는 장소는 여러 곳이 있다.

문 24. 다음 글에 나타난 화자의 심경으로 가장 적절한 것은?

Our whole tribe was poverty-stricken. Every branch of the Garoghlanian family was living in the most amazing and comical poverty in the world. Nobody could understand where we ever got money enough to keep us with food in our bellies. Most important of all, though, we were famous for our honesty. We had been famous for honesty for something like eleven centuries, even when we had been the wealthiest family in what we liked to think was the world. We put pride first, honest next, and after that we believed in right and wrong. None of us would take advantage of anybody in the world.

*poverty-stricken 가난에 시달리는

---

① peaceful and calm   ② satisfied and proud
③ horrified and feared ④ amazed and astonished

문 25. 다음 글의 내용과 가장 일치하지 않는 것은?

Despite the increasing popularity of consuming raw foods, you can still gain nutrients from cooked vegetables. For example, our body can absorb lycopene more effectively when tomatoes are cooked. (Keep in mind, however, that raw tomatoes are still a good source of lycopene.) Cooked tomatoes, however, have lower levels of vitamin C than raw tomatoes, so if you're looking to increase your levels, you might be better off sticking with the raw. Whether you decide to eat them cooked or raw, it's important not to dilute the health benefits of tomatoes. If you're buying tomato sauce or paste, choose a variety with no salt or sugar added — or better yet, cook your own sauce at home. And if you're eating your tomatoes raw, salt them sparingly and choose salad dressings that are low in calories and saturated fat.

*dilute 희석하다, 묽게 하다

---

① 토마토를 요리하여 먹었을 때, 우리의 몸은 리코펜을 더 효과적으로 흡수할 수 있다.
② 더 많은 비타민C를 섭취하고 싶다면 생토마토보다 조리된 토마토를 섭취하는 것이 낫다.
③ 토마토 소스를 구입하고자 한다면, 소금이나 설탕이 첨가되지 않은 것으로 골라야 한다.
④ 생토마토를 섭취 시, 소금을 적게 넣거나, 칼로리가 적은 드레싱을 선택하도록 한다.

해설편 ▶ P.135

2020
2월 22일 시행
법원직 9급

| 풀이 시간: ____:____ ~ ____:____ / 점수: ____점

문 1. 다음 밑줄 친 (A), (B), (C)의 각 괄호 안에서 문맥에 맞는 낱말로 가장 적절한 것은?

It's tempting to identify knowledge with facts, but not every fact is an item of knowledge. Imagine shaking a sealed cardboard box containing a single coin. As you put the box down, the coin inside the box has landed either heads or tails: let's say that's a fact. But as long as no one looks into the box, this fact remains unknown; it is not yet within the realm of (A) fact / knowledge . Nor do facts become knowledge simply by being written down. If you write the sentence 'The coin has landed heads' on one slip of paper and 'The coin has landed tails' on another, then you will have written down a fact on one of the slips, but you still won't have gained knowledge of the outcome of the coin toss. Knowledge demands some kind of access to a fact on the part of some living subject. (B) With / Without a mind to access it, whatever is stored in libraries and databases won't be knowledge, but just ink marks and electronic traces. In any given case of knowledge, this access may or may not be unique to an individual: the same fact may be known by one person and not by others. Common knowledge might be shared by many people, but there is no knowledge that dangles (C) attached / unattached to any subject.

	(A)	(B)	(C)
①	fact	With	unattached
②	knowledge	Without	unattached
③	knowledge	With	attached
④	fact	Without	attached

문 2. 다음 빈칸에 들어갈 말로 가장 적절한 것은?

Impressionable youth are not the only ones subject to _____. Most of us have probably had an experience of being pressured by a salesman. Have you ever had a sales rep try to sell you some "office solution" by telling you that 70 percent of your competitors are using their service, so why aren't you? But what if 70 percent of your competitors are idiots? Or what if that 70 percent were given so much value added or offered such a low price that they couldn't resist the opportunity? The practice is designed to do one thing and one thing only — to pressure you to buy. To make you feel you might be missing out on something or that everyone else knows but you.

① peer pressure
② impulse buying
③ bullying tactics
④ keen competition

문 3. 다음 밑줄 친 (A), (B), (C)의 각 괄호 안에서 문맥에 맞는 낱말로 가장 적절한 것은?

People with high self-esteem have confidence in their skills and competence and enjoy facing the challenges that life offers them. They (A) willingly / unwillingly work in teams because they are sure of themselves and enjoy taking the opportunity to contribute. However, those who have low self-esteem tend to feel awkward, shy, and unable to express themselves. Often they compound their problems by opting for avoidance strategies because they (B) deny / hold the belief that whatever they do will result in failure. Conversely, they may compensate for their lack of self-esteem by exhibiting boastful and arrogant behavior to cover up their sense of unworthiness. Furthermore, such individuals account for their successes by finding reasons that are outside of themselves, while those with high self-esteem (C) attempt / attribute their success to internal characteristics.

	(A)	(B)	(C)
①	willingly	deny	attempt
②	willingly	hold	attribute
③	unwillingly	hold	attempt
④	unwillingly	deny	attribute

문 4. 다음 글의 제목으로 가장 적절한 것은?

To be sure, no other species can lay claim to our capacity to devise something new and original, from the sublime to the sublimely ridiculous. Other animals do build things — birds assemble their intricate nests, beavers construct dams, and ants dig elaborate networks of tunnels. "But airplanes, strangely tilted skyscrapers and Chia Pets, well, they're pretty impressive," Fuentes says, adding that from an evolutionary standpoint, "creativity is as much a part of our tool kit as walking on two legs, having a big brain and really good hands for manipulating things." For a physically unprepossessing primate, without great fangs or claws or wings or other obvious physical advantages, creativity has been the great equalizer — and more — ensuring, for now, at least, the survival of Homo sapiens.

*sublime 황당한, (터무니없이) 극단적인
*Chia Pets 잔디가 머리털처럼 자라나는 피규어

① Where Does Human Creativity Come From?
② What Are the Physical Characteristics of Primates?
③ Physical Advantages of Homo Sapiens over Other Species
④ Creativity: a Unique Trait Human Species Have For Survival

문 5. 다음 글의 요지를 한 문장으로 요약하고자 한다. 빈칸 (A), (B)에 들어갈 말로 가장 적절한 것은?

"Most of bird identification is based on a sort of subjective impression — the way a bird moves and little instantaneous appearances at different angles and sequences of different appearances, and as it turns its head and as it flies and as it turns around, you see sequences of different shapes and angles," Sibley says, "All that combines to create a unique impression of a bird that can't really be taken apart and described in words. When it comes down to being in the fieldland looking at a bird, you don't take time to analyze it and say it shows this, this, and this; therefore it must be this species. It's more natural and instinctive. After a lot of practice, you look at the bird, and it triggers little switches in your brain. It looks right. You know what it is at a glance."

According to Sibley, bird identification is based on _____(A)_____ rather than _____(B)_____.

	(A)	(B)
①	instinctive impression	discrete analysis
②	objective research	subjective judgements
③	physical appearances	behavioral traits
④	close observation	distant observation

문 6. 주어진 글 다음에 이어질 글의 순서로 가장 적절한 것은?

As cars are becoming less dependent on people, the means and circumstances in which the product is used by consumers are also likely to undergo significant changes, with higher rates of participation in car sharing and short-term leasing programs.

(A) In the not-too-distant future, a driverless car could come to you when you need it, and when you are done with it, it could then drive away without any need for a parking space. Increases in car sharing and short-term leasing are also likely to be associated with a corresponding decrease in the importance of exterior car design.

(B) As a result, the symbolic meanings derived from cars and their relationship to consumer self-identity and status are likely to change in turn.

(C) Rather than serving as a medium for personalization and self-identity, car exteriors might increasingly come to represent a channel for advertising and other promotional activities, including brand ambassador programs, such as those offered by Free Car Media.

① (A) − (C) − (B)
② (B) − (C) − (A)
③ (C) − (A) − (B)
④ (C) − (B) − (A)

문 7. 주어진 글 다음에 이어질 글의 순서로 가장 적절한 것은?

> There is a wonderful story of a group of American car executives who went to Japan to see a Japanese assembly line. At the end of the line, the doors were put on the hinges, the same as in America.

> (A) But something was missing. In the United States, a line worker would take a rubber mallet and tap the edges of the door to ensure that it fit perfectly. In Japan, that job didn't seem to exist.
>
> (B) Confused, the American auto executives asked at what point they made sure the door fit perfectly. Their Japanese guide looked at them and smiled sheepishly. "We make sure it fits when we design it."
>
> (C) In the Japanese auto plant, they didn't examine the problem and accumulate data to figure out the best solution — they engineered the outcome they wanted from the beginning. If they didn't achieve their desired outcome, they understood it was because of a decision they made at the start of the process.

① (A) − (B) − (C) ② (A) − (C) − (B)
③ (B) − (A) − (C) ④ (B) − (C) − (A)

문 8. 다음 글의 빈칸 (A), (B)에 들어갈 말로 가장 적절한 것은?

> There has been much research on nonverbal cues to deception dating back to the work of Ekman and his idea of leakage. It is well documented that people use others' nonverbal behaviors as a way to detect lies. My research and that of many others has strongly supported people's reliance on observations of others' nonverbal behaviors when assessing honesty. _____(A)_____, social scientific research on the link between various nonverbal behaviors and the act of lying suggests that the link is typically not very strong or consistent. In my research, I have observed that the nonverbal signals that seem to give one liar away are different than those given by a second liar. _____(B)_____, the scientific evidence linking nonverbal behaviors and deception has grown weaker over time. People infer honesty based on how others nonverbally present themselves, but that has very limited utility and validity.

	(A)	(B)
①	However	What's more
②	As a result	On the contrary
③	However	Nevertheless
④	As a result	For instance

문 9. 다음 글의 밑줄 친 부분 중 어법상 틀린 것은?

> As soon as the start-up is incorporated it will need a bank account, and the need for a payroll account will follow quickly. The banks are very competitive in services to do payroll and related tax bookkeeping, ① starting with even the smallest of businesses. These are areas ② where a business wants the best quality service and the most "free" accounting help it can get. The changing payroll tax legislation is a headache to keep up with, especially when a sales force will be operating in many of the fifty states. And the ③ requiring reports are a burden on a company's administrative staff. Such services are often provided best by the banker. The banks' references in this area should be compared with the payroll service alternatives such as ADP, but the future and the long-term relationship should be kept in mind when a decision is ④ being made.

문 10. 다음 글의 밑줄 친 부분 중 어법상 틀린 것은?

> Many people refuse to visit animal shelters because they find it too sad or ① depressed. They shouldn't feel so bad because so many lucky animals are saved from a dangerous life on the streets, ② where they're at risk of traffic accidents, attack by other animals or humans, and subject to the elements. Many lost pets likewise ③ are found and reclaimed by distraught owners simply because they were brought into animal shelters. Most importantly, ④ adoptable pets find homes, and sick or dangerous animals are humanely relieved of their suffering.

문 11. 다음 밑줄 친 (A), (B), (C)의 각 괄호 안에서 문맥에 맞는 낱말로 가장 적절한 것은?

EQ testing, when performed with reliable testing methods, can provide you with very useful information about yourself. I've found, having tested thousands of people, that many are a bit surprised by their results. For example, one person who believed she was very socially responsible and often concerned about others came out with an (A) average / extraordinary score in that area. She was quite disappointed in her score. It turned out that she had very high standards for social responsibility and therefore was extremely (B) easy / hard on herself when she performed her assessment. In reality, she was (C) more / less socially responsible than most people, but she believed that she could be much better than she was.

	(A)	(B)	(C)
①	average	easy	less
②	average	hard	more
③	extraordinary	hard	less
④	extraordinary	easy	more

문 12. 다음 빈칸에 들어갈 말로 가장 적절한 것은?

A person may try to _____ by using evidence to his advantage. A mother asks her son, "How are you doing in English this term?" He responds cheerfully, "Oh, I just got a ninety-five on a quiz." The statement conceals the fact that he has failed every other quiz and that his actual average is 55. Yet, if she pursues the matter no further, the mother may be delighted that her son is doing so well. Linda asks Susan, "Have you read much Dickens?" Susan responds, "Oh, *Pickwick Papers* is one of my favorite novels." The statement may disguise the fact that *Pickwick Papers* is the only novel by Dickens that she has read, and it may give Linda the impression that Susan is a great Dickens enthusiast.

① earn extra money
② effect a certain belief
③ hide memory problems
④ make other people feel guilty

문 13. 다음 글의 내용을 한 문장으로 요약하고자 한다. 빈칸 (A), (B)에 들어갈 말로 가장 적절한 것은?

Whether we are complimented for our appearance, our garden, a dinner we prepared, or an assignment at the office, it is always satisfying to receive recognition for a job well done. Certainly, reinforcement theory sees occasional praise as an aid to learning a new skill. However, some evidence cautions against making sweeping generalizations regarding the use of praise in improving performance. It seems that while praise improves performance on certain tasks, on others it can instead prove harmful. Imagine the situation in which the enthusiastic support of hometown fans expecting victory brings about the downfall of their team. In this situation, it seems that praise creates pressure on athletes, disrupting their performance.

↓

Whether _____(A)_____ helps or hurts a performance depends on _____(B)_____.

	(A)	(B)
①	praise	task types
②	competition	quality of teamwork
③	praise	quality of teamwork
④	competition	task types

문 14. 다음 글의 밑줄 친 부분 중 어법상 틀린 것은?

As we consider media consumption in the context of anonymous social relations, we mean all of those occasions that involve the presence of strangers, such as viewing television in public places like bars, ① going to concerts or dance clubs, or reading a newspaper on a bus or subway. Typically, there are social rules that ② govern how we interact with those around us and with the media product. For instance, it is considered rude in our culture, or at least aggressive, ③ read over another person's shoulder or to get up and change TV channels in a public setting. Any music fan knows what is appropriate at a particular kind of concert. The presence of other people is often crucial to defining the setting and hence the activity of media consumption, ④ despite the fact that the relationships are totally impersonal.

문 15. 다음 글의 밑줄 친 부분 중 어법상 틀린 것은?

Many of us believe that amnesia, or sudden memory loss, results in the inability to recall one's name and identity. This belief may reflect the way amnesia is usually ① portrayed in movies, television, and literature. For example, when we meet Matt Damon's character in the movie *The Bourne Identity*, we learn that he has no memory for who he is, why he has the skills he does, or where he is from. He spends much of the movie ② trying to answer these questions. However, the inability to remember your name and identity ③ are exceedingly rare in reality. Amnesia most often results from a brain injury that leaves the victim unable to form new memories, but with most memories of the past ④ intact. Some movies do accurately portray this more common syndrome; our favorite *Memento*.

문 16. 다음 빈칸에 들어갈 말로 가장 적절한 것은?

Much is now known about natural hazards and the negative impacts they have on people and their property. It would seem obvious that any logical person would avoid such potential impacts or at least modify their behavior or their property to minimize such impacts. However, humans are not always rational. Until someone has a personal experience or knows someone who has such an experience, most people subconsciously believe "It won't happen here" or "It won't happen to me." Even knowledgeable scientists who are aware of the hazards, the odds of their occurrence, and the costs of an event _____.

① refuse to remain silent
② do not always act appropriately
③ put the genetic factor at the top end
④ have difficulty in defining natural hazards

문 17. 다음 글의 주제로 가장 적절한 것은?

The rise of cities and kingdoms and the improvement in transport infrastructure brought about new opportunities for specialization. Densely populated cities provided full-time employment not just for professional shoemakers and doctors, but also for carpenters, priests, soldiers and lawyers. Villages that gained a reputation for producing really good wine, olive oil or ceramics discovered that it was worth their while to specialize nearly exclusively in that product and trade it with other settlements for all the other goods they needed. This made a lot of sense. Climates and soils differ, so why drink mediocre wine from your backyard if you can buy a smoother variety from a place whose soil and climate is much better suited to grape vines? If the clay in your backyard makes stronger and prettier pots, then you can make an exchange.

① how climates and soils influence the local products
② ways to gain a good reputation for local specialties
③ what made people engage in specialization and trade
④ the rise of cities and full-time employment for professionals

문 18. 밑줄 친 the issue가 가리키는 내용으로 가장 적절한 것은?

Nine-year-old Ryan Kyote was eating breakfast at home in Napa, California, when he saw the news: an Indiana school had taken a 6-year-old's meal when her lunch account didn't have enough money. Kyote asked if that could happen to his friends. When his mom contacted the school district to find out, she learned that students at schools in their district had, all told, as much as $25,000 in lunch debt. Although the district says it never penalized students who owed, Kyote decided to use his saved allowance to pay off his grade's debt, about $74 — becoming the face of a movement to end lunch-money debt. When California Governor Gavin Newsom signed a bill in October that banned "lunch shaming," or giving worse food to students with debt, he thanked Kyote for his "empathy and his courage" in raising awareness of the issue. "Heroes," Kyote points out, "come in all ages."

① The governor signed a bill to decline lunch items to students with lunch debt.
② Kyote's lunch was taken away because he ran out of money in his lunch account.
③ The school district with financial burden cut the budget failing to serve quality meals.
④ Many students in the district who could not afford lunch were burdened with lunch debt.

문 20. 다음 글의 주제로 가장 적절한 것은?

In addition to controlling temperatures when handling fresh produce, control of the atmosphere is important. Some moisture is needed in the air to prevent dehydration during storage, but too much moisture can encourage growth of molds. Some commercial storage units have controlled atmospheres, with the levels of both carbon dioxide and moisture being regulated carefully. Sometimes other gases, such as ethylene gas, may be introduced at controlled levels to help achieve optimal quality of bananas and other fresh produce. Related to the control of gases and moisture is the need for some circulation of air among the stored foods.

① The necessity of controlling harmful gases in atmosphere
② The best way to control levels of moisture in growing plants and fruits
③ The seriousness of increasing carbon footprints every year around the world
④ The importance of controlling certain levels of gases and moisture in storing foods

문 19. 청고래에 관한 다음 글의 내용과 일치하지 않는 것은?

The biggest heart in the world is inside the blue whale. It weighs more than seven tons. It's as big as a room. When this creature is born it is 20 feet long and weighs four tons. It is way bigger than your car. It drinks a hundred gallons of milk from its mama every day and gains 200 pounds a day, and when it is seven or eight years old it endures an unimaginable puberty and then it essentially disappears from human ken, for next to nothing is known of the mating habits, travel patterns, diet, social life, language, social structure and diseases. There are perhaps 10,000 blue whales in the world, living in every ocean on earth, and of the largest animal who ever lived we know nearly nothing. But we know this: the animals with the largest hearts in the world generally travel in pairs, and their penetrating moaning cries, their piercing yearning tongue, can be heard underwater for miles and miles.

① 아기 청고래는 매일 100갤런의 모유를 마시고, 하루에 200파운드씩 체중이 증가한다.
② 청고래는 사춘기를 지나면서 인간의 시야에서 사라져서 청고래에 대해 알려진 것이 많지 않다.
③ 세계에서 가장 큰 심장을 지닌 동물이면서, 몸집이 가장 큰 동물이다.
④ 청고래는 일반적으로 혼자서 이동하고, 청고래의 소리는 물속을 관통하여 수 마일까지 전달될 수 있다.

문 21. 다음 글의 밑줄 친 부분 중 문맥상 낱말의 쓰임이 가장 적절하지 않은 것은?

Even if lying doesn't have any harmful effects in a particular case, it is still morally wrong because, if discovered, lying weakens the general practice of truth telling on which human communication relies. For instance, if I were to lie about my age on grounds of vanity, and my lying were discovered, even though no serious harm would have been done, I would have ① undermined your trust generally. In that case you would be far less likely to believe anything I might say in the future. Thus all lying, when discovered, has indirect ② harmful effects. However, very occasionally, these harmful effects might possibly be outweighed by the ③ benefits which arise from a lie. For example, if someone is seriously ill, lying to them about their life expectancy might probably give them a chance of living longer. On the other hand, telling them the truth could possibly ④ prevent a depression that would accelerate their physical decline.

문 22. 글의 흐름으로 보아 아래 문장이 들어가기에 가장 적절한 곳은?

> Water is also the medium for most chemical reactions needed to sustain life.

Several common properties of seawater are crucial to the survival and well-being of the ocean's inhabitants. Water accounts for 80-90% of the volume of most marine organisms. (①) It provides buoyancy and body support for swimming and floating organisms and reduces the need for heavy skeletal structures. (②) The life processes of marine organisms in turn alter many fundamental physical and chemical properties of seawater, including its transparency and chemical makeup, making organisms an integral part of the total marine environment. (③) Understanding the interactions between organisms and their marine environment requires a brief examination of some of the more important physical and chemical attributes of seawater. (④) The characteristics of pure water and sea water differ in some respects, so we consider first the basic properties of pure water and then examine how those properties differ in seawater.

문 23. (A), (B), (C)의 각 네모 안에서 문맥에 맞는 낱말로 가장 적절한 것은?

Here's the even more surprising part: The advent of AI didn't (A) diminish / increase the performance of purely human chess players. Quite the opposite. Cheap, supersmart chess programs (B) discouraged / inspired more people than ever to play chess, at more tournaments than ever, and the players got better than ever. There are more than twice as many grand masters now as there were when Deep Blue first beat Kasparov. The top-ranked human chess player today, Magnus Carlsen, trained with AIs and has been deemed the most computerlike of all human chess players. He also has the (C) highest / lowest human grand master rating of all time.

	(A)	(B)	(B)
①	diminish	discouraged	highest
②	increase	discouraged	lowest
③	diminish	inspired	highest
④	increase	inspired	lowest

문 24. 다음 글의 내용을 요약할 때 빈칸에 들어갈 말로 가장 적절한 것은?

Aesthetic value in fashion objects, like aesthetic value in fine art objects, is self-oriented. Consumers have the need to be attracted and to surround themselves with other people who are attractive. However, unlike aesthetic value in the fine arts, aesthetic value in fashion is also other-oriented. Attractiveness of appearance is a way of eliciting the reaction of others and facilitating social interaction.

⬇

Aesthetic value in fashion objects is _____.

① inherently only self-oriented
② just other-oriented unlike the other
③ both self-oriented and other-oriented
④ hard to define regardless of its nature

문 25. 글의 흐름으로 보아 아래 문장이 들어가기에 가장 적절한 곳은?

> The great news is that this is true whether or not we remember our dreams.

Some believe there is no value to dreams, but it is wrong to dismiss these nocturnal dramas as irrelevant. There is something to be gained in remembering. (①) We can feel more connected, more complete, and more on track. We can receive inspiration, information, and comfort. Albert Einstein stated that his theory of relativity was inspired by a dream. (②) In fact, he claimed that dreams were responsible for many of his discoveries. (③) Asking why we dream makes as much sense as questioning why we breathe. Dreaming is an integral part of a healthy life. (④) Many people report being inspired with a new approach for a problem upon awakening, even though they don't remember the specific dream.

해설편 ▶ P.143

삶의 순간순간이
아름다운 마무리이며
새로운 시작이어야 한다.

– 법정 스님

여러분의 작은 소리
에듀윌은 크게 듣겠습니다.

본 교재에 대한 여러분의 목소리를 들려주세요.
공부하시면서 어려웠던 점, 궁금한 점,
칭찬하고 싶은 점, 개선할 점, 어떤 것이라도 좋습니다.

에듀윌은 여러분께서 나누어 주신 의견을
통해 끊임없이 발전하고 있습니다.

에듀윌 도서몰 book.eduwill.net

• 부가학습자료 및 정오표: 에듀윌 도서몰 → 도서자료실
• 교재 문의: 에듀윌 도서몰 → 문의하기 → 교재(내용, 출간) / 주문 및 배송

2025 에듀윌 9급공무원 7개년 기출문제집 영어

발 행 일	2024년 12월 5일 초판
편 저 자	헤더진
펴 낸 이	양형남
펴 낸 곳	(주)에듀윌
I S B N	979-11-360-3480-9
등록번호	제25100-2002-000052호
주 소	08378 서울특별시 구로구 디지털로34길 55
	코오롱싸이언스밸리 2차 3층

www.eduwill.net
대표전화 1600-6700

9급공무원 공개경쟁채용 필기시험 답안지

컴퓨터용 사인펜으로 마킹하고 지우개로 지워서 사용하세요.

컴퓨터용 흑색사인펜만 사용

[필적감정용 기재]
*아래 예시문을 옮겨 적으시오

본인은 ○○○(응시자성명)임을 확인함

기 재 란

성	명
책	

※시험감독관 서명
(성명을 정자로 기재할 것)

책형 응시자 서명

성	명
자필성명	본인 성명 기재
응시직렬	
응시지역	
시험장소	

생 년 월 일

응 시 번 호

문번					1회독
1	①	②	③	④	⑤
2	①	②	③	④	⑤
3	①	②	③	④	⑤
4	①	②	③	④	⑤
5	①	②	③	④	⑤
6	①	②	③	④	⑤
7	①	②	③	④	⑤
8	①	②	③	④	⑤
9	①	②	③	④	⑤
10	①	②	③	④	⑤
11	①	②	③	④	⑤
12	①	②	③	④	⑤
13	①	②	③	④	⑤
14	①	②	③	④	⑤
15	①	②	③	④	⑤
16	①	②	③	④	⑤
17	①	②	③	④	⑤
18	①	②	③	④	⑤
19	①	②	③	④	⑤
20	①	②	③	④	⑤
21	①	②	③	④	⑤
22	①	②	③	④	⑤
23	①	②	③	④	⑤
24	①	②	③	④	⑤
25	①	②	③	④	⑤

(답안 마킹란은 동일한 형식으로 5개 영역에 걸쳐 문번 1~25, 선택지 ①②③④⑤, 각 "1회독" 표시와 함께 반복됨)

응시자 준수사항

□ 답안지 작성요령

※ 다음 사항을 준수하지 않을 경우에 발생하는 불이익은 응시자에게 귀책사유가 되므로 기재된 내용대로 이행하여 주시기 바랍니다.

1. 답안은 OCR 스캐너 판독결과에 따라 산출합니다. 모든 기재 및 표기사항은 반드시 〈보기〉의 올바른 표기 방식으로 답안을 작성해야 합니다.
   특히, 답안을 전부 채우지 않고 점만 찍어 표기한 경우, 번짐 등으로 두 개 이상의 답안에 표기된 경우, 농도가 옅어 컴퓨터용 사인펜을 사용하여 답안을 흐리게 표기한 경우 등에는 불이익(득점 등)을 받을 수 있으니 유의하시기 바랍니다.
   〈보기〉 올바른 표기: ● 잘못된 표기: ⊘⊗◑◐◍◌⦾⦿③

2. 성명란에는 연필, 사인펜 등 펜의 종류와 상관없이 예비표기를 하여 중복 답안으로 판독될 경우에는 불이익을 받을 수 있으므로 각별히 주의하시기 바랍니다.

3. 답안지를 받으면 상단에 인쇄된 성명, 응시직렬, 응시지역, 시험장소, 응시번호, 생년월일이 응시 본인의 정보와 일치하는지 확인하시기 바랍니다.

   가. (책 형) 응시자는 시험 시작 전 감독관의 지시에 따라 문제책 앞면에 인쇄된 책형을 확인한 후, 답안지 책형란에 해당 책형(1개)를 "●"로 표기하여야 합니다.
   ※ 책형 및 인적사항 기재란에 응시자의 답안과 동일한 내용을 필적으로 직접 작성해야 합니다.
   나. (필적감정용 기재) 예시문을 응시자 본인의 필적으로 직접 작성해야 합니다.
   다. (자필성명) 본인의 한글성명을 정자로 작성해야 합니다.
   다. (교체답안지 작성) 답안지를 교체받으면 반드시 교체답안지 상단 책형란에 해당 책형(1개)를 "●"로 표기하고, 필적감정용 기재란, 성명, 응시직렬, 응시지역, 시험장소, 응시번호, 생년월일을 빠짐없이 작성(표기)해야 하며, 잘못한 답안지는 1인 1매만 유효합니다.

4. 시험이 시작되면 문제책 표지의 과목순서와 일치 여부, 문제 누락·파손 등 문제책 인쇄상태를 반드시 확인하여야 합니다.

5. 답안은 반드시 문제책 표지의 과목순서에 맞추어 표기하여야 하며, 과목 순서를 바꾸어 표기한 경우에도 문제책 표지의 과목순서대로 채점되므로 각별히 유의하시기 바랍니다.

- 선택과목이 있는 행정직군 응시자는 본인이 응시표에 기재된 선택과목 순서에 따라 제1선택과목과 제2선택과목의 답안을 동일한 답안지에 순서대로 채점되므로 유의하시기 바랍니다.

6. 답안을 매 문항마다 반드시 하나의 답만을 골라 그 숫자에 "●"로 표기해야 하며, 답안을 잘못 표기하였을 경우에는 답안지를 교체하여 작성하거나 수정테이프만을 사용하여 수정할 수 있습니다.(수정액 및 수정스티커 등은 사용 불가)
   - 표기한 답안을 수정하는 경우에는 응시자 본인이 가져온 수정테이프를 사용할 수 있습니다.
   - 불량 수정테이프의 사용과 불완전한 수정처리로 인해 발생하는 문제는 응시자 본인에게 책임이 있으므로 주의하시기 바랍니다.

7. 답안지는 훼손·오염되거나 구겨지지 않도록 주의해야 하며, 특히 답안지 상단의 타이밍 마크(▮▮▮▮)를 절대 훼손해서는 안됩니다.

□ 부정행위 등 금지

※ 다음 사항을 위반한 경우에는 공무원임용시험령 제51조(부정행위자 등에 대한 조치)에 따라 그 시험의 정지, 무효, 합격취소, 5년간 공무원임용시험 응시자격정지 등의 불이익 처분을 받게 됩니다.

1. 시험시작 전까지 문제내용을 보아서는 안됩니다.

2. 시험시간 중 일체의 통신기기(휴대폰, 태블릿PC, 스마트시계, 이어폰, 등) 및 전자기기(전자계산기, 전자사전 등)를 소지할 수 없습니다.

3. 응시표 출력사항 외 시험과 관련된 내용이 인쇄 또는 메모된 응시표를 시험시간 중 소지하고 있는 경우 답안지 무효 처분을 받을 수 있으며, 특히 부정한 자료로 판단되는 경우에는 5년간 공무원 임용시험 응시자격 정지 처분을 받을 수 있습니다.

4. 시험종료 후에도 계속하여 답안을 작성하거나, 시험감독관의 답안지 제출 지시에 불응할 경우에는 무효처분을 받게 됩니다.

5. 답안 기재가 끝났더라도 시험종료 후 시험감독관의 지시가 있을 때까지 퇴실할 수 없으며, 사용한 모든 답안지는 반드시 제출해야 합니다.
   - 답안, 책형 및 인적사항 등 모든 기재(표기) 사항 작성 시 누락되는 항목이 없도록 유의하시기 바랍니다.

6. 그 밖에 공고문의 응시자 준수사항이나 시험감독관의 정당한 지시 등을 따르지 않을 경우 부정행위자로 간주될 수 있습니다.

에듀윌에서 꿈을 이룬
합격생들의 진짜 합격스토리

에듀윌 강의·교재·학습시스템의 우수성을
합격으로 입증하였습니다!

김○은 국가직 9급 일반행정직 최종 합격

에듀윌만의 탄탄한 커리큘럼 덕분에 공시 3관왕 달성

혼자서 공부하다 보면 지금쯤 뭘 해야 하는지, 내가 잘하고 있는지 걱정이 될 때가 있는데 에듀윌 커리큘럼은 정말 잘 짜여 있어 고민할 필요 없이 그대로 따라가면 되는 시스템이었습니다. 커리큘럼이 기본이론-심화이론-단원별 문제풀이-기출 문제풀이-파이널로 풍부하게 구성되어 인강만으로도 국가직, 지방직, 군무원 3개 직렬에 충분히 합격할 수 있었습니다. 혼자 공부하다 보면 내 위치를 스스로 가늠하기 어려운데, 매달 제공되는 에듀윌 모의고사를 통해서 제 수준이 어느 정도인지 파악할 수 있어서 좋았습니다.

신○은 국가직 9급 일반행정직 최종 합격

에듀윌 교수님들의 열정적인 강의는 업계 최고 수준!

에듀윌 교수님들의 강의가 열정적이어서 좋았습니다. 타사의 유명 행정법 강사분의 강의를 잠깐 들은 적이 있었는데, 그분이 기대만큼 좋지 못해서 열정적인 강의의 에듀윌로 돌아온 적이 있습니다. 그리고 수험생들은 금전적으로 좀 어려움이 있을 수밖에 없는데 에듀윌이 타사보다는 가격 대비 강의가 매우 뛰어나다고 생각합니다. 에듀윌 모의고사도 좋았습니다. 내가 맞혔는데 남들이 틀린 문제나 남들은 맞혔는데 내가 틀린 문제를 분석해줘서 저의 취약점을 알게 되고, 공부 방법에 변화를 줄 수 있는 계기를 마련해 줍니다. 에듀윌의 꼼꼼한 모의고사 시스템 덕분에 효율적인 공부를 할 수 있었습니다.

김○경 지방직 9급 사회복지직 최종 합격

초시생도 빠르게 합격할 수 있는 에듀윌 공무원 커리큘럼

에듀윌 공무원 커리큘럼은 기본 강의, 심화 강의, 문제풀이 강의가 참 적절하게 배분이 잘 되어 있었어요. 그리고 제가 공무원 시험에 대해서 하나도 몰랐는데 커리큘럼을 따라만 갔는데 바로 시험을 치를 수 있는 실력이 만들어진다는 것이 너무 신기한 경험이었습니다. 에듀윌 공무원 교재도 너무 좋았습니다. 기본서가 충실하게 만들어져 있어서 기본서만 봐도 기초를 쌓을 수 있었습니다. 그리고 기출문제집이나 동형 문제집도 문제 분량이 굉장히 많았어요. 이러한 꼼꼼한 교재 구성 덕분에 40대에 공부를 다시 시작했음에도 빠르게 합격할 수 있었어요.

다음 합격의 주인공은 당신입니다!

더 많은
합격스토리

합격자 수 2,100% 수직 상승!
매년 놀라운 성장

에듀윌 공무원은 '합격자 수'라는 확실한 결과로 증명하며
지금도 기록을 만들어 가고 있습니다.

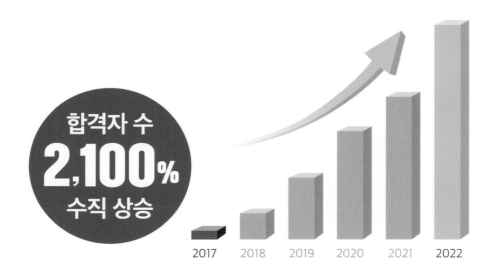

합격자 수
2,100%
수직 상승

2017 2018 2019 2020 2021 2022

합격자 수를 폭발적으로 증가시킨 합격패스

합격 시 수강료 100% 환급	+	합격할 때까지 평생 수강	+	교재비 부담 DOWN 에듀캐시 지원

※ 환급내용은 상품페이지 참고. 상품은 변경될 수 있음.

상품
페이지

* 2017/2022 에듀윌 공무원 과정 최종 환급자 수 기준

2025

에듀윌 9급공무원
7개년 기출문제집 영어

정답과 해설

eduwill

2025

에듀윌 9급공무원
7개년 기출문제집 영어

빠른 정답표 SPEED CHECK

2025 출제예상문제

1	2	3	4	5
①	③	④	②	③
6	7	8	9	10
②	④	④	①	③
11	12	13	14	15
②	②	④	④	②
16	17	18	19	20
④	④	②	②	②

인사혁신처 예시문제(1차)

1	2	3	4	5
①	②	④	①	①
6	7	8	9	10
④	③	③	②	②
11	12	13	14	15
③	④	④	①	①
16	17	18	19	20
③	③	②	②	③

인사혁신처 예시문제(2차)

1	2	3	4	5
③	②	③	④	②
6	7	8	9	10
②	②	①	④	①
11	12	13	14	15
③	①	①	③	②
16	17	18	19	20
②	②	②	④	③

2024 국가직 9급

1	2	3	4	5
③	②	①	④	③
6	7	8	9	10
②	①	④	①	④
11	12	13	14	15
③	③	②	④	②
16	17	18	19	20
④	③	①	②	①

2023 국가직 9급

1	2	3	4	5
②	②	③	④	③
6	7	8	9	10
④	④	③	①	①
11	12	13	14	15
②	②	④	④	①
16	17	18	19	20
②	④	①	②	①

2022 국가직 9급

1	2	3	4	5
①	②	②	②	①
6	7	8	9	10
④	①	④	②	③
11	12	13	14	15
①	②	③	②	④
16	17	18	19	20
③	④	④	①	③

2021 국가직 9급

1	2	3	4	5
①	②	②	④	④
6	7	8	9	10
②	④	③	④	④
11	12	13	14	15
④	②	②	③	②
16	17	18	19	20
①	③	③	③	①

2020 국가직 9급

1	2	3	4	5
①	④	②	①	④
6	7	8	9	10
②	②	③	①	④
11	12	13	14	15
④	②	③	②	③
16	17	18	19	20
④	④	②	①	②

2019 국가직 9급

1	2	3	4	5
②	②	④	②	②
6	7	8	9	10
①	②	②	②	③
11	12	13	14	15
④	②	④	②	④
16	17	18	19	20
①	③	④	③	④

2018 국가직 9급

1	2	3	4	5
①	①	②	③	①
6	7	8	9	10
②	④	④	②	③
11	12	13	14	15
②	④	②	①	④
16	17	18	19	20
①	②	②	④	④

지방직 9급

2024 지방직 9급

1	2	3	4	5	6	7	8	9	10	11	12	13	14	15	16	17	18	19	20
③	③	④	①	①	②	②	①	④	④	④	③	④	④	③	③	③	④	①	①

2023 지방직 9급

1	2	3	4	5	6	7	8	9	10	11	12	13	14	15	16	17	18	19	20
①	②	③	④	③	②	②	①	①	④	③	④	①	④	③	④	②	②	④	④

2022 지방직 9급

1	2	3	4	5	6	7	8	9	10	11	12	13	14	15	16	17	18	19	20
①	②	④	②	②	④	①	④	①	④	④	③	④	③	③	③	①	④	③	②

2021 지방직 9급

1	2	3	4	5	6	7	8	9	10	11	12	13	14	15	16	17	18	19	20
④	②	④	④	②	④	②	①	②	④	④	②	②	②	①	①	④	③	②	③

2020 지방직 9급

1	2	3	4	5	6	7	8	9	10	11	12	13	14	15	16	17	18	19	20
④	②	④	②	③	②	②	④	①	③	③	②	④	④	④	③	①	①	④	②

2019 지방직 9급

1	2	3	4	5	6	7	8	9	10	11	12	13	14	15	16	17	18	19	20
①	②	②	④	②	①	②	④	④	④	④	③	②	④	④	③	①	③	①	②

2018 지방직 9급

1	2	3	4	5	6	7	8	9	10	11	12	13	14	15	16	17	18	19	20
①	②	④	④	④	①	②	④	②	④	②	②	①	③	②	③	①	①	④	①

법원직 9급

2024 법원직 9급

1	2	3	4	5	6	7	8	9	10	11	12	13	14	15	16	17	18	19	20	21	22	23	24	25
①	②	③	②	③	④	①	②	②	①	②	④	④	①	③	④	②	②	②	④	②	①	②	①	④

2023 법원직 9급

1	2	3	4	5	6	7	8	9	10	11	12	13	14	15	16	17	18	19	20	21	22	23	24	25
③	②	③	④	②	③	③	②	①	②	③	③	②	④	②	④	①	②	③	③	③	③	①	④	③

2022 법원직 9급

1	2	3	4	5	6	7	8	9	10	11	12	13	14	15	16	17	18	19	20	21	22	23	24	25
①	①	①	③	④	①	①	①	③	④	④	①	③	③	④	②	③	①	①	④	③	②	③	①	③

2021 법원직 9급

1	2	3	4	5	6	7	8	9	10	11	12	13	14	15	16	17	18	19	20	21	22	23	24	25
④	②	④	④	②	④	④	④	①	②	④	①	②	②	①	①	④	①	②	①	②	③	②	②	②

2020 법원직 9급

1	2	3	4	5	6	7	8	9	10	11	12	13	14	15	16	17	18	19	20	21	22	23	24	25
②	①	②	④	①	②	①	②	④	①	②	②	①	③	③	②	②	④	③	③	④	②	③	③	④

2025

에듀윌 9급공무원
7개년 기출문제집

영어 | 해설편

합격을 당기는 전략

기출회독 최종점검

문제풀이 집중훈련

SPECIAL TEST

해설 &
출제 POINT

출제 POINT

Point 1 어휘는 필수 어휘를 기반으로 한 빈칸 어휘 추론 문제 출제 가능성이
높아졌다.

Point 2 문법은 동사와 준동사의 구분, 적절한 연결사에 따른 문장의 구조 이해
를 철저하게 정리해야 한다.

Point 3 독해는 늘어난 문항 수와 추론 관련 문제 비중의 증가가 예상된다.

출제비중 체크

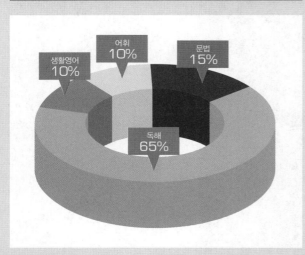

생활영어 10%
어휘 10%
문법 15%
독해 65%

맞힌 개수	/20문항	점수	/100점

취약영역 체크

문항	정답	영역	문항	정답	영역
1	①	어휘 > 빈칸	11	②	독해 > 세부내용 찾기
2	③	어휘 > 빈칸	12	②	독해 > 대의 파악
3	④	문법 > 동사의 형태	13	①	독해 > 대의 파악
4	②	문법 > 연결사	14	④	독해 > 세부내용 찾기
5	③	문법 > 연결사	15	④	독해 > 대의 파악
6	②	생활영어 > 회화	16	④	독해 > 글의 일관성 파악하기
7	④	생활영어 > 회화	17	④	독해 > 글의 일관성 파악하기
8	②	독해 > 세부내용 찾기	18	④	독해 > 글의 일관성 파악하기
9	①	독해 > 동의어	19	②	독해 > 빈칸의 내용 추론하기
10	③	독해 > 빈칸의 내용 추론하기	20	④	독해 > 빈칸의 내용 추론하기

⬇ 영역별 틀린 개수로 취약영역을 확인하세요!

어휘	/2	문법	/3	독해	/13	생활영어	/2

➡ 나의 취약영역: _____

※ 해당 회차는 〈1초 합격예측 서비스〉의 데이터 누적 기간이 충분하지 않아 오답률, 선지 선택률 기재를 생략하였습니다.

---

1 | 어휘 > 빈칸 | 답 ①

| 해석 | 유물 중 일부는 너무 ① 부서지기 쉽기 때문에 옮기는 데 시간이 더 걸릴 수도 있다.
① 부서지기 쉬운; 약한　　　　② 가상의; 실질적인
③ 상상의, 가상의　　　　　　④ 매력적인
| 정답해설 | ① 유물(relics)을 옮기는 데 시간이 더 걸릴 수 있다고 했는데, 유물이 가지고 있는 특성을 고려하면 주어진 선지 중에서는 '부서지기 쉬운'의 fragile이 문맥상 가장 적절하다.

어휘
relic 유물, 유적

2 | 어휘 > 빈칸 | 답 ③

| 해석 | 공직자 윤리법에 따라 대통령과 장관들, 그 밖의 고위 공직자들은 본인과 그들 가족들의 자산과 재산을 ③ 공개해야 한다.
① 수정[개정]하다　　　　　② 주장하다
③ 공개하다, 밝히다　　　　④ 제한[한정]하다
| 정답해설 | ③ 공직자 윤리법(law on government officials' ethics) 하에서 공무원들이 본인과 가족들의 자산과 재산을 어떻게 해야 할지 고려하면, 주어진 선지에서는 '공개해야' 할 것을 유추할 수 있다. 따라서 문맥상 '공개하다'의 의미인 disclose가 가장 적절하다.

어휘
ethics 윤리, 윤리학　　　　　　cabinet 내각, 각료

be subject to ~해야 한다, ~의 대상이다
asset 자산, 재산　　　　　　property 재산, 자산; 특성

3 | 문법 > 동사의 형태 > 수동태 | 답 ④

| 해석 | 20세기에는 뇌 질환 치료를 위한 의약품 개발을 통해 생긴 약간의 희망이 있었으며, 뇌 질환의 증상을 경감시킬 수 있는 많은 약물이 개발되었지만, 실제로는 그중 어떤 것도 치료된 것으로 여겨질 수 없다.
| 정답해설 | ④ 부사절을 이끄는 접속사 while의 주어는 many drugs이며, that ~ brain disorders는 주어이자 선행사인 many drugs를 수식하는 관계대명사절이다. 따라서 빈칸에는 동사가 와야 하므로 준동사인 ①과 ③은 정답에서 제외된다. develop이 '개발하다'의 의미일 때는 타동사이고, 빈칸에 이어 목적어가 없으므로 수동형 동사가 와야 함을 알 수 있다. 따라서 현재완료수동태 동사인 ④가 정답이다.

어휘
pharmaceutical 약학의, 약제의　　　treat 치료하다
alleviate 경감[완화]하다

4 | 문법 > 연결사 > 접속사 | 답 ②

| 해석 | 거의 대부분의 회사, 학교, 조직이 판매 수치, 수상 이력, 시험 점수와 같은 개인을 평가하는 수치의 관점에서 '높은 성과'를 측정하고 보상한다. 이 접근 방식의 문제는 이 방식이 우리가 '적자생존'의 세상에 살고 있

다는, 과학이 완전히 확인해 주었다고 생각하는 믿음에 바탕을 두고 있다는 점이다. 그러나 이 믿음은 정확하지 않다. 새로운 연구 덕분에 최고의 가능성을 성취하는 것은 적자생존이 아니라 가장 잘 어울리는 사람의 생존에 관한 것이라는 것을 우리는 이제 알고 있다.

| 정답해설 | ② 동사 is에 이어진 보어인 명사절을 이끌어야 하는 연결사인데, what은 명사절을 이끌 때 선행사를 포함한 관계대명사로 뒤에는 불완전한 절이 이어져야 한다. 완전한 절이 이어졌으므로 접속사 that으로 바꿔야 한다.

| 오답해설 | ① the vast majority는 부분 명사로, '부분 명사 of 명사'가 주어일 때, of 뒤의 명사에 동사의 수를 일치시켜야 한다. 따라서 companies, schools, and organizations에 동사의 수를 일치시켜 복수 동사인 measure가 올바르게 왔다.
③ 타동사 know의 목적어인 명사절을 이끄는 접속사로, 뒤에 완전한 절이 올바르게 이어졌다.
④ not과 호응하는 등위상관접속사로, 'not A but B'는 'A가 아니라 B'의 표현이다.

어휘

in terms of ~의 관점에서	metrics 측정 기준
résumé 이력(서)	accolades 포상, 표창
confirm 확인하다	survival of the fittest 적자생존
potential 잠재성	

---

5 문법 > 연결사 > 관계사 　　　　답 ③

| 해석 | 문화적 세계화는 인도에서 제작된 발리우드 영화와 홍콩에서 제작된 쿵푸 영화와 같이 아시아에서 다수의 중심지를 가진다. 그것들은 무려 17개 언어로 자막 처리가 되며 특정 디아스포라에 배급된다. 힌디어, 만다린어와 같은 언어들에 지배되는 이러한 문화적 장소들은 영어의 확산을 무시하고 저항한다. 따라서 일부 연구자들은 아시아 젊은이들이 문화적 세계화의 또는 서구로부터 퍼져 나온 '세계 문화'의 수동적 희생자라는 생각에 실증적으로 이의를 제기한다.

| 정답해설 | ③ which 다음에는 불완전한 절이 이어져야 하는데, 완전한 절이 이어졌다. 따라서 the idea의 동격절인 명사절을 이끄는 접속사 that으로 바꿔야 한다.

| 오답해설 | ① 명사 movies를 수식하는 과거분사로, 맥락상 '인도에서 만들어지는 발리우드 영화들'로 올바른 구조이다.
② 중간에 삽입된 관계대명사절(which ~ Mandarin'을 제외하면 주어는 These cultural spaces이므로 복수로 동사의 수일치가 이루어진 올바른 구조이다.
④ that은 선행사 world culture를 지칭하는 주격 관계대명사로, 이어지는 동사는 선행사의 수에 일치시켜야 하므로 단수로 수일치가 이루어진 올바른 구조이다.

어휘

globalization 세계화	multiple 다수의, 다양한
subtitle 자막 처리를 하다	distribute 배급하다
specific 특정한	dominate 지배하다
challenge 이의를 제기하다; 도전하다	
victim 희생자	

---

6 생활영어 > 회화 　　　　답 ②

| 해석 | Sue Ferguson: 그거 아세요? 교보문고가 다음 주에 그랜드 세일을 한대요.
Mike Owen: 와, 책을 저렴하게 살 수 있는 좋은 기회가 되겠네요.
Sue Ferguson: 네, 세일은 5일 동안 계속 될 거예요.
Mike Owen: 저도 소설 몇 권을 사야 하는데, 함께 가는 게 어때요?
Sue Ferguson: 좋아요. 그런데, 제 스케줄이 다음 주에 꽤 유연해요.
Mike Owen: 다음 주 수요일에 만나는 건 어때요? 괜찮으세요?
Sue Ferguson: ② 물론이죠. 당신이 필요로 하는 책들이 모두 있으면 좋겠네요.
① 네, 화요일부터 일요일까지 열어요.
② 물론이죠. 당신이 필요로 하는 책들이 모두 있으면 좋겠네요.
③ 맞아요. 그 책은 곧 출간될 거예요.
④ 걱정마세요. 당신을 위해 좋은 책을 찾아볼게요.

| 정답해설 | ② 서점에서 세일을 한다는 소식을 전하고 함께 서점을 가기로 약속을 정하는 상황이다. 빈칸 앞에서 Mike가 날짜를 제안하고 있으므로, 이에 대한 대답으로 수락 혹은 거절의 의사를 나타내야 한다. ②에서 수락의 Sure에 이어 책을 사고 싶어 하는 Mike에게 필요한 책들이 있기를 바란다고 덧붙이고 있으므로 정답으로 ②가 가장 적절하다.

어휘

at a bargain 염가로	flexible 유연한, 융통성 있는

---

7 생활영어 > 회화 　　　　답 ④

| 해석 | A: Jordan! 진정 좀 해줄래?
B: 엄마! 저는 아무것도 안 하고 있어요! 왜 그렇게 말씀하세요? 이 집에서 저만 애가 아니잖아요.
A: 너 뛰고 있었잖아, 아니야? 너무 시끄럽잖아. 엄마는 좀 쉬고 싶구나.
B: ④ 제가 아니에요. 시끄럽게 하고 있는 것은 John이에요.
① 엄마 말이 맞아요. 이 지역은 밤에 너무 시끄러워요.
② 자, 제 말을 들으세요. 복도에서 뛰지 마세요.
③ 조심하세요! 아이가 도로에 뛰어들고 있어요.
④ 제가 아니에요. 시끄럽게 하고 있는 것은 John이에요.

| 정답해설 | ④ 조용히 하라는 엄마의 말에 아들이 아무것도 하지 않고 있다고 하자 엄마가 뛰지 않았느냐고 말한다. 너무 시끄럽다는 엄마의 불평에 아들이 할 말로 ④가 가장 적절하다.

어휘

keep it down 소리를 줄이다, 조용히 하다

---

8 독해 > 세부내용 찾기 > 내용 불일치 찾기 　　　　답 ②

| 해석 | Clarence Foster 씨
월넛 크리크, 북 캘리포니아로 워터프론트 플라자 450동
우편번호 94596

친애하는 Foster씨:

제 남편과 제가 워터프론트 플라자로 옮긴 이틀 후인 11월 10일에 우리 집의 다음과 같은 문제점에 대해 저는 당신에게 전화했어요:
– 부엌 수납장과 가스레인지에 해충 창궐
– 현관문 페인트가 벗겨짐

– 부서진 침실 문

당신은 11월 17일까지 해충 방제를 실시하고, 현관문을 다시 칠하고, 침실 문을 수리할 수 있도록 보수 요원을 보내겠다고 제게 장담했습니다. 이제 그 날짜가 일주일이 지났고, 아무런 해결도 되지 않았네요.

이 상황을 해결하기 위해서, 저는 세 건의 수리 견적서 인증 사본을 정리하여 첨부했습니다. 만약 당신이 12월 3일까지 수리에 합의한 사항을 완료하지 않는다면, 저는 그 작업을 제 스스로 준비할 것이며 다음 달 집세에서 비용을 공제해 줄 것을 제안할 것입니다.

이 제안에 신속한 답변을 주시면 감사하겠습니다.

Samantha Bailey
① 그녀는 워터프론트 플라자에 온 지 얼마 되지 않았다.
② 그녀는 다음 달 집세를 내지 않을 것이다.
③ 그녀는 더 이상 수리를 기다릴 수 없다.
④ 그녀는 자기 집의 위생에 신경을 쓴다.
| 정답해설 | ② 다음 달 임대료에서 공사 비용을 공제할 것을 제안하는 것이지 집세를 내지 않겠다는 것은 아니므로 글의 내용과 일치하지 않는 것은 ②이다.

어휘

pest 해충, 유해 동물 　　　　　infestation 들끓음, 창궐
maintenance personnel 보수 요원, 정비 요원
remedy (결함 등의) 개선 방법, 구제(책); 치료, 처치
in an attempt to ~하려는 시도로 　　compile (자료 등을) 수집하다
certified 보증된 　　　　　　　　estimate 견적(액), 예정(액)
deduct (돈, 점수 등을) 공제하다 　　prompt 즉각적인, 신속한

9	독해 > 동의어	답 ①

| 해석 | 8번 해석과 동일
① 해결책 　　　　　　　　　② 피해
③ 치료 　　　　　　　　　　④ 도움
| 정답해설 | ① remedy는 '치료, 처치'의 의미 외에도 '(결함 등의) 개선 방법, 구제(책)'의 의미도 있다. 맥락상 '해결책'의 의미인 solution이 동의어로 가장 적절하다.

10	독해 > 빈칸의 내용 추론하기 > 빈칸 어구 추론	답 ③

| 해석 | 많은 놀라운 동물들이 있는 곳에서의 ③ 재미있는 가족 외출을 상상하시나요? Camperdown 동물원은 연중 내내 개방하며, 저희에게는 여러분의 방문을 고대하는 많은 행복한 동물들이 있습니다.

여러분은 Dundee에서 차로 약 15분 거리에 있는 아름다운 Camperdown Country 공원 안에서 저희를 찾으실 수 있습니다.

개방 시간
• 3월 ~ 9월
　매일 오전 10시 ~ 오후 4시 30분
　(마지막 입장 시간: 오후 3시 45분)
• 10월 ~ 2월
　매일 오전 10시 ~ 오후 3시 30분
　(마지막 입장 시간: 오후 2시 45분)

입장료
• 성인(18세 이상): 5달러 50센트
• 3세에서 17세의 어린이: 4달러 50센트
• 3세까지의 어린이: 2달러

14세 미만의 어린이들은 어른과 동행해야 합니다.

교육을 위한 관람, 단체 요금과 수업 또한 이용할 수 있습니다. 더 많은 정보를 원하신다면 저희의 교육을 맡아 진행하는 직원에게 361-243-4328로 전화하시면 됩니다.
① 사냥을 즐기기 원하다
② 별장 짓기를 꿈꾸다
③ 재미있는 가족 외출을 상상하다
④ 환경 운동을 하다
| 정답해설 | ③ 동물원을 소개하는 안내문이다. 동물원 위치, 개방 시간, 입장료 등이 상세하게 안내되어 있으므로, 빈칸에 들어갈 것으로 ③이 가장 적절하다.

어휘

all year round 일년 내내 　　　　　fancy 상상하다
outing 외출

11	독해 > 세부내용 찾기 > 내용 불일치 찾기	답 ②

| 해석 | 10번 해석과 동일
| 정답해설 | ② 10월의 마지막 입장 시간은 오후 2시 45분이므로, ②는 일치하지 않는 내용이다.

12	독해 > 대의 파악 > 요지·주장 찾기	답 ②

| 해석 | 수신: harris_hughes@norcross.com
발신: luckymichael85@norcross.com
날짜: 2024년 9월 18일
제목: 중요 공지사항

Harris Hughes씨에게,

저는 귀하가 Norcross Trading Company에 얼마나 귀중한지 알고 있기를 바랍니다. 이곳에서 고용된 6개월 동안에 주로 귀하의 열정과 행정 지원 때문에 전체 마케팅 부서는 현저한 향상을 증명했습니다.

그러나 매년 직원 성과를 평가하고 급여를 인상하는 것이 Norcross에서 우리의 정책입니다. 귀하가 아직 저희에게 고용된 지 첫 1년이 되지 않았기 때문에 저는 귀하의 요청을 받아 줄 수 없습니다.

올해 12월에 기꺼이 귀하와 만나서 귀하의 월급을 재검토하겠습니다. 그때 제가 귀하의 현재 급여를 인상하는 것을 고려하는 것이 적절할 것입니다.

귀하가 회사를 위해 훌륭하게 공헌해 주신 것에 다시 한번 감사드립니다.

Michael Sanderson
인사부 부장
① 급여 동결 결정에 항의하려고
② 임금 인상 요청을 거절하려고
③ 승진 누락 원인을 설명하려고
④ 임금 협상에 대해 안내하려고

| 정답해설 | ② 'I cannot accept your request.'와 I will be happy to meet with you and review your salary.'에서 봉급 인상 요청을 거절하고 있다는 것을 알 수 있으므로, 글의 목적으로 가장 적절한 것은 ②이다.

어휘

demonstrate 증명하다 marked 두드러진, 현저한
administrative 관리[경영]의, 행정(상)의
assess 평가하다

---

13 독해 > 대의 파악 > 주제 찾기 답 ①

| 해석 | 행동심리학은 그것의 중심적인 자극-반응 이론으로 특징지어지는데, 이 이론은 Pavlov가 종소리에 개가 침을 흘리도록 했을 때 확인했다. 자극-반응 이론은 얻고자 하는 결과가 무엇이든 간에 인간을 조건화되거나 길들여질 수 있는 일종의 기계로 여기며, 그저 정확한 자극을 찾아서 사용하기만 하면 된다. 그러나 S와 R 사이에 있는 그 하이픈에 많은 것이 생략되어 있다. 심리학의, 그리고 인간성의, 모든 풍부하고 중요한 부분이 단순한 인과의 논리에서 무시된다. 인간을 고작 통제할 수 있는 방식으로 특정한 자극에 반응하는 생물로 생각하는 것은 우리의 인간성을 손상시킨다. 그것은 정신을 무시하는데, 그것(정신)이야말로 심리학의 연구 주제이다. 우리는 조건화로만 설명할 수는 없는 그 이상의 존재이다. 우리의 삶에는 일련의 지정된 반응보다 더 많은 것이 있다. 유감스럽게도, 현대 심리학, 즉 과학으로서의 심리학의 많은 부분은 행동심리학과 그것에 수반되는 인간 경험의 빈곤화의 계통을 잇거나 그 영향을 받는다.
① 행동심리학의 문제와 한계
② 자극이 동일한 반응으로 이어지는 방식
③ 심리학이 행동 과학에 속하는 이유
④ 실험에서 감정 조작의 위험

| 정답해설 | ① 행동심리학은 자극에 대한 반응이라는 차원에서 인간의 행동을 설명하려 하는데, 이는 인간에 대한 풍부한 이해를 가로막는다는 내용이므로, 글의 주제로 ①이 가장 적절하다.

어휘

salivate 침을 흘리다 condition 조건화하다, 훈련시키다
disregard 무시하다 humanness 인간성
psyche 정신 attendant 수반되는
impoverishment 빈곤화, 궁핍함

---

14 독해 > 세부내용 찾기 > 내용 일치 찾기 답 ④

| 해석 | 플로깅 행사

플로깅에 대해 들어본 적 있으신가요? 플로깅은 줍는다는 뜻의 스웨덴 낱말인 'plocka upp'에서 왔고, 조깅과 쓰레기 줍기가 합쳐진 말입니다. 플로깅은 2016년 스웨덴에서 시작되었고 최근에 영국으로 건너와 새로운 자연 보호 운동이 되었습니다.

시간과 장소
• 매달 첫 번째 월요일 오전 9시
• East Twickenham, ETNA 센터 밖

준비물
• 그냥 운동화만 가져오세요. 그러면 다른 모든 장비는 우리가 제공합니다.
• 참가비는 없지만, 우리의 자연보호 활동을 위한 기부는 환영합니다.

※참가하기 위해 예약은 필요하지 않습니다.
더 많은 정보를 원하시면 www.environmenttrust.org를 방문해 주시기 바랍니다.

| 정답해설 | ④ There is no fee to participate, but you are welcome to donate toward our conservation work.에서 참가비는 무료지만 기부는 환영한다고 했으므로 안내문의 내용과 일치하는 것은 ④이다.

| 오답해설 | ① 플로깅은 스웨덴에서 시작된 자연 보호 운동이므로 운동 종목이라고 언급한 선지는 글의 내용과 일치하지 않는다.
② 플로깅은 걸으면서 쓰레기를 줍는 것이 아니라 달리면서 쓰레기를 줍는 것이므로 글의 내용과 일치하지 않는다.
③ 운동화를 제외한 나머지 모든 장비를 제공한다고 했으므로 글의 내용과 일치하지 않는다.

어휘

plogging 달리면서 쓰레기 줍기 combination 결합
litter 쓰레기 equipment 장비
participate 참가하다
conservation (자연 환경 · 사적 · 천연 자원 등의) 보호, 보존
reservation 예약

---

15 독해 > 대의 파악 > 제목 찾기 답 ④

| 해석 | 사랑하는 사람과 여행을 하기 전, 하는 도중, 한 후에 어떤 일이 일어나는지 고려해 보라. 만약 여러분이 휴가를 아주 미리 계획한다면, 여러분은 몇 달간 흥분된 기다림을 경험한다. 그 다음 여러분은 친구나 가족과의 여행을 실제로 경험하고, 수년간의 즐거운 추억이 뒤따른다. 이 모든 행복을 여러분 자신을 위해 새 셔츠를 사거나 혹은 심지어 새 차를 사는 값싼 전율과 비교해 보라. 여러분은 그 구매 직후에 행복에서의 작은 급증을 가질 수 있지만, 그러한 새 차를 사는 흥분은 다음 월요일 아침에 차량들 속에 앉아 있을 때 재빨리 사라진다. 여러분의 배우자와 함께 저녁 식사를 하러 나가거나 여러분의 아이를 운동 경기에 데려가는 것과 같은 사람과 사람 사이의 짧은 경험은 여러분의 재정적인 자원을 훨씬 더 낫게 사용하는 것이다.
① 당신의 행복을 위해 다른 사람에게 의존하지 말아라
② 기대를 낮추는 것이 행복의 비결이다
③ 혼자 혹은 누군가와 여행하기: 어떤 것이 더 나은가?
④ 다른 사람들과의 경험에 재원(財源)을 쓰라

| 정답해설 | ④ 물건을 사기 위해 재정적인 자원을 쓰기보다는 다른 사람들과 함께 하는 경험을 위해 그것을 사용하는 것이 훨씬 더 좋다는 내용의 글이므로, 제목으로 가장 적절한 것은 ④이다.

어휘

in advance 미리 anticipation 예상
cheap (값이) 싼, 돈이 적게 드는 purchase 구입, 구매
fade 사라지다
interpersonal 사람과 사람 사이의, 대인 관계의
financial 재정적인

16 독해 > 글의 일관성 파악하기 > 글의 흐름과 무관한 문장   답 ④

| 해석 | 카운터셰이딩(명암 역위(逆位)형 보호색)은 동물에게 위장을 제공하는 시각적으로 평평하게 하는 과정이다. 햇빛이 물체를 위에서 비출 때, 그 물체는 맨 위에서 가장 밝을 것이다. 물체의 색깔은 맨 아래로 향할수록 점차 더 어두운 색으로 음영이 생기게 될 것이다. 이러한 음영은 물체에 농도를 주고 보는 사람이 그것의 모양을 식별하게 해 준다. 따라서 비록 동물이 밑바탕과 정확하지만 균일하게 같은 색일지라도 빛이 비춰질 때 쉽게 눈에 띌 것이다. 그러나 대부분의 동물은 아랫부분보다 윗부분이 더 어둡다. 그들이 위에서 빛을 받을 때, 더 어두운 등은 밝아지고 더 밝은 복부는 음영이 생긴다. 따라서 동물은 하나의 색처럼 보이고 밑바탕과 쉽게 섞인다. ④ 이러한 이유로, 카운터셰이딩은 빛이 없는 환경에서 손실될 수 있다. 이러한 형태의 배색 또는 카운터셰이딩은 생물체의 모양의 시각적 인상을 파괴한다. 그것은 동물이 그것의 배경과 섞이게 해 준다.

| 정답해설 | ④ 카운터셰이딩은 기본적으로 동물은 아랫부분보다 윗부분이 어두운데, 위에서 빛을 받을 때 더 어두운 등은 밝아지고, 더 밝은 복부에 음영이 생김으로써 밑바탕과 쉽게 섞이는 현상이라고 ④ 이전에 설명하고 있다. ④에서 앞의 내용을 this reason으로 받아 빛이 없는 환경에서 카운터셰이딩이 손실된다고 했으나 카운터셰이딩 자체가 빛으로 인한 현상이므로 흐름상 맞지 않는 문장이다. ④에 이어진 문장의 This pattern of coloration이 맥락상 ④ 이전의 내용을 언급하고 있으므로 정답은 ④이다.

어휘

countershading 명암 역위(逆位)형 보호색: 햇빛 쪽은 어둡게 그늘 쪽은 밝게 변색시켜 은폐하는 현상   optical 광학의
flatten 평평하게 하다   camouflage 위장
illuminate 비추다   distinguish 구별하다
uniformly 균일하게   substrate 기질

17 독해 > 글의 일관성 파악하기 > 주어진 문장의 삽입   답 ④

| 해석 | 신경과학자인 David Eagleman은 'Sum'이라고 불리는 책을 썼는데, 그 책에서 각 장은 우리가 죽고 난 후에 일어나는 것에 대한 상상의 버전을 기술하고 있다. 특히 도발적인 마지막 장에서 그는 우리가 우리 삶의 마지막에 도달했을 때 마침내 우리의 전 생애를 분명히, 혹은 우리가 그렇다고 생각하면서 보는 시나리오를 묘사하고 있다. 그때 우리가 죽고 난 후에 우리는 우리의 삶을 거꾸로 다시 보게 된다. 우리가 우리의 여행을 다른 관점, 즉 끝에서부터 시작으로 보게 될 때, 각각의 사건은 완전히 다르게 보인다. 이때 우리는 우리가 믿었던 모든 것이 실제로 부정확하다는 것을 깨닫는다. 이것은 등장인물 중의 한 명이 장기 기억을 전혀 가지고 있지 않은 Christopher Nolan의 영화 'Memento'와 유사하다. ④ 그 이야기는 관객들에게 유사한 감정을 만들어 내기 위해 거꾸로 풀려간다. 더 이전의 장면들이 밝혀지면서, 관객들은 이전에 발생했던 것에 대한 자신들의 해석이 모두 틀렸다는 것을 깨닫는다.

| 정답해설 | ④ 주어진 문장의 The story는 영화 Memento의 이야기를 의미하고 a similar feeling은 자신들이 믿고 있던 것이 틀렸다는 것을 깨닫게 되는 느낌을 의미하므로, 주어진 문장은 ④에 위치하는 것이 적절하다.

어휘

neuroscientist 신경과학자   fanciful 상상의
provocative 도발적인, 자극적인   in reverse 거꾸로
perspective 관점   interpretation 해석

18 독해 > 글의 일관성 파악하기 > 글의 순서   답 ②

| 해석 | 많은 사람이 달력과 천문학에 대한 마야족의 관심을 잘 알고 있지만, 그들은 또한 날씨에 매료되기도 했다.
(B) 서기 1200년과 1400년 사이 언젠가 그들은 현재 멕시코 Cozumel에 Tumba del Caracol이라 불리는 등대를 건축했다. 마야족은 등대 안에 양초를 두었는데, 그것은 배들에게 육지에 접근했다는 것을 경고하는 전통적인 기능을 담당했다.
(A) 게다가 이 등대의 꼭대기에는 영리한 마야족이 다양한 조개껍데기를 전략적으로 두었다. 바람의 속도와 방향에 따라서 그 껍데기들은 다른 음조로 호각 소리를 내곤 했다.
(C) 어느 껍데기가 그리고 어떤 음조로 호각 소리를 내고 있는지, 그리고 어떤 상황이 폭풍우를 만들어 내는지에 대한 자신들의 지식에 따라서, 마야족은 카리브 해로부터 다가오는 폭풍우를 예측할 수 있었다고 말한다.

| 정답해설 | ② 마야족이 날씨에 관심이 있었다는 주어진 글의 내용에 대한 근거를 처음 시작하는 (B)가 이어진다. 건축한 등대 안에 양초를 두었다는 내용과 등대 꼭대기에 조개껍데기를 두었다는 내용인 (A)가 연결되고, 이 껍데기를 통해 카리브 해로부터 다가오는 폭풍우를 예측할 수 있었다는 (C)가 이어져야 한다.

어휘

fascinate 매료[매혹]하다   strategically 전략적으로
a variety of 다양한   seashell 조개껍데기
pitch 음조, 음률의 높이   lighthouse 등대
predict 예측[예견]하다

19 독해 > 빈칸의 내용 추론하기 > 빈칸 어구 추론   답 ②

| 해석 | 운전자로서 우리는 모두 같은 도로 규정을 적용받는다. 반짝거리는 새 스포츠카를 모는 부유한 사람도 속도위반에 대해 낡은 차를 모는 가난한 사람과 같은 대가를 지불한다. 사회적 지위에 상관없이 우리는 모두 같은 줄에 서서 차를 등록하거나 면허증을 갱신하려고 기다린다. 운전 중일 때 110파운드의 장애가 있는 사람은 230파운드의 보디빌더와 똑같은 기동성을 가지고 있다. 실제로 자동차는, 한때 집에 남겨졌던 여성, 시골 사람들, 그리고 장애가 있는 사람들을 포함한 일부 집단들에게 똑같은 기동성을 제공해 왔다. 이런 관점에서 보면, 차는 ② 훌륭한 평등 장치인 것처럼 보인다.
① 사치품
② 훌륭한 평등 장치
③ 지역의 상징
④ 성공의 측정

| 정답해설 | ② 차를 모는 사람이 부자이든 가난한 사람이든, 또는 장애가 있는 사람이든 건장한 사람이든 상관없이, 운전을 할 때는 모두 똑같은 도로 규정을 적용받고, 똑같은 기동성을 확보한다는 내용이다. 따라서 빈칸에 들어갈 말로 ②가 가장 적절하다.

어휘

speeding 속도위반   renew 갱신하다
disabled 장애를 가진   mobility 기동성
be left behind 뒤에 남게 되다   resident 거주자, 주민
disable (신체에) 장애를 입히다, 망가뜨리다

20　독해 > 빈칸의 내용 추론하기 > 빈칸 어구 추론　답 ④

| 해석 | 서비스의 무형적인 특성으로 인해서 소비자들은 ④ 서비스에 대한 최종 평가를 내릴 때 경험의 질에 강하게 의존할 수밖에 없다. 따라서 서비스 구매와 관련된 높은 수준의 위험 부담이 남아 있다. 예를 들어, 자동차를 사고자 하는 소비자들은 자동차를 시운전해 보고 그 모델에 관해 이용 가능한 소비자 성능 데이터를 검토해 보고 참고할 것이다. 이와는 반대로, 자동차를 단기간 빌리는 소비자들은 이용료 지불을 이행할 때까지 자신들이 구매하는 서비스를 평가할 수가 없다. 소비자들은 자동차를 빌리는 시점에서 결정을 내리기 전에 빌릴 가능성이 있는 자동차를 시운전해 볼 수 없다. 이와 비슷하게, 소비자들은 음식을 구매하기 전에 시식을 해 볼 수 없으므로 음식점을 선택할 때 위험을 무릅쓰게 된다.

① 대중 매체보다 입소문
② 전국 체인보다 지역 기업
③ 구매 결정을 이끄는 고가 제품
④ 서비스에 대한 최종 평가를 내릴 때 경험의 질

| 정답해설 | ④ 상품과 달리 서비스는 구매한 후에야 질을 평가 할 수 있어서 위험 부담이 있다는 내용이므로, 빈칸에 들어갈 것으로 ④가 가장 적절하다.

어휘

intangible 무형의, 만질 수 없는　associated with ~와 관련된
purchase 구매; 구입하다　consult 상의[상담]하다
prior to ~이전에

인사혁신처 예시문제

해설 &
기출분석 REPORT

출제 POINT

Point 1 핵심 문법인 동사와 준동사, 일치를 다루었으며, 문제의 난도는 낮지만 신유형에 대한 연습이 필요하다.

Point 2 빈칸 어휘 비중의 증가로 문맥을 파악하는 것이 관건이다.

Point 3 독해 지문은 평이한 수준이나 문항 수 증가와 지문이 길어짐에 따라 시간 안배 요령이 필수적이다.

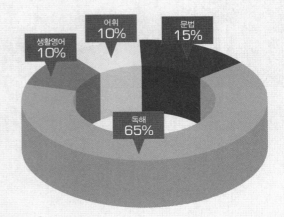

생활영어
10%

어휘
10%

문법
15%

독해
65%

▲ 1, 2차 예시문제 평균 출제비중

회차	총평	어휘	문법	독해	생활영어
1차	**평이한 난도의 신경향 문제 등장, 기본 학습이 철저하면 고득점 가능!** · 문법과 어휘 문항의 축소로 지엽적인 요소가 배제되어 철저한 기본학습이 필수임 · 실용문과 장문 독해가 추가되었으나 수능과 비슷한 유형으로 체감 난도 영향은 미미함 · 독해는 늘어난 문항 수에도 킬러 문항이 없는 쉬운 추론을 바탕으로 출제됨	10% (2문항)	15% (3문항)	65% (13문항)	10% (2문항)
2차	**1차와 동일한 영역별 문항 구성과 난도로 신경향 출제 기조 재점검!** · 문법과 어휘는 1차와 동일하게 가장 기본적인 요소들로 문제가 구성됨 · 대의 파악과 세부내용 찾기는 핵심 내용 파악으로 빠르게 해결 가능한 수준임 · 장문 독해와 실용문을 제외한 독해 지문은 상대적으로 짧은 편으로 무난한 소재와 단서 제시 등 고득점이 가능한 요소들을 갖춤	10% (2문항)	15% (3문항)	65% (13문항)	10% (2문항)

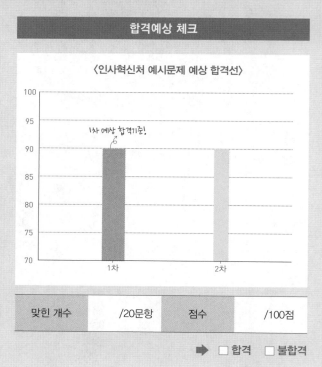

합격예상 체크		

〈인사혁신처 예시문제 예상 합격선〉

1차 예상 합격기준

맞힌 개수	/20문항	점수	/100점

➡ ☐ 합격 ☐ 불합격

취약영역 체크					
문항	정답	영역	문항	정답	영역
1	①	어휘 > 빈칸	11	③	독해 > 세부내용 찾기
2	②	어휘 > 빈칸	12	④	독해 > 세부내용 찾기
3	④	문법 > 동사의 형태	13	④	독해 > 세부내용 찾기
4	①	문법 > 동사의 형태	14	④	독해 > 대의 파악
5	①	문법 > 준동사	15	①	독해 > 대의 파악
6	④	생활영어 > 회화	16	③	독해 > 글의 일관성 파악하기
7	③	생활영어 > 회화	17	③	독해 > 글의 일관성 파악하기
8	③	독해 > 대의 파악	18	②	독해 > 글의 일관성 파악하기
9	②	독해 > 동의어	19	①	독해 > 빈칸의 내용 추론하기
10	②	독해 > 대의 파악	20	③	독해 > 빈칸의 내용 추론하기

⬇ 영역별 틀린 개수로 취약영역을 확인하세요!

어휘	/2	문법	/3	독해	/13	생활영어	/2

➡ 나의 취약영역: _____

※ 해당 회차는 〈1초 합격예측 서비스〉의 데이터 누적 기간이 충분하지 않아 오답률, 선지 선택률 기재를 생략하였습니다.

1 　어휘 > 빈칸 　　　　　　　　　답 ①

| 해석 | 최근, 전 세계적으로 흔히 '이상 기후'로 일컬어지는 ① 불규칙한 날씨 패턴이 점점 더 많이 관측되었다.
① 불규칙한　　　　　　　② 일관적인
③ 예측 가능한　　　　　　④ 효과[효력] 없는
| 정답해설 | ① 빈칸과 유사한 표현으로 abnormal(비정상적인)이 언급되었으므로 선지 중 irregular(불규칙한)가 가장 적절하다. 나머지 선지들은 weather를 수식하기 어색하거나 abnormal과 성격이 다른 어휘이므로 적절하지 않다.

어휘
refer to A as B A를 B로 언급하다　　abnormal 비정상적인

2 　어휘 > 빈칸 　　　　　　　　　답 ②

| 해석 | 대부분의 경제 이론은 사람들이 ② 이성적으로 행동한다고 가정한다. 그러나 이것은 그들이 종종 자신의 감정에 의존한다는 사실을 설명하지 못한다.
① 일시적인　　　　　　　② 이성적인
③ 자발적인　　　　　　　④ 상업의
| 정답해설 | ② 빈칸이 속한 첫 번째 문장에 이어진 연결사 however에 이어 사람들이 감정에 의존한다는 사실을 설명하지 못한다고 한 것으로 보아, 빈칸에는 emotions와 대비되는 어휘가 들어가야 함을 유추할 수 있다. 따라서 '이성적인'의 의미인 rational이 가장 적절하다.

어휘
account for ~을 설명하다　　　rely on ~에 의존하다

3 　문법 > 동사의 형태 > 시제 　　　　답 ④

| 해석 | 그녀가 학위를 마칠 때쯤이면, 자신의 연구 분야에 대한 귀중한 지식을 습득하게 될 것이다.
| 정답해설 | ④ 주절의 시제가 미래완료(will have acquired)이므로 빈칸에도 미래의 표현이 되어야 한다. by the time은 시간 부사절을 이끄는 접속사로 현재동사가 미래를 대신하므로 현재시제인 finishes가 정답이다.

어휘
degree 학위　　　　　　　acquire 취득[획득]하다, 입수하다
valuable 귀중한, 소중한

4 　문법 > 동사의 형태 > 시제 　　　　답 ①

| 해석 | 당신은 음성 체계, 단어 패턴 및 문장 구조에 대한 지식이 학생이 언어에서 유능해질 수 있도록 돕기에 충분하다고 결론을 내릴 수 있다. 그러나 우리 모두는 구조적으로 영어를 이해하지만 여전히 의사소통에 어려움을 겪는 언어 학습자들과 함께 일을 해왔다.
| 정답해설 | ① 접속사 that이 이끄는 절의 주어 knowledge와 호응하는 동사이므로 단수로 수일치가 되어야 한다. 시제를 고려해 현재시제인 is로 바꿔야 한다.

| **오답해설** | ② to help에 이어진 구조에서 준사역동사 help와 호응하는 목적보어로 원형부정사 become이 올바르게 왔다. to become 으로도 쓸 수 있다.

③ 동사 have worked를 수식하기 위해 부사로 올바르게 왔다.

④ '~에 어려움을 겪다'의 표현인 'have difficulty R-ing'의 구조로 올바르게 표현했다.

어휘

conclude 결론짓다　　　　　　　sufficient 충분한
competent 유능한　　　　　　　structurally 구조적으로
have difficulty R-ing ~에 어려움을 겪다

| **5** | 문법 > 준동사 > 동명사 | 답 ① |

| **해석** | 차들과 교통 체증을 넘어, 그녀는 한 곳에 그렇게 많은 사람들이 있는 것에 익숙해지는 데 시간이 좀 걸렸다고 말했는데, 사람들은 모두 매우 빨리 이동하고 있었다. "매사추세츠 주에서만 6백만 명이 넘는 사람들이 있다는 것과 비교하면, 호주에는 1천8백만 명의 사람들이 전 국가에 퍼져 있을 뿐이다."라고 그녀는 말했다.

| **정답해설** | ① get(be) used to + (대)명사/R-ing는 '~에 익숙해지다'의 표현으로 to는 전치사이다. 따라서 전치사의 목적어로 동사원형 have가 아닌 동명사 having이 되어야 한다.

| **오답해설** | ② '대명사 + of + 관계대명사'의 구조로 뒤에 동사 were moving이 있으므로 관계사가 필요하다. 이때 whom은 선행사인 many people을 지칭하고 전치사 of의 목적어가 되어야 하므로 목적격 whom으로 올바르게 왔다. 선행사에 이어진 문장인 and all of them(many people) were moving so fast에서 and와 them을 결합해 목적격 관계대명사 whom으로 바꾼 경우이다.

③ 유도부사 there가 이끄는 1형식 문장의 주어인 18 million people을 수식하는 과거분사구이다. spread out은 타동사구로 뒤에 목적어인 명사가 없고, 맥락상 사람들이 '퍼져 있는' 것이므로 수동의 과거분사로 올바르게 왔다. spread의 동사 변화는 spread-spread-spread이다.

④ 전치사 in에 이어진 목적어로 명사가 올바르게 왔다. alone이 형용사로 명사 뒤에서 수식할 때 '~만인, ~뿐인'의 의미로 구조와 맥락상 적절하다.

어휘

get used to ~에 익숙해지다　　　spread 분포하다; 펴다, 뻗다
compared to ~와 비교하여

| **6** | 생활영어 > 회화 | 답 ④ |

| **해석** | A: 안녕하세요. 서울에서 오클랜드로 가는 비행기를 예약하고 싶은데요.
B: 네. 특별히 염두에 둔 날짜가 있으신가요?
A: 네. 5월 2일에 출국해서 5월 14일에 귀국할 예정입니다.
B: 좋습니다. 일정에 맞는 비행 편을 찾았어요. 어떤 객실 등급으로 예약하시겠어요?
A: 이코노미 클래스면 충분합니다.
B: 좌석에 대한 다른 선호도가 있으신가요?
A: ④ 네, 저는 통로 쪽 좌석을 원합니다.
B: 좋습니다. 고객님의 항공편이 예약되었습니다.

① 네, 저는 비즈니스석으로 업그레이드하고 싶습니다.
② 아니오, 저는 편도 티켓을 구입하고 싶습니다.
③ 아니오, 저는 수하물이 없습니다.
④ 네, 저는 통로 쪽 좌석을 원합니다.

| **정답해설** | ④ 비행기 티켓을 예약하는 상황으로 좌석 등급에 대해 이미 그 이전에 이코노미석으로 결정했고, 그 외 좌석에 대한 선호도를 질문했으므로 빈칸에 들어갈 것으로 통로 쪽 좌석을 원한다고 언급한 ④가 가장 적절하다.

어휘

book a flight 비행편을 예약하다　　specific 특정한, 구체적인
preference 선호(도)

| **7** | 생활영어 > 회화 | 답 ③ |

| **해석** | Kate Anderson: 다음 주 금요일에 워크숍에 오시나요?
Jim Henson: 확실하지 않아요. 그날 병원 진료가 있어서요.
Kate Anderson: 오셔야 해요! 그 워크숍은 우리의 업무 효율성을 높여줄 수 있는 인공지능 툴에 관한 거예요.
Jim Henson: 와, 주제가 정말로 흥미롭네요.
Kate Anderson: 맞아요. 하지만, 워크숍 참석을 원한다면 자리 예약하는 것을 잊지 마시고요.
Jim Henson: 어떻게 하면 되나요?
Kate Anderson: ③ 게시판에 있는 설명대로 하세요.

① 당신은 노트북 컴퓨터를 가져오셔야 해요.
② 저는 이미 예약을 했어요.
③ 게시판에 있는 설명대로 하세요.
④ 당신은 진료를 위해 병원에 전화를 하셔야 해요.

| **정답해설** | ③ Kate가 Jim에게 워크숍 참석을 권유하는 대화문이다. 워크숍의 주제를 들은 후 Jim이 참석 방법을 물어보았으므로 이에 대한 대답으로 게시판 설명대로 하라고 언급한 ③이 정답으로 가장 적절하다.

어휘

appointment (모임·방문 등의) 약속　efficiency 효율(성), 능률
forget to + 동사원형 ~할 것을 잊다　reserve 예약하다
attend 참석하다

| **8** | 독해 > 대의 파악 > 글의 목적 | 답 ③ |

| **해석** | 수신: Clifton 지역 사무실
발신: Rachael Beasley
날짜: 6월 7일
제목: 동네의 과도한 소음

관련 당사자 앞

저는 이 이메일이 당신에게 잘 도착하기를 바랍니다. 저는 우리 동네, 특히 새로운 운동 경기장에서 나는 과도한 소음 수준에 대한 우려와 불만을 말하려고 글을 쓰고 있습니다.

Clifton 지역의 주민으로서, 저는 항상 우리 지역의 평온함에 감사해 왔습니다. 그러나 계속되는 소음 장애는 우리 가족의 안녕과 전반적인 삶의 질에 큰 영향을 미쳤습니다. 소음의 근원에는 사람들의 응원, 소리 지르는 선수, 호각 및 공의 충돌 등이 포함됩니다.

저는 당신이 이 문제를 살펴보고 소음 장애를 해결하기 위한 적절한 <u>조치</u>를 취할 것을 요청합니다. 이 문제에 관심을 가져주셔서 감사드리며, 우리 동네의 평온을 회복하는 데 도움이 되는 신속한 대응에 감사드립니다.

Rachael Beasley 드림

| 정답해설 | ③ 인근의 새로 생긴 스포츠 경기장에서 나오는 소음 방해에 대해 조치를 취해줄 것을 요청하는 글이므로 글의 목적으로 가장 적절한 것은 ③이다.

<mark>어휘</mark>

concern 관련되다; 우려, 걱정	frustration 불안, 좌절
appreciate 감사하다	disturbance 장애, 방해
look into ~을 살펴보다, 조사하다	appropriate 적절한
address 처리하다, 다루다	prompt 신속한
restore 회복하다	tranquility 고요, 평안

---

9 독해 > 동의어 　　　　　　　　　 답 ②

| 해석 | 8번 해석과 동일
① 운동, 동작　　　　　　　② 조치
③ 수준　　　　　　　　　　④ 계단

| 정답해설 | ② steps는 '조치, 단계, 걸음, 계단' 등 여러 의미가 있으나, 맥락상 '조치'의 의미가 가장 적절하므로 정답은 ②이다.

---

10 독해 > 대의 파악 > 빈칸 제목 추론 　　 답 ②

| 해석 | ② 우리의 활기찬 지역 행사를 기념하세요

다가오는 City Harbor Festival을 발표하게 되어 기쁘게 생각합니다. 이 축제는 우리가 공유하는 유산, 문화 및 지역 역량을 기념하기 위해 다양한 지역 사회를 하나로 모으는 연례 행사입니다. 여러분의 달력에 표시를 하고 신나는 주말을 위해 우리와 함께 하세요!

세부사항
- **날짜**: 6월 16일 금요일 – 6월 18일 일요일
- **시간**: 오전 10:00 – 오후 8:00 (금요일 및 토요일)
　　　　 오전 10:00 – 오후 6:00 (일요일)
- **위치**: City Harbor 공원, 메인 스트리트 및 주변 지역

하이라이트
- 라이브 공연
　축제장 곳곳의 여러 무대에서 다양한 라이브 음악, 춤, 연극 공연을 즐기세요.

- 푸드 트럭
　무료 샘플 시식뿐만 아니라 다양하고 맛있는 요리를 제공하는 다양하게 구비된 푸드 트럭과 함께 진수성찬을 즐기세요.

행사 및 활동의 전체 일정은 저희 웹사이트 www.cityharbourfestival.org를 방문하거나 (552) 234–5678로 축제 사무국에 문의하십시오.
① 귀하의 지역사회를 위한 안전 규정을 만드세요
② 우리의 활기찬 지역 행사를 기념하세요
③ 귀하의 흥미진진한 해양 경험을 계획하세요
④ 우리 도시의 유산을 재현하세요

| 정답해설 | ② (A)에 이어진 행사에 대해 지역사회를 하나로 모으는 연례 행사라고 언급하고, 일정 및 관련된 활동에 대해 설명하고 있는 글이므로 제목으로 가장 적절한 것은 ②이다.

<mark>어휘</mark>

upcoming 다가오는, 예정된	diverse 다양한
heritage 유산	theatrical 연극의, 극장의

---

11 독해 > 세부내용 찾기 > 내용 불일치 찾기 　 답 ③

| 해석 | 10번 해석과 동일

| 정답해설 | ③ 무료(free)라고 언급된 것은 요리 강습이 아닌 시식(free sample tasting)이므로 글의 내용과 일치하지 않는 것은 ③이다.

---

12 독해 > 세부내용 찾기 > 내용 불일치 찾기 　 답 ④

| 해석 | 세관 신고서에는 새로운 Enter-K 앱을 사용하세요.

공항에 도착하자마자 새로운 Enter-K 앱을 사용하세요. Enter-K가 제공하는 주목할 만한 특징 중 하나는 사전 세관 신고로, 이는 여행자에게 사전에 세관 신고서를 제출할 수 있는 옵션을 제공하며, 우리의 모든 국제 공항에서 시간을 절약할 수 있게 합니다. 진행 중인 여행자 현대화 기획의 일환으로, Enter-K는 장래에 국경 관련 기능을 추가로 도입하여 전반적인 해외 경험을 더욱 향상시킬 것입니다. 도착하기 전에 온라인으로 최신 버전의 앱을 다운로드하기만 하세요. 모바일 기기 사용이 불편한 분들을 위한 앱의 웹 버전도 있습니다.
① 여행자가 사전에 세관 신고를 할 수 있게 한다.
② 더 많은 기능이 나중에 추가될 것이다.
③ 여행자는 그것을 온라인으로 다운로드할 수 있다.
④ 개인 모바일 기기에서만 작동한다.

| 정답해설 | ④ 마지막 두 문장에서 온라인으로 최신 버전의 앱을 다운로드할 수 있다고 언급했고, 이런 모바일 기기 사용이 불편한 사람들을 위해 웹 버전도 있다고 했다. 따라서 모바일 기기에서만 작동한다고 한 ④는 글의 내용과 일치하지 않는다.

<mark>어휘</mark>

declaration (세관 등에의) 소득 · 물품의 신고	
notable 주목할 만한, 두드러진	feature 특징, 특성
submit 제출하다	in advance 사전에, 미리

---

13 독해 > 세부내용 찾기 > 내용 일치 찾기 　 답 ④

| 해석 | 노동 감독관 사무국(OLC)의 책무

OLC는 주 정부의 주된 노동 조정 기관이다. OLC는 최저 임금, 일반 임금 및 잔업 수당이 직원에게 지급되고 직원 휴식 및 점심 시간이 제공되도록 보장할 책임이 있다. 또한, OLC는 미성년자 고용에 대한 감독 권한을 가지고 있다. 노동 관련 문제를 효율적이고 전문적이며 효과적으로 해결하는 것이 이 사무국의 비전과 사명이다. 여기에는 고용주와 직원들에게 법에 따른 권리와 책임에 대해 교육하는 것이 포함된다. OLC는 근로자가 공정하게 대우받고 모든 근무 시간에 대해 보상받을 수 있도록 필요한 경우 조치를 시행한다.
① 직원들이 세금을 제대로 내도록 보장한다.
② 성인 노동자의 고용에 대해서만 감독 권한이 있다.
③ 고용주의 사업 기회를 장려한다.
④ 직원들이 부당한 대우를 받을 때 조치를 취한다.

| **정답해설** | ④ 마지막 문장에서 근로자가 공정하게 대우받고 모든 근무 시간에 대해 보상받을 수 있도록 조치를 취한다고 했으므로, 부당한 대우를 받을 경우에도 동일하게 할 것임을 유추할 수 있다. 따라서 글의 내용과 일치하는 것으로 ④가 적절하다. ①과 ③은 언급되지 않은 내용이고, ②는 미성년자 고용에도 권한이 있다고 했으므로 일치하지 않는다.

어휘

principal 제1의, 주요한	regulatory 조정력을 가진; 규제의
ensure 보증하다, 보장하다	authority 권한, 권위
minor 미성년자	enforcement 시행, 집행
compensate 보상하다	

---

14 독해 > 대의 파악 > 주제 찾기　　　　답 ④

| **해석** | 식품의약품안전처는 교차 감염의 결과로 식중독의 사례가 발생하고 있다고 주의를 당부했는데, 교차 감염은 음식을 준비하거나 식기를 사용하기 전, 사람들이 계란을 만지고 손을 씻는 것을 소홀히 하는 경우에 발생한다. 이러한 위험을 줄이기 위해, 식품의약품안전처는 계란을 냉장 보관하고 노른자와 흰자가 모두 단단해질 때까지 완전히 익혀야 한다고 권고했다. 지난 5년 동안, 7,400명이라는 많은 사람들이 살모넬라균에 의한 식중독을 겪었다. 살모넬라균은 따뜻한 온도에서 창궐하며, 섭씨 약 37도가 최적의 성장 조건이다. 날계란이나 덜 익은 계란을 섭취하고 비조리 음식과 조리 음식을 분리하지 않는 것이 살모넬라균 감염의 가장 흔한 원인으로 확인되었다. 살모넬라 관련 질병의 위험을 최소화하기 위해 식품 안전 조치의 우선순위를 정하고 적절한 조리 습관을 준수하는 것이 중요하다.
① 면역 체계에 계란 섭취의 이점들
② 살모넬라 감염에 대한 다양한 유형의 치료법
③ 따뜻한 온도에서 살모넬라균의 수명
④ 살모넬라 감염 예방을 위한 안전한 계란 취급

| **정답해설** | ④ 교차 감염으로 인한 식중독의 원인으로 계란을 언급하면서, 구체적인 감염 사례와 안전 조치를 서술하는 글이다. 살모넬라균에 의한 식중독을 언급하면서, 날계란과 덜 익은 계란을 섭취하는 것을 그 원인으로 언급했고, 마지막 문장에서 살모넬라 관련 질병의 위험을 최소화하기 위한 조언으로 글을 마무리하고 있으므로 글의 주제로 가장 적절한 것은 ④이다.

어휘

food poisoning 식중독	cross-contamination 교차 감염
neglect 소홀히 하다, 무시하다	utensil 식기, 기구
mitigate 줄이다; 완화하다	refrigerate 냉장하다
thoroughly 철저하게	
staggering (수량이) 엄청난, 막대한; 비틀거리는	
optimal 최선의, 최적의	prioritize 우선시하다
adhere to ~을 고수하다, 지키다	proper 적절한

---

15 독해 > 대의 파악 > 요지·주장 찾기　　　　답 ①

| **해석** | 교육 격차를 해소하기 위한 지속적인 노력에도 불구하고, 학생들 사이의 지속적인 성취 격차는 교육 시스템의 상당한 불평등을 계속 부각시키고 있다. 최근 자료에 따르면, 저소득층 학생들과 취약계층 학생들을 포함한 소외된 학생들은 학업 성적에서 계속해서 또래보다 뒤처지고 있다. 그 격차는 교육적 형평성과 사회적 이동성을 달성하는 데 어려움을 제기한다. 전문가들은 그들의 사회 경제적 지위나 배경에 관계없이 이러한 격차를 해소하고 모든 학생들을 위한 동등한 기회를 보장하기 위해 목표된 개입, 공평한 자원 배분 및 포괄적인 정책의 필요성을 강조한다. 지속적인 교육 격차 문제는 해결책을 찾기 위해 모든 교육 계층에서 다루어져야 한다.
① 우리는 지속적인 교육 불평등을 다루어야 한다.
② 교육 전문가들은 새로운 학교 정책에 집중할 필요가 있다.
③ 성취 격차를 줄이기 위해서는 새로운 교수법이 필요하다.
④ 가정의 수입은 교육의 논의에서 고려되어서는 안 된다.

| **정답해설** | ① 교육 격차를 해소하기 위한 노력에도 불구하고 학생들 사이의 지속적인 성취 격차가 있다고 언급한 후, 이에 대한 구체적인 사례를 통해 문제를 제기하는 글이다. 글의 뒷부분에서 이 문제를 해결하기 위해 전문가들이 관련 정책의 필요성을 강조한다고 했고, 마지막 문장에서 해결책을 찾기 위해 이 문제가 다루어져야 한다고 했으므로 글의 요지로 가장 적절한 것은 ①이다.

어휘

address 다루다, 해결하다	disparity 격차, 차이
persistent 지속하는; 끈기 있는	inequity 불평등
reveal 드러내다, 밝히다	marginalized 소외된
vulnerable 취약한	equity 공평, 공정
social mobility 사회적 이동성(사회의 다른 계층으로의 이동이 용이한 것)	
emphasize 강조하다	intervention 개입, 간섭
equitable 공평한; 공정[정당]한	allocation 할당, 배분
inclusive 포괄적인	bridge the gap 격차를 좁히다
irrespective of ~와는 상관없이	

---

16 독해 > 글의 일관성 파악하기 > 글의 흐름과 무관한 문장　　　　답 ③

| **해석** | 어린아이들의 모든 부모 혹은 보호자는 집에서 벗어나고 싶은 절실한 충동과 동네 공원으로의 짧은 여행의 마법 같은 회복 효과를 경험하게 될 것이다. 아마 이 지점에서는 그냥 스트레스를 해소하는 것 이상의 일이 벌어지고 있을 것이다. 아이들에게 있어 자연에 들어가는 이점은 매우 큰데, 이는 학업 성적 향상에서부터 기분과 집중력 향상에 이른다. ③ 야외 활동은 그들이 가족과 좋은 시간을 보내는 것을 어렵게 만든다. 어린 시절의 자연 체험은 또한 성인기의 환경보호주의를 끌어올릴 수 있다. 도심 녹지 공간에 출입하는 것은 아이들의 사회적 관계와 우정에 한몫을 할 수 있다.

| **정답해설** | ③ 어린아이들을 돌보는 성인들이 동네 공원에 가는 것만으로도 돌봄으로 인한 스트레스를 해소하는 것 이상의 장점이 있다고 언급하고, 그 이점들을 소개하는 글이다. 아이들이 자연과 접해서 얻는 이점으로 학업 성적 향상, 집중력 향상, 환경보호주의 육성, 사회적 관계와 우정 형성 등을 언급하고 있는데, ③에서 역접의 연결어 없이 야외 활동이 가족과 좋은 시간을 보내는 것을 어렵게 만든다는 부정적인 내용이 이어졌으므로 글의 흐름과 무관한 문장으로 ③이 가장 적절하다.

어휘

desperate 절실한, 필사적인; 절망적인	
urge 충동, 열망	restorative 회복시키는
let off steam 스트레스를 해소하다	boost 끌어올리다; 격려
environmentalism 환경 보호[보전]주의	

---

17 독해 > 글의 일관성 파악하기 > 주어진 문장의 삽입　　　　답 ③

| **해석** | 경제학자 Chay와 Greenstone은 1970년 대기 오염 방지법(Clean Air Act) 이후 대기 오염 정화의 가치를 평가했다. 1970년 이전에는 대기 오염에 대한 연방 정부의 규제가 거의 없었으며, 이 문제는 주 의원들의 의제

에서 중요하지는 않았다. 결과적으로, 많은 카운티에서는 오염에 대한 규제 없이 공장을 운영하도록 허가했으며, 일부 과하게 산업화된 카운티에서는 오염이 매우 높은 수치에 도달했다. ③ 특히, 많은 도시 카운티에서, 총 부유 분진의 양으로 측정한 대기 오염은 위험한 수치에 도달했다. 대기 오염 방지법은 특히 위험한 5가지 오염 물질의 높은 수치에 대한 지침을 제정했다. 1970년 법과 1977년 개정안 이후, 대기질이 개선되었다.

| **정답해설** | ③ 대기 오염 방지법 이전과 이후의 오염 수치에 대해 설명하는 글이다. 주어진 글에서 In particular를 통해 앞 문장과 비슷한 흐름의 내용이 더 첨가된 것을 유추할 수 있다. 총 부유 분진의 양으로 측정한 대기 오염이 위험한 수치에 도달했다고 했고 관련 내용이 먼저 언급된 부분이 ② 이후의 문장이므로, 주어진 문장이 들어가기에 가장 적절한 것은 ③이다.

어휘

federal 연방의	regulation 규제
agenda 의제, 안건	legislator 입법부의 의원, 입법자
suspended particles 부유 입자(분진)	
constitute 구성하다	dangerous 위험한
amendment (법령의) 개정[수정](안)	

---

18 독해 > 글의 일관성 파악하기 > 글의 순서   답 ②

| **해석** | 누군가 무슨 일이 일어났는지 보기도 전에, 나는 빵 덩어리를 셔츠 밑으로 밀어 넣고, 헌팅 재킷을 단단히 감싼 다음, 재빨리 걸어갔다.
(B) 빵의 열기에 피부가 타들어 갔지만, 생에 대한 집착으로 나는 그것을 더 꽉 움켜잡았다. 내가 집에 도착했을 때, 빵 덩어리들이 어느 정도 식었지만, 안쪽은 여전히 따뜻했다.
(A) 내가 그것들을 탁자 위에 떨어뜨리자, 여동생이 손을 뻗어 덩어리를 뜯어냈지만, 나는 여동생을 앉게 하고 어머니를 식탁에 앉히고 따뜻한 차를 따랐다.
(C) 나는 빵을 잘랐다. 우리는 한 조각씩, 한 덩어리를 다 먹었다. 그것은 건포도와 견과류로 가득 찬, 푸짐한 빵이었다.

| **정답해설** | ② 주어진 글에서 누가 볼세라 빵을 훔쳐 빠르게 달아나는 모습을 서술했으므로, 바로 빵을 탁자에 떨어뜨렸다는 (A)나, 빵을 잘랐다고 한 (C)보다는, 빵을 훔친 후 열기에도 빵을 꽉 쥐고 집에 도착한 모습을 서술한 (B)가 처음에 와야 한다. 이후에는 빵을 탁자에 떨어뜨리고, 빵을 잘라 가족이 먹었다는 내용이 이어지는 것이 자연스러우므로 글의 순서로 ②가 가장 적절하다.

어휘

witness 보다, 목격하다	shove 밀어 넣다
clutch ~을 꽉 쥐다	cling to ~을 고수하다
hearty 듬뿍 있는, 푸짐한	raisin 건포도

---

19 독해 > 빈칸의 내용 추론하기 > 빈칸 어구 추론   답 ①

| **해석** | 떨어지는 출산율은 이번 세기말까지 거의 모든 국가의 인구가 줄어드는 결과를 낳을 것으로 예상된다. 전 세계 출산율은 1950년에 4.7명이었으나, 2017년에 2.4명으로 절반 가까이 떨어졌다. 2100년까지는 1.7 이하로 떨어질 것으로 예상된다. 결과적으로, 일부 연구자들은 지구상의 인구수가 2064년쯤 97억 명으로 최고조에 달했다가 이번 세기말까지 88억 명으로 떨어질 것이라고 예측한다. 이러한 변화는 또한 인구의 상당한 고령화로 이어질 것이며, 태어나는 것만큼 많은 사람들이 80세에 이를 것이다. 그러한 인구통계학적 변화는 과세, 노인 의료, 간병 책임, 은퇴를 포함한 ① 미

래의 문제들에 대한 우려를 제기한다. 새로운 인구통계학적 환경으로의 '연착륙'을 확보하기 위해, 연구자들은 변화에 대한 세심한 관리의 필요성을 강조한다.
① 미래의 문제들에 대한 우려를 제기한다
② 역 연령 구조 현상을 완화한다
③ 감소된 결혼율 문제를 보충한다
④ 문제 해결을 위한 즉각적인 해결책을 제공한다

| **정답해설** | ① 빈칸 앞의 such a demographic shift의 구체적인 사례로 including에 이어진 과세, 노인 의료, 간병 책임, 은퇴 등이 언급되었으므로 이는 맥락상 미래의 문제들임을 유추할 수 있다. 출산율 저하로 인한 미래의 문제들에 대해 설명하는 글이므로, 빈칸에 들어갈 것으로 ①이 가장 적절하다.

어휘

fertility 출산; 비옥, 다산	shrinking 줄어드는, 감소하는
transition 변화, 전환	aging 고령화, 노화
demographic 인구통계(학)의	taxation 과세, 징세

---

20 독해 > 빈칸의 내용 추론하기 > 빈칸 어구 추론   답 ③

| **해석** | 많은 청취자들은 혼자만의 생각으로 인한 자신의 부주의에 대해 화자의 탓으로 돌린다: "누가 그런 인물의 말을 들을 수 있겠어? 그가 언젠가는 낭독 연설하는 것을 멈출까?" 좋은 청취자는 다르게 반응한다. 그 또한 화자를 보면서 생각할지도 모른다. "이 사람은 무능해. 거의 모든 사람이 그보다 더 잘 말할 수 있을 것 같아." 그러나 이런 처음의 유사성에서 그는 다른 결론으로 넘어가는데, "하지만 잠깐만, 나는 그의 성격이나 전달력에는 관심이 없어. 나는 그가 알고 있는 것을 알아내고 싶어. 이 사람이 내가 알아야 할 것들을 알고 있을까?"라고 생각한다. 본질적으로, 우리는 '우리 자신의 경험에 귀를 기울인다.' 우리가 그의 메시지를 제대로 이해하지 못하기 때문에 화자가 책임을 져야 하는가? 우리는 우리가 듣는 모든 것을 이해할 수는 없지만, 우리의 이해 수준을 높이는 확실한 한 가지 방법은 ③ 본질적인 우리의 책임을 지는 것이다.
① 말하는 사람이 알고 있는 것을 무시하다
② 말하는 사람의 성격을 분석하다
③ 본질적인 우리의 책임을 지다
④ 말하는 사람의 연설 전달 능력에 집중하다

| **정답해설** | ③ 많은 청자들이 자신의 부주의를 화자의 탓으로 돌린다고 언급하면서, 좋은 청자는 처음엔 비슷하게 반응하지만, 다른 사람들과는 달리 자신이 알 필요가 있는 것들을 말하는 사람이 알고 있는지 궁금해 한다고 설명한다. 화자의 메시지를 이해하지 못한다고 화자가 책임을 질 필요는 없으며, 결론은 청자의 책임이라는 것을 유추할 수 있으므로 빈칸에 들어갈 것으로 ③이 가장 적절하다.

어휘

blame A for B A를 B의 탓으로 돌리다
inattention 부주의   incompetent 무능한
delivery 전달
be equipped to ~할 준비가 되어 있다
comprehend 이해하다

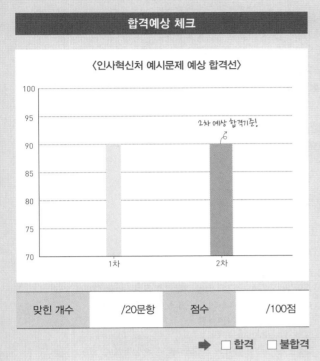

합격예상 체크		

〈인사혁신처 예시문제 예상 합격선〉

2차 예상 합격기준!

맞힌 개수	/20문항	점수	/100점

➡ ☐ 합격 ☐ 불합격

취약영역 체크					

문항	정답	영역	문항	정답	영역
1	③	어휘 > 빈칸	11	③	독해 > 세부내용 찾기
2	②	어휘 > 빈칸	12	①	독해 > 대의 파악
3	③	문법 > 준동사	13	④	독해 > 대의 파악
4	④	문법 > 연결사	14	③	독해 > 세부내용 찾기
5	②	문법 > 동사의 형태	15	②	독해 > 대의 파악
6	②	생활영어 > 회화	16	②	독해 > 글의 일관성 파악하기
7	③	생활영어 > 회화	17	②	독해 > 글의 일관성 파악하기
8	①	독해 > 세부내용 찾기	18	③	독해 > 글의 일관성 파악하기
9	④	독해 > 동의어	19	④	독해 > 빈칸의 내용 추론하기
10	①	독해 > 대의 파악	20	③	독해 > 빈칸의 내용 추론하기

⬇ 영역별 틀린 개수로 취약영역을 확인하세요!

어휘	/2	문법	/3	독해	/13	생활영어	/2

➡ 나의 취약영역: _____

※ 해당 회차는 〈1초 합격예측 서비스〉의 데이터 누적 기간이 충분하지 않아 오답률, 선지 선택률 기재를 생략하였습니다.

1	어휘 > 빈칸	답 ③

| 해석 | 큰 벽화를 전시하기 위해, 박물관 큐레이터는 ③ 충분한 공간이 있는지 확인해야 했다.
① 아늑한　　　　　　　　② 숨 막히는, 답답한
③ 충분한　　　　　　　　④ 답답한

| 정답해설 | ③ 벽화가 크다고(large) 했으므로, 벽화를 전시하기 위한 공간은 '충분해야' 함을 알 수 있다. 따라서 '충분한'의 의미인 ③이 가장 적절하다. stuffy와 cramped는 '답답한'의 의미로 정답에서 제외해야 한다.

어휘
exhibit 전시하다　　　　　　　mural 벽화
curator 전시 기획자, 큐레이터

2	어휘 > 빈칸	답 ②

| 해석 | 해결해야 할 문제가 많음에도 불구하고, 우리 시민들의 안전이 ② 최우선이라는 점을 강조하고 싶다.
① 비밀　　　　　　　　② 우선사항
③ 해결책　　　　　　　④ 기회

| 정답해설 | ② 접속사 even though가 이끄는 양보 부사절과 이어진 주절의 내용은 대비를 이루어야 한다. 부사절에서 해결해야 할 많은 문제가 있음에도 'I'가 강조하고 싶은 것이 주절에 이어진 것이므로 시민의 안전이 최고의 '우선사항'이라고 유추할 수 있다. 따라

서 빈칸에 들어갈 것으로 ②가 가장 적절하다.

어휘
emphasize 강조하다　　　　　safety 안전

3	문법 > 준동사 > 부정사	답 ③

| 해석 | 인구 과잉이 중요한 역할을 했을지도 모른다: 물 부족뿐 아니라 식량을 위해 마야인들이 의존했던 열대 우림 생태계에 대한 과도한 착취가 (문명의) 붕괴의 원인이었던 것으로 보인다.

| 정답해설 | ③ 동사가 현재 시제(seems)이고, 보어로 이어진 to부정사의 올바른 형태를 묻는 문제이다. contribute to는 자동사구이고 수동태로 전환할 수 없으므로 수동 구조인 ②와 ④는 정답에서 제외된다. 맥락상 마야 문명의 붕괴에 대한 내용은 '과거'의 사실이므로 본동사인 seems보다 앞선 시점의 표현으로 완료부정사를 써야 한다. 따라서 정답은 ③이다.

어휘
overpopulation 인구 과잉　　　exploitation 착취
collapse 붕괴, 쇠퇴

| **4** | 문법 > 연결사 > 관계사 | 답 ④ |

| **해석** | 내가 보기에 평화를 지키기 위해 고안된 어떤 국제기구라도 말뿐만 아니라 행동할 수 있는 힘을 가져야 할 것 같다. 사실, 나는 이것을 우연히가 아니라 의도적으로 전쟁을 피하는 국제 사회를 향한 어떤 진보의 중심 주제로 본다.

| **정답해설** | ④ 선행사 an international community를 수식하는 형용사절을 이끄는 관계사이다. 밑줄 뒤에 완전한 절이 이어졌으므로 선행사가 장소임을 고려해 관계부사 where로 바꿔야 한다.

| **오답해설** | ① 명사 organization을 수식하는 과거분사로, 구조와 맥락상 '고안되는' 것이므로 수동의 designed로 올바르게 왔다.

② not merely와 호응하는 접속사로 but also가 이어졌고, 병치 구조를 이끌어야 하므로 to talk와 호응해 to act가 온 올바른 구조이다.

③ 동사 see와 호응하는 표현으로 see A as B는 'A를 B로 보다'의 의미이다.

어휘

not merely(only) A but also B A뿐만 아니라 B도
see A as B A를 B로 보다   progress 진보, 발전
avoid 피하다   by chance 우연히
be design 고의로

| **5** | 문법 > 동사의 형태 > 수동태 | 답 ② |

| **해석** | 우리는 이미 디지털화된 세상에 도달했다. 디지털화는 전통적인 IT 기업뿐만 아니라 모든 분야에서 전반적으로 기업에 영향을 미친다. 새롭고 변화된 비즈니스 모델이 등장했다. 자동차는 앱을 통해 공유되고, 온라인으로 언어를 배우고, 음악은 스트리밍된다. 그러나 산업 또한 변화하고 있다. 3D 프린터는 기계 부품을 만들고, 로봇은 그것들을 조립하며, 공장 전체가 지능적으로 서로 연결되어 있다.

| **정답해설** | ② emerge는 자동사이므로 수동태로 전환할 수 없다. 맥락을 고려해 과거 시제인 emerged로 바꿔야 한다.

| **오답해설** | ① arrive는 자동사이므로 뒤에 목적어 없이 전치사 in이 나왔다. have와 함께 현재 완료시제로 쓰였다.

③ share는 타동사이므로 수동태로 전환할 수 있다. 밑줄에 이어 목적어가 없고 맥락상 수동태로 쓰이는 것이 적절하므로 진행수동태로 올바르게 표현했다.

④ are와 함께 수동태로 표현했으며, are connected에 이어 목적어에 해당하는 명사가 없으므로 구조와 맥락상 올바르다.

어휘

digitization 디지털화   across the board 전반적인
assemble 조립하다

| **6** | 생활영어 > 회화 | 답 ② |

| **해석** | Tim Jones: 안녕하세요, 회의실 중 하나를 빌리고 싶습니다.
Jane Baker: 관심에 감사드립니다. 회의 규모에 따라 이용하실 수 있는 다양한 공간들이 있어요. 5명에서 20명의 단체를 수용할 수 있습니다.
Tim Jones: 좋네요. 17명이 쓸 공간 하나가 필요하고요. 회의는 다음 달에 예정되어 있습니다.

Jane Baker: ② 회의의 정확한 날짜를 말해주시겠어요?
Tim Jones: 회의는 7월 15일 월요일에 있을 예정입니다. 그날 이용할 수 있는 회의실이 있을까요?
Jane Baker: 네, 있습니다. 회의실 하나를 예약해서 세부 내용들과 함께 확정 이메일을 보내드릴게요.

① 당신의 연락처를 알려주시겠습니까?
② 회의의 정확한 날짜를 말해주시겠어요?
③ 빔 프로젝터나 복사기가 필요하신가요?
④ 얼마나 많은 인원이 회의에 참석할 예정인가요?

| **정답해설** | ② 빈칸의 질문에 이어 회의의 정확한 날짜를 언급했으므로 빈칸에 들어갈 것으로 ②가 가장 적절하다.

어휘

accommodate 수용하다   reserve 예약하다
confirmation 확정, 확인

| **7** | 생활영어 > 회화 | 답 ③ |

| **해석** | A: 이 자전거에 대해 어떻게 생각해?
B: 와, 정말 멋져 보여! 방금 산 거야?
A: 아니, 이건 공유 자전거야. 시에서 자전거 공유 서비스를 시작했어.
B: 정말? 어떻게 작동하지? 내 말은, 내가 그 서비스를 어떻게 사용하지?
A: 간단해. ③ 자전거 공유 앱을 다운받고 온라인으로 결제하면 돼.
B: 복잡하게 들리진 않네. 이번 주말에 한 번 해볼까 봐.
A: 그런데, 이거 전기 자전거야.
B: 그래, 참으로 멋져 보여.

① 그것은 전기로 움직이기 때문에 에너지를 절약할 수 있어
② 그저 너의 자전거 주차 허가를 신청하면 돼
③ 자전거 공유 앱을 다운받고 온라인으로 결제하면 돼
④ 너의 안전을 위해 항상 헬멧을 써야 해

| **정답해설** | ③ A가 공유 자전거를 소개했고, B가 사용 방법을 묻고 있다. 따라서 빈칸에는 자전거 공유 앱을 다운받고 온라인으로 결제하라고 안내하고 있는 ③이 들어가는 것이 가장 적절하다.

어휘

launch 시작하다, 개시하다   complicated 복잡한
I can tell 그래 보여

| **8** | 독해 > 세부내용 찾기 > 내용 일치 찾기 | 답 ① |

| **해석** | **농업 마케팅 사무국**

임무
우리는 식품, 섬유 및 특수 작물의 국내 생산자를 위한 국내 및 국제 마케팅 기회를 창출하는 프로그램을 운영합니다. 우리는 또한 농업 산업에 가치 있는 서비스를 제공하여 전국 및 전 세계의 소비자를 위한 건강 식품의 품질과 가용성을 보장합니다.

비전
우리는 국내 및 국제 시장에서 전국 농산물의 전략적 마케팅을 촉진하면서 공정한 거래 관행을 보장하고 국내 식품, 섬유 및 특수 작물의 생산자, 상인 및 소비자의 이익을 위해 경쟁력 있고 효율적인 시장을 홍보합니다.

핵심 가치
• 정직과 진실성: 우리는 우리가 하는 모든 일에서 완전한 정직과 진실성을 기대하고 요구합니다.

- 독립성 및 객관성: 우리는 프로그램과 서비스에 대한 신뢰를 창출하기 위해 독립적이고 객관적으로 행동합니다.
① 국내 생산자들을 위한 마케팅 기회를 만든다.
② 전 세계적으로 건강 음식 섭취를 제한한다.
③ 생산자들보다 소비자들에게 이익을 주기 위해 헌신한다.
④ 결정을 내리기 전에 다른 기관으로부터의 명령을 받는다.

| 정답해설 | ① 임무에서 국내 생산자들을 위한 국내 및 국제 마케팅 기회를 창출하는 프로그램을 운영한다고 했으므로, 내용과 일치하는 것으로 ①이 가장 적절하다.

| 어휘 |
administer 운영하다, 관리하다   domestic 국내의
specialty 특산(품)   wholesome 건강에 좋은
facilitate 촉진하다; 수월하게 하다   integrity 진실성

---

9   독해 > 동의어   답 ④

| 해석 | 8번 해석과 동일
① 자유로운   ② 서로의, 공동의
③ 유익한   ④ 공정한

| 정답해설 | ④ fair는 '공정한, (날씨가) 좋은, 박람회' 등의 의미로 쓰인다. 맥락상 '공평한'의 의미이므로 의미가 가장 가까운 것은 '치우치지 않는, 공정한'의 impartial이 가장 적절하다.

---

10   독해 > 대의 파악 > 빈칸 제목 추론   답 ①

| 해석 | ① <u>Dimmesdale 호수가 죽어가고 있습니다</u>

가까운 이웃으로서, 당신은 호수를 구하는 방법을 배우고 싶을 것입니다.

아직 죽지 않았지만 Dimmesdale 호수는 이 끝을 향해 가고 있습니다. 그러니 그것의 아름다운 수역이 아직 살아 있는 동안 존중해주세요.

몇몇 헌신적인 사람들이 지금 호수를 구하기 위해 일하고 있습니다. 그들은 여러분에게 그것에 대해 말하기 위해 특별한 회의를 열고 있습니다. 오셔서 무엇이 행해지고 있고 어떻게 당신이 도울 수 있는지 배우세요. 이것은 여러분의 재산 가치에도 영향을 미칩니다.

누가 죽은 호수 근처에서 살고 싶을까요?

중앙 주정부 지역 기획 위원회의 후원으로

- 위치: Southern 주립 대학 맞은 편에 있는 Green City 공원 (우천 시: 대학 도서관 203호)
- 날짜: 2024년 7월 6일, 토요일
- 시간: 오후 2시

회의에 대한 문의는 웹사이트 www.planningcouncilsavelake.org를 방문하거나 (432) 345-6789로 사무실에 문의하십시오.
① Dimmesdale 호수가 죽어가고 있습니다
② 호수의 아름다움에 대한 찬양
③ Dimmesdale 호수의 문화적 가치
④ 호수가 대학에 주는 의미

| 정답해설 | ① 빈칸 (A)에 이어진 내용에서 Dimmesdale 호수가 죽어가고 있고, 호수를 구하기 위한 모임이 있다고 구체적으로 안내

하고 있다. 따라서 (A)에 들어갈 것으로 ①이 가장 적절하다.

| 어휘 |
dedicated 헌신적인, 열심인   property 재산
sponsor 후원하다   opposite 맞은편의; 정반대의

---

11   독해 > 세부내용 찾기 > 내용 불일치 찾기   답 ③

| 해석 | 10번 해석과 동일

| 정답해설 | ③ 우천 시에는 대학의 도서관 203호에서 회의가 열린다고 했으므로 글의 내용과 일치하지 않는 것은 ③이다.

---

12   독해 > 대의 파악 > 글의 목적   답 ①

| 해석 | 수신: cbsclients@calbank.com
발신: calbanks@calmail.com
날짜: 2024년 5월 7일
제목: 중요 공지

소중한 고객님들,

오늘날 세계에서, 사이버 범죄는 귀하의 보안에 심각한 위협이 됩니다. 신뢰할 수 있는 파트너로서, 우리는 귀하의 개인 정보 및 비즈니스 정보를 보호하는 데 도움을 드리고자 합니다. 여기 사이버 위협으로부터 자신을 보호하는 5가지 쉬운 방법이 있습니다.

1. 강력한 암호를 사용하고 자주 변경하십시오.
2. 소프트웨어 및 장치를 최신 상태로 유지하십시오.
3. 신속한 행동이나 민감한 정보를 제공하도록 압력을 가하는 수상한 이메일, 링크 또는 전화를 경계하십시오.
4. 이중 인증을 활성화하고 가능하면 언제든지 사용하십시오. 캘리포니아 은행 & 저축에 연락하실 때, 귀하의 신원을 확인하기 위해 OTP(One Time Passcode)를 사용하도록 요청받을 것입니다.
5. 귀하의 데이터를 정기적으로 백업하십시오.

저희의 보안 센터를 방문하여 온라인에서 안전하게 지낼 수 있는 방법에 대해 자세히 알아보십시오. 사이버 보안은 공동의 노력이라는 점을 기억하십시오. 함께 일함으로써, 저희는 우리 자신과 세계를 위해 더 안전한 온라인 환경을 구축할 수 있습니다.

캘리포니아 은행 & 저축
① 고객에게 사이버 위협으로부터 자신을 안전하게 지키는 방법을 알려주기 위해
② 고객에게 소프트웨어 및 장치를 업데이트하는 방법을 알려주기 위해
③ 고객에게 암호를 더 강하게 만드는 방법을 알려주기 위해
④ 고객에게 OTP를 보호하는 방법을 알려주기 위해

| 정답해설 | ① 메일 앞부분에서 사이버 범죄가 보안에 심각한 위협이 된다고 언급한 후, 그것으로부터 자신을 보호하는 5가지 방법을 소개하는 글이므로, 글의 목적으로 가장 적절한 것은 ①이다.

| 어휘 |
threat 위협   security 보안
safeguard 보호하다, 지키다   suspicious 수상한, 의심스러운
two factor authentication 이중 인증   verify 입증하다

13 독해 > 대의 파악 > 주제 찾기 　　　　답 ④

| 해석 | 지구에서 약 240마일 상공의 궤도를 돌고 있는 국제우주정거장은 세계의 야생 동물을 관찰하고 동물 추적 과학에 큰 변화를 일으키려는 노력에 동참하려고 한다. 2018년, 우주 유영을 하는 러시아 우주비행사들에 의해 설치된 궤도를 도는 전초 기지에 탑재된 대형 안테나와 다른 장비들이 테스트되고 있으며 올 여름 완전히 가동될 예정이다. 이 시스템은 이전의 추적 기술보다 훨씬 더 광범위한 데이터를 중계하여, 동물의 위치뿐만 아니라 생리기능 및 환경을 기록할 것이다. 이것은 과학자, 환경 보호론자 및 이동 중인 야생 동물을 면밀히 관찰해야 하는 사람들을 돕고 세계 생태계 건강에 대한 보다 자세한 정보를 제공할 것이다.
① 지구 생태계의 지속 가능성 평가
② 러시아 우주비행사들의 성공적인 훈련 프로젝트
③ 궤도를 도는 전초기지에서 행해진 동물 실험
④ 우주정거장에서의 혁신적인 야생 동물 관찰

| 정답해설 | ④ 첫 번째 문장이 주제문으로, 국제우주정거장에서 시행될 예정인 세계의 야생 동물 관찰과 동물 추적 과학에 대한 상세한 내용이 이어지고 있다. 따라서 글의 주제로 가장 적절한 것은 ④이다.

어휘

orbit 궤도를 돌다
revolutionize 혁명[대변혁]을 일으키다
outpost 전초 기지, 최선단　　　install 설치하다
astronaut 우주비행사　　　　　previous 이전의
log 일지[일기]에 기재하다　　　physiology 생리학
assist 돕다, 지원하다　　　　　conservationist 자연[환경] 보호론자

---

14 독해 > 세부내용 찾기 > 내용 불일치 찾기 　　　답 ③

| 해석 | Davis Williams 도서관 및 박물관은 11월에서 3월까지는 오전 9시부터 오후 5시까지, 4월에서 10월까지는 오전 9시부터 오후 6시까지 일주일 내내 운영됩니다. 온라인 티켓은 아래 링크에서 구매할 수 있습니다. 구매 후 확정 메일을 받게 됩니다(반드시 스팸 폴더를 확인하십시오). 구매에 대한 증명으로 이 확인서를 인쇄하거나 스마트 기기로 가져오십시오.

• 온라인 티켓: buy.davidwilliams.com/events

David Williams 도서관 및 박물관과 David Williams의 생가(국립 문화 유산 서비스가 운영)는 별도의 10달러 성인 입장권을 제공합니다. 생가 투어 티켓은 정상 영업 시간 동안 현장에서 구매할 수 있습니다.

• 휴관: 추수 감사절, 크리스마스 및 새해 첫날

David Williams 도서관 연구실에서 연구 수행은 일체 무료입니다.

자세한 내용은 1 (800) 333-7777로 문의하십시오.
① 도서관 및 박물관은 12월에 오후 5시에 문을 닫는다.
② 방문자는 현장에서 생가 투어 티켓을 구매할 수 있다.
③ Davis Williams의 생가는 연중무휴이다.
④ 도서관 연구실에서 무료로 연구할 수 있다.

| 정답해설 | ③ 추수 감사절, 크리스마스, 새해 첫날에는 휴관한다고 했으므로 연중무휴(open all year round)라고 한 ③은 글의 내용과 일치하지 않는다.

어휘

purchase 구매하다　　　　　confirmation 확인
separate 개별적인, 별개의　　on-site 현장의

---

15 독해 > 대의 파악 > 요지·주장 찾기 　　　답 ②

| 해석 | **동물 건강 긴급 상황**
동물 질병 발생에 대한 준비는 수십 년 동안 동물 건강 위원회(BOAH)의 최우선 과제였습니다. 전염성이 높은 동물 질병 발생은 공중 보건 또는 식품 안전 및 보안 결과뿐만 아니라 경제적으로 파멸적인 영향을 미칠 수 있습니다.

외래 동물 질병
외래 동물 질병(FAD)은 현재 국내에서 발견되지 않는 질병으로, 동물에게 심각한 질병이나 죽음을 초래하거나 다른 국가 및 주와의 무역 기회를 없앰으로써 광범위한 경제적 피해를 야기할 수 있습니다.

FAD 진단 훈련을 받은 몇몇 BOAH 수의사들이 FAD 의심 사례를 조사하기 위해 언제라도 시간을 낼 수 있습니다. FAD를 나타내는 임상 징후가 있는 동물의 보고가 접수되거나 진단 실험실에서 의심스러운 검사 결과를 확인하면 조사가 시작됩니다.
① BOAH는 FAD를 위한 수의사 훈련에 중점을 둔다.
② BOAH의 주요 목표는 동물 질병 전염병에 대응하는 것이다.
③ BOAH는 국제 무역 기회를 적극적으로 촉진한다.
④ BOAH는 FAD의 원인에 대한 실험실 연구를 주도하는 것을 목표로 하고 있다.

| 정답해설 | ② 첫 번째 문장(Preparedness for animal disease outbreaks has been a top priority for the Board of Animal Health (BOAH) for decades.)이 주제문으로, 동물 질병 발생에 대한 준비가 BOAH의 목표임을 알 수 있고, 이어지는 내용에서 외래 동물 질병에 대한 설명과 이에 대한 대응책이 구체적으로 나열되어 있으므로 글의 요지로 가장 적절한 것은 ②이다.

어휘

outbreak 발생, 발발　　　　　priority 우선순위
contagious 전염성의　　　　　devastating 지독한, 파괴적인
eliminate 제거하다, 없애다　　veterinarian 수의사
diagnose 진단하다　　　　　　investigation 조사
clinical 임상의　　　　　　　indicative 나타내는, 암시하는

---

16 독해 > 글의 일관성 파악하기 > 글의 흐름과 무관한 문장 　답 ②

| 해석 | 모든 학문 분야에서 나타나는 매우 일반적인 유형의 글쓰기 작업은 반응(reaction 혹은 response)이다. 반응 평론에서, 작가는 대개 시각적 또는 서면 자극인 '프롬프트(지시 메시지)'를 받아 이에 대해 생각하고 반응한다. ② 여러분의 주장을 효과적으로 방어할 수 있도록 신뢰할 수 있는 사실을 수집하는 것은 매우 중요하다. 이러한 유형의 글쓰기에 대한 일반적인 프롬프트 또는 자극에는 인용 부호, 문학 작품, 사진, 그림, 멀티미디어 프레젠테이션 및 뉴스가 포함된다. 반응은 작가의 감정, 의견, 그리고 특정 프롬프트에 대한 개인적인 관찰에 초점을 맞춘다. 반응 평론을 쓰는 당신의 임무는 두 가지인데, 프롬프트를 간략하게 요약하고 그것에 대한 개인적인 반응을 제공하는 것이다.

| 정답해설 | ② 매우 일반적인 유형의 글쓰기 작업으로 반응(reaction 혹은 response)을 제시하고, 반응 평론에 대해 상술하고 있는 글이다. ②번 문장은 주장을 효과적으로 방어할 수 있도록 신뢰할 수 있

는 사실을 수집하는 것에 대해 언급하고 있는데, 이는 반응 평론에 대한 내용이 아니므로 글의 흐름과 일치하지 않는다. ①번 문장에서 prompt를 언급했고, ③번 문장에서 Common prompts로 받아 구체적인 예시를 들어 설명하고 있으므로 ①에서 ③으로 가는 것이 자연스럽다. 따라서 흐름상 어색한 문장은 ②이다.

어휘

discipline 학문(분야)	prompt 자극, 촉진
stimulus 자극	reliable 신뢰할 만한
quote 인용 부호	literature 문학
twofold 두 부분[요소]으로 된; 이중의	

---

17 독해 > 글의 일관성 파악하기 > 주어진 문장의 삽입 답 ②

| 해석 | 적극 행동주의는 종종 개인과 집단이 원하는 목표를 달성하기 위해 실행하는 의도적이고, 활발하며, 정력적인 행동으로 정의된다. 어떤 사람들에게, 적극 행동주의는 정치적 또는 사회적 변화에 대한 인식된 필요성에 영향을 미치기 위해 이론적으로 또는 이념적으로 집중된 계획이다. ② 다른 사람들에게 있어서, 적극 행동주의는 논란의 여지가 있고 파괴적인데, 결국, 그것은 종종 사물의 질서에 직접적으로 이의를 제기하는 대립적인 활동으로 나타난다. 적극 행동주의는 불편하고, 때로는 불쾌하며, 거의 언제나 격렬하다. 또한 그것은 활동가의 존재와 헌신, 즉, 실행 가능한 전략을 개발하고 특정 문제에 집단적 스포트라이트를 집중시키며, 궁극적으로 사람들을 실행하게 하는 사람들이 없다면 발생하지 않는다. 한 저명한 학자가 제안하듯이, 유능한 활동가들도 때로는 큰 소리로 소란을 피운다.

| 정답해설 | ② 적극 행동주의에 대해 설명하는 글이다. 주어진 문장에서 For others라는 표현으로 보아 others 이전에 some에 대한 언급이 있어야 함을 유추할 수 있다. ① 다음에 For some이 있으므로, ②부터 주어진 문장을 삽입할 수 있다. ②에 이어진 내용으로 적극 행동주의의 부정적인 속성을 언급하고 있고, 주어진 문장에서 적극 행동주의가 논란의 여지가 있고 파괴적이라고 언급하면서 부정적으로 서술하고 있으므로 ②에 들어가는 것이 가장 적절하다.

어휘

activism 적극 행동주의	intentional 의도적인
vigorous 활발한	bring about ~을 일으키다, 초래하다
controversial 논란의 여지가 있는	disruptive 파괴적인
manifest 분명히 나타내다	confrontational 대립적인
strenuous 격렬한; 노력하는; 고생스러운	
noted 저명한, 유명한	make noise 소란을 피우다

---

18 독해 > 글의 일관성 파악하기 > 글의 순서 답 ③

| 해석 | Nick은 도끼로 그루터기에서 자른 몇 덩어리의 소나무로 불을 피웠다. 불 위로 그는 철사 그릴을 꽂아 자신의 부츠로 네 다리를 땅속으로 밀어 넣었다.

(C) Nick은 프라이팬을 불 위에 있는 그릴 위에 올려 놓았다. 그는 더 배가 고파졌다. 콩과 스파게티가 데워졌다. 그는 그것들을 젓고 섞었다.

(A) 그것들은 거품을 일으키기 시작했고, 표면으로 힘겹게 솟아오르는 작은 거품을 만들었다. 좋은 냄새가 났다. Nick은 토마토케첩 한 병을 꺼냈고 빵 네 조각을 잘랐다.

(B) 그 작은 거품들이 점점 빨리 나오고 있었다. Nick은 불 옆에 앉아 프라이팬을 들어 올렸다.

| 정답해설 | ③ Nick이 직접 불을 피워 음식을 준비하는 과정을 서

술하는 글이다. 주어진 문장에서 불을 피웠고 철사 그릴을 꽂았다고 했으므로, 다음에 Nick이 프라이팬을 그릴 위에 올려 놓았다고 서술한 (C)가 처음에 와야 한다. (C)의 뒤에서 언급한 the beans and spaghetti를 them으로 받았고, 맥락상 (A) 문장의 주어 They가 이와 일치하므로 (A)가 두 번째로 와야 한다. (A)에서 작은 거품들이 생긴다고 했고, 이를 주어 The little bubbles로 받아 서술한 (B)가 그 다음에 오는 것이 적절하므로 글의 순서로 가장 적절한 것은 ③이다.

어휘

stump (나무·식물의) 그루터기	stir 젓다, 섞다

---

19 독해 > 빈칸의 내용 추론하기 > 빈칸 어구 추론 답 ④

| 해석 | 기술 진보는 섬유와 같은 단일 산업에서 일자리를 파괴할 수 있다. 그러나 역사적 증거는 기술 진보가 전체적으로 한 국가의 실업을 초래하지는 않는다는 것을 보여준다. 기술 진보는 전체 경제에서 생산성과 소득을 증가시키고, 소득이 높아지면 재화에 대한 수요가 높아져 ④ 노동에 대한 수요가 높아진다. 결과적으로, 한 산업 분야에서 일자리를 잃은 근로자들은 다른 산업 분야에서 일자리를 찾을 수 있을 텐데, 비록 그들 중 많은 사람들에게 이것은 시간이 걸릴 수도 있고, 그들 중 일부는, 러다이트(산업 개혁 반대자)처럼, 자신들의 새로운 직업에서 결국 더 낮은 임금으로 끝날 수 있다.

① 증가된 실직 ② 직장에서 승진 지연
③ 더 큰 업무 만족도 ④ 더 높은 노동에 대한 수요

| 정답해설 | ④ 기술 진보가 일자리에 미치는 부정적인 내용을 언급한 후 However에 이어 긍정적인 내용이 이어지는 글이다. 따라서 빈칸에는 이와 관련된 긍정적인 내용이 들어가야 하므로 부정적이면서 관련성이 낮은 ①과 ②는 정답에서 제외된다. 빈칸 앞에서 기술 진보가 생산성과 소득을 증가시키고, 소득이 높아지면서 재화에 대한 수요가 올라간다고 했으므로, 노동에 대한 수요가 늘어날 것임을 유추할 수 있다. 따라서 빈칸에 들어갈 것으로 가장 적절한 것은 ④이다.

어휘

progress 진보, 발전	unemployment 실업
the Luddites [영국사] 러다이트: 산업 혁명 시대에 기계를 집단으로 파괴한 수공업자; 산업 개혁 반대자	wage 임금, 급여

---

20 독해 > 빈칸의 내용 추론하기 > 빈칸 어구 추론 답 ③

| 해석 | 석유를 대체할 만한 것은 없는데, 이는 석유가 세계 경제를 동반하면서 ③ 큰 호황과 깊은 불황을 겪기 쉬운 한 가지 이유이다. 우리가 가격에 따라 한 공급원에서 다른 공급원으로, 석탄, 천연가스 원자력 혹은 재생 가능 에너지를 통해 전기를 생산할 수 있는 반면, 석유는 운송에서 단연코 가장 우세한 연료로 남아 있다. 세계 경제가 활기를 띠면, 석유 수요가 증가하여 가격을 올리고 생산자들이 더 많은 양을 퍼내도록 장려한다. 결국, 그런 높은 가격은 경제 성장을 잠식하고 공급자가 과잉 생산함에 따라 수요를 감소시킨다. 가격이 폭락하고, 그 순환은 처음부터 다시 시작된다. 이는 가격이 폭락할 때 책임을 떠맡게 될 수 있는 생산업자들에게는 좋지 않은 일이며, 미래의 에너지 가격에 대해 불확실한 소비자들과 산업들에도 피해를 준다. 1990년대의 낮은 유가는 미국 자동차 회사들을 파멸을 초래하는 무사안일주의로 몰아넣었는데, 그들은 석유가 비싸졌을 때, 이용 가능한 효율적인 모델이 거의 없었다.

① 자동차 산업이 번창한다
② 그것은 국경 사이에 분열을 일으킨다
③ 그것은 큰 호황과 깊은 불황을 겪기 쉽다
④ 재생 가능 에너지에 대한 연구는 제한적이다

| **정답해설** | ③ 빈칸이 포함된 첫 번째 문장에서 석유를 대체할 만한 것은 없다고 한 데 이어, 다른 에너지 공급원과는 달리 석유가 가장 우세한 연료로 남아 있다고 했다. 이로 인해 세계 경제가 활기를 띠면 석유 수요가 증가하고, 이에 대해 가격이 올라가게 되는데, 이런 높은 가격은 다시 경제 성장을 잠식시키는 부정적인 결과가 이어지며 이 순환은 다시 시작된다고 서술했으므로, 빈칸에 들어갈 것으로 가장 적절한 것은 ③이다.

어휘

substitute 대용품, 대체   boom 호황
bust 파산, 불황   predominant 우세한, 지배적인
transportation 운송   heat up 활기를 띠다
hold the bag 공동 책임을 혼자 지게 되다
plummet 폭락하다
lull A into B A를 (안심시켜) B의 상태로 빠뜨리다
disastrous 파멸을 초래하는, 피해가 막심한
complacency 무사안일주의, 자기만족

포기하고 싶어질 때
왜 시작했는지를 기억하라.

국가직

해설 &
기출분석 REPORT

국가직 기출 POINT

Point 1 어휘는 기출 어휘와 기본 어휘를 기반으로 출제되고 있다.

Point 2 문법은 지엽적인 부분은 배제하고 핵심 문법인 동사, 준동사, 연결사 위주로 범위가 축소되고 있다.

Point 3 독해는 글의 일관성을 파악하는 것과 빈칸 유형의 문항 비중 증가로 맥락을 파악하는 것이 관건이다.

2025년 국가직 시험 대비전략

"기출 출제 요소 숙지 및 신경향 문제 적용 연습"

Point 1 인사혁신처 공개 예시문제에 등장한 유형을 반복해서 연습하는 것이 필요하다.

Point 2 필수요소와 기출요소를 통합해 정리 및 암기해야 한다.

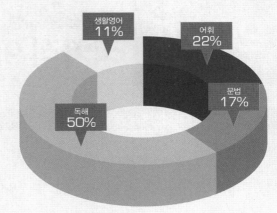

▲ 최근 7개년 평균 출제비중

연도	총평	어휘	문법	독해	생활영어
2024	**출제 전환을 앞둔 예비 시험, 평이한 출제 기조 유지!** · 동의어 비중이 높았으나 새로운 동사구의 등장으로 맥락 파악이 중요했음 · 문법은 기출 범위 내 출제가 대부분인 가운데, 지엽적인 문제(비교급 관용구)가 등장했음 · 공개된 신유형 문제(실용문과 안내문)와 다소 생소한 소재(그리스 비극, 고고학, 음모론 등)의 등장으로 독해 체감 난도가 상승했음	25% (5문항)	15% (3문항)	45% (9문항)	15% (3문항)
2023	**기출에 주목! 추론 영역 대비 여부가 당락을 결정!** · 추론형 문제의 출제 확대를 염두에 둔 문제가 다수 등장했음 · 어휘와 문법 모두 기출 범위 내에서 출제되었고 평이한 난도였음 · 독해의 경우 추론이 필요한 영역의 출제 비중이 높았음	20% (4문항)	15% (3문항)	50% (10문항)	15% (3문항)
2022	**기출 기반의 평이한 난도의 문제들, 실수는 치명적!** · 어휘와 문법은 평범하지만, 일부 관용구 등장으로 변별력을 확보함 · 까다로운 소재(과학, 경제 등)를 다룬 다수 문항의 독해로 체감 난도가 상승했음 · 독해의 경우 전년도와 동일한 9문항 출제로 풀이 시간의 부담이 감소했음	25% (5문항)	20% (4문항)	45% (9문항)	10% (2문항)
2021	**기본에 충실한 학습과 맥락 파악으로 고득점 완성!** · 문법에서 까다로운 요소들이 배제되었고, 동의어 출제 비중이 높아짐 · 기출범위 내의 새로운 동의어 출제로 맥락 파악이 관건 · 독해 문항이 9문항으로 축소되었으나 긴 지문으로 인한 핵심 내용 파악이 중요했음	20% (4문항)	20% (4문항)	50% (10문항)	10% (2문항)
2020	**구조에 대한 이해와 지문의 핵심을 파악해 풀이 시간 조절 고득점의 비결!** · 어휘는 평이한 수준의 동의어로 구성됨 · 문법의 경우 동사 부분에 대한 이해를 확인하는 문제들로 구성됨 · 독해의 경우 소재 자체는 평범하나 총 11지문으로 체감 난도는 상승했음	20% (4문항)	15% (3문항)	55% (11문항)	10% (2문항)
2019	**공무원 출제 전형을 따른 문제 구성과 난이도!** · 어휘와 문법 모두 기출 관련 범주 내에서 반복 출제됨 · 동사와 연결어에 집중된 문법 출제와 관용구가 포함된 영작문 문제가 등장했음 · 일부 장문의 독해 지문이 등장했지만, 평이한 소재로 실수만 없다면 고득점이 가능함	20% (4문항)	20% (4문항)	50% (10문항)	10% (2문항)
2018	**체감 난도 상승 요소들로 인한 기본기와 추론 능력이 무엇보다 중요!** · 동사와 준동사의 기본 개념 이해 여부를 묻는 문제가 집중됨 · 일부 까다로운 어휘의 등장으로 맥락 파악의 비중이 증가함 · 독해의 경우 다양한 주제와 더불어 전체적으로 긴 지문으로 시간 안배가 중요했음	20% (4문항)	15% (3문항)	55% (11문항)	10% (2문항)

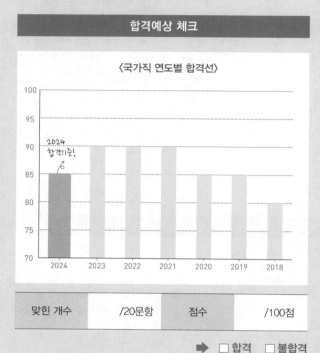

〈국가직 연도별 합격선〉

2024 합격기준

맞힌 개수	/20문항	점수	/100점

➡ ☐ 합격 ☐ 불합격

취약영역 체크

문항	정답	영역	문항	정답	영역
1	③	어휘 > 빈칸	11	③	생활영어 > 회화
2	②	어휘 > 동의어	12	②	독해 > 세부내용 찾기
3	①	어휘 > 동의어	13	③	독해 > 세부내용 찾기
4	④	어휘 > 동의어	14	④	독해 > 대의 파악
5	④	어휘 > 동의어	15	①	독해 > 대의 파악
6	②	문법 > 명사와 일치	16	④	독해 > 글의 일관성 파악하기
7	①	문법 > 형용사 · 부사 · 비교	17	③	독해 > 글의 일관성 파악하기
8	①	문법 > 명사와 일치	18	③	독해 > 글의 일관성 파악하기
9	②	생활영어 > 회화	19	②	독해 > 빈칸의 내용 추론하기
10	④	생활영어 > 회화	20	①	독해 > 빈칸의 내용 추론하기

⬇ 영역별 틀린 개수로 취약영역을 확인하세요!

어휘	/5	문법	/3	독해	/9	생활영어	/3

➡ 나의 취약영역:

※ 해당 회차는 〈1초 합격예측 서비스〉의 데이터 누적 기간이 충분하지 않아 오답률, 선지 선택률 기재를 생략하였습니다.

---

1 어휘 > 빈칸 답 ③

| 해석 | 분명히, 언어 기술의 어떤 측면도 학습이나 가르침에서 독립적이지 않다. 듣기, 말하기, 읽기, 쓰기, 보기, 그리고 시각적으로 표현하는 것은 서로 ③ 연관되어 있다.
① 뚜렷한, 확실한 ② 왜곡된
③ 서로 관계있는, 상관의 ④ 독립적인, 독자적인

| 정답해설 | ③ 언어 기술의 어떤 측면도 독립적이지 않다는 것은 기술의 면면들이 서로 '관련되어' 있다는 것임을 알 수 있으므로 빈칸에 들어갈 것으로 가장 적절한 것은 ③이다.

어휘
obviously 분명히, 명백히 aspect 측면
visually 눈에 보이게, 시각적으로 represent 표현[표시]하다; 대표하다

---

2 어휘 > 동의어 답 ②

| 해석 | 그 돈은 너무 빈틈없이 숨겨져 있어서 우리는 어쩔 수 없이 그 돈을 찾는 것을 포기했다.
① 사용된, 낭비된 ② 숨겨진
③ 투자된, 투입된 ④ 전달된, 배달된

| 정답해설 | ② 'so~ that…(매우 ~해서 …하다)'의 구문으로 주절에 이어 결과에 해당하는 부사절이 이어졌다. 종속절에서 어쩔 수 없이 돈을 찾는 것을 포기했다고 했으므로 돈이 '숨겨져' 있었음을 유추할 수 있다. '숨기다'의 표현인 hide의 과거분사 hidden이 동의어로 가장 적절하다.

어휘
conceal 은닉하다, 숨기다 cleverly 영리하게, 빈틈없이
be forced to + R 억지로 ~하다 abandon 포기하다, 버리다
search 조사, 탐색

---

3 어휘 > 동의어 답 ①

| 해석 | 비평가들을 진정시키기 위해, 무선 사업 업계는 드라이브 타임(출퇴근 운전 시간대) 라디오에서 1,200만 달러의 공공 교육 캠페인을 시작했다.
① 달래다, 진정시키다 ② 대항하다, 반대하다
③ 계몽하다, 교화하다 ④ 동화[일치]시키다

| 정답해설 | ① '목적'의 부사구에 이어진 문장에서 1,200만 달러가 투입된 공공 교육 캠페인을 시작했다고 했으므로 비평가들을 '진정시킬' 필요가 있었음을 유추할 수 있다. 따라서 appease의 동의어로 '진정시키다'의 표현인 soothe가 정답으로 가장 적절하다.

어휘
appease 달래다, 진정시키다 critic 비평가, 평론가
wireless industry 무선 산업 launch 시작하다; 출시하다; 발사하다

4 어휘 > 동의어 　　　　　　　　　　　　답 ④

| 해석 | 센터 관계자들은 그 문제들이 스타트업 운영에서 전형적인 것이라고 말하면서 그것들을 과소평가한다.
① 식별하다, 분간하다　　　　　② 불만을 느끼게 하다
③ 강조하다　　　　　　　　　　④ 과소평가하다, 경시하다
| 정답해설 | ④ play down에서 down은 '중요도가 떨어지다'라는 의미가 있으므로 목적어인 the troubles를 연결하면 '과소평가하다'의 underestimate가 동의어로 가장 적절함을 유추할 수 있다.

[어휘]
typical 전형적인; ~에 특유한, 상징적인
operation 운영; 작전; 수술

5 어휘 > 동의어 　　　　　　　　　　　　답 ④

| 해석 | 그녀는 부지런히 일했고 자신이 원하는 것을 얻으려는 배짱이 있었다.
① 걱정했다　　　　　　　　　② 운이 좋았다
③ 평판이 좋았다　　　　　　　④ 용감했다
| 정답해설 | ④ gut은 '소화관, 내장'의 의미이지만, 복수형인 guts로 쓰면 구어에서 '용기, 배짱'의 의미로 쓰인다. 맥락상 '배짱'의 표현이므로 동일한 표현으로 '용감한'의 의미인 courageous가 포함된 was courageous가 정답으로 가장 적절하다.

[어휘]
have the guts to do ~하는 용기가 있다
diligently 부지런히, 근면하게　　　　go for ~을 얻으려고 애쓰다

6 문법 > 명사와 일치 > 대명사 　　　　　　답 ②

| 해석 | 더 오래된 주택의 품질이 현대 주택의 품질보다 우수하다는 믿음에도 불구하고, 대부분의 20세기 이전 주택의 토대는 오늘날과 비교하여 엄청나게 얇팍하며, 벽돌과 석재 사이의 목재 구조 또는 석회 모르타르의 신축성 덕분에 세월의 시련을 견뎌냈다.
| 정답해설 | ② the quality를 지칭하는 대명사로 of modern houses의 수식을 받고 있다. the quality는 단수로 취급해야 하므로 those를 that으로 바꿔야 한다. 같은 문장 내의 명사를 다시 지칭하는 대명사가 'of + 명사', 형용사구, 분사구 등에 의해 수식을 받을 때는 that 혹은 those로 써야 한다.
| 오답해설 | ① despite는 '양보'의 전치사로 목적어로 명사나 명사 상당어구가 이어져야 한다. 명사 the belief가 이어졌으므로 올바른 구조이다.
③ compared to는 '~와 비교하여'의 의미로, 과거분사의 주체는 주어인 the foundations이다. 20세기 이전의 토대가 오늘날의 토대와 '비교되는' 것이므로 수동의 과거분사로 올바르게 표현했다.
④ 구조와 맥락상 their가 지칭하는 대상은 20세기 이전의 주택들(houses)이므로 복수로 수일치가 올바르게 이루어졌으며 소유격으로 명사 timber framework를 수식하고 있다.

[어휘]
quality 품질, 질; 특성　　　　　foundation 토대, 기초; 설립
shallow 얇은, 얕팍한; 피상적인; 천박한

compared to ~와 비교하여
stand the test of time 세월의 시련을 견뎌내다
flexibility 신축성, 유연성　　　　lime mortar 석회 모르타르

7 문법 > 형용사 · 부사 · 비교 > 비교 　　　답 ①

| 해석 | ① 그들은 글을 쓰는 것은 말할 것도 없고, 시를 읽는 것에도 관심이 없다.
② 주문이 확정되면, 당신의 주소로 배송하기 위해 주문품이 발송될 것이다.
③ 여객선이 정시에 출발하는 것을 전제로, 우리는 아침까지 항구에 도착해야 한다.
④ 외신 기자들은 수도에서의 짧은 체류 기간 동안 가능한 한 많은 뉴스를 다루기를 희망한다.
| 정답해설 | ① '~는 말할 것도 없이'의 표현으로 still more가 왔는데, still(much) more는 긍정문과 의문문에서 사용하며, 부정문에서는 still(much) less로 써야 한다. 긍정문과 부정문에 상관없이 쓸 수 있는 표현으로 let alone, not to speak of, to say nothing of, not to mention 등이 있다.
| 오답해설 | ② 접속사 once에 이어 과거분사가 왔으므로 once와 confirmed 사이에 '주어 + be동사'인 it is가 생략되었음을 알 수 있다. 생략된 주어는 이어진 주절의 주어인 the order와 일치하며, 주문은 '확정되는' 것이므로 수동태로 올바르게 표현했다.
③ provided that은 접속사 if의 대용표현으로 조건 부사절을 이끈다. 뒤에 완전한 절이 이어졌고, 맥락상 주절과 흐름이 자연스럽게 이어지므로 올바른 표현이다.
④ 'as 원급 as possible'의 표현으로 원급 much가 올바르게 쓰였다. news는 불가산 명사이므로 much의 수식을 받는다.

[어휘]
confirm 확정하다; 확인하다　　　　delivery 배송, 배달; 분만
on time 정각에, 제때에
capital 수도, 서울; 자본; 대문자; 주요한

8 문법 > 명사와 일치 > 일치 　　　　　　답 ①

| 정답해설 | ① 종속절의 주어는 the number이므로 단수동사 is로 수일치가 올바르게 이루어졌다. 'the number of + 복수명사'가 주어일 때 동사의 수는 the number에 일치시켜야 한다.
| 오답해설 | ② 과거 부사구인 two years ago와 호응하는 과거시제가 되어야 한다. 따라서 I've received를 I received로 바꿔야 올바른 문장이다.
③ 관계대명사 which에 이어 완전한 절이 이어졌으므로 틀린 문장이다. 구조상 which에 이어 불완전한 절이 와야 하며, 맥락상 '침대에서' 잠을 잤으므로 which he slept in, 혹은 전치사 in을 관계대명사 앞으로 빼서 in which he slept, 혹은 관계부사 where로 표현해야 올바른 문장이 된다.
④ each other는 상호 대명사이므로 명사 greetings에 바로 이어질 수 없다. 따라서 전치사 to로 연결해서 써야 올바른 문장이 된다.

[어휘]
applicant 지원자　　　　　　comfortable 편안한
exchange 교환하다, 맞바꾸다　　greeting 인사, 환영의 말

| 해석 | Brian: 안녕하세요, 시티투어에 대한 정보 좀 얻을 수 있을까요?
Ace Tour: 연락주셔서 감사합니다. 구체적으로 궁금한 점이 있으신가요?
Brian: ② 시티투어에 무엇이 포함되어 있나요?
Ace Tour: 도시의 모든 주요 명소들로 안내해 드려요.
Brian: 얼마인가요?
Ace Tour: 4시간에 1인당 50달러입니다.
Brian: 알겠습니다. 금요일 오후에 티켓 4장 예약할 수 있나요?
Ace Tour: 물론이죠. 바로 결제 정보를 보내드릴게요.
① 투어 시간은 얼마나 오래 걸리나요?
② 시티투어에 무엇이 포함되어 있나요?
③ 투어 패키지 목록이 있나요?
④ 괜찮은 관광 안내 책자를 추천해 줄 수 있나요?

| 정답해설 | ② 빈칸의 질문에 이어진 대답으로 '도시의 주요 명소들로 데리고 간다'고 했으므로 시티투어 프로그램의 내용이 무엇인지 물어보았음을 유추할 수 있다. 따라서 빈칸에 들어갈 것으로 ②가 가장 적절하다.

어휘

contact 연락을 취하다 / specific 구체적인, 특정한
book 예약하다 / payment 납부, 지급

| 해석 | A: 고맙습니다. 주문해 주셔서 감사합니다.
B: 천만에요. 항공 화물로 상품을 보내주실 수 있나요? 빨리 필요해서요.
A: 물론이죠. 바로 고객님 부서로 보내드릴게요.
B: 알겠습니다. 다음 주 초에 상품을 받을 수 있으면 해요.
A: 모든 것이 일정대로 진행된다면, 월요일까지 받으실 겁니다.
B: 월요일 좋네요.
A: 2주 이내에 지불 부탁드려요. 항공 화물 비용은 송장에 추가됩니다.
B: ④ 잠시만요. 운송비는 그쪽에서 부담하시는 것으로 생각했는데요.
A: 죄송합니다만 무료 운송 서비스는 더 이상 제공하지 않고 있어요.
① 그렇군요. 송장은 언제 받을 수 있을까요?
② 저희 부서가 2주 안에 결제를 못할 수도 있습니다.
③ 월요일에 당신의 회사 계좌로 대금을 보낼 수 있을까요?
④ 잠시만요. 운송비는 그쪽에서 부담하시는 것으로 생각했는데요.

| 정답해설 | ④ 항공 화물로 주문한 물품을 받는 상황을 확인하는 대화문이다. 빠른 배송을 위해 항공 화물을 요청했고, 받을 수 있는 있는 일정에 대한 소통까지 순조롭게 진행되었는데, 항공 화물은 비용이 추가로 지불될 예정이라는 A의 말에 이어진 B의 대답을 찾는 문제이다. 빈칸의 질문에 이어진 A의 대답에서 죄송하다는 유감의 표현과 함께 무료 운송 서비스가 더 이상 제공되지 않는다고 한 것으로 보아, 빈칸에는 운송비 부담에 대한 문제를 언급했음을 유추할 수 있다. 따라서 빈칸에 들어갈 것으로 ④가 가장 적절하다.

어휘

appreciate 감사하다 / freight 화물
invoice 송장, 청구서 / account 계좌; 시술, 서술, 설명
delivery 배송, 배달; 분만 / expense 비용, 지출

| 해석 | A: 휴대전화 찾았어요?
B: 안타깝지만 못 찾았어요. 여전히 찾고 있어요.
A: 지하철 분실물 보관소에 연락해 봤어요?
B: ③ 사실 아직 안했어요.
A: 저라면 먼저 그렇게 할 거예요.
B: 네, 당신 말이 맞아요. 새 휴대전화를 사기 전에 분실물 보관소에 확인해 볼게요.
① 전화기에 대해 물어 보려고 거기 갔었어요
② 오늘 아침에 사무실에 잠시 들렀어요
③ 사실 아직 안 했어요
④ 다 찾아봤어요

| 정답해설 | ③ 휴대전화를 지하철에서 분실한 것에 대한 후속 조치를 주제로 대화를 나누고 있는 상황이다. 지하철 분실물 보관소에 연락 여부를 묻는 질문에 대한 대답인 빈칸에 이어 A가 '자신은 그렇게 할 거라고' 아쉬움을 표현한 데에 이어 B가 분실물 보관소에 확인해 보겠다고 했으므로 아직까지 분실물 보관소에 가지 않았음을 나타내는 표현이 와야 한다. 따라서 빈칸에 가장 적절한 것은 ③이다.

어휘

look for 찾다 / lost and found office 분실물 보관소
stop by 잠시 들르다 / search 찾다, 수색하다

| 해석 | 노스이스턴 야생동물 박람회(NEWE)

2024년 3월 30일, 토요일, 입장권
- **가격:** 40달러
- **개장 시간:** 오전 10:00 – 오후 6:00

10세 이하 어린이는 무료입니다. 공연과 강연 입장은 선착순입니다. 모든 공연장은 날씨에 상관없이 개장합니다.

3월 20일은 2024 노스이스턴 야생동물 박람회의 온라인 입장권 구매 마지막 날입니다.

참고: NEWE 입장권 사전 구매가 모든 전시회 입장을 확실히 할 수 있는 최고의 방법입니다. NEWE 주최측은 행사장이 수용 인원에 도달하면, 현장 입장권 판매를 중단할 수 있습니다.

| 정답해설 | ② first-come, first-served가 선착순 입장의 의미이므로 본문의 내용과 일치한다.

| 오답해설 | ① Kids 10 and under are free를 통해 무료 입장이라는 것을 알 수 있다.
③ All venues open rain or shine을 통해 우천 여부와 상관없이 개장하는 것을 알 수 있다.
④ 마지막 문장에서 현장 티켓 판매(in-person ticket sales)가 중단될 수도 있다는 것으로 보아 온라인 외에 현장 판매도 이루어짐을 알 수 있다.

어휘

wildlife 야생동물 / exposition 전시회, 박람회
admission 입장 / entry 입장; 가입, 입회

lecture 강연, 연설
purchase 구입하다
guarantee 보장하다
in-person 직접

venue 장소, 현장
in advance 사전에, 미리
discontinue 중단하다
capacity 수용력

---

13 독해 > 세부내용 찾기 > 내용 불일치 찾기　　답 ③

| 해석 | 그리스 극작가 소포클레스의 비극들은 고전 그리스 희곡의 정점으로 여겨지게 되었다. 슬프게도, 그가 쓴 123개의 비극 중 7개만이 살아남았지만, 아마도 그중 가장 훌륭한 것은 '오이디푸스 왕'일 것이다. 이 희곡은 소포클레스가 테베의 신화상의 왕인 오이디푸스에 대해 집필한 세 작품 중 하나(다른 작품들은 '안티고네'와 '콜로누스의 오이디푸스'이다)였는데, 일괄적으로 테베 희곡으로 알려져 있다. 소포클레스는 이들 각각을 별개의 존재로 생각했으며, 이 작품들은 몇 년 간격으로 그리고 연대순을 벗어나 집필되고 제작되었다. '오이디푸스 왕'은 확립된 형식 구조를 따르며 고전 아테네 비극의 최고의 본보기로 여겨진다.
① 총 123편의 비극이 소포클레스에 의해 집필되었다.
② '안티고네'는 오이디푸스 왕에 대한 이야기이기도 하다.
③ 테베 희곡은 시간 순서대로 만들어졌다.
④ '오이디푸스 왕'은 고전적인 아테네 비극을 대표한다.

| 정답해설 | ③ out of chronological order로 보아 시간 순서를 벗어나 집필되었음을 알 수 있다. 따라서 in time order와 부합하지 않는 표현이다.

| 오답해설 | ① seven of 123 tragedies로 보아 오늘날까지 남은 건 7작품이지만 123작품을 집필했음을 알 수 있으므로 일치하는 내용이다.
② '오이디푸스 왕', '안티고네', '콜로누스의 오이디푸스'가 일괄적으로 테베 희곡으로 알려져 있다고 했으므로 본문과 일치하는 내용이다.
④ 마지막 문장의 the best example로 보아 '오이디푸스 왕'이 고전 아테네 비극을 대표한다(represents)고 볼 수 있으므로 일치하는 내용이다.

어휘
tragedy 비극
mythical 신화상의; 가공의, 상상의
conceive A as B A를 B라고 생각하다
separate 별개의, 독립된
be regarded as ~로 여겨지다
collectively 일괄하여; 전체적으로
chronological 연대기의

---

14 독해 > 대의 파악 > 주제 찾기　　답 ④

| 해석 | 한 사람이 하나의 문화 전체에 우리의 눈을 뜨게 해 줄 수 있다는 것은 믿기 힘들지만, 영국의 고고학자 Arthur Evans가 크레타 섬의 크노소스 궁전의 유물을 성공적으로 발굴하기 전까지 지중해의 위대한 미노스 문명은 사실보다는 전설에 가까웠다. 실제로 그 문명에서 가장 유명한 것은 신화 속에 나오는 미노스 왕의 궁전 아래에 살았다고 전해지는 반인반수(半人半獸)의 미노타우로스라는 신화 속 생명체였다. 하지만 Evans가 증명했듯이 이 왕국은 신화가 아니었다. 20세기 초 일련의 발굴 작업을 통해 Evans는 보석, 조각품, 도자기, 황소 뿔 모양의 제단, 미노스 문명의 삶을 보여 주는 벽화 등 기원전 1900년부터 1450년까지 정점을 찍었던 미노스 문명 시대의 유물들을 발견했다.
① 미노스 왕의 성공적인 발굴
② 미노스 시대의 유물 감상
③ 크레타 섬에 있는 궁전의 웅장함
④ 미노스 문화를 현실의 영역으로 가져오기

| 정답해설 | ④ 영국의 고고학자 Arthur Evans가 크레타 섬의 크노소스 궁전의 유물을 발굴함으로써 전설로 여겨졌던 미노스 문화를 사실로 입증되었다는 내용이므로 글의 주제로 ④가 가장 적절하다.

어휘
incredible 놀라운, 엄청난
responsible for ~에 책임이 있는, ~의 원인이 되는
archaeologist 고고학자
ruins 유적, 폐허
famed 유명한, 널리 알려진
excavation 발굴, 발굴물
carving 조각
altar 제단
excavate 발굴하다
the Mediterranean 지중해
realm 왕국; 영역
trove 귀중한 발견(물)
pottery 도기(류)

---

15 독해 > 대의 파악 > 제목 찾기　　답 ①

| 해석 | 나쁜 화폐 형태로 인한 좋은 화폐의 가치 저하는 귀금속 비율이 높은 주화가 더 낮은 가치의 귀금속으로 희석된 금이나 은을 더 낮은 비율로 재발행된 방식으로 나왔다. 이러한 불순물 섞기는 나쁜 주화를 위해 좋은 주화를 몰아냈다. 어느 누구도 좋은 주화를 쓰지 않고, 그것을 보관했기 때문에, 좋은 조화는 유통에서 밀려났고 저장되었다. 한편, 끝없는 전쟁과 그 외 방탕한 생활로 보물을 잃은, 대개 왕이었던 발행인이 그 배후에 있었다. 그들은 가능한 모든 좋은 오래된 주화를 모아서, 그것들을 녹이고 더 낮은 순도로 재발행하여 차액을 챙겼다. 왕이 적어도 일시적으로 자신의 국고를 보충하는 동안, 오래된 것(주화)을 계속 지니고 있는 것이 종종 불법이었음에도, 사람들은 그렇게 했다.
① 나쁜 화폐가 좋은 화폐를 대체하는 방식
② 좋은 주화의 요소
③ 주화를 녹이는 것은 어떨까?
④ 나쁜 화폐란 무엇인가?

| 정답해설 | ① 지문에서 귀금속 비율이 높은 주화는 보관하고, 불순물로 희석한 나쁜 주화를 유통시켰다고 했고, 이런 동향의 배후에 주화의 발행인인 왕이 있었다고 서술하였다. 따라서 글의 제목으로 ① '나쁜 화폐가 좋은 화폐를 대체하는 방식'이 가장 적절하다.

어휘
currency 화폐, 통화
precious 귀중한
dilute 희석하다, 묽게 하다
drive out 몰아내다, 쫓아내다
hoard 저장, 축적
treasure 보물, 보배
warfare 전쟁, 전투
melt down 녹여버리다
balance 나머지, 잔액; 균형
replenish 보충하다
debasement (품질·가치 등의) 저하
reissue 재발행하다
adulteration 불순물을 섞기, 불순품
circulation 유통; 순환; 발행부수
meanwhile 한편으로는
interminable 끝없는; 지루하게도 긴
dissolute 방탕한
purity 순도
illegal 불법[위법]의
treasury 재정; 국고

---

16 독해 > 글의 일관성 파악하기 > 글의 흐름과 무관한 문장　　답 ④

| 해석 | 반대되는 모든 증거에도 불구하고, NASA의 아폴로 우주 프로그램이 실제로 달에 사람을 착륙시킨 적이 없다고 진지하게 믿는 사람들이 있다. 이들은 달 착륙이 러시아와 필사적으로 경쟁하며, 체면을 잃을까 봐 두려워하는 정부에 의해 영속된 거대한 음모에 불과하다고 주장한다. 이러한 음모 이론가들은 미국이 우주 경쟁에서 러시아와 경쟁할 수 없다는 것을 알

고 있었기 때문에, 일련의 성공적인 달 착륙을 어쩔 수 없이 조작해야 했다고 주장한다. 음모론 옹호자들은 자신들이 증거로 여기는 몇 가지 부분을 인용한다. 그들의 주장에 결정적인 것은 우주비행사들이 지구 자기장에 갇혀진 방사능 지역인 밴 앨런대를 결코 안전하게 통과할 수 없었을 것이라는 것이다. ④ 그들은 또한 우주선의 금속 덮개가 방사선을 차단하도록 설계되었다는 사실을 지적한다. 만약 우주비행사들이 진정으로 그 대를 통과했다면, 음모론자들은 그들이 사망했을 것이라고 말한다.

| 정답해설 | ④ NASA의 아폴로 우주 프로그램에 관한 음모론에 관한 글이다. 음모론에 대한 근거로 우주 경쟁에서 러시아에 밀린 미국이 달 착륙 성공을 조작했다는 내용과 방사능 지역인 밴 앨런대를 안전하게 통과할 수 없었다는 내용이 이어진 가운데, ④에서 우주선의 금속 덮개가 방사선을 차단하도록 설계했다고 했는데, 이 경우 오히려 방사능대를 통과할 수 있다는 내용이므로 흐름과 무관하다. ④에 이어진 문장에서 그 대를 통과했다면 우주비행사들이 사망했을 것이라고 했으므로 이는 ③에 이어지는 내용임을 알 수 있다. 따라서 흐름과 무관한 문장은 ④이다.

어휘

contrary 반대의 것; 정반대의	nothing more than ~에 지나지 않는
conspiracy 음모	perpetuate 영속[영존]하게 하다
desperately 필사적으로	lose face 체면을 잃다
fake 날조[조작]하다; 위조[모조]의	advocate 옹호자, 지지자
crucial 결정적인; 중요한	astronaut 우주비행사
radiation 방사선, 방사능	magnetic field 자기장

---

17 독해 > 글의 일관성 파악하기 > 주어진 문장의 삽입 답 ③

| 해석 | 워싱턴 주 올림픽 반도의 가장 서쪽 지점에 있는 Ozette 마을에서 온 Makah 족의 구성원들은 고래를 사냥했다. 그들은 포획물을 선반 위와 훈제실에서 훈제했고 퓨젯 사운드 주변 및 밴쿠버 섬 인근의 이웃 부족들과 거래했다. Ozette는 그 지역에서 수천 년간 터를 잡아 온 원주민인 Makah 족이 거주하던 다섯 개의 주요 마을 중 하나였다. ③ 부족의 구전 역사와 고고학적 증거는 1500년에서 1700년 사이 어느 시점에 진흙 사태가 마을의 일부를 파괴하여 여러 채의 공동 가옥들을 덮고 내용물을 봉인했다고 시사한다. 그러지 않았으면(봉인되지 않았으면) 살아남지 못했을 바구니, 의류, 요, 포경 도구를 포함한 수천 개의 유물이 진흙 아래에 보존되었다. 1970년, 한 폭풍이 이런 공동주택과 인공 유물의 잔해를 드러나게 했던 해안 침식을 야기했다.

| 정답해설 | ③ 주어진 글에서 구전 역사와 고고학적 증거에 의하면 진흙 사태가 마을을 파괴해 가옥을 덮고 내용물을 봉인했다고 했으므로, 앞에는 the village에 대한 소개와 진흙 사태 이전의 마을의 상황에 대한 내용이 제시되어야 하고, 뒤에는 진흙 사태 이후의 결과가 언급되어야 함을 유추할 수 있다. 주어진 글의 mudslide가 ③에 이어진 문장의 under the mud에 연결되고, 수천 개의 유물들이 진흙 아래 보존되어 있었다고 했으므로 주어진 문장은 ③에 들어가는 것이 가장 적절하다.

어휘

tribe 부족	rack 선반
inhabit ~에 살다, 거주하다	indigenous 토착의, 고유의
millennia millennium(천년)의 복수형	oral 구두의, 구전의
archaeological 고고학적인	mudslide 진흙 사태
destroy 파괴하다	seal 봉인하다, 폐쇄하다

---

18 독해 > 글의 일관성 파악하기 > 글의 순서 답 ②

| 해석 | 영화와 스포츠 스타에 대한 관심은 스크린과 경기장에서의 그들의 성과를 넘어선다.
(B) 신문 칼럼, 전문 잡지, 텔레비전 프로그램 및 웹 사이트는 유명 할리우드 배우의 사생활을 때로는 정확하게 기록한다.
(A) 유니폼을 입지 않은 노련한 야구, 축구, 농구 선수들의 행동도 마찬가지로 대중의 관심을 끈다.
(C) 두 업계 모두 이러한 관심을 적극적으로 홍보하며, 이는 관객을 확대하고 수익을 증가시킨다. 그러나 그들을 구분하는 근본적인 차이가 있는데, 그것은 스포츠 스타가 생계를 위해 하는 일이 영화배우들이 하는 방식과는 다르게 진정성이 있다는 것이다.

| 정답해설 | ② 주어진 글에서 영화와 스포츠 스타에 대한 관심이 그들의 성과를 넘어서는 것이라고 서술했다. 따라서 성과 외의 다른 요소에 대해 서술하는 내용이 이어져야 하는데, (B)에서 각종 매체들의 할리우드 배우들의 '사생활(personal lives)'을 기록한다고 했으므로 주어진 글에 이어 가장 먼저 와야 한다. 배우들에 이어 스포츠 스타들의 행동도 대중의 관심을 끈다고 한 (A)가 그 다음에 이어져야 하며, 이때 (A)에 나오는 similarly를 통해 비슷한 흐름의 글인 (B)가 (A)보다 앞서야 함을 알 수 있다. 마지막으로 이 두 업계를 지칭하는 Both industries를 주어로 한 문장이 포함된 (C)가 이어지는 것이 문맥상 자연스럽다.

어휘

performance 성과; 수행	specialized 전문의, 특화된
celebrated 유명한, 저명한	accurately 정확하게, 틀림없이
expand 확대하다	revenue 수입, 세입
fundamental 근본적인, 기본적인	authentic 진정한

---

19 독해 > 빈칸의 내용 추론하기 > 빈칸 어구 추론 답 ②

| 해석 | ② 설득은 거의 모든 각계각층에서 나타난다. 거의 모든 주요 정치인들은 대중에게 어필하는 방법에 대한 조언을 제공하는 미디어 컨설턴트와 정치 전문가를 고용한다. 사실상 모든 주요 기업 및 특수 이익 단체는 의회 또는 주 정부 및 지방 정부에 자신들의 관심사를 표명하기 위해 로비스트들을 고용해 왔다. 거의 모든 지역 사회에서, 활동가들은 중요한 정책 문제에 대해 동료 시민들을 설득하려고 노력한다. 직장 역시 항상 사무실 정치와 설득을 위한 비옥한 토대가 되어 왔다. 한 연구에 따르면, 일반 관리자들은 자신의 시간의 80% 이상을 언어적 의사소통에 소비하고, 이 중 대부분은 동료 직원들을 설득하기 위한 목적으로 사용한다고 추정한다. 복사기의 등장으로, 사무실 설득을 위한 완전히 새로운 매체, 즉 복사 메모가 발명되었다. 펜타곤(美 국방부)만 해도 하루 평균 35만 쪽을 복사하는데, 이는 소설 1000권에 해당하는 분량이다.
① 기업인들은 훌륭한 설득 기술을 가져야 한다
② 설득은 거의 모든 각계각층에서 나타난다
③ 당신은 수많은 광고판과 포스터를 마주치게 된다
④ 대중 매체 캠페인은 정부에 유용하다

| 정답해설 | ② 빈칸에 이어 여러 단체와 여러 사람들 사이에서 이루어지는 설득(persuasion)의 유형들을 서술하고 있는 글이다. 정치인은 대중을, 기업과 특수 이익 단체는 정부를, 활동가들은 동료 시민을, 직장인들은 동료를 설득하기 위한 내용이 이어지고 있으므로 빈칸에 들어갈 것으로 가장 적절한 것은 ②이다.

어휘

politician 정치가	consultant 컨설턴트, 상담역, 고문
expert 전문가	virtually 사실상
policy issue 정책 문제	fertile 비옥한
persuasion 설득	estimate 추정하다
intent 의도, 의향	advent 등장, 출현, 도래
equivalent 동등한 것, 등가[등량]물	every walk of life 각계각층
encounter 만나다, 마주치다	

---

20   독해 > 빈칸의 내용 추론하기 > 빈칸 어구 추론   답 ①

| 해석 | 성인의 경우, 사회적 상호 작용은 주로 언어라는 수단을 통해 나타난다는 점에 주목하는 것이 중요하다. 성인 원어민 중 그 언어를 사용하지 않는 사람과 교류하는 데 기꺼이 시간을 쏟으려는 사람은 거의 없으며, 그 결과 성인 외국인은 유의미하면서 폭넓은 언어 교환에 참여할 기회는 거의 없기 마련이다. 반대로, 어린아이는 다른 아이들에게, 심지어 어른들에게도 쉽게 받아들여진다. 어린아이에게, 언어는 사회적 상호 작용에 그만큼 필수적이지 않다. 예를 들어, 소위 '평행 놀이'는 어린아이들 사이에서 흔하다. 아이들은 서로의 무리에 앉아서 그저 가끔씩 말을 하고 혼자 노는 것만으로도 만족할 수 있다. 성인들은 ① 사회적 상호 작용에서 언어가 중요한 역할을 하지 않는 상황에 있는 경우가 거의 없다.

① 언어는 사회적인 상호 작용에서 중요한 역할을 하지 않는다
② 자신들의 의견이 동료들에게 쉽게 받아들여진다
③ 그들이 다른 언어를 사용하도록 요청받다
④ 의사소통 능력이 대단히 요구된다

| 정답해설 | ① 성인의 사회적 상호 작용에서 언어가 중요하다는 글이다. 성인들은 자신의 언어를 사용하지 않는 사람과 사회적 상호 작용이 이루어지기 힘든 반면에 아이들은 언어가 중요하지 않으며, 그 예로 말을 가끔씩만 해도 평행 놀이로 만족할 수 있다는 내용이 이어졌다. 빈칸이 포함된 문장의 주어는 성인들(adults)이므로 앞에 전개된 내용으로 보아 언어가 사회적 상호 작용에서 중요하다는 내용이 되어야 하는데, 주절에 부정의 부사인 rarely가 있으므로, 빈칸에는 이와는 반대되는 내용이 들어가야 한다. 따라서 빈칸에 들어갈 말로 가장 적절한 것은 ①이다.

어휘

note 주목하다	interaction 상호 작용
be willing to + R 기꺼이 ~하다	devote A to B A를 B에 바치다
engage in ~에 참여하다	readily 쉽게
common 흔한, 일반적인	content 만족하는

합격예상 체크

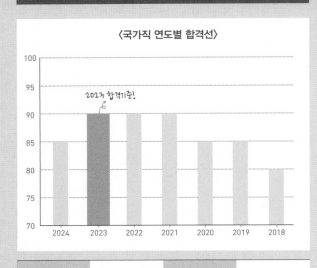

〈국가직 연도별 합격선〉

맞힌 개수	/20문항	점수	/100점

➡ ☐ 합격 ☐ 불합격

취약영역 체크

문항	정답	영역	문항	정답	영역
1	②	어휘 > 동의어	11	②	생활영어 > 회화
2	②	어휘 > 동의어	12	③	생활영어 > 회화
3	④	어휘 > 동의어	13	③	독해 > 대의 파악
4	①	어휘 > 동의어	14	①	독해 > 대의 파악
5	③	문법 > 명사와 일치	15	②	독해 > 대의 파악
6	④	문법 > 문장의 구조와 동사 유형	16	②	독해 > 빈칸의 내용 추론하기
7	②	문법 > 연결사	17	③	독해 > 글의 일관성 파악하기
8	④	독해 > 세부내용 찾기	18	③	독해 > 글의 일관성 파악하기
9	④	독해 > 세부내용 찾기	19	③	독해 > 글의 일관성 파악하기
10	①	생활영어 > 회화	20	①	독해 > 빈칸의 내용 추론하기

⬇ 영역별 틀린 개수로 취약영역을 확인하세요!

어휘	/4	문법	/3	독해	/10	생활영어	/3

➡ 나의 취약영역: _____

※ [정답해설]과 [오답해설] 선지의 50% 표시는 〈에듀윌 합격예측 풀서비스〉를 통해 수집된 선지 선택률을 나타냅니다.

1	어휘 > 동의어	오답률 18%	답 ②

| 해석 | 제인은 화려한 결혼식보다는 작은 결혼식을 하고 싶었다. 따라서 그녀는 가족과 친한 친구 몇 명을 초대하여 맛있는 음식을 먹고 즐거운 시간을 보낼 계획이었다.
① 3% 참견하기 좋아하는   ② 82% 친밀한, 가까운
③ 6% 사교적인, 외향적인   ④ 9% 사려 깊은, 신중한

| 정답해설 | ② intimate은 '친밀한'의 의미이며, 맥락상 스몰 웨딩을 위한 초대 대상으로 가족과 함께 언급되었으므로 '친밀한, 가까운'의 의미인 close가 동의어임을 유추할 수 있다.

어휘
intimate 친밀한; 개인적인   fancy 화려한, 근사한
pleasant 즐거운, 유쾌한

오답률 TOP 2			
2	어휘 > 동의어	오답률 51%	답 ②

| 해석 | 저렴한 비용과 건강상의 이점으로 인한 끊임없는 대중의 호기심과 소비자 요구는 기능성 식품에 대한 관심을 증가시켰다.
① 14% 빠른, 신속한   ② 49% 지속적인, 끊임없는
③ 24% 중요한, 상당한   ④ 13% 간헐적인, 주기적인

| 정답해설 | ② incessant에서 cease는 '중단하다, 그치다'의 의미이며, 형용사형 어미와 부정의 접두어인 'in-'이 앞에 있으므로 '끊임없는'의 의미임을 유추할 수 있다. 또한 대중의 관심과 소비자의 요구가 기능성 식품에 대한 관심을 증가시켰다고 했으므로 '끊임없는'

관심과 요구가 원인이 되었음을 알 수 있으므로 동의어로 ②가 적절하다.

어휘
incessant 끊임없는, 그칠 새 없는   curiosity 호기심
benefit 혜택, 이익   functional 기능상의

오답률 TOP 3			
3	어휘 > 동의어	오답률 50%	답 ④

| 해석 | 세계적인 전염병으로 인해 회사는 근로자에게 다양한 교육 프로그램을 제공하려는 계획을 연기해야 했다.
① 10% 공들여 마무리하다
② 22% 발표하다; 출시하다; 해방하다
③ 18% 수정하다, 변경하다
④ 50% 연기하다; 매달다, 걸다

| 정답해설 | ④ 보통 회사는 근로자들에게 교육 프로그램을 제공하는 것이 일반적이나, 세계적인 전염병을 이유로 들어 '연기해야' 했음을 유추할 수 있다. suspend는 '연기하다, 보류하다'의 의미이므로 동의어로 ④가 가장 적절하다.

어휘
hold off 연기하다; 막다   pandemic 전국[세계]적인 유행병
provide A with B A에게 B를 제공하다

4 어휘 > 동의어 | 오답률 39% | 답 ①

| 해석 | 새 주지사는 죄수를 석방하라는 고등법원의 판결을 따르겠다고 말했다.
① 61% 받아들이다, 승낙[수락]하다
② 6% 보고하다, 보도하다
③ 20% 연기하다, 미루다
④ 13% 발표하다, 알리다

| 정답해설 | ① 일반적으로 고등법원의 판결을 어떻게 해야 하는지 유추해 보면, 구속력이 있으므로 '따라야' 함을 알 수 있다. 주어진 선지에서 이와 가장 비슷한 어휘는 '수락하다'의 의미인 accept이므로 정답은 ①이다.

어휘
abide by (결정·제의 등에) 따르다, 동의하다
Regional Governor 주지사　　　　release 석방하다; 발표하다

5 문법 > 명사와 일치 > 일치 | 오답률 29% | 답 ③

| 해석 | (장기) 이식 기술의 발전으로 말기 장기 질환 환자의 수명이 연장될 수 있지만, 장기 이식술을 일단 심장이나 신장이 성공적으로 교체되면 끝나는 제한된 이벤트라는 생물 의학적 견해는 장기를 받는 경험을 좀 더 정확히 나타내주는 복잡하고 역동적인 과정을 감춘다고 주장한다.

| 정답해설 | ③ 71% conceal은 중간에 삽입된 관계대명사절 (which~replaced)을 배제하면, 접속사 that이 이끄는 절의 주어인 the biomedical view의 동사이므로 단수로 수일치 시켜야 한다. 따라서 conceals로 바꿔야 한다.

| 오답해설 | ① 5% 5형식 문장의 가목적어로 진목적어인 to extend~를 대신하고 있다.
② 8% 가주어 it과 호응하는 진주어인 명사절을 이끄는 접속사이다. that에 이어 완전한 절이 올바르게 이어졌다.
④ 16% 관계대명사절의 동사 represents를 수식하므로 동사를 수식할 수 있는 부사 accurately가 올바르게 왔다.

어휘
advance 발전, 진보　　　　　　transplant 이식
end-stage organ disease 말기 장기 질환
biomedical 생물 의학의　　　　transplantation [의학] 이식 (수술)
bounded 경계[한계, 제한]가 있는　kidney 신장, 콩팥
accurately 정확하게, 틀림없이

6 문법 > 문장의 구조와 동사 유형 > 동사와 문장의 5형식 | 오답률 44% | 답 ④

| 해석 | ① 모든 과제는 제때에 제출될 것으로 예상된다.
② 눈을 감자마자 나는 그녀에 대해 생각하기 시작했다.
③ 그 중개인은 그녀에게 즉시 주식을 사라고 권했다.
④ 머리에 연필 끝이 박힌 한 여성은 마침내 그것을 제거하게 되었다.

| 정답해설 | ④ 56% 동사 has had에 이어 목적어 it, 그 다음에 준동사인 remove가 왔으므로 구조와 문맥상 5형식 문장임을 알 수 있다. remove는 타동사이므로 뒤에는 remove의 목적어가 와야 하지만 없다는 점, 문맥상 그것(it)은 '제거되는' 것이므로 목적보어로 수동의 의미를 지닌 과거분사 removed로 바꿔야 한다.

| 오답해설 | ① 12% assignment는 가산명사이므로 복수형으로 쓸 수 있고 동사도 수일치가 올바르게 이루어졌다. turn in은 '제출하다'의 의미를 지닌 타동사구로, 과제들은 '제출되는' 것이므로 수동 부정사로 올바르게 표현되었다.
② 17% 'A하자마자 B했다'의 관용 표현으로 부정어구인 Hardly에 이어 과거완료시제에 대한 의문문의 어순으로 도치가 올바르게 이루어졌다. when에 이어진 절의 동사 began은 to부정사와 동명사 모두 목적어로 취할 수 있으며 과거시제로 올바르게 표현되었다. 'Scarcely~before', 'No sooner~than'과 바꿔 쓸 수 있다.
③ 15% 주절의 동사가 '권유'의 동사(recommended)이므로 종속절의 동사는 시제와 상관없이 'should + 동사원형'이 와야 한다. should는 생략이 가능하므로 동사원형 buy가 온 올바른 문장이다.

어휘
assignment 과제, 숙제; 할당　　turn in 제출하다
hardly A when B A하자마자 B하다　stock 주식
immediately 즉시, 곧　　　　　stick 찌르다
remove 제거하다, 없애다

오답률 TOP 1
7 문법 > 연결사 > 전치사 | 오답률 84% | 답 ②

| 정답해설 | ② 16% 문맥상 '완료'의 의미가 있는 절에 이어 '~까지'의 표현을 쓸 때는 by를 활용해서 써야 하며, '지속, 유지'의 의미가 있는 절에 이어질 때는 until을 써야 한다. finish를 통해 '완료'의 의미로 볼 수 있으므로 until을 by로 바꿔야 한다.

| 오답해설 | ① 25% 배수사를 활용한 비교구문으로 '배수사 as 원급 as'로 올바르게 표현했고, 비교대상 병치의 원칙에 따라 '그의 고양이'로 his cat을 대신할 수 있는 소유대명사인 his를 올바르게 썼다.
③ 44% '한 번 걸러'의 표현은 'every other + 단수명사'이므로 '이틀에 한 번'의 every other day로 올바르게 표현되었다.
④ 15% '~하는 편이 낫다'의 표현으로 '조동사 had better + 동사원형'이 적절하게 왔고, 조건절을 이끄는 접속사로 in case (that)가 올바르게 왔다.

어휘
every other 한 번 걸러　　　　had better + R ~하는 편이 낫다
in case (that) ~인 경우를 대비하여, ~라면

8 독해 > 세부내용 찾기 > 내용 불일치 찾기 | 오답률 25% | 답 ④

| 해석 | 여러분은 콜린은 충분히 섭취하고 있는가? 아마도 이 영양소는 당신의 레이더에도 잡히지 않을 것이다. 이제 콜린이 마땅히 받아야 할 관심을 받을 때이다. 최근의 한 연구에 따르면, 기가 막히게도 미국인의 90%가 콜린을 충분히 섭취하지 못하고 있다. 콜린은 모든 연령과 단계에서 건강에 필수적이며 특히 뇌 발달에 중요하다. 왜 우리는 충분히 얻지 않고 있는가? 콜린은 많은 다양한 음식들에서 발견되지만 적은 양으로 발견된다. 게다가, 콜린이 풍부한 음식들이 가장 인기 있는 음식은 아니다. 간, 달걀노른자, 리마콩을 생각해보라. 최근 미국에서 콜린 섭취량을 분석한 Taylor Wallace는 "우리 정부가 90년대 후반 이후로, 콜린에 대한 데이터를 검토하거나 정책을 수립하지 않았기 때문에 의료 전문가들 사이에서도 콜린에 대한 인식이 충분하지 않다."고 말한다.
① 대다수의 미국인들은 충분한 콜린을 섭취하지 못하고 있다.

② 콜린은 뇌 발달에 필요한 필수 영양소이다.

③ 간과 리마콩과 같은 음식들이 콜린의 좋은 공급원이다.

④ 콜린의 중요성은 미국에서 90년대 후반부터 강조되어 왔다.

| **정답해설** | ④ 75% 마지막 문장에서 90년대 후반 이후로 콜린에 대한 데이터를 검토하거나 정책을 수립하지 않았다고 했으므로 90년대 후반부터 콜린의 중요성이 강조되었다고 언급한 ④는 일치하지 않는 내용이다.

| **오답해설** | ① 5% 네 번째 문장인 A shocking 90 percent of Americans aren't getting enough choline, according to a recent study.로 보아 대다수의 미국인들이 충분한 콜린을 섭취하지 못하고 있음을 알 수 있다.

② 5% Choline is essential ~ and is especially critical for brain development.로 보아 콜린이 뇌 발달에 필수 영양소임을 알 수 있다.

③ 15% Plus, the foods that are rich in choline ~: think liver, egg yolks and lima beans.로 보아 간과 리마콩 등이 콜린이 풍부한 식품임을 알 수 있다.

어휘

choline [생화학] 콜린: 동식물의 레시틴 속에 있는 비타민 B 복합체

deserve (보수·도움·벌 등을) 받을 만하다

essential 필수적인; 본질적인

critical 중요한; 결정적인; 비판적인   egg yolk 달걀 노른자위

lima bean 리마콩   analysis 분석

intake 섭취

9　독해 > 세부내용 찾기 > 내용 일치 찾기　오답률 23%　답 ④

| **해석** | 일설에 따르면, 약 1700년경에 2,000개가 넘는 런던 커피 하우스가 있었고, 다른 어떤 업종보다 더 많은 건물을 차지하고 더 많은 임대료를 지불했다. 런던 커피하우스들은 페니 대학(penny universities)으로 알려지게 되었는데, 그 가격으로 커피 한 잔을 사서 특별한 대화를 들으며 여러 시간 동안 앉아있을 수 있었기 때문이다. 각 커피하우스는 다른 유형의 고객들을 전문으로 했다. 한 곳에서는 의사들과 상담할 수 있었다. 다른 곳들은 개신교도, 청교도, 카톨릭교도, 유대인, 지식인, 상인, 무역상, 휘그당원, 토리당원, 육군 장교, 배우, 변호사 혹은 성직자의 주문을 받았다. 커피하우스는 영국 최초의 평등주의적인 만남의 장소를 제공했는데, 이곳에서 한 남자는 알던 모르던 자신의 테이블 동료들과 수다를 떨었다.

① 커피 하우스의 수는 다른 어떤 사업체들의 수보다 적었다.

② 고객들은 커피 하우스에서 1시간 이상 머무를 수 없었다.

③ 종교인들은 대화를 하기 위해 커피 하우스에 모이지 않았다.

④ 사람들은 커피 하우스에서 모르는 테이블 동료들과 대화를 나눌 수 있었다.

| **정답해설** | ④ 77% 마지막 문장의 whether he knew them or not과 선지의 with unknown tablemates가 비슷한 표현으로 일치하는 문장이다.

| **오답해설** | ① 6% 첫 번째 줄에서 어느 업종보다 많은 건물을 차지하고 임대료를 지불했다고 했으므로 일치하지 않는 내용이다.

② 8% 본문의 for hours(여러 시간)로 보아 한 시간 이상 머물 수 있음을 알 수 있으므로 일치하지 않는 내용이다.

③ 9% 여러 종교를 믿는 사람들(Protestants~Jews)이 커피하우스에 드나들었다고 했으므로 내용과 일치하지 않는다.

어휘

by some accounts 일설에 따르면, 추정에 따르면

occupy 점령하다, 차지하다　　premises 양도 재산, 부동산, 토지

purchase 구매하다　　extraordinary 비범한, 특별한

specialize in ~을 전문으로 하다　clientele 고객, 단골; 의뢰인

physician 의사　　consult 상의[상담]하다

Protestant 프로테스탄트, 신교도　Puritan 청교도

Jew 유대인, 이스라엘인　　literati 지식인들, 학자들, 지식 계급

Whig 휘그당원　　Tory 토리당원

clergy 성직자들　　egalitarian 평등주의의; 평등주의자

오답률 TOP 2

10　생활영어 > 회화　오답률 51%　답 ①

| **해석** | A: 어제 약국에서 이 새로운 피부크림을 샀어. 이게 모든 주름을 없애고 너의 피부를 훨씬 더 젊어 보이게 할 거야.

B: ① 나는 안 살 거야.

A: 왜 그걸 믿지 않는 거야? 이 크림이 정말 효과가 있다고 몇몇 블로그에서 읽었어.

B: 그 크림이 피부에 좋다고 생각하지만, 크림을 사용해서 주름을 없애거나 마법처럼 더 젊어 보이는 것이 가능하다고 난 생각하지 않거든.

A: 넌 너무 비관적이야.

B: 아니, 난 그냥 현실적인 거지. 나는 네가 속고 있는 거라 생각해.

① 나는 안 살 거야.

② 너무 비싸다.

③ 나는 너를 도울 수 없어.

④ 믿거나 말거나, 그것은 사실이야.

| **정답해설** | ① 49% A가 구입한 피부크림에 대해 장점을 언급하고, B가 무언가 말한 후에 A가 자신이 말한 걸 왜 믿지 않느냐고 물어본 것으로 보아 B는 피부크림 효능과 관련한 부정적인 대답을 했음을 알 수 있다. 따라서 가격에 대해 언급한 ②나, 맥락상 적절하지 않은 ③과 ④는 정답이 아니므로 ①이 정답으로 가장 적절하다.

어휘

remove 제거하다, 없애다　　get rid of ~을 제거하다, 삭제하다

pessimistic 비관적인, 염세적인　gullible 속기 쉬운, 아둔한

11　생활영어 > 회화　오답률 40%　답 ②

| **해석** | A: 시내 관광을 하고 싶은데 어디로 가면 좋을까요?

B: 국립 미술관을 방문할 것을 강력히 제안해요.

A: 오, 그거 좋은 생각이네요. 그밖에 제가 무엇을 알아봐야 할까요?

B: ② 리버 파크로 가는 안내 여행이에요. 오후 내내 걸려요.

A: 그럴 시간은 없어요. 3시에 고객을 만나야 해서요.

B: 오, 알겠어요. 그러면 국립공원을 방문하는 건 어때요?

A: 좋은 생각이네요. 고마워요.

① 이것이 당신의 고객이 필요로 하는 지도입니다. 여기 있어요.

② 리버 파크로 가는 안내 여행이에요. 오후 내내 걸려요.

③ 가능한 한 빨리 확인해야 합니다.

④ 체크아웃 시간은 3시입니다.

| **정답해설** | ② 60% 미술관 방문을 권유받은 후 무엇을 더 알아봐야 할지 묻는 질문에 이어지는 대답을 찾는 문제이다. 빈칸에 이어 그럴 만한 시간이 없다고 말했으므로 관광과 시간에 대한 내용이 언급된 ②가 가장 적절하다.

어휘

client 고객, 손님

why don't you + 동사원형~? ~하는 것은 어때요?

12 생활영어 > 회화 [오답률 28%] 답 ③

| **해석** | ① A: 그가 마침내 히트 영화에 출연했어요!

B: 음, 그가 해냈네요.

② A: 지금 약간 피곤하네요.

　 B: 오늘은 여기까지만 해요.

③ A: 아이들이 생일 파티에 갈 거예요.

　 B: 따라서 그것은 식은 죽 먹기예요.

④ A: 그가 어제 왜 집에 일찍 갔는지 궁금해요.

　 B: 나는 그가 몸이 안 좋았다고 생각해요.

| **정답해설** | ③ [72%] 아이들이 생일 파티에 갈 거라고 말한 후에 이를 '쉽다'고 대답하고 있으므로 자연스럽지 않은 대화이다. a piece of cake은 '식은 죽 먹기, 누워서 떡 먹기'의 의미로 쉬운 일을 언급할 때 쓰는 표현이다.

어휘

call it a day 일과를 끝내다, 그만 하자고 말하다

a piece of cake 누워서 떡 먹기, 식은 죽 먹기

under the weather (몸이) 찌뿌드드한; 불쾌한

13 독해 > 대의 파악 > 제목 찾기 [오답률 30%] 답 ③

| **해석** | 사랑받는 느낌과 그것이 자극하는 생물학적 반응은 비언어적 신호, 즉 목소리의 어조, 얼굴 표정, 혹은 바르게 느껴지는 접촉에 의해 유발된다. 말이 아닌 비언어적 신호는 우리가 함께하는 사람이 우리에게 관심을 갖고, 이해하고, 존중한다고 우리에게 느끼게 한다. 우리가 그들과 함께 있을 때, 우리는 안전하다고 느낀다. 우리는 심지어 야생에서 비언어적 신호의 힘을 보기도 한다. 포식자의 추격을 피한 후, 동물들은 종종 스트레스 해소의 수단으로 서로를 킁킁거리며 문댄다. 이 신체 접촉은 안전의 안도감을 제공하고 스트레스를 완화시킨다.

① 야생 동물들은 어떻게 생각하고 느끼는가?

② 효과적으로 의사소통하는 것이 성공의 비결이다

③ 비언어적 소통이 말보다 더 중요하다

④ 언어적 단서: 감정 표현을 위한 기본 도구

| **정답해설** | ③ [70%] 핵심어는 비언어적인 신호(nonverbal cues)로, 말(spoken words)과 비교해 비언어적인 신호들이 하는 일과 힘에 대해 서술하고 있다. 비언어적인 신호에 대한 사례로 함께 하는 사람들의 비언어적인 신호와 야생의 동물들에게서 볼 수 있는 비언어적인 신호를 들어 사례를 설명하는 글이다. 따라서 글의 제목으로 가장 적절한 것은 ③이다.

어휘

stimulate 자극[격려]하다　　　　trigger 촉발하다, 유발하다

cue 단서, 신호　　　　　　　　　evade 피하다

chase 추적, 추격　　　　　　　　predator 포식자, 약탈자

muzzle ~에 코를 킁킁거리다; 재갈을 물리다; 억압하다

relief 안도, 완화　　　　　　　　reassurance 안심시키는 것[일]

relieve 완화시키다; 안심시키다

14 독해 > 대의 파악 > 주제 찾기 [오답률 30%] 답 ①

| **해석** | 명절이나 생일처럼, 자녀의 삶에 장난감과 선물이 쌓일 때가 있다. 당신은 이 시간을 이용해 사물에 대한 건전한 비의존성을 가르칠 수 있다. 장난감으로 자녀 주변을 둘러싸지 마라. 대신, 장난감을 바구니들에 정리하고, 한 번에 하나의 바구니를 꺼내고, 때때로 바구니들을 교대로 이용하라. 만약 소중한 물건이 잠시 치워진다면, 그것을 꺼내는 것은 즐거운 기억과 예상의 생생함을 만든다. 자녀가 잠시 동안 치워진 장난감을 요구한다고 가정해 보자. 당신은 한 물건에 대한 관심과 그 상황 속에 있는 경험을 이끌 수 있다. 만약 당신이 소유물을 잃어버리거나 망가뜨린다면, 당신의 자녀가 애착을 갖지 않는 태도를 발전시킬 수 있도록 좋은 태도("나는 그것을 가지고 있는 동안 감사했어!")의 모형을 만들고자 노력하라. 만약 그녀의 장난감 중 하나가 망가졌거나 분실되었다면, 자녀가 "나는 그것으로 재미있었어."라고 말하도록 도와라.

① 소유물에 대한 건전한 태도 형성

② 다른 사람들과 장난감을 공유하는 것의 가치를 배우기

③ 장난감을 질서 있는 방식으로 정돈하는 법을 가르치기

④ 바람직하지 않은 방식으로 행동하는 것에 대한 책임을 받아들이기

| **정답해설** | ① [70%] 두 번째 문장의 teach a healthy nondependency on things가 핵심 내용으로 이어서 명령문과 예시 등을 통해 구체적인 지침을 전달하고 있으므로, 주제로 가장 적절한 것은 ①이다. 본문의 healthy nondependency와 things를 정답에서 각각, healthy attitude와 possessions로 바꿔서 표현했다.

어휘

accumulate 축적하다, 모으다　　　nondependency 비의존성

arrange 정리하다; 배열하다　　　　rotate 순환시키다; 회전시키다

occasionally 가끔, 때때로　　　　　cherish 소중하게 여기다

outlook 전망; 견해, 시야　　　　　put away 치우다, 버리다

appreciate 감사하다; 인정하다; 이해하다

nonattachment 무집착

15 독해 > 대의 파악 > 요지·주장 찾기 [오답률 46%] 답 ②

| **해석** | 자녀의 자존감을 세우는 방법은 자녀들이 일을 얼마나 잘하는지 말해 주는 것이라는 '자존감 운동'에 의해 많은 부모들이 잘못 인도되어 왔다. 불행히도, 자녀에게 자신의 능력을 납득시키려고 노력하는 것은 실패할 가능성이 높은데, 인생은 성공과 실패를 통해 자신이 실제로 얼마나 유능하거나 무능력한지를 분명히 그들에게 말할 수 있는 방법이 있기 때문이다. 연구에 따르면 자녀를 칭찬하는 방법은 자녀의 발달에 강력한 영향을 미친다. 일부 연구원들은 자신의 노력에 비해 지능으로 칭찬을 받은 자녀들이 결과에 지나치게 집중하게 된다는 사실을 발견했다. 실패 후, 이 동일한 자녀들은 덜 지속적이었고, 즐거움을 덜 보였고, 실패를 능력 부족의 탓으로 돌렸으며, 미래에 성취하겠다는 노력도 제대로 수행하지 못했다. 지능에 대해 자녀들을 칭찬하는 것은 그들이 어려움을 두려워하게 만들었는데, 그들이 실패를 어리석음과 동일시하기 시작했기 때문이었다.

① 잦은 칭찬은 자녀들의 자존감을 높여 준다.

② 지능에 대한 칭찬은 부정적인 영향을 가져온다.

③ 자녀는 성공을 통해 실패에 대한 두려움을 극복해야 한다.

④ 부모는 과정보다는 결과에 집중해야 한다.

| **정답해설** | ② [54%] 핵심어는 자녀의 대한 자존감(self-esteem)으로, 부모들이 이를 잘못 인식해 왔다고 한 후, 칭찬의 방법이 자녀들에게 강한 영향을 미친다고 언급했다. 특별히 지능에 대한 칭찬은 자녀들이 결과에 과도하게 집중하게 한다고 하면서 부정적인 결과에 대해 서술했으므로 요지로 가장 적절한 것은 ②이다.

어휘

self-esteem 자존감, 자부심
convince A of B A에게 B를 납득[확신]시키다
competence 능력, 역량　　　　　unequivocally 명확하게
persist 지속하다; 고집하다
attribute A to B A를 B의 탓으로 돌리다
equate 동일시하다; 평균화하다　　stupidity 어리석음, 우둔함
compliment 찬사, 칭찬하는 말　　bring about 가져오다, 초래하다

16	독해 > 빈칸의 내용 추론하기 > 빈칸 어휘 추론
	오답률 43%　　답 ②

| 해석 | 최근 몇 년간 온라인 마케팅과 소셜 미디어 공유의 인기가 높아지면서 글로벌 브랜드에 대한 광고 표준화의 필요성이 높아졌다. 대부분의 대형 마케팅 및 광고 캠페인은 대규모의 온라인 활동을 포함한다. (인터넷으로) 접속하는 소비자들은 이제 인터넷과 소셜 미디어를 통해 국경을 쉽게 넘을 수 있게 되었고, 이는 광고주들이 통제 가능하고 질서정연한 방식으로 각색된 캠페인을 전개하는 것을 어렵게 만든다. 결과적으로, 대부분의 글로벌 소비자 브랜드들은 디지털 사이트를 국제적으로 관장한다. 예를 들어, 호주와 아르헨티나로부터 프랑스, 루마니아, 러시아에 이르기까지 전 세계의 코카콜라 웹사이트와 소셜 미디어 사이트는 놀라울 정도로 ② 획일적이다. 모두 친숙한 코카콜라의 붉은색, 상징적인 콜라병 모양, 코카콜라의 음악과 "Taste the Feeling" 테마를 특징으로 한다.

① 실험적인　　　　　　② 획일적인
③ 국소적인　　　　　　④ 다양한

| 정답해설 | ② ⌈57%⌉ 빈칸이 포함된 문장의 앞에서 as a result에 이어 글로벌 소비자 브랜드들이 디지털 사이트를 국제적으로 관장한다고 했고, 빈칸에 이어진 문장에서 전 세계적으로 코카콜라의 브랜드가 공유하는 특징들을 서술하고 있으므로 빈칸에 들어갈 말로 ②가 가장 적절하다.

어휘

boost 활성화하다; 늘리다　　　　zip 활기를 주다
roll out ~을 다량으로 만들어 내다　adapt 각색하다, 바꾸다; 적응하다
coordinate 관장하다; 조정하다

17	독해 > 글의 일관성 파악하기 > 글의 흐름과 무관한 문장
	오답률 23%　　답 ③

| 해석 | 5,000명의 미국인 근로자들과 500명의 미국 고용주들에 대한 월간 설문 조사에서, 하이브리드 워크(시간과 공간이라는 두 가지 요소에 대해 제약 없이 자유롭게 선택하여 탄력적으로 일하는 것)로의 거대한 전환은 사무직 및 지식 근로자에게 있어 매우 뚜렷하다. 새로운 기준은 사무실에서 일주일에 3일, 집에서 2일이며, 현장에서의 근무일수를 30% 이상 단축한다. 당신은 이 감축이 사무실 공간에 대한 수요를 크게 감소시킬 것이라고 생각할지도 모른다. 그러나 우리의 조사 자료는 사무실 공간의 평균 1%에서 2%의 감소를 시사하며, 이는 공간이 아닌 조밀도의 큰 감소를 의미한다. 우리는 그 이유를 이해할 수 있다. 사무실의 높은 조밀도는 불편하고 많은 근로자들은 책상 주변의 혼잡을 싫어한다. ③ 대부분의 직원들은 월요일과 금요일에 집에서 근무하기를 원한다. 조밀도에 대한 불편함은 로비, 주방, 특히 엘리베이터까지 확대된다. 조밀도를 줄이는 유일한 확실한 방법은 그만큼의 면적을 줄이지 않고 건물 내에서의 근무일을 줄이는 것이다. 우리의 조사 증거에 따르면 조밀도에 대한 불편함이 일반화되었다.

| 정답해설 | ③ ⌈77%⌉ 흐름상 어색한 문장 찾기 유형의 해법은 ①번 이전까지 제시된 문장을 통해 핵심어와 첫 번째 맥락을 찾는 것이

다. 하이브리드 워크로의 전환이 이루어졌다고 한 후에 이에 대한 구체적인 설명이 ①번 문장에서 이어졌고, ①번 문장의 내용을 상술한 문장이 ②번 문장이다. 이런 유형의 문제에서 문장의 주어의 전환이 이루어진 경우 그 문장이 정답인 경우가 많은데, ③번 문장의 주어는 most employees로 지문 전체의 핵심인 하이브리드 워크와 무관함을 알 수 있다. 내용 또한 공간의 조밀도와 무관하게 원하는 재택 근무요일에 대해 언급하고 있으므로 흐름상 어색한 문장은 ③이다.

어휘

abundantly 풍부하게, 많이; 매우　　emerging 신흥의, 떠오르는
norm 규범, 기준, 표준　　　　　　imply 암시하다, 함축하다
reduction 감소, 감축　　　　　　density 조밀도, 밀도
discomfort 불안, 불편　　　　　　footage 피트 수, 전체 길이
be here to stay 일상생활에 융합되다, 자리가 잡히다

18	독해 > 글의 일관성 파악하기 > 주어진 문장의 삽입
	오답률 37%　　답 ③

| 해석 | 이민 개혁은 정치적 지뢰밭이다. 광범위한 정치적 지원을 강요하는 거의 유일한 측면의 이민 정책은 불법 이민자의 유입을 제한하기 위해 멕시코와의 미국 국경을 지키겠다는 결의이다. 텍사스 보안관들은 최근 국경에서 감시하는 것을 돕기 위해 새로운 인터넷 사용법을 개발했다. ③ 그들은 불법 교차점으로 알려진 장소에 비디오카메라를 설치하고 카메라의 비디오 내용을 웹사이트에 실시간으로 올렸다. 국경 감시를 돕고 싶은 시민들은 온라인에 접속해 '가상 텍사스 보안관 부관' 역할을 할 수 있다. 만약 그들이 국경을 넘으려는 사람을 보면, 보안관실로 보고를 하는데, 이 보고는 때로는 미국 국경 순찰대의 도움을 받아 후속 조치가 취해진다.

| 정답해설 | ③ ⌈63%⌉ 주어진 문장의 삽입 유형은 먼저 제시된 문장에서 단서를 찾아야 한다. 주어진 문장의 They가 지칭하는 복수명사가 누구인지를 찾아야 하고, 내용을 통해 비디오카메라를 설치해야 하는 대상이 누구인지도 살펴봐야 한다. They로 받을 수 있는 대상에 대한 최초 언급은 ②에 이어진 문장의 주어인 Texas sheriffs이고 이들이 새로운 인터넷 사용법을 개발했다고 했으므로 제시된 문장의 내용이 이어져야 함을 알 수 있다. 따라서 정답은 ③이다.

어휘

immigration reform 이민 개혁
minefield 지뢰 부설 지역; (비유) 보이지 않는 위험이 많은 장소
resolve 결의, 결심　　　　　　secure 확보하다; 보호하다
illegal 불법적인, 위법인　　　　install 설치하다
crossing 교차점　　　　　　　virtual 가상의; 실질적인
deputy (보안관의) 부관

19	독해 > 글의 일관성 파악하기 > 글의 순서　오답률 27%　답 ③

| 해석 | 모든 문명은 정부 행정에 의존한다. 아마도 고대 로마만큼 이것을 잘 보여 주는 문명은 없을 것이다.
(B) 사실 '문명'이라는 단어 자체는 '시민'을 뜻하는 라틴어 civis에서 유래했다.
(C) 라틴어는 고대 로마의 언어였는데, 고대 로마의 영토는 지중해 분지에서 북쪽의 영국 일부와 동쪽의 흑해까지 뻗어 있었다.
(A) 그렇게 큰 지역을 통치하기 위해서, 현재 이탈리아 중부에 기반을 둔 로마인들은 효과적인 정부 행정 시스템을 필요로 했다.

| **정답해설** | ③ [73%] 주어진 문장에서 모든 문명이 정부 행정에 의존한다고 언급한 후 고대 로마의 사례를 들었다. 따라서 '문명'에 대한 기원을 서술한 (B)가 온 후, (B)에서 언급한 라틴어가 고대 로마의 언어임을 설명한 (C)가 온 후, (C)에서 고대 로마의 넓은 영토에 대한 내용을 an area that large로 받은 (A)가 이어지는 것이 자연스러우므로 정답은 ③이다.

어휘

civilization 문명   administration 행정, 정부; 경영
exemplify ～을 예증[실증]하다; ～의 예가 되다
territory 영토, 영역
stretch from A to B A로부터 B에 뻗어 있다, 달하다
rule 통치하다

---

20   독해 > 빈칸의 내용 추론하기 > 빈칸 어구 추론
               오답률 48%   답 ①

| **해석** | 지난 50년 동안, 심리학의 모든 주요 하위 학문 분야는 교육이 점점 전문화되고 초점이 좁아짐에 따라 점점 더 서로 고립되어 왔다. 일부 심리학자들이 오랫동안 주장해 온 것처럼, 심리학 분야가 과학적으로 성숙하고 발전하려면 다른 부분들(예를 들면, 신경 과학, 발달, 인지, 성격 및 사회)이 다시 전체적이고 통합되어야 한다. 과학은 이론적 구조를 단순화하여 별개의 주제가 이론적으로 그리고 경험적으로 통합될 때 발전한다. 과학 심리학은 다양한 하위 영역의 심리학자들 사이의 협력을 장려하여 그 분야가 지속적인 분열보다는 조화를 이루도록 도울 것이다. 이런 식으로, 과학 심리학은 한 학문분야 하의 모든 주요한 분파/파벌을 그 분야 내에서 통합함으로써 전체적으로 심리학의 모형으로 작용할 수 있다. 과학 심리학이 ① 통일된 관점에서 자원을 결합하고 과학을 연구하는 방법에 대한 모학문(parent discipline)에 대한 모델이 될 수 있다면 그것은 결코 작은 위업이 아니며 전혀 중요도가 적지 않다(매우 중요하다).

① 통일된 관점에서   ② 역동적인 측면에서
③ 역사를 통해   ④ 정확한 증거로

| **정답해설** | ① [52%] 첫 번째 문장과 두 번째 문장을 통해 하위 학문 분야가 통합되어야 함을 강조하고 있다. 특히 심리학 분야가 과학적으로 성숙하려면 다른 부분들이 통합되어야 하고, 이때 과학은 별개의 주제가 통합될 때 발전한다고 서술하고 있으므로 빈칸에는 관련 표현인 unified가 언급된 ①이 가장 적절하다.

어휘

subdiscipline 학문 분야의 하위 구분
isolated 분리[격리]된; 고립된   disparate 다른, 이종의
cognitive 인식의, 인지의   integrate 통합하다
empirically 경험에 의거하여, 실증적으로
collaboration 협력, 협업   coherence 일관성, 일치, 조화
fragmentation 분열, 붕괴   template 모형, 원형; 형판
fraction 파편; 분수   faction 당파, 파벌

2022

4월 2일 시행
국가직 9급 (㉮책형)

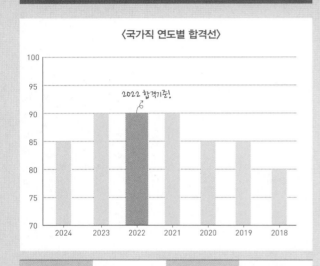

합격예상 체크

〈국가직 연도별 합격선〉

2022 합격기준

맞힌 개수	/20문항	점수	/100점

➡ ☐ 합격 ☐ 불합격

취약영역 체크

문항	정답	영역	문항	정답	영역
1	①	어휘 > 동의어	11	④	생활영어 > 회화
2	②	어휘 > 동의어	12	③	생활영어 > 회화
3	④	어휘 > 동의어	13	②	문법 > 형용사·부사·비교
4	②	어휘 > 빈칸	14	④	문법 > 준동사
5	①	어휘 > 빈칸	15	②	독해 > 빈칸의 내용 추론하기
6	①	문법 > 동사의 형태	16	②	독해 > 빈칸의 내용 추론하기
7	④	독해 > 세부내용 찾기	17	③	독해 > 대의 파악
8	②	문법 > 명사와 일치	18	④	독해 > 글의 일관성 파악하기
9	①	독해 > 대의 파악	19	①	독해 > 대의 파악
10	③	독해 > 글의 일관성 파악하기	20	③	독해 > 글의 일관성 파악하기

⬇ 영역별 틀린 개수로 취약영역을 확인하세요!

어휘	/5	문법	/4	독해	/9	생활영어	/2

➡ 나의 취약영역: _____

※ [정답해설]과 [오답해설] 선지의 50% 표시는 〈에듀윌 합격예측 풀서비스〉를 통해 수집된 선지 선택률을 나타냅니다.

---

1 어휘 > 동의어 오답률 19% 답 ①

| 해석 | 수년간 형사들은 쌍둥이 형제의 갑작스러운 실종에 대한 수수께끼를 풀려고 노력해 왔다.
① 81% 해결하다
② 4% 만들다; 창조하다
③ 9% 모방하다
④ 6% 공표하다; 광고[선전]하다

| 정답해설 | ① 주어인 형사(detectives)가 갑작스러운 실종의 미스터리를 어떻게 할 것인가를 생각하면 정답을 유추할 수 있다. 수수께끼를 '해결'하는 것이 형사의 일이므로 동의어로 ①이 가장 적절하다.

어휘

detective 형사, 탐정, 수사관
sudden 갑작스러운
unravel 해결하다; (실 등을) 풀다
disappearance 실종; 소멸, 소실

---

2 어휘 > 동의어 오답률 29% 답 ②

| 해석 | 그 부부가 부모 노릇을 경험하기도 전, 침실 네 개가 딸린 그들의 집은 불필요하게 호화로워 보였다.
① 5% 숨겨진
② 71% 호화로운, 사치스러운
③ 20% 빈, 비어 있는
④ 4% 단단한; 고체의

| 정답해설 | ② 자녀가 생기기 전에 4개의 침실이 딸린 집은 다소 '호화로워' 보일 수 있음을 유추할 수 있고, 나머지 선지의 어휘들은 맥락상 적절하지 않다. 따라서 동의어로 ②가 가장 적절하다.

어휘

opulent 호화로운; 부유한; 풍부한   parenthood 어버이의 입장[신분]

---

3 어휘 > 동의어 오답률 28% 답 ④

| 해석 | 사장은 우리가 그렇게 짧은 기간에 이미 전체 예산을 쓴 것을 보고 화를 냈다.
① 6% 매우 만족했다
② 17% 매우 놀랐다
③ 5% 극도로 차분해졌다
④ 72% 극도로 화가 났다

| 정답해설 | ④ 짧은 기간 동안 전체 예산을 쓴 것에 대한 사장의 반응을 생각해 보면, 대단히 화가 났음에 틀림없다. hit the roof는 분노가 천장을 뚫고 나오는 이미지를 연상시키므로 동의어로 ④가 가장 적절하다. hit the ceiling도 동일한 표현이다.

어휘

hit the roof(ceiling) 화가 치밀다, 발끈 화를 내다
entire 전체[전부]의   budget 예산, 재정

---

4 어휘 > 빈칸 오답률 48% 답 ②

| 해석 | 마우스 포테이토는 텔레비전의 카우치 포테이토와 ② 동일한 것이다: 그들은 카우치 포테이토가 텔레비전 앞에서 하는 것과 거의 같은 방식으로 컴퓨터 앞에서 많은 여가 시간을 보내는 경향이 있는 사람이다.
① 12% 기술자; 전문가
② 52% 동등한 것, 등가물
③ 13% 네트워크, 조직
④ 23% 모의실험; 가장, 겉치레

| 정답해설 | ② 마우스 포테이토와 카우치 포테이토를 비교한 글이다. 부연 설명에서 컴퓨터와 텔레비전이라는 대상만 다를 뿐 그 앞에서 많은 여가 시간을 보낸다는 점에서 동일하다는 것을 알 수 있

으므로 빈칸에 들어갈 표현으로 '등가물'의 의미인 ②가 정답으로 가장 적절하다.

어휘

mouse potato 인터넷에 중독된 사람, 컴퓨터광
couch potato 소파에 앉아 TV만 보며 많은 시간을 보내는 사람
tend to + R ~하는 경향이 있다   a (great) deal of 다량의(= much)

| **5** | 어휘 > 빈칸 | 오답률 48% | 답 ① |

| **해석** | 메리는 남아메리카에 가기 전에 스페인어를 ① 복습하기로 결심했다.
① 52% 복습하다
② 12% 끝까지 듣다; 듣고 분간하다
③ 26% 변호하다, 변명하다; 지지하다
④ 10% 해고하다

| **정답해설** | ① 남아메리카를 가기 전에 스페인어로 '무엇'을 해야 할지를 생각해 보면, 그것을 배우거나 복습하는 등의 표현이 빈칸에 들어가야 함을 알 수 있다. '배우다'의 표현이 없으므로 '(잊혀져 가는 것을) 복습하다'의 표현인 ①이 정답으로 가장 적절하다.

어휘

decide to + R ~하겠다고 결심하다

오답률 TOP 1

| **6** | 문법 > 동사의 형태 > 수동태 | 오답률 67% | 답 ① |

| **해석** | ① 말은 개별적인 필요와 일의 성격에 따라 먹여야 한다.
② 좁은 길을 걷는 동안에 내 모자가 바람에 날아가 버렸다.
③ 그녀는 일을 하는 내내 주로 정치 풍자 만화가로 알려져 왔다.
④ 어린 아이들조차도 일을 잘했다는 칭찬을 받는 것을 좋아한다.

| **정답해설** | ① 33% feed는 타동사이므로 수동태인 be fed에 이어 목적어가 없으므로 구조와 문맥상 올바른 구조이다. a horse를 대명사로 받을 때 단수인 its로 적절하게 일치시켰다.

| **오답해설** | ② 32% 접속사 while에 이어진 현재분사 walking의 주체는 주절의 주어인 my hat과 일치하지 않으므로, while I was walking~으로 바꿔야 한다.
③ 22% 능동태 동사 has known에 이어 목적어가 없고 문맥상 '정치 풍자 만화가로서 알려진' 것이므로 수동태 동사 has been known으로 바꿔야 한다.
④ 13% 과거분사 done을 수식하기 위해 형용사 good이 아닌 부사인 well로 바꿔야 한다.

어휘

according to ~에 따라   nature 성격, 본질; 자연
narrow 좁은   political cartoonist 정치 풍자 만화가
compliment 칭찬하다

| **7** | 독해 > 세부내용 찾기 > 내용 불일치 찾기 | 오답률 19% | 답 ④ |

| **해석** | 움베르토 에코는 이탈리아의 소설가이자 문화 평론가, 그리고 철학자였다. 그는 소설에서 기호학을 성경적 분석, 중세 연구 및 문학 이론과 결합한 역사적 미스터리인 1980년 소설 '장미의 이름'으로 널리 알려져 있다. 그는 나중에 '푸코의 진자'와 '전날의 섬'을 포함한 다른 소설들을 썼다. 그는 또한 번역가였다: Raymond Queneau의 저서 'Exercices de style'을

이탈리아어로 번역했다. 그는 산마리노 공화국 대학교의 미디어학과 창립자였다. 그는 2016년 2월 19일 밤, 2년 동안 앓고 있던 췌장암으로 밀라노의 집에서 사망했다.
① '장미의 이름'은 역사 소설이다.
② 에코는 책을 이탈리아어로 번역했다.
③ 에코는 한 대학의 학과를 설립했다.
④ 에코는 암으로 병원에서 사망했다.

| **정답해설** | ④ 81% 마지막 문장의 He died at his Milanese home of pancreatic cancer~로 보아 밀라노에 있는 자신의 집에서 사망했으므로 ④가 일치하지 않는 문장이다.

| **오답해설** | ① 7% 두 번째 문장의 He is widely known for his 1980 novel *The Name of the Rose*, a historical mystery~와 일치하는 내용이다.
② 5% 네 번째 문장 Eco was also a translator: he translated Raymond Queneau's book *Exercices de style* into Italian.와 일치하는 내용이다.
③ 7% 다섯 번째 문장 He was the founder of the Department of Media Studies at the University of the Republic of San Marino.와 일치하는 내용이다.

어휘

be known for ~으로 알려져 있다   historical 역사의, 역사에 관한
semiotics 기호학; [의학] 증후학   pendulum 추, 진자
translator 번역가, 역자; 통역   founder 설립자, 창시자
pancreatic cancer 췌장암

| **8** | 문법 > 명사와 일치 > 일치 | 오답률 45% | 답 ② |

| **해석** | 좋은 출발점을 찾으려면 최초의 현대 전기 배터리가 개발된 1800년으로 돌아가야 한다. 이탈리아의 알레산드로 볼타는 은, 구리 및 아연의 결합이 전류를 생성하는 데 이상적이라는 것을 발견했다. Voltaic pile(전기 쟁반)이라고 불리는 개선된 설계는 바닷물에 적신 판지로 만든 얇은 판 사이에 이 금속들로 만든 얇은 판들을 쌓아서 만들었다. 볼타의 연구에 대한 이야기들로 인해 그는 나폴레옹 황제 앞에서 시연을 하도록 요청받았다.

| **정답해설** | ② 55% 주절의 동사 found의 목적어인 접속사 that이 이끄는 절의 동사이다. 주어는 a combination이므로 단수로 수일치시켜 was로 바꿔야 한다.

| **오답해설** | ① 23% 선행사 1800에 이어 전치사 during과 함께 쓰인 관계대명사로 '전치사 + which'에 이어 완전한 절이 올바르게 이어졌다.
③ 7% 주어인 명사 design을 서술하는 수동분사구문으로, 과거분사 called에 이어 명사 a Voltanic pile이 이어졌으므로 5형식 문장에서 파생된 분사구문임을 알 수 있다.
④ 15% 접속사 that이 이끄는 부사절과 호응하는 표현으로 전체적으로 '매우 ~해서 …하다'의 의미이다. such에 이어 명사 talk가 적절하게 이어졌다. such와 달리 so는 형용사 혹은 부사를 수식한다.

어휘

combination 조합, 결합   copper 구리
zinc 아연   electrical current 전류
enhanced 향상된, 개선된

Voltanic pile [전기] 예전 볼타(Volta) 전지(電池)에서 전류를 생성하는 금속판의 층[파일]

stack 쌓아올리다, 겹겹이 쌓다　　　　soak 흡수하다, 담그다

demonstration 시연; 증명; 시위

9　독해 > 대의 파악 > 제목 찾기　　오답률 51%　　답 ①

| 해석 | 레이저는 빛이 전자와 상호 작용하는 방식으로 인해 가능하다. 전자는 특정 원자 혹은 분자의 특징인 특정 에너지 준위 혹은 상태로 존재한다. 에너지 준위는 핵 주변에 있는 고리 혹은 궤도로 상상할 수 있다. 외륜 전자는 내륜 전자보다 높은 에너지 준위에 있다. 전자는 에너지 주입 즉, 예를 들어 섬광에 의해 더 높은 에너지 준위에 부딪힐 수 있다. 전자가 외부 준위에서 내부 준위로 떨어질 때 '과잉' 에너지가 빛으로 방출된다. 방출되는 빛의 파장이나 색은 방출되는 에너지의 양과 확실히 관련이 있다. 사용되는 특정한 레이저광선을 발하는 물질에 따라, 빛의 특정 파장이 흡수되어 (전자에 에너지를 공급하거나 자극시키기 위해) 특정 파장이 방출된다(전자가 초기 준위로 다시 떨어질 때).

① 레이저는 어떻게 만들어지는가?
② 레이저는 언제 발명되었는가?
③ 레이저는 어떤 전자를 방출하는가?
④ 전자는 왜 빛을 반사하는가?

| 정답해설 | ① 49% 첫 번째 문장에서 레이저가 가능한 이유로 빛이 전자와 상호 작용하는 방식을 언급한 후, 전자에 대해 상술하고 있다. 이에 대한 구체적인 과정을 서술하는 글이다. 전자가 외부 준위에서 내부 준위로 떨어질 때 '과잉' 에너지가 빛으로 방출되고, 결국 이 빛이 레이저가 되는 것임을 알 수 있으므로, 글의 제목으로 가장 적절한 것은 ①이다.

어휘
interact with ~와 상호 작용하다　　　electron [화학·물리] 전자
energy level [물리] 에너지 준위(準位); 활동 능력
atom [물리] 원자　　　molecule [화학·물리] 분자
nucleus [화학] 핵; [물리] 원자핵　　　bump up 부딪히다, 마주치다
injection 주입, 투입　　　give off 방출하다, 발산하다
wavelength [물리] 파장; 주파수　　　emit 내뿜다, 방출하다
release 방출하다; 발표하다; 해방하다
depending on ~에 따라　　　initial 처음의, 초기에

10　독해 > 글의 일관성 파악하기 > 글의 흐름과 무관한 문장　　오답률 25%　　답 ③

| 해석 | 용수권 시장은 인구 증가가 부족으로 이어지고 기후 변화가 가뭄과 기근을 야기함에 따라 발전할 가능성이 있다. 그러나 그 시장은 지역적이고 윤리적인 무역 관행에 기반할 것이며 대부분의 상품 무역과 다를 것이다. 비방하는 사람들은 물을 거래하는 것이 비윤리적이거나 심지어 인권 침해라고 주장하지만, 이미 용수권은 오만에서 호주에 이르는 전 세계의 건조한 지역에서 사고 팔린다. ③ 증류수를 마시는 것은 유익할 수 있지만, 특히 미네랄이 다른 공급원에 의해 보충되지 않는다면 모든 사람에게 최선의 선택은 아닐 수 있다. Ziad Abdelnour는 "우리는 물이 사실상 지금의 10년과 그 이후로 새로운 금으로 변할 것이라고 강력히 믿는다."고 말했다. "스마트 머니가 이런 방향으로 공격적으로 움직이는 것은 당연하다."

| 정답해설 | ③ 75% 지문 전체적으로 용수권 시장에 대한 설명이 이어지는데, ③의 문장의 주어는 '증류수'로 이어 증류수가 이익이 될 수 있지만 모든 사람들에게 최고의 선택이 아니라는 내용으로 흐름과 동떨어진 내용이 이어지고 있다. ④번 문장에서 금융전문가

가 한 말을 인용해 물이 새로운 금과 마찬가지이며 스마트 머니가 이 방향으로 가는 것이 당연하다며 용수권 거래에 대한 내용을 언급하고 있으므로 ②에 이어져야 함을 알 수 있다. 따라서 흐름상 어색한 문장은 ③이다.

어휘
water right (강·호수·관개용수의) 수리[용수]권
shortage 부족, 결핍　　　drought 가뭄; 고갈, 결핍
famine 기근, 굶주림　　　ethical 윤리적인, 도덕적인
commodity 상품
detractor 중상[비방]을 일삼는 사람, 험담꾼
breach 위반, 침해　　　arid 건조한; 불모의
distilled water 증류수　　　beneficial 유익한, 이익이 되는
supplement 보완하다, 채우다
smart money 스마트 머니, 고수익을 위해 장세의 변화에 따라 신속하게 움직이는 자금

11　생활영어 > 회화　　오답률 15%　　답 ④

| 해석 | A: 대학 구내식당이 메뉴를 바꿨다고 들었어.
B: 응, 막 확인했지.
A: 그리고 새로운 요식업체를 들였다던데.
B: 맞아, 샘스 케이터링이야.
A: ④ 저번 메뉴랑 뭐가 달라?
B: 디저트 선택이 더 많아. 그리고, 일부 샌드위치가 없어졌대.

① 가장 좋아하는 디저트가 뭐야
② 그들의 사무실이 어디에 있는지 알아
③ 메뉴에 내 도움이 필요해
④ 저번 메뉴와 무엇이 달라

| 정답해설 | ④ 85% 대학 구내식당의 요식업체가 바뀐 것에 대한 대화문으로 빈칸에 이어 구체적인 메뉴에 대한 내용이 이어지고 있으므로, 지난번 업체 메뉴와 무엇이 다른지를 묻는 ④가 가장 적절하다.

어휘
cafeteria 구내식당　　　caterer 요리 조달업체, 요식업자
remove 제거하다, 없애다

12　생활영어 > 회화　　오답률 8%　　답 ③

| 해석 | A: 안녕하세요. 무엇을 도와드릴까요?
B: 네, 스웨터를 찾고 있어요.
A: 저기, 이건 가을 컬렉션의 최신 스타일이에요. 어떠세요?
B: 멋지네요. 얼마죠?
A: 제가 가격을 확인해 볼게요. 120달러네요.
B: ③ 그것은 제가 생각하는 가격대를 조금 벗어나네요.
A: 그러면 이 스웨터는 어때요? 지난 시즌에 나온 건데, 50달러로 할인 판매 중이에요.
B: 좋네요! 한 번 입어볼게요.

① 저는 그것과 어울리는 바지 한 벌도 필요해요.
② 그 재킷은 저를 위한 완벽한 선물이네요.
③ 그것은 제가 생각하는 가격대를 조금 벗어나네요.
④ 토요일에는 저녁 7시까지 문을 엽니다.

| 정답해설 | ③ 92% 점원이 스웨터의 가격을 말한 후에 B의 대답에 이어 저렴한 다른 스웨터를 권하고 있는 것으로 보아 B가 가격이

생각보다 비싸다는 말을 했음을 유추할 수 있다. 따라서 정답은 ③이 가장 적절하다.

어휘

gorgeous (아주) 멋진
on sale 세일 중인, 할인 판매 중인
try on 입어 보다, 신어 보다
go with ~와 어울리다
price range 가격대, 가격 폭

오답률 TOP 2

13 문법 > 형용사 · 부사 · 비교 > 비교 　오답률 56%　답 ②

| 정답해설 | ② 44% 부정어구와 비교급이 결합된 최상급의 표현으로 more precious와 호응하는 접속사로 as가 아닌 than이 와야 한다.
| 오답해설 | ① 16% 문장 전체적으로 가주어 it, 진주어 to learn, 의미상의 주어로 for us가 온 구조이며, 부정의 강조 표현으로 by no means가 적절하게 쓰였다.
③ 33% '아무리 ~해도 지나치지 않다'는 조동사 can의 관용적 표현으로 cannot과 더불어 과도함의 표현인 too가 적절하게 쓰였다.
④ 7% 타동사 believes의 목적어로 선행사를 포함한 관계대명사 what이 이끄는 명사절이 왔으며, what에 이어 타동사 say의 목적어가 없는 불완전한 절이 올바르게 이어졌다.

어휘

by no means 결코 ~하지 않다
precious 귀중한, 소중한
cannot ~ too… 아무리 ~해도 지나치지 않다

오답률 TOP 2

14 문법 > 준동사 > 분사구문 　오답률 56%　답 ④

| 정답해설 | ④ 44% 주어인 동명사 sitting과 함께 'with + 명사 + 분사'의 분사구문이 결합된 문장으로 다리(the legs)는 '꼬아진' 것이므로 타동사 cross의 과거분사인 crossed로 수동의 의미를 나타내야 한다.
| 오답해설 | ① 16% 완료분사구문이 포함된 문장으로, 잠을 이룰 수 없는 것보다 커피를 마셨던 것이 이전 시점(과거)이므로 having drunk로 올바르게 표현했다. '커피 세 잔'의 표현으로 조수사 three cups of가 물질명사 coffee를 적절하게 수식했다. 이어진 절의 동사 fall은 불완전자동사이므로 보어로 서술적 형용사 asleep이 왔다.
② 23% 분사구문 being의 생략된 주어가 이어지는 절의 주어인 she와 동일해야 하므로 올바른 문장이다.
③ 17% 비인칭 독립분사구문으로, 모든 점은 '고려되는' 것이므로 타동사 consider에서 파생한 과거분사 considered가 수동의 의미로 적절하게 쓰였다.

어휘

fall asleep 잠이 들다
consider 고려하다, 생각하다
qualified 자격을 갖춘
period 기간, 시기
blood pressure 혈압

---

15 독해 > 빈칸의 내용 추론하기 > 연결어 추론 　오답률 39%　답 ②

| 해석 | 사망한 사람들과의 관계 유지에 대한 신념은 문화에 따라 다르다. 예를 들어, 고인과의 관계를 유지하는 것은 일본 종교 의식에서 받아들여지고 유지된다. 그러나 애리조나의 호피 인디언들 사이에서, 고인은 가능한 한 빨리 잊혀지고 삶은 평소처럼 계속된다. (A) 사실상, 호피족의 장례식은 인간과 영혼 사이의 결렬로 끝난다. 애도의 다양성은 두 이슬람 사회 – 한 곳은 이집트에, 다른 하나는 발리에 – 보다 더 명확한 곳은 없다. 이집트의 이슬람교도들 사이에서 유족들은 비슷한 슬픈 이야기를 언급하고 자신의 슬픔을 표현하는 사람들에 의해 둘러싸여, 충분히 그들의 슬픔에 대해 생각하는 분위기가 조성된다. (B) 이와는 대조적으로 발리에서는 유족인 이슬람 교도들은 슬퍼하기보다는 오히려 웃고 즐거워하도록 권장된다.

　　(A)　　　　　(B)
① 그러나　　　비슷하게, 유사하게
② 사실상　　　대조적으로
③ 따라서　　　예를 들어
④ 마찬가지로　결과적으로

| 정답해설 | ② 61% (A) 앞에서 호피족 사이에서 고인은 빠르게 잊혀진다고 언급했고, (A)에 이어 호피 장례식이 살아 있는 사람들과 영혼 사이의 결렬로 끝난다고 하면서 실질적인 언급을 했으므로 (A)에는 In fact가 적절하다. (B)에는 애도의 다양성에 대해 서술하면서 이집트와 발리의 차이점에 대해 언급하는 부분이므로 대조의 표현인 By contrast가 적절하다. 따라서 정답은 ②이다.

어휘

tie 관계, 인연; 속박
the deceased 고인
sustain 지속하다; 견디다
religious 종교적인
ritual 의식, 제사
funeral 장례식
break-off 결렬
mortal 인간; 죽을 운명의, 인간의
diversity 다양성, 상이점
grieve 슬퍼하다, 애도하다
bereaved 사별한, 유족이 된
at length 충분히, 마침내
grief 슬픔, 애도
tragic 비극적인, 슬픈

---

16 독해 > 빈칸의 내용 추론하기 > 빈칸 어휘 추론 　오답률 27%　답 ④

| 해석 | 과학자들은 오래 전부터 높은 기온이 그린란드의 빙상에서 표면 용융의 원인이라는 것을 알고 있었다. 그러나 새로운 연구에 따르면 아래에서 얼음을 공격하기 시작한 또 다른 위협이 발견되었다: 광대한 빙하 아래에서 이동하는 따뜻한 바닷물이 빙하를 훨씬 더 빨리 녹게 하고 있다. 이 연구 결과는 그린란드 북동부에 있는 빙하 79N(Nioghalvfjerdsfjorden Glacier)의 많은 '빙설' 중 하나를 연구한 연구원들에 의해 네이처 지오사이언스誌에 발표되었다. 빙설은 육지의 얼음에서 떨어지지 않은 상태로 물 위에 떠 있는 길쭉한 얼음조각이다. 이 과학자들이 연구한 거대한 빙설은 거의 50마일 길이이다. 이 조사는 대서양의 따뜻한 물이 빙하 쪽으로 직접 흐를 수 있는 너비 1마일 이상의 해류를 밝혀냈고 이는 많은 양의 열을 얼음과 접촉시키고 빙하의 용융을 ④ 가속화했다.

① 분리하는
② 지연시키는
③ 방해하는
④ 가속화하는

| 정답해설 | ④ 73% 첫 번째 문장에서 높은 기온이 그린란드 빙상의 표면 용융의 원인이라는 것을 과학자들이 알고 있다고 했고, 이어서 또 다른 위협이 발견되었다고 하면서 빙하 아래에서 흐르는 따뜻한 해수에 대해 서술하고 있다. 연구 결과를 통해 대서양의 따뜻한 물이 빙하로 흘러 들어가는 해류를 밝혀냈다고 했고, 이에 대

한 결과로 얼음이 열과 접촉했다고 했으므로 빙하 용융이 '가속화되는' 것을 유추할 수 있다. 따라서 빈칸에 들어갈 것으로 ④가 가장 적절하다.

어휘
contribute to 원인이 되다, 기여하다　melting 용융, 용해
ice sheet (극지 등의) 빙상(氷床), 대륙 빙하 잡지
threat 위협　　　　　　　　　　underneath 아래의
glacier 빙하
ice tongue 빙설, 해안선에서 돌출된 길고 좁은 얼음판
float 뜨다, 떠다니다

17　독해 > 대의 파악 > 제목 찾기　　오답률 26%　답 ③

| 해석 | 다른 문화권의 사람들은 세상을 다르게 보는가? 한 심리학자가 물고기와 다른 수중 물체의 사실적인 애니메이션 장면을 일본과 미국 학생들에게 보여주고 그들이 본 것을 보고하도록 요청했다. 미국인과 일본인은 중점을 두는 물고기에 대해 동일한 수의 언급을 했지만, 일본인은 물, 암석, 거품 및 무자력의 식물과 동물을 포함한 배경 요소에 대해 60% 이상 더 많은 언급을 했다. 게다가, 일본인과 미국인 참가자가 활동적인 동물과 관련된 운동에 대해 동일한 수의 언급을 한 반면, 일본인 참가자는 무자력의 배경 대상과 관련된 관계에 대해 거의 두 배나 많은 언급을 했다. 아마도 가장 현저하게, 일본인 참가자의 첫 번째 문장은 환경을 언급하는 문장일 가능성이 높았지만, 미국인의 첫 번째 문장은 중점을 두는 물고기를 언급하는 문장일 가능성이 세 배 높았다.
① 일본인과 미국인 사이의 언어 장벽
② 뇌 속에서 사물과 배경의 연관성
③ 인식의 문화적 차이
④ 세부 지향적인 사람들의 우월성

| 정답해설 | ③ 74% 첫 번째 문장이 주제문으로, 질문에 이어 이에 대한 일본 학생들과 미국 학생들을 대상으로 한 한 심리학자의 실험을 통해 문화에 따라 사물을 인식하는 방식이 다르다는 것을 서술하고 있다. 따라서 글의 제목으로 가장 적절한 것은 ③이다. 주제 문장의 different cultures와 view가 정답에서 각각 cultural differences와 perception으로 표현되었다.

어휘
reference 언급; 참조, 참고　　　focal 초점의, 초점에 있는; 중요한
inert 자력으로 행동할 수 없는; 불활성의
participant 참가자　　　　　　　involve 관련되다; 포함하다
refer to 언급하다

18　독해 > 글의 일관성 파악하기 > 주어진 문장의 삽입
　　　　　　　　　　　　　　　　오답률 51%　답 ④

| 해석 | 사람들은 다른 방식으로 중력, 즉 지포스(g-force)에 노출될 수 있다. 그것은 등을 찰싹 맞는 것처럼 신체의 일부분에만 영향을 미치면서 국부에 그치게 할 수 있다. 그것은 또한 자동차 충돌에서 버텨지는 강한 힘과 같은 순간적인 것일 수도 있다. 세 번째 유형의 지포스는 지속되거나 적어도 몇 초 동안 지속된다. 지속적이고 몸 전체에 걸친 지포스는 사람들에게 가장 위험하다. 신체는 대개 지속적인 지포스보다 국부적이거나 순간적인 지포스를 더 잘 견딜 수 있는데, 이는 혈액이 다리로 들어가서 나머지 신체의 산소를 빼앗기 때문에 치명적일 수 있다. 앉아 있거나 서 있는 대신 몸이 수평이거나 누워있는 동안 적용하는 지포스는 다리가 아닌 뒤쪽에 피가 고이기 때문에 사람들에게 더 견딜 수 있는 경향이 있다. ④ 따라서 혈액과 생

명을 주는 산소는 심장이 뇌로 순환시키기가 더 쉽다. 우주비행사나 전투기 조종사 같은 몇몇 사람들은 지포스에 대한 신체의 저항력을 높이기 위해 특별한 훈련을 받는다.

| 정답해설 | ④ 49% 제시된 문장에서 결과를 유도하는 thus와 함께 산소가 뇌로 순환하기에 더 쉽다는 긍정적인 내용이 이어졌다. 따라서 이 문장 앞에는 이런 결과를 도출할 수 있는 상황이 서술되어야 하는데, blood가 처음으로 언급된 부분 이후에 주어진 문장이 삽입되어야 함을 알 수 있다. 혈액이 다리로 들어가는 것이 치명적이라고 서술한 후, 신체가 수평일 때 다리보다는 신체 뒷부분에 피가 고여 사람들이 더 버틸 만하다고 언급한 후에 제시된 문장이 들어가는 것이 자연스러우므로 정답은 ④이다.

어휘
expose 노출하다, 드러내다　　　　gravitational force 중력
localize 국부에 그치게 하다　　　　slap 때리다
momentary 순간적인　　　　　　　endure 견디다, 참다
sustain 지속하다, 지탱하다　　　　withstand 견디다, 이겨내다
deadly 치명적인　　　　　　　　deprive A of B A로부터 B를 빼앗다
apply 적용하다; 이용하다　　　　　horizontal 바로 누운; 수평의
tolerable 참을 수 있는, 견딜 만한　astronaut 우주비행사
undergo 경험하다, 겪다　　　　　　resistance 저항, 내성

오답률 TOP 3
19　독해 > 대의 파악 > 요지·주장 찾기　오답률 55%　답 ①

| 해석 | 만약 누군가가 당신에게 제안을 하고 당신이 그 제안의 일부에 대해 진심으로 걱정한다면, 당신은 대개 당신의 모든 변경 내용을 한 번에 제안하는 것이 더 낫다. "월급이 좀 적네요. 어떻게 좀 해주실 수 있나요?" 그러고 나서 일단 그녀가 그것에 대해 애를 쓰면, 다시 와서 "고마워요. 이제 내가 원하는 두 가지 다른 일들이 있는데요..."라고 말하지 마시오. 당신이 처음에 한 가지만 요구한다면, 그녀는 그것을 얻는 것이 당신이 그 제안을 받아들일 준비를 하게 (혹은 최소한 결정을 하게) 만들 것으로 생각할지도 모른다. 당신이 계속 "그리고 한 가지 더…"라고 말한다면, 그녀는 관대하거나 이해심 많은 기분으로 남아 있을 것 같지 않다. 게다가, 만약 당신이 하나 이상의 요청이 있다면, 당신이 원하는 – A, B, C, 그리고 D; 모든 것을 단순하게 언급하지 마라; 또한 당신에게 있어 각각의 상대적인 중요성을 알려주어라. 그렇지 않으면, 그녀는 당신이 가장 적은 가치를 매기는 두 가지를 선택할 수도 있는데, 그것들은 당신에게 주기가 꽤 쉽고, 그녀는 자신이 당신에게 적당히 응대했다고 느낄 수 있기 때문이다.
① 다수의 사안은 연속으로 하지 말고 동시에 협상하라.
② 성공적인 협상을 위해 민감한 주제를 피하라.
③ 협상을 위한 적절한 때를 선택하라.
④ 연봉 협상을 할 때 너무 직접적으로 하지 마라.

| 정답해설 | ① 45% 협상에 대한 지문으로 첫 번째 문장에서 모든 변경 내용을 동시에 진행하라고 언급한 후 이에 대한 구체적인 예를 들어 설명하고 있다. 따라서 글의 요지로 가장 적절한 것은 ①이다.

어휘
legitimately 합법적으로
be concerned about ~에 대해 근심하다
better off 더 나은; 유복한　　　　　generous 관대한
relative 상대적인; 관련이 있는
meet halfway 적당히 응대하다, 요구를 어느 정도 들어주다

20 독해 > 글의 일관성 파악하기 > 글의 순서 오답률 28% 답 ③

| 해석 | 오늘날, 라마르크는 적응이 어떻게 진화로 이어지는지에 관한 그의 잘못된 설명으로 인해 부당하게 기억되고 있다. 그는 한 생물체가 특정 신체 부위를 사용하거나 사용하지 않음으로써 특정한 형질을 발전시킨다고 제안했다.

(B) 라마르크는 이러한 형질이 자손에게 전해진다고 생각했다. 라마르크는 이러한 생각을 '획득형질 유전'이라고 불렀다.

(C) 예를 들어, 라마르크는 캥거루의 강력한 뒷다리는 선조들이 점프를 통해 다리를 강화한 다음 그 획득된 다리의 힘을 자손에게 물려준 결과라고 설명할지도 모른다. 그러나 획득된 형질은 유전되기 위해서는 특정 유전자의 DNA를 어떻게든 변형해야만 할 것이다.

(A) 이런 일이 발생한다는 증거는 없다. 그럼에도 불구하고 라마르크는 생물이 자신의 환경에 적응할 때 진화가 발생한다는 것을 제시했음에 주목하는 것이 중요하다. 이러한 생각은 다윈을 위한 발판을 마련하는 데 도움이 되었다.

| 정답해설 | ③ 72% (B)의 these characteristics는 주어진 문장의 마지막 줄의 certain characteristics를 지칭하므로 (B)가 처음에 와야 한다. (B)에서 라마르크가 제안한 특정한 형질이 자손에게 전해진다고 하는 내용에 이어 이에 대한 구체적인 사례를 서술한 (C)가 그 다음에 이어져야 한다. 마지막으로 (A)에 서술한 내용에 대한 증거는 없지만 결국 라마르크의 생각이 다윈을 위한 발판을 마련하는 데 도움이 되었다는 결론으로 이어지는 것이 자연스럽다. 따라서 정답은 ③이다.

어휘

adaptation 적응, 순응
inheritance 유전, 상속
hind 뒤쪽의
modify 변경하다, 변형하다

characteristic 독특한, 특징적인
acquired 획득한, 후천적인
offspring 자손; (짐승의) 새끼

합격예상 체크

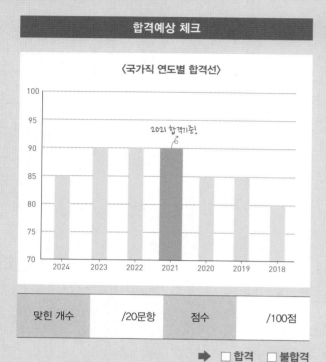

〈국가직 연도별 합격선〉

2021 합격기준!

맞힌 개수	/20문항	점수	/100점

➡ ☐ 합격　☐ 불합격

취약영역 체크

문항	정답	영역	문항	정답	영역
1	①	어휘 > 동의어	11	①	생활영어 > 회화
2	②	어휘 > 동의어	12	②	생활영어 > 회화
3	②	어휘 > 동의어	13	④	독해 > 세부내용 찾기
4	④	어휘 > 빈칸	14	④	문법 > 특수구문
5	④	독해 > 세부내용 찾기	15	②	문법 > 명사와 일치
6	②	문법 > 동사의 형태	16	①	독해 > 빈칸의 내용 추론하기
7	③	독해 > 대의 파악	17	①	독해 > 빈칸의 내용 추론하기
8	①	문법 > 연결사	18	④	독해 > 글의 일관성 파악하기
9	④	독해 > 글의 일관성 파악하기	19	④	독해 > 대의 파악
10	④	독해 > 글의 일관성 파악하기	20	①	독해 > 대의 파악

⬇ 영역별 틀린 개수로 취약영역을 확인하세요!

어휘	/4	문법	/4	독해	/10	생활영어	/2

➡ 나의 취약영역: _____

※ [정답해설]과 [오답해설] 선지의 50% 표시는 〈1초 합격예측 서비스〉를 통해 수집된 선지 선택률을 나타냅니다.

1　어휘 > 동의어　　오답률 29%　답 ①

| 해석 | 사회적 관행으로서의 프라이버시는 다른 사회적 관행과 함께 개인의 행동을 형성하므로 사회생활의 중심이다.
① 71% ~와 결합하여, 짝지어
② 19% ~와 비교하여
③ 4% ~대신에
④ 6% ~의 경우에는; ~에 대비하여
| 정답해설 | ① conjunction은 '결합', '[문법] 접속사'의 의미이다. combination은 '조합, 결합'의 의미로 conjunction과 동의어로 볼 수 있으므로 맥락상 동의어로 가장 적절한 것은 ①이다.

어휘

in conjunction with ~와 함께, ~와 연대하여
privacy 사생활, 개인정보　　practice 관행
individual 개인적인, 개개의　　central 중심[중앙]의

2　어휘 > 동의어　　오답률 36%　답 ②

| 해석 | 재즈의 영향은 매우 널리 퍼져서 대부분의 대중음악은 재즈에 양식적인 뿌리를 두고 있다.
① 12% 속이는, 현혹시키는
② 64% 도처에 존재하는, 편재하는
③ 20% 설득력 있는
④ 4% 피해가 막심한
| 정답해설 | ② 문장 전체적으로 'so~ that…(매우 ~해서 …하다)'의 구조로, pervasive는 원인에 해당되고, that이 이끄는 부사절의

내용은 대부분의 대중음악 양식의 뿌리가 재즈 덕분이라고 했으므로, 재즈의 영향력이 컸음을 알 수 있다. 따라서 '골고루 미치는, 퍼지는'의 pervasive와 동의어로 ubiquitous가 가장 적절하다. 어근 'ubique'는 everywhere(모든 곳)의 의미이다.

어휘

pervasive 퍼지는, 골고루 미치는; 배어드는
influence 영향
owe A to B A에 대해 B의 신세를 지고 있다

3　어휘 > 동의어　　오답률 45%　답 ②

| 해석 | 이 소설은 사업을 시작하기 위해 학교를 그만두는 제멋대로인 10대 청소년에 대해 화가 난 부모에 관한 것이다.
① 13% 냉담한, 무감각한
② 55% 짜증난, 화가 난
③ 17% 평판이 좋은, 유명한
④ 15% 자신 있는; 확신하는
| 정답해설 | ② 학교를 그만두려는 제멋대로인 십대 자녀에 대해 부모가 어떤 입장인지를 생각하면, vexed는 '화가 난'의 의미임을 유추할 수 있다. annoy는 '화나게 하다, 짜증나게 하다'의 의미를 지닌 동사로 과거분사 annoyed가 vexed와 동의어임을 알 수 있으므로 정답은 ②이다.

어휘

vexed 신경질나는, 화나는　　unruly 제멋대로인, 다루기 힘든
quit 그만두다

4 어휘 > 빈칸 | 오답률 26% | 답 ④

| 해석 | 한 무리의 젊은 시위자들이 경찰서에 ④ <u>침입</u>하려고 시도했다.
① 16% 늘어세우다; 결속시키다
② 3% (소리·빛·냄새 등을) 발하다, 발산하다; 나누어 주다
③ 7% 계속하다; 진행시키다
④ 74% 침입하다, 난입하다

| 정답해설 | ④ 주어가 시위 참가자들이므로 이들이 경찰서에 '침입하려고' 하는 것이 가장 자연스럽다. 따라서 빈칸에 들어갈 말로 가장 적절한 것은 ④이다.

어휘
demonstrator 시위 운동(참가)자   attempt to + R ~하려고 시도하다

5 독해 > 세부내용 찾기 > 내용 일치 찾기 | 오답률 21% | 답 ④

| 해석 | 수입 노동의 가장 악명 높은 사례는 당연히 대서양 노예무역인데, 이 무역은 1,000만 명에 달하는 노예가 된 아프리카인들을 신대륙으로 데려와 농장에서 일하게 했다. 그러나 유럽인들이 가장 큰 규모로 노예 제도를 시행했을지 모르지만, 그들은 노예를 그들의 공동체로 데려온 유일한 사람들은 전혀 아니었다: 일찍이 고대 이집트인들은 노예 노동을 피라미드를 짓기 위해 이용했고, 초기 아랍 탐험가들은 종종 노예 무역상이었으며, 아랍의 노예 제도는 20세기까지 계속되었고, 실제로 여전히 몇 군데에서 계속되고 있다. 아메리카 대륙에서는 일부 원주민 부족이 다른 부족의 구성원을 노예로 삼았고, 노예 제도는 특히 식민지 시대 이전에 많은 아프리카 국가에서 하나의 관례였다.
① 아프리카 노동자들은 자발적으로 신대륙으로 이주했다.
② 유럽인들은 노예노동을 이용한 최초의 사람들이었다.
③ 아랍 노예 제도는 더 이상 어떤 형태로도 존재하지 않는다.
④ 노예 제도는 아프리카 국가에서도 존재했다.

| 정답해설 | ④ 79% 마지막 문장 ~slavery was also an institution in many African nations, especially before the colonial period.로 보아 아프리카에서도 노예 제도가 있었음을 알 수 있다.

| 오답해설 | ① 8% 첫 번째 문장에서 노예 노동을 가장 악명 높은 수입 노동으로 지칭한 것으로 보아 자발적으로(voluntarily) 이주한 것이 아님을 알 수 있으므로 ①은 일치하지 않는 내용이다.
② 7% 유럽인들보다 앞서 고대 이집트인들과 아랍 탐험가들이 노예 노동을 이용했다고 했으므로 일치하지 않는다.
③ 6% Arabic slavery continued into the twentieth century and indeed still continues in a few places.를 통해 현재도 여전히 아랍 노예 제도가 존재하고 있다고 했으므로 일치하지 않는 내용이다.

어휘
notorious 악명높은   enslave 노예로 만들다
plantation 농장, 조림지   by no means 결코 ~하지 않다
explorer 탐험가   tribe 부족, 종족
institution 관습, 사회 제도; 기관, 협회
colonial 식민지의   voluntarily 자발적으로

6 문법 > 동사의 형태 > 시제 | 오답률 46% | 답 ②

| 해석 | ① 이 안내서는 당신이 홍콩 어디를 방문해야 하는지 알려주고 있다.
② 나는 대만에서 태어났지만, 일을 시작한 이후로 한국에서 살아왔다.
③ 소설이 너무 흥미진진해서 나는 시간 가는 줄 모르고 버스를 놓쳤다.
④ 서점들에 더 이상 신문이 없다는 것이 놀라운 것은 아니지 않은가?

| 정답해설 | ② 54% 접속사 since가 이끄는 부사절이 과거시제로 과거부터 현재에 이르는 시점의 표현을 위해 현재완료시제로 표현된 올바른 문장이다.

| 오답해설 | ① 9% 수여동사 tells에 이어진 간접목적어 you, 직접목적어로 의문부사 where가 이끄는 명사절이 이어진 문장이다. 간접의문문의 어순은 '의문사 + 주어 + 동사~'가 되어야 하므로 where you should visit~으로 바꿔야 한다.
③ 25% 전체적으로 'so~ that… (매우 ~해서 …하다)'의 구조로, 주절의 보어인 excited는 사람의 상태를 서술할 때 쓰는 감정타동사에서 파생된 과거분사이다. 소설은 '흥미를 주는' 것이므로 현재분사 exciting으로 바꿔야 한다.
④ 12% 부가의문문은 주절인 It's not surprising에 호응해야 하므로, 동사는 be동사로 쓰고, 주절이 부정문이므로 긍정문으로 바꿔야 한다. 따라서 is it?으로 바꿔야 한다.

어휘
lose track of ~을 잊어버리다, 놓치다
carry (상품을) 취급하다, 팔고 있다

7 독해 > 대의 파악 > 제목 찾기 | 오답률 31% | 답 ③

| 해석 | 바다에서 따뜻해지는 온도와 산소 손실은 참치와 능성어부터 연어, 탈곡 상어, 해덕(북대서양산 대구)과 대구에 이르기까지 수백 종의 물고기 종을 이전에 생각했던 것보다 훨씬 더 줄어들게 할 것이라고 새로운 연구 결과가 결론내렸다. 보다 따뜻한 바다는 신진대사를 가속화하기 때문에 물고기, 오징어 그리고 다른 해수호흡 동물들은 바다에서 더 많은 산소를 끌어낼 필요가 있기 마련이다. 동시에, 따뜻해지는 바다는 이미 바다의 많은 부분에서 산소의 가용성을 줄이고 있다. 브리티시 컬럼비아 대학의 2인조 과학자들은 물고기의 몸이 아가미보다 더 빨리 자라기 때문에, 이 동물들은 결국 정상적인 성장을 지속할 수 있는 충분한 산소를 얻을 수 없는 지경에 이르게 될 것이라고 주장한다. "우리가 발견한 것은 물고기의 체적이 수온이 섭씨 1도 상승할 때마다 20~30퍼센트 감소한다는 것입니다."라고 저자인 William Cheung은 말한다.
① 어류는 이제 그 어느 때보다 빨리 자란다
② 산소가 해양온도에 미치는 영향
③ 기후 변화로 세계의 어류가 줄어들 수도 있다
④ 해양 동물이 낮은 신진대사로 어떻게 살아남는가

| 정답해설 | ③ 69% 첫 번째 문장 Warming temperatures and loss of oxygen in the sea will shrink hundreds of fish species~가 주제문으로 이를 표현한 ③이 정답이다. warming temperatures and loss of oxygen이 선지에서 climate change로 표현되었다.

어휘
shrink 줄다, 감소하다   metabolism 신진대사, 물질대사
availability 유용성, 유효성   gill 아가미
sustain 지속하다

8 문법 > 연결사 > 관계사 　　　오답률 47% 　답 ③

| 해석 | 도시 농업(UA)은 오랫동안 도시에 설 자리가 없는 변두리 활동으로 치부되어 왔지만, 그 잠재력은 실현되기 시작하고 있다. 사실, UA는 식량 자립에 관한 것이다: 그것은 일자리를 창출하는 것을 포함하고 있으며, 특히 가난한 사람들을 위한 식량 불안정에 대한 반응이다. 많은 사람들이 믿는 것과는 달리, UA는 모든 도시에서 발견되며, 때때로 숨겨져 있고, 때로는 명백하다. 주의 깊게 보면, 큰 도시에서 사용되지 않는 공간은 거의 없다. 귀중한 공터는 거의 비어있지 않으며 종종 공식적으로, 또는 비공식적으로 인수되어 생산적으로 만들어진다.

| 정답해설 | ③ 53% 전치사 to의 목적어인 명사절을 이끌어야 한다. 뒤에 타동사 believe의 목적어가 없으므로 명사절을 이끌면서 불완전한 절이 이어지는 선행사를 포함한 관계대명사 what이 적절하다.

| 오답해설 | ① 7% realize는 타동사로 밑줄에 이어 목적어인 명사가 없다는 점과, 잠재성은 '실현되는' 것이므로 수동부정사로 표현된 올바른 문장이다.

② 14% 타동사 involve는 동명사를 목적어로 취하는 동사이므로 올바른 구조이다.

④ 26% 등위접속사 and를 두고 is often taken over에 병치된 구조이다. 5형식 문장의 수동태로 is made에 이어 목적보어인 형용사 productive가 왔으며, 주어인 valuable vacant land를 서술한다.

어휘

dismiss 무시하다, 해고하다	fringe 주변, 가장자리
self-reliance 자립	insecurity 불안정
contrary to ~에 반해서, ~와 상반되는	
idle (물건이) 사용되지 않고 있는, 쉬고 있는; 나태한, 게으른	
take over 인수하다; 인계받다; 빼앗다	

9 독해 > 글의 일관성 파악하기 > 주어진 문장의 삽입 　　　오답률 26% 　답 ④

| 해석 | 기록보관소는 오디오에서 비디오, 신문, 잡지 및 인쇄물에 이르는 자료들의 보고이며, 이는 기록보관소를 모든 역사 탐정 조사에 필수 불가결하게 만든다. 도서관과 기록보관소는 같은 것처럼 보일지 모르지만, 그 차이는 중요하다. 기록보관소의 수집물은 거의 항상 1차 자료로 구성되는 반면, 도서관에는 2차 자료가 포함되어 있다. 한국 전쟁에 대해 더 많이 알기 위해, 당신은 역사책을 위해 도서관에 갈 것이다. 만약 당신이 한국 전쟁 군인들이 쓴 정부 논문이나 편지를 읽고 싶다면, 당신은 기록보관소에 갈 것이다. 정보를 찾고 있는 경우에는, 거기에 당신을 위한 기록 보관소가 있을 가능성이 있다. 많은 주 및 지역 기록보관소는 공공 기록을 저장하고 있는데, 그것은 놀랍고 다양한 자료들이다. ④ 예를 들어 뉴저지 주의 기록보관소에는 3만 세제곱 피트 이상의 종이와 2만 5천 릴의 마이크로 필름이 보관되어 있다. 주의 기록보관소에 대한 온라인 검색은 입법부의 의사록보다 훨씬 더 많은 것을 포함하고 있다는 것을 빠르게 보여줄 것이다. 세부적인 토지 보조금 정보, 구시가지 지도, 범죄 기록, 행상인 면허 신청서와 같은 기이한 것들이 있다.

| 정답해설 | ④ 74% For example에 이어 뉴저지 주의 기록보관소에 대한 내용이 이어지고 있다. ④의 앞 문장으로 보아, many state and local archives에 대한 구체적인 사례로 주어진 문장의 뉴저지 주의 기록보관소가 이어진 것을 알 수 있으므로 ④가 정답이다.

어휘

archive 기록보관소, 문서국	indispensable 필수적인
investigation 조사, 연구	
the minutes (회의 · 위원회 등의) 의사록	
legislature 의회의, 입법부	oddity 괴상한 사람
peddler 판매원	license application 면허 신청

10 독해 > 글의 일관성 파악하기 > 글의 흐름과 무관한 문장 　　　오답률 16% 　답 ④

| 해석 | 번아웃(극도의 피로)이라는 용어는 업무의 압박에서 나오는 '소진'을 말한다. 번아웃은 일상 업무 스트레스 요인과 같은 결과가 직원들에게 해를 끼치는 만성 질환이다. 번아웃에 대한 가장 널리 채택된 개념화는 Maslach와 그녀의 동료들이 인적 서비스 종사자에 대한 연구에서 개발했다. Maslach는 번아웃을 세 가지 상호 관련 차원으로 구성된 것으로 본다. 첫 번째 차원—감정적 탈진—은 정말로 번아웃 현상의 핵심이다. 노동자들은 피로, 좌절, 지치거나 직장에서 또 하나의 하루를 마주할 수 없을 때 감정적인 피로로 고통 받는다. 번아웃의 두 번째 차원은 개인적인 성취의 부족이다. 번아웃 현상의 이러한 측면은 자신을 실패로 보고, 직무요건을 효과적으로 달성할 수 없는 노동자를 말한다. ④ 감정 노동자들은 신체적으로 지쳐있지만 동기부여가 높은 상태로 직장에 들어간다. 번아웃의 세 번째 차원은 비인격화이다. 이 차원은 일의 일부로써 다른 사람들(예를 들어, 고객, 환자, 학생)과 대인관계로 의사소통해야 하는 근로자에게만 관련이 있다.

| 정답해설 | ④ 84% 번아웃에 대한 정의를 내린 후 이를 세 가지 차원으로 분류해 서술한 글이다. 각각의 차원에 대한 설명에서 번아웃이 부정적으로 서술되고 있는 가운데, ④의 내용이 긍정적으로 서술되었으므로 글의 흐름상 어색한 문장임을 알 수 있다.

어휘

burnout 번아웃, 극도의 피로; 소진　refer to 언급하다	
wear out 소진되다	
take a toll on 피해를 주다, 해를 끼치다	
conceptualization 개념화	
human service worker 인적서비스 종사자	
used up 지쳐 빠진; 써서 낡은	
depersonalization 주체감 상실; 비인격화; 몰개성화	
relevant 관련 있는, 적절한	

11 생활영어 > 회화 　　　오답률 8% 　답 ①

| 해석 | A: 어젯밤에 여기 있었나요?
B: 네, 마감 교대 근무를 했어요. 왜요?
A: 주방이 오늘 아침에 엉망이었어요. 스토브에 음식이 튀어 있었고 얼음 쟁반은 냉동실에 없었고요.
B: 제가 청소 체크리스트를 검토하는 것을 잊은 것 같네요.
A: 청결한 주방이 얼마나 중요한지 아시잖아요.
B: 죄송해요. ① 이런 일이 다시 없도록 할게요.

① 이런 일이 다시 없도록 할게요.
② 지금 계산서를 원하시나요?
③ 그게 바로 내가 어제 잊었던 이유예요.
④ 주문을 제대로 받으셨는지 확실히 해 주세요.

| 정답해설 | ① 92% B가 마감 교대 근무 시 청소 체크리스트를 소홀히 한 것에 대해 사과를 하고 있으며, 이어지는 빈칸에는 이런 일이 앞으로 없도록 하겠다는 다짐의 표현인 ①이 들어가는 것이 맥락상 가장 적절하다.

어휘

closing shift 마감 교대[근무]조　　spatter 튀기다
go over 검토하다

| **12** | 생활영어 > 회화 | 오답률 15% | 답 ② |

| 해석 | A: 감기약 좀 드셨어요?
B: 아니요, 그냥 코를 많이 풀었어요.
A: 비강 스프레이 좀 뿌려봤어요?
B: ② 아니요, 비강 스프레이를 좋아하지 않아서요.
A: 효과가 엄청 좋은데요.
B: 감사하지만 사양할게요. 저는 코에 뭐든 넣는 것을 좋아하지 않아서 그
　걸 사용해 본 적이 없네요.
① 네, 하지만 도움이 되지 않았어요.
② 아니요, 비강 스프레이를 좋아하지 않아서요.
③ 아니요, 약국이 문을 닫았어요.
④ 네, 얼마나 많이 써야 하죠?

| 정답해설 | ② 85% 감기로 코를 많이 풀었다는 B에게 A가 비강 스
프레이를 뿌려봤냐고 물은 것에 대한 대답이 빈칸에 와야 한다. 빈
칸에 이어 A가 효과가 있다고 했음에도 B가 죄송하지만 사양하겠
다는 부정적인 대답을 했으므로 빈칸에 들어갈 표현으로 ②가 가장
적절하다.

어휘

blow one's nose 코를 풀다　　nose spray 비강 스프레이
work 작용하다, 효과가 있다　　pharmacy 약국

| **13** | 독해 > 세부내용 찾기 > 내용 불일치 찾기 | 오답률 11% | 답 ④ |

| 해석 | 사막은 지구 육지 면적의 5분의 1 이상을 차지하고 있으며, 모든
대륙에서 발견된다. 연간 25cm(10인치) 미만의 비가 내리는 곳은 사막으로
간주된다. 사막은 건조지라고 불리는 더 넓은 부류의 지역의 일부분이다.
이러한 지역들은 "수분 부족"하에 존재하며, 이는 그 지역들이 연간 강수량
보다 증발을 통해 수분을 더 많이 잃을 수 있음을 의미한다. 사막이 뜨겁다
는 일반적인 개념에도 불구하고, 추운 사막도 있다. 세계에서 가장 큰 뜨거
운 사막인 아프리카 북부의 사하라 사막은 낮 동안 최고 섭씨 50도(화씨
122도)의 기온에 이른다. 하지만 아시아의 고비 사막이나 세계에서 가장 큰
남극과 북극의 극지 사막처럼 일부 사막은 항상 춥다. 다른 사막들은 산악
성이다. 사막들은 약 20%만이 모래로 덮여 있다. 칠레의 아타카마 사막과
같은 가장 건조한 사막은 연간 강수량이 2mm(0.08인치) 미만인 곳들이 있
다. 그러한 환경은 너무 혹독하고 딴 세상이어서 과학자들은 심지어 화성의
생명체에 대한 단서를 찾기 위해 그것들을 연구하기도 했다. 반면에, 몇 년
에 한 번씩 유난히 비가 오는 기간은 '엄청난 개화기'를 만들어 낼 수 있는
데, 심지어 아타카마 사막도 야생화로 뒤덮인다.
① 각 대륙에 최소 하나의 사막이 존재한다.
② 사하라 사막은 세계에서 가장 큰 뜨거운 사막이다.
③ 고비 사막은 추운 사막으로 분류된다.
④ 아타카마 사막은 비가 가장 많이 내리는 사막 중 하나이다.

| 정답해설 | ④ 89% 아타카마 사막이 가장 건조한 사막이라고 했으
므로 비가 가장 많이 내리는 사막들 중의 하나라고 서술한 ④는 글
의 내용과 일치하지 않는다.

| 오답해설 | ① 6% 첫 번째 문장의 they are found on every
continent.로 보아 각 대륙에 최소의 하나의 사막이 존재함을 알 수
있다.

② 2% The largest hot desert in the world, northern Africa's
Sahara, reaches temperatures~로 보아 사하라 사막이 세계에
서 가장 큰 뜨거운 사막임을 알 수 있다.

③ 3% some deserts are always cold, like the Gobi Desert in
Asia~로 보아 고비 사막은 추운 사막임을 알 수 있다.

어휘

deficit 적자, 결손　　　　　evaporation 증발
precipitation 강수(량)　　　　mountainous 산악의, 산이 많은
otherworldly 내세의, 저승의　　blanket 뒤덮다

| **14** | 문법 > 특수구문 > 도치 | 오답률 39% | 답 ④ |

| 정답해설 | ④ 61% love는 동명사와 to부정사 모두를 목적어로 취
하는 완전타동사이며, and에 이어 긍정의 동의의 표현으로 'so + 대
동사 + 주어'의 어순으로 왔다. loved를 대신해야 하므로 대동사로
did가 온 올바른 문장이다.

| 오답해설 | ① 21% look forward to는 '~를 고대하다'의 표현으로
to는 전치사이므로 동사원형 receive가 아니라 동명사 receiving으
로 바꿔야 한다.

② 9% rise는 자동사이므로 목적어를 취할 수 없다. 구조와 문맥을
　고려할 때 my salary를 목적어로 받을 수 있는 타동사 'raise'로
　바꿔야 한다.

③ 9% worth는 목적어를 취하는 형용사이므로 worth에 이어 동
　명사 considering이 와야 한다. '~할 만한 가치가 있다'의 표현
　으로 'be worth R-ing', 'be worthy of R-ing', 'be worthy to be
　p.p.' 등으로 쓸 수 있다.

어휘

look forward to + (대)명사/R-ing ~를 기대하다, 고대하다
be worth R-ing ~할 만한 가치가 있다

| **15** | 문법 > 명사와 일치 > 관사 | 오답률 43% | 답 ② |

| 정답해설 | ② 57% '매우 ~해서 …하다'의 표현으로 'such~
that…'의 구문이 쓰였고, 주절에서 단수명사 meteor storm을 수식하
는 어순이 'such a 형용사 + 명사'의 어순으로 올바르게 표현되었다.

| 오답해설 | ① 15% 접속사 as if는 '마치 ~처럼'의 의미로 양태부
사절을 이끌며, 주어진 우리말의 양보부사절을 이끌 수 없다. 따라
서 보어인 형용사 rich가 문장의 맨 앞에 나온 점을 감안하면, 접속
사 as 혹은 though로 바꿔야 한다. Though you may be rich에서
보어 rich를 문장의 맨 앞으로 이동시켜 Rich as(though) you may
be로 전환한 구조이다.

③ 11% 동사 keep이 '방해하다'의 표현으로 쓰일 때는 전치사
　from과 함께 써야 한다. 따라서 Her lack of a degree kept her
　from advancing.으로 바꿔야 한다.

④ 17% 전치사 on의 목적어로 접속사 if가 이끄는 명사절이 올 수
　없다. 또한 if는 or not과 함께 쓸 수 없으므로 if를 whether로
　바꿔야 한다. if(~인지 아닌지)가 이끄는 명사절은 타동사의 목
　적어일 때에 한해 쓴다.

어휘

sincere 진실한, 진정한	meteor 유성, 별똥별
keep A from R-ing A가 ~하는 것을 막다	
death penalty 사형	abolish 폐지하다, 없애다

---

16 독해 > 빈칸의 내용 추론하기 > 빈칸 어구 추론

오답률 15% | 답 ①

| 해석 | 소셜 미디어, 잡지, 쇼윈도우는 매일 사람들에게 구매할 물건들을 퍼붓고, 영국 소비자들은 그 어느 때보다도 더 많은 옷과 신발을 사고 있다. 온라인 쇼핑은 고객이 생각 없이 쉽게 구매할 수 있다는 것을 의미하며, 주요 브랜드는 2~3번 착용한 후 버리는 일회용 아이템처럼 취급할 수 있는 매우 저렴한 옷을 제공한다. 영국에서는 평균적인 사람이 1년에 1,000파운드 이상을 새 옷에 쓰는데, 이는 수입의 약 4%에 해당한다. 많은 것처럼 들리지는 않겠지만, 그 수치는 사회와 환경에 대한 훨씬 더 걱정스러운 두 가지 현상을 숨긴다. 첫째, 그 많은 소비 지출은 신용카드를 통해서이다. 영국 사람들은 현재 성인 한 명당 약 670파운드의 빚을 신용카드 회사에 지고 있다. 이는 평균 의상 예산의 66%에 해당한다. 또한 사람들이 가지고 있지 않은 돈을 쓸 뿐만 아니라, ① 그들이 필요로 하지 않는 물건을 사기 위해 돈을 사용하고 있다. 영국은 일 년에 30만 톤의 의류를 버리는데, 그중 대부분은 매립지로 들어간다.

① 그들이 필요로 하지 않는
② 생활필수품인
③ 곧 재활용 될
④ 다른 사람들에게 물려줄 수 있는

| 정답해설 | ① 85% 걱정스러운 현상(worrying trends)을 언급한 후, 이에 대한 구체적인 사례가 이어지고 있다. 따라서 빈칸에는 부정적인 흐름을 이끄는 어구가 들어가야 하므로 ①이 정답이다. 나머지 선지들은 긍정적인 흐름의 내용이므로 문맥상 들어갈 수 없다.

어휘

bombard 폭격하다, 공격하다	disposable 처분할 수 있는
approximately 거의, 대략	wardrobe 의상
budget 예산, 재정	landfill 매립

---

17 독해 > 빈칸의 내용 추론하기 > 빈칸 어휘 추론

오답률 44% | 답 ②

| 해석 | 청구 가격이 확실히 높기 때문에 파인다이닝의 절대적인 전제조건은 탁월함이다. 운영자는 레스토랑을 효율적으로 만들기 위해 가능한 모든 것을 할 수 있지만, 손님들은 여전히 신중하고 개인적인 서비스를 기대한다. 고도로 숙련된 요리사가 주문에 따라 준비하고 전문 서버가 가져다 주는 그런 음식들 말이다. 이 서비스는 문자 그대로 노동이기 때문에, 생산성에서 간신히 수지를 맞추는 개선만 가능하다. 예를 들어, 요리사, 서버 또는 바텐더는 인간 수행의 한계에 도달하기 전에 제한된 수준으로만 더 빨리 움직일 수 있다. 따라서 효율성을 향상시켜 적당한 절감만 가능하므로 가격 상승이 ② 불가피해진다. (가격이 오르면 소비자들이 더욱 안목이 있게 되는 것은 경제학의 원칙이다.) 따라서, 고급 식당의 고객들은 우수성을 기대하고 요구하며 기꺼이 지불할 것이다.

① 익살맞은, 웃기는
② 불가피한, 필연적인
③ 터무니없는, 불합리한
④ 상상도 할 수 없는, 믿을 수 없는

| 정답해설 | ② 56% 파인다이닝의 전제조건인 탁월함에 대한 손님들의 기대로 인해 수지 개선이 어려운 점을 서술한 후, 결국 이로

인해 가격 상승이 불가피하다는 내용이 이어졌다. 따라서 빈칸에 들어갈 것으로 가장 적절한 것은 ②이다.

어휘

prerequisite 필요조건	manual labor 노동일
marginal 하찮은, 근소한; 가장자리의	
moderate 보통의, 중간의	escalation 확대, 강화
inevitable 불가피한, 필연적인	axiom 이치, 격언
discriminating 구별하는, 안목 있는	clientele 고객
ludicrous 터무니없는	preposterous 터무니없는
inconceivable 상상도 할 수 없는	

오답률 TOP1
18 독해 > 글의 일관성 파악하기 > 글의 순서

오답률 51% | 답 ③

| 해석 | 확실히, 인간의 언어는 원숭이와 유인원의 명백히 제한된 발성으로부터 두드러진다. 또한, 그것은 동물의 다른 어떤 형태의 의사소통을 훨씬 능가하는 정교함을 보여준다.

(C) 심지어 우리와 가장 가까운 영장류들도 몇 년 동안 집중적인 훈련을 받은 후에도 초보적인 의사소통 체계 이상의 것을 얻을 수 없는 것 같다. 언어의 복잡성은 확실히 종 특유의 특성이다.

(A) 그렇긴 하지만, 인간 언어에 크게 미치지 못할지라도, 그럼에도 불구하고 많은 종들은 자연환경에서 인상적으로 복잡한 소통 체계를 보여준다.

(B) 그리고 그들은 인간과 함께 길러졌을 때와 같이 인공적인 환경에서 훨씬 더 복잡한 체계를 배울 수 있다.

| 정답해설 | ③ 49% 주어진 문장에서 인간의 언어가 원숭이와 유인원의 발성보다 우수하다는 점을 서술한 후에, 비슷한 맥락으로 (C)에서 유인원들이 훈련을 받은 후에도 복잡한 의사소통은 불가능하다는 것을 서술하고 있다. 상대적으로 (A)와 (B)는 영장류들도 소통 체계를 가질 수 있다는 비슷한 내용이 서술되어 있는데, (C)와는 대조적인 내용이므로 이를 연결할 수 있는 대조의 연결사 That said로 시작하는 (A)가 먼저 나오고 이후에 비슷한 흐름의 내용을 And로 연결한 (B)가 이어지는 것이 자연스럽다.

어휘

stand out 눈에 띄다	vocalization 발성
rudimentary 근본적인	trait 특성
that said 그렇긴 하지만	
fall short of ~에 미치지 못하다, 부족하다	
context 맥락, 문맥	primate 영장류
rudimentary 가장 기본적인	

오답률 TOP2
19 독해 > 대의 파악 > 주제 찾기

오답률 50% | 답 ④

| 해석 | 20세기 후반 사회주의는 서구와 개발도상국의 상당 지역에서 모두 퇴조하고 있었다. 시장 자본주의의 진화에 있어서 이 새로운 단계 동안, 세계 무역 패턴은 점점 더 연결되었고, 정보 기술의 발전은 규제가 완화된 금융 시장이 몇 초 안에 국경을 넘나드는 막대한 자본 흐름을 바꿀 수 있다는 것을 의미했다. '세계화'는 무역을 촉진하고 생산성 향상을 촉진하고 가격을 낮추었지만, 비평가들은 그것이 저임금 노동자들을 착취했고, 환경적 우려에 무관심했으며, 제3세계를 독점적인 자본주의 형태에 종속시켰다고 주장했다. 이 과정에 저항하기를 원했던 서구 사회의 많은 급진주의자들은 소외된 좌파 정당들보다는 자발적인 단체, 자선단체, 그리고 다른 비정부 단체들에 합류했다. 환경 운동 자체는 세계가 상호 연결되어 있다는 인식에서 비롯되었고, 확산된다면 언제든지 분노한 국제적인 이해 단체가 출현했다.

① 과거 개발도상국에서 세계화의 긍정적인 현상
② 20세기 사회주의의 쇠락과 자본주의의 출현
③ 세계 자본시장과 좌파 정치 단체의 갈등
④ 세계 자본주의의 착취적 특성과 그것에 대한 다양한 사회적 반응

| **정답해설** | ④ 50% 시장 자본주의의 진화에 따른 여러 가지 현상들을 서술하고 있는 글이다. 세계화에 대한 부정적인 결과들이 나열되었고, 이 과정에서 이에 저항하는 단체들이 출현했다고 했으므로 이 글의 주제로 가장 적절한 것은 ④이다.

어휘

socialism 사회주의	retreat 후퇴하다, 철수하다
interlink 연결되다	deregulate 규제를 철폐하다
allege 주장하다, 진술하다	indifferent 무관심한, 무심한
marginalized 소외된	diffuse 퍼지다, 퍼뜨리다
coalition 연합, 연대, 단체	affirmative 긍정의, 긍정하는
conflict 갈등	exploitative 착취적인

---

20 독해 > 대의 파악 > 심경   오답률 20%   답 ①

| **해석** | 이글거리는 한낮의 태양 아래, 최근 발굴된 자갈 더미에서 노란 달걀 모양의 돌이 눈에 띄었다. 호기심에서 열여섯 살의 광부 Komba Johnbull은 그것을 집어 들고 납작하고 피라미드 같은 표면을 만지작거렸다. Johnbull은 다이아몬드를 본 적이 없었지만, 큰 발견이라도 엄지손톱보다 크지 않을 것이라는 것을 충분히 알고 있었다. 그래도 그 돌은 다른 사람의 의견을 들어볼 수 있을 만큼 이례적이었다. 그는 소심하게 정글 깊숙한 곳에서 진흙을 파고 있는 경험이 많은 광부 중 한 명에게 그것을 가져갔다. 탄광 반장은 돌을 보고 눈을 크게 떴다. "주머니에 넣어." 그가 속삭였다. "계속 파헤쳐." 그 나이 든 광부는 그들이 무언가 큰 것을 발견했다고 누군가 생각한다면 위험할 수 있다고 경고했다. 그래서 Johnbull은 해질녘까지 자갈을 계속 삽질하면서 가끔 그의 주먹에 있는 무거운 돌을 움켜잡기 위해 잠시 멈췄다. 그럴 수도 있을까?

① 신나고 흥분한
② 고통스럽고 괴로운
③ 오만하고 확신에 찬
④ 초연하고 무관심한

| **정답해설** | ① 80% 소년 광부인 Johnbull이 다이아몬드로 추정되는 돌을 발견한 후 나이가 있는 광부의 조언에 따라 그 돌을 주머니에 넣은 후 흥분하고 초조한 상태로 일을 계속하는 모습을 서술하고 있는 글이므로 정답은 ①이다.

어휘

blazing 맹렬한, 격렬한	unearth 발굴하다
gravel 자갈	sheepishly 순하게, 소심하게
pit 탄광; 구덩이, 구멍	shovel 삽질하다; 삽

합격예상 체크

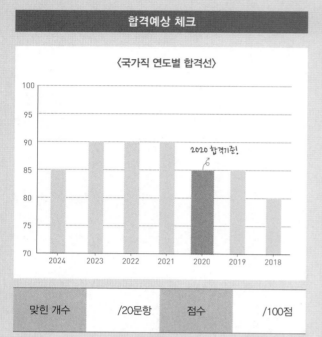

〈국가직 연도별 합격선〉

2020 합격기준

맞힌 개수	/20문항	점수	/100점

➡ ☐ 합격 ☐ 불합격

취약영역 체크

문항	정답	영역	문항	정답	영역
1	①	어휘 > 동의어	11	④	생활영어 > 회화
2	④	어휘 > 동의어	12	③	생활영어 > 회화
3	③	어휘 > 동의어	13	②	독해 > 빈칸의 내용 추론하기
4	①	어휘 > 동의어	14	③	독해 > 대의 파악
5	④	문법 > 문장의 구조와 동사 유형	15	④	독해 > 글의 일관성 파악하기
6	②	문법 > 동사의 형태	16	④	독해 > 글의 일관성 파악하기
7	③	문법 > 문장의 구조와 동사 유형	17	④	독해 > 글의 일관성 파악하기
8	②	독해 > 대의 파악	18	③	독해 > 세부내용 찾기
9	①	독해 > 대의 파악	19	①	독해 > 빈칸의 내용 추론하기
10	④	독해 > 세부내용 찾기	20	②	독해 > 빈칸의 내용 추론하기

⬇ 영역별 틀린 개수로 취약영역을 확인하세요!

어휘	/4	문법	/3	독해	/11	생활영어	/2

➡ 나의 취약영역: _____

※ [정답해설]과 [오답해설] 선지의 50% 표시는 〈1초 합격예측 서비스〉를 통해 수집된 선지 선택률을 나타냅니다.

---

1 어휘 > 동의어 　　오답률 33%　답 ①

| 해석 | 솔직한 소비자 평가 및 가격대와 함께 전자레인지 모델과 스타일에 대한 광범위한 목록은 가전제품 비교 웹사이트에서 얻을 수 있다.

① 67% 솔직한
② 10% 논리적인
③ 11% 함축적인
④ 12% 열정적인

| 정답해설 | ① 가전제품 비교 웹사이트에서 이용 가능한 내용들이 나열되어 있다. 전자레인지 모델, 스타일, 가격과 함께 소비자 리뷰가 제시되었고, 이 중 소비자 리뷰를 수식할 수 있는 표현으로 맥락상 '솔직한'이 가장 적절하다. 따라서 candid의 동의어로 ①이 가장 적절하다.

어휘

candid 솔직한　　　　　extensive 광범위한
review 평가, 리뷰　　　　appliance 가전제품
comparison 비교

---

2 어휘 > 동의어 　　오답률 46%　답 ④

| 해석 | 옐로스톤이 사실상 화산 작용에 의해 만들어졌다는 것은 오래전부터 알려져 있었고, 화산에 대한 한 가지 사실은 그것들이 보통 눈에 잘 띈다는 것이다.

① 6% 수동적인
② 15% 증기가 많은; 공허한
③ 25% 위험한
④ 54% 눈에 띄는, 주목할 만한

| 정답해설 | ④ 화산이 주는 이미지를 생각해 보면 다른 일반 지형과

비교했을 때 특별하다는 것을 유추할 수 있고, conspicuous를 분석하면 con(완전히) + spicuous(보이다)의 조합으로 '잘 보이는, 눈에 잘 띄는'의 의미이다. 따라서 동의어로 가장 적절한 것은 ④이다.

어휘

conspicuous 눈에 잘 띄는　　　volcanic 화산 작용에 의해 만들어진
volcano 화산　　　　　　　　generally 보통, 일반적으로

---

3 어휘 > 동의어 　　오답률 18%　답 ③

| 해석 | 그는 도시를 속속들이 알고 있기 때문에 너에게 그곳에 가는 방법을 말해줄 수 있는 최적의 인물이다.

① 3% 결국
② 8% 문화적으로
③ 82% 철저하게, 완전히
④ 7% 잠정적으로; 시험삼아

| 정답해설 | ③ inside out을 있는 그대로 해석하면 '안팎으로'의 의미이다. 따라서 그 도시를 안팎으로 알고 있다는 것은 '완전히' 알고 있다는 것으로 볼 수 있으므로 동의어로 ③이 가장 적절하다.

어휘

inside out 속속들이, 완전히

오답률 TOP 1

4 어휘 > 동의어 　　오답률 62% 　답 ①

| 해석 | 그 길을 따라 줄곧 판지, 눈, 그리고 색판지에 새겨진 문구를 포함해, 그 팀을 예우하려는 많은 소박한 시도들이 있었다.
① 38% 예우하다, 존경하다　② 24% 구성하다
③ 10% 알리다, 공표하다　④ 28% 참여하다, 가입하다

| 정답해설 | ① 사람들이 판지와 색판지에 문구를 새겨 팀에게 무엇을 했을지를 생각하면, 좋은 의도임을 알 수 있다. 예우의 표현임을 유추할 수 있으므로 동의어로 ①이 가장 적절하다. tribute는 '찬사, 감사의 표시'의 의미이다.

어휘

pay tribute to ~에게 경의를 표하다　homespun 손으로 만든, 소박한
etch 뚜렷이 새기다　　　　cardboard 판지, 마분지
construction paper 색판지, 색도화지

5 문법 > 문장의 구조와 동사 유형 > 문장의 구성과 종류
　　오답률 47% 　답 ④

| 해석 | ① 대도시의 교통은 소도시의 교통보다 더 분주하다.
② 내가 다음 주에 해변에 누워있을 때, 당신을 생각할 것이다.
③ 건포도는 한때 비싼 음식이었고, 부유한 사람들만이 그것을 먹었다.
④ 색의 채도는 색상이 얼마나 많은 회색을 포함하고 있는지와 관련이 있다.

| 정답해설 | ④ 53% 전치사 to의 목적어로 명사절인 '의문사 + 주어 + 동사'가 간접의문문의 어순으로 올바르게 왔다. 이때 의문사는 종속절의 동사인 타동사 contains의 목적어로 how much gray가 의문사가 포함된 명사로 본다.

| 오답해설 | ① 11% 접속사 than에 이어진 비교 대상은 소도시의 교통(the traffic)이 되어야 하므로 of a small city의 한정을 받는 지시대명사로 단수 명사인 that이 와야 한다.
② 11% 주절에 이어 접속사 when이 이끄는 시간부사절에서 현재동사가 미래를 나타내야 하므로 will be lying은 am lying으로 바꿔야 한다.
③ 25% 문맥상 두 번째 문장의 주어는 '부유한 사람들'이 되어야 한다. 따라서 명사 wealth가 아닌 형용사 wealthy로 바꿔야 하며, 'the + 형용사'는 '~한 사람들'의 의미이다.

어휘

raisin 건포도　　　　intensity 채도, 선명도; 강도
be related to ~와 관련이 있다　contain 함유하다, 포함하다

오답률 TOP 3

6 문법 > 동사의 형태 > 시제 　오답률 57% 　답 ②

| 정답해설 | ② 43% 주절의 동사가 '명령'의 동사인 command가 왔고, 종속절이 당위성의 의미가 있으므로 종속절의 동사는 시제 일치 예외로 'should + 동사원형'이 와야 하며, 이때 조동사 should는 생략이 가능하다. 따라서 should가 생략되고 동사원형 cease만 남은 올바른 문장이다. cease는 자동사로 쓸 수 있는 동사이다.

| 오답해설 | ① 20% raise는 타동사로 동사가 능동태이므로 목적어가 이어져야 한다. 목적어가 없고, 문맥상 문제들이 '생겨난' 것으로 보아 수동태 have been raised로 바꿔야 한다.

③ 18% 관계대명사 that이 이끄는 종속절의 동사는 주절과 시제 일치가 되어야 하므로 미래시제인 will blow는 올 수 없다. 문맥상 시제 차이가 크게 있지 않으므로 주절과 일치시켜 과거동사인 blew로 바꿔야 한다.
④ 19% 우리말과 영작문의 주어가 일치하고, survive는 능동의 의미로 '~로부터 살아남다'의 의미가 있으므로 수동태로 전환할 필요가 없다. are survived by를 survive로 바꿔야 한다.

어휘

several 몇몇의　　　　due to ~에 기인하여
committee 위원회　　　harsh 혹독한

오답률 TOP 2

7 문법 > 문장의 구조와 동사 유형 > 동사와 문장의 5형식
　　오답률 61% 　답 ③

| 정답해설 | ③ 39% 전치사의 목적어인 promoting의 대상은 문장 전체의 목적어인 him으로, 문맥상 '승진되는' 것이므로 수동 동명사인 being promoted로 바꿔야 한다.

| 오답해설 | ① 14% 주어와 목적어가 동일한 대상이므로 목적어로 재귀대명사인 themselves가 올바르게 왔다.
② 31% '~하지 않을 수 없다'의 표현으로 'have no choice but to + 동사원형'의 구조로 올바르게 영작된 문장이다. 이때 but은 전치사로, 전치사의 목적어로 to부정사가 이어진 구조이다.
④ 16% 가주어 it과 호응하는 진주어로 to부정사 두 개(to assemble and take apart~)가 병치 구조로 올바르게 왔다. 두 번째 to는 생략이 가능하다. easy는 난이형용사로 가주어와 진주어를 활용해 표현하며, 진주어로 접속사 that이 이끄는 명사절을 쓸 수 없음에 유의해야 한다.

어휘

adapt 적응하다, 맞추다
have no choice but to + R ~하지 않을 수 없다
prohibit A from R-ing A가 ~하는 것을 막다
assemble 조립하다; 집합시키다　take apart 분해하다, 해체하다

8 독해 > 대의 파악 > 요지·주장 찾기 　오답률 7% 　답 ②

| 해석 | 다른 사람의 생각을 듣는 것은 — 당신 자신과 세상 안에 있는 당신의 위치에 대해서 뿐만 아니라 — 세상에 대해 당신이 믿는 이야기가 온전한 것인지 아닌지를 알 수 있는 유일한 방법이다. 우리는 모두 우리의 신념을 검토하고 그것들을 공개적으로 토의하고 그것들이 호흡하도록 둘 필요가 있다. 다른 사람들이, 특히 우리가 기본적이라고 여기는 개념에 대해 말해야 하는 것을 듣는 것은 우리 마음과 가슴의 창문을 여는 것과 같다. 의견을 말하는 것은 중요하다. 그러나 듣지 않고 의견을 말하는 것은 냄비와 팬을 함께 세게 두드리는 것과 같다: 비록 그것이 당신에게 관심을 갖게는 할지라도 당신을 존중하게 하지는 못할 것이다. 대화가 의미를 갖게 되도록 하는 데 있어 세 가지 전제 조건이 있다. 1. 당신이 무엇을 말하고 있는지 알아야 하고, 이는 당신이 독창적인 견해를 가지며 진부하고 독창성 없는 미리 만들어 낸 주장을 그대로 따라하지 않는다는 것을 의미한다. 2. 당신은 당신이 이야기하고 있는 사람들을 존중하고 비록 당신이 그들의 입장에 동의하지 않더라도 진정으로 그들을 예의바르게 대하려고 한다. 3. 당신은 계속하여 좋은 유머와 분별력을 가지고 주제에 대한 자신의 관점을 다루면서 상대방이 말하는 것을 들을 만큼 똑똑하고 충분한 정보가 있어야 한다.

① 우리는 다른 사람들을 설득하는 데 좀 더 단호해져야 한다.
② 우리는 대화를 잘하기 위해서 듣고 의견을 말해야 할 필요가 있다.
③ 우리는 우리가 보는 세상에 대한 믿음을 바꾸는 데 주저한다.
④ 우리는 우리가 선택한 것만 듣고 다른 의견들을 무시하려고 애쓴다.

| **정답해설** | ② 93% 이 글은 대화를 잘하기 위해서 다른 사람의 생각을 듣는 것의 중요성에 대해 말하고 있다. 글의 첫 번째 문장이 주제문으로 다른 사람의 생각을 듣는 것이 당신이 믿는 것들에 대해 확인할 수 있는 유일한 방법이며, 다른 사람들의 의견을 듣는 것은 열린 자세로 대화에 임하는 것이라고 말하고 있다. 그 이후에는 이에 대한 부연 설명이 이어진다. 듣지 않고 말하는 것은 시끄럽게 떠들기만 하는 것이라 말한 후, 의미 있는 대화를 위해서 필요한 세 가지 전제 조건을 제시한다. 따라서 글의 요지로 가장 적절한 것은 ②이다.

어휘

intact 온전한, 손상되지 않은	air out 공표하다, 퍼뜨리다; 환기하다
regard A as B A를 B라고 여기다	foundational 기초를 이루는, 기본의
prerequisite 필요[전제] 조건	worn-out 닳아 해진, 진부한
hand-me-down 값싼, 퇴물의	pre-fab 조립식의
authentically 확실하게	perspective 관점, 견해
uninterrupted 연속적인, 끊임없는	discernment 인식, 식별[통찰]력

---

9 독해 > 대의 파악 > 제목 찾기   오답률 20%   답 ①

| **해석** | 미래는 불확실할지 모르지만, 기후 변화, 바뀌는 인구 통계, 지정학 같은 어떤 것들은 명백하다. 유일한 보장은 변화가 있을 것이라는 점인데 그 변화는 멋질 수도, 끔찍할 수도 있다. 현재와 미래에 예술이 어떤 도움이 될지 뿐만 아니라 이러한 변화에 예술가들이 어떻게 반응할지는 고려해볼 가치가 있다. 보고서는 2040년까지 인간이 초래한 기후 변화의 영향은 피할 수 없을 것이고, 20년 후 예술과 삶의 중심에서 큰 이슈가 될 것이라고 제시하고 있다. 미래의 예술가들은 포스트 휴먼과 포스트 인류세(人類世)의 가능성 — 인공지능(AI), 우주에 있는 인간의 식민지, 그리고 잠재적 파멸과 씨름할 것이다. #미투(MeToo)와 흑인 민권 운동(Black Lives Matter : 흑인 생명도 중요하다)을 둘러싼 예술에서 볼 수 있는 정체성의 정치학은 환경 결정론, 경계 정치, 이주가 훨씬 더 뚜렷해지면서 성장하게 될 것이다. 예술은 점점 더 다양해질 것이고 우리가 기대하는 것만큼 '예술처럼 보이지' 않을 수도 있다. 미래에, 모두가 보는 온라인에서의 가시적인 우리의 삶에 우리가 싫증나게 되고 우리의 사생활이 거의 없어지면, 익명성이 명성보다 더 바람직할지도 모른다. 수천 또는 수백만의 '좋아요'와 '팔로워'들 대신에, 우리는 진실성과 관계에 굶주리게 될 것이다. 예술은 결국 개인보다는 좀 더 집단적이고 경험적이게 될 수 있다.
① 예술은 미래에 어떤 모습일까?
② 지구 온난화는 우리의 삶에 어떤 영향을 미칠까?
③ 인공지능이 환경에 어떤 영향을 미칠까?
④ 정치 운동으로 인해 어떤 변화가 일어날까?

| **정답해설** | ① 80% 첫 번째 문장에서 '미래 변화'라는 토픽을 제시하고 있고, 글 전반적으로 art, artist라는 키워드가 반복되고 있다. 세 번째 문장에서 '예술가들이 현재와 미래에 이러한 변화에 어떻게 반응할지를 고려해 볼 가치가 있다'라고 주제문을 제시하고, 이후에 구체적인 예시를 제시하고 있다. 기후 변화가 예술에서 큰 이슈가 될 것이고, 미래의 인공지능 등과 씨름할 것이고, 미투와 흑인 민권 운동, SNS 등의 예시를 통해 변화에 반응하는 예술의 모습을 설명하고 있다. 따라서 글의 제목으로 가장 적절한 것은 ①이다.

어휘

undeniable 부정할 수 없는, 틀림없는	
demographics 인구통계	geopolitics 지정학
guarantee 보증(서); 보장하다	wrestle with ~와 맞붙다, 고심하다
doom 운명, 파멸; ~할 운명에 처해 있다	
identity 정체성; 신원	weary 피곤한, 지친
anonymity 익명	starve 굶주리다
authenticity 확실성, 신뢰성	experiential 경험상의, 경험에 의한

---

10 독해 > 세부내용 찾기 > 내용 불일치 찾기   오답률 12%   답 ④

| **해석** | 미국 연방헌법 수정조항 제2조는 "잘 규율된 시민군은 자유로운 주의 안보에 필수적이므로, 무기를 소장하고 휴대하는 국민의 권리는 침해될 수 없다."라고 명시한다. 연방대법원 판결들은 이 수정조항을 인용하면서 총기를 규제하기 위한 주(州 정부)의 권리를 지지해 왔다. 그러나 2008년의 무기를 소유하고 휴대할 수 있는 개인의 권리를 확인하는 결정에서 법원은 권총을 금지하고 권총을 가정에서 안전장치를 해 두거나 분해해 둘 것을 규정하는 워싱턴 DC의 법을 기각했다. 많은 총기 지지자들은 소유권을 천부의 권리이며 이 국가 유산의 중요한 부분으로 여긴다. 스위스에 기반을 두고 있는 Small Arms Survey의 2007년 보고서에 따르면 전 세계 인구의 5퍼센트 미만을 가진 미국은 전 세계 민간인 소유 총기의 약 35~50퍼센트를 가지고 있다. 미국은 1인당 총기에서 첫째를 차지한다. 미국은 또한 세계의 가장 발전된 국가들 중에서 가장 높은 총기에 의한 살인율을 가지고 있다. 그러나 많은 총기 소유권 지지자들은 이 통계들이 인과 관계를 나타내지 못하며 총기 살인이나 다른 총기관련 범죄가 1990년대 초의 높은 기록들 이후로 줄어들고 있다고 지적한다.
① 2008년에 미국 연방 대법원은 권총을 금지하는 Washington DC의 법을 뒤집었다.
② 많은 총기 옹호자들은 총기의 소유는 천부의 권리라고 주장한다.
③ 가장 발전된 국가들 중에서 미국은 가장 높은 총기 살인율을 가지고 있다.
④ 미국에서 총기 관련 범죄는 최근 30년 넘게 꾸준하게 증가하고 있다.

| **정답해설** | ④ 88% 마지막 문장에서 보면 미국의 총기 관련 범죄 기록은 1990년대 초에 가장 높았고 그 이후로 줄어들고 있다고 언급하고 있으므로 글의 내용과 일치하지 않는다.

| **오답해설** | ① 3% 세 번째 문장에서 법원이 권총의 휴대를 금하는 Washington DC의 법을 기각했다고 언급하고 있으므로 글의 내용과 일치한다.
② 4% 네 번째 문장에서 많은 총기 옹호자들이 총기의 소유권을 천부의 권리라고 여긴다고 언급하고 있으므로 글의 내용과 일치한다.
③ 5% 일곱 번째 문장에서 미국은 또한 세계의 가장 발전된 국가들 중에서 가장 높은 총기에 의한 살인율을 가지고 있다고 언급하고 있으므로 글의 내용과 일치한다.

어휘

the Amendment (美) 헌법 수정조항	constitution 헌법
infringe 침해하다, 위반하다	uphold 지지[후원]하다
regulate 규제[규정]하다; 조절[조정]하다	
firearm (라이플 · 권총 등의) 소형 화기	
confirm 확인하다; 확신하다	
disassemble 분해하다, 해체하다	ban 금지하다
heritage 유산, 세습 재산	advocate 옹호하다, 지지하다
homicide 살인(죄)	per capita 1인당
statistics 통계 자료, 통계학	proponent 지지자; 제안자

11 생활어 > 회화 | 오답률 16% | 답 ④

| 해석 | ① A: 납입 기한이 언제인가요?
B: 다음 주까지 내셔야 합니다.
② A: 이 짐을 부쳐야 하나요?
B: 아니오, 비행기에 실어도 될 만큼 충분히 작네요.
③ A: 우리 언제 어디서 만날까요?
B: 8시 30분에 당신의 사무실로 태우러 갈게요.
④ A: 제가 요리 대회에서 입상했어요.
B: 당신이 없었다면, 저는 못했을 거예요.

| 정답해설 | ④ 84% A가 요리 대회에서 입상했다고 했으므로 B는 축하의 인사를 건네는 것이 적절하다. B의 내용은 상을 탄 A가 도움을 준 사람에게 건넬 수 있는 표현이므로 적절하지 않다.

12 생활어 > 회화 | 오답률 4% | 답 ③

| 해석 | A: 전화주셔서 감사합니다. 로얄 포인트 호텔 예약부입니다. 제 이름은 Sam입니다. 무엇을 도와드릴까요?
B: 안녕하세요, 객실 하나 예약하고 싶어요.
A: 두 가지 타입이 있어요. 디럭스룸과 럭셔리 스위트룸입니다.
B: ③ 그것들의 차이가 무엇일까요?
A: 우선, 스위트룸은 매우 넓습니다. 침실 외에 주방, 거실과 식당이 있어요.
B: 비싸겠네요.
A: 음, 1박에 200달러가 넘습니다.
B: 그러면, 디럭스룸으로 할게요.
① 더 필요한 것이 있으십니까
② 객실 번호를 알려주시겠어요
③ 그것들의 차이가 무엇일까요
④ 객실에 반려동물이 들어갈 수 있나요

| 정답해설 | ③ 96% 두 가지 객실 유형을 들은 후에 질문을 했고, 이에 대한 대답으로 스위트룸에 대한 설명을 들은 것으로 보아 빈칸에는 객실 유형의 차이점에 대해 질문을 했음을 유추할 수 있다. 따라서 빈칸에 들어갈 것으로 ③이 가장 적절하다.

어휘
reservation 예약   in addition to ~이외에, ~뿐 아니라

13 독해 > 빈칸의 내용 추론하기 > 연결어 추론 | 오답률 36% | 답 ②

| 해석 | 홈스쿨링을 지지하는 사람들은 아이들이 안전한 사랑의 환경에 있을 때 더 잘 배운다고 믿는다. 많은 심리학자들은 집을 가장 자연적인 학습 환경으로 보고 있으며, 원래 집은 학교가 설립되기 훨씬 전부터 교실이었다. 홈스쿨링을 하는 학부모들은 자녀의 교육을 관찰할 수 있고 전통적인 학교 환경에서는 부족한 관심을 아이들에게 줄 수 있다고 주장한다. 학생들은 또한 무엇을 공부할지, 언제 공부할지를 선택할 수 있어서 그들 자신만의 속도로 학습할 수 있다. (A) 대조적으로 홈스쿨링에 대한 비판자들은 교실에 있지 않은 아이들은 또래와의 상호 작용이 거의 없기 때문에 중요한 사회적 기술을 배우는 것을 놓친다고 말한다. 하지만, 몇몇 연구들은 가정에서 교육받은 아이들이 그들의 행복에 신경을 쓰는 부모들의 지도와 함께 그들은 가정의 편안함과 안전 속에서 더 많은 시간을 보냈기 때문에 다른 학생들만큼 사회적이고 정서적인 발달에 있어서 잘하는 것같이 보인다는 것을 보여주었다. (B) 그럼에도 불구하고, 홈스쿨링에 대한 많은 비판자들은 아이들을 효과적으로 가르칠 수 있는 부모의 능력에 대해 우려를 제기해 왔다.

(A)	(B)
① 따라서	그럼에도 불구하고
② 대조적으로	그럼에도 불구하고
③ 따라서	그것과 반대로
④ 대조적으로	게다가

| 정답해설 | ② 64% 홈스쿨링에 대한 찬반 입장에 대한 내용의 글이다. (A) 앞에서는 홈스쿨링 지지자들의 입장이 설명되고 있다. 홈스쿨링은 안전한 사람의 환경에서 학습이 이루어지고 부모의 관심이 주어지며 학생들은 자신만의 속도로 학습할 수 있다는 홈스쿨링의 장점이 설명되고 있고 (A) 뒤에는 홈스쿨링을 비판하는 비판자들의 입장이 나오고 있으므로 빈칸 (A)에는 대조의 연결어 In contrast가 오는 것이 가장 적절하다. 빈칸 (A) 문장에서 홈스쿨링에 대한 비판자들의 의견으로 홈스쿨링은 또래와의 상호 작용이 없어서 사회적 기술을 배우지 못한다고 말하고 나서 though 문장에서 이를 반박하는 내용으로 홈스쿨링을 하는 아이들이 사회적이고 정서적인 발달을 잘하고 있다는 것을 보여준다는 연구를 제시하여 홈스쿨링의 긍정적인 측면을 서술하고 다시 빈칸 (B) 뒤에서 홈스쿨링에 대한 비판자들의 의견이 다시 제시되므로 빈칸 (B)에는 역접, 대조의 연결어가 쓰인 In spite of this가 오는 것이 가장 적절하다. 따라서 두 가지를 모두 충족하는 ②가 가장 적절하다.

어휘
advocate 옹호자, 지지자   secure 안전한, 안정된
miss out 놓치다   peer 동료, 또래
comfort 안심, 위로   guidance 지도, 안내

14 독해 > 대의 파악 > 주제 찾기 | 오답률 22% | 답 ③

| 해석 | 많은 사람들에게, 일은 강박이 되었다. 사람들이 급료를 받고 하는 일 외에 아이들, 취미 활동, 애완동물, 또는 어떤 종류의 생활을 위해서든 시간을 내려고 애를 쓰면서 그것은 극도의 피로, 불행, 그리고 남녀의 불평등을 유발했다. 하지만 점차, 젊은 근로자들이 반발하고 있다. 그들 중 더 많은 이들이 유연성을 기대하고 요구한다 — 예를 들어, 원격 근무, 늦은 출근이나 이른 퇴근, 또는 운동이나 명상을 위해 시간을 낼 수 있는 것처럼 일상적인 문제들과 더불어, 신생아를 위한 유급 휴가와 넉넉한 휴가 기간. 그들 삶의 나머지 부분이 특정한 장소나 시간에 얽매이지 않은 채, 전화기 상에서 벌어진다 — 일이라고 해서 다를 것이 있겠는가?
① 당신의 급여를 인상하는 방법들
② 불평등을 줄이는 것에 대한 강박관념
③ 유연 근무제에 대한 늘어나는 요구
④ 긴 휴가를 누리는 삶의 장점

| 정답해설 | ③ 78% 첫 번째와 두 번째 문장에서 많은 사람들이 근무 이외의 개인적인 생활을 위해 시간을 내려고 애쓰면서 일은 강박이 되어 피로감과 불행을 유발한다고 말한다. But으로 시작하는 세 번째 문장부터 내용이 전환되어, 이런 상황에 반발해 젊은 근로자들이 근무의 유연성을 요구한다는 내용이 전개된다. 그 예로, 출산 관련 유급 휴가, 긴 휴가 기간, 출퇴근 시간의 유연성, 여가 확보 등이 제시된다. 따라서 글의 주제로 ③이 가장 적절하다.

어휘
obsession 강박관념   burnout 번아웃, 극도의 피로
gender inequity 성 불평등
struggle to + R ~하려고 분투하다, 노력하다

paycheck 봉급, 급료
meditation 명상, 숙고

flexibility 유연성, 융통성

---

15 독해 > 글의 일관성 파악하기 > 글의 순서   오답률 17%   답 ③

| 해석 | 과거의 연구는 잦은 심리적 스트레스를 경험하는 것이 심혈관 질환, 즉 미국에서 20세 이상의 사람들 거의 절반에게 발생하는 병의 중요한 위험 요인이 될 수 있다는 것을 보여주었다.
(C) 잦은 스트레스의 한 가지 원인은 운전으로, 교통 체증 또는 미숙한 운전자들에게 흔히 동반되는 불안과 관련된 스트레스 요인이다.
(A) 그런데, 이 말은 매일 운전하는 사람들이 심장 질환에 걸리게 되어 있다는 뜻일까, 또는 운전의 스트레스를 덜어줄 간단한 방법이 있을까?
(B) 새로운 연구에 따르면, (그런 방법이) 있다. 연구원들은 운전하면서 음악을 듣는 것이 심장 건강에 영향을 미치는 스트레스를 덜어주는 데 도움이 된다고 말했다.

| 정답해설 | ③ 83% 주어진 문장은 과거의 연구에 따르면 잦은 스트레스가 심혈관 질환의 중요한 위험 요인이 될 수 있다고 설명한다. 여기서 언급된 잦은 스트레스를 (C)에서 받아서, 잦은 스트레스의 한 가지 원인으로 운전을 든다. 이 내용을 (A)의 this로 받아서, 그렇다면 운전을 하는 사람은 심장 질환에 걸릴 수밖에 없다는 뜻인지 묻고 운전의 스트레스를 줄일 수 있는 방법이 있는지 질문한다. 그 질문을 받아 (B)에서 새로운 연구에 따르면 운전 중 음악을 듣는 방법이 효과적이라고 대답한다. 따라서 글의 순서로 가장 적절한 것은 ③이다.

어휘
cardiovascular 심장 혈관의
accompany 수반하다, 동반하다
relieve 경감[완화]시키다; 안심시키다

associated with ~와 관련된
ease 완화하다, 덜어주다

---

16 독해 > 글의 일관성 파악하기 > 글의 흐름과 무관한 문장
오답률 29%   답 ④

| 해석 | 뇌는 가까운 환경에서 위협을 인지하면, 신체에 복잡한 일련의 사건들을 일으킨다. 뇌는 화학적 호르몬을 혈류로 분비하는 기관인 다양한 분비샘에 전기적 메시지를 보낸다. 혈액은 그 다음에 다양한 것들을 하도록 유도되는 다른 기관들로 이 호르몬들을 재빨리 이동시킨다. 예를 들어, 신장 위의 부신은 신체의 스트레스 호르몬인 아드레날린을 분출한다. 아드레날린은 온몸을 이동하면서 눈을 크게 뜨고 위험 징후들을 살피고, 혈액과 부수적인 호르몬들이 계속 흘러가도록 심장을 더 빠르게 펌프질하고, 그리고 골격근을 긴장시켜 위험에 반격하거나 위험으로부터 달아날 준비를 하는 것과 같은 일들을 한다. 이 전체 과정은 신체가 생명을 구하기 위해 싸우거나 달아나도록 준비시키기 때문에 투쟁 도피 반응이라고 불린다. ④ 인간들은 다양한 호르몬의 분비를 조절하기 위해 분비샘들을 의식적으로 통제한다. 일단 이 반응이 시작되고 나면, 그것을 무시하는 것이 불가능한데, 호르몬들은 논리적으로 설득되지 않기 때문이다.

| 정답해설 | ④ 71% 이 글은 뇌가 주변에서 위험을 인지했을 때 신체가 어떤 일련의 반응을 보여 주는지 설명하는 내용이다. 뇌가 다양한 분비샘과 기관에 메시지를 보내면 호르몬이 혈류로 분비되어 혈액이 호르몬을 다양한 기관으로 이동시켜 여러 반응을 불러일으킨다는 것이다. 그 예로 ①~③은 아드레날린의 분비와 그로 인한 신체 반응에 관해 설명하는 데에 비해, ④는 인간이 호르몬 분비샘을 의식적으로 통제할 수 있다는 내용이어서 글의 전체적인 흐름에

서 벗어난다. ④의 다음 문장에서 호르몬은 논리적으로 설득되지 않는다는 내용상 호르몬 분비를 조절한다는 ④는 글의 흐름상 어색하다.

어휘
perceive 인지하다, 인식하다
gland [생리·식물] 선(腺), 샘
adrenal glands 부신
tense 긴장시키다; 팽팽한
lash out 강타하다; 채찍질하다
release 방출; 석방, 해방

initiate 시작하다, 개시하다
prompt 자극하다, 촉발하다
kidney 신장, 콩팥
skeletal 골격의
consciously 의식적으로
reason with ~를 설득하다

---

17 독해 > 글의 일관성 파악하기 > 주어진 문장의 삽입
오답률 38%   답 ④

| 해석 | 1903년에 프랑스의 화학자 Edouard Benedictus는 어느 날 딱딱한 바닥에 유리 플라스크를 떨어뜨려 깨뜨렸다. 하지만 놀랍게도 플라스크는 산산조각 나지 않았고, 원래 형태의 대부분을 여전히 유지했다. 그는 플라스크를 조사했을 때 (그 플라스크) 안쪽에 얇은 막의 코팅이 있다는 것을 알아냈는데, 코팅은 그 플라스크가 가지고 있던 콜로디온 용액의 잔여물이었다. 그는 이 특이한 현상을 노트에 적어두었지만, 몇 주 뒤에 자동차 사고에서 날아오는 자동차 앞 유리에 크게 다친 사람들에 관한 신문 기사를 읽을 때까지는 그것에 관해 더 생각하지 않았다. ④ 그가 그 유리 플라스크에 관한 자신의 경험을 기억해낸 것은 바로 그때였고, 재빨리 그는 특별한 코팅이 자동차 앞 유리에 적용되면 그것이 산산조각 나지 않을 것이라고 상상했다. 그로부터 얼마 지나지 않아, 그는 세계 최초의 안전유리를 생산하는 데 성공했다.

| 정답해설 | ④ 62% 이 글은 프랑스의 화학자가 유리 플라스크를 떨어뜨렸지만, 완전히 부서지지 않은 것을 보고 플라스크 안에 발린 코팅 용액의 존재를 알아냈고, 나중에 신문 기사를 읽다가 이 일을 떠올려 이 용액을 자동차 유리창에 적용했다는 내용이다. 주어진 문장에서 유리 플라스크와 관련된 경험을 then he remembered 라고 했으므로 그 이전까지는 기억하지 못했다고 볼 수 있다. ③에서 그는 유리 플라스크에 관한 내용을 기록해 두었지만 한동안 잊어버렸다고 했고 ④에서 그가 안전유리 생산에 성공했다고 설명하므로, 주어진 문장이 들어갈 가장 적절한 위치는 ④이다.

어휘
shatter 산산이 부서지다
residue 잔여물
windshield (자동차 앞부분의) 방풍 유리
be applied to ~에 적용되다

retain 유지하다

---

18 독해 > 세부내용 찾기 > 내용 불일치 찾기   오답률 29%   답 ③

| 해석 | Croatia의 Dubrovnik는 혼란 상태이다. 그것의 주요 관광 명소가 80피트의 중세 벽로로 둘러싸인 해안가의 Old Town이기 때문에 이 달마티안 지역 해안 도시는 방문객들을 잘 흡수하지 못한다. 그리고 유람선들이 이곳에 정박할 때면 관광객 군단은 Old Town을 탱크톱을 입은 관광객들이 마을의 석회암으로 포장된 거리를 활보하는 불길한 분위기로 변화시킨다. 그렇다, Dubrovnik 시에서는 유람선 관광을 억제하기 위해 적극적으로 노력해 왔지만, 어떠한 것도 Old Town을 계속되는 관광객 무리로부터 구해낼 수 없다. 설상가상으로, 여분의 돈을 벌도록 하는 유혹은 Old Town의 많은 집주인들이 그들의 장소를 에어비앤비로 바꾸도록 자극했고, 그 마을의 벽으로 둘러진 지역을 하나의 거대한 호텔로 만들었다. 당신은 Old Town에

서 지역 주민들처럼 '진정한' Dubrovnik를 경험하기를 원하는가? 이곳에서 그것을 발견하지는 않을 것이다. 절대로.

| 정답해설 | ③ 71% 네 번째 문장에서 Dubrovnik 시에서는 유람선 관광을 억제하기 위해 적극적으로 노력해 왔다고 했으므로 글의 내용과 일치하지 않는다.

| 오답해설 | ① 2% 두 번째 문장에서 Dubrovnik의 주요 관광 명소가 80피트의 중세 벽돌로 둘러싸인 해안가의 Old Town이라고 했으므로 글의 내용과 일치한다.

② 19% 세 번째 문장에서 유람선들이 정박할 때면 Old Town은 탱크톱을 입은 관광객들이 마을을 활보하는 불길한 분위기가 된다고 했으므로 글의 내용과 일치한다.

④ 8% 여러분의 돈을 벌고자 하는 유혹으로 인해 벽으로 둘려진 지역이 거대한 호텔이 되었다고 했으므로 글의 내용과 일치한다.

어휘

mess 엉망, 혼란	attraction 관광 명소
dock 정박하다; 부두	miasma 불길한 분위기, 악영향
limestone 석회석, 석회암	proactive 적극적인
curb 억제하다	perpetual 영구적인
to make matters worse 설상가상으로	
lure 유혹; 유혹하다	authentic 진정한

---

19 독해 > 빈칸의 내용 추론하기 > 빈칸 어휘 추론
오답률 43% 답 ①

| 해석 | 유기체가 살아 있을 때, 그것은 주변의 공기로부터 이산화탄소를 흡수한다. 그 이산화탄소의 대부분은 탄소12로 이루어져 있지만, 소량은 탄소14로 구성된다. 따라서 살아 있는 유기체는 언제나 매우 작은 양의 방사성 탄소인 탄소14를 포함한다. 살아 있는 유기체 옆에 놓인 감지기는 그 유기체 안의 탄소14에 의해서 방출되는 방사능을 기록한다. 그 유기체가 죽으면 그것은 더는 이산화탄소를 흡수하지 않는다. 어떠한 새로운 탄소14도 추가되지 않으며, 기존의 탄소14는 천천히 붕괴되어 질소로 바뀐다. 시간이 지날수록 탄소14의 양은 천천히 (A) 감소한다. 시간이 지나면서, 탄소14로부터 점점 더 적은 양의 방사능이 생산된다. 따라서 유기체에서 감지되는 탄소14의 방사능의 양은 그 유기체가 얼마나 오랫동안 (B) 죽어 있었는지에 관한 측정법이다. 이 유기체의 연대를 결정하는 이러한 방식은 탄소14 연대측정법이라고 불린다. 탄소14의 붕괴는 고고학자들이 한때는 살아 있었던 물질들의 연대를 측정하도록 해준다. 남아있는 방사능의 양을 측정하는 것이 대략적인 연대를 알려준다.

	(A)	(B)
①	감소한다	죽은
②	증가한다	살아 있는
③	감소한다	생산적인
④	증가한다	활동하지 않는

| 정답해설 | ① 57% (A) 새로운 탄소14가 추가되지 않으며 기존의 탄소14는 붕괴되어 질소로 변환된다고 했으므로 탄소14의 양은 점차적으로 '감소하게' 됨을 유추할 수 있다.

(B) 빈칸의 뒤에서 명확한 근거가 등장한다. 탄소14 연대측정법을 통해 유기체의 연대를 측정할 수 있다고 설명한다. 유기체의 연대를 측정할 수 있다는 것은 그 유기체가 어느 연대에 존재했는지, 즉 그 유기체가 얼마나 오랜 기간 '죽은' 상태로 묻혀 있었는지를 알 수 있다는 의미이다. 따라서 빈칸에는 dead가 들어와야 함을 유추할 수 있다.

어휘

carbon dioxide 이산화탄소	be made of ~로 만들어지다
consist of ~로 구성되다	radioactive carbon 방사성 탄소
detector 탐지기	radiation 방사, 방출
give off 방출하다	decay 붕괴하다, 쇠퇴하다
nitrogen 질소	
carbon dating 방사성 탄소 연대 측정	
archaeologist 고고학자	approximate 대략의

---

20 독해 > 빈칸의 내용 추론하기 > 빈칸 어구 추론
오답률 27% 답 ②

| 해석 | 과거와 현재의 모든 생물들은 이미 사라졌거나 혹은 멸종하게 될 것이다. 그러나, 지구상 생물의 38억년이라는 역사에 걸쳐 각각의 종들이 사라져 감에 따라, 새로운 종들이 이들을 대신하기 위해, 혹은 새로이 생겨난 자원을 소비하기 위해 불가피하게 등장해 왔다. 몇몇 매우 단순한 유기체로부터 엄청난 수의 복잡한 다세포적 형태가 이 거대한 기간 동안 진화해 왔다. 19세기 영국의 자연학자인 찰스 다윈이 '미스터리 중의 미스터리'라고 언급했던 새로운 종의 기원은 인간이 지구를 함께 공유하는 이 놀라운 ② 생물체들의 다양성을 형성하는 것을 담당했던 자연적인 종 분화 과정이다. 비록 분류학자들이 현재 150만의 생존하는 종들을 분간하고 있을지라도 실질적 숫자는 아마도 천만에 가까울 것이다. 이러한 다수(많은 종)들의 생물학적 상태를 인식하는 것은 무엇이 하나의 종을 구성하고 있는지에 관한 명확한 이해를 요구하는데, 이것은 진화생물학자들이 아직 보편적으로 수용될 수 있는 정의에 합의하지 못했음을 볼 때, 쉬운 일이 아니다.

① 생물학자들의 기술
② 생물체들의 다양성
③ 멸종한 유기체들의 목록
④ 멸종 위기종들의 모음

| 정답해설 | ② 73% 지구상에 존재하는 생물 종들의 다양성의 기원에 관한 글이다. 역사상 수많은 종들이 사라지고 새로운 종들이 생겨났다는 일반적인 진술로 글이 시작된 후, 세 번째 문장에서 단순한 유기체로부터 수많은 복합적인 생물체가 진화했다는 글의 소재와 주제가 등장한다. 그리고 이러한 새로운 종이 출현한 기원은 사실상 종 분화의 자연적인 과정이라고 언급한다. 이러한 종 분화의 자연적인 과정은 바로 빈칸의 내용을 만드는 것을 담당하였다고 설명하는데, 빈칸 앞의 this를 통해 빈칸의 내용이 이미 앞에서 언급된 내용임을 유추할 수 있다. 종 분화의 과정이란 앞 문장에서 설명했던 단순 유기체로부터 엄청난 수의 복합 유기체(a great number of complex, multicellular forms)가 진화하는 과정을 말하는데, 이를 통해 빈칸에는 이러한 종 분화 과정이 살아 있는 생물체들의 다양성에 관련이 있다는 내용이 오는 것이 적합하다. 그 이후에 분류학자마다 다름에 대한 언급을 통해, 빈칸에 종들의 다양성에 관한 언급이 나와야 하는 것임을 좀 더 확실하게 알 수 있으므로 ②가 들어가는 것이 적절하다.

어휘

vanish 사라지다, 소멸되다	inevitably 필연적으로, 불가피하게
exploit 활용하다; 착취하다	multicellular 다세포의
immense 굉장한, 거대한	refer to A as B A를 B라고 언급하다
speciation 종(種) 형성, 종 분화	taxonomist 분류학자
have yet to + R 아직 ~하지 않았다	definition 정의

합격예상 체크

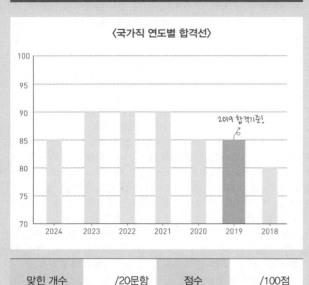

〈국가직 연도별 합격선〉

2019 합격기준

맞힌 개수	/20문항	점수	/100점

➡ ☐ 합격 ☐ 불합격

취약영역 체크

문항	정답	영역	문항	정답	영역
1	①	어휘 > 동의어	11	④	독해 > 세부내용 찾기
2	②	어휘 > 동의어	12	②	독해 > 글의 일관성 파악하기
3	④	생활영어 > 회화	13	③	독해 > 대의 파악
4	②	생활영어 > 회화	14	③	어휘 > 동의어
5	②	문법 > 형용사·부사·비교	15	①	어휘 > 동의어
6	①	문법 > 형용사·부사·비교	16	①	독해 > 빈칸의 내용 추론하기
7	②	문법 > 준동사	17	④	독해 > 글의 일관성 파악하기
8	④	문법 > 동사의 형태	18	③	독해 > 빈칸의 내용 추론하기
9	④	독해 > 대의 파악	19	②	독해 > 세부내용 찾기
10	③	독해 > 대의 파악	20	④	독해 > 글의 일관성 파악하기

⬇ 영역별 틀린 개수로 취약영역을 확인하세요!

어휘	/4	문법	/4	독해	/10	생활영어	/2

➡ 나의 취약영역: _____

※ [정답해설]과 [오답해설] 선지의 50% 표시는 〈1초 합격예측 서비스〉를 통해 수집된 선지 선택률을 나타냅니다.

1 어휘 > 동의어   오답률 29% 답 ①

| 해석 | 'Natural Gas World' 구독자들은 이 업계에서 무슨 일이 일어나고 있는지에 대해 정확하고 신뢰할 만한 핵심 사실들과 수치를 받게 될 것이고, 따라서 그들은 무엇이 그들의 사업에 영향을 줄지를 충분히 **구별할 수** 있다.

① 71% 구별하다 ② 6% 강화하다
③ 12% 약화시키다, 쇠퇴시키다 ④ 11% 포기하다, 버리다

| 정답해설 | ① Natural Gas World라는 간행물을 통해 정확하고 믿을 만한 자료를 받아볼 수 있게 되었으므로 구독자들은 이에 대한 결과로 무엇이 사업에 영향을 줄지에 대해 '알 수 있음'을 유추할 수 있다. discern은 '식별하다'의 의미이므로 동의어로 ①이 가장 적절하다.

어휘

subscriber 구독자 reliable 신뢰할 만한, 믿을 만한
accurate 정확한 discern 구별하다, 식별하다
concern 관여하다

2 어휘 > 동의어   오답률 36% 답 ②

| 해석 | 여자 1,500미터 경기의 은메달리스트인 West 씨는 경기 내내 **돋보였다.**

① 29% 압도되었다 ② 64% 인상적이었다
③ 3% 우울했다 ④ 4% 긍정적이었다

| 정답해설 | ② 64% West 씨는 은메달리스트이므로 경기력이 훌륭했음을 유추할 수 있다. stood out은 말 그대로 일렬로 서 있는 중에 열외로 서 있음을 나타내므로 이는 다른 사람들보다 '탁월하다'는 의미임을 알 수 있다. 따라서 동의어로 가장 적절한 것은 '인상적이었다'의 표현인 ②이다.

어휘

stand out 두드러지다, 뛰어나다 overwhelm 압도하다
impressive 인상적인, 인상(감명) 깊은 depressed 우울한
optimistic 낙관적인, 낙관하는

3 생활영어 > 회화   오답률 13% 답 ④

| 해석 | ① A: 내가 해외여행을 가려고 하는데 다른 나라에 머무는 것이 익숙하지가 않아.
B: 걱정하지 마. 넌 곧 익숙해질 거야.
② A: 나는 사진 콘테스트에서 상을 받고 싶어.
  B: 넌 확실히 그럴 거야. 행운을 빌게!
③ A: 가장 친한 친구가 세종시로 이사 갔어. 그녀가 너무 그리워.
  B: 그래. 네가 어떤 기분인지 알겠다.
④ A: 당신과 잠시 이야기할 수 있나요?
  B: 신경 쓰지 마세요. 제가 지금 매우 바빠서요.

| 정답해설 | ④ 87% mind는 '꺼리다, 싫어하다'의 의미로, 의문문의 동사가 mind인 경우, No, Not at all 등으로 대답하면 '꺼리지 않는다, 괜찮다'의 의미가 되어 자연스럽다. Never mind는 '신경

쓰지 마세요'의 표현이므로 맥락상 적절하지 않으며, 이 경우 지금 매우 바쁘다고 했으므로, I'm 앞에 유감의 표현인 I'm sorry 혹은 I'm afraid를 추가하는 것이 자연스럽다.

어휘

get accustomed to ~에 익숙해지다
in no time 당장, 곧
keep one's fingers crossed 행운을 빌다, 바라다
Never mind 신경 쓰지 마, 아무것도 아니다, 됐어

---

4 생활영어 > 회화　　오답률 3%　답 ②

| 해석 | A: 딤섬 좀 드시겠어요?
B: 네, 고맙습니다. 맛있어 보이네요. 안에 뭐가 들었죠?
A: 이것은 돼지고기와 다진 채소가 들어있고, 저것은 새우가 들어있어요.
B: 그리고, 음, ② 그것들을 어떻게 먹나요?
A: 이렇게 젓가락으로 하나를 집어 들고서 소스에 담그세요. 쉬워요.
B: 네, 한번 해 볼게요.
① 얼마인가요
② 어떻게 먹나요
③ 얼마나 매운가요
④ 어떻게 조리하나요

| 정답해설 | ② 97% 딤섬 시식을 추천받았고, 빈칸에 이어 A가 젓가락을 이용해 딤섬을 먹는 방법을 설명하고 있으므로, 빈칸에 들어갈 표현으로 먹는 방법을 물어보는 ②가 가장 적절하다.

어휘

chopped 잘게 썬; 개조한, 개조된　　pick up 집다, 들다; 태워주다
give it a try 시도하다

---

5 문법 > 형용사·부사·비교 > 형용사　　오답률 35%　답 ②

| 정답해설 | ② 65% shy of는 '~이 모자란'의 의미이므로 우리말의 '5분이나 지난 후'에 적절한 영작이 아니다. 따라서 shy of 대신 전치사 past, after 등으로 대체해야 한다.

| 오답해설 | ① 12% 명사 teacher 다음에 목적격 관계대명사 who(that)가 생략된 구조로 I told you about이 선행사인 문장 전체의 주어인 The new teacher를 수식하고 있다. 따라서 동사는 단수인 is로 받았으며 '~출신이다'의 표현으로 be from이 적절하게 왔다.

③ 14% 관계대명사 what이 이끄는 명사절이 문장 전체의 주어로 주어진 우리말에 일치하며, 문장 전체의 동사는 명사절이 주어로 왔으므로 단수 was lurking으로 수일치가 올바르게 이루어진 문장이다.

④ 9% reach는 타동사이므로 목적어가 바로 이어졌으며, '16세의'의 표현으로 '수량표현-단위명사의 단수형'이 적절하게 왔다.

어휘

shy of ~이 모자란　　　　　　urgent 긴급한, 급박한
lurk 숨어 기다리다, 잠복하다　　coral reef 산호초
summit 정상, 정점; 정상 회담

---

6 문법 > 형용사·부사·비교 > 형용사　　오답률 39%　답 ①

| 정답해설 | ① 61% 우리말은 '(한 나라가 가지고 있는) 개인용 컴퓨터가 가장 많은 나라'를 지칭하지만 영작문은 per person이 '1인당'의 의미이므로 '1인당 가장 많은 컴퓨터를 가지고 있는 나라'가 되므로 올바른 영작문이 아니다. 따라서 주어진 문장에 맞는 영작은 The country with the largest number of personal computers~가 되어야 한다.

| 오답해설 | ② 8% 관계대명사 what이 이끄는 명사절이 문장 전체의 주어이므로 동사도 단수인 was로 수일치가 이루어졌다. amaze는 감정타동사로 주어의 내용이 '놀라움을 주는' 것에 해당되므로 능동의 현재분사인 amazing이 보어로 적절하게 왔다.

③ 15% 긍정인 문장에 이어 동의를 표현할 때, 'So + 대동사 + 주어'의 어순으로 와야 한다. 앞 문장의 동사가 be동사이므로 대동사 역시 be동사 are로 올바르게 표현되었다.

④ 16% '은퇴 후부터'의 표현으로 '~이후로'의 의미의 접속사 since를 썼으며, 이때 since 다음에는 과거의 한 시점을 표현해야 하므로 과거동사로 올바르게 왔다. 주절의 시제는 과거부터 현재까지의 시점을 표현하면서 진행의 느낌을 더해 현재완료 진행시제로 올바르게 표현된 문장이다.

어휘

from time to time 때때로, 종종　　amazing 놀라운, 대단한
wooden 나무로 된, 목재의　　　　retire 은퇴하다

오답률 TOP 2

7 문법 > 준동사 > 분사　　오답률 49%　답 ②

| 해석 | 가축은 인간이 이용할 수 있는 가장 오래되고 가장 효율적인 '기계'이다. 가축은 인간의 등과 팔에 진 부담을 없애준다. 다른 기술들과 함께 이용되어, 동물은 보조 식품(고기와 우유의 단백질)으로써 그리고 짐을 나르고 물을 길어 올리며, 곡식을 으깨는 기계로서 인간의 생활수준을 아주 상당히 끌어올렸다. 동물은 아주 확실하게 도움이 되었으므로, 사람들은 수세기에 걸쳐 인간이 그들이 기르는 동물의 수와 질을 늘릴 것이라는 것을 발견할 것이라 기대했을 것이다. 놀랍게도 이것은 일반적으로 그러한 경우는 아니었다.

| 정답해설 | ② 51% utilize는 타동사이므로 능동의 현재분사 뒤에는 목적어가 이어져야 한다. 구조상 목적어가 없다는 점과 분사구문의 생략된 주어는 이어진 문장의 주어 animals와 일치하므로 문맥상 '동물들이 다른 기법들과 함께 이용되는' 것이므로 수동의 과거분사 Utilized로 바꿔야 한다.

| 오답해설 | ① 5% 형용사 available이 이끄는 형용사구가 명사 machines를 수식하는 올바른 구조이다.

③ 14% to부정사의 형용사적 용법으로 명사 machines를 수식하고 있다.

④ 30% 전치사 of가 뒤에 이어진 명사 benefit와 결합하여 형용사구로 문장의 보어 역할을 하고 있다. 'of + 명사'는 형용사구이며, 문장의 보어 역할을 하거나, 혹은 명사를 수식한다.

어휘

domesticated 길들인, 가축화한　　strain 압력, 압박
supplementary 보충의, 보완의　　obviously 분명히, 명백히

8 | 문법 > 동사의 형태 > 수동태 | 오답률 37% | 답 ④

| 해석 | 신화는 어떤 문화의 종교적, 철학적, 도덕적 그리고 정치적 가치를 구현하며 어떤 면에서는 설명을 돕는 이야기이다. 신들과 초자연적 존재들에 대한 이야기를 통해, 신화는 자연 세계에서 발생하는 것들을 이해하려 시도한다. 일반적인 관례와는 달리, 신화는 '거짓'을 의미하지 않는다. 가장 개괄적인 면에서, 신화는, 대개 이야기들의 전체적 집단인데, 허구일 뿐만 아니라 사실일 수도 혹은 부분적으로 사실일 수 있다; 그러나 정확함의 정도와 상관없이, 신화는 빈번히 한 문화의 가장 깊은 믿음을 표현한다. 이 정의에 따르면, '일리아드'와 '오디세이', '코란', '구약 성경'과 '신약 성경'은 모두 신화로 언급될 수 있다.

| 정답해설 | ④ 63% refer to A as B(A를 B로 언급하다)의 표현으로, refer to는 타동사이므로 능동태인 경우 목적어인 명사가 이어져야 한다. 밑줄 친 부분은 조동사 can에 이어진 능동 구조임에도 목적어가 없으므로 구조와 문맥상 수동태가 되어야 함을 알 수 있다. 따라서 be referred to as로 바꿔야 한다.

| 오답해설 | ① 19% help는 목적어로 to부정사를 취할 수 있으므로 올바른 구조이다. 주어는 A myth이므로 수일치 역시 올바르게 이루어졌다.

② 9% try는 to부정사를 목적어로 취하는 동사로 '~하고자 노력하다'의 표현으로 구조와 문맥상 적절하다.

③ 9% 주격 관계대명사 that에 이어 동사가 이어진 구조로 삽입구 (usually whole groups of stories)를 제외하면 선행사는 stories임을 알 수 있다.

어휘

narrative 이야기, 담화	embody 구체화하다, 구현하다
contrary to ~에 반해, ~와 상반되는	
falsehood 거짓말, 허언; 기만	regardless of ~와 상관없이
accuracy 정확, 정밀	refer to A as B A를 B로 언급하다

9 | 독해 > 대의 파악 > 제목 찾기 | 오답률 17% | 답 ④

| 해석 | 지도 제작 기술은 많은 새로운 응용 분야에 사용되고 있다. 생물학 연구자들은 DNA의 분자구조('유전자 지도 제작')를 탐구 중이고, 지리 물리학자들은 지구 핵의 구조 지도를 제작하고 있으며, 해양학자들은 대양저의 지도를 제작하고 있다. 컴퓨터 게임은 규칙, 위험, 그리고 보상이 변하는 다양한 상상의 '땅'과 레벨을 가지고 있다. 컴퓨터화는 현재 특수한 상황을 자극하는 인공 환경인 '가상 현실'로 현실에 도전하는데, 이는 훈련과 오락에 유용할 수 있다. 지도 제작 기법은 또한 아이디어 영역에서 이용된다. 예를 들어, 아이디어들 사이의 관계는 소위 개념도를 이용해 보여질 수 있다. 일반적인 혹은 '중심적인' 아이디어로 시작해, 관련된 아이디어들은 연결될 수 있고 주요 개념을 중심으로 하나의 망을 형성한다. 이것은 어떤 전통적 정의에 의한 지도가 아니라 그것을 만들기 위해 지도 제작의 도구와 기법이 이용된 것이며, 여러 가지 점에서 그것은 지도와 유사하다.

① 컴퓨터화 된 지도 對 전통적 지도
② 지도 제작은 어디에서 시작하는가?
③ DNA 비밀로 가는 길을 찾는 것
④ 새로운 영역의 지도 제작

| 정답해설 | ④ 83% 지도 제작 기술이 전통적인 지도를 넘어 많은 새로운 응용 분야에 적용되고 있다고 서술하고 있으며 첫 문장에 이어 여러 영역에서의 지도 제작 기술이 응용되는 사례들을 나열하고 있다. 따라서 정답은 ④이다.

어휘

application 응용, 적용; 지원(서)	geophysicist 지구 물리학자
oceanographer 해양학자	computerization 컴퓨터화
virtual reality 가상 현실	artificial 인공적인, 인위적인, 거짓된
realm 영역, 범위	cartography 지도 제작

10 | 독해 > 대의 파악 > 요지·주장 찾기 | 오답률 22% | 답 ③

| 해석 | 성과 피드백을 전달할 때, 여러분은 피드백을 받는 사람의 이전 성과와 빈도, 양, 내용을 설계하는 데 있어 그 사람의 장래의 잠재성에 대한 당신의 평가를 고려해야 한다. 성장의 잠재성이 있는 성취도가 높은 사람에게, 피드백은 그들을 자극해 개선조치를 취할 정도로 잦아야 하지만, 피드백이 통제를 하는 것으로 느끼고 그들의 주도권을 빼앗을 만큼 너무 자주해서는 안 된다. 자신의 일에 정착했고 발전에 대한 제한된 잠재성을 지닌 그만그만한 성과를 내는 사람들은 매우 적은 양의 피드백이 필요한데, 그들은 자신의 임무를 알고 무엇이 행해질 필요가 있는가를 인식하면서 과거에 믿을 만하면서 꾸준한 행동 양식을 보여 주었기 때문이다. 성과가 형편없는 사람들에게 – 즉, 그들의 성과가 발전하지 않는다면 직장에서 사라질 필요가 있는 사람들 – 피드백은 자주 이루어져야 하고 매우 구체적이어야 하며, 피드백에 대한 행동과 일시적 해고 혹은 해고와 같은 부정적 제재 사이의 연관성이 명확하게 이루어져야 한다.

① 피드백 시간을 잘 정해라.
② 부정적인 피드백을 (사람에 따라) 바꿔라.
③ 피드백을 그 사람에게 맞춰라.
④ 목표 지향적인 피드백을 피하라.

| 정답해설 | ③ 78% 성과에 대한 피드백을 전달할 때, 전달받는 대상의 성취도의 정도에 따라 피드백을 다르게 해야 한다는 내용이므로 정답은 ③이다.

어휘

prod 자극하다, 찌르다	
take corrective action 올바른 조치를 취하다	
sap 빼앗다	initiative 주도권; 계획, 진취성
adequate 적절한	sanction 제재
lay off 임시 해고하다	explicit 명확한

11 | 독해 > 세부내용 찾기 > 내용 불일치 찾기 | 오답률 10% | 답 ④

| 해석 | Langston Hughes는 미주리 주의 Joplin에서 태어났고 링컨 대학을 졸업했는데, 그 대학에서는 많은 아프리카계 미국인 학생들이 그들의 학문적 수양을 추구했다. 18세의 나이에, Hughes는 그의 가장 유명한 시들 중 하나인 'Negro Speaks of Rivers'를 발표했다. 창의적이고 실험적이었던 Hughes는 그의 작품에 실제 사투리를 포함시켰고, 블루스와 재즈의 리듬과 감정을 포용하기 위해 전통적인 시적 형식을 변경했으며, 흑인 하층민 문화의 요소를 반영하는 등장인물과 주제를 만들었다. 심각한 내용을 유머러스한 문체로 융합하는 그의 능력으로, Hughes는 자연스럽고 재치 있는 방식으로 인종 편견을 공격했다.

| 정답해설 | ④ 90% 마지막 문장에서 유머러스한 문체로 인종 편견을 공격했다고 했으므로 글의 내용과 일치하지 않는 것은 ④이다.

어휘

pursue 추구하다, 추진하다	discipline 수양, 훈련
incorporate 포함하다	authentic 진짜의, 실제의
dialect 사투리, 방언	adapt 적응시키다; 각색하다
embrace 포용하다, 수용하다	cadence 억양
fuse 융합하다; 녹이다	racial prejudice 인종 편견

12 독해 > 글의 일관성 파악하기 > 글의 흐름과 무관한 문장
오답률 26% 답 ②

| 해석 | 2007년에, 사람들의 가장 큰 우려는 '너무 커서 파산할 수 없는' 것이었다. 월스트리트 은행들은 엄청난 정도의 규모로 성장했고 금융 제도의 활력의 너무 중심부에 있게 되었으므로 어떤 합리적인 정부도 은행들이 파산하게 할 수는 없었다. 그들이 보호받는 위치에 있다는 것을 인지하여, 은행들은 주택 시장에 과도하게 돈을 거는 위험을 무릅썼고 더 복잡한 금융 파생 상품들을 만들어냈다. ② 비트코인과 이더리움 같은 새로운 가상 화폐들은 돈이 어떻게 작용할 수 있고 바뀌는가에 대한 우리의 생각을 철저히 변화시켰다. 그 결과는 1929년도의 경제 붕괴 이후의 가장 최악의 금융 위기였다. 2007년 이후 몇 년간, '너무 커서 파산할 수 없는 것'의 딜레마를 다루는 데 있어 큰 발전을 이루어왔다. 은행들은 이전보다 더 잘 자본화되었다. 규제들은 규모가 큰 기관들의 정기적인 압박 테스트를 실시한다.

| 정답해설 | ② 74% 첫 번째 문장의 은행들의 규모와 파급력이 너무 커서 파산시킬 수 없다는 내용에 이어 은행들이 실시한 내용들, 결과 등이 서술되었다. ②의 가상화폐의 등장이 사람들의 생각을 바꾸어 놓았다는 이야기는 전체 흐름에 맞지 않으며, 특히 ②에 이어진 ③의 내용이 이전의 내용에 연계되어 있으므로 글의 흐름과 맞지 않는 문장은 ②이다.

| 어휘 |
staggering 휘청거리는; 충격적인　　rational 합리적인, 이성적인
complicated 복잡한　　　　　　derivative 파생 상품, 파생물
radically 철저히; 원래는; 급진적으로
regulator 단속 기관

13 독해 > 대의 파악 > 주제 찾기
오답률 2% 답 ③

| 해석 | 두 사람이 같은 날 같은 법률 회사에서 일을 시작한다고 가정해보자. 한 사람은 매우 단순한 이름을 가지고 있다. 나머지 한 사람은 매우 복잡한 이름을 가지고 있다. 그들이 일을 하는 다음 16년 이상의 시간에 걸쳐, 더 단순한 이름을 가진 사람이 더 빠르게 법조계 계층을 올라갈 것이라는 꽤나 많은 증거가 있다. 그들은 커리어 중반에 더 빠르게 파트너십을 달성할 것이다. 그리고 로스쿨을 졸업한 후 대략 8~9년차쯤에, 더 단순한 이름을 가진 사람들은 대략 7~10퍼센트 정도 파트너가 될 가능성이 더 있는데, 이는 두드러진 결과이다. 우리는 모든 종류의 다른 대안적 설명을 제거하고자 애쓴다. 예를 들어, 우리는 그것이 외래성에 대한 것이 아니라는 것을 보여 주고자 하는데, 외국 이름들은 발음하기에 더 어려운 경향이 있기 때문이다. 하지만 당신이 그저 정말로 내집단에 속한 앵글로 아메리칸 이름을 지닌 백인 남성들을 볼지라도, 당신은 앵글로 이름을 지닌 그런 백인 남성들 중에서도 만약 그들의 이름이 우연스럽게도 더 단순하다면, 그들이 더 올라갈 가능성이 있다. 따라서 단순성은 이름에 있어 다양한 결과를 결정하는 하나의 핵심적인 특징이다.
① 법적 이름의 발전
② 매력적인 이름의 개념
③ 단순한 이름의 장점
④ 외국 이름의 뿌리

| 정답해설 | ③ 98% 지문 전체적으로 더 단순한 이름을 지닌 사람이 사회적 계층에서 더 빠르게 상승할 수 있다는 내용을 서술하고 있으므로 정답은 ③이다.

| 어휘 |
hierarchy 계급, 계층　　　　attain 달성하다, 성취하다
eliminate 제거하다　　　　　alternative 대안적인, 대체의
rise up 올라가다, 솟아나다　　simplicity 간단, 단순(성)

14 어휘 > 동의어
오답률 30% 답 ③

| 해석 | 학교 교육은 미국의 모든 어린이들에게 의무적이지만 취학해야 하는 연령대는 주마다 다르다.
① 11% 상호 보완적인　　② 15% 체계적인, 조직적인
③ 70% 의무적인　　　　④ 4% 획기적인, 혁신적인

| 정답해설 | ③ 미국의 학교 교육에 대한 이야기로, 첫 번째 문장에 이어 but으로 연결된 내용이 취학 연령은 주마다 다르다고 했다. 따라서 빈칸에는 동일하게 적용되면서 맥락상 가장 적절한 것은 당위성의 의미를 가져야 하므로 정답은 ③이다. compulsory는 동사 compel과 어근이 동일하며, compel이 '강요하다'의 의미이므로 이를 통해 뜻을 유추할 수 있다.

| 어휘 |
compulsory 강제적인, 의무적인　　complementary 상호 보완적인
systematic 체계적인, 조직적인　　mandatory 의무적인; 법에 정해진
innovative 획기적인, 혁신적인

오답률 TOP 1
15 어휘 > 동의어
오답률 71% 답 ①

| 해석 | 그 배우는 활동 중에 많은 혼란을 겪었음에도, 결코 어느 누구에게도 그녀가 불행하다고 드러내지 않았다.
① 29% 폭로하다
② 40% 해방하다; (총 등을) 발사하다; 봐주다
③ 10% 완화하다, 누그러지다
④ 21% 실망시키다; 감소시키다

| 정답해설 | ① let이 포함된 동사구의 의미를 묻는 문제이다. disclose는 닫힌(close) 상태에서 벗어나는(dis-) 것이므로 '드러내다, 폭로하다'의 의미이다. let은 '~하도록 두다'의 의미로, let on은 '~위에 두다'이므로 결국 '드러내다'의 표현임을 유추할 수 있다.

| 어휘 |
turmoil 소란, 혼란　　　　　disclose 드러내다, 폭로하다
let on 폭로하다
let off 해방하다; (총 등을) 발사하다; 봐주다
let up 완화하다, 누그러지다　　let down 감소시키다; 실망시키다

16 독해 > 빈칸의 내용 추론하기 > 연결어 추론
오답률 38% 답 ①

| 해석 | 선지자들은 그들의 산업 분야에서 새로운 기술의 잠재성을 알아보는 최초의 사람들이다. 근본적으로, 그들은 그들 스스로를 경쟁사에 있는 수많은 상대방들보다 더 똑똑하다고 여기는데, 매우 자주 그들은 그러하다. 실로, 그들이 경쟁 우위에 있어 활용하기 원하는 것은 다름 아닌 먼저 사물을 이해하는 그들의 능력이다. 그런 장점은 그밖에 어느 누군가 그것을 발견하지 못할 때만 생길 수 있다. (A) 따라서 그들은 광범위한 목록의 산업 참조 자료를 갖춘 충분히 시험된 제품을 구입하는 것을 기대하지 않는다. 정말로, 그러한 참조 자료 기반이 존재한다면, 그것은 실제로 그들의 흥미를 떨어뜨릴 수 있는데, 이는 어쨌든, 이 기술에 대해 그들이 이미 늦었다는 것을 나타내는 것이다. (B) 반면에, 실용주의자들은 다른 기업에 있는 그들의 동료의 경험에 몹시 가치를 둔다. 그들이 구입할 때 그들은 광범위한 참조 자료들을 기대하고 자신이 속한 산업 분야의 다른 기업들로부터 많은 것들이 나오기를 바란다.

	(A)	(B)
①	따라서	반면에
②	그러나	게다가
③	그럼에도	동시에
④	게다가	결론적으로

| **정답해설** | ① `62%` (A)에서 새로운 기술을 가장 먼저 알아보는 선지자들에 대한 내용에 이어 (A) 다음에 그 결과인 이미 시험된 제품을 구입하는 것을 기대하지 않는다는 내용이 이어졌으므로 therefore가 적절하다.

(B)는 주어가 pragmatists로 이는 visionary와는 대조적인 개념이므로 on the other hand가 적절하다.

어휘

visionary 선지자; 예지력 있는
competitive advantage 경쟁 우위
reference 참고, 참조 (자료)
pragmatist 실용주의자

leverage 활용하다; 영향력
come about 일어나다, 발생하다
turn off 끄다; 흥미를 없애다

---

17 독해 > 글의 일관성 파악하기 > 주어진 문장의 삽입

오답률 32% | 답 ④

| **해석** | 수세기 동안, 인간은 하늘을 올려다보고 우리 행성의 영역 너머로 무엇이 존재할까 궁금해했다. 고대 천문학자들은 우주에 대해 더 많은 것을 알기를 바라며 밤하늘을 관찰했다. 더 최근에는, 일부 영화들이 외계에서 인간의 생명 유지 가능성을 탐구했고 반면에 다른 영화들은 외계 생명체가 우리 행성(지구)을 방문했는지에 대해 의문을 품었다. 우주비행사 유리 가가린이 1961년 우주를 여행한 최초의 인간이 된 이후, 과학자들은 지구 대기권 너머 환경이 어떠한지 그리고 우주여행이 인간의 몸에 어떤 영향을 미치는지에 대해 연구했다. 대부분의 우주비행사들이 우주에서 몇 개월 이상 보내지는 않지만, 많은 우주비행사들은 그들이 지구로 귀환했을 때, 생리적이면서 심리적인 문제를 겪는다. ④ 이런 병들 중 일부는 단기적이지만 다른 병들은 장기적일 수 있다. 모든 우주비행사들의 2/3 이상이 우주여행 동안 멀미로 고통받는다. 무중력 환경에서, 몸은 위아래를 구별할 수 없다. 몸 내부의 균형 체계는 뇌에 혼란스러운 신호를 보내는데, 이는 며칠 동안 유지되는 메스꺼움을 초래할 수 있다.

| **정답해설** | ④ `68%` 제시문의 Some of these ailments가 지칭하는 대상이 앞에 언급되어야 하는데 ③에 이어진 문장에서 우주비행사들이 지구 귀환 이후 생리적이면서 심리적인 문제를 겪는다고 했으므로, problems가 제시문의 these ailments임을 알 수 있다. 따라서 정답은 ④이다.

어휘

realm 영역, 범주
sustain 유지하다, 지탱하다
astronaut 우주비행사
physiological 생리적인, 생리학의
motion sickness 멀미
differentiate 구별하다, 분간하다

astronomer 천문학자
extraterrestrial 외계의
atmosphere 대기; 분위기
ailment 질병
gravity free 무중력
nausea 메스꺼움

---

18 독해 > 빈칸의 내용 추론하기 > 빈칸 어구 추론

오답률 40% | 답 ③

| **해석** | 모든 것의 역사에 대해 왜 신경을 쓰는가? ③ 오늘날, 우리는 우리의 세상에 대해 단편적으로 가르치고 배운다. 문학 수업에서 당신은 유전자에 대해 배우지 않고 물리 수업에서 당신은 인간의 진화에 대해 배우지 않는다. 따라서 당신은 부분적인 세계관을 갖게 된다. 그것은 교육에서 '의미'를 발견하는 것을 어렵게 만든다. 프랑스 사회학자인 에밀 뒤르켐은 이런 방향 상실감과 무의미를 '아노미'라고 불렀고 그는 그것이 절망, 심지어 자살을 초래할 수 있다고 주장했다. 독일의 사회학자인 막스 베버는 세상의 '각성'에 대해 이야기 했다. 과거에, 사람들은 세계에 대한 통합적 시야를 가지고 있었는데, 그 시야는 보통 그들 자신의 종교적 전통의 기원에 대한 이야기에 의해 제공된다. 그런 통합적 시야는 목적, 의미, 심지어 세계와 삶에 대한 각성을 주었다. 그러나 오늘날, 많은 작가들은 무의미에 대한 감각은 과학과 이성의 세계에서 불가피하다고 주장해 왔다. 현대성이란 무의미함을 의미하는 것 같다.

① 과거에, 역사 연구는 과학으로부터의 각성을 요구했다.
② 최근에, 과학은 우리에게 많은 교묘한 재주와 의미를 제공했다.
③ 오늘날, 우리는 우리의 세상에 대해 단편적으로 가르치고 배운다.
④ 최근에, 역사는 여러 범주로 나누어졌다.

| **정답해설** | ③ `60%` 첫 번째 문장에서 모든 것의 역사에 대해 신경 쓸 필요가 없다고 반어적으로 표현한 후 빈칸에 이어 각 학문의 분야에서 다른 학문 분야의 내용에 대해 배우지 않는다고 서술하고 이 결과 세상에 대한 부분적인 시야를 갖게 된다고 했으므로 빈칸에는 ③이 가장 적절하다.

어휘

bother 신경 쓰다, 애를 쓰다; 괴롭히다
disorientation 방향 상실감
disenchantment 각성
rationality 이성, 합리성

despair 절망(하다), 체념(하다)
inevitable 불가피한, 필연적인

오답률 TOP 3

19 독해 > 세부내용 찾기 > 내용 불일치 찾기

오답률 42% | 답 ②

| **해석** | 가장 오래된 정부주도 급식 프로그램은 1900년 무렵 유럽에서 시작되었다. 미국에서 급식 프로그램은 대공황 이후 존재하는데, 그때 잉여 농산물 사용에 대한 필요성과 빈곤층의 어린이들에게 급식을 하는 것에 대한 관심이 결합되었다. 2차 세계대전 동안과 그 이후에, 폭발적으로 늘어난 일하는 여성의 수는 더 폭넓은 프로그램에 대한 필요성을 부채질했다. 점심을 준비하는 것과 같은, 예전에 가정의 기능이었던 일은 학교 급식 체계로 전환되었다. '전국 급식 프로그램'은 이러한 노력들의 결과이다. 그 프로그램은 학령 어린이들에게 연방 차원으로 지원된 식사를 제공하도록 설계되었다. 2차 세계대전 종전부터 1980년대까지, 학교 급식에 대한 기금 지원은 꾸준히 늘어났다. 오늘날 그것은 미국 전역의 거의 10만 개 이상의 학교에서 어린이들에 식사를 제공하도록 도움을 준다. 그것의 첫 번째 기능은 모든 학생들에게 영양이 있는 점심을 제공하는 것이고, 두 번째는 가난한 어린이들에게 아침 식사와 점심 식사 모두 영양가 있는 음식을 제공하는 것이다. 오히려, 한때 가정의 기능이었던 것의 대체물로써 학교 급식 서비스의 역할은 확대되어 왔다.

① 일하는 여성의 수의 증가는 급식 프로그램의 확대를 활성화시켰다.
② 미 정부는 식량부족에도 불구하고 대공황 동안 가난한 어린이들에게 급식을 하기 시작했다.
③ 미국의 학교 급식 서비스는 현재 가난한 가정의 어린이들에게 급식하는 것을 돕는다.
④ 점심을 제공하는 기능은 가정에서 학교로 이동되었다.

| 정답해설 | ② 58% ② when the need to use surplus agricultural commodities was joined to concern for feeding the children of poor families로 보아 식량 부족이 아니라 잉여 식량을 사용하려고 하는 목적이 결합되었다고 했으므로 despite the food shortage는 지문과 일치하지 않는 내용이다.

어휘

surplus 잉여; 과잉   commodity 상품, 물품
fuel 부채질하다; 연료   shift 변화하다, 전환하다
federally 연방차원에서, 연방적으로   nutritious 영양분이 많은

---

20 독해 > 글의 일관성 파악하기 > 글의 순서 [오답률 33%] 답 ④

| 해석 | 한국은 지구에서 가장 인터넷에 연결된 국가라는 것을 자랑한다.
(B) 사실상, 다른 어떤 나라도 그렇게 완전히 인터넷을 받아들이지는 않았다.
(C) 하지만 무수히 많은 (인터넷에) 빠져 있는 사용자들이 그들 스스로를 컴퓨터 스크린으로부터 떼어 놓을 수 없다는 것을 알게 되면서 언제든 웹에 접근할 수 있는 것은 대가를 치르게 되었다.
(A) 이러한 중독은 최근 몇 년 동안 한국에서 국가적 문제가 되었는데, 인터넷 사용자들이 여러 날 동안 계속 온라인 게임을 한 후에 극도의 피로로 급사하기 시작했기 때문이었다. 점점 더 많은 학생들이 온라인에 머무느라 학교를 빠지는데, 이는 현재의 격렬하게 경쟁적인 사회에서 매우 자기 파괴적인 행동이다.

| 정답해설 | ④ 67% 제시문의 한국이 인터넷 강국이라는 내용 다음에는 이와 연관된 내용인 (B)가 이어져야 한다. 이 부분을 such ready access to the Web으로 지칭한 (C)가 이어지는 것이 적절하며, (C)에서 언급된 '중독된 사용자들(obsessed users)'에 대한 내용이 (A)의 주어인 this addiction으로 연결되었음을 알 수 있으므로 정답은 ④이다.

어휘

boast of ~을 뽐내다, 자랑하다   embrace 포용하다, 받아들이다
legions of 수많은   obsessed 중독된
addiction 중독
exhaustion 고갈, 소진; 기진맥진, 극도의 피로

합격예상 체크

〈국가직 연도별 합격선〉

| | 맞힌 개수 | /20문항 | 점수 | /100점 |

➡ ☐ 합격 ☐ 불합격

취약영역 체크

문항	정답	영역	문항	정답	영역
1	①	생활영어 > 회화	11	④	독해 > 글의 일관성 파악하기
2	①	독해 > 빈칸의 내용 추론하기	12	④	독해 > 대의 파악
3	②	독해 > 대의 파악	13	②	독해 > 세부내용 찾기
4	③	문법 > 동사의 형태	14	①	어휘 > 동의어
5	①	어휘 > 동의어	15	④	어휘 > 동의어
6	②	어휘 > 빈칸	16	④	독해 > 글의 일관성 파악하기
7	④	독해 > 글의 일관성 파악하기	17	②	독해 > 세부내용 찾기
8	②	생활영어 > 회화	18	②	독해 > 빈칸의 내용 추론하기
9	②	독해 > 세부내용 찾기	19	④	독해 > 글의 일관성 파악하기
10	③	문법 > 준동사	20	④	문법 > 형용사 · 부사 · 비교

⬇ 영역별 틀린 개수로 취약영역을 확인하세요!

| 어휘 | /4 | 문법 | /3 | 독해 | /11 | 생활영어 | /2 |

➡ 나의 취약영역: _____

※ [정답해설]과 [오답해설] 선지의 50% 표시는 〈1초 합격예측 서비스〉를 통해 수집된 선지 선택률을 나타냅니다.

---

1 생활영어 > 회화　　　　오답률 17%　답 ①

| 해석 | A: 부탁 좀 드려도 될까요?
B: 네, 무슨 일이시죠?
A: 출장으로 공항에 가야 하는데, 제 차가 좀처럼 시동이 걸리지 않네요. 저 좀 태워 주시겠어요?
B: 물론이죠. 어제 거기에 도착해야 하죠?
A: 늦어도 6시까지 가야 해요.
B: 지금 4시 30분이네요. ① 시간이 촉박하네요. 바로 출발해야겠어요.
① 시간이 촉박하네요
② 나는 방심했어요
③ 반짝이는 모든 것이 금은 아니에요
④ 이미 지나간 일이에요

| 정답해설 | ① 83% 6시까지 공항에 도착해야 하는데 현재 시간이 4시가 넘었고, 빈칸에 이어 바로 출발해야 한다는 표현으로 미루어 정답은 '시간이 촉박하다'의 표현인 ①이 가장 적절하다.

어휘
cut it close (시간 · 돈 등을) 최소한으로 줄이다, 시간이 빠듯하다
take one's eyes off the ball 방심하다
All that glitters is not gold. 반짝이는 모든 것이 금은 아니다.
water under the bridge 지나가 버린 일, 과거지사

---

2 독해 > 빈칸의 내용 추론하기 > 빈칸 어구 추론

오답률 26%　답 ①

| 해석 | 상실에 대한 두려움은 인간이라는 존재가 가지고 있는 기본적인 부분이다. 두뇌에게, 손실은 위협이고 우리는 자연적으로 그것을 피하기 위한 조치를 취한다. 그러나 우리는 그것을 무기한으로 피할 수는 없다. 상실을 마주하는 한 가지 방법은 주식 거래자의 관점을 가지는 것이다. 주식 거래자는 손실의 가능성을 게임의 일부로서 받아들이지 경기의 목적으로서 받아들이지 않는다. 이 사고를 인도하는 것은 포트폴리오 접근법이다. 이득과 손실은 둘 다 발생하지만, 가장 중요한 것은 결과의 전반적인 포트폴리오이다. 포트폴리오 접근 방식을 채택하면 손실이라는 것은 훨씬 더 큰 그림의 작은 일부라는 것을 알기 때문에 당신은 ① 개인적 손실에 대해 덜 연연하게 될 것이다.
① 개인적인 손실에 대해 덜 연연하게
② 당신의 투자에 덜 관심을 갖게
③ 손실을 더욱 싫어하게
④ 주식 시장의 변동에 더욱 민감하게

| 정답해설 | ① 74% 손실을 극복하는 방법으로써 제안된 주식 거래자의 관점에 따르면, 최종 결과에 해당하는 큰 그림의 관점에서 보면 순간적인 손실은 일종의 부분에 해당하는 것이므로, 과정에 해당하는 개인적인 손실에 덜 연연하게 될 것이라는 ①이 가장 적절하다.

어휘
threat 위협, 위험　　　indefinitely 무기한으로, 영구히
perspective 관점, 시각　　　outcome 결과

embrace 포용하다, 받아들이다   averse 싫어하는
fluctuation 동요, 변동

| **3** | 독해 > 대의 파악 > 제목 찾기 | 오답률 7% | 답 ② |

| 해석 | 지난 수년간에 걸친 여행 동안, 우리 인간들이 얼마나 많이 과거에 살고 있는지를 나는 알아챘다. 무언가가 분명해지자마자, 그것은 과거가 된다는 것을 고려할 때, 과거는 계속해서 우리 주변에 있다. 우리 주변 환경, 우리 가정, 우리 환경, 우리 건축, 우리의 생산물들은 모두가 과거의 구조물들이다. 우리는 우리 시대 및 우리 집단적 의식의 일부를 이루는 것, 즉 우리가 사는 동안 만들어졌던 것들과 더불어 살아야 한다. 물론, 우리가 우리 시대 동안 관련이 있고 착상된 우리 주변의 모든 것을 소유할 선택이나 통제력을 지니고 있지는 못하지만, 우리가 진정 통제하고 있는 것은 우리가 살고 있는 시대를 반영하는 것이어야 하고 또 현재를 전달해야 한다. 현재는 우리가 지닌 모든 것이고, 그래서 우리가 그것에 더 많이 둘러싸여 있을수록, 우리는 우리 자신의 존재와 참여를 그만큼 더 많이 인식하게 된다.
① 여행: 과거의 유산 추적하기
② 현재 당신을 둘러싸고 있는 시간에 대해 성찰하라
③ 숨겨진 삶의 현시(現示)
④ 미래 삶의 건축

| 정답해설 | ② 93% 네 번째 문장 We should live with~ 이하에서 언급한 내용을 통해 필자의 주장을 펼치고 있으며, Of course 이후의 내용에서 '현재'에 강조점을 두고 있으므로 정답으로 ②가 가장 적절하다.

어휘

considering that ~ ~라는 사실을 고려해 보건대
the minute ~하자마자   manifest 명백히 하다, 명시하다
construct 구성 (개념), 구성물, 구조물
relevant 적절한, 관련된   conceive 상상하다, 착상하다
reflection 반사, 반영   trace 추적하다, 행방을 찾아내다
legacy 유산, 유증(재산)   reflect on ~을 심사숙고하다
manifestation 명시, 표명   futuristic 미래의, 미래지향적인

| **4** | 문법 > 동사의 형태 > 수동태 | 오답률 36% | 답 ③ |

| 해석 | 숲들의 아름다움과 풍부함이 없는 삶을 상상한다면 그것은 어려울 것이다. 그렇지만, 과학자들은 우리가 우리 숲을 당연하게 여길 수 없다는 것을 경고하고 있다. 일부 추정치들에 따르면, 벌목은 세계의 자연 수풀들 중 자그마치 80%의 상실을 초래했다고 한다. 현재, 벌목은 세계적인 문제이고, 태평양의 온대 우림과 같은 야생 지역들에 영향을 주고 있다.

| 정답해설 | ③ 64% result in은 자동사구이므로 수동태로 전환할 수 없다. 따라서 has resulted in으로 바뀌야 한다.

| 오답해설 | ① 5% 가주어 it과 호응하여 쓰인 진주어로 to부정사의 명사적 용법이다.
② 17% for와 함께 쓰여 숙어로 '당연한'의 의미로 쓰인다.
④ 14% 분사구문을 이끄는 현재분사로 생략된 주어는 앞 문장의 주어 deforestation이며, 능동형이므로 목적어 wilderness regions를 취한 올바른 구조이다.

어휘

take~ for granted ~을 당연시하다 estimate 추산치, 추정치
deforestation 벌목, 남벌
wilderness 황무지, 사람이 살지 않는 땅, 광대한 곳
temperate rainforest 온대 우림

| **5** | 어휘 > 동의어 | 오답률 32% | 답 ① |

| 해석 | 전설적인 다큐멘터리 영화 제작자인 Robert J. Flaherty는 토착민들이 어떻게 식량을 채집하는지를 보여주고자 하는 시도를 했다.
① 68% 토착의   ② 9% 탐욕스러운
③ 16% 가난한, 빈곤한   ④ 7% 순회하는, 이리저리 이동하는

| 정답해설 | ① 한 전설적인 다큐 영화 제작자가 보여주고자 노력했던 것이 무엇임을 유추해야 하는데, 식량을 채집하는 방법을 보여주려 했으므로 일반적인 현대인들이 아닌 '토착 원주민'임을 알 수 있다. 따라서 동의어로 가장 적절한 것은 ①이다.

어휘

indigenous 토착의   legendary 전설적인, 믿기 어려운
gather 모으다, 채집하다

오답률 TOP 2

| **6** | 어휘 > 빈칸 | 오답률 45% | 답 ② |

| 해석 | 음악을 듣는 것은 결코 록 스타가 되고자 ② 하는 것이 아니다. 누구든지 음악을 들을 수 있지만, 음악가가 되는 것은 재능을 요한다.
① 16% ~와 동등하게
② 55% ~과 거리가 먼, ~와 전혀 다른
③ 12% ~을 조건으로
④ 17% ~의 전조인

| 정답해설 | ② 음악을 듣는 것과 음악인이 되는 것과의 관계를 유추하는 문제이다. 두 번째 문장에서 어느 누구도 음악을 들을 수는 있지만 음악가가 되기 위해서는 재능이 필요하다고 했으므로 빈칸에는 부정적인 표현이 들어가야 한다. 따라서 정답으로 ②가 가장 적절하다.

어휘

talent 재능

| **7** | 독해 > 글의 일관성 파악하기 > 글의 흐름과 무관한 문장 | 오답률 35% | 답 ④ |

| 해석 | 생물학자들은 벼가 – 현재보다 1주 이상 긴 – 최대 2주 동안 물속에 잠겨 생존할 수 있게 하는 유전자를 발견했다. 일주일 이상 동안 물속에 있는 식물들은 산소가 없어지고 시들어서 죽는다. 과학자들은 그들의 발견이 홍수에 취약한 지역에서 작물의 수확을 증가시킬 것으로 기대한다. 아시아의 홍수 발생 가능성이 높은 지역의 쌀 재배자들은 과도하게 수분이 많은 논으로 인해 매년 약 10억 달러의 손실을 보고 있다. 그들은 새로운 유전자가 태풍 및 장마철에 발생하는 재정적 피해를 줄이고 예외적으로 엄청난 수확을 가져오는 더욱 견실한 쌀 품종을 가져올 것으로 기대한다. ④ 이것은 도시화의 피해자이며, 농작물이 부족한 취약한 지역의 사람들에게 두려운 소식이다. 10억 명의 사람들이 주요 식단을 제공받을 수 있도록 하기 위해서는 쌀 생산량이 향후 20년 동안 30% 증가해야 한다.

| 정답해설 | ④ 65% 쌀을 개량하여 홍수와 계절의 영향을 덜 받도록 연구 중이라는 긍정적 서술에 이어 이것은 두려운 소식이라는 부정적 서술이 역접의 연결어 없이 이어져 있으므로 ④가 정답이다.

어휘

identify 식별하다   submerge 잠수하다, 담그다
deprive A of B A로부터 B를 빼앗다 perish 사라지다, 죽다
prolong 연장하다, 길어지다   susceptible 민감한; 감염되기 쉬운

waterlogged 물에 잠긴, 물로 흥건한
strain (동식물의) 변종; (근육의) 긴장
dreadful 무서운, 가혹한   vulnerable 취약한, 영향 받기 쉬운
yield 수확, 산출량   staple 주요한; 주산물

---

8   생활영어 > 회화   오답률 37%   답 ②

| 해석 | A: 운전하는 방법 알아요?
B: 물론이죠. 저 운전 잘해요.
A: 저에게 운전하는 방법 알려줄 수 있어요?
B: 임시 운전면허증을 가지고 있나요?
A: 네, 지난주에 막 땄어요.
B: 운전을 해 보신 적은 있나요?
A: 아니요, 하지만 ② 발을 담가보고(운전하고) 싶어서 참을 수가 없네요.
① 다음을 기약하다
② 발을 담그다, 처음으로 해 보다
③ 오일을 교체하다
④ 펑크 난 타이어를 교체하다

| 정답해설 | ② 63% A가 B에게 운전을 가르쳐 달라고 요청하는 상황으로, B가 운전해 본 경험을 물어봤을 때, A가 No라고 했음에도 '기다릴 수 없다(can't wait~)'고 한 것으로 보아 운전하고 싶다는 표현이 빈칸에 들어가야 함을 알 수 있다. get one's feet wet은 '시작하다'의 의미로 맥락상 가장 적절하다.

어휘
learner's permit 임시 운전면허증

오답률 TOP 3

9   독해 > 세부내용 찾기 > 내용 일치 찾기   오답률 44%   답 ②

| 해석 | 상어는 치아와 같은 물질로 만든 비늘로 덮여 있다. 이 부드러운 비늘은 상어를 보호하고 물속에서 빠르게 헤엄칠 수 있도록 도와준다. 상어는 헤엄칠 때 이 비늘을 움직일 수 있다. 이 운동은 물의 항력을 감소시키는 데 도움이 된다. 앨라배마 대학교의 항공 우주 엔지니어인 Amy Lang은 백상아리의 동족인 청상아리의 비늘을 연구한다. Lang과 그녀의 팀은 청상아리의 비늘이 몸의 다양한 부분의 크기와 유연성에 따라 다른 것을 발견했다. 예를 들어, 신체의 측면에 있는 비늘은 한쪽 끝이 가늘고 다른 쪽 끝은 좁아진다. 이러한 비늘은 가늘기 때문에 매우 쉽게 움직인다. 그것들은 상어 주변의 물의 흐름에 적응하고 공기의 힘을 줄이기 위해 위로 올리거나 평평하게 할 수 있다. Lang은 상어 비늘이 항공기처럼 공기의 저항을 겪는 기계의 설계에 영감을 줄 수 있다고 생각한다.
① 상어는 헤엄치는 동안 스스로를 보호하기 위해 항상 움직이지 않는 비늘이 있다.
② Lang은 청상아리의 비늘이 물속에서 항력을 줄이기 위해 활용된다는 것을 밝혔다.
③ 청상아리는 몸 전체에 동일한 크기의 비늘을 가지고 있다.
④ 항공기의 과학적 설계는 상어 비늘에 영감을 받았다.

| 정답해설 | ② 56% Lang and her team discovered that ~ They can turn up or flatten to adjust to the flow of water around the shark and to reduce drag.를 통해 ②가 지문의 내용과 일치함을 알 수 있다.

어휘
flexible 유연한; 융통성 있는   relative 친척; 동족; 상대적인
tapered (끝으로 갈수록) 점점 가늘어진, 좁아진

---

flatten 평평하게 하다   adjust 조정하다, 적응하다
drag 항력(抗力); 끌기   inspire 영감을 주다; 격려하다

10   문법 > 준동사 > 분사   오답률 41%   답 ③

| 해석 | 집중은 어떤 일들을 해내는 것을 의미한다. 많은 사람들이 좋은 아이디어를 가지고 있지만 그것들을 실행에 옮기지는 않는다. 예를 들어, 내게 기업가의 정의는 그 새로운 아이디어를 실행할 수 있는 능력을 혁신 및 독창성과 결합시킬 수 있는 사람이다. 삶에 있어서 중심이 되는 이분법이란 당신에게 흥미를 주거나 심려를 끼치는 문제들에 대해 당신이 긍정적인지 부정적인지에 관한 것이라고 어떤 사람들은 생각한다. 낙관적인 시선을 가지는 것이 나은지 비관적인 시선을 가지는 것이 나은지에 대한 이 질문에 쏟아지는 관심은 많다. 내 생각에 더 나은 질문은 당신이 그것에 대해 뭔가를 할 것인지 아니면 인생이 그냥 지나치게 놔둘지 묻는 것이다.

| 정답해설 | ③ 59% 명사 attention을 수식하는 분사구로 pay는 타동사이므로 paying에 이어 목적어가 와야 하는데 없는 점, 맥락상 관심은 '받는' 것이므로 수동의 과거분사 paid로 바꿔야 한다.

| 오답해설 | ① 4% 타동사 mean의 목적어로 동명사가 왔고, getting의 목적어 stuff, 목적격보어인 과거분사 done이 이어졌다. 일은 '행해지는' 것이므로 목적격보어로 수동의 의미를 지닌 과거분사 done이 이어진 올바른 구조이다.

② 18% that은 선행사 issues를 지칭하는 주격 관계대명사로, 이어서 선행사에 수를 일치시켜 복수동사인 interest와 concern이 병치된 올바른 구조이다. 능동태이므로 뒤에 목적어인 you가 이어졌다.

④ 19% let은 등위접속사 or로 보아 동사원형 do와 병치된 동사원형이자, 사역동사이므로 목적어인 명사 life에 이어 목적격보어로 원형부정사인 pass가 이어진 올바른 구조이다.

어휘
definition 정의   entrepreneur 기업인, 기업가
combine 결합하다   innovation 혁신
ingenuity 창의력   execute 실행하다
dichotomy 이분법, 양분   optimistic 낙관적인
pessimistic 비관적인

---

11   독해 > 글의 일관성 파악하기 > 글의 흐름과 무관한 어휘   오답률 15%   답 ④

| 해석 | 대부분의 사람들은 말하기를 좋아하는 반면에, 듣기를 좋아하는 사람은 거의 없다. 하지만 잘 듣는 것은 모든 사람들이 높이 평가해야 할 대단한 재능이다. 뛰어난 경청가들은 더 많이 듣기 때문에 더 많이 알고 대부분의 사람들보다 그들 주변의 돌아가는 상황에 대해 더 민감한 경향이 있다. 게다가, 뛰어난 경청가들은 판단하고 비판하기보다는 수용하고 인내하는 경향이 있다. 따라서, 그들은 대부분의 사람들보다 적수들이 더 적다. 사실상, 그들은 아마 가장 사랑받는 사람일 것이다. 그러나, 그러한 일반론에도 예외는 있다. 예를 들어, John Steinback은 탁월한 경청가였다고 알려졌지만, 그는 그가 글의 소재로 쓴 몇몇 사람들로부터 미움을 받았다. 의심할 여지없이 그의 듣는 능력은 글을 쓸 수 있는 능력에 기여했다. 그럼에도, 그의 경청의 결과는 그를 ④ 인기 없게(→ 인기 있게) 만들지 않았다.

| 정답해설 | ④ 85% 일반적으로 경청하는 사람들은 가장 사랑받는 사람들이라고 서술한 데 이어, 경청가였음에도 미움을 받았던 사례로 John Steinback을 언급했다. 따라서 그의 경청의 결과는 인기

가 없게 했다는 것을 유추할 수 있는데, 빈칸 앞에 부정의 표현인 didn't가 있으므로 이를 감안하면 unpopular는 popular로 바꿔야 함을 알 수 있다. 따라서 정답은 ④이다.

어휘
rare (한정적) 대단한; 드문, 진귀한　treasure 소중히 하다
be inclined to + R ~하는 경향이 있다
tolerate 참다, 견디다　　　generality 일반 원리, 일반론
contribute to ~에 기여하다

---

12 독해 > 대의 파악 > 주제 찾기　　오답률 19%　답 ④

| 해석 | 걱정은 흔들 목마와 같다. 당신이 아무리 빨리 간다고 하더라도, 당신은 어느 곳으로도 움직이지 않는다. 걱정은 완전한 시간 낭비이고, 마음에 너무 많은 혼란을 일으켜 그 어떤 것도 명확하게 생각할 수 없다. 걱정을 멈추는 방법을 배우는 것은 먼저 당신이 집중하는 어떤 것에든 에너지를 쏟아야 한다는 것을 이해함으로써이다. 따라서 당신 자신이 걱정을 하게 더 내버려 둘수록, 일이 잘못될 가능성이 더 많아진다! 걱정하는 것은 그토록 몸에 밴 습관이 되어서 그것을 피하려면 당신 스스로가 의식적으로 달리 행동하도록 단련시켜야 한다. 당신이 걱정이라는 감정에 북받칠 때마다, 생각을 멈추고 다른 생각으로 전환하라. 당신이 정말로 일어나기를 바라는 일에 좀 더 생산적으로 집중하고 당신의 인생에 이미 일어났던 근사한 것들에 대해 생각하면 더 멋진 것들이 당신에게 올 것이다.
① 걱정은 삶에 어떤 영향을 미치는가?
② 걱정은 어디에서 유래하는가?
③ 우리는 언제 걱정해야 하는가?
④ 우리는 걱정에 어떻게 대처하는가?

| 정답해설 | ④ 81% 걱정을 흔들 목마에 비유해 걱정에 대한 부정적인 견해를 제시하고, 뒷부분에서 걱정에 대처하는 방법을 설명하는 글이다. 따라서 글의 주제로 가장 적절한 것은 ④이다.

어휘
clutter 혼란 (상태), 잡동사니　energize 기운을 북돋우다, 격려하다
ingrain 뿌리 깊은, 깊이 배어든　conscious 의식하는
have a fit of ~이 북받치다
dwell on ~을 곰곰이 생각하다; ~을 상세히 말하다
originate from ~에서 기원하다, 비롯하다
cope with ~에 대처하다, ~을 극복하다

---

13 독해 > 세부내용 찾기 > 내용 불일치 찾기　오답률 13%　답 ②

| 해석 | Macaulay Honors College(MHC) 학생들은 높은 수업료에 대해 걱정하지 않는다. 무료이기 때문이다. Macaulay와 소수의 다른 서비스 아카데미, 근로 연계 단과대, 단과대학교 및 음악학교는 학생의 100%가 4년 동안 학비 전액 장학금을 수령한다. Macaulay 학생들은 연구, 서비스 경험, 유학 프로 그램 및 인턴십을 추구하기 위해 노트북과 7500 달러의 '기회 자금'을 받는다. Macaulay Honors College의 학장인 Ann Kirschner는 "가장 중요한 것은 무료 수업이 아니라 등 뒤에 빚진 부담없이 공부할 수 있는 자유입니다."라고 말한다. 그녀는 "부채 부담은 학생들이 대학에서 내리는 결정을 손상시키므로, 우리는 그들에게 자유로운 기회를 제공하고 있습니다."라고 말한다. 모든 학생들에게 무료 수업료를 제공하는 학교는 드물다. 그러나 더 많은 수의 기관이 높은 성적의 등록자에게 장학금을 제공한다. 인디애나 대학교 블루밍턴 캠퍼스와 같은 기관에서는 우수한 성적 학점(GPA) 및 반 석차를 갖춘 우수한 학생에게 자동으로 상을 수여한다.

| 정답해설 | ② 87% Macaulay students also receive a laptop

---

and \$7,500 in "opportunities funds" to pursue research, service experiences, study abroad programs and internships. 를 통해 컴퓨터 외에 7,500달러의 기회 자금이 제공된다고 했으므로 ②는 지문의 내용과 일치하지 않는다.

어휘
tuition 등록금, 수업료　　conservatory 음악 학교, 예술 학교
research 연구　　　　　burden 부담, 짐, 책임
compromise 손상시키다; 타협하다　enrollee 등록자

---

14 어휘 > 동의어　　　오답률 36%　답 ①

| 해석 | 경찰은 그 범죄 사건에 대해 조사를 하는데 7개월을 보냈지만, 그 범인의 신원을 판단할 수 없었다.
① 64% 죄인, 범죄자, 원흉
② 10% 딜레탕트, (문학·예술의) 아마추어 애호가
③ 11% (남부 인도·미얀마의) 최하층민, 천민
④ 15% (민중) 선동가, 선동 정치가

| 정답해설 | ① 경찰이 범죄 사건 조사로 수개월을 보냈음에도 불구하고, malefactor의 신원을 판단할 수 없었다고 했으므로 조사의 대상인 malefactor는 '범인, 범죄자'의 의미임을 알 수 있다. male은 '악한', factor는 '행하는 사람'의 의미임을 고려하면 범죄자의 의미를 쉽게 유추할 수 있다. 따라서 동의어로 가장 적절한 것은 ①이다.

어휘
spend + 시간 + R-ing ~하느라 시간을 보내다
crime case 범죄 사건　　　identity 신원

---

15 어휘 > 동의어　　　오답률 21%　답 ④

| 해석 | 언뜻 보기에 그의 친구들이 단지 거머리들에 불과해 보임에도 불구하고, 그들은 좋을 때나 나쁠 때나 그가 의지할 수 있는 사람들인 것으로 밝혀졌다.
① 5% 즉시, 당장　　　　② 12% 때때로, 이따금
③ 4% 즐거운 때에　　　④ 79% 좋을 때나 나쁠 때나

| 정답해설 | ④ through thick and thin은 사냥할 때 빽빽한(thick) 덤불을 지나갈 때나, 덤불이 드문드문 있는(thin) 곳을 지나는 상황에서 유래한 표현으로, 어떤 어려움이나 장애물에도 변함없이 함께한다는 의미로 확대된 표현이다. 따라서 동의어로 가장 적절한 것은 ④이다.

어휘
through thick and thin 때를 가리지 않고, 좋을 때나 안 좋을 때나
at first glance 언뜻 보기에　　leech 거머리
depend on ~에 의존하다; ~에 달려 있다

---

16 독해 > 글의 일관성 파악하기 > 주어진 문장의 삽입　오답률 31%　답 ④

| 해석 | 말에 대한 우리의 지각과 발화는 시간이 지나면서 변한다. 우리가 오랜 기간 동안 우리가 원래 살던 곳을 떠나야 한다면, 우리 주변의 새로운 억양이 이상하다는 우리의 인식은 단지 일시적일 것이다. 점차적으로 우리는 다른 사람들이 억양을 가지고 있다는 느낌을 잃어버릴 것이고 새로운 규범에 맞게 우리의 말 패턴을 수용하기 시작할 것이다. 모든 사람들이 같은 정도로 이것을 하는 것은 아니다. ④ 일부 사람들은 원래의 억양과 사투리

단어, 문구 및 몸짓을 매우 자랑스럽게 여긴다. 반면에 다른 사람들은 더 이상 '군중에서 눈에 띄지 않도록' 말하기 습관을 변경함으로써 새로운 환경에 빠르게 적응한다. 그들이 이것을 의식적으로 하는지 아닌지에 대해서는 논쟁의 여지가 있으며 개별적으로 다를 수 있지만, 언어와 관련이 있는 대부분의 과정과 마찬가지로 변화는 아마도 우리가 이를 인식하기 전에 발생하고 비록 우리가 알지라도 발생하지 않을 수 있다.

| 정답해설 | ④ [69%] 'Not all people do this to the same degree.'에 이어 사람에 따라 다르다는 내용의 제시문이 들어가야 하므로 정답은 ④이다.

어휘

perception 지각, 인식	temporary 일시적인; 임시의
accommodate 수용하다	dialect 방언, 사투리
stand out 두드러지다; 뛰어나다	open to debate 논쟁의 여지가 있는
have to do with ~와 관련이 있다	be aware of ~을 인지하다, 깨닫다

---

17 독해 > 세부내용 찾기 > 내용 불일치 찾기 [오답률 28%] 답 ②

| 해석 | 불면증은 일시적, 급성 또는 만성으로 분류할 수 있다. 일시적인 불면증은 1주일 미만 동안 지속된다. 그것은 다른 장애, 수면 환경의 변화, 수면의 타이밍, 심한 우울증 또는 스트레스로 인해 야기될 수 있다. 졸음과 정신 운동 능력의 손상과 같은 그것에 따른 결과들은 수면 부족과 유사하다. 급성 불면증은 1개월 미만의 기간 동안 지속적으로 잘 수 없다는 것이다. 급성 불면증은 수면을 시작하거나 유지하는 데 어려움이 있거나 얻은 수면이 상쾌하지 않은 때에 나타난다. 이러한 문제들은 적절한 기회와 수면 환경에도 불구하고 발생하며 또 주간에 기능을 발휘하는 것을 손상시킬 수 있다. 급성 불면증은 또한 단기간의 불면증 또는 스트레스 관련 불면증으로도 알려져 있다. 만성 불면증은 한 달 이상 지속된다. 그것은 다른 장애로 인해 발생할 수 있으며, 혹은 그것이 주요 장애가 될 수 있다. 스트레스 호르몬 수치가 높거나 사이토카인 수준이 바뀌면 다른 사람들보다 만성 불면증이 더 많이 생긴다. 그 영향들은 원인에 따라 다를 수 있다. 근육 피로, 환각 및/혹은 정신적 피로를 포함할 수 있다. 만성 불면증은 또한 복시(複視)를 유발할 수 있다.

① 불면증은 지속 기간에 따라 분류될 수 있다.
② 일시적 불면증은 부적절한 수면 환경에 의해서만 발생한다.
③ 급성 불면증은 일반적으로 스트레스와 관련된 것으로 알려져 있다.
④ 만성 불면증 환자는 환각으로 고통받을 수 있다.

| 정답해설 | ② [72%] 세 번째 문장을 통해 부적절한 수면 환경 외에도 다른 요인들이 있음을 알 수 있으므로 정답은 ②이다.

어휘

insomnia 불면증	transient 일시적인
acute 예민한, 급성인	chronic 만성적인, 상습적인
disorder 장애, 질환	impaired 손상된
psychomotor 정신 운동(성)의	performance 성적, 실행
sleep deprivation 수면 부족	consistently 시종일관으로, 모순 없이
initiate 개시하다, 시작하다	refreshing 상쾌한, 마음이 시원한
cytokine 사이토카인	hallucination 환각
mental fatigue 정신 피로	double vision 복시(複視)

---

18 독해 > 빈칸의 내용 추론하기 > 빈칸 어구 추론 [오답률 43%] 답 ②

| 해석 | 뭄바이의 Everonn Education 창업자인 Kisha Padbhan은 자신의 사업을 일종의 국가 건설로 보고 있다. 인도의 학령 인구 2억 3천만(유치원부터 대학까지)은 세계에서 가장 큰 규모 중 하나이다. 정부는 교육에 830억 달러를 쓰지만 심각한 격차가 있다. "교사가 충분하지 않고 교사 훈련 기관이 충분하지 않습니다."라고 Kisha는 말한다. "인도 외딴 지역의 어린이들에게 부족한 것은 좋은 선생님을 만나고 양질의 콘텐츠를 접하는 것입니다." Everronn의 해결책은? 그것은 ② 가상 교실을 통해 격차를 해소하도록 양방향 비디오 및 오디오와 함께 위성 네트워크를 사용한다. 그것은 인도의 28개 주 중 24개 주에 1,800개의 단과대와 7,800개의 학교에 미친다. 그것은 디지털화된 학교 수업부터 장래의 엔지니어를 위한 입학 시험 준비에 이르기까지 모든 것을 제공하며 구직자를 위한 교육도 제공한다.

① 교사 연수 시설의 질적 향상을 위해
② 가상 교실을 통해 격차를 해소하도록
③ 학생들이 디지털 기술에 익숙해지도록
④ 전국적으로 자격을 갖춘 강사를 발굴하도록

| 정답해설 | ② [57%] '인도의 외딴 지역의 어린이들에게 부족한 것은 좋은 선생님을 만나고 양질의 콘텐츠를 접하는 것입니다'라는 부분에서 지역 간의 교육 격차를 해소하는 것이 Everonn Education의 목표임을 알 수 있으므로 정답은 ②이다.

어휘

founder 설립자	gap 간격, 차이
satellite network 인공위성 네트워크	digitize 디지털화하다
prep 예습, 준비	
bridge the gap 격차를 줄이다, 좁히다	
virtual 가상의, 인터넷의; 실질적인	qualified 자격이 있는, 적임의

---

19 독해 > 글의 일관성 파악하기 > 글의 순서 [오답률 46%] 답 ③

| 해석 | 한 개인이 신체 기능들의 전자 측정치들을 관찰함으로써 자율적인 혹은 무의식적인 신체 기능들에 대한 어떠한 자발적인 통제력을 얻게 해주는 것을 가능하게 하는 기술이 생체 자기 제어(biofeedback)로 알려져 있다.
(B) 심박동수, 혈압, 그리고 피부의 온도와 같은 다양한 변수들을 측정하기 위하여 전자 감지기들이 신체의 다양한 부위들에 부착된다.
(A) 그런 변수가 (예를 들어, 혈압을 낮추는 것과 같이) 바람직한 방향으로 움직일 때, 그것은 시각적이거나 청각적인 디스플레이, 즉 텔레비전 세트, 측정기, 또는 조명과 같은 장비에 피드백이 생겨나게 만든다.
(C) 생체 자기 제어 훈련은 어떤 사람이 그런 디스플레이를 유발했던 사고의 패턴이나 행동들을 재생함으로써 바람직한 반응을 만들도록 가르친다.

| 정답해설 | ③ [54%] 제시문에 이어 생체 자기 제어 기술을 실행하는 첫 번째 단계를 서술한 (B)가 온 후에, (B)에서 언급된 'such variables'를 지칭한 것이 (A)의 'such a variable'임을 알 수 있으므로 (A)가 이어져야 하며, 여러 가지 파생되는 피드백을 언급한 것에 이어 (C)에서 이에 대한 결과를 서술하고 있으므로 정답은 ③이다.

어휘

voluntary 자발적인, 임의의	involuntary 무심결의, 무의식적인
biofeedback 생체 자기 제어	electronic sensor 전자 감지기
variable 변수; 가변적인	heart rate 심박동수
trigger 야기하다, 유발하다	reproduce 재생하다, 재현하다

| 20 | 문법 > 형용사·부사·비교 > 비교 | 오답률 42% | 답 ④ |

| 정답해설 | ④ 58% 'not so ~ as'의 구조이므로 동등비교의 표현이 되어야 함을 알 수 있다. 따라서 비교급 stingier는 원급인 stingy로 바꿔야 한다.

| 오답해설 | ① 14% 'be good at R-ing'는 '~하는 데 익숙하다'의 표현으로 주어진 우리말과 일치하는 표현이며, 타동사구 get across는 '이해시키다'의 표현이므로 주어진 우리말과 일치한다.

② 14% 우리말은 비교급을 이용한 최상급의 표현이므로 '비교급 than any other + 단수명사'의 구조로 올바르게 표현되었다.

③ 14% 문장 전체 주어는 동명사 making이므로 단수로 동사의 수가 올바르게 일치되었고, 전치사 with의 목적어인 the person을 목적격 관계대명사 that이 생략된 you are speaking to가 수식하고 있는 올바른 구조이다.

어휘

be good at R-ing ~에 익숙하다, 능숙하다

get across 이해시키다   stingy 인색한

지방직

해설 &
기출분석 REPORT

지방직 기출 POINT

Point 1 어휘는 기출 어휘를 기반으로 출제되나 최근 난도는 하향하고 있는 추세이다.

Point 2 문법은 문법 요소에 대한 기본적인 응용력을 요구하는 문제로 출제되고 있다.

Point 3 독해는 비슷한 유형이 계속 출제되고 있기에 유형별 풀이법을 숙지하고 있는 것이 중요하다.

2025년 지방직 시험 대비전략

"달라진 출제 경향에도 집중력과 시간 안배를 통해 고득점 달성!"

Point 1 인사혁신처 공개 예시문제에 기반하여 취학 유형을 파악하고 집중적으로 연습해야 한다.

Point 2 늘어난 독해 비중을 대비하여 유형별 핵심 내용을 파악하고 빠른 정답 찾기 연습이 필요하다.

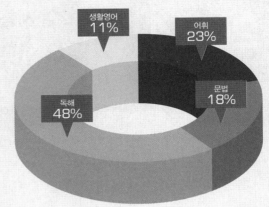

▲ 최근 7개년 평균 출제비중

생활영어 11%
어휘 23%
문법 18%
독해 48%

연도	총평	어휘	문법	독해	생활영어
2024	**역대급 낮은 난도의 시험, 실수가 당락을 가른다!** · 국가직과 전년도 지방직 대비 난도 하락으로 정확한 문제 풀이가 합격의 관건임 · 문법과 어휘 모두 기출 범위 내에서 출제됨 · 국가직에 이어 공개된 신유형 문제(업무 이메일 등)가 일부 도입됨	25% (5문항)	15% (3문항)	45% (9문항)	15% (3문항)
2023	**기본과 기출에 충실한 학습으로 고득점 완성이 가능한 시험!** · 전 영역에 걸쳐 평이한 난도의 출제로 합격선이 높아짐 · 문법과 어휘는 기출 출제 범위 내의 문제들로 구성됨 · 독해 문항 수는 9문항으로 감소하고, 지문 자체의 길이가 전년도 대비 줄어듦	25% (5문항)	15% (3문항)	45% (9문항)	15% (3문항)
2022	**공무원 출제 전형을 따른 문제 구성과 난이도!** · 기출 어휘들 위주로 출제가 이루어졌고, 동사구에 대한 이해가 요구됨 · 문법은 지엽적인 부분을 배제하고 출제 빈도가 높은 부분(일치, 준동사, 관계사 등)으로 문제가 구성됨 · 독해는 비교적 긴 10개 문항으로 출제되었으나, 소재 자체의 난도는 높지 않음	20% (4문항)	20% (4문항)	50% (10문항)	10% (2문항)
2021	**예년과 비교해 역대급 최저 난도, 실수가 없어야 합격!** · 어휘에서 다수의 빈칸 추론(3문항) 출제로 맥락 파악이 중요함 · 문법은 영작문 길이가 긴 편이나 문제 자체는 기출 범위 내 평범한 수준임 · 독해 문제 감소(전년도와 동일하게 9문항)와 평이한 소재로 풀이 부담이 감소함	25% (5문항)	20% (4문항)	45% (9문항)	10% (2문항)
2020	**기출에 기반한 문법 이해와 어휘 추론 능력이 고득점 요소!** · 출제되지 않았던 동사구와 표현의 등장으로 추론의 중요성 대두됨 · 문법은 일치, 동사, 관계사 등 출제 빈도가 높은 문법 중심의 학습이 중요함 · 독해에서 일관성과 빈칸 추론 문항의 비중은 높으나 난도는 평이했음	25% (5문항)	20% (4문항)	45% (9문항)	10% (2문항)
2019	**독해 난도 대폭 상승으로, 체감 난도의 상승과 더불어 합격선은 낮아질 듯!** · 먼저 치러진 국가직 대비 모든 영역에 걸쳐 문제 난도가 상승함. · 문법과 어휘, 생활영어는 평이하게 출제된 편으로 충실한 학습 필요함 · 독해는 긴 지문, 까다로운 유형의 문항 비중 증가, 논리적 사고를 요구하는 소재를 다른 지문으로 난도가 대폭 상승함	20% (4문항)	15% (3문항)	55% (11문항)	10% (2문항)
2018	**기출 핵심 요소를 볼 수 있는 눈과 정확한 순발력이 요구되는 시험** · 어휘는 대부분 평이한 난도지만, 관용어구나 동사구에 대한 이해도가 필요함 · 지엽적인 부분의 비중이 줄어들고, 일치와 시제, 동사 등의 기출 핵심 부분의 출제 비중이 증가함 · 전체적으로 긴 독해 지문으로 시간 조절에 대한 연습이 필요함	20% (4문항)	20% (4문항)	50% (10문항)	10% (2문항)

합격예상 체크

〈지방직 연도별 합격선〉

2024 합격기준!

맞힌 개수	/20문항	점수	/100점

➡ ☐ 합격 ☐ 불합격

취약영역 체크

문항	정답	영역	문항	정답	영역
1	②	어휘 > 동의어	11	②	생활영어 > 회화
2	②	어휘 > 동의어	12	③	독해 > 세부내용 찾기
3	①	어휘 > 동의어	13	④	독해 > 세부내용 찾기
4	①	어휘 > 동의어	14	③	독해 > 대의 파악
5	③	어휘 > 빈칸	15	③	독해 > 대의 파악
6	④	문법 > 연결사	16	③	독해 > 글의 일관성 파악하기
7	③	문법 > 연결사	17	④	독해 > 글의 일관성 파악하기
8	②	문법 > 문장의 구조와 동사 유형	18	④	독해 > 글의 일관성 파악하기
9	④	생활영어 > 회화	19	④	독해 > 빈칸의 내용 추론하기
10	④	생활영어 > 회화	20	①	독해 > 빈칸의 내용 추론하기

⬇ 영역별 틀린 개수로 취약영역을 확인하세요!

어휘	/5	문법	/3	독해	/9	생활영어	/3

➡ 나의 취약영역: _____

※ [정답해설]과 [오답해설] 선지의 50% 표시는 〈에듀윌 합격예측 풀서비스〉를 통해 수집된 선지 선택률을 나타냅니다.

1	어휘 > 동의어	오답률 19%	답 ②

| 해석 | 셰익스피어의 희극은 많은 유사성을 공유하지만, 그것들은 또한 서로 현저하게 다르다.
① 5% 부드럽게; 조용히
② 81% 분명히, 명백히
③ 8% 가까스로
④ 6% 식별할 수 없게

| 정답해설 | ② 동사 differ from을 수식하는 부사로, 맥락상 '~와 현저하게 다르다'의 의미가 가장 자연스러움을 알 수 있다. 따라서 markedly와 의미가 가장 가까운 것은 '분명히'의 의미인 obviously가 정답이다.

어휘
markedly 현저하게, 두드러지게   similarity 유사성
differ from ~와는 다르다

오답률 TOP 2

2	어휘 > 동의어	오답률 57%	답 ②

| 해석 | 제인은 진한 다크티를 따르고 그것을 우유로 희석했다.
① 10% 물로 씻다
② 43% 약화시키다
③ 21% 연결하다
④ 26% 발효되다

| 정답해설 | ② 진한 다크티에 부드러운 우유를 넣었을 때 차가 어떻게 될 것인가를 생각하면, 강한 맛이 순화될 것임을 유추할 수 있다. dilute는 '희석하다'의 의미로 이와 가장 의미가 유사한 것으로 '약화시키다'의 의미인 weaken의 과거형인 weakened가 가장 적절하다.

어휘
dilute 희석시키다   pour out 붓다, 쏟다

3	어휘 > 동의어	오답률 35%	답 ①

| 해석 | 수상은 육아수당이나 연금 삭감을 배제한 것으로 여겨진다.
① 65% 배제된
② 13% 뒷받침된
③ 10% 굴복한; 제출된
④ 12% 위임된, 권한을 부여받은

| 정답해설 | ① rule out은 규정 등에 의해 외부에(out) 두는 것이므로 유추하면 '배제하다'의 의미임을 알 수 있다. exclude는 외부에(ex-) 두고 닫는다(clude)는 의미로 ' 못 들어오게 하다' 즉, '배제하다, 제외하다'의 의미이다. 따라서 rule out과 의미가 가장 가까운 것은 exclude이다.

어휘
rule out 배제하다, 제외하다
benefit (보험 회사 · 공제 조합 등의) 수당, 혜택
pension 연금

4	어휘 > 동의어	오답률 26%	답 ①

| 해석 | 우리가 깜짝 파티를 계획하고 있다는 것을 누설한다면, 아버지는 너에게 질문을 멈추지 않을 거야.
① 74% 드러내다, 폭로하다
② 11% 관찰하다; 준수하다
③ 5% 믿다
④ 10% 소유하다

| **정답해설** | ① 깜짝 파티를 계획 중인 상황에서 무엇을 했을 때 아버지가 끊임없이 질문을 하게 될지에 대해 생각해 보면, 그 사실을 알게 되었을 때임을 유추할 수 있다. 따라서 let on은 '누설하다'의 의미임을 알 수 있고, '드러내다, 밝히다'의 의미인 reveal이 의미상 가장 가깝다.

어휘
let on 폭로하다, 누설하다　　　stop R-ing ~을 중단하다, 멈추다

| **5** | 어휘 > 빈칸 | 오답률 25% | 답 ③ |

| **해석** | 슈퍼마켓의 자동문은 가방이나 쇼핑 카트가 있는 고객의 출입을 ③ 수월하게 한다.
① 8% 무시하다　　　② 7% 용서하다
③ 75% 수월하게 하다　　④ 10% 과장하다

| **정답해설** | ③ 슈퍼마켓의 자동문은 짐이나 쇼핑 카트가 있는 고객들의 출입에 어떤 영향을 줄지에 대해 생각해 보면, '수월하게' 함을 유추할 수 있다. 따라서 빈칸에 들어갈 것으로 가장 적절한 것은 facilitate이다.

어휘
automatic 자동의　　　　　　entry 입구, 입장, 등장
exit 출구; 퇴장

| **6** | 문법 > 연결사 > 접속사 | 오답률 28% | 답 ④ |

| **해석** | 당신이 지금 읽고 있는 책의 많은 장점 중 하나는, 저자가 집필하면서 심리학에 대한 자신의 접근 방식을 정리하고 있었기에, 매우 복잡한 작업인 '의미의 지도'로 진입하도록 한다는 점이다.

| **정답해설** | ④ 72% because of는 전치사구이므로 목적어로 명사나 명사 상당어구가 와야 한다. 뒤에 '주어 + 동사'의 절이 이어졌으므로 이유 부사절을 이끄는 접속사 because로 바꿔야 한다.

| **오답해설** | ① 7% 형용사 many의 수식을 받는 명사이므로 복수형으로 올바르게 왔다.
② 10% 문장 전체의 주어는 one이므로 호응하는 동사로 단수인 is가 올바르게 수일치가 이루어졌다.
③ 11% 관계대명사 which에 이어진 내용으로 보아 선행사는 'Maps of Meaning'이고, comma(,)를 통해 계속적 용법임을 알 수 있으므로 which가 온 것은 적절하다. 주격 관계대명사로 뒤에 동사(is)부터 시작하는 불완전한 절이 올바르게 이어졌다.

어휘
virtue 장점, 미덕　　　　　complex 복잡한
author 저자　　　　　　　psychology 심리학

| **7** | 문법 > 연결사 > 관계사 | 오답률 33% | 답 ③ |

| **해석** | ① 프로젝트에 너무 많은 돈을 쓰지 않도록 계획해야 한다.
② 내 개는 지난 달에 사라졌고 그 이후로는 보이지 않았다.
③ 내가 돌보는 딸이 있는 사람들이 떠나가는 것이 슬프다.
④ 여행 중에 책을 샀는데, 집에 있는 것보다 두 배나 비쌌다.

| **정답해설** | ③ 67% 접속사 that이 이끄는 절의 주어 the people을 수식하는 관계대명사절을 who가 이끌고 있다. who는 주격 관계대

명사이므로 뒤에는 동사부터 시작되는 불완전한 절이 이어져야 하는데, 명사 daughter에 이어 '주어 + 동사(I look after)'가 이어지므로 daughter를 한정할 수 있는 소유격 관계대명사 whose로 바꿔야 한다.

| **오답해설** | ① 12% plan의 목적어로 to부정사가 왔고, 준동사의 부정은 준동사 바로 앞에 not을 붙이므로 올바른 구조이다.
② 12% disappear는 자동사이며, 과거 부사구인 last month와 호응해 과거시제로 올바르게 시제일치가 이루어졌다.
④ 9% 동등비교 as expensive as 앞에 배수사가 결합해 '두 배만큼 비싼'의 의미로 올바른 표현이다. it was에 이어진 비교구문으로 주격보어로 형용사 expensive가 올바르게 왔다.

어휘
disappear 사라지다　　　　look after ~을 돌보다

오답률 TOP 1

| **8** | 문법 > 문장의 구조와 동사 유형 > 동사와 문장의 5형식 | | |
| | | 오답률 64% | 답 ② |

| **정답해설** | ② 36% mention은 4형식 동사가 아닌 3형식 동사이므로 목적어는 하나만 와야 한다. 따라서 '~에게'의 표현으로 me를 to me로 바꿔야 한다. 주절의 동사가 과거이므로 종속절의 동사로 '과거에서의 미래'의 표현으로 'would + 동사원형'이 온 것과, 왕래발착 동사인 leave가 진행시제로 쓰이면 가까운 미래를 나타냄으로 시제일치는 올바르게 이루어진 문장이다.

| **오답해설** | ① 23% 5형식 문장으로 목적어인 to work here를 목적격보어인 exciting 뒤로 보내고 목적어 자리에 가목적어인 it을 삽입한 올바른 문장이다. 또한 진목적어인 to work here는 '흥미를 주는' 것이므로 능동의 현재분사 exciting이 목적보어로 온 것 또한 적절하다.
③ 12% 5형식 문장으로 불완전타동사 want와 호응하는 목적보어로 to부정사가 올바르게 왔다.
④ 29% 명사 teacher를 수식하는 형용사로 skillful과 experienced가 병치되었고, 우리말로 보아 과거 사실의 반대되는 표현인 '~했을 텐데'의 표현으로 'would have + p.p.'가 적절하게 왔다.

어휘
mention 언급하다　　　　　skillful 능숙한
experienced 경험 많은　　　treat 대하다, 대우하다; 치료하다
otherwise 다르게, 달리; 그렇지 않으면

| **9** | 생활영어 > 회화 | 오답률 18% | 답 ④ |

| **해석** | A: 찰스, 다가오는 행사를 위해 의자가 더 필요할 것 같아요.
B: 정말요? 의자는 이미 충분하다고 생각했는데요.
A: 매니저가 350명 이상이 올 거라고 나에게 말했어요.
B: ④ 제가 예상했던 것보다 훨씬 더 많네요.
A: 맞아요. 나도 약간 놀랐어요.
B: 그러면 의자를 더 주문해야 할 것 같네요. 감사해요.
① 매니저가 행사에 참석할지가 궁금해요.
② 350명 이상이 올 거라고 생각했어요.
③ 그게 사실은 많은 인원은 아니에요.
④ 제가 예상했던 것보다 훨씬 더 많네요.

| 정답해설 | ④ 82% 다가오는 행사를 위한 의자가 충분할 줄 알았던 상황에서 A가 350명 이상이 참석하게 되었다는 점을 언급했고, 빈칸에 이어 A도 '역시' 놀랐다고 말한 것으로 보아, 빈칸에서 B는 예상보다 더 많은 인원이 참석한다는 표현을 했을 것으로 유추할 수 있다. 따라서 빈칸에 들어갈 말로 가장 적절한 것은 ④이다.

어휘

upcoming 다가오는, 예정된

10	생활영어 > 회화	오답률 13%	답 ④

| 해석 | A: 어제 회의에서 언급하신 문서를 받을 수 있나요?
B: 물론이죠. 문서 제목이 뭔가요?
A: 제목은 기억나지 않지만, 지역 축제에 관한 것이었어요.
B: 아, 무엇을 말씀하시는 건지 알겠어요.
A: 좋아요. 그것을 저에게 이메일로 보내주실 수 있나요?
B: 제가 그것을 가지고 있지 않아요. Park 씨가 그 프로젝트를 담당하고 있으니, 그분이 가지고 있을 거예요.
A: ④ 알려주셔서 감사합니다. 그에게 연락해 볼게요.
B: 행운을 빌어요. 원하시는 문서를 받으시길 바랄게요.
① 그가 사무실에 있는지 확인해 주실 수 있나요?
② Park 씨가 당신에게 다시 이메일을 보냈어요.
③ 당신은 주민 축제에 오시나요?
④ 알려주셔서 감사합니다. 그에게 연락해 볼게요.

| 정답해설 | ④ 87% A가 필요한 문서에 대해 B에게 요청을 했고, B는 그 문서를 자신이 아닌 Park 씨가 가지고 있다고 했으므로, 이 이야기를 듣고 A가 한 말을 유추해야 한다. 빈칸에 이어 B가 문서를 받기를 바란다고 언급했으므로 A는 Park 씨에게 연락을 해 보겠다고 했을 것을 추측할 수 있다. 따라서 빈칸에 들어갈 말로 가장 적절한 것은 ④이다.

어휘

refer to 말하다, 언급하다
in charge of ~을 담당하는, ~에 책임이 있는
contact 연락을 취하다

11	생활영어 > 회화	오답률 16%	답 ②

| 해석 | A: 안녕하세요. 다음 주 화요일에 있을 발표에 대한 질문을 해도 될까요?
B: 자원봉사 프로그램 홍보에 관한 발표를 말씀하시는 건가요?
A: 네. 어디에서 발표를 하나요?
B: 확인해 볼게요. 201호실이네요.
A: 그렇군요. 강의실에서 제 노트북을 사용할 수 있나요?
B: 물론이죠. 강의실에 컴퓨터가 있지만, 원하시면 본인 것을 사용하셔도 돼요.
A: ② 발표 예행연습은 언제 할 수 있을까요?
B: 저희는 발표 2시간 전에 강의실에서 만날 수 있어요. 괜찮으실까요?
A: 네. 정말 감사합니다!
① 컴퓨터 기술자가 한 시간 전에 여기에 왔어요.
② 발표 예행연습은 언제 할 수 있을까요?
③ 우리 프로그램을 위한 자원봉사자를 더 모집해야 할까요?
④ 제 노트북을 강의실에 두고 가기에 마음이 편치 않아요.

| 정답해설 | ② 84% 다음 주 화요일에 있을 발표에 관해 A가 B에게 질문을 하고 있는 상황이다. A가 빈칸 내용을 언급한 후, B는 발표 2시간 전에 강의실에서 만날 수 있다고 하였으므로, 빈칸에는 발표 전에 미리 만나야 하는 것과 관련된 내용이 언급되어야 한다. 따라서 빈칸에 들어갈 말로 가장 적절한 것은 ②이다.

어휘

presentation 발표
rehearsal 예행연습, 리허설
comfortable 편안한
technician 기술자
recruit 모집하다

12	독해 > 세부내용 찾기 > 내용 불일치 찾기	오답률 13%	답 ③

| 해석 | 수신: reserve@metropolitan.com
발신: BruceTayor@westcity.com
날짜: 2024년 6월 22일
제목: 행사장 시설

안녕하세요,

Metropolitan Conference Center에 대한 정보를 요청하기 위해 글을 씁니다. 저희는 올해 9월에 3일간의 콘퍼런스를 위한 장소를 찾고 있습니다. 귀사의 주 회의실에 200명 이상의 대표자를 수용할 수 있는 충분한 공간이 필요하며, 회의를 위한 소회의실 3곳도 필요합니다. 각 회의실에는 wi-fi도 필요합니다. 저희는 오전과 오후 중간에 마실 수 있는 커피가 필요하며, 3일 동안 점심식사를 위해 귀사의 식당도 예약하고 싶습니다.

더불어, Metropolitan 고객이나 대규모 단체를 위한 할인 요금이 적용되는 현지 호텔이 있는지 알려주실 수 있을까요? 매일 밤 100명 이상의 대표자가 묵을 수 있는 숙소가 필요합니다.

귀사의 답장을 기다리겠습니다.

안부를 전하며,

행사 매니저 Bruce Taylor 드림

| 정답해설 | ③ 87% 두 번째 단락 마지막 문장(we would also like to book your restaurant for lunch on all three days)에서 3일간 '점심식사'를 위해 식당을 예약하고 싶다고 언급하였다. 따라서 글의 내용과 일치하지 않는 것은 ③이다.

어휘

venue 장소
delegate 대표자, 대리인
accommodation 숙박
conference 회의, 회견
available 이용 가능한
look forward to R-ing ~를 기대하다, 고대하다

13	독해 > 세부내용 찾기 > 내용 불일치 찾기	오답률 26%	답 ④

| 해석 | 역사가들에 따르면, 넥타이의 역사는 1660년으로 거슬러 올라간다. 그 해 크로아티아에서 온 한 무리의 병사들이 파리를 방문했다. 이 병사들은 루이 14세가 매우 존경했던 전쟁 영웅들이었다. 그들이 목에 두른 색색의 스카프에 깊은 인상을 받은 왕은 Royal Cravattes라고 하는 연대를 만들어 크로아티아 군인들을 기리기로 결정했다. 'cravat(크라바트; 남성이 목에 두른 스카프)'라는 단어는 'Croat(크로아티아인)'라는 단어에서 유래했다. 이 연대의 모든 병사들은 목에 화려한 스카프나 크라바트를 두르고 다녔다. 이 새로운 스타일의 넥웨어는 영국으로 전파되었다. 곧 모든 상류층 남성들

이 크라바트를 착용하고 있었다. 일부 크라바트는 매우 극단적이었다. 때때로, 크라바트는 너무 높아서 남자가 온몸을 돌리지 않고는 머리를 움직일 수 없을 정도였다. 크라바트는 격자무늬부터 레이스까지 많은 다양한 재료로 제작되었고, 그것은 어떤 경우에도 어울렸다.

① 한 무리의 크로아티아 군인들이 1660년에 파리를 방문했다.
② Royal Cravattes는 스카프를 착용한 크로아티아 군인들을 기리기 위해 만들어졌다.
③ 일부 크라바트는 남자가 머리를 자유롭게 움직이기에는 너무 불편했다.
④ 크라바트를 만드는 데 사용된 재료들은 제한적이었다.

| **정답해설** | ④ 74% 마지막 문장에서 크라바트가 격자무늬부터 레이스까지 많은 다양한 재료(many different materials)로 제작되었다고 했으므로, 글의 내용과 일치하지 않는 것은 ④이다.

어휘

date back to ～까지 거슬러 올라가다
impressed 감명 받은
honor 존경하다, 예우하다
cravat 넥타이; 크라바트(17세기에 남성이 목에 두른 스카프)
extreme 극단적인, 극심한
be made of ～로 구성되다
lace 레이스
occasion (특정한) 때(time); 행사

scarves 스카프(scarf의 복수형)
regiment [군사] 연대
at times 때때로, 가끔
plaid 격자무늬
suitable 적합한, 적절한

---

14 독해 > 대의 파악 > 주제 찾기 오답률 40% 답 ③

| **해석** | 최근 몇 년 동안 라틴 아메리카는 엄청난 양의 풍력, 태양열, 지열 및 바이오 연료 에너지 자원을 활용하는 데 큰 발전을 이루었다. 라틴 아메리카의 전력 부문은 이미 석유에 대한 의존도를 점차 낮추기 시작했다. 라틴 아메리카는 2015년에서 2040년 사이에 전력 생산량을 거의 두 배로 늘릴 것으로 예상된다. 실제로 라틴 아메리카의 신규 대규모 발전소 중 석유를 연료로 사용하는 발전소는 전혀 없을 것이며, 이는 다양한 기술을 위한 장을 열어준다. 예전부터 석유를 수입했던 중앙아메리카와 카리브해의 국가들은 21세기 초 10년간의 높고 불안정한 유가를 겪은 후 가장 먼저 석유 기반 발전소로부터 탈피했다.

① 라틴 아메리카의 석유 산업 호황
② 라틴 아메리카의 전력 사업 쇠퇴
③ 라틴 아메리카의 재생 에너지 발전
④ 라틴 아메리카의 석유 기반 자원에 대한 적극적인 개발

| **정답해설** | ③ 60% 최근 라틴 아메리카가 풍력, 태양열, 지열 및 바이오 연료 에너지와 같은 재생 에너지 분야에서 큰 발전을 이루어 전력 생산에 대한 석유 의존도를 크게 줄였고, 향후에는 거의 석유에 의존하지 않을 것이라는 내용의 글이다. 따라서 글의 주제로 적절한 것은 ③이다.

어휘

stride 진보, 발전
incredible 엄청난, 놀라운
biofuel 생물 연료
output 발전량, 생산량, 출력
volatile 불안정한; 휘발성의
advancement 발전, 진보
aggressive 적극적인; 공격적인

exploit 활용하다, 착취하다
geothermal 지열의
gradually 점진적으로, 차차
power plant 발전소
booming 급속히 발전하는
renewable 재생 가능한; 갱신 가능한
exploitation 개발, 개척; 착취

---

15 독해 > 대의 파악 > 제목 찾기 오답률 38% 답 ③

| **해석** | 모든 조직에는 임무를 수행하는 데 사용할 수 있는 자원이 있다. 당신의 조직이 업무를 얼마나 잘 수행하는지는 부분적으로는 당신이 그 자원을 얼마나 많이 보유하고 있는지에 따라 결정되지만, 대부분은 사람과 돈과 같이 당신이 보유한 자원을 얼마나 잘 활용하느냐에 따라 결정된다. 만약 당신이 조직의 인사와 안건, 그리고 자동적으로 발생하지 않는 조건의 통제권을 갖는다면, 조직의 리더로서 당신은 항상 이러한 자원의 활용을 더 효율적이고 효과적으로 만들 수 있다. 당신의 인력과 자금을 신중하게 관리하고, 가장 중요한 것을 가장 중요한 것으로 처리하고, 훌륭한 결정을 내리고, 당신이 직면한 문제를 해결함으로써, 당신은 당신에게 주어진 것을 최대한 활용할 수 있다.

① 조직 내 자원 교환하기
② 외부 통제를 설정하는 리더의 능력
③ 자원을 최대한 활용하기: 리더의 방식
④ 조직의 기술적 역량: 성공의 장벽

| **정답해설** | ③ 62% 조직 내에서 주어진 자원을 효율적이고 효과적으로 활용하는 것에 있어서 리더의 역할과 방식이 중요함을 강조하는 글이다. 따라서 글의 제목으로 적절한 것은 ③이다.

어휘

resource 자원
effective 효과적인
provided that 만일 ～이라면, ～을 전제로
personnel 전 직원, 인원
treat 다루다, 처리하다
external 외부의, 밖의
make the most of ～을 최대한 활용하다
capacity 능력, 수용력

efficient 효율적인
agenda 의제, 과제
encounter 만나다, 마주치다
barrier 장벽, 장애물

---

16 독해 > 글의 일관성 파악하기 > 글의 흐름과 무관한 문장 오답률 42% 답 ③

| **해석** | 비판적 사고는 감정적이지 않은 과정처럼 들리지만, 감정 그리고 심지어는 격렬한 반응을 관여할 수 있다. 특히, 우리는 자신의 의견이나 신념과 모순되는 증거를 싫어할지도 모른다. 만약 증거가 도전적인 방향을 가리키면, 그것은 예상치 못한 분노감, 좌절감 혹은 불안감을 일으킬 수 있다. 학계는 전통적으로 스스로를 논리적이며 감정이 없다고 간주하기를 좋아하기 때문에, 감정이 드러날 경우, 이는 특히 힘들어질 수 있다. ③ 예를 들어, 같은 정보를 여러 관점에서 바라보는 것은 중요하지 않다. 그러한 상황에서 당신의 감정을 관리할 수 있는 것은 유용한 기술이다. 당신이 침착함을 유지하고 근거를 논리적으로 제시할 수 있다면, 당신은 자신의 관점을 설득력 있는 방식으로 더 잘 주장할 수 있을 것이다.

| **정답해설** | ③ 58% 비판적 사고에 있어 감정이 드러나지 않을 수 없으며, 반대되는 의견에 부딪히면 여러 감정이 드러나게 되므로 감정을 잘 관리하여 자신의 의견을 설득력 있게 주장해야 한다는 내용의 글이다. 따라서 글의 흐름상 어색한 문장은 여러 관점에서 같은 정보를 바라보는 것이 중요치 않다는 내용의 ③이다.

어휘

engage 종사[관여]시키다, 끌다
contradict 모순되다
rouse 불러일으키다, 자극하다
logical 논리적인, 타당한
circumstance 상황, 환경

passionate 격렬한; 열정적인
challenging 도전적인; 힘든
frustration 좌절
point of view 관점, 견해
convincing 납득이 가는, 설득력 있는

| **해석** | 컴퓨터 보조 언어 학습(CALL)은 연구와 실습의 한 분야로서 흥미롭기도 하고 좌절감을 주기도 하다.

(B) 그것은 복잡하고 역동적이며 빠르게 변화하기 때문에 흥미로우며, 동일한 이유로 좌절감을 준다.

(C) 기술은 언어 학습 영역에 차원들을 보태고, 그것을 자신들의 전문적인 실무에 적용하고자 하는 사람들에게 새로운 지식과 기술을 요구한다.

(A) 그러나 기술은 너무 빠르게 변화해서 CALL 지식과 기술은 그 분야의 속도를 따라잡기 위해 지속적으로 갱신되어야 한다.

| **정답해설** | ③ 57% 주어진 글은 컴퓨터 보조 언어 학습이 흥미와 좌절감을 동시에 준다는 내용으로, 그 뒤에는 그러한 감정을 주는 이유를 설명하는 (B)가 와야 한다. 이어서, 언어 학습 영역에서 기술이 새로운 차원을 더해 주어 실무에 적용하길 원하는 사람들에게 새로운 지식과 기술이 필요하다는 흥미와 관련된 내용의 (C)가 온 다음, Yet을 통해 (C)에서 언급한 Technology를 the technology로, new knowledge and skills를 CALL knowledge and skills로 받아 기술이 너무 빨리 변화해서 따라잡으려면 컴퓨터 보조 언어 학습의 지식과 기술도 끊임없이 갱신되어야 한다는 (A)가 오는 것이 자연스럽다. 따라서 글의 순서로 적절한 것은 ③이다.

어휘

frustrating 좌절감을 주는   dimension 차원
domain 분야, 영역, 범위   constantly 끊임없이, 계속

| 18 | 독해 > 글의 일관성 파악하기 > 주어진 문장의 삽입 | 오답률 26% | 답 ④ |

| **해석** | 인어공주는 선실의 작은 창문 바로 앞까지 헤엄쳐 올라왔고, 파도가 그녀를 들어 올릴 때마다, 그녀는 투명한 유리를 통해 옷을 잘 차려입은 사람들의 무리를 볼 수 있었다. 그들 중에는 크고 짙은 눈을 가진, 그곳에서 가장 잘생긴 사람인 젊은 왕자가 있었다. 그날은 그의 생일이었고, 그것이 바로 그토록 흥이 있던 이유였다. 그 젊은 왕자가 선원들이 춤을 추고 있는 갑판으로 나왔을 때, 100개 이상의 폭죽이 하늘로 올라갔다가 휘황찬란하게 하늘을 낮처럼 밝게 만들었다. 인어공주는 너무 놀라서 물속으로 들어갔다. ④ 그러나 그녀는 재빨리 다시 고개를 밖으로 내밀었다. 그리고 보아라! 마치 하늘에 있는 모든 별들이 그녀 위로 떨어지는 것 같았다. 그녀는 그런 불꽃놀이를 결코 본 적이 없었다.

| **정답해설** | ④ 74% 주어진 문장은 인어공주(she)가 '다시' 고개를 밖으로 내밀었다는 내용이므로, 이전에는 그녀가 처음으로 고개를 밖으로 내민 상황과 물속으로 다시 들어간 상황이 모두 나와야 한다. ④의 앞 문장에서 그녀가 물속으로 들어갔다고 언급되므로, 주어진 문장과 But으로 자연스럽게 연결된다. 따라서 주어진 문장이 들어갈 위치로 적절한 것은 ④이다.

어휘

glitter 반짝이는 빛, 찬란함   startled ~에 놀란

| 19 | 독해 > 빈칸의 내용 추론하기 > 빈칸 어휘 추론 | 오답률 34% | 답 ① |

| **해석** | Javelin 리서치는 모든 밀레니얼 세대가 현재 동일한 삶의 단계에 있는 것은 아니라는 사실에 주목했다. 모든 밀레니얼 세대가 세기가 전환될 무렵에 태어났지만, 그 중 일부는 아직 성인 초기에서 새로운 직업과 정착

하고자 씨름하고 있다. 반면, 나이가 더 많은 밀레니얼 세대는 집이 있고 가정을 꾸리고 있다. 당신은 아이가 생기면 관심사와 우선순위가 어떻게 달라질지 상상할 수 있으므로, 마케팅 목적을 위해 이 세대를 Y.1 세대와 Y.2 세대로 나누는 것이 유용하다. 두 집단은 문화적으로 다를 뿐만 아니라, 매우 다른 재정적 삶의 단계에 있기도 하다. 더 어린 집단은 이제 막 구매력을 보여주기 시작한 금융 초보자들이다. 후자의 집단은 신용 기록이 있고, 첫 주택 담보 대출을 받았을 수도 있으며, 어린 자녀들을 양육하고 있다. Y.1 세대와 Y.2 세대 간 우선순위와 요구의 ① 차이는 매우 크다.

① 차이   ② 감소
③ 반복   ④ 능력

| **정답해설** | ① 66% 같은 밀레니얼 세대 내에서도 문화적으로나, 재정적으로나 관심사와 우선순위가 매우 다른 두 집단으로 나뉜다는 내용의 글이다. 지문 전체적으로 Y.1 세대와 Y.2 세대 간의 차이를 상세하게 설명하고 있으므로, 빈칸에 들어갈 말로 가장 적절한 것은 ①이다.

어휘

wrestle with ~로 고심하다, ~와 씨름하다
settle down 정착하다, 안정되다   priority 우선순위
split 쪼개다   mortgage 주택 담보 대출, 융자

오답률 TOP 3

| 20 | 독해 > 빈칸의 내용 추론하기 > 빈칸 어구 추론 | 오답률 50% | 답 ① |

| **해석** | 자유 시장에서의 비용 압력은 기존 및 미래의 수력 발전 계획에 다른 영향을 미친다. 비용 구조상, 기존 수력 발전소는 언제나 수익을 내기 마련이다. 미래 수력 발전 계획에 대한 계획안과 건설은 단기적인 과정이 아니기 때문에, 낮은 전력 생산 비용에도 불구하고, 그것은 인기 있는 투자는 아니다. 대부분의 민간 투자자들은 ① 더 단기적인 기술에 자금을 대는 것을 선호하는데, 이는 기존 수력발전소가 캐시카우(큰 돈벌이가 되는 일)처럼 보이는데도 불구하고 아무도 새로운 곳에 투자하지 않으려는 역설적인 상황으로 이어진다. 공공 주주/소유주(주, 시, 지자체)가 참여하는 경우, 그들은 공급 안정성의 중요성을 인식하고 장기적인 투자도 중요하게 생각하기 때문에 상황은 매우 다르게 보인다.

① 더 단기적인 기술
② 모든 첨단 산업
③ 공익 증진
④ 전력 공급 강화

| **정답해설** | ① 50% 필자에 따르면, 수력 발전소의 높은 수익 창출 가능성에도 불구하고 새로운 발전소를 짓는 데 오랜 시간이 필요하기 때문에 민간 투자자들은 이에 투자하지 않는다. 따라서 민간 투자자들은 장기적인 투자를 꺼리는 것을 알 수 있으므로, 상대적으로 더 단기적인 투자를 선호한다고 볼 수 있다. 또한, 마지막 문장에서 공공 주주/소유주는 장기적인 투자를 중요시한다고 언급했으므로, 빈칸에는 단기적인 투자와 관련된 내용이 와야 함을 알 수 있다. 따라서 빈칸에 들어갈 말로 적절한 것은 ①이다.

어휘

liberalize (법률 등을) 완화하다; 관대해지다
existing 기존의, 현존하는   scheme 계획, 설계
investment 투자   private 민간의, 개인의
paradoxical 역설적인, 모순적인   shareholder 주주(株主); 출자자
municipality 지방 자치제   involved 관련된
appreciate ~의 진가를 인정하다, 이해하다

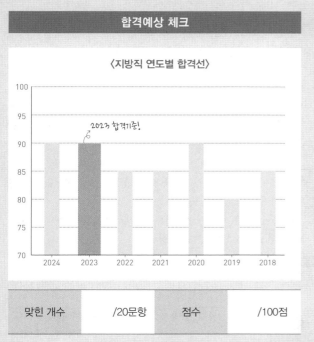

맞힌 개수	/20문항	점수	/100점

➡ ☐ 합격 ☐ 불합격

취약영역 체크

문항	정답	영역	문항	정답	영역
1	②	어휘 > 동의어	11	③	생활영어 > 회화
2	④	어휘 > 동의어	12	②	독해 > 대의 파악
3	①	어휘 > 동의어	13	②	독해 > 대의 파악
4	①	어휘 > 동의어	14	④	독해 > 대의 파악
5	④	어휘 > 빈칸	15	④	독해 > 세부내용 찾기
6	③	문법 > 연결사	16	④	독해 > 글의 일관성 파악하기
7	③	문법 > 형용사·부사·비교	17	②	독해 > 글의 일관성 파악하기
8	①	문법 > 문장의 구조와 동사 유형	18	②	독해 > 글의 일관성 파악하기
9	④	생활영어 > 회화	19	①	독해 > 빈칸의 내용 추론하기
10	③	생활영어 > 회화	20	③	독해 > 빈칸의 내용 추론하기

➡ 영역별 틀린 개수로 취약영역을 확인하세요!

어휘	/5	문법	/3	독해	/9	생활영어	/3

➡ 나의 취약영역: _____

※ [정답해설]과 [오답해설] 선지의 50% 표시는 〈에듀윌 합격예측 풀서비스〉를 통해 수집된 선지 선택률을 나타냅니다.

1	어휘 > 동의어	오답률 45%	답 ②

| 해석 | 우리의 프로젝트에 대한 추가적인 설명은 다음 발표에서 제공 될 것이다.
① 9% 필수인, 요구되는 ② 55% 다음의, 그 후의
③ 13% 진보한, 선진의 ④ 23% 보충의, 추가의

| 정답해설 | ② 추가적인 설명이 미래의 시점에 있을 발표에서 제공될 예정이라고 했으므로, presentation을 수식하는 표현은 '미래'와 연관된 표현이 적절할 것이다. sub-은 '밑에'의 의미이고, sequ-는 '계속되다'의 의미가 있으므로 이 부분을 종합하면 동의어로 following이 적절함을 유추할 수 있다.

어휘
subsequent 다음의, 뒤이은　further 그 이상의, 더 추가된
explanation 설명　presentation 발표

2	어휘 > 동의어	오답률 37%	답 ④

| 해석 | 풍습(풍속)은 한 집단의 구성원이 다른 사람들에게 예의를 보여주기 위해 따르기로 예상되 관습이다. 예를 들어, 재채기를 할 때 "실례합니다"라고 말하는 것이 미국의 풍습(풍속)이다.
① 10% 자선; 자비심 ② 20% 겸손; 굴욕감
③ 7% 대담; 뻔뻔함 ④ 63% 공손함, 예의

| 정답해설 | ④ 밑줄 친 어휘 courtesy의 예시로, 재채기를 할 때 '실례합니다'라고 말한다는 것을 제시했으므로 이는 '예절'에 대한 내용

임을 알 수 있다. 따라서 동의어로 politeness가 적절하다.

어휘
courtesy 예의바름, 공손함　folkway 풍속(풍습), 민속, 사회적 관행
custom 관습　sneeze 재채기하다

3	어휘 > 동의어	오답률 34%	답 ①

| 해석 | 이 아이들은 건강에 좋은 음식을 먹으며 자랐다.
① 66% 기르다; 올리다; (돈을) 모으다
② 10% 충고하다, 조언하다
③ 10% 관찰하다; 준수하다; 말하다
④ 14% 지배하다; 억제[제어]하다

| 정답해설 | ① 아이들과 건강한 음식으로 이루어진 식단의 관계를 생각해 보면, 아이들은 건강한 음식으로 '키워지는' 것을 유추할 수 있다. 따라서 bring up의 동의어로 raise가 적절하며, raise가 가지고 있는 여러 가지 의미를 정리해서 맥락상 가장 적절한 것을 찾을 수 있도록 해야 한다.

어휘
bring up 키우다, 양육하다　diet 식단, 음식

4   어휘 > 동의어   오답률 26%   답 ①

| 해석 | 노예 제도는 미국에서 19세기가 되어서야 비로소 폐지되었다.

① 74% 폐지하다   ② 8% 동의하다, 승낙하다
③ 9% 비난하다   ④ 9% 정당화하다

| 정답해설 | ① 현재 미국에 노예 제도는 없으므로, 맥락상 19세기까지는 노예 제도가 있었음을 유추할 수 있다. 밑줄 앞에 not이 있으므로 이를 고려하면 do away with는 '폐지하다'의 의미가 되어야 함을 알 수 있다. 따라서 동의어로 수동태 문장임을 감안해 과거분사인 abolished가 와야 한다.

어휘

do away with ~을 폐지하다, 제거하다
not A until B B에 이르러서야 비로소 A하다

오답률 TOP 3

5   어휘 > 빈칸   오답률 46%   답 ④

| 해석 | 유권자들은 그들이 명확히 보고 이해할 수 있도록 선거 과정에 보다 많은 ④ 투명성이 있어야 한다고 요구했다.

① 16% 기만, 사기   ② 14% 융통성; 유연성
③ 16% 경쟁; 대회, 시합   ④ 54% 투명도; 명백

| 정답해설 | ④ 유권자들이 요구하는 내용은 '당위성'의 의미가 되어야 한다. 따라서 선거에서 중요한 점이 무엇인지를 생각해보면 정답은 '투명성'의 의미인 transparency임을 알 수 있다.

어휘

voter 유권자   demand 요구하다
election 선거

---

6   문법 > 연결사 > 접속사   오답률 42%   답 ③

| 해석 | 스포츠에서 승리할 것으로, 그리고 상대방보다 우월할 것으로 예상되는 팀이 시합에서 지는 한 가지 이유는 그 우월한 팀이 상대방을 자신의 지속적인 성공에 위협적인 것으로 인식하지 못했을 수도 있다는 것이다.

| 정답해설 | ③ 58% 보어인 명사절을 이끄는 연결사로 what에 이어 불완전한 절이 이어져야 한다. 완전한 절이 이어졌으므로 구조와 문맥을 고려해 접속사 that으로 바꿔야 한다.

| 오답해설 | ① 8% 맥락상 선행사인 upsets를 수식하는 관계사절을 이끌며, in which에 이어 완전한 절(the team이 주어, loses가 동사, the contest가 목적어)이 올바르게 이어졌다.

② 17% 수동의 의미를 지닌 과거분사로 명사 the team을 수식한다.

④ 17% perceive A as B의 B로 목적어인 their opponents를 서술하는 현재분사이다. 문맥상 상대방이 '위협을 주는' 것이므로 능동의 현재분사로 올바르게 표현되었다.

어휘

upset 예상 밖의 승리   supposedly 아마
opponent 상대방, 경쟁자   perceive 인지하다
threatening 위협적인

오답률 TOP 1

7   문법 > 형용사·부사·비교 > 형용사   오답률 61%   답 ③

| 해석 | ① 나는 오늘 아침에 갔어야 했는데, 몸이 좀 안 좋았다.
② 요즘 우리는 예전만큼 돈을 저축하지 않는다.
③ 구조대는 살아 있는 사람을 발견하게 되어 기뻤다.
④ 미술 평론가가 그 그림을 주의 깊게 보았다.

| 정답해설 | ③ 39% alive는 서술적 형용사로 명사를 전치 수식하지 않는다. 명사 앞에서 수식할 수 있는 같은 의미의 형용사 living을 써야 하므로 a living man으로 바꿔야 한다.

| 오답해설 | ① 14% should have p.p.는 '~했어야만 했다'의 의미로 과거의 이루지 못한 일에 대한 유감을 나타낸다. but에 이어진 문장과 시제일치를 이루었고 문맥상 적절한 표현이다.

② 22% 동등비교의 표현으로 'as + 원급 + as'의 구조이다. 접속사 as에 이어 과거의 습관을 나타내는 조동사 used to가 왔으며 현재와 과거를 비교하는 구문이다.

④ 25% look at은 타동사구이므로 수동태 전환이 가능하다. 'The art critic looked로 전환한 문장이다.

어휘

rescue squad 구조대

---

8   문법 > 문장의 구조와 동사 유형 > 동사와 문장의 5형식   오답률 44%   답 ①

| 정답해설 | ① 56% 5형식 문장의 수동태로 능동태 문장의 목적어인 us를 서술하는 목적보어는 touching인데 문맥상 우리는 '감동을 받는' 것이므로 수동의 과거분사인 touched로 바꿔야 한다.

| 오답해설 | ② 12% 보어인 a good one에서 one은 계획을 지칭하며, 주어인 the plan과 동일 대상이 아닌 동일한 종류이므로 대명사 one으로 올바르게 받았다.

③ 12% 시간부사절을 이끄는 접속사 while 다음에 'they were'가 생략된 문장으로 능동의 현재분사 drinking으로 올바르게 왔다.

④ 20% 목적어인 him은 프로젝트에 '적합한' 것이므로 형용사로 굳어진 과거분사 suited가 목적보어로 적절하게 왔다.

어휘

apart from ~은 제쳐 놓고, ~이외에   suited 적합한, 알맞은

---

9   생활영어 > 회화   오답률 18%   답 ④

| 해석 | A: 죄송하지만, 좀 도와주시겠어요?
B: ④ 물론이죠. 무엇을 도와드릴까요?
A: 인사부를 찾고 있어요. 10시에 약속이 있어서요.
B: 3층에 있습니다.
A: 어떻게 거기에 갈 수 있나요?
B: 저기 코너에서 엘리베이터를 타세요.
① 우리가 이 상황을 어떻게 처리해야 할지 모르겠네요.
② 누가 책임자인지 말씀해 주시겠습니까?
③ 네. 이 근처에서 도움이 좀 필요할 것 같아요.
④ 물론이죠. 무엇을 도와드릴까요?

| 정답해설 | ④ 82% A가 도움을 요청했으므로, 빈칸에는 수락 혹은 거절의 내용이 들어가야 한다. 빈칸에 이어진 A의 대화에서 구체적

인 요청의 내용이 제시되었으므로 빈칸에는 '수락'의 표현이 적절하며, 따라서 정답은 ④이다.

어휘
give a hand 도와주다, 거들어주다   personnel department 인사부
appointment 약속; 임명

---

10 생활영어 > 회화   오답률 12%   답 ③

| 해석 | A: 마지막으로 사무실을 나간 사람이 당신이었죠?
B: 네, 무슨 문제라도 있나요?
A: 오늘 아침에 사무실 조명과 에어컨이 켜져 있었어요.
B: 정말이요? 오, 이런. 지난밤에 전원을 끄는 걸 잊었나봐요.
A: 아마 밤새도록 켜져 있었을 것 같아요.
B: ③ 죄송해요. 앞으로는 더 조심할게요.
① 걱정하지 마세요. 이 기계는 잘 작동합니다.
② 맞아요. 모든 사람이 당신과 함께 일하는 것을 좋아해요.
③ 죄송해요. 앞으로는 더 조심할게요.
④ 너무 안타깝네요. 퇴근이 늦어서 피곤하시겠어요.

| 정답해설 | ③ 88% 조명과 에어컨의 전원을 끄지 않은 사실에 대해 A가 언급하고 있으므로, 빈칸에는 이에 대한 '사과'의 내용이 적절하다. 따라서 정답은 ③이다.

어휘
forget to + R ~할 것을 잊다
turn off (등불·라디오·텔레비전을) 끄다

---

11 생활영어 > 회화   오답률 13%   답 ③

| 해석 | ① A: 머리를 어떻게 하고 싶으세요?
B: 머리 색깔이 좀 지겨워요. 염색이 하고 싶어요.
② A: 지구 온난화를 늦추기 위해 우리는 무엇을 할 수 있을까요?
B: 우선, 우리는 더 많은 대중교통을 이용할 수 있어요.
③ A: 안나, 당신이에요? 오랜만이네요! 이게 얼마만이예요?
B: 차로 한 시간 반 정도 걸렸어요.
④ A: 폴이 걱정돼요. 불행해 보여요. 제가 어떻게 해야 하죠?
B: 내가 당신이라면, 그가 자신의 문제에 대해 말할 때까지 기다릴 거예요.

| 정답해설 | ③ 87% A가 오랜만에 만난 친구에게 안부를 물었는데, B는 차로 1시간 반 정도 걸렸다고 언급하고 있으므로 자연스럽지 않은 대화이다. How long has it been?은 시간의 길이를 묻는 것이 아니라 '안부'의 표현이다.

어휘
be tired of ~에 질리다, 신물나다

---

12 독해 > 대의 파악 > 제목 찾기   오답률 32%   답 ②

| 해석 | 유명 작가인 다니엘 골먼은 인간관계의 과학에 일생을 바쳤다. 그의 저서 'Social Intelligence'에서 그는 우리의 두뇌가 얼마나 사교적인지 설명하기 위해 신경 사회학로부터 나온 결과들에 대해 논의한다. 골먼에 따르면, 우리는 다른 사람과 관계를 맺을 때마다 다른 사람의 뇌에 끌린다. 우리의 관계를 깊게 하기 위해, 다른 사람들과 의미 있는 연결성에 대한 인간의 욕구는 우리 모두가 갈망하는 것이다. 그러나 우리가 그 어느 때보다 외롭다는 것을 시사하는 수많은 기사와 연구가 있으며, 외로움은 이제 세계적인 보건 전염병이다. 특히, 호주에서는, 국가 라이프라인 조사에 따르면, 조

사 대상자의 80% 이상이 우리 사회가 더 외로운 곳이 되고 있다고 믿고 있다. 그러나, 우리의 두뇌는 인간 상호 작용을 갈망한다.
① 외로운 사람들
② 사교적인 두뇌
③ 정신 건강 조사의 필요성
④ 인간 연결성의 위험

| 정답해설 | ② 68% 다니엘 골먼의 저서를 통해 인간이 사교적인 뇌를 가지고 있고, 현재 세계적으로 외로움이라는 병이 퍼져 있지만, 그럼에도 인간적인 상호 작용을 갈망한다는 것이 글의 주제이다. 따라서 이를 간결하게 정리한 ②가 제목으로 가장 적절하다.

어휘
dedicate A to B A를 B에게 바치다, 헌신하다
sociable 사교적인
engage with ~와 관계맺다, ~와 연관짓다
connectivity 접속 가능성   crave 갈망[열망]하다
epidemic 유행병, 전염병

---

13 독해 > 대의 파악 > 주제 찾기   오답률 22%   답 ②

| 해석 | 확실히 어떤 사람들은 이점을 가지고 태어난다(예를 들어, 기수의 신체 크기, 농구 선수의 키, 음악가의 귀). 그러나 수년에 걸쳐 신중하고 의도적인 연습에 헌신하는 것만이 그러한 이점을 재능으로, 그리고 그러한 재능을 성공으로 바꿀 수 있다. 같은 종류의 헌신적인 연습을 통해, 그러한 이점을 가지고 태어나지 않은 사람들은 자연이 그들의 손이 닿는 곳에서 약간 더 멀리 놓은 재능을 개발할 수 있다. 예를 들어, 수학에 대한 재능을 타고난 것이 아니라고 느낄지라도, 신중하고, 의도적인 연습을 통해 수학 능력을 크게 향상시킬 수 있다. 혹은, 여러분이 자신을 '선천적으로' 수줍다고 생각한다면, 사교적 기술을 개발하기 위한 시간과 노력을 기울이면 사교 행사에서 활기, 우아함, 편안함을 가지고 사람들과 상호 작용할 수 있다.
① 어떤 사람들이 다른 사람들보다 유리한 점
② 재능 육성을 위한 부단한 노력의 중요성
③ 수줍은 사람들이 사회적 상호 작용에서 겪는 어려움
④ 자신의 장단점을 이해할 필요성

| 정답해설 | ② 78% 특정 직업에 대한 타고난 신체적 장점을 타고난 사람들에 대해 언급한 후 Yet에 이어 헌신적인 연습을 통해 타고나지 않아도 재능을 개발할 수 있다는 것이 이 글의 주제이다. 따라서 주제로 가장 적절한 것은 ②이다.

어휘
jockey (경마의) 기수   dedication 헌신, 전념
mindful 신경을 쓰는, 주의하는   deliberate 의도적인; 신중한
significantly 현저하게, 상당히   interact with ~와 상호 작용하다
social occasion 사교 행사

---

14 독해 > 대의 파악 > 요지·주장 찾기   오답률 32%   답 ④

| 해석 | Roossinck 박사와 그녀의 동료들은 식물 실험에 널리 사용되는 식물에서 한 바이러스가 가뭄에 대한 내성을 증가시킨다는 것을 우연히 발견했다. 관련 바이러스에 대한 그들의 추가 실험은 그것이 15종의 다른 식물 종들에게도 사실이라는 것을 보여주었다. Roossinck 박사는 현재 다양한 식물에서 내열성을 증가시키는 또 다른 유형의 바이러스를 연구하기 위한 실험을 하고 있다. 그녀는 다른 종류의 바이러스가 숙주에게 주는 이점에 대해 더 깊이 이해하기 위해 연구를 확장하기를 희망한다. 그것은 많은 생명체들이 자급자족하기보다는 공생에 의존한다는 점점 증가하는 생물학

자들의 견해를 뒷받침하는 데 도움이 될 것이다.
① 바이러스는 생물학적 존재의 자급자족을 보여준다.
② 생물학자들은 식물에 바이러스가 없도록 하기 위한 모든 것을 해야 한다.
③ 공생 원칙은 감염된 식물에 적용될 수 없다.
④ 바이러스는 때때로 숙주에게 해를 끼치기보다는 좋은 일을 한다.

| **정답해설** | ④ [68%] 식물 실험에서 바이러스가 가뭄에 대한 내성을 증가시킨다는 발견에 이어, 추가 실험을 통해 다른 식물들에도 이런 결과가 동일했다는 내용이 글 앞부분에서 언급되고 있다. 이어서 다른 유형의 바이러스도 비슷한 영향을 미치는지에 대한 실험을 확장하고 싶다는 내용이 이어졌으므로 요지로 가장 적절한 것은 ④이다.

어휘

by chance 우연히, 운 좋게	resistance 내성, 저항
drought 가뭄, 한발	botanical 식물의[에 관한]
tolerance 내성; 관용	rely on ~에 의존하다
symbiosis 공생	self-sufficient 자급자족하는

---

15 독해 > 세부내용 찾기 > 내용 불일치 찾기 [오답률 12%] 답 ④

| **해석** | 메이플 시럽을 만드는 전통적인 방법은 흥미롭다. 사탕단풍나무는 매년 봄 많은 수액을 생산하는데, 그 시기에 땅에는 여전히 많은 눈이 있다. 사탕단풍나무에서 수액을 채취하기 위해, 농부가 특수 칼로 나무껍질에 틈새를 만들고, 그 위에 '꼭지'를 얹는다. 그러고 나서 농부는 꼭지에 수액 통을 매달고 나면, 수액이 그 속으로 뚝뚝 떨어진다. 그 수액은 모아져서 달콤한 시럽이 남아 있을 때까지 끓여지는데, 40갤런의 사탕단풍나무 '수액'이 1갤런의 시럽을 만든다. 수액 통도 많고, 수증기도 많고, 일도 많다. 그렇다고 해도, 대부분의 메이플 시럽 생산자들은 수액 통을 손으로 모아 수액을 끓여서 시럽으로 만드는 가족 농부들이다.

| **정답해설** | ④ [88%] 마지막 문장의 'most of maple syrup producers are family farmers who collect the buckets by hand~'로 보아 기계로 하는 것이 아닌 손으로(by hand) 수액 통을 수거하므로 내용과 일치하지 않는 것은 ④이다.

어휘

sap 수액	slit 틈, 기다란 구멍
bark 나무 껍질	tap (통 등의) 마개; (통의) 꼭지
drip 뚝뚝 떨어지다	by hand 손으로, 수제로

---

16 독해 > 글의 일관성 파악하기 > 글의 흐름과 무관한 문장
[오답률 36%] 답 ④

| **해석** | 나는 한때 단편소설 쓰기 강좌를 들은 적이 있는데, 그 과정에서 한 유력 잡지의 저명한 편집자가 우리 반 학생들에게 말했다. 그는 매일 책상에 올라오는 수십 개의 이야기 중 어느 하나라도 집어 들고 몇 단락을 읽고 나면 저자가 사람을 좋아하는지 아닌지를 느낄 수 있다고 말했다. "작가가 사람을 좋아하지 않으면 사람들은 그의 이야기를 좋아하지 않을 거예요"라고 그는 말했다. 편집자는 소설쓰기 강연 동안 사람들에게 관심을 갖는 것의 중요성을 계속 강조했다. ④ 위대한 마술사인 Thurston은 무대에 오를 때마다 스스로에게 이렇게 말했다고 한다. "성공했으므로 나는 감사해." 강연이 끝나자, 그는 이렇게 결론을 내렸다. "다시 한번 말하지만, 성공적인 이야기 작가가 되려면 사람들에게 관심을 가져야 합니다."

| **정답해설** | ④ [64%] 글의 주제는 작가로서 성공을 하려면 작가 스스로가 사람들에게 관심을 가져야 한다는 것이다. 그런데 ④번 문

장의 주어로 마술사인 Thurston이 오면서 그가 인용한 말이 언급되는데, 이는 글쓰기와 관련이 없다. ④에 이어진 문장에서 다시 주제를 언급한 내용이 이어졌고, 문맥상 he는 Thurston이 아닌 강연자인 편집장이므로, 글의 흐름상 어색한 문장은 ④이다.

어휘

renowned 유명한, 저명한	dozens of 수십 개의
grateful 감사하는, 고마운	

---

17 독해 > 글의 일관성 파악하기 > 글의 순서 [오답률 24%] 답 ②

| **해석** | 불과 몇 년 전만 해도 인공지능(AI)에 대한 모든 대화는 종말론적인 예측으로 끝나는 것 같았다.
(B) 2014년, 이 분야의 한 전문가는 AI로 우리가 악마를 소환하고 있다고 말했고, 노벨상을 수상한 물리학자는 AI가 인류의 종말을 초래할 수 있다고 말했다.
(A) 그러나 최근에는 상황이 변하기 시작했다. AI는 무서운 검은색 상자에서 사람들이 다양한 용도로 사용할 수 있는 것으로 변했다.
(C) 이러한 변화는 이러한 기술들이 마침내 업계에서, 특히 시장 기회를 위해 규모에 따라 탐구되고 있기 때문이다.

| **정답해설** | ② [76%] 주어진 문장에서 인공지능에 대한 부정적인 언급이 온 후, 이에 대한 구체적인 사례로 (B)의 내용이 언급되었다. 그러나 (A)의 however에 이어 인공지능에 대한 긍정적인 생각의 변화가 생겼음을 언급하면서, 이에 대한 이유로 (C)의 내용이 이어진다. 따라서 정답은 ②이다. 각 단락에서 제시된 단서로, 주어진 문장의 예시를 위해 (B)에는 구체적인 연도인 'In 2014'가 언급되었고, (A)에는 이전의 내용과 반대되는 서술을 하기 위해 접속부사 however가 왔으며, (A)의 change가 (C)의 주어 'This shift'로 연결되었다.

어휘

apocalyptic 종말론적인, 계시의	prediction 예측, 예언
expert 전문가	summon 소환하다
demon 악마	
spell ~이 되다, ~의 결과를 초래하다	
scary 무서운, 두려운	

[오답률 TOP 2]
18 독해 > 글의 일관성 파악하기 > 주어진 문장의 삽입
[오답률 52%] 답 ②

| **해석** | 회계 분기가 막 끝났다. 당신의 상사가 당신에게 이번 분기의 매출 면에서 당신이 얼마나 잘했는지 묻기 위해 들른다. 당신의 성과를 어떻게 설명하겠는가? 훌륭하다고? 좋았다고? 끔찍하다고? 누군가가 객관적인 성과 측정 기준 (예를 들어, 이번 분기에 당신이 얼마나 많은 매출을 올렸는지)에 대해 질문할 때와 달리 주관적으로 성과를 설명하는 방법은 종종 명확하지 않다. 정답은 없다. ② 그러나 이러한 자기 평가에 대한 요구는 누군가의 경력 기간 내내 널리 퍼져 있다. 학교 지원서, 입사 지원서, 면접, 성과 평가, 회의에서 자신의 성과를 주관적으로 설명해야 하고 그 목록은 계속 이어진다. 당신의 성과를 설명하는 방법은 소위 자기 홍보의 수준이다. 자기 홍보는 일의 보편적인 부분이므로, 자기 홍보를 더 많이 하는 사람들이 고용되고, 승진되고, 급여 인상이나 보너스를 받을 수 있는 더 좋은 기회를 가질 수 있다.

| **정답해설** | ② [48%] 자신의 성과를 설명하는 방법에 대해 서술한 글로, 객관적인 성과 측정 방법이 명확하지 않다고 언급한다. ②에

이어 구체적으로 주관적인 자기 성과에 대한 사례들이 이어지고 있으므로 주어진 문장은 ②에 들어가야 한다. 주어진 문장의 requests의 예들이 ②에 이어진 문장의 school applications, job applications 등에 해당되므로 이를 근거로 정답을 찾을 수 있다.

어휘

fiscal quarter 회계 분기	in terms of ~의 관점에서
objective 객관적인	metric 측정 기준
application 지원, 응모	
self-assessment 과세액 자기 평가, 자진 신고 납세	
pervasive 퍼지는, 스며드는	raise (임금·물가 등의) 인상

---

19 독해 > 빈칸의 내용 추론하기 > 빈칸 어휘 추론

오답률 24%   답 ①

| 해석 | 우리는 불안의 시대에 살고 있다. 불안해하는 것은 불편하고 무서운 경험이 될 수 있기 때문에 우리는 그 순간에 불안을 줄이는 데 도움이 되는 의식적 또는 무의식적인 전략, 즉 영화나 TV 프로그램 시청, 식사, 비디오 게임 및 과로에 의존한다. 게다가, 스마트폰은 낮이든 밤이든 언제든지 기분 전환하게 한다. 심리학 연구는 기분 전환이 일반적인 불안 회피 전략으로 작용한다는 것을 보여주었다. 그러나 ① 역설적이게도 이러한 회피 전략은 결국 불안을 더욱 악화시킨다. 불안해하는 것은 유사(流砂)에 빠지는 것과 같다. 더 많이 맞붙을수록 더 깊이 가라앉는다. 실제로, 연구는 "당신이 저항을 하면, 계속 지속된다"라는 유명한 문구를 강력하게 뒷받침한다.

① 역설적으로
② 다행스럽게
③ 중립적으로
④ 독창적으로

| 정답해설 | ① [76%] 불안의 시대에 불안을 회피하는 여러 가지 전략을 언급한 후 빈칸에 이어 이런 전략들이 불안을 더욱 악화시킨다는 부정적인 내용이 이어졌으므로 빈칸에 들어갈 말로 가정 적절한 것은 ①이다.

어휘

anxiety 불안, 걱정	resort to ~에 의지하다
conscious 의식하고 있는	unconscious 무의식의
strategy 전략	
distraction 기분 전환, 오락; 주의 산만	
avoidance 회피	in the long run 결국
quicksand 유사(流砂): 사람이나 물건이 빨려 들어가는 유동성 모래; 유동적이고 위험한 상태	
resist 저항[반항]하다	persist 지속하다

---

20 독해 > 빈칸의 내용 추론하기 > 빈칸 어구 추론

오답률 28%   답 ③

| 해석 | 여러분은 얼마나 많은 다양한 방법으로 정보를 얻는가? 어떤 사람들은 대답으로 문자 메시지, 음성 메시지, 종이 문서, 일반 메일, 블로그 게시물, 다양한 온라인 서비스에 대한 메시지 등 6가지 종류의 통신을 말할 수 있다. 이들 각각은 일종의 받은 편지함이며, 각각은 지속적으로 처리되어야 한다. 그것은 끝없는 과정이지만, 피곤하거나 스트레스를 받을 필요는 없다. 여러분의 정보 관리를 보다 관리 가능한 수준으로 낮추고 생산적인 영역으로 만드는 것은 ③ 여러분이 가지고 있는 받은 편지함의 수를 최소화함으로써 시작된다. 메시지를 확인하거나 유입되는 정보를 읽기 위해 가야 하는 모든 장소는 받은 편지함이며, 더 많은 것(받은 편지함)을 가질수록, 모든 것을 관리하기가 더 어려워진다. 필요한 방식으로 여전히 작동할 수 있도록 가능한 한 가장 작은 수로 받은 편지함 개수를 줄여라.

① 한 번에 여러 가지 목표 설정하기
② 들어오는 정보에 몰두하기
③ 여러분이 가지고 있는 받은 편지함의 수를 최소화함
④ 관심 있는 정보를 선택하기

| 정답해설 | ③ [72%] 빈칸 앞에서 여러 종류의 받은 편지함에 대해 언급한 후, 빈칸에 이어진 내용에서 받은 편지함 개수를 줄이라고 조언하고 있으므로, 정보 관리를 관리 가능한 수준으로 낮추고 생산적인 영역으로 만드는 것은 편지함을 최소화해야 하는 것임을 유추할 수 있다. 따라서 빈칸에 들어갈 가장 적절한 것은 ③이다.

어휘

in-box 받은 메일함, 미결 서류함
on a continuous basis 연속적으로
exhausting 지치게 하는, 소모적인
manageable 조작[관리]할 수 있는; 처리하기 쉬운

합격예상 체크

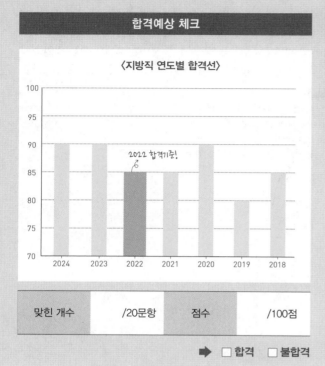

〈지방직 연도별 합격선〉

2022 합격기준!

| 맞힌 개수 | /20문항 | 점수 | /100점 |

➡ ☐ 합격 ☐ 불합격

취약영역 체크

문항	정답	영역	문항	정답	영역
1	②	어휘 > 동의어	11	③	독해 > 글의 일관성 파악하기
2	①	어휘 > 동의어	12	③	독해 > 글의 일관성 파악하기
3	④	어휘 > 동의어	13	④	독해 > 대의 파악
4	④	어휘 > 빈칸	14	④	독해 > 글의 일관성 파악하기
5	②	문법 > 명사와 일치	15	③	독해 > 세부내용 찾기
6	②	문법 > 연결사	16	③	독해 > 세부내용 찾기
7	①	문법 > 문장의 구조와 동사 유형	17	①	독해 > 대의 파악
8	①	문법 > 동사의 형태	18	①	독해 > 빈칸의 내용 추론하기
9	④	생활영어 > 회화	19	④	독해 > 빈칸의 내용 추론하기
10	④	생활영어 > 회화	20	②	독해 > 빈칸의 내용 추론하기

⬇ 영역별 틀린 개수로 취약영역을 확인하세요!

| 어휘 | /4 | 문법 | /4 | 독해 | /10 | 생활영어 | /2 |

➡ 나의 취약영역: _____

※ [정답해설]과 [오답해설] 선지의 50% 표시는 〈에듀윌 합격예측 풀서비스〉를 통해 수집된 선지 선택률을 나타냅니다.

---

1 어휘 > 동의어   오답률 12%   답 ②

| 해석 | 학교 교사들은 학생들의 다른 능력 수준에 대처하기 위해 융통성이 있어야 한다.
① 4% 강한, 튼튼한
② 88% 융통성 있는, 유연한
③ 3% 정직한, 솔직한
④ 5% 열정적인; 격렬한

| 정답해설 | ② 당위성의 동사 have to로 보아 flexible은 교사가 가져야 할 소양임을 알 수 있는데, 학생들의 다양한 능력 수준에 대처하는 데 있어 필요한 것은 융통성이므로 정답은 flexible의 동의어인 adaptable이 가장 적절하다.

어휘
flexible 융통성 있는, 유연한   cope with ~에 대처하다

---

2 어휘 > 동의어   오답률 47%   답 ①

| 해석 | 작물 수확량은 달라지는데, 일부 지역에서는 늘고 다른 지역에서는 감소한다.
① 53% 변하다, 달라지다
② 5% 거절하다; 감소하다
③ 33% 확대하다
④ 9% 포함하다, 포괄하다

| 정답해설 | ① 작물 수확량을 서술할 수 있는 표현이 되어야 하는데, 이어지는 분사구문에서 일부 지역에서는 늘고 다른 지역에서는 감소하고 있다고 했으므로 지역에 따라 다르다는 것을 유추할 수 있다. 따라서 동의어로 change가 가장 적절하다.

어휘
vary 다양하다, 다르다; 바꾸다, 변경하다
crop 작물   yield 수확; 산출하다; 포기하다

오답률 TOP 2
3 어휘 > 동의어   오답률 57%   답 ④

| 해석 | 나는 내 교육에 관해서는 어느 누구에게도 열등감을 느끼지 않는다.
① 3% ~의 위험에 처한
② 14% ~에도 불구하고
③ 40% ~에 찬성하여
④ 43% ~에 있어서, ~에 관하여

| 정답해설 | ④ 명사 respect는 '존경, 관계, 관련' 등 다양한 의미를 지니고 있다. I는 다른 어느 누구에게도 열등감을 느끼지 않는다고 했으므로 my education과 연결했을 때 '교육과 관련해서'임을 유추할 수 있다. 따라서 동의어로 in terms of가 가장 적절하다.

어휘
with respect to ~에 대한, ~에 관한

---

4 어휘 > 빈칸   오답률 25%   답 ④

| 해석 | 때때로 우리는 다음 월급날 훨씬 전에 돈을 ④ 다 써버린다.
① 7% 바뀌다, 변하다
② 6% 처음부터 다시 하다
③ 12% 참다, 견디다
④ 75% ~을 다 써버리다, ~이 동나다

| **정답해설** | ④ 다음 급여일 전에 사람들이 돈을 어떻게 하는지에 대해 생각해 보면, 돈을 쓰거나 저축하는 것인데, 문맥상 '다 써버리다'의 표현이 선지 중에서 가장 적절함을 알 수 있다. 따라서 run out of가 정답이다.

어휘
payday 봉급[급료, 지불]일

| **5** | 문법 > 명사와 일치 > 일치 | 오답률 30% | 답 ② |

| **해석** | ① 그는 나에게 왜 내가 매일매일 돌아왔는지 물었다.
② 아이들이 일년 내내 원하던 장난감들이 최근에 폐기되었다.
③ 그녀는 도움의 손길을 내밀 준비가 언제나 되어 있는 사람이다.
④ 곤충들은 자주 우리에게는 명확하지 않은 냄새에 끌린다.

| **정답해설** | ② 70% Toys 다음에 목적격 관계대명사(that/which)가 생략된 문장으로 문장 전체 주어는 선행사인 Toys이다. 따라서 호응하는 주절의 동사는 복수로 수일치가 되어야 하므로 has를 have로 바꿔야 한다. 또한 discard는 타동사로 장난감이 '폐기되는' 것이므로 수동태로 바꿔야 한다. 따라서 has recently discarded는 have recently been discarded로 바꿔야 한다.

| **오답해설** | ① 11% 4형식 문장으로 me는 간접목적어, 의문부사 why가 이끄는 명사절이 직접목적어로 왔다. 간접의문문의 어순은 '의문사 + 주어 + 동사~'이고 주절의 동사가 과거동사(asked)이므로 종속절의 동사 역시 과거(kept)로 시제일치가 올바르게 이루어졌다.

③ 12% who는 선행사인 someone을 지칭하는 주격 관계대명사로 이어지는 동사의 수는 선행사의 수에 일치시켜야 한다. 단수로 수일치가 올바르게 이루어진 문장이다.

④ 7% 명사 scents를 주격 관계대명사절이 수식하는 구조로, that에 이어진 동사가 선행사인 scents와 수일치가 이루어진 올바른 구조이다.

어휘
discard 폐기하다   attract 끌어당기다
obvious 분명한, 명백한

| **6** | 문법 > 연결사 > 접속사 | 오답률 56% | 답 ② |

| **해석** | ① 당신의 종이의 양쪽에 글씨를 쓸 수 있다.
② 나의 집은 안정감, 따뜻함, 사랑의 느낌을 나에게 준다.
③ 자동차 사고 건수가 증가하고 있다.
④ 당신이 무엇을 하려고 하는지 알았더라면 나는 당신을 막았을 것이다.

| **정답해설** | ② 44% 전치사 of의 목적어로 명사가 병치되었는데, warm은 형용사이므로 명사인 warmth로 바꿔야 한다.

| **오답해설** | ① 13% both는 2(two)를 지칭하는 형용사이자 명사로 쓸 수 있다. 따라서 both가 수식하는 명사로 복수명사인 sides가 이어진 올바른 구조이다.

③ 20% 주어는 the number이므로 동사의 수일치가 단수로 일치된 올바른 문장이다. the number of는 '~의 수'의 의미이다.

④ 23% 가정법 과거완료 문장으로 조건절의 동사로 had + p.p.

(had realized)가, 주절의 동사로 조동사과거 + have + p.p. (would have stopped)가 왔다. 접속사 if를 생략하면서 주어와 조동사 had가 도치된 올바른 문장이다.

어휘
security 안전; 보안   on the rise 증가 중인
intend ~할 작정이다

| **7** | 문법 > 문장의 구조와 동사 유형 > 문장의 구성과 종류 | 오답률 47% | 답 ① |

| **정답해설** | ① 53% 'afford to + 동사원형'은 '~할 만한 여유가 있다'의 의미로 주어진 우리말은 바꿔 말하면 '~을 낭비할 만한 여유가 없다'이므로 영작문은 부정문이 되어야 한다. 따라서 can을 can't로 바꿔야 한다.

| **오답해설** | ② 10% fade는 자동사로 '사라지다'의 의미가 있으므로 주어진 우리말에 맞는 올바른 영작문이다.

③ 13% '~하는 것 외에는 대안이 없다'는 바꿔 말하면 '~하지 않을 수 없다'의 표현이다. 'have no alternative/choice but to + 동사원형'의 구조로 올바르게 표현했으며, but은 목적어로 to부정사를 취하는 전치사이며, '~을 제외하고'의 의미이다.

④ 24% 'in + 수량 시간 명사'는 '~후에'의 의미로 미래 부사구로 쓸 수 있다. 따라서 주어진 우리말에 알맞은 영작문이다.

어휘
afford to + R ~할 여유가 있다   fade 사라지다, 흐려지다
have no alternative(choice) but to + R ~하지 않을 수 없다
resign 사임하다   aim to + R ~하는 것을 목표로 하다

| **8** | 문법 > 동사의 형태 > 시제 | 오답률 40% | 답 ① |

| **정답해설** | ① 60% 'A 하자마자 B하다'를 'No sooner~ than…'의 구조로 표현했다. no sooner에 이어 과거완료 동사가 의문문의 어순으로 도치되어야 하므로 I have finishing~을 had I finished~로 바꿔야 한다.

| **오답해설** | ② 11% 미래의 당위성의 표현으로 must의 대용 표현인 have to를 활용해 'will have to + 동사원형'으로 올바르게 영작한 문장이다.

③ 22% 비례식의 표현으로 관계대명사 what의 관용 표현이 올바르게 쓰였다. A is to B what C is to D는 'A와 B의 관계는 C와 D의 관계와 같다'의 의미이다.

④ 7% 등위접속사 but을 두고 과거동사가 병치된 문장으로 두 번째 동사로 온 end up R-ing는 '결국 ~하다'의 의미로 주어진 우리말과 일치하는 영작문이다.

어휘
sooner or later 조만간
A is to B what C is to D A와 B의 관계는 C와 D의 관계와 같다
end up R-ing 결국 ~하게 되다   accounting firm 회계법인

9 생활영어 > 회화 | 오답률 19% | 답 ④

| 해석 | ① A: 나는 이 신문이 독선적이지 않아서 좋아요.
B: 그게 바로 발행부수가 가장 많은 이유예요.
② A: 잘 차려입은 그만한 이유가 있나요?
   B: 네, 오늘 중요한 구직 면접이 있어요.
③ A: 저는 연습 중에는 공을 똑바로 칠 수 있는데 게임에서는 못해요.
   B: 저한테도 항상 일어나는 일이에요.
④ A: 캔버스에 그리고 싶은 특정한 대상이 있나요?
   B: 고등학생 때 나는 역사를 잘 못했어요.

| 정답해설 | ④ 81% A가 그림을 그리고 싶은 대상이 있는지를 물었는데 B는 자신이 고등학생 때 역사를 못했다고 대답을 하고 있으므로 어색한 대화이다. subject는 '주제, 대상'의 의미와 더불어 '과목'의 의미가 있는 점을 응용한 문제이다.

어휘
opinionated 독단적인, 의견을 고집하는
circulation 발행 부수

10 생활영어 > 회화 | 오답률 25% | 답 ④

| 해석 | A: 이봐! 지리 시험은 어떻게 됐어?
B: 나쁘지 않아, 고마워. 끝나서 그저 기뻐! 너는 어때? 과학 시험은 어떻게 됐어?
A: 아, 정말 잘 됐어. ④ 네가 도와줘서 얼마나 고마운지 몰라. 너에게 한 턱 낼게.
B: 천만에. 그래서 다음 주에 예정된 수학 시험을 준비하고 싶어?
A: 물론이지. 같이 공부하자.
B: 좋아. 나중에 보자.
① 이 일로 네가 자책하는 것은 말이 안 돼
② 여기서 너를 볼 줄은 몰랐어
③ 사실, 우리는 매우 실망했어
④ 네가 도와줘서 얼마나 고마운지 몰라

| 정답해설 | ④ 75% 빈칸에 이어 한 턱 내겠다고 했으므로, 빈칸에 들어갈 표현은 '감사'가 되어야 한다. 따라서 가장 적절한 것은 ④이다.

어휘
geography 지리(학)   owe 빚을 지다
treat 한턱 내기

11 독해 > 글의 일관성 파악하기 > 글의 순서 | 오답률 32% | 답 ③

| 해석 | 시각장애인들에게 우편물을 분류하거나 빨래를 많이 하는 것과 같은 일상적인 일은 난제이다.
(B) 하지만 그들이 볼 수 있는 사람의 눈을 '빌릴' 수 있다면 어떨까?
(A) 그것이 Aira 이면에 숨겨진 생각인데, Aira는 수천 명의 사용자가 스마트폰이나 Aira의 전용 안경을 사용하여 주문자 자신의 주변 상황을 실시간으로 스트리밍할 수 있게 해주는 새로운 서비스이다.
(C) 24시간 이용할 수 있는 Aira 에이전트는 질문에 답하거나, 물건을 설명하거나, 위치를 통해 사용자를 안내할 수 있다.

| 정답해설 | ③ 68% 주어진 문장에서 시각 장애인들이 겪는 어려움을 제시한 이후, (B)에서 역접의 접속사 But에 이어 볼 수 있는 사람의 눈을 빌릴 수 있다는 가정을 하는 내용이 나온 후, 이 내용을 대명사 that으로 받아 Aira에 대해 서술하는 (A)가 이어지는 것이 자연스럽다. Aira라는 a new service에 대해 (A)에서 언급한 후,

구체적으로 Aira가 할 수 있는 일을 서술한 (C)가 마지막에 오는 것이 자연스러우므로 정답은 ③이다.

어휘
sort 분류하다, 정렬하다   on-demand 청구[요구]가 있는 즉시
proprietary 소유자의; 전매특허의; 사유의

오답률 TOP1
12 독해 > 글의 일관성 파악하기 > 주어진 문장의 삽입 | 오답률 58% | 답 ③

| 해석 | 비유는 두 가지가 매우 근본적인 여러 측면에서 유사하다고 주장되는 수사적 표현이다. 비록 두 가지가 크게 다르기도 하지만, 구조, 부분의 관계, 혹은 수행하는 본질적인 목적은 비슷하다. 장미와 카네이션은 비슷하지 않다. 그것 둘 다 줄기와 잎을 가지고 있으며 둘 다 붉은 색일 수 있다. 그러나 그들은 같은 방식으로 이러한 속성을 보여주는데, 그들은 같은 속(屬)이다. ③ 그러나 심장을 펌프에 비교하는 것은 진정한 비유이다. 이것들은 서로 다른 것들이지만 기계 장치, 밸브 소지, 압력 증가 및 감소 기능, 유체 이동 능력 등 중요한 특성을 공유한다. 그리고 심장과 펌프는 다른 방식과 다른 맥락에서 이러한 특성을 보여준다.

| 정답해설 | ③ 42% 제시된 문장에서 접속부사 however가 왔으므로 앞 문장과는 다른 내용이 이어져야 하며, 펌프를 심장과 비교하고 있으므로 이어진 문장에서는 이에 대한 구체적인 내용이 와야 함을 유추할 수 있다. ③ 이전까지는 장미와 카네이션의 비유에 대한 내용이 서술되었고, ③ 이후에 이어진 문장의 these가 지칭하는 것과 내용은 심장과 펌프에 대한 것임을 알 수 있으므로 주어진 문장이 들어가기에 가장 적절한 곳은 ③이다.

어휘
analogy 비유, 유추
figure of speech 비유적 표현, 수사적 표현
assert 주장하다, 단언하다   fundamental 근본적인; 중요한
dissimilar 다른, 닮지 않은   analogous 유사한, 비슷한
genus [생물] (분류상의) 속(屬)   comparison 비교
disparate 종류가 다른, 이종의   apparatus 장치, 기구, 기관

13 독해 > 대의 파악 > 제목 찾기 | 오답률 30% | 답 ④

| 해석 | 효율성을 최적화 할 수 있는 영역 중 하나는 증가하는 개인의 생산성을 통한 노동력이다. 개별 생산성은 직원이 주어진 시간에 처리하는 작업량(생산된 제품, 고객 서비스)으로 정의된다. 최적의 성능을 보장하기 위한 적절한 장비, 환경 및 교육에 투자했는지 확인하는 것 외에도, 여러분은 직원들이 현대의 에너지 소모원인 멀티태스킹을 끝내도록 장려함으로써 생산성을 높일 수 있다. 연구에 따르면 당신이 다른 프로젝트를 동시에 수행하려고 할 때 작업을 완료하는 데 25~40% 더 오래 시간이 걸린다. 더 생산적이기 위해서는, 컨설팅 기업인 The Energy Project의 비즈니스 개발 담당 부사장인 Andrew Deutscher는 "일정 기간 동안 한 가지 일을 중단 없이 수행하십시오."라고 말한다.
① 인생에서 더 많은 선택권을 만드는 방법
② 일상적인 신체 활동을 향상시키는 방법
③ 멀티태스킹은 더 나은 효율성을 위한 해답이다
④ 더 큰 효율성을 위해 한 번에 한 가지 일을 하라

| 정답해설 | ④ 70% 핵심어는 '개인의 생산성(individual productivity)을 통한 노동력'으로 이에 대한 장점을 서술하고 있는 글이다. 이와 반대로 멀티태스킹의 부정적인 측면을 서술한 후에 컨설팅 기업의

임원의 말로 글이 전달하는 바를 확실하게 마무리하고 있으므로 글의 제목으로 가장 적절한 것은 ④이다.

어휘
optimize 최적화하다
put an end to ~에 종지부를 찍다, 그치다
drain 소모, 유출; 배수
uninterrupted 연속적인, 끊임없는
simultaneously 동시에, 일제히
sustained 지속적인; 한결같은

---

14 독해 > 글의 일관성 파악하기 > 글의 흐름과 무관한 문장
오답률 45% 답 ③

| 해석 | 훌륭한 논쟁을 하는 기술은 인생에서 중요하다. 하지만 자녀에게 이를 가르치는 부모는 거의 없다. 우리는 아이들에게 안정된 가정을 주고 싶어서 형제들이 말다툼을 하는 것을 막고, 우리는 닫힌 문 뒤에서 언쟁을 한다. 그러나 아이들이 결코 논쟁에 노출되지 않는다면, 우리는 결국 그들의 창의력을 제한할 수 있다. ③ 아이들은 평화로운 환경에서 많은 칭찬과 격려로 자유롭게 브레인스토밍 할 때 가장 창의적이다. 대단히 창의적인 사람들은 종종 긴장감 넘치는 가정에서 자란다는 것이 밝혀졌다. 그들은 주먹다짐이나 인신공격에 둘러싸여 있는 것이 아니라 진정한 논쟁에 둘러싸여 있다. 30대 초반의 성인이 상상력이 풍부한 이야기를 쓰도록 요청받았을 때, 가장 창의적인 이야기는 25년 전에 부모가 가장 갈등을 겪은 사람들에게서 나왔다.

| 정답해설 | ③ 55% 논쟁(argument)이 창의력을 이끈다는 관점으로 서술한 글이다. ③에 이어진 문장에서 아이들이 가장 창의적인 경우로 자유롭게 브레인스토밍을 할 수 있을 때라고 한 점은 흐름과 일치하지 않고, ④번 문장의 내용은 ②에 이어지는 것이 자연스러우므로 흐름상 가장 어색한 문장은 ③이다.

어휘
sibling 형제자매
fistfight 주먹다짐
conflict 갈등, 분쟁
tension 긴장
insult 상해, 모욕적 언동

---

15 독해 > 세부내용 찾기 > 내용 불일치 찾기
오답률 21% 답 ③

| 해석 | 크리스토퍼 놀란은 영어에서 상당히 저명한 아일랜드 작가이다. 태어날 때부터 뇌가 손상된 놀란은 음식을 삼키는 데 어려움을 겪을 정도로 몸의 근육을 거의 통제하지 못했다. 그는 혼자 앉을 수 없기 때문에 휠체어에 묶여 있어야 한다. 놀란은 알아들을 만한 말소리를 내지 못한다. 하지만 다행스럽게도, 그의 뇌 손상은 지능이 손상되지 않는 정도였고 청력도 정상이었다. 그 결과, 그는 어렸을 때 언어를 이해하는 법을 배웠다. 그러나 그가 처음으로 자신의 말을 표현할 수단을 얻었던 것은 많은 해가 지나고 나서, 그가 10살이 되고 나서, 그리고 그가 읽는 법을 배우고 난 후였다. 그는 글자를 가리키기 위해 머리에 붙어 있는 막대기를 사용함으로써 이렇게 했다. 그가 아직 10대일 때 시집과 단편집을 묶은 전권인 'Dam-Burst of Dreams'를 만든 것은 바로 이런 글자 하나하나를 가리키는 '유니콘' 방식이었다.

| 정답해설 | ③ 79% 'Fortunately, though, his brain damage was such that Nolan's intelligence was undamaged and his hearing was normal~'를 통해 말소리를 내지는 못했지만 청력이 정상이라고 했으므로 글의 내용과 일치하지 않는 것은 ③이다.

어휘
renown 명성, 유명
utter 말하다
strap 끈으로 묶다; 채찍질하다
attach 부착하다, 붙이다

---

16 독해 > 세부내용 찾기 > 내용 불일치 찾기 오답률 22% 답 ③

| 해석 | 많은 가톨릭 국가에서 아이들은 종종 성인의 이름을 따서 이름이 지어진다. 실제로 일부 사제들은 부모가 드라마 스타나 축구 선수를 따라 자녀의 이름을 짓는 것을 허락하지 않을 것이다. 개신교 국가들은 이 부분에 대해 더 자유로운 경향이 있다. 그러나 노르웨이에서는 아돌프와 같은 특정 이름들은 완전히 금지된다. 아프리카와 같이 유아 사망률이 매우 높은 국가에서는, 부족들은 생존 가능성이 늘어나기 시작하는 5세가 되었을 때만 자녀의 이름을 짓는다. 그때까지, 그들은 그들의 나이로 불린다. 극동 지방의 많은 국가들은 자녀에게 그들의 출생 상황이나 자녀에 대한 부모의 기대와 희망을 설명하는 독특한 이름을 부여한다. 일부 호주 원주민은 지혜, 창의력 혹은 결단력을 어떻게 해서든 입증한 중요한 경험의 결과로 평생 동안 이름을 계속 바꿀 수 있다. 예를 들어, 어느 날, 그들 중 하나가 매우 잘 춤을 추면, 그는 자신에게 '최고 댄서' 혹은 '가벼운 발'로 이름을 바꾸기로 결정할 수 있다.
① 많은 가톨릭 국가에서 아이들은 종종 성인의 이름을 따서 이름이 지어진다.
② 어떤 아프리카 아이들은 다섯 살이 되어야 비로소 이름이 지어진다.
③ 이름을 바꾸는 것은 호주 원주민 문화에서 완전히 용납될 수 없다.
④ 다양한 문화권에서 아이들의 이름을 다른 방식으로 짓는다.

| 정답해설 | ③ 78% 'Some Australian aborigines can keep changing their name throughout their life as the result of some important experience~'에서 호주 원주민이 중요한 경험의 결과로 평생 동안 이름을 바꿀 수 있다고 했으므로 글의 내용과 일치하지 않는 문장은 ③이다.

어휘
protestant 개신교, 신교도
infant mortality 유아 사망률
ban 금지하다
determination 결심, 결정

---

17 독해 > 대의 파악 > 요지·주장 찾기 오답률 38% 답 ①

| 해석 | 젊은이들이 '히피(hippie)'나 '스트레이트(straight)' 패션으로 옷을 입는 경향이 있었던 1970년대 초반에 이뤄진 한 연구에서, 실험자들은 히피나 스트레이트 복장을 하고 캠퍼스에 있는 대학생들에게 전화를 걸기 위해 10센트짜리 동전을 달라고 요청했다. 실험자가 학생과 같은 방식으로 옷을 입었을 때, 그 경우, 요청은 3분의 2 이상의 경우에 승인되었다. 학생과 요청자가 다르게 옷을 입었을 때, 10센트 짜리 동전은 절반보다 더 적은 경우로 제공되었다. 또 다른 실험은 비슷한 타인들에 대한 우리의 긍정적인 반응이 얼마나 자동적일 수 있는지를 보여주었다. 반전 시위에 참가한 시위자들은 비슷한 복장을 한 요청자의 탄원서에 서명하고 먼저 읽으려고 애쓰지 않고 서명할 가능성이 더 높은 것으로 밝혀졌다.
① 사람들은 자신처럼 옷을 입는 사람들을 도울 가능성이 더 크다.
② 정장 차림은 청원서에 서명할 가능성을 높인다.
③ 전화 통화를 하는 것은 다른 학생들과 어울리는 효율적인 방법이다.
④ 1970년대 초의 일부 대학생들은 그들의 독특한 패션으로 감탄의 대상이 되었다.

| 정답해설 | ① 62% 실험의 내용을 통해 비슷한 옷차림의 실험자가 요구하는 것을 받아들일 가능성이 더 있다는 사실을 보여주고 있으므로 글의 요지로 가장 적절한 것은 ①이다.

어휘
don (옷을) 입다, (모자 등을) 쓰다
grant 부여하다, 승인하다
marcher 데모 참가자, 도보 행진자
bother 신경 쓰다, 걱정하다
attire 의상, 복장
dissimilarly 같지 않게, 다르게
petition 청원, 호소

독해 > 빈칸의 내용 추론하기 > 연결어 추론

오답률 14%   답 ①

| 해석 | 지속시간은 빈도와 반비례 관계를 공유한다. 친구를 자주 보게 되면 만남의 지속시간은 더 짧아지기 마련이다. 반대로 친구를 자주 보지 못하면 방문의 지속시간이 보통 크게 늘어난다. (A) 예를 들어, 매일 친구를 만나는 경우, 방문 시간은 낮아질 수 있는데, 사건이 전개될 때 일이 어떻게 진행되는지를 따라잡을 수 있기 때문이다. 그러나 친구를 1년에 두 번만 본다면, 방문 시간은 더 길어질 것이다. 오랫동안 보지 못했던 친구와 식당에서 저녁을 먹었던 때를 떠올려보자. 당신은 아마 각자의 생활을 따라잡느라 몇 시간을 보낼 것이다. 만약 여러분이 정기적으로 그 사람을 본다면, 동일한 저녁 식사 시간은 상당히 더 짧을 것이다. (B) 반대로, 낭만적인 관계에서 커플, 특히 새로 생겨난 커플은 가능한 한 많은 시간을 서로 보내고 싶기 때문에 빈도와 지속시간이 매우 높다. 그 관계의 강도 또한 매우 높을 것이다.

(A)	(B)
① 예를 들어	반대로
② 그럼에도 불구하고	게다가
③ 그러므로	결과적으로
④ 같은 방법으로	그래서

| 정답해설 | ① 86% 지속시간이 빈도와 반비례 관계라는 것을 서술한 후 A에 이어 구체적인 예시를 들어주고 있으므로 (A)에는 For example이 와야 한다. (B)에는 그 이전에 친구와의 관계에서 시간과 빈도가 반비례한다는 사례가 전개된 것과는 달리, 낭만적인 관계에서는 빈도와 지속시간이 둘 다 높은 사례가 이어졌으므로 Conversely가 가장 적절하다. 따라서 ①이 정답이다.

어휘

duration 지속시간, 기간   inverse 반대의, 역의
catch up on 뒤쳐진 일을 보충하다   intensity 강도

독해 > 빈칸의 내용 추론하기 > 빈칸 어구 추론

오답률 47%   답 ②

| 해석 | 가장 자주 사용되는 선전 기법 중 하나는 선전가의 견해가 일반인의 견해를 반영하고 대중의 최선의 이익을 위해 일하고 있음을 대중에게 납득시키는 것이다. 육체노동자 청중에게 말하는 정치인은 소매를 걷어 올리고, 넥타이를 풀고, 군중의 특정 관용구를 이용하고자 할지도 모른다. 그는 심지어 자신이 '그 사람들 중 하나'라는 인상을 주기 위해 의도적으로 언어를 부정확하게 사용할 수도 있다. 이 기법은 또한 정치인의 견해가 연설을 듣고 있는 군중의 생각과 같다는 인상을 주기 위해 미사여구를 사용한다. 노동계 지도자들, 기업가들, 장관들, 교육자들, 그리고 광고주들은 ② 우리와 같은 평범한 사람들로 보임으로써 우리의 신뢰를 얻기 위해 이 기법을 이용해 왔다.
① 미사여구를 초월한
② 우리와 같은 평범한 사람들
③ 다른 사람들과 다른 점
④ 군중보다 더 나은 교육을 받은

| 정답해설 | ② 53% 첫 번째 문장에서 선전 기법의 목표로 선전가가 일반 대중을 위해 일하고 있음을 납득시키는 것이라고 했고, 이에 대한 사례로 정치인들이 육체노동자 청중을 위해 그들과 비슷한 모습을 의도적으로 연출하고 있다는 내용이 이어졌다. 따라서 빈칸에 들어갈 것으로 가장 적절한 것은 이런 내용을 반영한 ②가 가장 적절하다.

어휘

propaganda 선전 (활동); (비격식) 유언비어
convince 설득하다, 납득시키다   undo 풀다, 벗다; 원상태로 돌리다
specific 특정한; 구체적인
glittering generality (정치가·광고 등의) 미사여구

독해 > 빈칸의 내용 추론하기 > 빈칸 어휘 추론

오답률 39%   답 ②

| 해석 | 롤러코스터가 트랙의 첫 번째 상승 경사로를 오를 때, 그것은 위치 에너지를 만들고 있다 – 그것이 지상 위로 더 높이 올라갈수록, 중력의 힘은 더 강해질 것이다. 롤러코스터가 상승 경사로의 꼭대기에 이르러 하강을 시작할 때, 위치 에너지는 운동 에너지가 된다. 흔한 오해는 롤러코스터가 트랙을 따라 에너지를 잃는다는 것이다. 그러나 에너지 보존의 법칙이라고 불리는 물리학의 중요한 법칙은 에너지가 결코 생성되거나 파괴될 수 없다는 것이다. 그것은 한 형태에서 다른 형태로 바뀔 뿐이다. 트랙이 다시 오르막길을 올라갈 때마다, 그 기구의 운동 에너지인 추진력은 그것들을 위쪽으로 이동시키는데, 이는 위치 에너지를 생성하고 롤러코스터는 반복적으로 위치 에너지를 운동 에너지로 변환했다가 다시 반대로 한다. 승차가 끝나면 롤러코스터 기구는 두 표면 사이에 ② 마찰을 일으키는 브레이크 장치에 의해 속도가 느려진다. 이 움직임은 그것들을 뜨겁게 만들며, 이는 운동 에너지가 제동 중에 열 에너지로 바뀐다는 것을 의미한다. 탑승자는 롤러코스터가 트랙의 끝에서 에너지를 잃는다고 잘못 생각할 수 있지만, 에너지는 다른 형태로 혹은 다른 형태로부터 변할 뿐이다.
① 중력   ② 마찰
③ 진공   ④ 가속

| 정답해설 | ② 61% 글 전체적으로 특정 에너지가 사라지는 것이 아니라 형태가 바뀔 뿐이라는 내용을 서술하고 있다. 롤러코스터의 예를 통해 트랙에서 상승할 때는 위치 에너지로, 하강할 때는 운동 에너지로, 승차가 끝나면 열 에너지로 바뀌는 과정을 설명하고 있는데, 빈칸은 열 에너지로 바뀌는 부분에 대한 설명으로 기구가 속도가 느려지려면 표면 사이의 '마찰(friction)'이 발생하는 것이 자연스럽다. 따라서 빈칸에 들어갈 것으로 가장 적절한 것은 ②이다.

어휘

potential energy 위치 에너지   gravity 중력
crest (산 등의) 꼭대기에 이르다   descent 하강
kinetic energy 운동 에너지   misperception 오해
conservation 보존   momentum 추진력, 힘, 기세
convert 전환하다, 바꾸다

<table>
<tr><td colspan="3">**합격예상 체크**</td></tr>
</table>

합격예상 체크

〈지방직 연도별 합격선〉

	2024	2023	2022	2021	2020	2019	2018

2021
합격기준!

맞힌 개수	/20문항	점수	/100점

➡ ☐ 합격 ☐ 불합격

취약영역 체크

문항	정답	영역	문항	정답	영역
①	④	어휘 > 동의어	11	①	생활영어 > 회화
2	③	어휘 > 빈칸	12	③	생활영어 > 회화
3	①	어휘 > 빈칸	13	②	독해 > 세부내용 찾기
4	②	어휘 > 빈칸	14	②	독해 > 글의 일관성 파악하기
5	④	어휘 > 동의어	15	③	문법 > 동사의 형태
6	④	문법 > 문장의 구조와 동사 유형	16	②	독해 > 빈칸의 내용 추론하기
7	②	문법 > 문장의 구조와 동사 유형	17	②	독해 > 빈칸의 내용 추론하기
8	②	문법 > 동사의 형태	18	①	독해 > 대의 파악
9	④	독해 > 대의 파악	19	②	독해 > 빈칸의 내용 추론하기
10	①	독해 > 글의 일관성 파악하기	20	②	독해 > 글의 일관성 파악하기

⬇ 영역별 틀린 개수로 취약영역을 확인하세요!

어휘	/5	문법	/4	독해	/9	생활영어	/2

➡ 나의 취약영역: _____

※ [정답해설]과 [오답해설] 선지의 50% 표시는 〈1초 합격예측 서비스〉를 통해 수집된 선지 선택률을 나타냅니다.

1	어휘 > 동의어	오답률 11%	답 ④

| 해석 | 충동적 구매를 하는 많은 사람들에게는 무엇을 사느냐보다 구매 행위 자체가 만족으로 이어진다.

① 3% 쾌활함, 원기 ② 2% 자신감; 신뢰
③ 6% 고요, 평안 ④ 89% 만족, 충족

| 정답해설 | ④ 충동적인 구매자들에 대한 서술로, rather than의 의미상 than에 이어진 그들이 구매하는 물건보다는 구매하는 행위가 더 중요함을 알 수 있다. 따라서 주어진 선지에서 '만족'의 의미인 satisfaction이 동의어로 가장 적절하다. gratification은 '만족, 희열'의 의미이다.

어휘

gratification 만족, 희열 compulsive 충동적인, 강박관념의
purchase 구입하다 lead to ~로 이어지다, ~을 이끌다

2	어휘 > 빈칸	오답률 7%	답 ③

| 해석 | 세계화는 더 많은 나라들이 그들의 시장을 개방하게 하고, 더 높은 ③ 효율성과 더 낮은 비용으로 재화와 용역을 자유롭게 교환할 수 있게 한다.

① 3% 멸종, 소멸 ② 2% 침체, 불황; 우울증
③ 93% 효율성, 능률 ④ 2% 주의, 경계

| 정답해설 | ③ 세계화에 대한 내용으로 전체적으로 긍정적인 서술을 하고 있다. 따라서 빈칸에는 '긍정적인' 어휘가 들어가야 하므로 선지 중 흐름과 맥락상 efficiency가 가장 적절하다.

어휘

globalization 세계화 trade 교환하다; 교역[거래]하다
goods and services 재화와 용역

오답률 TOP 2

3	어휘 > 빈칸	오답률 64%	답 ①

| 해석 | 우리는 번아웃(극도의 피로)의 대가를 잘 알고 있다. 에너지, 동기부여, 생산성, 참여, 헌신은 직장과 가정에서 모두 타격을 입을 수 있다. 그리고 많은 ① 해결책들은 상당히 직관적이다. 규칙적으로 플러그를 뽑아라. 불필요한 회의를 줄여라. 운동하라. 낮에 작은 휴식 시간을 잡아라. 때때로 떠날 여유가 없기 때문에 직장을 떠나 있을 여유가 없다고 생각하더라도 휴가를 보내라.

① 36% 해결법; 파악; 곤경 ② 34% 손상, 피해
③ 12% 상, 포상 ④ 18% 문제; 합병증

| 정답해설 | ① 번아웃으로 인한 결과를 앞 부분에서 제시하고 빈칸이 포함된 문장에 이어 명령문으로 번아웃에 대한 해결책들을 제시하고 있다. 따라서 빈칸에는 '해결책'의 의미인 fixes가 가장 적절하다.

어휘

burnout 극도의 피로, 소모 motivation 동기부여
engagement 참여, 연대 commitment 헌신; 위임, 약속
intuitive 직관력 있는 afford ~할 여유가 있다

| **4** | 어휘 > 빈칸 | 오답률 36% | 답 ② |

| 해석 | 정부는 새로운 세금 정산 제도로 인한 세금 부담 증가에 대해 샐러리맨들을 달래기 위한 방법을 모색하고 있다. 대통령은 지난 월요일 대통령 보좌관들과의 회의에서 참석자들이 대중과 더 많은 의사소통 채널을 개방할 것을 ② 요구했다.

① 3% ~이 되다; ~에게 떨어지다
② 64% 요구하다
③ 23% 집다; 태워주다; 회복하다
④ 10% 거절하다; 줄이다

| 정답해설 | ② 정부가 세금 부담 증가에 대해 샐러리맨들을 달래기 위한 방법을 모색중이라고 했고, 이에 대해 대통령이 참석한 회의에서 대통령이 해결책으로 제시할 수 있는 내용으로 대중과의 소통 채널 개방을 '요구했음'을 유추할 수 있다. 따라서 빈칸에 들어갈 것으로 called for가 가장 적절하다.

어휘

soothe 달래다, 진정시키다
tax settlement 세금 정산
arise from ~에서 발생하다
aide 측근, 보좌관

| **5** | 어휘 > 동의어 | 오답률 42% | 답 ④ |

| 해석 | 중국 서예를 공부할 때, 한자어의 기원과 원래 어떻게 쓰였는지에 대한 것을 배워야 한다. 그러나 그 나라의 예술적 전통에서 자라난 사람들을 제외하고는 그 미적 중요성은 이해하기가 매우 어려운 것 같다.

① 17% 둘러싸다, 포위하다; 포함하다
② 9% 침범하다
③ 16% 검사하다, 조사하다
④ 58% 이해하다; 꽉 쥐다

| 정답해설 | ④ apprehend는 여러 가지 의미로 자주 쓰이는 동사이다. 이 문제에서 자신의 나라에서 자라난 사람이 아닌 경우, 미적 중요성에 대해 어려울 수 있는 점이 무엇일까 생각해 보면, '이해하기'가 쉽지 않음을 유추할 수 있다. 따라서 apprehend는 '이해하다'의 의미이며 동의어로 grasp가 가장 적절하다.

어휘

apprehend 이해하다; 체포하다; 염려하다
calligraphy 서법, 서예
significance 중요성; 의미
aesthetic 미학의, 심미안이 있는

| **6** | 문법 > 문장의 구조와 동사 유형 > 동사와 문장의 5형식 | 오답률 36% | 답 ④ |

| 정답해설 | ④ 64% 주절의 동사 saw는 5형식 문장에서 지각동사이므로 호응하는 목적보어로 원형부정사 혹은 현재분사가 와야 한다. 따라서 moved를 move나 moving으로 바꿔야 한다.

| 오답해설 | ① 4% 'It is hard to read his novels'에서 진주어인 to부정사의 목적어인 his novels를 가주어 it의 자리로 옮긴 문장으로 올바른 구조이다.

② 18% '~해봐야 소용없다'의 표현으로 동명사를 활용한 관용표현인 'It is no use R-ing'로 올바르게 영작한 문장이다. 'try to + 동사원형'은 '~하고자 노력하다'의 의미로 주어진 우리말과 일치하는 표현이다.

③ 14% 주어인 my house는 페인트칠이 되는 것이므로 수동태로 표현했고, '5년마다'로 'every five years' 혹은 'every fifth year'로 써야 하므로 올바른 문장이다.

어휘

It is no use R-ing ~하는 것은 소용없다

오답률 TOP 3

| **7** | 문법 > 문장의 구조와 동사 유형 > 동사와 문장의 5형식 | 오답률 62% | 답 ② |

| 정답해설 | ② 38% 수동 관계이고 동사가 let일 때 목적보어는 'be + p.p.'로 써야 한다. 따라서 distract는 be distracted로 바꿔야 한다.

| 오답해설 | ① 25% 목적어와 목적보어가 수동관계일 때 목적보어는 과거분사가 와야 하므로 arrested로 올바르게 표현되었다.

③ 4% 목적어와 목적보어가 능동관계이고, let과 호응하는 목적보어로 원형부정사가 와야 하므로 know로 올바르게 표현된 문장이다.

④ 33% 목적어와 목적보어가 능동관계이므로, had와 호응하는 목적보어로 원형부정사 phone과 ask가 and를 두고 병치된 올바른 문장이다. 두 번째 동사인 ask는 5형식 문장에서 호응하는 목적보어로 to부정사가 와야 하므로 them에 이어 to donate로 올바르게 표현되었다.

어휘

authorities 당국
distracted 주의가 산만한, 마음이 산란해진
donate 기부하다, 기증하다
arrest 체포하다

| **8** | 문법 > 동사의 형태 > 시제 | 오답률 58% | 답 ② |

| 해석 | ① 상냥한 딸이 갑자기 예측할 수 없게 되었다.
② 그녀는 새로운 방법을 시도했고, 말할 필요도 없이 다른 결과가 나왔다.
③ 도착하자마자 그는 새로운 환경을 최대한 이용했다.
④ 그는 자신이 하고 싶은 일에 대해 나에게 말할 만큼 편안함을 느꼈다.

| 정답해설 | ② 42% 문장 전체적으로 주어 she에 이어 과거동사 attempted와 had가 병치구조로 시제일치가 이루어졌고, '~는 말할 필요도 없이'의 표현으로 needless to say가 적절하게 온 올바른 문장이다.

| 오답해설 | ① 7% become은 불완전자동사이므로 보어로 부사 unpredictably가 올 수 없으므로 형용사 unpredictable로 바꿔야 한다.

③ 28% 'upon R-ing'는 '~하자마자'의 표현으로 전치사의 목적어로 arrived가 올 수 없다. 따라서 동명사 arriving으로 바꿔야 한다.

④ 23% 부사 enough가 이끄는 to부정사가 형용사를 수식할 때 '형용사 enough to + 동사원형'이 되어야 하므로 'He felt comfortable enough to tell me~'로 바꿔야 한다.

어휘

unpredictable 예측할 수 없는
take advantage of ~을 이용하다, 활용하다
needless to say 말할 필요도 없이

9 독해 > 대의 파악 > 제목 찾기   오답률 29%   답 ④

| 해석 | '전환'의 정의는 디지털 전환을 사회적 현실 속에서 디지털화의 역할에 집중할 수 있는 분석 전략으로 제시한다. 분석적 관점에서 디지털 전환은 디지털화의 사회적 의미를 분석하고 논의할 수 있게 한다. 따라서 '디지털 전환'이라는 용어는 한 사회 내에서 디지털화의 역할에 초점을 맞춘 분석적 접근을 의미한다. 언어적 전환이 언어를 통해 현실이 구축된다는 인식론적 가정에 의해 정의된다면, 디지털 전환은 디지털화에 의해 사회적 현실이 점점 더 정의되고 있다는 가정에 기초한다. 소셜 미디어는 사회적 관계의 디지털화를 상징한다. 개인은 소셜 네트워킹 사이트(SNS)에서 정체성 관리에 점점 더 많이 관여하고 있다. SNS는 다방향적인데, 사용자들이 서로 연결하여 정보를 공유할 수 있다는 의미이다.
① SNS에서의 정체성 재구축
② 언어적 전환 대 디지털 전환
③ 디지털 시대의 정보 공유 방법
④ 사회 현실의 맥락 안에서의 디지털화

| 정답해설 | ④ 71% 첫 번째 문장에서 전환의 정의를 사회적 현실에서의 디지털화로 전환되는 것으로 연결해 언급한 후, 디지털 전환에 대해 상술하고 있으므로 정답은 ④이다.

어휘
definition 정의, 개념 / analytical 분석적인
perspective 관점, 시각 / societal 사회의, 사회 활동의
center on ~에 집중되다 / assumption 가정, 추측
polydirectional 다방향적인

10 독해 > 글의 일관성 파악하기 > 글의 순서   오답률 25%   답 ①

| 해석 | 지구 기후 변화에 대한 우려가 커지면서 화석 연료 추출 소비에 반대하는 캠페인뿐만 아니라 재생 가능 에너지를 지원하는 캠페인도 조직하도록 활동가들에게 동기를 부여했다.
(C) 영국 정부가 재생 에너지 산업의 성장을 빠르게 가속화하지 못하는 것에 좌절한 환경 운동가들은 1년에 2,500가구에 의해 사용되는 양의 전기를 생산할 것으로 추정되는 2,000명 이상의 회원을 가진 지역사회 소유의 단체인 웨스트밀 풍력 농장 협동조합을 결성했다. 웨스트밀 풍력 농장 협동조합은 지역 시민들에게 웨스트밀 태양광 협동조합을 설립하도록 고무했다.
(A) 이 태양광 협동조합은 1,400가구에 전력을 공급할 수 있는 충분한 에너지를 생산하여 국내 최초의 대규모 태양광 농장 협동조합이 되었으며, 회원들의 말로는 태양광 발전이 "일반인들이 옥상뿐만 아니라 공공시설에서도 깨끗한 전력을 생산할 수 있는 지속 가능하고 '민주적인' 에너지 공급의 새로운 시대"를 상징한다는 것을 가시적으로 상기시켜준다.
(B) 마찬가지로 미국의 재생 에너지 애호가들은 "참여하는 공공시설 고객이 집단 소유한 중규모 시설을 통해 깨끗한 전력을 제공하는 모델"을 개척한 회사인 청정에너지 공동체를 설립했다.

| 정답해설 | ① 75% 주어진 문장에서는 지구의 기후 변화에 대해 걱정이 커지면서 재생 에너지를 지지하기 위한 캠페인을 조직하도록 동기 부여를 하고 있다는 내용에 이어서 (C)를 통해 영국의 재생 에너지 운동을 소개하고, (A)에서 태양광 발전 협동조합에 대한 설명을 이어간 후에, (B)에서 비슷한 미국의 재생 에너지 단체까지 소개하는 것이 자연스러우므로 정답은 ①이다.

어휘
concern 우려, 걱정 / extraction 추출
consumption 소비
renewable 재생 가능한, 회복할 수 있는

frustrated 낙담한, 좌절한 / inability 무능력, 불가능
onshore 연안의 / cooperative 협동조합
sustainable 지속 가능한, 고갈되지 않는
ordinary 일반적인, 평범한 / utility 공공시설; 유용, 유익

11 생활영어 > 회화   오답률 8%   답 ①

| 해석 | A: 주말 잘 보냈어?
B: 응, 꽤 괜찮았어. 우린 영화 봤어.
A: 오! 무슨 영화 봤는데?
B: 인터스텔라. 진짜 좋았어.
A: 진짜? ① 어떤 부분이 가장 좋았는데?
B: 특수효과. 환상적이었어. 다시 본다고 해도 상관없을 것 같아.
① 어떤 부분이 가장 좋았는데?
② 가장 좋아하는 영화 장르는 뭐야?
③ 그 영화 전 세계적으로 홍보됐어?
④ 그 영화 비싸?

| 정답해설 | ① 92% 영화 감상에 대한 대화로 빈칸에 이어 'The special effects'라고 하면서 환상적이라고 극찬을 하고 있으므로 A가 좋았던 점에 대해 물었음을 알 수 있다. 따라서 빈칸에 가장 적절한 것은 ①이다.

어휘
mind 꺼리다, 싫어하다 / costly 값이 비싼

12 생활영어 > 회화   오답률 32%   답 ③

| 해석 | ① A: 오늘 해야 할 연설 때문에 너무 긴장돼.
B: 침착함을 유지하는 게 제일 중요해.
② A: 그거 알아? 민수랑 유진이가 결혼한대!
B: 잘됐네! 언제 결혼하는 거야?
③ A: 2개월 방학이 일주일 정도 지났어. 새 학기가 코앞으로 왔어.
B: 내 말이. 방학이 너무 오랫동안 계속됐어.
④ A: '물'을 프랑스어로 뭐라 그래?
B: 생각이 날 듯 말 듯한데 기억이 안 나.

| 정답해설 | ③ 68% A는 휴가가 빨리 지나 아쉬운 느낌에 대해 이야기 하는데, B는 휴가가 너무 오랫동안 계속됐다고 했으므로 둘의 대화가 어색함을 알 수 있다.

어휘
nervous 긴장되는, 불안한 / stay cool 침착하다, 냉정을 유지하다
tie the knot 결혼하다 / around the corner 가까이에, 코앞에

13 독해 > 세부내용 찾기 > 내용 불일치 찾기   오답률 15%   답 ②

| 해석 | 여자들은 수다를 떨기에 능숙하며, 언제나 사소한 일에 대해서만 이야기한다고 적어도 남자들은 항상 그렇게 생각해 왔다. 그러나 일부 새로운 연구는 여성이 여성과 대화할 때 그들의 대화는 경박함과는 거리가 멀며, 남성들이 다른 남성들과 대화할 때보다 더 많은 주제(최대 40개 주제)를 다루고 있다고 제시한다. 여성의 대화는 건강에서부터 집, 정치, 패션, 영화, 가족, 교육, 관계 문제 등 다양하지만 스포츠는 눈에 띄게 없다. 남성은 보다 제한된 범위의 주제를 갖는 경향이 있으며, 가장 인기 있는 주제는 일, 스포츠, 농담, 자동차 및 여성이다. 1,000명 이상의 여성을 인터뷰한 심리학자 페트라 보인튼 교수에 따르면, 여성들도 대화에서 한 주제에서 다른 주제로 빠르게 움직이는 경향이 있는 반면, 남자들은 보통 한 주제에 더 오랜 기간

동안 집착한다고 한다. 직장에서, 이러한 차이는 남성들에게 유리할 수 있는데, 그들은 다른 문제들을 제쳐두고 논의되고 있는 주제에 완전히 집중할 수 있기 때문이다. 한편, 그것은 회의 중에 여러 가지를 동시에 논의해야 할 때 집중하기가 어려울 때가 있다는 뜻이기도 하다.

| 정답해설 | ② 85% 대화에 있어 여성과 남성의 차이에 관한 글로, 세 번째 문장에서 여성들의 대화 주제 범위가 다양하지만 그 중 스포츠는 눈에 띄게 없다고 언급했으므로 글의 내용과 일치하지 않는 것은 ②이다.

어휘

gossiping 잡담, 수다 trivial 사소한, 하찮은
frivolous 하찮은, 경박한
range from A to B A에서 B의 범위에 이르다
stick to 고수하다, 충실하다 put aside 치우다, 한쪽에 두다

| 14 | 독해 > 글의 일관성 파악하기 > 글의 흐름과 무관한 문장 | 오답률 17% | 답 ② |

| 해석 | 15세기에는 과학, 철학, 마술 사이에는 차이가 없었다. 세 가지 모두 '자연 철학'이라는 일반적인 표제 아래 있었다. 자연 철학의 발전의 중심은 고전 작가들의 회복이었고, 가장 중요한 것은 아리스토텔레스의 작품이었다. ② 인본주의자들은 그들의 지식을 퍼뜨리기 위한 인쇄기의 힘을 재빨리 깨달았다. 15세기 초에 아리스토텔레스는 철학과 과학에 관한 모든 학문적 고찰의 기초가 되었다. 아리스토텔레스는 아랍어 번역과 아베로, 아비케나의 논평에서 살아남아 인류의 자연계와의 관계에 대한 체계적인 관점을 제공했다. 그의 『물리학』, 『형이상학』, 『기상학』과 같은 현존하는 텍스트들은 학자들에게 자연 세계를 창조한 힘을 이해할 수 있는 논리적 도구를 제공했다.

| 정답해설 | ② 83% 15세기 자연 철학 발전의 중심이 되었던 아리스토텔레스에 대해 서술하는 글이다. 따라서 인쇄기의 힘을 빠르게 깨달은 인문주의자들에 내용인 ②는 글의 흐름상 적절하지 않은 문장이다.

어휘

divide 분할, 분배 speculation 사색, 고찰; 투기
commentary 주석, 논평 perspective 관점; 시작
metaphysics 형이상학 meteorology 기상학

| 15 | 문법 > 동사의 형태 > 조동사 | 오답률 58% | 답 ③ |

| 해석 | ① 지진에 따른 화재는 보험업계에 특별한 관심사다.
② 워드 프로세서는 과거에 타이피스트의 궁극적인 도구로 간주되었다.
③ 현금예측에 포함된 소득 요소는 회사의 사정에 따라 달라질 것이다.
④ 세계 최초의 디지털 카메라는 1975년 이스트맨 코닥 사(社)에서 스티브 사슨이 만들었다.

| 정답해설 | ③ 42% vary는 자동사로 조동사 will에 이어 동사원형 2개가 나란히 올 수 없다. 따라서 will be vary를 will vary로 바꿔야 한다.

| 오답해설 | ① 32% following은 현재분사로 주어인 명사 fire를 수식하고 있으며 보어로 형용사구인 of special interest가 올바르게 이어졌다. 'of + 명사'는 형용사구이다.

② 22% 수동태 동사에 이어 to be가 이어졌으므로 5형식 문장의 수동태임을 알 수 있다. 'they considered word processors to be the ultimate tool~'에서 목적어인 word processors를 주어

로 이동시켜 수동태로 전환한 문장이며 주어인 they는 일반인 주어이므로 by them으로 전환된 후 생략된 문장이다.

④ 4% 1975년이라는 과거 시점에 이루어진 일이므로 시제일치가 올바르게 이루어졌으며 'Steve Sasson at Eastman Kodak created the world's first digital camera in 1975'를 수동태로 전환한 문장이다.

어휘

insurance 보험, 보험업 forecast 예상, 예측

오답률 TOP 1

| 16 | 독해 > 빈칸의 내용 추론하기 > 빈칸 어휘 추론 | 오답률 68% | 답 ② |

| 해석 | 역사적으로 높은 성장률에서 중국 경제의 둔화는 오랫동안 다른 곳에서의 성장을 ② 짓누를 것으로 예상되어 왔다. 예일대 스티븐 로치는 "30년 동안 10%로 성장해 온 중국은 세계 경제를 앞으로 나아가게 한 많은 것에 강력한 연료 공급원이었다"라고 말했다. 성장률은 공식 수치인 7%대로 둔화되었다. "그것은 확실한 감속이다"라고 로치가 덧붙였다.

① 가속하다 ② 짓누르다, 내리누르다
③ 이끌다, 일으키다 ④ 결과적으로 ~가 되다

| 정답해설 | ② 32% 빈칸에 이어진 내용에서 중국의 성장률이 둔화되었다는 부정적인 묘사가 있으므로 빈칸에는 목적어인 성장(growth)을 '짓눌렀다'는 부정적인 동사구가 들어가야 한다. 따라서 선지에서 맥락상 가장 적절한 것은 weigh on이다.

어휘

concrete 확실한; 구체적인 deceleration 감속

| 17 | 독해 > 빈칸의 내용 추론하기 > 빈칸 어휘 추론 | 오답률 42% | 답 ④ |

| 해석 | 점점 더 많은 리더들이 원격으로 또는 컨설턴트와 프리랜서들뿐만 아니라 전국이나 전 세계에 흩어져 있는 팀들과 함께 일하기 때문에, 당신은 그들에게 더 많은 ④ 자율성을 주어야 할 것이다. 신뢰를 많이 줄수록 다른 사람들이 당신을 더 신뢰한다. 나는 직무 만족과 사람들이 누군가가 모든 단계에서 그들을 따라다니지 않고도 업무를 완전히 수행할 수 있는 권한 사이에는 직접적인 상관관계가 있다고 확신한다. 신뢰하는 사람들에게 책임을 주는 것은 조직을 더 원활하게 운영하게 할 뿐만 아니라 당신이 더 큰 문제에 집중할 수 있도록 시간을 더 많이 벌어줄 수 있다.

① 일 ② 보상
③ 제한 ④ 자율성

| 정답해설 | ④ 58% 함께 업무를 하는 사람들에게 신뢰와 책임감을 주어야 한다고 서술하고 있다. 더 많은 권한을 부여받은 사람들은 일을 더 완벽하게 처리할 수 있으며, 그것이 직무 만족과 연관된다고 했고, 신뢰하는 사람에게 책임을 맡기는 것이 조직을 더 원활하게 만들고 본인에게 더 많은 시간을 주어 더 큰 문제에 집중할 수 있게 만든다고 했으므로, 빈칸에 들어갈 말로 가장 적절한 것은 ④이다.

어휘

remotely 멀리서, 간접적으로 scatter 분산시키다, 흩뜨리다
consultant 상담역, 고문 bestow 수여하다, 주다
convinced 확신하는 empower 권한을 주다
execute 실행하다; 집행하다; 처형하다
restriction 제한, 규제 autonomy 자율성, 자치

18 독해 > 대의 파악 > 요지·주장 찾기　오답률 45%　답 ①

| 해석 | 몬트리올의 에미누-엘-베스 솔롬 사원의 선임 랍비인 리사 그루시코우는 "유대교에서는 주로 우리의 행동에 의해 정의된다"라고 말한다. "당신은 사실상 앉아 있는 공상적인 개혁가가 될 수는 없다" 이 개념은 유대인의 틱쿤 올람 개념과 관련이 있는데, 그것은 '세상을 수리하는 것'으로 번역된다. 인간으로서의 우리의 일은 "깨진 것을 고치는 것이다. 우리 자신과 서로를 돌볼 뿐만 아니라 우리 주변에 더 나은 세상을 건설하는 것도 우리에게 의무가 있다"라고 그녀는 말한다. 이 철학은 선함을 봉사에 기반을 둔 것으로 개념화한다. "내가 좋은 사람인가?"라고 묻는 대신 "세상에서 내가 어떤 좋은 일을 하는가?"라고 묻고 싶을 것이다. 그루시코우의 사원은 이런 믿음들을 공동체 안팎에서 행동으로 옮기게 한다. 예를 들어, 그들은 1970년대에 베트남 출신의 두 난민 가족을 캐나다로 오게 하기 위해 후원했다.
① 우리는 세상을 치유하기 위해 노력해야 한다.
② 공동체는 피난처 역할을 해야 한다.
③ 우리는 선함을 믿음으로 개념화해야 한다.
④ 사원은 공동체에 기여해야 한다.

| 정답해설 | ① 55% 인간으로서 우리의 일은 망가진 것을 고치는 것 즉, 더 나은 세상을 만드는 것이라 했으며 자신이 세상에 무슨 도움이 되는지 질문해야 한다고 언급했으므로, 글의 요지로 가장 적절한 것은 ①이다.

어휘
Judaism 유대교　　　　　define 정의하다, 규정하다
rabbi 랍비, 유대교 율법학자　　relate to ~와 관련되다
translate 번역하다, 해석하다
incumbent 의무로서 지워지는; 현직의
conceptualize 개념화하다　　sponsor 후원하다
refugee 난민; (국외) 망명자

19 독해 > 빈칸의 내용 추론하기 > 연결어 추론　오답률 47%　답 ③

| 해석 | 고대 철학자들과 영적 교사들은 긍정적인 것과 부정적인 것, 낙관적인 것과 비관적인 것, 성공을 위한 노력과 실패와 불확실성에 대한 개방성에서 비롯된 안전의 균형을 맞출 필요성을 이해했다. 스토아학파는 '악의 사전 계획' 또는 최악의 시나리오를 의도적으로 시각화할 것을 권고했다. 이것은 미래에 대한 불안을 줄이는 경향이 있다. 현실에서 상황이 얼마나 나쁘게 진행될 수 있는지를 냉정하게 상상할 때, 당신은 보통 당신이 대처할 수 있다고 결론짓는다. (A) 게다가, 당신이 현재 즐기고 있는 관계와 소유물을 잃을지도 모른다고 상상하는 것은 당신이 지금 가지고 있는 것에 대한 감사를 증가시킨다고 그들은 언급했다. (B) 반면에, 긍정적인 사고는 현재의 즐거움을 무시하면서 항상 미래로 기울어진다.

　　　(A)　　　　　(B)
① 그럼에도　　　게다가
② 게다가　　　　예를 들어
③ 게다가　　　　반면에
④ 그러나　　　　결론적으로

| 정답해설 | ③ 53% 이 글은 부정적 사고를 권고하는 스토아 학파의 견해를 서술하고 있다. (A) 앞에서 최악의 상황을 가정하는 경우, 이것이 미래에 대한 불안감을 감소시키는 경향이 있다고 했고, 현실에서 상황이 악화되었을 경우 대처가 가능하다고 했다. 이는 (A) 뒤의 현재 누리고 있는 관계나 소유물이 없어질 수도 있다고 가정하는 내용과 이어지므로 (A)에는 Besides가 적절하다. (B) 뒤에 서는 긍정적인 생각이 현재의 기쁨을 무시하고 미래에 기댄다고 했으므로, (B) 앞에 나온 내용과는 반대임을 알 수 있다. 따라서 (B)에는 by contrast가 적절하다.

어휘
optimism 낙관주의　　　　　pessimism 비관주의
strive 노력하다, 애쓰다　　　　the Stoics 스토아 학파
premedition 미리 계획하기　　deliberately 의도적으로; 신중히
visualize 시각화하다　　　　　possession 소유, 재산
gratitude 감사, 고마움

20 독해 > 글의 일관성 파악하기 > 주어진 문장의 삽입　오답률 49%　답 ②

| 해석 | 일중독자들은 왜 그들의 일을 그렇게 즐기는가? 주로 일하는 것이 몇 가지 중요한 이점을 제공하기 때문이다. 그것은 사람들에게 생계를 꾸려 나가는 급여를 제공한다. ② 그리고 일하는 것은 재정적인 안정보다 더 많은 것을 제공한다. 그건 사람들에게 자신감을 제공한다. 그들은 도전적인 작품을 제작했을 때 만족감을 느끼고 "내가 그걸 만들었다."라고 말할 수 있다. 심리학자들은 일은 또한 사람들에게 정체성을 준다고 주장한다; 그들은 자기와 개인주의에 대한 의미를 얻을 수 있도록 일한다. 또한 대부분의 직업은 사람들에게 다른 사람들을 만나는 사회적으로 용인된 방법을 제공한다. 일을 하는 것은 긍정적인 중독이라고 말할 수 있다. 일 중독자는 일에 대해 강박적일 수 있지만 중독은 안전하고 이롭기조차 한 것으로 보인다.

| 정답해설 | ② 51% 주어진 문장은 일이 재정적 안정 이상을 제공한다는 내용이다. ② 앞에서 재정적 안정을 의미하는 급여에 관한 내용이 나왔고, ② 뒤에 자신감을 준다는 내용이 이어졌는데, 바로 이 자신감이 주어진 문장의 재정적 안정 이상을 의미함을 알 수 있다. 따라서 주어진 문장이 들어갈 위치로 가장 적절한 것은 ②이다.

어휘
provide A with B A에게 B를 제공하다
earn a living 생계를 꾸리다　　identity 정체성; 신원
individualism 개인주의; 개성　　addiction 중독, 과몰입
compulsive 강박관념의, 강제적인

합격예상 체크

맞힌 개수	/20문항	점수	/100점

➡ ☐ 합격 ☐ 불합격

취약영역 체크

문항	정답	영역	문항	정답	영역
1	②	어휘 > 빈칸	11	②	생활영어 > 회화
2	②	어휘 > 동의어	12	②	생활영어 > 회화
3	④	어휘 > 동의어	13	①	문법 > 준동사
4	①	어휘 > 동의어	14	④	독해 > 대의 파악
5	③	문법 > 동사의 형태	15	④	독해 > 글의 일관성 파악하기
6	④	어휘 > 동의어	16	③	독해 > 빈칸의 내용 추론하기
7	②	문법 > 연결사	17	①	독해 > 대의 파악
8	③	문법 > 명사와 일치	18	③	독해 > 글의 일관성 파악하기
9	①	독해 > 빈칸의 내용 추론하기	19	④	독해 > 글의 일관성 파악하기
10	③	독해 > 대의 파악	20	④	독해 > 세부내용 찾기

⬇ 영역별 틀린 개수로 취약영역을 확인하세요!

어휘	/5	문법	/4	독해	/9	생활영어	/2

➡ 나의 취약영역: _____

※ [정답해설]과 [오답해설] 선지의 ▢50%▢ 표시는 ⟨1초 합격예측 서비스⟩를 통해 수집된 선지 선택률을 나타냅니다.

1　어휘 > 빈칸　　　오답률 40%　답 ②

| 해석 | 플라스틱 병의 문제는 ② 절연 처리가 되지 않았다는 점인데, 따라서 온도가 상승하기 시작할 때 물도 또한 데워질 것이다.
① ▢9%▢ 위생적인　　　　② ▢60%▢ 절연 처리가 된
③ ▢26%▢ 재활용 가능한　　④ ▢5%▢ 방수의

| 정답해설 | ② 플라스틱 병에 대한 문제점을 찾아야 하는 문제이다. 빈칸에 이어 결과를 나타내는 두 번째 문장에서 온도가 상승하면서 물도 가열된다고 하였으므로, 플라스틱 병은 절연 처리가 되지 않았음을 유추할 수 있다. 빈칸 앞의 not을 고려해 빈칸에는 '절연 처리가 된'의 표현인 insulated가 가장 적절하다.

[어휘]
issue 문제, 쟁점　　　　　　temperature 온도

▢오답률 TOP 2▢
2　어휘 > 동의어　　　오답률 51%　답 ②

| 해석 | 그 잔인한 장면들은 다른 상황이었다면 그녀의 마음에 파고들지 않았을 생각을 야기했다.
① ▢8%▢ 돌보다　　　　　② ▢49%▢ 불러 일으키다
③ ▢11%▢ 보충하다, 보상하다　④ ▢32%▢ ~와 계속 연락하다

| 정답해설 | ② touch off는 '(로켓·총포 등을) 발사하다; (폭발물에) 점화하다' 등의 의미가 있는데, 건드렸을 때(touch) 발사가 되어 이탈(off)하는 모습을 생각하면, '(분노·사건 등을) 유발하다, 일으

키다'의 의미가 될 수 있음을 유추할 수 있다. 따라서 맥락상 동의어로 가장 적절한 것은 give rise to이다.

[어휘]
touch off 야기하다　　　　cruel 잔인한
otherwise 다른 상황에서는, 그렇지 않으면

3　어휘 > 동의어　　　오답률 29%　답 ④

| 해석 | 작가가 글을 쓰는 과정에서 채택하는 전략은 주의 과부화로 인한 어려움을 완화하는 데 도움이 될 수 있다.
① ▢10%▢ 보완하다　　　② ▢14%▢ 가속하다
③ ▢5%▢ 계산하다　　　④ ▢71%▢ 완화하다

| 정답해설 | ④ 작가가 택하는 전략은 작가에게 유리한 내용이 되어야 한다. 따라서 동사 alleviate의 목적어로 부정적인 의미의 the difficulty가 왔으므로 전략은 어려움을 '완화하는' 것이 되어야 함을 유추할 수 있다. 따라서 동의어로 relieve가 가장 적절하다.

[어휘]
alleviate 완화하다　　　　strategy 전략
adopt 채택하다; 입양하다　attentional overload 주의 과부하

4 어휘 > 동의어 　　　오답률 30%　　답 ①

| 해석 | 그 학교 불량배는 학급에서 다른 학생들에 의해 꺼려지는 것이 어떠한지를 알지 못했다.

① 70% 피하다　　　　　　② 9% 경고하다
③ 12% 처벌하다　　　　　④ 9% 모방하다

| 정답해설 | ① 학교 불량배가 알지 못할 만한 일이 무엇인가를 생각해 보면, 평소 자신이 다른 학생들에게 생각 없이 가하는 행동 중 하나일 것이다. shun은 '피하다, 꺼리다' 등의 의미가 있으므로 동의어로 avoid가 가장 적절하다.

어휘
shun 피하다　　　　　　　school bully 학교 불량배

오답률 TOP 1
5 문법 > 동사의 형태 > 시제 　　오답률 53%　　답 ③

| 해석 | ① 은하계의 수십 억 개의 별들 중에, 얼마나 많은 별들이 생명을 잉태할 수 있을까?
② 크리스마스 파티는 정말로 재미있어서 나는 완전히 시간 가는 줄 몰랐다.
③ 나는 지금 바로 떠나야만 하는데 오늘 정오에 일을 시작할 것이기 때문이다.
④ 그들은 더 어렸을 때 훨씬 더 많이 책을 좋아했었다.

| 정답해설 | ③ 47% 이유 부사절의 at noon today는 미래를 나타내는 부사구이다. 동사는 왕래발착동사인 start의 현재 진행시제로, 현재 혹은 현재 진행시제가 미래를 대신할 수 있으므로 올바른 문장이다.

| 오답해설 | ① 21% 동사(are able to hatch)의 주체는 stars이므로, 셀 수 있는 복수명사임을 감안하면 how much가 아닌 how many가 되어야 한다. much는 셀 수 없는 명사에 대해 쓰는 표현이다.

② 20% party는 '흥분하는' 것이 아니므로, excited는 적절하지 않다. 감정타동사 excite에서 파생한 현재분사 exciting이 '재미있는, 흥미를 주는'의 의미이므로 exciting으로 바꿔야 한다.

④ 12% used to가 조동사일 때 뒤에는 동사원형이 와야 한다. 문맥상 과거의 지속적 상태를 나타내고 있으므로 used to love로 바꿔야 한다.

어휘
hatch life 생명을 잉태하다　　　lose track of ~을 잊어버리다, 놓치다

6 어휘 > 동의어 　　　오답률 38%　　답 ④

| 해석 | 프란체스카가 여름휴가 동안 집에서 머무는 것을 강하게 주장한 후, 불편한 침묵이 저녁 식사 테이블위에 드리웠다. 로버트는 자신의 거창한 계획에 대해 그녀에게 말하는 것이 적절한 때인지에 대해 확신이 서지 않았다.

① 15% ~에 반대했다　　　② 17% ~에 대해 꿈꾸었다
③ 6% 완전히 배제했다　　　④ 62% 강하게 주장했다

| 정답해설 | ④ 프란체스카가 여름휴가를 집에서 보내겠다고 무언가를 한 뒤에 불편한 침묵이 있었고, 로버트는 거창한 계획을 말해야 할지에 대해 고민하고 있으므로, 프란체스카의 의지가 확고함을 알 수 있다. 따라서 선지 중 맥락상 가장 적절한 것은 strongly suggested

임을 알 수 있다. make a case for는 '~해야 한다고 말하다, 주장하다'의 의미이다.

어휘
make a case for ~을 강하게 주장하다
grandiose 웅장한, 장엄한

오답률 TOP 3
7 문법 > 연결사 > 관계사 　　오답률 49%　　답 ②

| 정답해설 | ② 51% 전치사 to의 목적어로 선행사를 포함한 복합관계대명사절이 이어졌다. 관계대명사의 격은 뒤에 이어지는 절에서 결정하는데, 주어 없이 동사 completes가 이어졌으므로 whomever는 주격 복합관계대명사인 whoever로 바꿔야 한다.

| 오답해설 | ① 13% 수리가 무료가 아니었던 것은 과거시점으로, 만료되었던 것은 그 이전의 시점이므로 대과거 had expired로 시제 일치가 올바르게 이루어졌다. '무료의' 표현으로 free of charge가 적절하게 쓰였다.

③ 20% 주어진 우리말과 last month, now로 보아 혼합가정법 시제가 되어야 함을 알 수 있다. 조건절은 과거의 사실을 나타내기 위해 가정법 과거완료인 had asked로 표현했고, 주절은 현재의 사실을 나타내기 위해 가정법 과거인 would be로 올바르게 표현한 문장이다.

④ 16% 우리말과 last year로 보아 전체적으로 과거시제로 일치가 이루어졌고, '설상가상으로'의 표현으로 관계대명사 what의 관용 표현인 what was worse로 올바르게 표현된 문장이다.

어휘
warranty 보증, 담보　　　　　expire 만료되다
free of charge 무료인　　　　　pass away 죽다

8 문법 > 명사와 일치 > 일치 　　오답률 38%　　답 ③

| 해석 | 엘리자베스 테일러는 아름다운 보석들을 보는 눈이 있었고 수년에 걸쳐 일부 엄청난 보석들을 모았으며, 한번은 '여자는 언제나 더 많은 다이몬드를 원할 수 있다'고 말했다. 2011년에 그녀의 최고급 보석들이 1억 1,590만 달러를 벌어들인 크리스티 사(社)에 의한 한 저녁 경매에서 판매가 되었다. 그날의 저녁 경매 동안 팔린 그녀의 가장 가치 있는 소장품들 중에 불가리에 의해 만들어진 1961년판 보석 시계가 있었다. 손목에 휘감긴 뱀의 모습으로 디자인되었고, 머리와 꼬리는 다이아몬드로 덮였으며, 두 개의 최면을 거는 듯한 에메랄드 눈을 가지고 있는데, 작아서 눈에 띄지 않는 장치가 작은 석영으로 된 시계를 드러내기 위해 날카로운 턱을 연다.

| 정답해설 | ③ 62% 'among + 명사'의 부사구가 문장의 앞으로 오면서 주어와 동사의 도치가 이루어진 문장이다. 따라서 밑줄 친 동사의 주어는 뒤에 이어진 timepiece이므로 단수인 was로 바꿔야 한다.

| 오답해설 | ① 15% 현재분사로 뒤에 목적어로 인용문이 이어졌고, 생략된 주어는 문장 전체 주어인 Elizabeth Taylor로, 문맥상 테일러가 말하는 것이므로 자연스럽다.

② 11% 선행사 auction을 지칭하는 주격 관계대명사로 뒤에 동사가 이어진 올바른 구조이다.

④ 12% 'with + 명사 + 과거분사'의 구조로, 명사 head and tail은

다이아몬드로 '덮인' 것이므로 수동의 과거분사로 올바르게 표현되었다.

어휘

amass 축적하다, 모으다   possession 소유, 재산
hypnotic 최면 상태의
discreet 작아서 눈에 띄지 않는; 신중한

---

9 독해 > 빈칸의 내용 추론하기 > 연결어 추론   오답률 23%   답 ①

| 해석 | 적극적인 행동은 타인들의 권리를 침해하지 않는 직접적이고 적절한 방식으로 여러분의 권리를 옹호하고 여러분의 생각과 감정들을 표현하는 것을 포함한다. 그것은 상대방이 여러분의 관점을 이해하도록 만드는 것의 문제이다. 적극적인 행동 수완을 보여주는 사람들은 좋은 대인 관계를 유지하면서 편안함과 자신감으로 갈등이 있는 상황들을 다룰 수 있다. (A) 대조적으로, 공격적인 행동은 대놓고 타인들의 권리를 침해하는 방식으로 여러분의 생각과 감정을 표현하고 여러분의 권리를 옹호하는 것을 포함한다. 공격적인 행동을 보여주는 사람들은 타인의 권리는 그들의 권리보다 부차적인 것이 틀림없다고 믿는 것 같다. (B) 따라서 그들은 좋은 대인 관계를 유지하는 데 어려움을 겪는다. 그들은 통제력을 유지하기 위해 방해를 하고, 빠르게 이야기하며, 타인을 무시하고, 빈정거리나 다른 형태의 폭언을 사용하기 쉽다.

(A)	(B)
① 대조적으로	따라서
② 마찬가지로	더욱이
③ 그러나	한편으로는
④ 따라서	또 한편으로는

| 정답해설 | ① 77% (A) 이전까지는 적극적인 행동에 대한 내용이 긍정적으로 서술되었는데, (A) 이후에는 공격적인 행동에 대한 부정적인 서술이 이어졌으므로 '대조'의 연결사인 In contrast가 적절하다. (B)에는 그 이전에 공격적인 행동을 하는 사람들의 성향이 서술되었고, 이후에는 이로 인한 좋은 대인관계 형성의 어려움이 이어졌으므로, 논의를 매듭짓는 Thus가 적절하다.

어휘

assertive behavior 적극적인 행동   stand up for ~을 옹호하다, 지지하다
appropriate 적절한   violate 위반하다, 침해하다
assurance 보장, 확신, 자신   aggressive behavior 공격적인 행동
subservient 부차적인, 종속하는   interrupt 방해하다
sarcasm 빈정거림, 비아냥   verbal abuse 폭언

---

10 독해 > 대의 파악 > 주제 찾기   오답률 8%   답 ③

| 해석 | 태블릿 컴퓨터에서 이용 가능한 전자책 애플리케이션들은 터치스크린 기술을 채택한다. 일부 터치스크린은 마주보며 있는 두 개의 전자 충전 금속 표면을 덮는 유리판이 특징이다. 스크린에 닿았을 때, 두 개의 금속 표면은 압력을 느끼고 연결되게 한다. 이 압력은 전자 신호를 컴퓨터에 보내고 그것은 접촉을 명령으로 전환한다. 이러한 버전의 터치스크린은 감압식 스크린으로 알려져 있는데, 스크린이 손가락의 압력에 반응을 하기 때문이다. 다른 태블릿 컴퓨터는 유리판 아래에 있는 단일 전기화 금속층이 특징이다. 사용자가 스크린을 터치할 때, 전류의 일부가 유리를 통해 사용자의 손가락으로 넘어간다. 전하가 이동할 때, 컴퓨터는 전력의 상실을 명령으로 해석하고 사용자가 바라는 기능을 실행한다. 이런 유형의 스크린은 정전식 스크린으로 알려져 있다.
① 사용자가 어떻게 새로운 기술을 배우는가

② 전자책이 태블릿 컴퓨터상에서 어떻게 작용하는가
③ 터치스크린 기술이 어떻게 작동하는가
④ 터치스크린이 어떻게 발전해 왔는가

| 정답해설 | ③ 92% 전자책 애플리케이션들이 터치스크린 기술을 이용한다고 한 후, 터치스크린 종류와 이에 대한 기능 실행에 대한 내용들이 이어지고 있다. 따라서 정답은 ③이 가장 적절하다.

어휘

application 애플리케이션, 응용 프로그램
feature 특징을 이루다   make contact 연결되다
translate 옮기다; 번역하다   resistive screen 감압식 스크린
electrified 전기가 통하는   transfer 옮기다; 바꾸다
interpret 해석하다, 설명하다   carry out ~을 실행하다
capacitive screen 정전식 스크린

---

11 생활영어 > 회화   오답률 10%   답 ②

| 해석 | A: 에이, 하나 더 왔네! 정크 메일이 너무 많아!
B: 그러게 말이야. 나는 하루에 10개 이상의 정크 메일을 받아.
A: 그것들이 오는 것을 막을 수 있을까?
B: 완전히 차단할 수 있을 것 같지는 않아.
A: ② 우리가 할 수 있는 일은 없을까?
B: 글쎄, 설정에 필터를 설치할 수는 있지.
A: 필터라고?
B: 응. 필터는 일부 스팸 메일들을 제거할 수 있어.
① 너는 자주 이메일을 쓰니
② 우리가 할 수 있는 일은 없을까
③ 너는 어떻게 이런 훌륭한 필터를 만들었니
④ 내가 이메일 계정을 만드는 것을 도와줄 수 있어

| 정답해설 | ② 90% 정크 메일 수신에 대한 대화문으로 A가 무언가를 물어본 후에 B가 해결책 하나를 제안하고 있으므로, 빈칸에 들어갈 표현으로 ②가 가장 적절하다.

어휘

stop A from R-ing A가 ~하는 것을 막다
completely 완전히   filter 필터, 여과 장치
weed out 제거하다, 추려내다

---

12 생활영어 > 회화   오답률 15%   답 ②

| 해석 | ① A: 지금 몇 시인지 아세요?
B: 미안해요. 요즘에 바빠서요.
② A: 이봐요, 어디 가고 있어요?
B: 우리는 식료품점에 가고 있어요.
③ A: 내가 이것을 하는 것을 도와줄 수 있어요?
B: 좋아요, 당신을 위해 박수를 쳐 줄게요.
④ A: 내 지갑 본 사람 있어요?
B: 오랜만이네요.

| 정답해설 | ② 85% be off는 '중지되다'의 의미도 있지만 '떠나다, 출발하다'의 의미도 있으므로 문맥상 ②가 가장 적절하다.

어휘

be headed ~으로 향하다   be off 떠나다
give a hand 도와주다, 거들어주다
clap (손뼉을) 치다; (연기·연사 등에) 박수갈채를 보내다

| 13 | 문법 > 준동사 > 동명사 | 오답률 32% | 답 ① |

| 정답해설 | ① 68% '~했던 것을 후회하다'의 표현은 regret의 목적어로 동명사 혹은 완료동명사가 와야 한다. 따라서 to tell은 telling 혹은 having told로 바꿔야 한다. 'regret to + 동사원형'은 '~하게 되어 유감이다'의 의미이다.

| 오답해설 | ② 5% 비교 대상인 그의 경험과 그녀의 경험으로 접속사 than에 이어 her experience를 한 단어로 표현한 소유대명사 hers로 올바르게 표현되었다.

③ 11% remind A of B의 구조로 주어진 우리말과 일치하는 문장이다.

④ 16% 주절의 목적어 people을 주격관계대명사 who가 이끄는 절이 수식하는 문장으로, who에 이어 선행사인 people에 수일치가 이루어진 동사 look이 적절하게 왔으며, look과 호응하는 신체 부위를 언급하는 표현으로 in the eye가 올바르게 왔다.

어휘
remind A of B A에게 B를 상기시키다   conversation 대화

| 14 | 독해 > 대의 파악 > 제목 찾기 | 오답률 8% | 답 ④ |

| 해석 | 루이 14세는 그의 위대함의 가치를 보여주는 궁전을 필요로 했고, 따라서 베르사유에 거대한 새로운 궁전을 짓기로 결정했는데, 그곳에는 작은 사냥 막사 하나가 있었다. 거의 50년간의 노력이 이루어진 후, 이 작은 사냥 막사는 4분의 1마일 길이의 거대한 궁전으로 바뀌었다. 강으로부터 물을 가져오고, 습지대의 물을 배수시키기 위해 운하를 팠다. 베르사유는 유명한 거울의 방과 같은 정교한 방들로 꽉 차 있는데, 거울의 방에는 17개의 거대한 거울들이 17개의 큰 창문 맞은편에 서 있고, 아폴로의 방에는 순은으로 된 왕좌가 있다. 아폴로, 주피터, 넵튠과 같은 수백여 점의 그리스 신들의 조각상들이 정원에 있는데, 각각의 신은 루이 14세의 얼굴을 지니고 있다!
① 그리스 신들의 진짜 얼굴
② 거울의 방 대(對) 아폴로의 방
③ 운하가 베르사유에 단지 물보다 더 많은 것을 가져왔을까?
④ 베르사유: 초라한 오두막으로부터 대궁전으로

| 정답해설 | ④ 92% 루이 14세가 작은 사냥 막사가 있는 베르사유를 대궁전으로 바꾸는 과정과 베르사유 궁전에 있는 유명한 방들에 대해 서술하고 있는 지문이므로 정답은 ④가 가장 적절하다.

어휘
worthy of ~의 가치가 있는   hunting lodge 사냥 막사
canal 운하   drain 배수하다, 배출시키다
elaborate 정교한, 공을 들인   statue 조각상

| 15 | 독해 > 글의 일관성 파악하기 > 글의 흐름과 무관한 문장 | 오답률 37% | 답 ③ |

| 해석 | 철학자들은 인류학자들이 철학에 대해 가지고 있는 것만큼 인류학에 대해 관심이 있지 않았다. 자신의 연구에 인류학적 연구를 고려하는 영향력 있는 현대 철학자들은 거의 없다. 사회 과학 철학을 전문으로 하는 사람들은 인류학적 연구에서 나온 사례들을 고려하거나 분석할 수 있지만, 이것은 대개 개념적 포인트 혹은 인식론적 구별을 설명하기 위해 혹은 인식론적이거나 윤리적 함의를 비판하기 위해 한다. ③ 사실, 우리 시대의 위대한 철학자들은 자주 인류학과 심리학과 같은 다른 분야로부터 영감을 얻는다. 철학과 학생들은 인류학을 거의 공부하지 않거나 진지한 관심을 보여주지

않는다. 그들은 과학의 실험적 방법에 대해 배울 수 있지만 인류학적 현장 조사에 대해 거의 배우지 않는다.

| 정답해설 | ③ 63% 첫 번째 문장에서 철학자들이 인류학에 대해 관심이 없다는 내용 뒤에 이에 대한 구체적인 언급이 이어지고 있는 지문이다. 그러다가 ③에 이어진 문장에서 위대한 철학자들이 인류학과 심리학과 같은 다른 분야에서 영감을 받는다는 정반대의 내용이 대조의 연결사 하나 없이 이어지고 있고, ④에 이어진 문장에서 철학과 학생들도 인류학을 공부하지 않거나 진지한 관심을 보여주지 않는다는 ③ 이전의 흐름과 이어지는 내용이 서술되었으므로 흐름상 어색한 문장은 ③이다.

어휘
concerned with ~에 관심이 있다   anthropology 인류학
contemporary 현대의; 동시대의
take ~ into account ~을 고려하다, 참작하다
specialize in ~를 전문으로 하다   conceptual 개념의
epistemological 인식론적인   distinction 구별, 차이
implication 함의, 함축   fieldwork 현장 조사

| 16 | 독해 > 빈칸의 내용 추론하기 > 빈칸 어구 추론 | 오답률 48% | 답 ③ |

| 해석 | 우리 모두는 무언가를 상속받는다: 어떤 경우, 그것은 돈, 부동산 혹은 어떤 물건 – 할머니의 웨딩드레스 혹은 아버지가 지녔던 도구 세트와 같은 가보 – 와 같은 물건일 수 있다. 그러나, 그 외에도. 우리 모두는 다른 무언가를 상속받는데, 이는 ③ 훨씬 덜 구체적이고 명확하지 않은 것, 우리가 충분히 그것을 인지조차 할 수 없는 그런 것이다. 그것은 일상 업무를 하는 방식일 수도, 혹은 우리가 특정한 문제를 해결하거나 스스로 도덕적 문제를 결정하는 방식일 수 있다. 그것은 명절을 지키는 특별한 방식일 수도 혹은 특정한 날에 소풍을 가는 전통일 수도 있다. 그것은 우리의 사고에 중요하거나 중심적인 무언가 일 수 있고, 혹은 우리가 무심코 오랫동안 받아들여 왔던 사소한 무언가일 수도 있다.
① 우리의 일상생활과 대단히 관련이 없는
② 우리의 도덕 기준에 반하는
③ 훨씬 덜 구체적이고 명확하지 않은
④ 대단히 금전적인 가치를 지닌

| 정답해설 | ③ 52% 빈칸에 이어진 내용은 사실상 동격의 내용으로 '우리가 완전히 알아차리지 못하는 것'과 비슷한 선지를 찾아야 한다. 또한, 빈칸을 포함한 문장에 이어진 내용에서 이 부분에 대한 구체적인 내용들이 언급되고 있는데, 이로 보아 ③이 가장 적절하다.

어휘
inherit 물려받다, 상속받다   property 재산, 부동산; 특성
be aware of ~을 인지하다, 알아차리다
keep a holiday 명절을 보내다   casually 무심코

| 17 | 독해 > 대의 파악 > 요지·주장 찾기 | 오답률 47% | 답 ① |

| 해석 | 진화론적으로, 살아있기를 바라는 어떤 종이든 주의 깊게 자신의 자원들을 관리해야 한다. 그것은 음식과 다른 물건들에 대한 첫 번째 요구는 기르는 사람에게 그리고 전사와 사냥꾼들에게, 그리고 나서 심는 사람들과 건축하는 이들에게, 그리고 확실히 아이들에게 가는데, 노인들에게 남는 게 별로 없는 상태가 되며, 이들은 그들이 기여하는 것보다 더 많은 것을 소비하는 것처럼 보일 수 있다. 하지만 현대 의학이 기대 수명을 연장하기 전 조차, 평범한 가족들은 조부모, 심지어 증조부모들을 포함하고 있었다. 그것은 노인

들이 물질적으로 소비하지만, 그들은 행동함으로 그들 주위에서 종종 소용돌이치는 소동에 대해 대등하게 만들고 추론적인 핵심을 되돌려주기 때문이다.
① 노인들은 가족에 기여를 해 왔다.
② 현대 의학은 노인의 역할에 초점을 맞춰 왔다.
③ 한 가정에서 자원을 잘 할당하는 것은 가족의 번창을 결정한다.
④ 대가족은 제한된 자원의 비용을 들이게 된다.

| **정답해설** | ① ⌊53%⌋ 음식과 물건들에 대한 요구는 최종적으로 적은 부분이 노인에게 간다는 내용이 서술된 후 역접의 접속사 But에 이어지는 내용에서 가족에서 노인이 하는 긍정적인 역할을 서술하고 있으므로, 요지로 가장 적절한 것은 ①이다.

어휘

evolutionarily 진화론적으로; 점진적으로
goodies 썩 매력 있는 것
contribute ~에 기여하다, ~의 원인이 되다
life expectancy 기대 수명   ordinary 평범한
old folk 노인   level 대등하게 만들다
tumult 소동, 혼란   swirl 소용돌이치다

---

18 독해 > 글의 일관성 파악하기 > 글의 순서   [오답률 27%]   답 ③

| **해석** | 요즘 시계는 우리의 삶을 너무 많이 지배하고 있어서 시계가 없는 삶을 상상하기는 힘들다. 산업화 이전에, 대부분의 사회는 시간을 말하기 위해 태양 혹은 달을 이용했다.
(B) 기계 시계가 처음 등장했을 때, 그것들은 즉시 인기를 끌었다. 시계 혹은 손목시계를 지니는 것이 유행이었다. 사람들은 시간을 말하기 위한 이런 새로운 방식을 언급하기 위해 'of the clock' 혹은 'o'clock'이라는 표현을 만들었다.
(C) 이런 시계들은 장식적이었지만 언제나 유용하지는 않았다. 이는 마을, 지방 그리고 심지어 인근 마을이 시간을 말하는 다른 방식을 가지고 있기 때문이었다. 여행자들은 한 장소에서 다른 장소로 이동할 때 반복해서 시계를 재설정해야만 했다. 미국에서, 1860년대에 대략 70개의 다른 시간대가 있었다.
(A) 점점 더 늘어나는 철도망에 있어서 시간 기준이 없다는 사실은 큰 불행이었다. 자주, 그저 몇 마일 떨어져 있는 역들이 다른 시간대에 시계를 설정했다. 여행자들에게는 큰 혼란이 있었다.

| **정답해설** | ③ ⌊73%⌋ 지문 전체에서 시계(clock)의 출현과 발전에 대한 내용이 시간 순으로 이어지고 있다. 따라서 제시된 문장에 이어 시계가 처음으로(first) 등장했던 시기를 서술한 (B)가 처음에 오고, 이 문장에 언급된 mechanical clocks를 these clocks로 받아 문장을 시작한 (C)가 그 다음에 오는 것이 적절하다. (C)에는 1860년대의 미국이 매우 다른 시간대를 가지고 있다는 점을 언급했고, (A)에서는 이는 큰 불행이라고 언급하면서 여행자들에게 혼란을 초래했다는 결과가 이어졌으므로 마지막에 (A)가 와야 한다.

어휘

dominate 지배하다, 장악하다   fashionable 유행의, 최신식인
refer to 언급하다, 말하다   disaster 큰 불행, 재난, 재해

---

19 독해 > 글의 일관성 파악하기 > 주어진 문장의 삽입
[오답률 45%]   답 ④

| **해석** | 밀레니얼 세대는 자주 현대에, 가장 빈곤하고, 가장 재정적으로 부담을 지닌 세대라는 꼬리표가 달린다. 그들 중 많은 이들이 대학을 졸업해서 미국이 지금까지 본 것 중 가장 최악의 노동시장으로 진입했는데, 휘청

거릴 정도의 학자금 부채를 덤으로 짊어지고 말이다. 놀랄 것도 없이, 밀레니얼 세대는 인생에서 비슷한 단계에 X세대가 그랬던 것보다 부를 덜 쌓았는데, 주된 이유로는 집을 소유한 사람들이 거의 없기 때문이다. 그러나 지금까지 다른 세대의 미국인들이 무엇을 저축하는지에 대한 가장 상세한 그림을 제공하는 새롭게 이용 가능한 자료들은 그러한 평가를 복잡하게 한다. 그렇다, 1965년과 1980년 사이에 태어난 X세대들은 더 높은 순(純)자산을 가지고 있다. ④ 그러나 또한 1981년에서 1996년 사이에 태어난 밀레니얼 세대가 동일한 연령인 22세에서 37세에 X세대가 그랬던 것보다 더 공격적으로 은퇴를 위해 저축을 하고 있다는 분명한 증거가 있다. 그리고 그것은 많은 사람들이 생각하는 것보다 그들이 더 나은 재정 상태에 있게 할 것이다.

| **정답해설** | ④ ⌊55%⌋ 주어진 문장에서 역접의 접속사 But이 있으므로 이전의 내용과 주어진 문장의 내용은 대조적인 점을 고려한다. 이어진 문장에서 밀레니얼 세대가 공격적으로 저축을 하고 있다는 확실한 증거가 있다고 했으므로, 그 이전에는 밀레니얼 세대에 대한 부정적인 점이, 이후에는 공격적으로 저축을 하는 것에 대한 긍정적일 수 있는 결과가 이어져야 함을 알 수 있다. ④ 이전까지는 밀레니얼 세대보다 X세대가 물질적으로 더 나은 위치에 있다는 내용이 서술되고 있는데, ④에 이어지는 내용에서 사람들이 생각하는 것보다 더 나은 자산을 가지고 있을 수 있다고 했으므로, 마지막 문장의 them은 이미 물질적 풍요가 있는 X세대가 아닌 밀레니얼 세대를 지칭하는 것임을 알 수 있다. 따라서 정답은 ④이다.

어휘

millennials 밀레니얼, 1980~2000년 사이에 태어난 세대
label 꼬리표를 달다, ~라고 부르다   staggering 비틀거리는, 휘청거리는
to boot 덤으로, 게다가   accumulate 축적하다, 쌓아올리다
assessment 평가   net worth 순자산

---

20 독해 > 세부내용 찾기 > 내용 불일치 찾기   [오답률 22%]   답 ④

| **해석** | 수천 년 동안 산호와 다른 암초 생물의 분해로부터 쌓인 탄산염 모래는 산호초의 틀을 위한 건축 재료이다. 그러나 이 모래는 해수의 화학적 구성에 민감하다. 대양이 이산화탄소를 흡수하면서, 대양은 산성화되고, 어느 시점에서, 탄산염 모래는 용해되기 시작한다. 세계의 대양들은 인간이 방출하는 이산화탄소의 대략 3분의 1을 흡수해 왔다. 모래가 용해되는 속도는 위에 있는 해수의 산성화와 강력하게 관련이 있었고, 해양 산성화에 대한 산호의 성장보다 10배 더 민감했다. 다시 말해서, 해양 산성화는 산호의 성장보다 더 산호초 모래의 분해에 영향을 줄 것이다. 이것은 아마도 자신의 환경을 바꾸고 부분적으로 해양 산성화에 적응하는 산호의 능력을 반영할지도 모르지만, 반면에 모래의 분해는 적응할 수 없는 지구 화학적 과정이다.
① 산호초의 틀은 탄산염 모래로 만들어진다.
② 산호는 해양 산성화에 부분적으로 적응할 수 있다.
③ 인간이 방출한 이산화탄소는 세계 해양 산성화의 원인이 된다.
④ 해양 산성화는 산호초 모래의 분해보다 더 많이 산호의 성장에 영향을 미친다.

| **정답해설** | ④ ⌊78%⌋ 'In other words, ocean acidification will impact the dissolution of coral reef sands more than the growth of corals.'로 보아 ④의 내용이 일치하지 않음을 알 수 있다.

어휘

carbonate sands 탄산염 모래   breakdown 붕괴, 분해
coral 산호   dissolve 용해시키다, 분해하다
acidity 산성, 산도   acidification 산성화
adjust 조정하다, 조절하다   geochemical 지구 화학적인

2019
6월 15일 시행
지방직 9급 (Ⓐ책형)

합격예상 체크

〈지방직 연도별 합격선〉

맞힌 개수	/20문항	점수	/100점

➡ ☐합격 ☐불합격

취약영역 체크

문항	정답	영역	문항	정답	영역
1	①	어휘 > 동의어	11	④	어휘 > 동의어
2	①	어휘 > 동의어	12	①	어휘 > 동의어
3	④	생활영어 > 회화	13	③	독해 > 빈칸의 내용 추론하기
4	③	생활영어 > 회화	14	④	독해 > 빈칸의 내용 추론하기
5	④	문법 > 준동사	15	④	독해 > 글의 일관성 파악하기
6	②	문법 > 동사의 형태	16	③	문법 > 동사의 형태
7	②	독해 > 글의 일관성 파악하기	17	①	독해 > 세부내용 찾기
8	②	독해 > 세부내용 찾기	18	③	독해 > 세부내용 찾기
9	②	독해 > 대의 파악	19	①	독해 > 빈칸의 내용 추론하기
10	④	독해 > 글의 일관성 파악하기	20	②	독해 > 빈칸의 내용 추론하기

➡ 영역별 틀린 개수로 취약영역을 확인하세요!

어휘	/4	문법	/3	독해	/11	생활영어	/2

➡ 나의 취약영역: _____

※ [정답해설]과 [오답해설] 선지의 50% 표시는 〈1초 합격예측 서비스〉를 통해 수집된 선지 선택률을 나타냅니다.

---

1 어휘 > 동의어 오답률 43% 답 ①

| 해석 | 나는 이 문서들을 이제 죽어서 묻힌 감성적인 유물로 보게 되었는데, 그것은 발굴될 필요가 있었다.

① 57% 파내다, 발굴하다
② 9% 싸다, 묶다, 포장하다
③ 30% 지우다, 없애다
④ 4% 기념하다, 축하하다

| 정답해설 | ① 'I'는 문서들을 '유물'로 본다고 했고, 유물이나 유적은 발굴이 되어야 하는 것들이므로 excavated의 동의어로 exhume이 가장 적절하다. ex-는 '밖으로'의 의미이고, humus는 '흙, 땅'을 의미하므로 exhume은 '파다, 발굴하다'의 의미임을 유추할 수 있다.

어휘
excavate ∼을 파다, 발굴하다   relics 유물, 유적
sensibility 감성, 정서   bury 묻다

---

2 어휘 > 동의어 오답률 32% 답 ①

| 해석 | 롤러코스터를 타는 것은 감정적 난폭운전일 수 있다: 당신이 안전벨트를 맬 때 초조한 기대감, 당신이 위로, 위로, 위로 올라갈 때 오는 의문과 후회, 그리고 차가 첫 번째 하강할 때 몰려오는 완전한 아드레날린.

① 68% 완전한; 말하다
② 18% 무서운, 두려운
③ 10% 가끔의, 때때로의
④ 4% 관리할 수 있는; 다루기 쉬운

| 정답해설 | ① 롤러코스터를 탈 때, 과정에 따른 감정을 묘사하는 글이다. 롤러코스터가 올라갔다가 급격히 하강할 때 느낄 수 있는 감정을 생각해 보면, 아드레날린이 상당히 분출될 것을 알 수 있

다. 따라서 이 상황에 따른 adrenaline을 수식할 수 있는 형용사로 '완전한'의 의미인 utter가 동의어로 가장 적절하다.

어휘
sheer 순전한, 완전한   joy ride 드라이브, 난폭하게 운전하기
nervous 긴장되는, 불안한   anticipation 기대, 예상
strapped 끈으로 묶인

---

3 생활영어 > 회화 오답률 8% 답 ④

| 해석 | ① A: 우리 점심 몇 시에 먹나요?
B: 정오 전에 준비가 될 거예요.
② A: 당신에게 여러 차례 전화를 했어요. 왜 받지 않았죠?
  B: 오, 제 휴대폰이 꺼져 있었나 봐요.
③ A: 이번 겨울에 휴가를 가실 건가요?
  B: 아마도요. 아직 정하지 않았어요.
④ A: 안녕하세요. 당신의 전화를 못 받아서 죄송해요.
  B: 메시지를 남기시겠어요?

| 정답해설 | ④ 92% A가 전화를 받지 못한 것에 대해 사과하고 있는데, B는 메시지를 남길 것인지 물어보고 있으므로 대화의 흐름이 어색하다. 보통 사과를 하는 경우에는 '괜찮아요'의 표현으로 That's all right.가 적절하다.

어휘
turn off (전원을) 끄다   miss one's call 전화를 받지 못하다
leave a message 메시지를 남기다

| **4** | 생활영어 > 회화 | 오답률 35% | 답 ③ |

| **해석** | A: 안녕하세요. 돈을 약간 환전해야 해서요.

B: 네. 어떤 통화가 필요하세요?

A: 달러를 파운드로 바꾸려고요. 환율이 어떻게 되나요?

B: 환율은 1달러 당 0.73파운드입니다.

A: 좋네요. 수수료도 받으시나요?

B: 네, 4달러의 소액 수수료를 받습니다.

A: ③ 환매 방침은 어떻게 되나요?

B: 저희는 무료로 다시 환전을 해 드립니다. 영수증을 가지고 오시기만 하세요.

① 이것은 비용이 얼마나 드나요

② 이것에 대해 내가 얼마나 지불해야 하나요

③ 환매 방침은 어떻게 되나요

④ 신용카드를 받으시나요

| **정답해설** | ③ 65% 빈칸의 질문에 대한 답변으로 B가 무료로 환전을 해준다고 하면서 영수증을 가지고 오라고 했으므로, A는 환전한 돈을 다시 재환전할 때에 관해 물어봤음을 유추할 수 있다. 따라서 빈칸에는 되사기 정책에 관해 묻는 ③이 가장 적절하다.

어휘

exchange money 환전하다   currency 통화
convert A into B A를 B로 전환하다, 바꾸다
commission 수수료; 위임, 위탁   buy-back 매입, 되사기
receipt 영수증

| **5** | 문법 > 준동사 > 분사 | 오답률 21% | 답 ④ |

| **해석** | 매년, 27만 명이 넘는 보행자들이 전 세계의 도로에서 목숨을 잃는다. 많은 사람들이 언제나 그렇듯이 집을 떠나 다시는 돌아오지 않는다. 전 세계적으로 보행자들은 모든 도로 교통 사망자의 22%를 차지하고 일부 국가에서는 이 비율이 모든 도로 교통 사망자의 3분의 2만큼 높다. 수백만 명의 보행자들이 치명상을 당하지는 않지만, 그들 중 일부는 영구 장애로 남는다. 이런 사고들은 경제적 어려움뿐만 아니라 많은 고통과 슬픔을 야기한다.

| **정답해설** | ④ 79% injure는 '부상을 입히다'의 의미로 타동사이다. injuring은 능동형인데, 뒤에 목적어가 없고, 주어인 보행자들은 '부상을 입는' 것이므로 수동의 과거분사 injured로 바꿔야 한다.

| **오답해설** | ① 2% 주어는 pedestrians로 복수명사이므로 동사도 복수형으로 수일치가 올바르게 이루어졌다. 매년 발생하는 일을 언급하므로 현재의 사실을 전달하는 현재시제로 표현했다.

② 14% 이 문장에서 조동사 would 뒤에는 동사원형 leave가 생략되었고, 문맥상 자동사이므로 뒤에 이어진 to return은 to부정사의 부사적 용법임을 알 수 있다. 문맥상 부사 never와 함께 '결코 ~하지 않게 되다'이므로 부사적 용법의 '결과'의 표현으로 볼 수 있다.

③ 5% 동사 is에 이어진 보어로 형용사 high가 왔으며 동등비교의 구조로 표현되었다. 'as + 원급 + as'의 구조가 올바르다.

어휘

pedestrian 보행자; 평범한, 시시한   constitute 구성하다
fatality 사망자; 치사성; 운명   grief 슬픔, 비탄
hardship 고난, 어려움

| **6** | 문법 > 동사의 형태 > 수동태 | 오답률 55% | 답 ② |

| **해석** | ① 그 문서는 그녀 자신의 목적을 위해 회사 자금을 쓴 것에 대해 그녀를 비난했다.

② 의심을 불러일으키지 않도록 하기 위해 그 수사는 최대한 주의를 기울여 다루어져야 했다.

③ 과정의 속도를 내는 다른 방법은 새로운 시스템으로의 전환을 이룰 것이다.

④ 화석 연료를 연소하는 것이 기후 변화의 주요한 원인들 중 하나이다.

| **정답해설** | ② 45% 주절에 이어진 부사절이 '부정'의 의미가 포함된 목적부사절이다. 접속사 lest는 이미 not을 포함한 표현으로 긍정문이 뒤에 이어졌고, 이때 종속절의 동사는 'should + 동사원형'이 되어야 하는데, should는 생략이 가능하다. 따라서 should가 생략되고 수동태 동사가 남은 올바른 문장이다.

| **오답해설** | ① 8% charge A with B는 'A를 B라는 점에서 비난하다(책망하다)'의 표현이다. 전치사 with의 목적어로 use가 왔는데, 뒤에 명사 the company's money가 이어졌으므로 이를 목적어로 받을 수 있는 동명사 using으로 바꿔야 한다.

③ 22% 동사가 수동태(would be made)인데 뒤에 명사 the shift가 이어졌으므로 구조와 문맥상 능동태인 would make로 바꿔야 한다.

④ 25% '~들 중 하나'의 표현은 'one of the + 복수명사'이므로 cause는 복수명사인 causes로 바꿔야 한다. 또한 명사 cause를 수식하는 표현으로 lead보다는 현재분사 leading이 자연스럽다.

어휘

charge A with B A를 B로 비난하다 investigation 조사, 연구
utmost 최대한, 극도의

| **7** | 독해 > 글의 일관성 파악하기 > 글의 순서 | 오답률 59% | 답 ② |

| **해석** | 우리를 괴롭힐 수 있는 생각이 하나 있다: 모든 것이 아마도 다른 모든 것에 영향을 미치므로, 어떻게 우리가 사회 세계를 이해할 수 있을까? 하지만 우리가 그 걱정에 짓눌린다면, 우리는 결코 진전을 이루지 못할 것이다.

(A) 내가 익숙한 모든 학문은 그것을 이해하기 위해 세상에 대한 캐리커처를 그린다. 현대 경제학자는 모형들을 만듦으로써 이렇게 하는데, 그 모형들은 저 외부에 있는 현상에 대한 설명들이 의도적으로 제거되어져 있다.

(C) 내가 "제거되었다"라고 하면 정말로 제거된 것을 의미한다. 우리 경제학자들 사이에서는 현실의 그런 측면들이 어떻게 작용하고 상호 작용하는지 이해할 수 있게 해주기를 바라면서 한두 가지 인과적 요인들에 초점을 맞추고 다른 모든 것은 배제하는 것은 드문 일은 아니다.

(B) 경제학자인 존 메이너드 케인스는 우리의 논제를 이렇게 묘사했다: "경제학은 현 시대와 관련된 모형을 선택하는 기술과 결합된 모형의 관점에서 생각하는 과학이다."

| **정답해설** | ② 41% 제시문에서 우리가 사회 세계를 어떻게 이해할 수 있을지에 대한 의문을 던지고, (A)에서 이에 대한 필자가 친숙한 규율을 서술하고 있다. 제시문의 make sense of the social world를 (A)에서 in order to make sense of it으로 받았으므로 (A)가 먼저 오는 것이 자연스럽다. 필자의 생각을 전개한 (C)가 이어진 이후, 이 주제에 대해 설명한 경제학자의 말을 인용해 내용을 마무리하는 (B)가 이어지는 것이 적절하므로 정답은 ②이다.

어휘

haunt 괴롭히다; 머리에서 떠나지 않다
make sense of ~을 이해하다 　　discipline 학문; 규율; 훈육
deliberately 의도적으로, 고의로
strip (down) A of B A로부터 B를 제거하다
relevant 관련된 　　　　　　contemporary 현대의; 동시대의
causal 원인의, 인과관계의

---

8 독해 > 세부내용 찾기 > 내용 일치 찾기　오답률 9%　답 ②

| 해석 | 대략 50만 년 전, 선사시대 사회는 정신적 장애와 신체적 장애를 명확히 구별하지 않았다. 단순한 두통에서 경련성 발작까지 비정상적인 행동은 고통 받는 사람의 몸에 살거나 통제하는 악령들의 탓으로 여겨졌다. 역사가들에 의하면, 이 고대인들은 많은 형태의 병을 악령에 사로잡힘, 주술, 또는 분노한 조상 영혼의 명령의 탓으로 돌렸다. '악마학'이라 불리는 이러한 믿음 체계 속에서, 희생자는 보통 적어도 그 불행에 대해 일부 책임을 져야 했다. 석기 시대의 동굴인들은 천공이라고 하는 외과수술법으로 행동 장애를 치료했을지도 모른다고 제기되었는데, 이 수술에서 악령이 빠져나갈 수 있는 구멍을 만들기 위해 두개골의 일부가 잘려나갔다. 사람들은 악령이 떠날 때, 그 사람은 자신의 정상적인 상태로 돌아올 거라 믿었을지도 모른다. 놀랍게도, 천공이 있는 두개골은 치유된 것으로 밝혀졌는데, 이는 일부 환자들이 이 극도로 조잡한 수술에서 살아 남았다는 걸 나타낸다.
① 정신적 장애는 명백히 신체적 장애와 구별되었다.
② 비정상적인 행동은 한 개인에게 영향을 주는 악령이 원인이라고 믿어졌다.
③ 두개골에는 악령이 사람의 몸에 들어가도록 구멍이 만들어졌다.
④ 어떤 동굴인들도 천공으로부터 생존하지 못했다.

| 정답해설 | ② 91% 두 번째 문장 'Abnormal behaviors, from simple headaches to convulsive attacks, were attributed to evil spirits'를 통해 ②가 내용과 일치함을 알 수 있다.

어휘

prehistoric 선사시대의 　　　　distinguish 구별하다
attack 발병; 공격; 비난
attribute A to B A를 B의 탓으로 돌리다
afflict 괴롭히다 　　　　　　demonic 악령의
sorcery 마법, 마술 　　　　　behest 명령, 지령
offended 노한, 기분이 상한 　　trephine 천공하다
crude 조잡한, 거친

---

9 독해 > 대의 파악 > 주제 찾기　오답률 38%　답 ②

| 해석 | 디지털 혁명이 전국의 뉴스룸에 근본적인 변화를 일으키게 됨에 따라, 기자들에게 주는 나의 조언이 있다. 나는 25년 동안 기자였기 때문에 여섯 번 정도의 기술적 라이프 사이클을 겪었다. 가장 극적인 변화들은 지난 6년 동안에 왔다. 이는 내가 더욱 잦은 빈도로 진행하면서 뭔가를 만들어가고 있음을 의미한다. 뉴스 업계에 있어 많은 시간 동안 우리는 우리가 무엇을 하고 있는지 알지 못한다. 우리는 아침에 출근을 하고, 누군가는 "세금 정책, 이민, 기후 변화에 관해(하나를 골라서) 글을 써주시겠습니까?"라고 말한다. 신문들이 하루에 한 번씩 마감이 있었을 때, 우리는 기자는 아침에는 배우고 밤에는 가르친다고 말했다 – 그 기자가 약 24시간 전에는 알지 못했던 주제에 관해 내일의 독자들에게 알려주는 기사를 쓰는 것 말이다. 이제 이것은 오히려 마치 정시에는 배우고 30분에는 가르치는 것에 가깝다. 예를 들어, 나는 또한 정치 팟캐스트를 운영 중이고, 대통령 전당대회 동안, 우리는 어느 곳에서나 실시간 인터뷰를 하기 위해 그것을 사용해야만 한다. 나는 그저 점점 더 대본 없이 일하고 있다.
① 교사로서의 기자

② 기자와 즉흥성
③ 정치학에서의 기술
④ 저널리즘과 기술의 분야들

| 정답해설 | ② 62% 필자는 언론인으로서 디지털 혁명으로 인한 변화를 겪으며 느끼는 소회를 서술하고 있다. 과거에는 하루에 한번 마감을 하고, 아침에는 배우고 밤에는 기사를 썼지만, 현재는 팟캐스트를 운영하면서 대본 없이 일하고 있다고 서술하고 있으므로 가장 적절한 주제는 ②이다.

어휘

transformation 변화; 전환 　　　top of the hour 정시
bottom of the hour 30분
presidential convention 대통령 전당대회

오답률 TOP 3
10 독해 > 글의 일관성 파악하기 > 글의 흐름과 무관한 문장
　오답률 63%　답 ④

| 해석 | 역사상 아이들의 놀이터는 시골의 황야, 들판, 개울과 언덕, 그리고 마을과 시내, 도시의 도로, 거리, 그리고 공터였다. 놀이터라는 용어는 아이들이 자유롭고 자발적인 게임을 하기 위해 모인 모든 장소를 말한다. 불과 지난 수십 년 동안 아이들은 비디오 게임, 문자, 그리고 소셜 네트워크에 대한 열광이 커짐에 따라 이런 자연적인 놀이터가 비어졌다. 미국 시골에서조차 어른을 동반하지 않은 채, 자유로운 방식으로 돌아다니는 아이들은 거의 없다. ④ 학교 밖에 있을 때, 아이들은 모래를 파거나, 요새를 짓고, 전통 게임을 하고, 등산하거나, 혹은 공놀이를 하면서 동네에서 흔히 발견된다. 그들은 계곡, 언덕 그리고 들판의 자연적 지형에서 빠르게 사라지고 있고 도시 아이들과 마찬가지로, 오락을 위해 실내에서 앉아 하는 사이버 장난감으로 눈을 돌리고 있다.

| 정답해설 | ④ 37% 핵심어는 아이들의 놀이터(children's playgrounds)로 시대를 거쳐 놀이터의 장소나 형태가 달라지는 모습을 서술하는 지문이다. ④는 아이들의 놀이터가 아닌 아이들이 동네 밖에서 하는 여러 가지 놀이에 대해 구체적으로 서술하고 있으므로 글의 흐름과 일치하지 않는 문장이다.

어휘

refer to ~을 말하다, 언급하다 　spontaneous 자발적인, 자연스러운
roam 돌아다니다, 배회하다 　　　range 방목하다
terrain 지형, 지세 　　　　　　counterpart 상대방, 대응하는 대상
turn to ~에 의지하다 　　　　　sedentary 앉은 자세의, 앉아 지내는

---

11 어휘 > 동의어　오답률 45%　답 ④

| 해석 | 지겨운 오후 강의 도중에는 시간이 천천히 흐르는 것 같으며 뇌가 큰 즐거움을 주는 일에 몰두할 때에는 시간이 빨리 흐르는 것으로 느껴진다.
① 25% 강화된 　　　　　② 11% 무관심한
③ 9% 안정된 　　　　　④ 55% 열중하는

| 정답해설 | ④ 시간의 상대성에 대한 내용으로 지겨운 오후 강의는 시간이 천천히 흐른다고 했으므로, 시간이 빠르게 흐르는 경우는 뇌가 즐거움을 주는 일에 '몰두할' 때임을 유추할 수 있다. 따라서 engrossed in의 동의어로 preoccupied with가 가장 적절하다.

어휘

engross 몰두시키다, 열중시키다 　trickle 느릿느릿한 움직임
lecture 강의 　　　　　　　　enhance 강화하다, 향상시키다

apathetic 무관심한, 냉담한
stabilize 안정시키다; ~을 일정한 수준으로 유지하다
preoccupy 열중하게 하다, ~의 마음을 빼앗다

---

12 어휘 > 동의어 ⌈오답률 53%⌉ 답 ①

| 해석 | 정부가 독자들을 통제하고자 시도함에 따라 이러한 일일 업데이트는 그들이 시장을 따라잡는 것을 돕기 위해 만들어졌다.
① ⌈47%⌉ ~에 정통하다, 잘 알다
② ⌈12%⌉ ~에 영감을 받다
③ ⌈22%⌉ ~을 믿고 있다
④ ⌈19%⌉ ~를 멀리하다, 가까이 하지 않다

| 정답해설 | ① 일일 업데이트가 독자들로 하여금 시장 상황과 관련해 도움을 주기 위해 만들어졌다고 했으므로, keep abreast of의 의미는 '~에 뒤지지 않다'의 의미임을 유추할 수 있다. acquaint는 '정통하게 하다, 알리다'의 의미이므로 be acquainted with가 동의어로 가장 적절하다.

어휘
keep abreast of ~에 뒤지지 않고 따라가다

---

13 독해 > 빈칸의 내용 추론하기 > 빈칸 어휘 추론 ⌈오답률 9%⌉ 답 ③

| 해석 | 1840년대에 아일랜드 섬은 기근에 시달렸다. 아일랜드는 인구를 먹일 충분한 식량을 생산할 수 없었기 때문에 약 백만 명의 사람들이 (A) 기아로 죽었다; 그들은 단지 살아남기 위해 먹을 것이 충분하지 않았다. 이 기근은 또 다른 125만 명의 사람들이 (B) 이민을 가도록 야기했다; 많은 사람들은 그들의 고향 섬에서 미국으로 떠났다; 나머지는 캐나다, 호주, 칠레, 그리고 다른 나라들로 갔다. 기근 전에 아일랜드의 인구는 약 6백만 명이었다. 엄청난 식량 부족 후에 약 4백만이 되었다.

	(A)	(B)
①	탈수	추방되다
②	트라우마	이민 오다
③	기아	이민 가다
④	피로	구류되다

| 정답해설 | ③ ⌈91%⌉ (A)에는 빈칸 앞에서 충분한 식량을 생산할 수 없었으므로 죽음의 원인은 starvation임을 알 수 있다. (B)에는 빈칸에 이어진 서술에서 미국, 캐나다, 호주, 칠레 등의 다른 나라로 이주했다는 내용이 이어지므로 emigrate가 적절하다.

어휘
famine 기근
starvation 기아; 궁핍
immigrate 이민하다, 와서 살다
detain 붙들다; 구류하다
dehydration 탈수; 건조
deport 추방하다
emigrate 이민가다

---

14 독해 > 빈칸의 내용 추론하기 > 연결어 추론 ⌈오답률 45%⌉ 답 ④

| 해석 | 오늘날 가상 현실(VR) 경험의 시각적 요소를 만드는 기술은 널리 접근 가능하고 저렴한 방향으로 진척되고 있다. 하지만 강하게 작용하기 위해서는, 가상 현실은 시각적인 것 이상의 것이 필요하다. 여러분이 듣고 있는 것이 설득력 있게 보고 있는 것과 부합하지 (A) 않는다면, 가상의 경험은 무너진다. 농구 시합을 예로 들어보자. 만약 선수, 코치, 아나운서, 그리고 관중이 모두 코트 가운데에 앉아 있는 것처럼 들린다면, 텔레비전으로 경기를 보는 게 더 낫다. – 당신은 "거기"에 있다는 느낌만을 가지게 될 것이다.
(B) 유감스럽게도, 오늘날의 음향 기기와 널리 사용되는 녹음과 재생 방식은 먼 행성의 전장, 코트사이드의 농구 시합, 혹은 거대한 공연장의 첫 번째 줄에서 들리는 교향곡 소리를 설득력 있게 재현하는 작업에 그저 적절하지 않다.

	(A)	(B)
①	~라면	반대로
②	~하지 않으면	결과적으로
③	~라면	유사하게
④	~하지 않으면	유감스럽게도

| 정답해설 | ④ ⌈55%⌉ (A)에는 이어지는 주절에서 가상의 경험이 무너진다는 부정적인 내용이 이어지므로 듣고 있는 것이 보고 있는 것과 부합하지 '않아야' 의미가 자연스럽다. 따라서 부정의 의미를 담은 조건절을 이끄는 접속사인 unless가 적절하다. (B)에는 빈칸 앞에서 가상 현실의 경험을 통해 농구 경기장에 있는 듯한 경험을 한다면 텔레비전으로 경기를 보아도 된다고 했지만 빈칸에 이어진 문장에서는 기술이 재현을 하는데 부적합하다고 했으므로, 아쉬움을 전달하는 부사 Unfortunately가 적절하다.

어휘
affordable 입수 가능한; (가격 등이) 알맞은
inadequate 부적절한, 불충분한

---

15 독해 > 글의 일관성 파악하기 > 주어진 문장의 삽입 ⌈오답률 34%⌉ 답 ④

| 해석 | 행복한 두뇌는 단기간에 집중하는 경향이 있다. 사정이 그렇다면, 최종적으로 장기 목표를 달성하는 데에 어떤 단기 목표를 달성할 수 있을지를 고려하는 것은 좋은 생각이다. 예를 들어, 만약 여러분이 6개월 안에 30파운드를 빼기를 원한다면, 여러분은 어떤 단기 목표를 거기에(최종 감량) 도달하게 할 더 작은 무게 증가량을 빼는 것과 연관 지을 수 있는가? 아마 그것은 매주 2파운드를 뺄 때마다 당신 스스로에게 보상하는 것만큼 간단한 일일 것이다. ④ 그와 동일한 생각이 직장에서 성과를 향상하는 것과 같은 어느 목표에도 적용될 수 있다. 전체적인 목표를 더 작고 단기적인 부분으로 나눔으로써, 우리는 직업에서 목표의 거대함에 압도되는 대신 점진적인 성취에 초점을 맞출 수 있다.

| 정답해설 | ④ ⌈66%⌉ 제시문의 'the same thinking'에 대한 구체적인 내용이 마무리되는 부분을 찾아야 하는데, 장기 목표를 세울 때 단기 목표에 대해 생각해야 한다는 내용에 이어 체중을 빼는 것에 대한 사례가 이어지고 있다. 이 사례를 제시문의 'the same thinking'으로 받아 직업으로 연결했으므로 정답은 ④이다.

어휘
apply 적용하다
that being the case 이러한 실정이니
associate A with B A를 B와 연관시키다
increment 증가량
overwhelmed 압도된
rewarding 보람 있는
profession 직업, 직종

16 문법 > 동사의 형태 > 수동태 　오답률 27%　답 ③

| 정답해설 | ③ 73% marry는 타동사이므로 전치사와 함께 쓸 수 없다. 따라서 has married to를 has married나 has been married to로 바꿔야 한다. for more than two decades와 호응하는 시제로 현재완료로 표현한 것은 올바르다.

| 오답해설 | ① 6% '~하고 싶은 경우'의 표현으로 구접속사 in case (that)로 올바르게 표현되었다.

② 14% '~하느라 바쁘다'의 표현으로 'be busy R-ing'로 적절하게 표현되었다.

④ 7% to부정사의 형용사적 용법으로 to read가 명사 a book을 수식하고 있으며, to부정사의 의미상의 주어로 for my son이 삽입된 올바른 문장이다.

어휘
be busy R-ing ~하느라 바쁘다　　decade 10년

17 독해 > 세부내용 찾기 > 내용 불일치 찾기 　오답률 20%　답 ①

| 해석 | 19세기에 가장 존경 받는 건강 및 의료 전문가들 모두 질병은 나쁜 공기에 대한 근사한 용어인 "미아즈마(독기)"에 의해 야기되었다고 주장했다. 서구 사회의 건강관리 체계는 이런 추정을 기반으로 했다: 질병을 예방하기 위해, 창문은 방 안 혹은 밖에 더 많은 미아즈마가 있는지에 따라 열려 있거나 닫혀 있었다; 신사는 나쁜 공기가 있는 지역에 살지 않으므로 의사들은 질병을 옮길 수 없다고 믿어졌다. 그 이후 세균에 대한 개념이 나타났다. 어느 날, 모든 사람들은 나쁜 공기가 당신을 아프게 한다고 믿었다. 그러고 나서 거의 하룻밤 사이에, 사람들은 질병의 진짜 원인인 미생물과 박테리아라 불리는 보이지 않는 것들이 존재한다는 것을 인식하기 시작했다. 이런 질병에 대한 새로운 관점은 외과 의사들이 소독제를 채택하고 과학자들이 백신과 항생제를 발명함에 따라 의학에 엄청난 변화들을 가져왔다. 하지만 그만큼 중요하게, 세균에 대한 개념은 일반 사람들에게 그들 자신의 삶에 영향을 주는 힘을 주었다. 이제, 건강을 유지하고 싶다면, 손을 씻고 물을 끓이고 음식을 철저히 조리하고 그리고 베인 상처와 찰과상을 아이오딘으로 닦으면 된다.

① 19세기에 창문을 여는 것은 미아즈마의 밀도와 무관했다.

② 19세기에 신사들은 나쁜 공기가 있는 곳에서 살지 않는다고 믿었다.

③ 백신은 사람들이 미생물과 박테리아가 질병의 진짜 원인이라는 것을 깨달은 후에 발명되었다.

④ 상처와 찰과상을 닦는 건 사람들이 건강을 유지하는 데 도움을 줄 수 있다.

| 정답해설 | ① 80% 두 번째 문장 'to prevent diseases, windows were kept open or closed, depending on whether there was more miasma inside or outside the room~'을 통해 창을 기준으로 실내 혹은 실외의 미아즈마가 더 많거나 적다고 생각했음을 알 수 있으므로 ①은 지문과 일치하지 않는다.

어휘
fancy 근사한, 화려한　　　　assumption 가정, 추정
inhabit 거주하다, 서식하다　　invisible 눈에 보이지 않는
antiseptics 소독제　　　　momentously 긴히, 중요하게
thoroughly 철저히　　　　scrape 긁힌 자국, 생채기
iodine 아이오딘, 요오드

18 독해 > 세부내용 찾기 > 내용 불일치 찾기 　오답률 13%　답 ③

| 해석 | 추종자들은 리더십 등식의 중요한 부분이지만 그들의 역할이 항상 인정받는 것은 아니다. 사실 오랫동안 "리더십의 흔한 관점은 리더가 적극적으로 주도하고 나중에 추종자라고 불리는 부하들이 수동적이고 순종적으로 따르는 것이다." 시간이 지나면서 특히 지난 세기에는 사회적 변화가 추종자에 대한 사람들의 관점들을 형성했고 리더십 이론들은 추종자들이 리더십 과정에서 수행하는 점진적으로 적극적이고 중요한 역할을 인식했다. 오늘날 추종자들이 수행하는 중요한 역할을 받아들이는 것이 자연스러워 보인다. 리더십의 한 측면은 특히 이와 관련하여 주목할 만하다: 리더십은 한 그룹의 모든 구성원들 사이에서 공유되는 사회적 영향 과정이다. 리더십은 특정한 위치나 역할에 있는 누군가가 가하는 영향에만 국한되지 않는다; 추종자들도 리더십 과정의 일부이다.

① 오랜 기간 동안 리더는 적극적으로 주도하고 추종자들이 수동적으로 따랐던 것으로 이해되었다.

② 부하에 대한 사람들의 관점은 사회 변화에 의해 영향을 받았다.

③ 추종자들의 중요한 역할은 오늘날에도 여전히 부정되고 있다.

④ 리더와 추종자들 둘 다 리더십 과정에 참여한다.

| 정답해설 | ③ 87% 'Today it seems natural to accept the important role followers play.'로 보아 오늘날에도 추종자들에 대한 중요한 역할을 인정하고 있음을 알 수 있으므로 ③은 지문과 일치하지 않는다.

어휘
equation 등식, 방정식　　　subordinate 부하, 하급자
obediently 고분고분하게, 공손하게　exert (힘·능력 등을) 발휘하다

오답률 TOP 1
19 독해 > 빈칸의 내용 추론하기 > 빈칸 어구 추론 　오답률 66%　답 ①

| 해석 | 엄밀한 의미에서의 언어는 그 자체로 이중적인 층을 이룬다. 단일 소음은 그저 가끔씩 의미가 있다: 대부분 다양한 말소리는 다른 색의 아이스크림이 녹아서 서로 섞이는 것처럼, 혼합되어 겹쳐지는 사슬이 될 때에만 논리적인 메시지를 전달한다. 새소리에서도 ① 개별적인 음조는 종종 거의 가치가 없다. 순서가 중요하다. 인간과 조류 둘 다에서, 이 특화된 음성 체계의 통제는 뇌의 절반, 보통 왼쪽 부분에 의해 행해지고 이 체계는 비교적 삶의 초기에 학습된다. 그리고 많은 인간의 언어들이 방언을 가지고 있는 것처럼 몇몇 새 종들도 그렇다: 캘리포니아에서는 흰관참새가 지역마다 너무 다른 노랫소리를 가지고 있어서 캘리포니아 사람들은 이 참새의 소리를 들어 보면 그들이 그 주의 어디에 있는지 알 수 있을 것이다.

① 개별적인 음조는 종종 거의 가치가 없다

② 리듬감 있는 소리가 중요하다

③ 방언은 중요한 역할을 한다

④ 음향 장치는 존재하지 않는다

| 정답해설 | ① 34% 엄밀한 의미에서 언어에 대한 정의를 내린 후 단일 소음이 가끔씩만 의미가 있을 뿐이라고 했고, 다양한 말소리는 아이스크림의 비유를 들어 설명하고 있다. 이때 아이스크림이 녹아서 서로 섞이는 것을 언어에서는 혼합되었을 때 논리적인 메시지를 전달한다고 했으므로 정답은 ①이 되며, 빈칸 이후에는 이에 대한 구체적인 사례로 흰관참새를 들어 서술하고 있다.

어휘
proper (명사 뒤에서) 엄밀한 의미에서, 진정한; 적합한
overlap 겹치다, 포개다　　　sequence 순서, 배열
sparrow 참새

| 해석 | 노벨상 수상자인 심리학자 다니엘 카네만은 인간이 이상적인 의사결정자라는 개념을 뒤집으면서 경제학에 대한 세계의 사고방식을 변화시켰다. 그 과정에서 그의 학문을 넘나드는 영향력은 의사들이 의학적 결정을 내리고 투자자들이 월 가(街)에서 위험을 평가하는 방식을 바꾸었다. 한 논문에서 카네만과 그의 동료들은 큰 전략적 결정을 내리는 과정의 개요를 잡았다. "중재 평가 프로토콜" 혹은 MAP로 명시된 이들이 제시한 접근법은 간단한 목표를 지닌다: 선택이 많은 개별 요인들에 의해 알려질 수 있을 때까지 배짱을 기반으로 한 의사결정을 미루는 것. "MAP의 본질적 목표 중 하나는 기본적으로 직관을 ② 미루는 것이다."라고 카네만이 '더 포스트'와의 최근 인터뷰에서 말했다. 구조화된 과정은 이전에 택해진 여섯 개에서 일곱 개의 속성을 바탕으로 분석하고, 각각에 대해 별도로 논의하고, 상대적 백분위 점수를 할당하고, 그리고 그러한 점수를 이용하여 전체론적 판단을 내리는 것을 요구한다.

① 개선하다　　　　　　② 미루다
③ 소유하다　　　　　　④ 수월하게 하다

| 정답해설 | ② 36% 심리학자 다니엘 카네만의 새로운 개념이 경제학뿐만 아니라 다른 분야에도 영향을 미쳤다는 내용에 이어 그의 구체적인 이론으로 큰 전략적 결정을 내리는 과정을 서술하고 있는 글이다. 빈칸 이전에 이에 대한 설명에서 그의 접근법의 목표는 배짱을 기반으로 한(gut-based) 의사결정을 미루는(put off) 것이라고 했으므로, 빈칸에는 put off와 동일한 표현인 delay가 적절하다. 따라서 정답은 ②이다.

어휘

upend 뒤엎다
strategic 전략적인
put off ~을 연기하다, 미루다
intuition 직관
holistic 전체론의, 전체론적인

outline 요점을 말하다; 윤곽을 그리다
mediate 중재하다, 조정하다
gut 배짱, 용기; 내장
attribute 특성, 속성

합격예상 체크

〈지방직 연도별 합격선〉

2018 합격기준!

맞힌 개수	/20문항	점수	/100점

➡ ☐ 합격 ☐ 불합격

취약영역 체크

문항	정답	영역	문항	정답	영역
1	①	어휘 > 동의어	11	②	생활영어 > 회화
2	②	어휘 > 동의어	12	①	독해 > 대의 파악
3	④	문법 > 연결사	13	②	독해 > 글의 일관성 파악하기
4	④	문법 > 준동사	14	①	생활영어 > 회화
5	④	어휘 > 동의어	15	④	독해 > 빈칸의 내용 추론하기
6	③	어휘 > 빈칸	16	③	독해 > 대의 파악
7	②	문법 > 동사의 형태	17	①	독해 > 빈칸의 내용 추론하기
8	①	문법 > 동사의 형태	18	①	독해 > 세부내용 찾기
9	③	독해 > 글의 일관성 파악하기	19	①	독해 > 글의 일관성 파악하기
10	②	독해 > 대의 파악	20	①	독해 > 빈칸의 내용 추론하기

⬇ 영역별 틀린 개수로 취약영역을 확인하세요!

어휘	/4	문법	/4	독해	/10	생활영어	/2

➡ 나의 취약영역: _____

※ [정답해설]과 [오답해설] 선지의 ▢50% 표시는 〈1초 합격예측 서비스〉를 통해 수집된 선지 선택률을 나타냅니다.

1	어휘 > 동의어	오답률 20%	답 ①

| 해석 | 의사의 가장 중요한 임무는 해를 끼치지 않는 것이다. 다른 어떤 것도 — 심지어 치료조차도 — 그것만큼 중요하지 않다.
① ▢80% 최고의, 주요한   ② ▢8% 맹세한, 선서한
③ ▢9% 성공한, 잘된   ④ ▢3% 신비의, 불가사의한

| 정답해설 | ① 의사의 가장 중요한 임무는 해를 끼치지 않는 것이라고 했으므로 paramount의 의미와 동일한 것은 '최고의'의 의미인 chief가 가장 적절하다.

▢어휘

paramount 최고의, 가장 중요한   duty 임무, 직무
physician 의사
take second place ~에 비해서 그렇게 중요하지 않다

2	어휘 > 동의어	오답률 20%	답 ②

| 해석 | 북극으로 여행하는 것에 대해 사람들이 두려워하는 것은 이상한 것이 아니다.
① ▢7% 야망을 품다   ② ▢80% 두려워하다
③ ▢11% 기진맥진하다   ④ ▢2% 슬퍼하다

| 정답해설 | ② get cold feet을 직역하면 '발이 얼다'의 의미이다. 추운 날씨로 인해 발이 얼 수도 있지만, 추운 지방인 북극으로 가는 여행에 대해 사람들이 가질 수 있는 생각을 고려해 보면, '두려워서 꼼짝 못하다'의 의미임을 유추할 수 있다. 따라서 become afraid가

정답이다.

▢어휘

get cold feet 겁을 먹다, 긴장하다   unusual 특별한, 이상한

3	문법 > 연결사 > 관계사	오답률 26%	답 ④

| 해석 | 나는 Mrs. Ferrer의 신원 보증에 대한 당신의 요청에 대한 회신으로 글을 씁니다. 그녀는 지난 3년간 나의 비서로 일했고 훌륭한 직원이었습니다. 나는 그녀가 당신의 직무 내용 설명서에서 언급된 모든 요건들을 충족하고, 많은 면에서 그것들을 능가할 것이라 믿습니다. 나는 그녀의 완벽함을 의심할 만한 이유가 전혀 없습니다. 따라서 당신이 광고하는 그 자리에 대해 Mrs. Ferrer를 추천하는 바입니다.

| 정답해설 | ④ ▢74% 명사 post에 이어 관계대명사 what이 이끄는 명사절은 올 수 없다. 따라서 post를 수식하는 형용사절을 이끌면서 타동사 advertise의 목적어가 없는 불완전한 절을 이끌 수 있는 관계대명사 that 혹은 which로 바꿔야 한다.

| 오답해설 | ① ▢4% 일정 시간을 나타내는 표현으로 현재완료로 표현된 동사 has worked와 적절하게 호응한다.
② ▢9% 명사 requirements를 수식하는 과거분사로 문맥상 요구 조건들이 '언급되어지는' 것이므로 올바른 표현이다.
③ ▢13% 명사 reason을 수식하는 to부정사의 형용사적 용법이다.

▢어휘

reference 추천인, 추천서   exceed 능가하다

| **4** | 문법 > 준동사 > 분사 | 오답률 30% | 답 ④ |

| **정답해설** | ④ 70% 분사구문의 생략된 주어는 날씨를 나타내는 비인칭 주어 it이고, 이어진 문장의 주어 I와 일치하지 않으므로 독립분사구문으로 표현해야 한다. 따라서 It being cold outside로 바꿔야 한다.

| **오답해설** | ① 11% 'all of the + 명사'가 주어로 오면 동사의 수는 명사에 일치시켜야 한다. information은 셀 수 없는 명사이므로 단수 동사인 was로 수일치가 올바르게 이루어졌다.

② 10% '~했어야만 했는데'의 표현은 'should have + p.p.'이므로 주어진 우리말과 일치하는 표현이다.

③ 9% 도착한 시점보다 영화가 시작한 것이 이전 시점이므로 과거완료인 had started로 올바르게 표현되었다.

어휘

false 거짓의, 허위의   apologize 사죄하다, 사과하다

오답률 TOP1

| **5** | 어휘 > 동의어 | 오답률 64% | 답 ④ |

| **해석** | 최첨단 접근이 두렵다고 느끼는 학생은 그가 구식의 방식들로 배울 수 있었을지도 모르는 것보다 덜 배운다.

① 5% 우스운, 유머러스한   ② 37% 친화적인, 친절한
③ 22% 편리한, 간편한   ④ 36% 무서운, 위협적인

| **정답해설** | intimidating은 관계대명사의 목적보어로, 목적어인 the state-of-the-art approach를 서술해야 한다. 동사가 '덜 배운다'이므로, intimidating은 부정적인 의미임을 유추할 수 있고, 주어진 선지에서 ④를 제외한 나머지는 모두 긍정적인 의미이다. 따라서 정답은 '무서운'의 뜻인 frightening이 가장 적절하다. intimidating은 '겁먹게 하는'의 의미이다.

어휘

intimidating 겁먹게 하는, 협박하는
state-of-the-art 최첨단 기술을 이용한
approach 접근, 접근법

| **6** | 어휘 > 빈칸 | 오답률 42% | 답 ③ |

| **해석** | 에어컨이 현재 수리중이기 때문에, 사무실 직원들은 오늘 선풍기로 ③ 변통해야 한다.

① 23% 제거하다
② 13% ~을 놓다, ~에서 손을 놓다
③ 58% 변통하다, 때우다
④ 6% ~와 관계를 끊다

| **정답해설** | ③ 접속사 since가 이끄는 '이유' 부사절에서 에어컨이 수리중이라고 했으므로, 사무실 직원들은 에어컨 대신 선풍기로 지내야 함을 유추할 수 있다. 따라서 '변통하다'의 표현인 make do with가 빈칸에 들어갈 것으로 가장 적절하다.

어휘

electric fan 선풍기

| **7** | 문법 > 동사의 형태 > 가정법 | 오답률 33% | 답 ② |

| **해석** | ① 부디 내가 지난주에 당신에게 준 이메일 주소로 나에게 연락하세요.

② 물이 없다면, 지구상의 모든 살아 있는 동물들이 멸종할 텐데.

③ 노트북 컴퓨터는 사무실에서 멀리 떨어져 있는 사람들이 계속해서 작업을 할 수 있도록 한다.

④ 그들이 실수를 더 많이 설명하려고 하면 할수록 그들이 하는 이야기는 더욱 안 좋게 들렸다.

| **정답해설** | ② 67% 가정법 과거시제의 문장으로 조건절에서 if가 생략되면서 주어 it과 동사 were가 도치된 문장이다. 조건절의 동사는 were, 주절의 동사는 would be로 시제일치가 올바르다.

| **오답해설** | ① 9% contact는 타동사이므로 전치사 to 없이 목적어 me를 바로 받아야 한다

③ 15% 5형식 문장으로 불완전타동사 allow와 호응하는 목적보어로 to부정사인 to continue가 올바르게 이어졌다. 이때 목적어인 people을 주격 관계대명사 who가 이끄는 형용사절이 수식하고 있고 who에 이어지는 동사의 수는 people에 일치시켜 복수 동사인 are로 바꿔야 한다.

④ 9% 'the 비교급 주어 + 동사~, the 비교급 주어 + 동사~'의 구문으로 worst는 최상급의 표현이므로 worse로 바꿔야 한다.

어휘

extinct 멸종된

| **8** | 문법 > 동사의 형태 > 시제 | 오답률 37% | 답 ① |

| **정답해설** | ① 63% 과거를 나타내는 부사구인 a few days ago와 호응하여 동사가 과거로 올바르게 표현되었으며 'to see off~'는 to부정사의 부사적 용법으로 주어진 우리말과 일치하는 표현이다. see off는 '배웅하다'의 의미를 지닌 타동사구이다.

| **오답해설** | ② 8% '~인 체하다'의 표현은 make believe이다. 따라서 it을 삭제해야 한다.

③ 21% 'look forward to R-ing'의 표현으로 to는 전치사이므로 go를 going으로 바꿔야 한다.

④ 8% anything은 '흥미를 주는' 것이므로 능동의 의미를 지닌 현재분사 interesting으로 바꿔야 한다.

어휘

see off 배웅하다   spoiled 버릇없는
make believe ~인 체하다
look forward to R-ing ~를 기대하다, 고대하다

| **9** | 독해 > 글의 일관성 파악하기 > 글의 흐름과 무관한 문장 | 오답률 21% | 답 ③ |

| **해석** | 르네상스 시대의 주방은 정교한 연회를 만들기 위해 함께 일하는 일손에 대한 분명한 위계질서가 있었다. 맨 위에는 우리가 본 바대로, 주방뿐만 아니라 식당을 책임지고 있는 scalco, 혹은 급사장이 있었다. 식당은 집사에 의해 지휘되는데, 그는 은식기와 식탁보를 담당하고, 연회의 처음부터 끝까지 — 처음에는 차가운 요리, 샐러드, 치즈, 그리고 과일 등 전채요리부터 음식의 끝에는 당과 등의 후식까지 — 요리를 차려내는 역할을 한다. ③ 이 정교한 장식과 서빙은 식당에서 '고객 접대하는 영업부서(the front of

the house)'라고 불린다. 주방은 보조 요리사와 빵과 과자 요리사, 주방 보조를 이끄는 주방장에 의해 지휘된다.

| **정답해설** | ③ [79%] 첫 문장을 통해 지문이 전체적으로 주방과 식당을 관장하는 위계질서의 체계를 설명하고 있으므로 장식과 서빙에 대해 서술하고 있는 ③은 흐름과 일치하지 않는다.

어휘

definite 확실한, 분명한   hierarchy 계급, 계층
elaborate 정교한, 정성을 들인   banquet 연회, 만찬
scalco 식탁에서 고기를 잘라주는 사람, 집사
steward 집사장
supervise 감독하다, 지휘하다   in charge of ~을 맡아서, 담당하여
                                          butler 집사

---

10 독해 > 대의 파악 > 요지·주장 찾기   [오답률 35%]   답 ②

| **해석** | 내 학생들은 단지 중요한 사람들을 더 만나면 자신의 업무가 향상될 것이라고 종종 믿는다. 그러나 당신이 가치 있는 것을 이미 세상에 내어 놓지 않았다면 그 사람들과 교제하는 것이 현저히 어렵다. 그것은 조언자와 후원자의 호기심을 자극한다. 업적은 당신이 뭔가를 가질 수 있는 것뿐만 아니라 줄 것이 있음을 보여준다. 인생에서 훌륭한 사람을 아는 것은 분명 도움이 된다. 그러나 그들이 얼마나 열심히 당신을 지지하는지 혹은 당신을 위해 자신들을 얼마나 희생할 수 있는지는 당신이 제공해야 하는 것에 달려 있다. 강력한 인맥을 구축하는 것이 당신으로 하여금 인맥 전문가가 되기를 요구하는 것은 아니다. 그것은 단지 당신이 무언가에 전문가일 것을 요구한다. 좋은 관계를 맺으면 경력을 쌓을 수 있다. 훌륭한 일을 한다면, 그 연결은 더 쉬울 것이다. 명함이 아닌 통찰력과 결과물이 말하게 하라.
① 성공적인 경력을 위해서는 후원이 필요하다.
② 좋은 인맥을 구축하는 것은 성취에서부터 시작된다.
③ 강력한 인맥이 당신의 성취를 위한 전제조건이다.
④ 인맥에서 전문가가 되면 당신의 통찰력과 결과물은 커진다.

| **정답해설** | ② [65%] 두 번째 문장 'But it's remarkably hard to engage with those people unless you've already put something valuable out into the world.'가 주제문이므로 글의 요지로 가장 적절한 것은 ②이다.

어휘

pique 불쾌감; 자극하다   bat ~을 치다; ~을 상세히 논의하다
stick one's neck out 위험 등에 노출되다
sponsorship 후원, 지원   prerequisite 필요조건, 전제 조건

---

11 생활영어 > 회화   [오답률 3%]   답 ②

| **해석** | A: 제 컴퓨터가 이유 없이 방금 꺼졌어요. 다시 켤 수도 없네요.
B: 충전해 봤어요? 단순히 배터리가 방전되었을지도 몰라요.
A: 물론 충전해 봤죠.
B: ② 그러면 가장 가까운 서비스센터를 방문해 보세요.
A: 그래야겠지만 제가 너무 게을러서요.
① 당신의 컴퓨터를 고치는 방법을 몰라요.
② 그러면 가장 가까운 서비스센터를 방문해 보세요.
③ 글쎄요. 문제에 대해 그만 생각하고 자러 가세요.
④ 제 형이 기술자니 당신의 컴퓨터를 고쳐 볼 거예요.

| **정답해설** | ② [97%] 컴퓨터가 꺼졌고 배터리 충전에도 켜지지 않고 있으므로 그 다음 조치가 이어져야 하는데 빈칸에 이어진 대답에서 게을러서 그렇게 못한다고 했으므로 서비스센터 방문을 권했음을 유추할 수 있다.

어휘

shut down (기계가) 멈추다[정지하다]
charge 충전하다   lazy 게으른

---

12 독해 > 대의 파악 > 심경   [오답률 2%]   답 ①

| **해석** | 내 얼굴은 백지장처럼 하얘졌다. 나는 내 손목시계를 보았다. 시험은 지금이면 거의 끝났을 것이다. 나는 완전히 공황 상태로 시험장에 도착했다. 나는 자초지종을 설명하려고 시도했지만, 나의 문장과 설명하려는 몸짓은 너무 혼란스러워서 아주 확실한 인간 토네이도에 불과했다. 나의 산만한 설명을 관두게 하려는 시도로, 그 시험 감독관은 나를 빈자리로 데려가 시험 책자를 내 앞에 놓았다. 그는 의문스러운 듯이 나와 시계를 보다가 가 버렸다. 나는 필사적으로 잃어버린 시간을 보충하려고 노력했고, 미친 듯이 유추와 문장 완성 문제들을 허둥지둥 풀어 나갔다. "15분 남았습니다." 파멸의 목소리가 교실 앞에서 공표되었다. 대수 방정식, 산술 계산, 기하학 도형들이 내 눈 앞을 헤엄쳐 갔다. "시간 다 되었습니다! 연필을 내려놓으세요."
① 긴장하고 걱정하는
② 신나고 쾌활한
③ 차분하고 단호한
④ 안전하고 느긋한

| **정답해설** | ① [98%] 시험장에 늦어 당황한 상태로 시험을 치르게 된 화자의 상황을 설명하는 글이다. 따라서 화자의 심경으로 가장 적절한 것은 ①이다.

어휘

absolute 절대적인   panic 공황, 공포
descriptive 서술적인   confused 혼란한, 당황한
nothing more than ~에 지나지 않은
convincing 그럴싸한, 설득력이 있는   curb 억제하다, 막다
distracting 집중할 수 없는   proctor 시험 감독관
desperately 필사적으로   make up for ~을 보충하다, 보상하다
analogy 유추; 유사, 일치   doom 운명
declare 선언[공표]하다   algebraic equation 대수 방정식
arithmetic calculation 산술 계산   geometric diagram 기하학 도형

오답률 TOP3

13 독해 > 글의 일관성 파악하기 > 글의 순서   [오답률 51%]   답 ②

| **해석** | 당신의 건강을 감시하고 추적하는 장치들은 점점 더 모든 연령대의 사람들에게 인기를 얻고 있다.
(B) 하지만, 지역사회 거주 노인들 중 특히 가정 내에 돌보는 사람이 없는 경우 이러한 기술들은 생명을 구할 수도 있다.
(A) 예를 들어, 낙상은 65세 이상 성인들에게 있어 사망의 주된 원인이다. 낙상 경보는 수년 동안 있어 왔던 대중적인 노인 양로 기술이지만 지금은 개선되었다.
(C) 이 단순한 기술은 노인이 넘어지는 순간, 자동으로 911이나 가까운 가족 구성원에게 알려 준다.

| **정답해설** | ② [49%] 주어진 문장은 건강을 감시 및 추적하는 장치들이 인기를 얻고 있다는 내용이다. (B)의 these technologies는 주어진 문장의 devices를 지칭하므로 주어진 문장에 이어 (B)가 와야 한다. 그 후에 (A)에서 노인들의 주요 사망 원인인 낙상을 예로 들어 낙상 경보 기술에 대한 언급으로 이어져야 하며, (C)의 This simple technology는 (A)에서 언급한 낙상 경보 기술(Fall alerts)을 지칭하므로 ②가 정답이다.

---

14 생활영어 > 회화　　　　오답률 8%　　답 ①

| 해석 | A: 우리의 신혼여행으로 어디 가고 싶어?
B: 우리가 가 보지 않은 곳으로 가자.
A: 그러면 하와이에 가는 것은 어때?
B: ① 언제나 거기에 가고 싶었어.
① 언제나 거기에 가고 싶었어.
② 한국이 살기에 근사한 장소 아니니?
③ 좋아! 그곳에서의 지난 여행이 멋졌어!
④ 아, 너는 이미 하와이에 다녀왔음에 틀림없구나.

| 정답해설 | ① 92% 둘이 가보지 못한 곳으로 하와이를 추천했으므로 이에 동감하는 표현으로 ①이 적절하다. ③과 ④는 하와이에 다녀온 적이 있는 것에 대한 이야기이므로 적절하지 않고, 신혼여행에 대한 이야기를 하고 있는 중이므로 사는 곳에 대한 이야기인 ② 역시 적절하지 않다.

| 어휘 |

Why don't we + 동사원형~? ~하는 것은 어때?

---

15 독해 > 빈칸의 내용 추론하기 > 빈칸 어구 추론
　　　　　　　　　　　　　　　　오답률 23%　　답 ④

| 해석 | 성공하는 사람들의 비결은 보통 그들이 한 가지에 완전히 집중할 수 있다는 것이다. 그들은 그들의 머릿속에 많은 걸 가지고 있더라도, 그들은 많은 책무들이 서로 방해하기는커녕 훌륭한 내적 질서를 이루는 방법을 찾아냈다. 그리고 이러한 질서는 꽤 단순하다: ④ 가장 중요한 것을 먼저 한다. 이론상으로는 꽤 명확해 보이지만 일상생활에서 그것은 다소 달라 보인다. 당신은 우선순위에 따라 결정하려 노력했을지도 모르지만 당신은 매일의 사소한 일들과 모든 예측하지 못한 방해물로 인해 실패했다. 예를 들어, 다른 사무실로 도망침으로써, 그리고 어떤 방해물도 방해하도록 허용하지 않음으로써 방해들을 분리하라. 당신이 당신의 우선순위에 있는 한 가지 과제에 집중할 때, 당신은 심지어 당신이 가지고 있으면서도 알지 못했던 당신의 에너지를 발견할 것이다.
① 빠를수록 좋다
② 하지 않는 것보다는 늦더라도 하는 것이 낫다
③ 눈에서 멀어지면 마음에서도 멀어진다
④ 가장 중요한 것을 먼저 한다

| 정답해설 | ④ 77% 우선순위에 따라 방해물을 허용하지 않고 한 가지 과제에 집중하라고(concentrate on the one task of your priorities) 했으므로 빈칸에 들어갈 말로 가장 적절한 것은 ④이다.

| 어휘 |

concentrate on ~에 집중하다　　commitment 책임, 책무; 약속
impede 방해하다　　　　　　　　quite 꽤, 상당히; 지극히
trivial 사소한, 하찮은　　　　　unforeseen 예기치 않은, 뜻하지 않은
distraction 주의 산만, 방심; 기분전환
disturbance 방해, 교란　　　　　get in the way 방해가 되다

---

16 독해 > 대의 파악 > 제목 찾기　　오답률 19%　　답 ③

| 해석 | 과학자들의 도움으로 상업적 수산업은 그것이 계속되려면 어업이 과학적으로 이루어져야 함을 알아냈다. 물고기 개체 수에 대한 조업 경쟁 없이, 물고기의 수는 예상 가능한 풍부한 수준에 도달하여 그대로 유지될 것이다. 유일한 변동은 먹이의 이용가능성, 적절한 온도 등과 같은 자연 환경 요인 때문일 것이다. 만약 어업이 이러한 물고기를 잡도록 발전되고 어획량이 작다면, 그 개체 수는 유지될 수 있다. 북해의 고등어가 좋은 예이다. 만약 우리가 어장을 늘리고 매년 더 많은 물고기를 잡는다면, 매년 잡는 모든 물고기를 대체할 수 있는 이상적인 수준 아래로 개체 수를 줄이지 않도록 신중해야 한다. 만약 우리가 '최대 유지 생산량'이라고 하는 이러한 정도로 물고기를 잡는다면, 우리는 가능한 한 가장 많은 어획량을 해마다 유지할 수 있다. 우리가 너무 많이 잡는다면, 우리가 어업을 할 수 없을 때까지 물고기의 수는 매년 줄어들 것이다. 과도하게 남획된 물고기 사례로는 대서양의 흰긴수염고래와 북대서양의 넙치가 있다. 연 최대 어획량을 유지하기 위해 꼭 정확한 양의 물고기를 잡는 것은 과학인 동시에 기술이다. 우리가 물고기 개체 수를 더 잘 이해하도록 돕고, 개체 수를 고갈시키지 않고 최대한 이용하는 방법에 대한 연구는 끊임없이 진행되고 있다.
① 상업적 어업을 거부하라
② 수산업으로 간주되는 양식 어업
③ 왜 어업에 과학이 필요한가?
④ 남획된 물고기들: 불법 어업의 사례

| 정답해설 | ③ 81% 과학과 기술의 도움으로 물고기 개체 수에 대한 우려 없이 어업을 지속할 수 있다는 내용의 글이므로, 글의 제목으로 가장 적절한 것은 ③이다.

| 어휘 |

predictable 예측할 수 있는, 당연한　abundance 풍부, 다량
fluctuation 변동, 동요　　　　　　　availability 유용성
proper 적절한
sustainable 지속 가능한, 유지할 수 있는

---

17 독해 > 빈칸의 내용 추론하기 > 연결어 추론
　　　　　　　　　　　　　　　　오답률 43%　　답 ①

| 해석 | 테러리즘은 유효하게 작용할까? 911 테러는 알카에다에게는 막대한 전술적인 성공이었는데, 부분적인 이유는 이것이 세계의 언론의 중심지이며 미국의 실질적인 수도에서 일어난 공격을 수반했고, (A) 그것으로 인해 이 사건의 가능한 한 가장 폭넓은 언론 보도를 확보했기 때문이다. 만약 테러리즘이 당신이 많은 사람들이 시청하기를 원하는 극장의 한 형태라면 인간 역사에서 911 테러보다 더 많은 전 세계 시청자들에 의해 시청된 사건은 없을 것이다. 그 당시 911 테러가 진주만 공습과 어떻게 같은 것인지에 대해 많은 토론이 있었다. 그것들 모두 미국을 중대한 전쟁으로 끌어들인 기습공격이었기 때문에 그것들은 실제로 유사했다. 그러나 그것들은 또한 다른 의미에서 유사했다. 진주만 기습은 제국주의 일본의 '전술적인' 대성공이었지만 그것은 '전략적인' 실패로 이어졌다. 진주만 공습 이후 4년 만에 일본 제국은 폐허가 되었으며, 완전히 패배했다. (B) 유사하게, 911 테러는 알카에다의 '전술적인' 대성공이었지만 이 역시 오사마 빈 라덴에게 '전략적인' 큰 실패로 판명났다.

　　　　(A)　　　　　　(B)
① 그것으로 인해　　유사하게
② ~에 반하여　　　따라서
③ ~에 반하여　　　다행히
④ 그것으로 인해　　이와 반대로

| 정답해설 | ① 57% (A)에는 앞부분이 원인에 해당하고 뒤는 결과에 해당하므로, thereby가 적절하고, (B)에는 그 앞에 일본의 진주

만 공격에 대한 설명이, 그 이후에는 비슷한 결과를 빚은 911 테러 공격에 대한 설명이 이어졌으므로 similarly가 적절하다.

어휘

tactical 전술의
coverage 보도, 방송
utterly 완전히, 철저히

ensure 보장하다, 확실하게 하다
lie in ruins 폐허가 되어 있다
defeat 패배시키다, 이기다

---

18 독해 > 세부내용 찾기 > 내용 불일치 찾기 오답률 23% 답 ①

| **해석** | 우리는 중국 과학자들이 아기만으로부터가 아니라 모든 자손들로부터 치명적인 혈액 질환을 제거하기 위해 인간 배아를 변형시켰을 때 종으로서 새로운 단계에 진입했다. 연구원은 이 과정을 '생식계열 변형'이라고 부른다. 미디어는 '디자이너 아기'라는 문구를 좋아한다. 그러나 우리는 그것을 있는 그대로 우생학이라고 부를 수 있다. 그리고 우리 인류는 우리가 그것을 사용하기를 원할지 여부를 결정해야 한다. 지난달 미국에서 과학 기관이 관여했다. 국립 과학원과 미국 국립 의학원 공동위원회는 '합리적인 대안이 없을 때' 심각한 질병을 일으키는 유전자를 겨냥한 배아 조작을 승인했다. 그러나 이미 건강한 아이들을 더 강하고 키를 더 크게 만드는 것과 같은 '향상'을 위해 조작하는 것은 더 조심스러워졌다. 그것은 공개 토론을 권장했고 의사들은 '이번에 진행하지 말아야' 한다고 말했다. 위원회는 주의를 촉구할 정당한 이유가 있었다. 우생학의 역사는 억압과 불행으로 가득 차 있다.
① 의사들은 향상을 위한 배아 조작을 즉시 진행하도록 권장되었다.
② 최근에 미국의 과학 연구 기관이 우생학에 관한 토론에 참여했다.
③ 중국 과학자들은 심각한 혈액 장애를 예방하기 위해 인간 배아를 변형했다.
④ '디자이너 아기'는 생식계열 변형 과정의 또 다른 용어다.

| **정답해설** | ① 77% 혈액 장애와 같은 질병을 위한 배아 조직이 아니라 '향상'을 위한 조작은 논쟁 중이라고 했으므로 지문의 내용과 일치하지 않는 것은 ①이다.

어휘

alter 바꾸다, 변경하다
fatal 치명적인
germline 생식 계열
weigh in 의견을 제시하다
be wary of ~을 경계하다

embryo 배아, 태아
descendant 후손
modification 변경, 수정
endorse 승인하다; 배서하다
urge 촉구하다, 요구하다

---

19 독해 > 글의 일관성 파악하기 > 주어진 문장의 삽입
오답률 13% 답 ④

| **해석** | 고대 올림픽은 운동선수들에게 우리의 현대 경기처럼 자신의 체력과 우월을 증명할 수 있는 기회를 제공했다. 고대 올림픽 경기는 약자를 제거하고 강한 사람을 찬양하기 위해 고안되었다. 우승자들은 극단으로 내몰렸다. 현대와 마찬가지로 사람들은 익스트림 스포츠를 좋아했다. 가장 인기 있는 경기 중 하나가 33번째 올림피아드에서 추가되었다. 이것은 판크라티온으로, 레슬링과 권투의 극단적인 혼합이었다. 그리스 단어 pankration은 '모든 힘'을 의미한다. 남자들은 금속 징이 달린 가죽 끈을 착용했고, 이는 상대방에게 끔찍한 일이 될 수 있었다. 이 위험한 형태의 레슬링에는 시간이나 체중의 제한이 없었다. 이 경기에는 두 가지 규칙만 적용된다. 첫째, 레슬링 선수는 엄지손가락으로 눈을 후벼 팔 수 없었다. 두 번째로 그들은 물어뜯을 수 없었다. 다른 것은 공정한 플레이로 간주되었다. 경기는 권투 경기와 동일한 방법으로 결정되었다. 선수들은 두 사람 중 하나가 쓰러질 때까지 계속되었다. ④ 둘 다 항복하지 않으면 한 사람이 쓰러질 때까지 주먹을 교환했다. 최강의 선수들만이 이 경기에 도전했다. 상대방의 손가락을 부러뜨려 자신의 별명을 얻은 'Mr. Fingertips'와 레슬링을 하는 것을 상상해보라!

| **정답해설** | ④ 87% 주어진 문장에서 경기의 승패가 결정되는 마지막 순간을 서술했고 neither에 해당하는 대상은 ④ 이전의 contenders이므로, ④가 정답이다.

어휘

eliminate 제거하다
opponent 반대자, 상대, 적수
contender 경쟁자, 도전자

glorify 찬미하다; 미화하다
gouge 후벼 파다
surrender 항복하다, 포기하다

오답률 TOP2

20 독해 > 빈칸의 내용 추론하기 > 빈칸 어구 추론
오답률 58% 답 ①

| **해석** | 우리 시대에는 인간에 대한 그것만의 삶과 규칙을 가진 것은 시장의 법칙뿐만 아니라 과학과 기술의 발전도 있다. 여러 가지 이유로 오늘날의 과학의 문제와 구조는 너무 커서 과학자가 자신의 문제를 선택하지 않는다. 그러나 문제들은 과학자에게 강요된다. 그가 한 가지 문제를 해결하면 그 결과가 더 안전하거나 확실한 것이 아니라, 해결된 단일 문제 대신 열 개의 다른 새로운 문제가 펼쳐진다. 그 문제들은 과학자가 그 문제를 풀도록 강요한다. 그래서 그는 계속해서 빠른 속도로 나아가야 한다. 산업 기술에 대해서도 마찬가지다. 과학의 속도는 기술의 속도를 강제한다. 이론 물리학은 우리에게 원자력을 강요한다. 그래서 핵분열 폭탄의 성공적인 생산은 우리에게 수소 폭탄 제조를 강요한다. 우리는 문제를 선택하지 않고, 우리는 그 결과물을 선택하지 않는다. 우리는 밀쳐지고, 우리는 강요당한다. 무엇에 의해? 시스템을 초월하는 목적과 목표를 가지고 있지 않고 ① 사람을 시스템의 부속물로 만드는 시스템에 의해서이다.
① 사람을 시스템의 부속물로 만든다
② 거짓된 안전 의식을 창출한다
③ 창조적인 도전으로 인간에게 영감을 준다
④ 과학자들이 시장 법칙을 통제할 수 있도록 권한을 부여한다

| **정답해설** | ① 42% 지문 중반부의 'They force him to solve them; he has to go ahead at an ever-quickening pace'를 통해 과학자들이 문제를 푸는 것이 아니라, 유례없는 문제들이 새로운 과제를 과학자들에게 강요한다고 했으므로 정답은 ①임을 알 수 있다.

어휘

pace 속도, 페이스
fission bomb 핵분열 폭탄, 원자 폭탄
transcend 초월하다, 넘다
empower 권한을 주다

atomic 원자력의, 원자 폭탄의

appendix 부속물, 부록

법원직

해설 &
기출분석 REPORT

법원직 기출 POINT

Point 1 최근 몇 년간 영역별 문항 수와 난도 변화가 잦아 최신 기출문제를 반드시 풀어봐야 한다.

Point 2 문법 문항 비중이 줄어들었고 기본 개념과 기출 요소들 위주로 출제되고 있어 필수 문법을 반드시 숙지해야 한다.

Point 3 독해의 지문 길이가 길어지고 까다로운 유형의 비중 증가로 난도가 상승하여 시간 안배가 중요하다.

2025년 법원직 시험 대비 전략

"맥락 추론과 시간 안배가 고득점의 해법!"

Point 1 유형별 독해 풀이법을 숙지하고 많은 문제를 풀어보는 것이 필요하다.

Point 2 다양한 소재의 지문을 계속 풀어보면서 정해진 시간 안에 문제를 효율적으로 푸는 연습해야 한다.

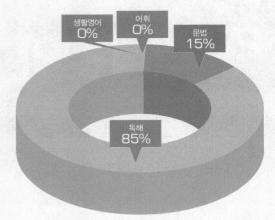

생활영어 0% 어휘 0% 문법 15% 독해 85%

▲ 최근 5개년 평균 출제 비중

연도	총평	어휘	문법	독해	생활영어
2024	**난도 상향의 요소를 갖춘 시험, 철저한 영역별 고득점 전략 필수!** · 전년도에 이어 문법 문항 비중이 축소하고 상대적으로 독해 문항이 증가함 · 쉬운 유형으로 분류되는 대의 파악 문항 수 축소로 난도가 올라감 · 글의 일관성, 세부내용 문항의 증가로 인한 맥락 파악과 시간 안배가 중요함	0% (0문항)	12% (3문항)	88% (22문항)	0% (0문항)
2023	**유형에 따른 시간 안배가 관건, 문제가 요구하는 핵심 파악이 중요!** · 문법의 문항 비중이 축소하고 핵심 문법에 대한 이해도를 요구함 · 상대적으로 독해 문항의 비중이 늘어나 유형에 따른 시간 안배가 중요함 · 세부 내용과 일관성 유형의 비중 증가로 변별력 확보	0% (0문항)	12% (3문항)	88% (22문항)	0% (0문항)
2022	**독해는 평이한 난도, 문법 문항 비중 증가가 변수!** · 문법 문항 증가(5문항)로, 문법 요소와 구조에 대한 이해도가 요구됨 · 비교적 간단한 어휘 관련 독해 문항의 증가로 빠른 맥락 파악이 필수임 · 문법과 독해 전체적으로 평이한 난도로 쉽게 정답을 찾을 수 있는 수준임	0% (0문항)	20% (5문항)	80% (20문항)	0% (0문항)
2021	**지문의 길이는 줄었지만 전년 대비 전체적인 난도는 상승!** · 문법은 동사와 준동사, 연결사 등 필수 요소들 위주로 평이한 난도로 출제됨 · 다양한 유형의 독해에 대한 맞춤형 풀이법을 익혀 시간을 조절하는 것이 중요함 · 지문 길이는 전년 대비 줄어든 편이나 소재와 내용에 대한 철저한 이해가 필요함	0% (0문항)	16% (4문항)	84% (21문항)	0% (0문항)
2020	**압도적인 어휘 관련 독해 비중, 맥락 파악이 고득점 여부 결정!** · 문법은 4문항으로 동사와 준동사 위주의 평이한 난도로 출제됨 · 어휘 관련 독해(어휘 선택, 요약문, 빈칸 어휘 등) 문항의 비중이 최대 · 상대적으로 지문의 난도는 평해 제대로 된 출제 의도 파악한다면 고득점 가능	0% (0문항)	16% (4문항)	84% (21문항)	0% (0문항)

〈법원직 연도별 합격선〉

| 맞힌 개수 | /25문항 | 점수 | /100점 |

➡ ☐ 합격 ☐ 불합격

취약영역 체크

문항	정답	영역	문항	정답	영역
1	④	독해 > 글의 일관성 파악하기	14	③	독해 > 글의 일관성 파악하기
2	①	독해 > 빈칸의 내용 추론하기	15	①	독해 > 글의 일관성 파악하기
3	②	독해 > 세부내용 찾기	16	④	독해 > 세부내용 찾기
4	②	독해 > 빈칸의 내용 추론하기	17	②	독해 > 글의 일관성 파악하기
5	④	독해 > 세부내용 찾기	18	②	문법 > 분사, 관계사, 일치
6	②	독해 > 밑줄 어휘	19	②	독해 > 세부내용 찾기
7	④	독해 > 요약	20	④	문법 > 준동사
8	④	독해 > 밑줄 어휘	21	④	독해 > 빈칸의 내용 추론하기
9	①	독해 > 글의 일관성 파악하기	22	①	독해 > 밑줄 어구
10	③	문법 > 명사와 일치	23	②	독해 > 대의 파악
11	②	독해 > 세부내용 찾기	24	①	독해 > 대의 파악
12	②	독해 > 글의 일관성 파악하기	25	④	독해 > 세부내용 찾기
13	②	독해 > 대의 파악			

⬇ 영역별 틀린 개수로 취약영역을 확인하세요!

| 어휘 | /0 | 문법 | /3 | 독해 | /22 | 생활영어 | /0 |

➡ 나의 취약영역: _____

※ 해당 회차는 〈1초 합격예측 서비스〉의 데이터 누적 기간이 충분하지 않아 오답률, 선지 선택률 기재를 생략하였습니다.

| **1** | 독해 > 글의 일관성 파악하기 > 글의 순서 | 답 ④ |

| 해석 | 이제 우리는 첨단 AI와 생명공학을 모두 포함하는 다가오는 기술의 물결에 직면하면서 전환점의 가장자리에 서 있다. 우리는 이전에 결코 그러한 변화 잠재성을 지닌 기술을 목격한 적은 없는데, 이는 경외심을 불러일으키기도 하고 위압적이기도 한 방식으로 우리의 세계를 재편성할 가능성이 있다.

(C) 한편으로, 이러한 기술의 잠재적 이점들은 방대하고 심오하다. AI를 통해, 우리는 우주의 비밀을 풀고, 오랫동안 우리가 이해할 수 없던 질병을 치료하고, 상상력의 한계를 넓히는 새로운 형태의 예술과 문화를 창조할 수 있다.

(B) 생명공학으로, 우리는 질병을 치료하고 농업을 변화시키기 위해 생명을 가공할 수 있는데, 이는 더 건강하고 지속 가능한 세상을 만들 수 있다. 그러나 다른 한편으로, 이러한 기술에 대한 잠재적 위험은 동일하게 광대하고 심오하다.

(A) AI를 통해, 우리가 통제할 수 없는 시스템을 만들 수 있고, 우리가 이해하지 못하는 알고리즘에 좌우되는 우리 자신을 발견할 수 있다. 생명공학을 통해, 우리는 생명의 구성 요소를 조작할 수 있고, 잠재적으로 개인과 생태계 전체 모두에 의도치 않은 결과를 초래할 수 있다.

| 정답해설 | ④ AI와 생명공학이 우리에게 가져올 잠재성에 대한 글이다. 주어진 글에서 AI와 생명공학이 우리에게 경외심과 더불어 위압감을 준다고 했고, 우리의 세계를 재편성할 것이라고 언급했다. 따라서 이에 대한 구체적인 내용들이 이어져야 하는데, On the one hand(한편으로)가 이야기를 시작하기에 좋은 연결어이므로 (C)가 처음에 오는 것이 자연스럽다. (C)에서는 AI의 장점에 대해 서술하고 있고, 그 다음에 (B)의 앞부분에서는 생명공학의 장점에 대해 서술하고 있으므로 (C)에 이어 (B)가 와야 한다. (B)의 뒷부분에서 On the one hand와 호응하는 On the other hand(다른 한편으로)가 오면서 이러한 기술이 주는 위험이 있다고 언급했고, (A)에서 AI와 생명공학의 단점에 대해 서술하고 있으므로 글의 순서로 가장 적절한 것은 ④이다.

어휘

daunting 위협적인, 벅찬   profound 심오한, 지대한
tackle (문제 등으로) 대결하다   transform 변형시키다, 바꾸다
sustainable 지속 가능한
at the mercy of ~의 처분대로, ~의 마음대로
manipulate 조종하다, 조작하다

| **2** | 독해 > 빈칸의 내용 추론하기 > 빈칸 어구 추론 | 답 ① |

| 해석 | 새로운 예술작업 기술에 대한 논란은 새로운 것이 아니다. 많은 화가들은 카메라의 발명을 혐오했는데, 그들은 카메라를 인간 예술성의 훼손으로 여겼다. 19세기 프랑스의 시인이자 예술 평론가인 샤를 보들레르는 사진술을 '예술의 가장 치명적인 적'이라고 불렀다. 20세기에는 디지털 편집 도구와 컴퓨터를 이용한 디자인 프로그램이 인간 협력자들의 기술을 너무 적게 요구한다는 이유로 예술 순수주의자들에 의해 비슷하게 무시되었다. 새로운 종의 AI 이미지 생성 도구들을 다르게 만드는 것은 그저 그것들이

최소한의 노력으로 아름다운 예술 작품을 제작할 수 있다는 것만은 아니다. 그것은 그것들이 작용하는 방식이다. 이러한 도구들은 오픈 웹에서 수백만 개의 이미지를 모은 다음, 알고리즘이 해당 이미지의 패턴과 관계를 인식해서 동일한 스타일로 새로운 이미지를 생성하도록 교육함으로써 만들어진다. 그것은 자신의 작품을 인터넷에 업로드하는 예술가들이 자신도 모르게 ① 자신들의 알고리즘 경쟁자들을 훈련시키는 데 도움을 줄 수 있다는 것을 의미한다.

① 자신들의 알고리즘 경쟁자들을 훈련시키는 데 도움을 주는
② AI가 만든 예술의 윤리에 대한 논쟁을 불러일으키는
③ 창의적 과정의 일환으로써 디지털 기술을 수용하는
④ 독창적인 창작물을 제작하기 위해 인터넷 활용 기술을 습득하는

| 정답해설 | ① 새로운 예술작업 기술에 대한 논란은 새로운 것이 아니라는 글이다. 과거에는 카메라의 경우를 언급했고, 20세기에는 AI(인공지능)에 대해 서술하고 있다. 글 중반부터 AI의 이미지 생성과정에 대해 설명하면서 오픈 웹상의 수백만 개의 이미지를 모아 알고리즘이 해당 이미지의 패턴과 관계를 인식해 새로운 이미지를 만들어낸다고 했다. 따라서 예술가들이 인터넷에 자신의 작품을 업로드한다면, 이를 AI가 사용해서 다시 새로운 창작물을 만들어 낼 것임을 유추할 수 있다. 따라서 빈칸에 들어갈 것으로 가장 적절한 것은 ①이다. 정답의 알고리즘 경쟁자들은 맥락상 AI를 지칭함을 알 수 있다.

| 어휘 |
recoil 움찔하다, 뒷걸음치다
debasement (품질·가치·인격 등의) 저하, 타락
artistry 예술성
dismiss 무시하다, 일축하다
scrape 긁어내다; 상처나게 하다
competitor 경쟁자
mortal 죽을 운명의, 치명적인
collaborator 협력자, 합작자
unwittingly 무심코, 무의식적으로

3 독해 > 세부내용 찾기 > 내용 불일치 찾기 답 ②

| 해석 | 1890년 8월 26일, 하와이의 와이키키 근처에서 태어난 Duke Kahanamoku는 하와이 서퍼이자 수영 선수로 미국에게 3개의 올림픽 금메달을 안겨 주었으며, 수년 동안 세계에서 가장 위대한 자유형 수영 선수로 여겨졌다. 그는 아마도 플러터 킥을 개발한 것으로 가장 널리 알려져 있었는데, 플러터 킥은 대체로 시저스 킥을 대체했다. Kahanamoku는 1913년 7월 5일과 1917년 9월 5일 사이에 100야드 자유형에서 전반적으로 인정받은 3개의 세계 기록을 세웠다. 100야드 자유형에서, Kahanamoku는 1913년 미국 실내 경기 챔피언이었고 1916-17년과 1920년에는 야외경기 타이틀을 보유자였다. 그는 1912년 스톡홀름 올림픽에서 100미터 자유형 경기에서 우승했고 그 승리를 벨기에 앤트워프에서 열린 1920년 올림픽에서 되풀이했는데, 그 올림픽에서 그는 800미터 계주 경주에서 승리한 미국 팀의 일원이었다. Kahanamoku는 또한 서핑에 뛰어났으며, 그 스포츠(서핑)의 우상들 중 하나로 여겨졌다. 1920년대 중반부터는 때때로, Kahanamoku는 영화배우이기도 했다. 1932년부터 1961년까지, 그는 호놀룰루시와 카운티의 보안관이었다. 그는 1961년부터 사망할 때까지 하와이 주의 유명인사에 대한 공식 의전을 담당하며 유급으로 재직했다.

| 정답해설 | ② He was perhaps most widely known for developing the flutter kick, which largely replaces the scissors kick.를 통해 시저스 킥을 대체하는 플러터 킥을 개발한 것으로 널리 알려져 있음을 알 수 있으므로 반대로 언급한 ②는 글의 내용과 일치하지 않는다.

| 어휘 |
universally 보편적으로
personage 저명인사, 명사
triumph 승리

4 독해 > 빈칸의 내용 추론하기 > 빈칸 어휘 추론 답 ②

| 해석 | 아이들이 교실에 가져오는 이해도는 이미 저학년일 때 상당히 강할 수 있다. 예를 들어, 일부 아이들은 둥근 지구가 팬케이크처럼 생겼다고 상상함으로써 평평한 지구에 대한 선입견을 계속 유지하는 것으로 밝혀졌다. 이 신선한 이해에 대한 구성은 아이들이 어떻게 사람들이 지구 표면 위에 서 있거나 걸을 수 있는지를 설명하는 데 도움이 되는 지구 모형에 의해 유도된다. 많은 어린 아이들은 8분의 1이 4분의 1보다 더 크다는 개념을 단념하는 데 어려움을 겪는데, 8이 4보다 더 큰 수이기 때문이다. 만약 아이들이 백지상태였다면, 그저 그들에게 지구는 둥글다거나 4분의 1이 8분의 1보다 더 크다고 말해주는 것만으로 ② 충분할 것이다. 그러나 그 아이들은 이미 지구와 숫자에 대한 개념을 가지고 있기 때문에, 그러한 생각들을 변형시키거나 확장하기 위해서는 직접적으로 다루어져야 한다.

① 친숙한
② 충분한
③ 부적절한
④ 관련이 없는

| 정답해설 | ② 아이들이 사실과 다른 참신한 개념을 갖는 이유에 대해 설명한 글이다. 아이들이 지구가 평평하다고 하거나 8분의 1이 4분의 1보다 더 크다고 생각하는 사례를 들었고, 이런 생각을 갖게 된 원인으로 아이들이 이미 지구와 숫자에 대한 개념이 어느 정도 있기 때문이라고 했다. 빈칸이 포함된 문장에서 아이들이 백지상태였다면 그저 그들에게 '사실(지구는 둥글다 혹은 4분의 1이 8분의 1보다 더 크다 등)'을 언급하는 것만으로 '충분할' 것이라고 유추할 수 있다. 따라서 빈칸에 들어갈 것으로 가장 적절한 것은 ②이다.

| 어휘 |
preconception 선입견; 예상, 예측
have trouble R-ing ~에 어려움을 겪다
give up 포기하다, 단념하다
blank slate 백지상태
transform 변형시키다, 바꾸다
notion 개념
address 다루다, 처리하다

5 독해 > 세부내용 찾기 > 내용 불일치 찾기 답 ④

| 해석 | 도시 농업(urban agriculture)이라고도 알려진 도시 농업(urban farming)은 옥상, 버려진 건물 및 지역의 정원 같은 공간을 활용하여, 도시 환경 내에서 먹거리를 재배하는 것을 포함한다. 이러한 지속 가능한 관행은 그것이 식량 공급 및 지역 경제에서 중요한 역할을 하는 많은 아프리카 및 아시아 도시들뿐만 아니라 뉴욕, 시카고, 샌프란시스코, 런던, 암스테르담, 베를린을 포함해 전세계적으로 견인력을 얻고 있다. 도시 농업은 운송 배기가스 배출을 최소화함으로써 탄소 발자국을 줄이는 데 도움이 될 뿐만 아니라, 도시 지역의 신선하고 건강한 식품에 대한 접근성을 높인다. 그것은 일자리를 창출하고 지역사회 내에서 계속 이익을 가져옴으로써 지역 경제를 강화한다. 더욱이, 도시 농장은 도시 경관을 향상시키고, 대기질을 개선하며, 물을 절약하고, 교육 기회를 제공하고, 생물 다양성을 촉진하고, 자연과 사람들을 연결하며, 현지에서 식량을 생산함으로써 식량 안보를 향상시키는데, 이는 도시를 자연재해와 같은 혼란에 더 회복력 있게 만든다.

| 정답해설 | ④ 마지막 문장 'Additionally, urban farms enhance cityscapes, ~and improve food security by producing food locally, making cities more resilient to disruptions like natural disasters.'의 뒷부분에서 도시 농업이 자연재해와 같은 혼란에 대

해 도시를 더 회복력 있게 만든다고 했으므로, 글의 내용과 일치하지 않는 것은 ④이다.

[어휘]

urban farming 도시 농업   agriculture 농업
abandoned 버려진, 유기된   sustainable 지속 가능한
crucial 결정적인, 중요한
carbon footprint 탄소 발자국(개인이나 단체가 직간접적으로 발생시키는 온실 기체의 총량)
conserve 보존하다   biodiversity 생물 다양성
resilient 회복력 있는; 탄력이 있는   disruption 혼란, 붕괴

---

6   독해 > 밑줄 어휘 > 어휘 추론   답 ②

| 해석 | 인간 본성에 대한 개념이나 이론은 과학에서 독특한 위치를 차지한다. 우리는 우주에 대한 우리의 이론에 의해 우주가 바뀔 것이라고 걱정할 필요가 없다. 행성들은 우리가 어떻게 생각하든, 어떻게 행성들에 대해 이론화하든 상관하지 않는다. 그러나 우리는 인간 본성에 대한 우리의 이론에 의해 인간 본성이 바뀔 것을 걱정해야만 한다. 40년 전, 저명한 인류학자는 인간은 '완성되지 않은 동물(unfinished animal)'이라고 말했다. 그가 의미하는 것은 우리를 둘러싼 사회의 산물인 인간의 본성을 갖는 것이 인간의 본성이라는 것이다. 그런 인간의 본성은 발견되기보다는 오히려 창조된다. 우리는 사람들이 살고 있는 제도들을 설계함으로써 인간 본성을 '설계한다.' 따라서 우리는 우리가 어떤 종류의 인간 본성을 설계하는 데 도움을 주고 싶은지 자문해 보아야 한다.
① 불완전한 발달 단계에 갇힌
② 생물학에 의해 고정되기보다는 오히려 사회에 의해 형성되는
③ 환경적인 배경으로부터 유례없이 자유로운
④ 동물적인 면과 영적인 면 모두 가지고 태어난

| 정답해설 | ② 밑줄에 포함된 문장 뒤에 인간 본성에 대한 정의를 내린 문장이 나오는데, '그런 인간의 본성은 발견되기보다는 오히려 창조된다'고 했으므로 인간의 본성은 타고나서 '발견되는' 것이 아니라 살아가면서 형성이 되어 '창조되는' 것으로 볼 수 있으므로 unfinished animals가 의미하는 바로 가장 적절한 것은 ②이다.

[어휘]

cosmos 우주   theorize 이론을 세우다
distinguished 저명한, 뛰어난   anthropologist 인류학자
unfinished 미완성의
institution 제도, 관례; 설립, 제정; 시설

---

7   독해 > 요약   답 ④

| 해석 | 패시브 하우스는 쾌적한 상태를 보장하고 에너지 비용을 크게 줄이기 위해, 건축 물리학의 정밀도를 사용하는 건물 설계의 표준이자 진보적인 방법이다. 그것은 설계 과정에서 모든 어림짐작을 제거한다. 그것은 국가 건축 규정이 하려고 했던 것을 한다. 패시브 하우스 방식은 '빌드빌리티(시공성)'에 영향을 미치지 않지만, 설계와 성능의 차이를 좁히고 정부 규제보다 훨씬 더 높은 수준의 편안함과 효율성을 제공하며, 온전히 선의로 그럭저럭 달성해 왔다. 우리가 패시브 하우스 방식을 사용할 때, 우리는 단열과 자유롭게 사용할 수 있는 일광을 가장 합리적인 방법으로 그리고 편안함과 에너지 효율성 모두에 적합한 양으로 사용하는 방법을 배운다. 이것은, 내가 믿건대, 좋은 설계의 기본이며, 우리의 주거와 직장의 발전에서 우리가 해야 할 다음 단계이다. 우리가 손아귀에 쥐고 있는 개선들은 잠재적으로 인류와 지구에 변화를 가져올 수 있다.

↓

패시브 하우스는 쾌적함과 에너지 효율성을 보장하기 위해 정확한 건축 물리학을 이용하고, 이는 전통적인 규제들을 (A) 능가하고 (B) 지속 가능한 설계를 위한 변화시키는 잠재성을 제공한다.

     (A)   (B)
① 지속되는   지속 가능한
② 지속되는   지속 불가능한
③ 능가하는   지속 불가능한
④ 능가하는   지속 가능한

| 정답해설 | ④ (A)에 들어갈 것에 대한 근거는 글의 중간에 있는 'they close the gap between design and performance and deliver a much higher standard of comfort and efficiency than government regulations'에서 찾을 수 있는데, 요약문의 전통적인 규제(traditional regulations)는 지문의 정부 규제(government regulations)를 지칭하는 것임을 알 수 있다. 이런 정부 규제보다 훨씬 더 수준 높은 쾌적함과 효율성의 기준을 전달한다고 했으므로 (A)에는 '능가하는'의 supassing이 적절하다. 또한 글의 뒷부분에서 패시브 하우스 방식이 우리의 주거와 직장의 발전에서 우리가 해야 할 다음 단계라고 언급하면서 결국 이로 인한 개선들이 변화를 가져온다고 했으므로 맥락상 (B)에는 '지속 가능한'의 sustainable이 적절하다. 따라서 정답은 ④이다.

[어휘]

Passive House 패시브 하우스: 단열재 등을 이용해 내부 열이 밖으로 새어 나가는 것을 막음으로써 에너지 사용량을 절감하는 집(외부 에너지원을 적극적으로 활용하지 않고 내부의 에너지를 보존한다는 의미에서 붙은 이름)
precision 정확, 정밀   remove 제거하다
regulation 규제, 규정   buildability 시공성
efficiency 능률, 효율   intention 의도
insulation 단열   sensible 합리적인, 분별 있는
grasp 꽉 쥐기[움켜잡기]   transformative 변화시키는

---

8   독해 > 밑줄 어휘 > 어휘 추론   답 ④

| 해석 | 오늘날, 세상에는 오직 한 종의 인간, 호모 사피엔스만이 남아 있다. 그러나 그 한 종은 유전적으로 99.9% 이상 동일하다는 사실에도 불구하고, 다양한 이질적인 환경에 적응해 왔다. 그리고 어느 정도의 인간의 유전적 변이는 각 사회가 그 자체만의 독특한 환경에 적응한 결과이지만, 각 사회가 그렇게 적응하면서 이룬 문화적 적응은 차례로 그 사회의 유전적 구성에 대해 어느 정도 더 많은 변화를 요구할 것이다. 다시 말해, 우리는 우리의 지역 생태계와 너무 얽혀 있기 때문에 우리 인간은 환경으로부터 우리가 의존하게 되는 다양한 자원을 추려낼 때, 환경을 바꿀 뿐만 아니라 이어서 우리가 그렇게 바꿔버린 환경도 우리를 변화시킨다. 그리고 이는 때때로 우리에게 지대한 생물학적 부담을 가하고 있다. 그러한 세계의 지역들로, 예를 들어, 환경의 이용에 북유럽의 소의 가축화가 포함되고, 또는 동아프리카인 성인의 유당 내성(유아기를 지나 우유를 소화할 수 있는 능력)을 ④ 감소시켰다(→ 증가시켰다).

| 정답해설 | ④ 유일한 인간 종인 호모 사피엔스가 유전적으로 거의 완전히 동일함에도 다양한 이질적인 환경에 적응해 왔다는 내용의 글이다. 중간에 인간은 환경을 바꾸기도 하지만 인간이 바꿔버린 환경이 우리를 바꿔버린다는 내용이 나오면서, 이는 우리에게 생물학적 부담을 가한다고 했다. 이에 대한 사례로 환경을 이용해 소를 가축화하고, 이로 인해 소에서 나오는 우유를 섭취함으로써 유당에

대한 내성이 오히려 증가했음을 유추할 수 있다. 따라서 ④의 reduced를 increased로 바꿔야 한다.

어휘

genetically 유전적으로	identical 동일한
adapt 적응[순응]하다; 각색하다	disparate 다른, 공통점이 없는
exact (남에게) 구하다, 요구하다	entangled 얽힌, 연루된
cull 고르다, 추려내다	exert (힘·능력 등을) 쓰다, 발휘하다
exploitation 이용, 착취	domestication 길들이기
tolerance 내성; 관용	infancy 유아기

---

9 독해 > 글의 일관성 파악하기 > 글의 순서   답 ①

| **해석** | 우리가 일상생활을 하는 방식에 중요한 역할을 하는 은유 하나를 잠시 생각해 보자: 시간은 돈이다.

(A) 우리는 흔히 시간을 마치 돈인 것처럼 말하는데, 예를 들어, 일상적인 표현으로는 '너는 내 시간을 낭비하고 있어', '이 장치는 네가 일할 몇 시간을 절약해 줄 거야', '너는 주말을 어떻게 보낼 거니?', '나는 이 관계에 많은 시간을 투자했어.' 등이 있다.

(B) 모든 은유는 눈에 보이거나 보이지 않는 것을 중개한다. 이것은 시간이 어떻게 돈과 같은지를 강조하고, 어떻게 그렇지 않은가를 모호하게 한다. 따라서 시간은 우리가 낭비하거나 잃을 수 있는 것이 되고, 우리가 나이가 들수록 줄어들게 된다. 그것은 매우 직선적이고 질서정연한 방식으로 추출된다.

(C) 그러나 이 은유는 우리가 하고 있는 일에 대한 우리의 참여에 따라, 시간이 어떻게 빨라지거나 느려질 수 있는지와 같은 중요한 현상학적 측면을 드러내지 못한다. 대신, 우리는 시간을 예를 들어, 하천처럼 매우 유동적이라고 생각할 수 있는데, 이는 우리는 시간이 돈이라는 세계관을 채택하는 정도로 이것을 놓치고 있다는 생각이다.

| **정답해설** | ① 주어진 글에서 '시간은 돈이다'라는 은유를 제시했고, 이 은유를 직접적으로 받은 내용이 (A)에 이어져 있으므로 (A)가 처음에 와야 한다. 관련된 여러 은유들이 열거가 되었으므로, (C)의 주어인 This metaphor로 시작하는 문장이 바로 올 수 없다. 따라서 두 번째로 모든 은유가 눈에 보이는 것과 보이지 않는 것을 중개한다는 내용의 (B)가 이어지는 것이 자연스럽다. (B)의 뒷부분에서 시간이 매우 직선적이고 질서정연한 방식으로 추상화된다고 언급했고, 이를 This metaphor로 받은 (C)가 그 다음에 이어져야 한다. 따라서 글의 순서로 적절한 것은 ①이다.

어휘

metaphor 은유	significant 중요한; 상당한
invest 투자하다	visible 눈에 보이는
invisible 눈에 보이지 않는	highlight 강조하다
diminish 줄이다	abstract 추출하다; 발췌하다; 추상적인
linear 직선 모양의	disclose 드러내다; 폭로하다
phenomenological 현상학의, 현상의	
engagement 참여	
conceive (생각·목적·감정 등을) 마음에 품다; 상상하다	
lose sight of ~을 잊다, 놓치다	adopt 채택하다; 입양하다

---

10 문법 > 명사와 일치 > 대명사   답 ③

| **해석** | 그의 마지막 생각은 아내를 위한 것이었다. "그는 그녀가 그것을 거의 버티지 못할까 걱정이다."라고 Burnet에게 말했는데, 그는 지난 며칠 동안 그와 함께 있도록 허락된 주교였다. 그가 그녀에 대해 말할 때 그의 눈에 눈물이 고였다. 마지막 날이 왔고, Russell 부인은 아버지에게 영원히 작별을 고하기 위해 세 명의 어린아이들을 데리고 왔다. '어린 Fubs'는 단지 9살이었고, 그녀의 여동생 Catherine은 7살, 아기는 3살이었는데, 그 아기는 너무 어려서 그의 상실을 깨닫지 못했다. 그는 그들 모두에게 침착하게 키스를 하고, 돌려보냈다. 그의 아내는 남아서 그들의 마지막 식사를 함께 했다. 그러고는 둘은 아무 말 없이 키스를 나누었고, 그녀는 조용히 그를 떠났다. 그녀가 가버렸을 때, Russel 경은 완전히 무너졌다. "그녀가 나에게 얼마나 큰 축복이었는지!" 그가 외쳤다. "내 아이들을 그런 엄마의 보살핌에 맡기는 것은 나에게 큰 위안입니다. 그녀는 아이들을 위해 자신을 돌보겠다고 약속했지요. 그녀는 그것을 해낼 거예요."라고 그는 단호하게 덧붙였다. 레이디 Russell은 다시는 결코 그를 환영하지 못할 슬픈 집에 무거운 마음으로 돌아왔다. 1683년 7월 21일, 그녀는 미망인이었고, 그녀의 아이들은 아버지가 없었다. 그들은 칙칙한 런던 집을 떠나 시골에 있는 오래된 수도원으로 갔다.

| **정답해설** | ③ 맥락상 주어인 she와 동일한 대상이므로 재귀대명사인 herself로 바꿔야 한다.

| **오답해설** | ① 부정 부사로 조동사 뒤에 적절하게 왔다.

② 완전한 절에 이어 동사를 수식하는 부사로 calmly가 적절하게 왔다.

④ 선행사인 the sad home을 수식하는 형용사절을 이끄는 관계대명사로 '전치사 + which'의 구조이므로 뒤에 완전한 절이 올바르게 이어졌다.

어휘

bear 참다, 견디다	bishop 주교
comfort 위안, 위로	for one's sake ~를 위해
resolutely 단호히, 결연히	dreary 황량한, 쓸쓸한
abbey 대수도[수녀]원	

---

11 독해 > 세부내용 찾기 > 내용 불일치 찾기   답 ②

| **해석** | 프리랜서와 부업에 종사하는 사람들의 노동력을 가리키는 긱 이코노미는 미국에서 빠르게 성장하고 있으며, 2022년 맥킨지 조사에서, 36%의 취업자가 독립 근로자로 확인되었고, 이는 2016년의 27%에서 증가한 것이다. 이 노동 인구에는 변호사와 같은 고소득 전문직에서부터 배달 기사와 같은 저임금 역할에 이르기까지 다양한 직업이 포함된다. 그것이 제공하는 유연성과 자율성에도 불구하고, 대부분의 독립 근로자는 보다 안정적인 고용을 원한다. 62%는 고용 안정과 혜택에 대한 우려로 정규직을 선호한다. 긱 이코노미 근로자들이 직면하고 있는 문제들로 의료, 주택 및 기타 기본적인 요구에 대한 제한된 접근 등이 포함되는데, 이것은 정부의 지원에 상당히 의존하는 것들이다. 기술적 진보는 독자적인 작업의 증가를 촉진하여 원격 및 프리랜서 작업을 보다 접근 가능하고 매력적으로 만들었다. 이러한 추세는 인플레이션 및 고용 시장 역학과 같은 광범위한 경제적 압력을 반영하여, 개인이 생존, 유연성 혹은 즐거움을 위해 긱 경제 근무를 선택하도록 영향을 준다.

| **정답해설** | ② 글의 중간에서 'Despite the flexibility and autonomy it offers, most independent workers desire more stable employment'를 통해 유연성과 자율성에도 불구하고 대부분의 독립 근로자들은 더 안정적인(more stable) 고용을 원한다고 했으므로 ②은 글의 내용과 일치하지 않는다.

어휘

gig economy 긱 이코노미, 임시적 선호 경제(일자리에 계약직이나 프리랜서 등을 주로 채용하는 현상)

refer to ~을 언급하다, 말하다   flexibility 유연성, 융통성
autonomy 자율성   stable 안정적인
permanent 영구적인, 영원한   assistance 원조, 도움
facilitate 촉진하다; 수월하게 하다

---

12   독해 > 글의 일관성 파악하기 > 글의 순서   답 ②

| 해석 | 우리는 분류를 통해 세상을 알고 관계를 맺게 된다.

(B) 일반적인 의사소통은 이 기능에 대한 가장 즉각적인 표현이다. 우리는 소리와 말을 통해 사물을 언급하고, 우리가 개념이라고 부르는 것들에 아이디어를 붙인다.

(C) 우리가 하는 분류 중 일부는 암묵적으로 남아 있고, 다른 것들은 관습, 법률, 정치 혹은 과학에 의해 명시적으로 관리된다. 동일한 것들에 대한 분류 체계의 적용은 상황과 용도에 따라 다르다.

(A) 예를 들어, 한 동물 종에 대한 개념은 어떤 환경에서는 민간전승과 신화로, 다른 환경에서 하나의 상세한 법적 구조로, 또 다른 환경에서는 과학적 분류 체계로 묘사된 것으로 가장 잘 생각될 수 있다.

| 정답해설 | ② 주어진 문장에서 우리가 분류를 통해 세상을 알고 관계를 맺게 된다고 했으므로, 뒤에는 이에 대한 구체적인 내용이 이어져야 한다. 분류에 대한 일반적인 개념을 설명한 (B)가 처음에 와야 하는데, 지칭어인 this faculty는 주어진 문장의 내용임을 알 수 있다. (A)에는 for instance가 있지만 내용이 (B)에 대한 예시라고 볼 수 있으므로 (B)에 이어지기에는 맥락상 적절하지 않다. 따라서 분류를 암묵적인 것과 명시적인 것으로 나눈 (C)의 내용이 이어진 후 이에 대한 예시로 (A)가 이어지는 것이 가장 적절하다.

어휘

relate to ~와 관련되다   ordinary 평범한, 일반적인
faculty 능력, 재능   explicitly 명시적으로, 솔직하게
folklore 민간전승, 민속

---

13   독해 > 대의 파악 > 심경   답 ②

| 해석 | 지금은 새벽 3시이고, 우리는 유타 주 남부에서 북부로 이동하고 있다. 사막의 건조한 한기에서 고산 겨울의 차가운 강풍으로 날씨가 변하는 시기다. 얼음이 길을 차지한다. 눈송이들이 작은 곤충들처럼 앞유리에 휙 부딪치고, 처음에는 몇 개, 그 다음에는 너무 많아서 길이 사라진다. 우리는 폭풍의 중심부로 밀고 들어간다. 밴이 미끄러지고 덜컹거린다. 바람은 맹렬하고, 창밖의 경치는 순백이다. Richard가 차를 한쪽에 세운다. 그는 우리가 더 이상 갈 수 없다고 말한다. 아버지가 운전대를 잡고, Richard는 조수석으로, 엄마는 내 옆에, Audrey는 매트리스에 누워 있다. 아버지는 고속도로에 진입하고, 요점을 말하려는 듯 빠르게 가속을 해서 Richard보다 속도를 두 배로 올렸다. 엄마가 묻는다. "더 느리게 운전해야 하지 않아요?" 아빠가 씩 웃는다. "나는 우리 천사들이 날 수 있는 속도보다 더 빨리 운전하지는 않아요." 밴은 여전히 가속하고 있다. 50마일로, 그 다음은 60마일로. Richard는 타이어가 미끄러질 때마다 손 마디가 하얗게 되도록 손으로 팔걸이를 움켜쥐고 긴장한 채 앉아 있었다. 엄마는 옆으로 누운 채, 내 옆에 얼굴을 묻고, 밴이 뒷바퀴가 옆으로 미끄러질 때마다, 공기를 조금씩 들이마시다가 아빠가 바로 잡아서 다시 차선으로 돌아올 때, 숨을 참는다. 그녀는 너무 경직되어 있어서 산산조각이 날지도 모른다고 나는 생각한다. 내 몸은 그녀의 몸과 함께 긴장한다. 우리는 함께 충격에 대해 백 번을 버틴다.
① 신나고 아주 기쁜

② 걱정하고 두려워하는
③ 신중하지만 안정된
④ 편안하고 느긋한

| 정답해설 | ② 새벽에 악천우 속에서 Richard가 운전대를 아버지에게 넘겨준 후 아버지의 난폭운전으로 모든 가족이 불안한 상태를 서술하는 글이다. tensely, his knuckles bleaching, holding her breath 등의 표현으로 보아 화자의 심경으로 가장 적절한 것은 ②이다.

어휘

chill 냉기, 한기   alpine 고산(高山)의, 높은 산의
flick 가볍게 치다, 휙 튀기다   furious 격렬한; 격노한
pull over 차를 길가에 대다   grin 밝게 생긋[방긋] 웃다
knuckle 손가락 관절[마디]   bleach 바래게[희게] 하다
slip 미끄러지다   rigid 경직된; 엄격한
shatter 산산이 부서지다   brace 떠받치다

---

14   독해 > 글의 일관성 파악하기 > 주어진 문장의 삽입   답 ③

| 해석 | COVID-19 동안 도시 봉쇄 정책은 수많은 테이크아웃, 채소 쇼핑, 지역사회 공동 구매, 그리고 다른 사업들의 급속한 성장을 촉진시켰다. 라스트 마일 배송은 유행병 동안 중요한 생계 지원이 되었다. 동시에, 바이러스는 에어로졸을 통해 전염될 수 있기 때문에, 라스트 마일 배송을 위한 비접촉 배송의 필요성이 점차 높아지면서, 무인 물류 이용이 어느 정도 가속화되고 있다. ③ 그러나 현재 무인 배송의 적용에는 많은 문제들이 있다. 예를 들어, 커뮤니티 공간은 지원 물류 인프라가 부족해 무인 택배 시설 운영에 적합하지 않다. 게다가, 현재 기술로는 배송 과정을 완료할 수 없어 무인 배송 노드 도킹을 돕기 위한 인력은 물론 관련 공간의 협업이 필요하다.

| 정답해설 | ③ 주어진 문장에서 역접의 연결어인 However에 이어 현재의 무인 배송 적용에 많은 문제점들이 있었다고 했으므로, 뒤에는 문제점들에 대한 구체적인 내용이 나와야 함을 유추할 수 있다. ③ 이전에는 라스트 마일 배송에 대한 설명이 이어졌고 부정적인 언급이 없으므로 그 이전에는 주어진 문장이 들어갈 수 없다. ③에 이어 For example에 이어 부정적인 내용이 이어졌고, 주어진 문장의 unmanned distribution에 대해 다시 언급하며 부정적인 내용이 이어지고 있으므로 주어진 문장이 들어가기에 적절한 곳은 ③이다.

어휘

lockdown 봉쇄   facilitate 촉진시키다; 수월하게 하다
takeaway 테이크아웃, 집에 사 가지고 가는 요리
epidemic 유행병   transmit 전염시키다; 전송하다
logistics 물류, 택배   infrastructure 기반 시설
collaboration 협업, 협동   relevant 적절한; 관계가 있는
personnel 인력
node [컴퓨터] 노드: 네트워크의 분기점이나 단말 장치의 접속점

---

15   독해 > 글의 일관성 파악하기 > 글의 순서   답 ①

| 해석 | 사람들은 이해하고자 하는 욕구가 어떤 대가를 치르더라도 설득하고자 하는 욕구보다 우선하는 진정한 관점의 교환에 별로 관심이 없다.

(B) 사실에서 벗어난 의견은 평가절하, 명예훼손, 모욕, 혹은 심지어 물리적인 충동을 동반한다. 만약 당신이 소셜 미디어 네트워크에서 벌어지는 '토론'을 살펴본다면, 사람들이 의견을 교환하는 방식에서 명백한 품격의 하락을 보기 위해 난민 위기나 테러와 같은 불쾌한 문제를 바라볼 필요조차 없다.

(A) 하지만 갈등은 그저 행동하라는 압력에 대한 인기 없는 원천만은 아니다. 또한 그것에는 많은 에너지가 내재되어 있는데, 이는 능숙한 접근법의 도움으로 긍정적인 변화, 즉 개선을 만들어 내기 위해 이용될 수 있다. 기본적으로 오늘날의 불행은 더 나은 미래를 향한 경쟁의 출발점이다.

(C) 갈등에 대한 건설적인 해결책을 찾는 데 성공했을 때, 그리고 몹시 힘든 설명 과정이 끝날 때, 성공적인 결과가 모든 노력을 기울일 가치가 있다는 것을 깨달았을 때, 여러분은 아마도 자신의 경험을 통해 이것을 알게 될 것이다.

| **정답해설** | ① 주어진 문장에서 이해하고자 하는 욕구에 대해 관심이 없다고 했는데, 이에 대한 하나의 예로 (B)에서 사실에서 벗어난 의견이 동반하게 되는 부정적인 요소들이 언급되는 것이 자연스럽다. (C)에는 this라는 지칭어가 있는데, 뒤에 이어진 내용으로 보아 this는 '긍정적인' 요소임을 알 수 있으므로 (B)에 이어 (C)는 올 수 없음을 알 수 있으며, (A)의 역접의 접속사 Yet에 이어진 내용에서 긍정적인 요소를 찾아볼 수 있다. (A)에서 갈등이 부정적인 요소뿐만 아니라 긍정적인 변화를 만들어 내기 위해 이용될 수 있다고 했고, 그 다음에 (C)가 이어지는 것이 자연스럽다. 따라서 글의 순서로 적절한 것은 ①이다.

어휘

genuine 진정한
take precedence 우위에 서다, 우선하다
convince 설득하다, 확신시키다　deviate 벗어나다, 빗나가다
insult 모욕적 언동　confrontation 대결, 직면
conflict 갈등, 충돌　clarification 설명, 해명
harness 이용하다; (태양열·물·바람 등을) 동력화하다
misery 고통, 불행

16　독해 > 세부내용 찾기 > 내용 불일치 찾기　답 ④

| **해석** | Belus Smawley는 그의 부모님과 6명의 남매들과 함께 농장에서 자랐다. 1학년 시절에, 그는 키가 크고 다른 어떤 소년보다 더 높이 점프할 수 있었고, 농장에서 떡갈나무의 더 높은 가지들에 터치하면서 도약 능력을 향상시키려고 노력했다. 이것은 그의 최초의 점프 숏 시도가 일어난 곳이라고 언급할 수 있는 지점이다. Belus Smawley가 그의 숏을 규칙적으로 사용하기 시작했을 때, 그는 득점 선두가 되었다. 18세의 나이에, 그는 AAU18 농구팀에 한 자리를 받게 되었다. 그는 이후 고등학교를 졸업하고 애팔래치아 (역사와 체육 교육을 전공하며) 주립대학교에서 전미 체육 장학금을 받았다. 그는 해군에 입대하기 전까지 선수 겸 코치가 되었다. 그는 그들의 농구팀에서 뛰기 시작했으며 점프숏을 정교하게 다듬었다. 그는 결혼하여 고등학교 교사와 농구 코치로 일하거나, 여러 팀에서 전업으로 NBA 농구 경력을 쌓았다. 결국 그는 가족과 교육 경력에 중점을 두어, 중학교의 교장이 되었다.

| **정답해설** | ④ 글의 뒷부분의 'He got married and either worked as a high school teacher and basketball coach or further pursued his NBA basketball career playing fulltime for several teams.'에서 한 팀이 아니라 여러 팀(several temas)에서 활동했다고 했으므로 Belus Smawley에 대한 내용과 일치하지 않는 것은 ④이다.

어휘

sibling (남녀의 구별 없이) 동기, 형제자매
limb (나무의) 큰 가지　major in ~를 전공하다
principal 교장

17　독해 > 글의 일관성 파악하기 > 주어진 문장의 삽입　답 ②

| **해석** | 인간은 대부분의 다른 종에 비해 눈에 띄게 크고 눈에 보이는 공막 (눈의 흰자위)을 가지고 있으며, 그 결과 우리는 우리의 주의가 향하는 방식, 또는 적어도 시선을 향하는 방식에 독특하게 노출된다. 진화생물학자들은 '협력적 눈 가설'을 통해 이것이 오류가 아니라 하나의 특징임에 틀림없다고 주장해 왔는데, 그것은 협력이 하나의 종으로서 우리의 생존에 몹시 중요하다는 사실을 가르침에 틀림없다는 것이다. 그리고 이는 공유된 관심의 이점들이 어느 정도의 사생활이나 재량권의 손실을 능가한다는 점이다. ② 그렇다면 우리가 우리의 기관들로부터 비슷한 것을 기대하고 싶어하는 것, 즉, 그들이 무엇을 보고 있다고 생각하는지 뿐만 아니라, 특히 그들이 어디를 보고 있는지를 아는 것을 이해할 수 있을 것이다. 기계 학습에서 이 개념은 '특징'이라는 이름으로 등장하는데, 이는 만약 하나의 시스템이 어떤 이미지를 보고 그것을 어떤 범주에 할당한다면, 아마도 그 이미지의 어떤 부분들이 그 결정을 내리는 데 있어서 다른 부분들보다 더 중요하거나 더 영향력이 있을 것이라는 개념이다. 만약 이미지의 이러한 중요한 부분을 강조 표시하는 일종의 '열지도'를 볼 수 있다면, 우리는 시스템이 우리가 생각하는 방식으로 작동하는지 확인하기 위해 일종의 온전한 검사로 사용할 수 있는 얼마간의 중요한 진단 정보를 얻을 수 있을지도 모른다.

| **정답해설** | ② 글의 앞부분에서 눈의 공막을 예시로 들어 이것은 오류가 아닌 하나의 특징으로, 인간에게 있어 협력이 생존에 중요하다는 사실을 알려주는 것이라고 했다. ①에 이어 진화생물학자들이 공막에 대한 주장을 언급했으므로 ①에는 들어갈 수 없다. 주어진 문장에서는 우리의 기관들(our machines)로부터 비슷한 것을 기대하고 싶어 하는 것이 이해할 만하다는 내용이 나왔고, ②에 이어 This idea is machine learning~이 언급되었으므로 주어진 문장 다음에 이에 대한 구체적인 설명이 이어진 것으로 볼 수 있다. 따라서 주어진 문장이 들어가기에 가장 적절한 곳은 ②이다.

어휘

relative to ~에 관하여, ~에 비례하여　gaze 시선[눈길]
feature 특징, 특성
bug 미생물, 세균; [컴퓨터] 버그(프로그램 내의 오류와 불량)
presumably 아마, 추정하건대　determination 결심, 결단력
obtain 얻다, 획득하다　diagnostic 진단(상)의
sanity 온전한 정신; 판단의 건전함

18　문법 > 분사, 관계사, 일치　답 ②

| **해석** | 관개평야(물을 끌어 댄 평야) 기후는 벽화에서 엿볼 수 있다. 여름의 태양은 딱딱한 땅 위에 내리쬐고, 왕 자신은 커다란 우산으로 그늘을 피한다. 종종 존재하는 전쟁도 생생하게 새겨져 있다. 기원전 878년 경에 세 명의 남자가 아마도 체포된 도시에서 도망치는 모습이 묘사된다. 긴 로브를 입은 그들은 유프라테스 강으로 뛰어드는데, 한 사람은 수영을 하고 다른 사람들은 가슴에 구명 부표를 안고 있다. 긴 베개처럼, 구명 부표는 공기로 팽창된 동물의 가죽으로 이루어져 있다. 난민들의 손이 부풀어 오른 구명 부표를 움켜쥐고 있고, 부표에 공기를 불어넣는 데 많은 시간을 소비하기 때문에, 그들은 다리로 수영해야만 떠 있을 수 있다. 그들이 강가 반대편에 도달했는지는 결코 알 수 없을 것이다.

| **정답해설** | ② (A) flee는 자동사이므로 수동태로 전환해 쓸 수 없다. 완전한 절에 이어 분사구문이 이어졌는데, flee의 주체는 문장의 주어인 three men이 '(스스로) 도망가는' 것이므로 과거분사가 아닌 현재분사 fleeing이 올바르다.

(B) the Euphrates River가 선행사로 왔고, 관계사에 이어 완전한 절이 이어졌으므로 관계부사 where가 와야 한다.

(C) 주어는 the hands이므로 복수 동사인 are로 수일치가 되어야 한다.

어휘

irrigate 관개하다, 물을 대다	glimpse 잠깐[언뜻] 보다
mural 벽화	flee 도망가다
lifebuoy 구명 부표	inflate 부풀리다, 팽창시키다
refugee 난민, 피난자	afloat 물 위에 떠서
opposite 맞은편의, 반대쪽의	

---

19 독해 > 세부내용 찾기 > 내용 불일치 찾기   답 ②

| 해석 | 네덜란드인들이 17세기에 지금의 뉴욕시인 곳에 도착했을 때, Lenape(델라웨어족)라고 알려진 원주민들과의 만남은 역사적 기록에 따르면, 처음에는 대체로 우호적이었다. 그들은 땅을 공유하고, 비버 모피를 위해 총, 구슬, 양모를 교환했다. 네덜란드인들은 1626년에 르나페 원주민으로부터 Manahatta섬을 '구입하기도' 했다. 그 거래는 결국은 뉴암스테르담 주변에 벽을 건설하면서 시행되었는데, 르나페 원주민이 고향을 떠나 강제 집단 이주를 시작하는 계기가 되었다. 1660년대에 지도에 등장하기 시작한 이 벽은 아메리카 원주민과 영국인들을 막기 위해 지어졌다. 이는 결국 월 스트리트가 되었고 Manahatta는 Manhattan이 되었다. Manhattan에서 Wickquasgeck으로 알려진 르나페 원주민의 무역로의 일부가 Brede weg가 되었고, 훗날 Broadway가 되었다. 르나페 원주민은 오늘날 뉴욕시의 지형을 형성하는 데 도움을 주었지만, 그들의 유산의 다른 흔적들은 모두 사라졌다.

| 정답해설 | ② 'The Dutch even "purchased" Manahatta island from the Lenape in 1626. The transaction, enforced by the eventual building of wall around New Amsterdam~'에서 르나페 원주민으로부터 네덜란드인이 Manahatta섬을 구입하고 이를 뉴암스테르담 주변에 벽을 건설하면서 실행했다고 했으므로, 벽을 세운 것은 원주민이 아닌 네덜란드인이었다는 것을 알 수 있다. 따라서 글의 내용과 일치하지 않는 것은 ②이다.

어휘

encounter 만남, 접촉	indigenous 토착의; 타고난
amicable 우호적인	purchase 구입하다
transaction 거래; 업무	legacy 유산
vanish 사라지다	

---

20 문법 > 준동사 > 분사   답 ④

| 해석 | 오늘날, 우리는 매스 미디어와 그것이 지탱하는 유명인사 문화가 새로운 형태의 공공성을 창출했다는 것을 당연하게 여기는데, 이를 통해 우리는 우리가 결코 만난 본 적이 없는 사람들과 친밀한 관계를 맺을 수 있다. 미디어 기술로 인해, 우리는 유명한 사람들과 더 가까워지고, 그들과 친밀감을 느끼는 착각을 즐길 수 있게 되었다. 어느 정도까지, 우리는 유명인을 주관화하고, 무의식적으로 그들을 우리의 의식의 일부로 만들었는데, 이는 마치 그들이 실제로 친구인 것처럼 말이다. 유명인사들은 우리의 내면생활에서도 영구적으로 자리를 차지하고, 우리의 몽상과 환상, 행동 지침, 야망의 중심이 된다. 현재, 사실상, 유명인사 문화는 우리의 정서에 영구적으로 일부가 될 수 있는데, 우리 중 많은 사람들이 정신적 짐의 일부로 그들과 그들의 특성, 그리고 그들과의 관계를 지니고 있기 때문이다.

| 정답해설 | ④ become 앞에는 완전한 절이 있으므로 연결어 없이 become이 올 수 없다. 결국은 앞 문장 전체를 수식하는 분사구문이 되어야 하는데, become이 자동사이므로 현재분사 becoming으로 바꿔야 한다.

| 오답해설 | ① 선행사 new forms of publicness에 이어진 관계대명사로, '전치사 + which'에 이어 완전한 절이 와야 한다. 뒤에 완전한 절이 이어졌으므로 올바른 구조이다. with의 목적어인 people을 목적격 관계대명사가 생략된 관계대명사절(that we have never met)이 수식하고 있으므로, 완전한 절임을 알 수 있다.

② bring은 타동사이므로 수동태 전환이 가능하다. 선행사 media techonologies를 수식하는 관계대명사절의 동사로 구조와 맥락상 올바르다. Thanks to media technologies that we are brought에서 목적격 관계대명사 that이 생략된 구조이다.

③ 완전한 절에 이어 부사절을 이끄는 접속사로 뒤에 완전한 절이 올바르게 이어졌다. '마치 ~처럼'의 의미이며, 가정법 과거시제를 적용해 과거동사 were가 왔으며, 이 경우 '현재'로 해석해야 한다.

어휘

sustain 지탱하다, 유지하다	publicness 공공성
intimate 친밀한, 사적인	illusion 착각, 환각
intimacy 친밀, 친교	internalize ~을 내면[주관]화하다
consciousness 의식	take residence 자리를 잡다
trait 특징, 특성	luggage 짐, 수하물

---

21 독해 > 빈칸의 내용 추론하기 > 빈칸 어구 추론   답 ②

| 해석 | 축제는 전 세계적으로 전통, 유산 및 공동체 정신을 보여 주는 중요한 문화 행사이다. 그것들은 다양성을 기념하는 플랫폼 역할을 하며, 각 축제는 브라질의 카니발이나 인도의 디 왈리와 같은 독특한 전통을 반영한다. 축제는 또한 미국의 독립 기념일이나 프랑스의 혁명 기념일과 같은 역사적인 순간을 기린다. 또한, 그것들은 개인적, 문화적 정체성을 강화하는 관습과 의식을 보존하면서 공유 활동을 통해 강력한 공동체 유대를 육성한다. 축제는 사회적 가치를 반영하고 지역 공예와 예술을 홍보하며, 영성(靈性)을 높이고 관광을 유치하여 문화 교류와 이해를 용이하게 한다. 인도의 홀리(Holi)와 같은 계절 축제는 자연 주기와 일치하며, 소생의 시간을 축하한다. 궁극적으로, 축제에 참여하는 것은 지역사회와 개인의 정체성을 강화하여 ② 다양성을 중시하고 상호 존중과 이해를 장려하는 국제적인 담론에 기여한다.

① 참가자들이 일상의 걱정과 고통을 잊게 한다
② 다양성을 중시하고 상호 존중과 이해를 장려한다
③ 사람들이 개인의 삶과 사회적 삶의 연결고리를 끊을 수 있게 한다
④ 축제가 사람들이 스스로를 어떻게 생각하는지 결정하는 것을 막는다

| 정답해설 | ② 축제에 대해 정의를 내리고 역할에 대해 서술하는 글이다. 첫 문장에서 축제는 중요한 문화 행사이며, 다양성을 기념하는 플랫폼 역할을 한다고 했다. 이후에는 이에 대한 구체적인 사례로 세계의 축제들을 언급해 이해를 돕고 있다. 따라서 빈칸에는 이와 관련된 내용으로 다양성과 상호 존중, 이해를 언급한 ②가 빈칸에 들어갈 것으로 가장 적절하다.

어휘

significant 중요한; 상당한	showcase 소개하다, 전시하다
heritage 유산	reflect 반영하다

historical 역사적인　　　　preserve 보존하다
customs 관습　　　　　　ritual 의식, 제례
identity 정체성　　　　　　foster 육성하다, 기르다
societal 사회의　　　　　　craft 공예
spirituality 영성(靈性); 숭고함　facilitate 용이하게 하다; 촉진시키다
align with ~와 일렬로 맞추다
renewal 소생, 재생; 재건; 갱신

22　독해 > 밑줄 어구 > 어구 추론　　　　답 ①

| 해석 | 인생은 우여곡절로 가득 차 있다. 어느 날, 당신은 모든 것을 알아낸 것처럼 느낄지도 모른다. 그러다가, 한순간에 커브 볼을 맞기도 한다. 이런 감정은 당신 혼자만 느끼는 건 아니다. 모든 사람은 자신만의 문제들에 직면해야 한다. 문제를 극복하는 방법을 배우는 것은 여러분이 압박을 받는 상황에서도 중심을 잡고 침착함을 유지하도록 도움을 줄 것이다. 모든 사람들은 인생에서 문제에 직면하는 방법에 대한 자신만의 좋아하는 방식이 있다. 하지만, 상황이 어려워질 때, 따라야 할 몇 가지 좋은 조언과 요령도 있다. 도움을 요청하는 것을 부끄러워할 필요는 없다. 사랑하는 사람, 낯선 사람, 멘토 혹은 친구에게 의존하기로 선택하든 하지 않든, 성공하도록 돕고 싶은 사람들이 있다. 당신은 마음을 열고 기꺼이 지지를 받아들여야 한다. 당신을 도우러 오는 사람들은 진심으로 당신을 돌본다. 당신이 그것을 필요로 할 때 도움을 받는 것에 마음을 열어라.

| 정답해설 | ① 인생은 우여곡절로 가득 차 있고, 어려운 문제들에 직면할 때 극복할 수 있는 방법으로 도움을 요청하라고 조언하는 글이다. 따라서 커브 볼을 맞는다는 것이 의미하는 바로 가장 적절한 것은 ①이다. 밑줄 친 문장에 이어 challenges에 대한 언급이 있는데, curve ball에 대한 구체적인 표현임을 유추할 수 있다.

어휘
figure out 알아내다, 생각해 내다　　preference 선호, 애호
aid 도움, 지원, 원조

23　독해 > 대의 파악 > 요지·주장 찾기　　　　답 ②

| 해석 | 사회적 지배는 개인이나 집단이 주로 경쟁 상황에서 타인의 행동을 통제하거나 지시하는 상황을 말한다. 일반적으로, 개인이나 집단은 '미래의 상호 작용 과정이나 경쟁 상황의 결과에 대한 예측이 이루어질 때' 지배적이라고 한다. 지배 관계를 평가하고 할당하는 기준은 상황에 따라 다를 수 있다. 이용 가능한 데이터를 간략하게 요약하기는 어렵지만, 일반적으로 지배적인 개체들은 종속적인 개체들과 비교했을 때, 종종 더 많은 이동의 자유를 가지고, 음식 접근의 우선 순위를 가지며, 고품질의 휴식 장소를 얻고, 유리한 그루밍 관계를 누리며, 한 집단에서 더 많이 보호받는 부분을 차지하고, 더 높은 수준의 짝을 얻고, 다른 그룹 구성원의 관심을 조절하며, 스트레스와 질병에 대한 저항력이 더 큰 것으로 드러났다. 그렇지 않다는 주장에도 불구하고, 개인의 우세 상태와 평생 번식 성공 사이의 관계가 얼마나 강력한지는 분명하지 않다.

| 정답해설 | ② 사회적 지배에 대해 설명하는 글이다. 일반적인 지배의 개념을 서술한 후, 지배적인 관계를 평가하고 할당하는 기준은 상황에 따라 다를 수 있다고 언급한 후 이에 대해 구체적인 내용을 들어 설명하고 있다. 마지막 문장에서 개인의 우세 상태와 평생 번식 성공 사이의 관계가 얼마나 강력한지는 명확하지 않다(not clear)고 했으므로, 가장 잘 요약한 것은 ②이다.

---

dictate 지시하다　　　　　prediction 예측, 추정
criteria 기준, 평가(criterion의 복수형)
assess 평가하다　　　　　assign 할당하다
summarize 요약하다　　　　subordinate 하위[하급]의; 종속의
priority 우선하는 것　　　　groom (가죽, 털 등을) 다듬다
command 명령하다, 지휘하다　regulate 조절하다; 규제하다
resistance 저항　　　　　assertion 주장, 단언
status 상태; 지위, 신분　　　reproductive 번식[생식]의; 복사하는

24　독해 > 대의 파악 > 주제 찾기　　　　답 ①

| 해석 | 마음 챙김 명상은 일반적으로 안전하지만, 공황 발작이나 정신병과 같은 부작용으로 인해 우려가 생겨나는데, 공황 발작이나 정신병은 학술 연구에서는 거의 보고되지 않고 이해가 부실하게 이루어진다. 비평가들은 조직과 교육 시스템에 의한 마음 챙김을 신속하게 채택하는 것은 부적절하게 사회 문제를 개인에게 전가시킬 수 있다고 주장하며, 개인적인 스트레스는 환경 오염이나 직장에서 곤란한 상황과 같은 체계적인 원인을 다루기보다는 명상 부족으로 인한 것이라고 말한다. Ronald Purser 교수와 같은 비평가들은 마음 챙김을 개인이 변화를 추구할 수 있는 권한을 부여하는 대신, 불리한 조건에 더 순응하게 만들 수 있다고 말한다. 이러한 우려에도 불구하고, 비판은 마음 챙김 자체에 반대하는 것이 아니라, 변화에 저항하는 실체에 의한 보편적인 해결책으로서의 홍보에 반대한다. 마음 챙김의 이점과 위험에 대한 보다 철저한 이해를 위해서는, 장기적이고 엄격하게 관리된 연구가 필수적이다.
① 마음 챙김 명상의 폭넓은 채택의 안전과 사회적 함의와 관련된 비판
② 개인의 스트레스를 완화하고 사회적, 문화적 혼란을 막기 위해 취해지는 사회적, 국가적 조치
③ 개별적인 문제라기보다 사회적 문제의 해결에 선행해야 하는 마음 챙김의 기본 요소
④ 부적절하게 수행된 명상과 명상 부족으로 인해 개인과 사회가 직면하는 단점들

| 정답해설 | ① 마음 챙김 명상에 대한 내용으로 처음부터 부작용에 대한 언급을 하고 있다. 비평가들의 견해를 통해 마음 챙김이 사회 문제를 개인에게 전개시킬 수 있다는 점, 불리한 조건에 더 순응하게 만들 수 있다는 점 등을 서술하고 있고, 마지막 문장에서 마음 챙김에 대한 이점과 위험을 철저하게 이해하기 위해 연구가 필수적이라고 했으므로 글의 주제로 가장 적절한 것은 ①이다.

어휘
mindfulness 마음 챙김　　　meditation 명상
panic attack 공황 발작　　　adoption 채택
inappropriately 부적절하게　shift 옮기다, 이동하다
address 다루다, 처리하다　　pollution 오염
adverse 불리한; 반대하는　　resistant 저항하는
thorough 철저한　　　　　rigorously 엄격히, 엄밀히

25　독해 > 세부내용 찾기 > 내용 불일치 찾기　　　　답 ④

| 해석 | 말수가 적고 겸손한 사람인 Mike Mansfield는 종종 기억되고 싶지 않다고 말했다. 하지만, 그의 매혹적인 인생 이야기와 엄청난 공헌은 따르는 모든 사람들에게 영감을 준다. Mike Mansfield는 1903년 3월 16일 뉴욕에서 태어났다. Mike가 7살이었을 때, 어머니가 돌아가신 후, 아버지는 그와 그의 두 여동생을 몬태나 주의 Great Falls로 보내 그곳에서 이모와 삼촌에 의해 길러졌다. 14세 때, 그는 제1차 세계 대전 동안 미 해군에 입대하

기 위해 자신의 나이를 속였다. 훗날, 그는 육군과 해병대에서 복무했으며, 이는 그를 필리핀과 중국으로 보내 아시아에 대한 평생의 관심을 일깨우게 되었다. Mlke Mandfield의 정치 경력은 1942년 그가 미국 하원의원에 당선되면서 시작되었다. 그는 몬태나 제1관할구에서 다섯 번의 임기를 보냈다. 1952년에, 그는 미국 상원에 선출되어 1958년, 1964년 및 1970년에 재선되었다. 민주당 다수당 원내 총무로 선출된 그는 1961년 상원 다수당 원내대표로 선출되었다. 그는 1977년 상원에서 은퇴할 때까지 그 역량을 발휘했으며, 역사상 다른 다수당 원내 대표보다 더 오래 역임했다.

| 정답해설 | ④ In 1952, he was elected to the U.S. Senate and re-elected in 1958, 1964 and 1970.에서 상원의원에 3번 당선이 되었으므로, 5번 당선되었다고 언급한 ④는 글의 내용과 일치하지 않는다. 다만, ④의 뒤에서 언급한 가장 긴 다수당 원내대표를 역임했다는 내용은 마지막 문장으로 보아 내용과 일치한다. 하지만 선지의 일부 내용이 본문과 다른 것은 틀린 것으로 보아야 하므로 정답은 ④이다.

어휘

modesty 겸손, 소박함
enlist ~에 입대하다
launch 시작하다
capacity 역량, 능력

fascinate 매료시키다
awaken 각성하다, 깨닫다
term 임기

합격예상 체크

〈법원직 연도별 합격선〉

2023 합격기준

맞힌 개수	/25문항	점수	/100점

➡ □ 합격 □ 불합격

취약영역 체크

문항	정답	영역	문항	정답	영역
1	③	독해 > 세부내용 찾기	14	④	독해 > 대의 파악
2	②	문법 > 명사와 일치	15	②	독해 > 글의 일관성 파악하기
3	②	독해 > 세부내용 찾기	16	②	독해 > 글의 일관성 파악하기
4	①	독해 > 빈칸의 내용 추론하기	17	①	문법 > 동사의 형태
5	②	독해 > 요약	18	②	독해 > 대의 파악
6	③	문법 > 연결사	19	③	독해 > 세부내용 찾기
7	③	독해 > 글의 일관성 파악하기	20	③	독해 > 대의 파악
8	②	독해 > 글의 일관성 파악하기	21	②	독해 > 밑줄 어휘
9	④	독해 > 세부내용 찾기	22	②	독해 > 빈칸의 내용 추론하기
10	②	독해 > 글의 일관성 파악하기	23	①	독해 > 글의 일관성 파악하기
11	④	독해 > 글의 일관성 파악하기	24	④	독해 > 대의 파악
12	②	독해 > 글의 일관성 파악하기	25	③	독해 > 세부내용 찾기
13	③	독해 > 세부내용 찾기			

⬇ 영역별 틀린 개수로 취약영역을 확인하세요!

어휘	/0	문법	/3	독해	/22	생활영어	/0

➡ 나의 취약영역: _____

※ 해당 회차는 〈1초 합격예측 서비스〉의 데이터 누적 기간이 충분하지 않아 오답률, 선지 선택률 기재를 생략하였습니다.

1 　독해 > 세부내용 찾기 > 내용 불일치 찾기　　답 ③

| 해석 | 27세의 Henry Molaison은 1950년대에 약 10년간 쇠약하게 만드는 발작을 겪었다. 1953년 9월 1일, Molaison은 발작을 멈추게 하려고 외과 의사들이 뇌의 각 면에서 조직의 한 부분을 제거하도록 허용했다. 수술은 효과가 있었지만, Molaison은 새로운 기억을 형성할 수 없는 영구적인 기억 상실증 상태로 남았다. 이 비극적인 결과는 20세기 뇌 과학에서 가장 중요한 발견 중 하나로 이어졌는데, 학습과 기억과 같은 복잡한 기능이 뇌의 특정 영역과 연결되어 있다는 발견이었다. Molaison은 그의 사생활을 보호하기 위한 연구에서 'H.M.'으로 알려지게 되었다. William Scoville은 Molaison과 비슷한 수술을 받은 다른 9명의 환자를 연구하여, 내측 측두엽의 일부를 제거했던 사람들만이 기억 문제, 특히 최근의 기억에 있어 문제를 경험한다는 것을 발견했다. 그는 뇌의 특정 구조가 정상적인 기억에 필수적이라는 것을 발견했다. Molaison의 삶은 처음의 연속이었는데, 그가 전에 했던 일은 하나도 기억할 수 없었기 때문이었다. 하지만, 그는 시간이 지남에 따라 새로운 운동 기술을 습득할 수 있었다. Molaison에 대한 연구는 신경과학자들이 그가 2008년 사망한 후에도 의식과 무의식에 관련된 뇌의 연결조직을 더 탐구할 수 있게 해 주었다.

| 정답해설 | ③ 수술 이후 기억을 상실해 이후의 삶이 새로움의 연속이라고 했으므로 조금씩 기억할 수 있다는 것은 일치하지 않는다. 또한 However, he was able to acquire new motor skills over time으로 보아 기억은 상실했지만 새로운 운동 능력은 얻을 수 있었다고 했으므로 글의 내용과 일치하지 않는 것은 ③이다.

어휘
debilitate 약화시키다　　　　　tragic 비극적인, 참혹한
specific 특정한; 구체적인　　　surgery 수술
conscious 의식의　　　　　　　unconscious 무의식의

2 　문법 > 명사와 일치 > 일치　　답 ②

| 해석 | 인간은 우리가 살고 있는 생물군계의 미생물, 식물, 동물로부터 얻을 수 있는 실질적인 이익을 넘어서는 타고난 자연 친화력을 가지고 있다. 풍경, 식물, 동물의 형태를 띤 자연이 우리의 행복에 좋다는 생각은 오래되었고 Charles Darwin이나 그 이전까지 거슬러 올라갈 수 있다. 이 개념은 심리학자 Erich Fromm에 의해 생명애(生命愛)라고 불렸고, 하버드 대학의 개미 생물학자인 Edward O. Wilson과 Stephen Kellert에 의해 연구되었다. 1984년에 Wilson은 'Biophilia'를 출간했으며, 그것에 이어 또 다른 책인 Kellert와 Wilson이 편집한 'The Biophilia Hypothesis'가 뒤따랐다. 그들의 생명애 가설은 인간이 자연 환경에 있고자 하는 보편적인 욕구를 가지고 있다는 것이다.

| 정답해설 | ② 문장 전체 주어는 관계대명사절(that~and animals)이 수식하는 The idea이므로 단수로 수일치시켜야 한다. 따라서 is로 바꿔야 한다.

| 오답해설 | ① 선행사 biomes를 수식하는 관계대명사이다. '전치사 + which' 뒤에 1형식 구조의 완전한 절이 이어졌으므로 올바르다.
③ 완전한 절에 이어진 분사구문으로 생략된 주어는 another book,

The Biophilia Hypothesis로 구조와 맥락상 적절하다. being edited에서 being이 생략된 구조이다.

④ 문장 전체의 보어인 명사절을 이끄는 접속사로 뒤에 완전한 절이 이어진 올바른 구조이다.

어휘

inborn 타고난
derive from ~에서 유래하다
biophilia 생명애(生命愛)
universal 보편적인

tangible 명백한; 유형의
microbe 미생물; 병원균
hypothesis 가설, 가정

| **3** | 독해 > 세부내용 찾기 > 내용 불일치 찾기 | 답 ② |

| **해석** | 지구상의 생명체는 7억 2천만 년 전에 시작된 크라이오제니아기(극저온 시대)에 생존 가능성에 대한 극단적인 시험에 직면했다. 지구는 8천 5백만 년의 대부분의 기간 동안 얼어 있었다. 그러나 생명체는 '눈덩이 지구'라고 불리는 이 기간 동안 어떻게든 살아남았다. 과학자들은 이 시기의 시작을 더 잘 이해하려고 노력하고 있다. 그들은 태양의 복사에너지가 하얀 대륙 빙하에 반사되면서 태양의 온기가 행성 표면에 도달하는 양이 크게 감소했다고 믿는다. 또한, 그들은 검은 이판암에서 발견되어 해초로 확인된 화석은 살기 적합한 수중 환경이 그들이 한때 믿었던 것보다 그 당시에 더 널리 퍼져 있었다는 표시라고 말했다. 일부 연구 결과는 지구가 오히려 눈이 녹는 '슬러시 볼 지구'에 가깝다는 견해를 뒷받침한다. 이는 가장 초기 형태의 복합 생명체가 한때 단단하게 얼어붙은 것으로 생각되었던 지역에서 생존하는 것을 가능하게 해 준다. 연구자들은 가장 중요한 발견은 이른바 '빙하기'의 후반기에 얼음이 없는 개빙(開氷) 구역 환경이 존재했다는 것이라고 말했다. 이 결과는 세계의 바다가 완전히 얼지 않았다는 것을 보여 준다. 그것은 다세포 생물이 생존할 수 있는 서식 가능한 피난처 영역이 존재했음을 의미한다.

| **정답해설** | ② They believe a greatly reduced amount of the sun's warmth reached the planet's surface as its radiation bounced off the white ice sheets.에서 태양의 온기가 행성 표면에 크게 감소했다고 믿는다고 했으므로 글의 내용과 일치하지 않는 것은 ②이다.

어휘

survivability 생존 가능성
radiation 방사, 복사(작용); 복사에너지
bounce off ~을 맞고 튕겨나가다
shale 이판암(泥板巖)
refuge 피난

ice sheet 대륙 빙하, 빙상
widespread 널리 퍼진, 만연한

| **4** | 독해 > 빈칸의 내용 추론하기 > 빈칸 어구 추론 | 답 ① |

| **해석** | 지구 온도가 상승함에 따라, 해수면도 상승하여 전 세계적으로 연안 지역을 위협하고 있다. 놀랍게도, 굴과 같은 작은 생물들조차도 ① 우리의 방어수단이 될 수 있다. 굴은 자신들의 생태계와 서식 생물들의 건강에 파급 효과를 지닌 핵심종이다. 성체 굴 하나만으로 하루에 최대 50갤런의 물을 여과시켜, 수로를 더 깨끗하게 할 수 있다. 건강한 굴 암초는 또한 수백 가지의 다른 해양 생물을 위한 거주지를 제공하는데, 이는 생물 다양성과 생태계 균형을 촉진시킨다. 해수면 상승이 잦은 범람으로 이어지면서, 굴 암초는 폭풍을 완화하고 더 많은 연안 침식으로부터 보호하는 벽 역할을 한다.

① 우리의 방어수단이 될 수 있다
② 비상 식량이 될 수 있다
③ 미세 플라스틱에 오염될 수 있다
④ 지역 주민들의 소득을 올릴 수 있다

| **정답해설** | ① 지구 온도가 상승하고 해수면이 상승함에 따라 연안 지역이 위험하다고 언급한 후, 이런 상황에서 굴이 하는 역할을 유추해야 하는 글이다. 빈칸에 이어진 내용에서 굴이 물 여과를 통해 수로를 깨끗하게 하고 다른 해양 생물을 위한 거주지를 제공한다고 했고, 마지막 문장에서 연안 침식으로 보호하는 벽 역할을 한다고 했으므로, 빈칸에 들어갈 말로 가장 적절한 것은 ①이다.

어휘

threaten 위협하다
keystone species 핵심종
biodiversity 생물 다양성
buffer 완화하다

oyster 굴
inhabitant 서식 동물; 주민
pervasive 퍼지는, 골고루 미치는
erosion 침식

| **5** | 독해 > 요약 | 답 ② |

| **해석** | 현대 과학에 따르면, 혀의 다른 부분이 특정한 맛을 담당한다고 주장하는 미각 지도에 대한 미신은 부정확하다. 미각 지도는 1900년대 초, 독일 과학자 David Hänig의 실험에서 유래되었는데, 이 실험은 혀가 가장자리를 따라 맛에 가장 민감하고 중앙은 별로 그렇지 않다는 것을 발견했다. 그러나 시간이 흐르면서 이것은 단맛이 혀 앞쪽에 있고 쓴맛이 뒤쪽에 있으며, 짠맛과 신맛이 측면에 있다고 주장하기 위해 잘못 해석되었다. 실제로, 다른 맛들은 혀 전체에 있는 미뢰에 의해 감지된다. 미뢰는 장기간의 학습과 연관성을 기반으로 특정 음식을 갈망하거나 싫어하게 만들도록 함께 작용한다. 예를 들어, 우리 조상들은 영양소와 손쉬운 열량을 위해 과일을 필요로 했고, 따라서 우리는 자연스럽게 단맛에 이끌리는 반면, 일부 식물의 쓴맛은 독성에 대한 경고 역할을 한다. 물론, 동물계의 다른 종들도 고유의 미각 능력을 지니고 있는데, 육식 동물은 과일을 먹지 않으므로 인간처럼 당분을 갈망하지는 않는다.

↓

혀의 다른 부분이 특정한 맛을 담당한다는 주장은 현대 과학에 의해 (A) 거짓인 것이 밝혀졌고, 맛 선호도는 (B) 진화의 역사에 의해 영향을 받는다.

	(A)	(B)
①	정확한	진화의
②	거짓의	진화의
③	거짓의	심리학상의
④	정확한	심리학상의

| **정답해설** | ② (A)에는 첫 문장에서 혀의 다른 부분이 특정한 맛을 담당한다고 주장하는 미각지도를 '미신(myth)'이라고 언급했으므로 비슷한 의미의 형용사 false가 적절하다. (B)에는 맛 선호도에 대한 사례로 우리 인간 조상들이 영양소와 손쉬운 열량을 위해 과일을 필요로 하다 보니 단맛에 이끌리게 되었고, 육식 동물은 과일을 먹지 않으므로 인간처럼 당분을 갈망하지 않는다는 것이 언급되었으므로, 이는 진화와 관련된 내용임을 알 수 있다. 따라서 정답으로 가장 적절한 것은 ②이다.

어휘

originate 시작하다
sour 신, 시큼한
association 연관, 관련
carnivore 육식 동물

misinterpret 오역하다; 오해하다
crave 갈망(열망)하다
toxicity 독성

6 　문법 > 연결사 > 관계사 　　　　　답 ③

| 해석 | 언어는 사람들이 서로 의사소통하는 주요 수단이다. 대부분의 동물들이 의사소통을 하지만, 인간의 말은 다른 동물들의 의사소통 체계보다 더 복잡하고, 더 창의적이며, 더 광범위하게 사용된다. 언어는 인간이 되는 것이 무엇을 의미하는지에 대한 본질적이고 모든 문화의 기본적인 부분이다. 언어 인류학은 언어와 문화에 대한 언어의 관계를 이해하는 것과 관련된다. 언어는 우리가 당연하게 여기는 놀라운 것이다. 우리가 말할 때, 우리는 우리의 몸, 즉 폐, 성대, 입, 혀, 입술을 사용하여 다양한 음색과 음조의 소리를 낸다. 그리고, 어찌된 일인지, 우리와 다른 사람들이 함께 이것을 할 때, 우리는 같은 언어를 말할 때에만 서로 의사소통을 할 수 있다. 언어 인류학자들은 언어 간의 차이와 언어가 어떻게 구조화되고, 학습되고, 사용되는지를 이해하고 싶어 한다.

| 정답해설 | ③ 선행사를 포함한 관계대명사 what이 이끄는 절은 명사절이므로 앞에 있는 명사 an amazing thing과 나란히 쓸 수 없다. what에 이어 목적어가 없는 불완전한 절이 이어진 것은 올바르나, 선행사인 명사 thing을 수식할 형용사절을 이끌어야 하므로 관계대명사 that 혹은 which로 바꿔야 한다.

| 오답해설 | ① which는 선행사 means를 지칭하는 관계대명사로 맥락상 적절하며, by which에 이어 완전한 절이 이어졌으므로 올바른 구조이다.

② 주어인 human speech와 동사 is에 이어 형용사가 병치된 문장이다. complex, creative에 이어 used가 왔고, 과거분사는 형용사의 기능을 할 수 있는데, 맥락상 인간의 말은 '사용되는' 것이므로 수동의 과거분사로 올바르게 왔다.

④ 주어가 we and others이므로 복수로 수일치가 올바르고, do는 타동사이므로 뒤에 목적어인 this가 올바르게 이어졌다.

어휘
anthropology 인류학자	be concerned with ~와 관련되다
relation 관계	take ~ for granted ~를 당연히 여기다
vocal cords 성대	

7 　독해 > 글의 일관성 파악하기 > 주어진 문장의 삽입 　답 ③

| 해석 | 사람들은 병에 걸릴지도 모른다는 두려움이나 거액의 진찰료 때문에 병원이나 의료 센터에 접근하는 것을 주저하게 되었다. 이것은 그들이 인터넷상의 검증되지 않은 정보 자료를 바탕으로 자가 진단하게 만든다. 이것은 종종 잘못 진단되고 부적절한 의약품이 복용되면 그 사람의 정신적, 육체적 건강에 해로운 영향을 미친다는 것을 증명한다. ③ 의료 챗봇은 이 문제를 해결하고 가정에서 편안하게 사람들을 위한 적절한 진단과 조언을 보장하기 위해 마련되었다. 진단의 심각성에 따라, 챗봇은 일반 의약품 치료를 처방하거나 검증된 의료 전문가에게 올려보낸다. 크고 다양한 증상, 위험 요소, 치료에 대해 훈련받은 대화형 챗봇이 사용자의 건강 관련 질의를 처리할 수 있는데, 특히 COVID-19의 경우에 그러하다.

| 정답해설 | ③ 주어진 문장에서 의료 챗봇이 언급되고 등장한 이유에 대해 언급했으므로, 이후에는 챗봇에 대한 구체적인 기능이 나와야 함을 유추할 수 있다. ③ 이전까지는 여러 이유로 병원에 가지 않고, 인터넷상의 자료로 자가 진단 후 잘못된 과정을 통해 건강에 해를 끼친다는 내용이므로 주어진 문장이 들어갈 수 없다. ③ 이후에 주어로 챗봇이 나오면서 실제로 하는 기능들이 언급되었으므로 주어진 문장이 들어가기에 가장 적절한 곳은 ③이다.

어휘
hesitant 주저하는, 망설이는	contract (병에) 걸리다
consultation 상담, 자문, 협의	diagnosis 진단
unverified 증명[입증]되지 않은	misdiagnose 오진하다
improper 부적절한	comfort 위로, 위안; 위로하다
prescribe 처방하다; 규정하다	
over the counter 의사의 처방 없이도 합법적으로 약방에서 팔 수 있는	
query 질문, 질의	

8 　독해 > 글의 일관성 파악하기 > 글의 순서 　　답 ②

| 해석 | 스포츠 팬 우울증은 많은 열렬한 스포츠 팬들에게 영향을 미치는 실제적인 현상인데, 특히 실망하거나 패배할 때 그렇다.

(B) 많은 팬들에게, 자신이 좋아하는 팀이나 선수들에 대한 감정적인 투자는 매우 열렬해서, 지거나 기대에 미치지 못하는 것은 슬픔, 좌절감, 심지어 우울증의 감정으로 이어질 수 있다. 연구에 따르면 스포츠 팬 우울증은 정신적, 육체적 건강에 부정적인 영향을 미칠 수 있다.

(A) 팬들은 스트레스 수치의 증가, 불안이나 우울증에 걸릴 위험의 증가뿐만 아니라 식욕 및 수면 질의 감소를 겪을 수 있다. 스포츠 팬 우울증에 기여할 수 있는 많은 요인들이 있는데, 팀의 성공에 대한 개인 투자, 특정 팀을 지지하는 사회적 압박, 남의 시선을 끄는 스포츠 이벤트에 흔히 수반되는 강렬한 언론 보도 및 조사 등이 포함된다.

(C) 스포츠 팬 우울증의 부정적인 영향을 완화하기 위해서는, 팬들이 스포츠에 대한 건강한 시각을 유지하고 궁극적으로 그저 게임이라는 것을 기억하는 것이 중요하다. 운동과 같은 자기 관리 활동에 참여하는 것, 사랑하는 사람들과 시간을 보내는 것, 그리고 정신 건강 전문가의 도움을 구하는 것도 도움이 될 수 있다.

| 정답해설 | ② 주어진 문장에서 스포츠 팬 우울증에 대해 정의를 내리고 이에 대한 설명이 이어지는 글이다. (B)에서 많은 팬들이 스포츠 팬 우울증을 겪는 과정에 대해 상세하게 설명하고 있으므로 (B)가 먼저 와야 한다. (B)의 뒷부분에서 스포츠 팬 우울증이 정신과 신체 건강에 부정적인 영향을 미칠 수 있다는 연구 결과를 언급했는데, (C)에서 이에 대한 해결책을 제시했고, (A)에서는 우울증을 일으키는 요인들을 상세하게 나열했으므로 (C)보다는 부정적인 흐름이 이어지는 (A)가 와야 한다. 마지막으로 스포츠 팬 우울증의 부정적인 영향을 완화시키기 위한 조언을 하고 있는 (C)가 오는 것이 자연스러우므로 정답은 ②이다.

어휘
depression 우울증	defeat 패배
investment 투자	intense 강렬한, 격렬한
frustration 좌절	contribute to ~에 기여하다
coverage (뉴스의) 취재 범위; 보도	scrutiny 조사
accompany 동반하다	mitigate 완화하다
perspective 관점, 견해	

9 　독해 > 세부내용 찾기 > 내용 불일치 찾기 　　답 ④

| 해석 | Roald Dahl(1916~1990)은 웨일즈에서 노르웨이인 부모 사이에 태어났다. 그는 어린 시절을 영국에서 보냈고, 18세에 아프리카의 Shell Oil Company로 일하러 갔다. 제2차 세계 대전이 발발하자, 왕립 공군에 합류하여 전투기 조종사가 되었다. 26세에 그는 워싱턴 D.C.로 이주했고, 그가 글을 쓰기 시작한 곳은 다름 아닌 그곳에서였다. 전쟁에서의 모험을 구술한 그의 첫 번째 단편 소설은 The Saturday Evening Post에서 구입했고, 길고

저명한 활동이 시작되었다. 성인을 위한 작가로 자리매김한 후, Roald Dahl은 가족과 함께 영국에 살면서 1960년에 동화를 쓰기 시작했다. 그의 첫 번째 이야기는 자신의 자녀들의 즐거움을 위해 쓰여졌는데, 그의 많은 책들이 자녀들에게 헌정된 것이다. Roald Dahl은 현재 우리 시대의 가장 사랑받는 이야기꾼 중 하나로 여겨진다.

| **정답해설** | ④ After establishing himself as a writer for adults, Roald Dahl began writing children's stories in 1960 while living in England with his family.에서 가족과 함께 영국에서 살면서 글을 썼다고 했으므로, 가족과 떨어져 혼자 살면서 글을 썼다고 한 ④는 글의 내용과 일치하지 않는다.

어휘

recount 이야기하다, 묘사하다　　illustrious 걸출한, 뛰어난
be dedicated to ~에 전념하다　　beloved 사랑받는, 소중한

10　독해 > 글의 일관성 파악하기 > 글의 흐름과 무관한 문장　답 ②

| **해석** | 지속 가능한 새로운 에너지원 분야에서 가장 흥미로운 발견 중 하나는 해파리의 바이오 솔라 에너지이다. 과학자들은 이 동물의 형광 단백질이 현재의 광전기성 에너지보다 더 지속 가능한 방식으로 태양 에너지를 생산하는 데 사용될 수 있다는 것을 발견했다. 이 에너지는 어떻게 재생되는가? 이 과정은 해파리의 형광 단백질을 에너지를 생성해서 그것을 작은 장치로 전송하는 태양 전지로 변환하는 것을 포함한다. ② 무분별한 태양광 발전으로 자연환경이 훼손되고 있다는 지적이 끊이지 않았다. 이러한 생명체를 천연 에너지원으로 사용하는 것의 주된 장점은 그것들이 화석 연료를 사용하지 않거나 제한된 자원을 사용해야 하는 청정한 대안이라는 점이다. 이 프로젝트는 현재 아직 시험 단계에 있지만, 이 에너지원은 확대될 것이고 점점 더 보편화되고 있는 소형 전자 장치 유형에 동력 공급하기 위한 친환경적인 대안이 될 것이다.

| **정답해설** | ② 지속 가능한 새로운 에너지원으로 해파리에서 나오는 바이오 솔라 에너지를 언급했고, 이 에너지의 생성 방식과 장점에 대해 설명하는 글이다. 친환경적인 에너지원으로써 전체적으로 긍정적인 관점에서 서술하는 가운데, 역접이나 대비의 연결사 없이 ②에서 관련 없는 태양광 발전에 의해 자연환경이 훼손되고 있다는 비판이 있다고 했으므로 글의 흐름과 관계없는 문장으로 ②가 가장 적절하다.

어휘

sustainable 지속 가능한　　jellyfish 해파리
fluorescent 형광성의　　protein 단백질
transfer 넘겨주다, 옮기다　　constant 일관적인, 지속적인
reckless 무모한　　trial 실험, 시도

11　독해 > 글의 일관성 파악하기 > 글의 순서　답 ④

| **해석** | 인간의 차원에서, 암소는 단순해 보인다. 당신이 소에게 풀을 먹이면, 그것은 우유로 갚는다. 그것은 암소와 몇몇 포유류(대부분 풀을 소화하지 못하는)에게만 국한된 비결의 속임수이다.
(C) 당신은 이 과정을 이용하기 위해 자세한 내용을 이해할 필요는 없는데, 이것은 풀에서 우유로의 직접적인 변화이며, 생물학보다는 화학이나 연금술에 더 가깝다. 그것은 그 나름대로 마법이긴 하지만, 안정적으로 작용하는 것은 다름 아닌 이성적인 마법이다. 당신에게 필요한 전부는 약간의 풀과 암소, 그리고 몇 세대에 걸친 실용적인 노하우뿐이다.
(B) 하지만 현미경으로 보면, 모든 것이 더 복잡해진다. 가까이서 볼수록, 더

복잡해진다. 우유는 하나의 물질이 아니라, 많은 것들이 섞여 있는 것이다. 풀은 너무나 복잡해서 우리는 아직도 그것을 완전히 이해하지 못한다.
(A) 암소의 복잡성은 훨씬 더 크다. 특히 암소(황소도 함께)는 새로운 세대의 송아지를 만들 수 있다. 이것은 인간의 차원에서는 간단한 것이지만, 미시적인 수준에서는 표현할 수 없을 정도로 복잡하다.

| **정답해설** | ④ 주어진 글에서 암소가 풀을 먹고 우유를 만들어 낸다는 (인간의 차원에서) 단순한 현상을 언급한 후, 여기에는 속임수가 있다고 마무리하고 있다. 따라서 그 다음에는 이 과정이 단순하지 않다는 내용이 올 것이라 유추할 수 있는데, 주어진 글을 the process로 지칭한 (C)가 처음에 오는 것이 적절하다. 이 과정을 풀에서 우유로의 직접적인 변화라고 칭하면서 이는 생물학이 아닌 화학이나 연금술에 가깝다고 언급한 후, (B)에서 접속사 though에 이어 현미경을 통해 보면 복잡한 과정이라고 서술하는 내용이 이어지는 것이 자연스럽다. (C)에서는 (B)의 흐름에 연결되는 내용이 이어지고 있으므로 글의 순서로 가장 적절한 것은 ④이다.

어휘

digest 소화하다　　exploit 이용하다, 착취하다
straightforward 직접의, 솔직한　　transformation 변화, 변형
rational 합리적인, 이성적인　　complicated 복잡한
complexity 복잡성　　microscopic 미시적인, 미세한

12　독해 > 글의 일관성 파악하기 > 주어진 문장의 삽입　답 ②

| **해석** | 코로나19의 확산으로 원격근무를 가로막고 있던 문화 · 기술 장벽이 허물어졌다. 원격근무가 지속될 가능성에 대한 한 가지 분석에 따르면 선진국의 인력 중 20~25%가 일주일에 3~5일 범위 내에서 집에서 일할 수 있었다. 이것은 COVID-19 이전보다 4~5배 더 많은 원격근무이다. ② 하지만 여기서 절반 이상의 근로자들이 원격 근무를 할 기회가 거의 없거나 아예 없다는 점은 주목할 가치가 있다. 또한 원격으로 수행할 수 있는 모든 업무가 그래야만 하는 것은 아니다. 예를 들어, 협상, 브레인스토밍 및 민감한 피드백 제공은 원격으로 수행할 때, 덜 효과적일 수 있는 활동이다. 그러면, 원격근무에 대한 전망은 근무 환경, 업무 및 당면 업무에 따라 달라지므로, 일부 업무는 현장에서, 일부는 원격으로 진행되는 혼합체 근무 환경은 지속될 가능성이 높다. 혼합체 세계에서 지속 가능한 성과와 복지를 열기 위해서는, 성과와 생산성의 주도적인 동인(動因)이 보상이 아니라, 직원들에게 제공되는 목적의식이어야 한다.

| **정답해설** | ② 주어진 문장에서 But에 이어 절반 이상의 인력이 원격근무의 기회가 거의 없거나 아예 없었다고 했으므로, 이전에는 원격근무가 실행되고 있다는 내용이 있어야 한다. ② 앞에서 COVID-19 이전보다 이후에 원격근무 비율이 늘었다고 언급했고, ②에 이어 부연의 연결사인 Moreover에 이어 모든 근무가 원격으로 이루어질 필요는 없다고 했으므로 흐름의 전환을 이끄는 주어진 문장은 ②에 들어가는 것이 가장 적절하다.

어휘

flatten (건물 등을) 쓰러뜨리다; 평평하게 하다
barrier 장벽　　stand in the way of ~을 훼방 놓다
negotiation 협상, 협의　　outlook 전망
setup 설립, 설치　　persist 지속하다
sustainable 지속 가능한　　purpose 목적
compensation 보상

13 독해 > 세부내용 찾기 > 내용 불일치 찾기   답 ③

| 해석 | Sigmund Freud는 19세기 말, 오스트리아 비엔나에서 정신과 의사였다. 그는 자신의 '대화 치료'를 통해 많은 신경증 환자를 치료했다. 이런 유형의 치료를 위해, Freud는 그저 환자들이 자신들을 괴롭히는 어떤 것에 대해서도 그에게 말하도록 했다. 환자를 치료하는 동안, 그는 환자의 과거에 의식적으로 기억하지 못하는 사건이 있었음에도, 이러한 사건이 환자의 현재 행동에 영향을 줄 수 있음을 깨닫기 시작했다. Freud는 과거의 기억이 숨겨져 있는 장소를 무의식이라고 칭했다. 무의식의 이미지는 한 사람의 꿈이나 그 사람의 행동을 통해 나타날 수 있다. Freud는 1899년에 무의식과 꿈에 관한 그의 이론에 관한 책을 썼다. 그 책의 제목은 'The Interpretation of Dreams(꿈의 해석)'이었다.

| 정답해설 | ③ he began to realize that although there were events in a patient's past that she or he might not remember consciously, these events could affect the person's actions in her or his present life.에서 기억이 나지 않는 과거가 환자의 현재의 삶에서 행동에 영향을 미칠 수 있다는 것을 깨달았다고 했으므로, ③은 글의 내용과 일치하지 않는다.

어휘

nervous 신경 과민의; 신경성의   bother 괴롭히다, 성가시게 하다
consciously 의식적으로   interpretation 해석, 이해

14 독해 > 대의 파악 > 요지·주장 찾기   답 ④

| 해석 | 모든 감정은 우리 자신과 상황에 대해 무언가를 말해 준다. 그러나 때때로 우리는 우리가 느끼는 것을 받아들이기가 어렵다고 생각한다. 예를 들어, 우리가 질투심을 느끼는 것처럼, 특정한 방식으로 느끼는 것에 대해 우리 자신을 판단할지도 모른다. 하지만 우리가 그런 방식으로 느껴서는 안 된다고 생각하는 대신에, 우리가 실제로 어떻게 느끼는지를 알아차리는 것이 더 낫다. 부정적인 감정을 피하거나 우리가 느끼는 방식을 모르는 척하는 것은 역효과를 낳을 수 있다. 어려운 감정들을 마주하지 않고 우리가 왜 그런 감정을 느끼는지 이해하려고 노력하지 않는다면, 어려운 감정들을 지나가게 하고 그것들이 사라지게 하는 것은 더 어렵다. 당신은 감정에 연연할 필요도, 당신이 어떻게 느끼는가에 대해 끊임없이 이야기할 필요도 없다. 감정적 인식은 감정이 생겨날 때, 단순히 자신의 감정을 인식하고 존중하며 받아들이는 것을 의미한다.

| 정답해설 | ④ 모든 감정이 우리 자신과 상황에 대해 무언가를 말해 준다고 언급한 후, 이에 대한 구체적인 내용을 전개하는 글이다. 첫 문장에 이어진 But 다음에 우리가 느끼는 것을 받아들이는 것이 힘들다고 언급한 후, 또 한번 더 But에 이어 어떻게 우리가 느끼는가에 주목하는 것이 더 낫다며, 감정에 대한 우리의 대처 방식을 서술하고 있다. 마지막 문장이 주제문으로, 감정적 인식은 감정이 생겨날 때 인식하고 존중하고 받아들이는 것이라고 했으므로 글의 요지로 가장 적절한 것은 ④이다.

어휘

jealous 질투하는, 시기하는   avoid 회피하다
fade 사라지다, 흐려지다   dwell on ~을 곰곰이 생각하다
constantly 끊임없이, 계속   awareness 인식, 자각

15 독해 > 글의 일관성 파악하기 > 글의 순서   답 ②

| 해석 | 입법 수준에서, 거대 기술 기업들이 기술 자원과 혁신에 대해 그렇게 철통 같은 장악력을 가져야 할 이유는 없다.

(B) 사적인 그리고 개인적인 수준에서, 그들이 당신의 삶을 통제해야 할 이유도 없다. 정책, 정치 및 우리의 개인 생활에서, 우리의 데이터가 가장 높은 입찰자에게 팔리고, 우리의 자녀가 온라인 게임에 중독되며, 우리의 삶이 메타버스에서 살게 될 것이라는 것이 불가피한 것으로 받아들여서는 안된다.

(C) 자유로운 사람으로서, 우리는 우리가 소비하는 디지털 제품의 종류와 수량에 대해 '절대적인' 통제를 행사할 권리가 있다. 특별히, 부모들은 자신들의 자녀들에게 어떤 기술 제품이 가는지 통제해야 한다.

(A) Daily Wire의 Matt Walsh가 지적했듯이, 예를 들어, 당신이 자녀에게 스마트폰을 사주지 않으면, 아이는 스마트폰을 갖지 못할 것이다. 감독 없이 모든 충동에 빠져들도록 만드는 장비를 자녀의 손에 쥐어줄 필요는 없다.

| 정답해설 | ② 주어진 글에서는 입법 수준에서, 거대 기술 기업들이 기술 자원과 혁신에 있어 장악력을 가져야 할 이유는 없다고 했는데, 이후 이어지는 내용을 보면, 입법과 기업 간의 관계가 아님을 알 수 있다. 따라서 비슷한 맥락으로, 사적인 그리고 개인적인 수준에서의 통제에 관한 시작이라고 볼 수 있는 (B)가 처음에 와야 함을 알 수 있다. (A)에는 자녀에게 스마트폰을 쥐어주는 것에 대한 사례이므로 (B)에 이어지기보다는 (C)의 뒷부분에서 부모가 어떤 기술 제품이 자녀들에게 가는가를 통제해야 한다고 했으므로 (C)에 이어 (B)의 사례가 언급되어야 함을 알 수 있다. 따라서 정답은 ②이다.

어휘

ironclad 철갑을 입힌, 견고한   inevitable 불가피한
bidder 입찰자, 협상자
be addicted to ~에 빠지다, 탐닉하다
metaverse 메타버스(특히 온라인 게임에서 3D 가상 세계)
be entitled to ~의 자격이 있다   indulge 탐닉하다, 빠지다
impulse 충동, 자극   supervision 감독, 관리

16 독해 > 글의 일관성 파악하기 > 주어진 문장의 삽입   답 ③

| 해석 | 지구 온난화는 인간이 감수해야 할 현실이다. 이것은 인식해야 할 매우 중요한 문제인데, 왜냐하면, 지구상에서 인간의 존재에 영향을 미치는 모든 변수들 중에서, 지구상의 생명체에게 가장 중요하고 지구 온난화에 의해 가장 위협받는 것은 다름 아닌 식품 안전이기 때문이다. 미래의 식품 안전은 기후 변화, 생장기 내의 날씨 가변성, 다른 주변 환경에 더 적합화된 품종의 개발, 그리고 이러한 품종이 그들의 유전적인 가능성을 변화하는 기후 환경하에서 펼칠 수 있도록 하는 효과적인 적응 전략 개발 능력에 의해 부과되는 생물적인 그리고 비생물적인 스트레스의 결합에 좌우될 것이다. ③ 이것들은 미래의 기후를 예측하는 우리의 능력의 불확실성 때문에 대처하기에 불가능할 수도 있는 문제들처럼 보일 수도 있다. 그러나 이러한 문제들은 또한 우리에게 토양-식물-대기 상호 작용에 대한 우리의 이해를 높이고, 이 지식을 활용하여 우리가 세계의 모든 지역에서 식품 안전이라는 궁극적인 목표를 어떻게 달성할 수 있는지에 대한 이해를 향상시키는 기회를 제공한다.

| 정답해설 | ③ 주어진 문장의 주어인 These가 지칭하는 대상이 이전에 나와야 하는데, These가 대처하는 것이 불가능한 '문제들'이라고 했으므로 뒤에는 이에 대한 구체적인 내용이나 해결책이 제시될 거라고 유추할 수 있다. 이 글은 지구 온난화와 이에 따른 식품 안전

에 대한 내용을 다루고 있고, ③ 이전까지 미래의 식품 안전에 대한 전망을 서술하고 있다. ③ 뒤에 나오는 역접의 접속사 However에 이어 주어로 these challenges가 왔으므로 전에 challenges가 언급되어야 하는데, 주어진 문장에서 challenges가 언급되었으므로, 정답은 ③이 가장 적절하다. 이후에는 식품 안전에 관련된 문제점들에 대한 긍정적인 전망이 이어졌다.

어휘

live with 감수하다, 참고 지내다　　parameter 변수, 매개 변수
paramount 최고의, 뛰어난　　threaten 위협하다
combination 조합, 결합　　impose 부과하다
adaptation 적응, 순응; 각색

17　문법 > 동사의 형태 > 수동태　　답 ①

| 해석 | 인류학자 Paul Ekman은 1970년대에 인간은 분노, 두려움, 놀람, 혐오, 기쁨, 슬픔 등 6가지 기본 감정을 경험한다고 제시했다. 그러나 감정의 정확한 수는 논쟁의 여지가 있으며, 일부 연구자들은 4가지뿐이라고 말하고, 다른 사람들은 27개씩이나 포함한다. 게다가, 과학자들은 감정이 모든 인간 문화에 보편적인지, 아니면 우리가 감정을 가지고 태어났는지 혹은 경험을 통해 배우는지에 대해 논쟁한다. 이러한 의견 차이에도 불구하고, 감정은 뇌의 특정 영역에서 활동의 분명한 산물이다. 편도체와 대뇌 피질은 감정과 가장 밀접하게 연결된 두 가지 대표적인 뇌 조직이다. 뇌 깊숙한 곳에 있는 한 쌍의 아몬드 모양의 조직인 편도체는 감정, 감정적 행동, 동기부여를 통합한다. 그것은 두려움을 해석하고, 친구와 적을 구별하고, 사회적 보상과 그것을 얻는 방법을 식별하는 데 도움이 된다. 혐오의 경험은 당신을 독이나 상한 음식을 섭취하는 것으로부터 보호할지도 모른다.

| 정답해설 | ① 명사에 이어 disputing이 왔고, 이어서 전치사 with에 이어 목적어인 명사가 이어졌다. 즉, However에 이어진 절이 없는 상태이므로, disputing은 준동사가 아닌 본동사가 되어야 한다. disputes는 타동사로 뒤에 목적어인 명사가 없다는 점과 맥락상 감정의 정확한 수는 '논의되는' 것이므로 수동태가 되어야 한다. 맥락상 과거에서 현재에 이르는 현재완료시제 혹은 현재의 상태를 나타내는 현재시제 모두 가능하며, 수를 고려해 has been disputed로 바꿔야 한다. 뒤에 이어진 with 분사구문에서 suggesting 다음에는 명사절을 이끄는 접속사 that이 생략된 구조이다.

| 오답해설 | ② 전치사 despite의 목적어로 명사 these disagreements가 이어진 올바른 구조이다.

③ 분사 linked를 수식하는 품사로 '밀접하게'라는 의미의 부사 closely가 적절하게 왔다.

④ and 앞에 있는 social rewards를 지칭하는 대명사가 복수형으로 올바르게 왔다.

어휘

anthropologist 인류학자　　disgust 혐오
dispute 논쟁　　debate 논쟁, 토론
universal 보편적인　　representative 대표적인
integrate 통합하다　　interpret 해석하다
distinguish 구별하다　　foe 적
attain 달성하다　　ingest 섭취하다
spoiled 상한; 버릇 없는

18　독해 > 대의 파악 > 주제 찾기　　답 ②

| 해석 | 당신은 성공적인 앵커가 되고 싶은가? 만약 그렇다면, 이것을 명심하라. 앵커로서 개인은 뉴스 방송, 특별 보도 및 기타 유형의 뉴스 프로그램 중에 시청자에게 뉴스와 정보를 전달하도록 요청받기 마련이다. 여기에는 뉴스 사건들, 즉흥 진행, 대본이 없을 때 속보를 효과적으로 전달하는 것이 포함된다. 앵커의 의무는 또한 이야기를 수집하고 집필하는 것을 포함한다. 앵커는 대본을 명확하고 효과적으로 전달할 수 있어야 한다. 강력한 집필 기술, 확고한 뉴스 판단 및 강력한 시각적 이야기 전달력이 필수 기술이다. 이러한 인물은 업무의 규칙적인 부분으로써 정보원을 육성하고 새로운 정보를 찾는 자발적인 사람이어야 한다. 속보가 발생할 때, 즉흥 진행과 속보를 설명하는 능력뿐 아니라, 생방송 보도 기술 또한 중요하다.
① 생방송 뉴스 제작의 어려움
② 뉴스 앵커가 되기 위한 자질
③ 언론인의 사회적 역할의 중요성
④ 올바른 여론 형성의 중요성

| 정답해설 | ② 글의 첫 번째 문장과 두 번째 문장의 주제문이다. 성공적인 앵커가 되고 싶은지 물어보고, 성공적인 앵커가 갖추어야 할 자질들에 대해 상세하게 설명한 글이다. 따라서 글의 주제로 가장 적절한 것은 ②이다.

어휘

anchor (美) 뉴스 캐스터, 보도 프로 담당 아나운서
interpret 해석하다
ad lib 즉흥적으로 말하다, 준비 없이 하다
script 대본　　　　　　　　　　cultivate 기르다, 육성하다

19　독해 > 세부내용 찾기 > 내용 불일치 찾기　　답 ③

| 해석 | 현대 조각은 일반적으로 프랑스 조각가 오귀스트 로댕의 작품으로 시작된 것으로 여겨진다. 종종 인상파 조각가로 여겨지는 로댕은 예술적 전통에 반항하는 것을 시도하지 않았지만, 그는 전통적인 범주와 기법을 거부하는 자신의 조각품을 만드는 것에 새로운 방식을 도입했다. 특히, 로댕은 복잡하고, 격동적이고, 깊이 감추어진 표면을 점토로 만들었다. 그가 인상파 화가로 자칭하지는 않았지만, 그의 작품에서 사용한 활기찬 몸짓 표현은 종종 인상파 화가들에게 전형적이었던 찰나의 순간을 포착하기 위한 빠른 몸짓의 붓놀림과 비유되곤 한다. 로댕의 가장 독창적인 작품은 신화와 우화라는 전통적인 주제에서 벗어났는데, 이는 극도의 사실주의에 입각해 인체를 만들고 개인의 특성과 운동능력을 찬양하는 것이었다.

| 정답해설 | ③ 조각가 로댕을 인상파 화가와 비유해 작품을 만드는 방식에 있어 유사성에 대해 서술한 글이다. While he never self-identified as an Impressionist, the vigorous, gestural modeling he employed in his works is often likened to the quick, gestural brush strokes aiming to capture a fleeting moment that was typical of the Impressionists.에서 로댕이 인상파로서 자칭하지는 않았다고 했으므로 글의 내용과 일치하지 않는 것은 ③이다.

어휘

rebel against ~에 저항하다　　incorporate 포함하다, 통합하다
novel 새로운, 참신한　　defy 거부하다
turbulent 사나운, 난폭한　　vigorous 활발한, 박력 있는
liken 비유하다　　fleeting 순식간의, 덧없는
depart from ~에서 떠나가다
in favor of ~에 찬성하여; ~에 유리하게
celebrate 찬양하다, 기념하다

20 독해 > 대의 파악 > 주제 찾기 답 ③

| 해석 | 화장품은 사진 인물 묘사와 매우 밀접하게 연관되어 일부 사진 안내서는 그것들에 대한 비결이 포함되어 있다. 미국의 사진작가들도 때때로 화장품을 사용해 원판과 인화를 수정하고, 연지의 흔적으로 여성의 얼굴에 생기를 불어넣었다. 어두운 피부를 가진 몇몇 고객들은 더 환하게 보이게 만드는 사진을 요청했다. 1935년 아프리카계 미국인 신문에 실린 피부 미백제 광고는 이 제품이 사진작가들이 만들어 내는 것과 똑같은 티 없는 더 밝은 피부를 만들어 낼 수 있다고 약속함으로써 이러한 관행을 보여주었다. 얼굴에 주의를 끌고 화장품 사용을 장려함으로써, 인물 사진 촬영은 부드럽고 종종 밝은색 피부에 대한 미적 평가를 높였다.

① 과도한 화장품 사용에 대한 부작용
② 사진작가에 의해 조장된 화장품 남용
③ 얼굴이 더 나아 보이기 위한 활발한 화장품 사용
④ 사진술 발전으로 인한 감소된 화장품 사용

| 정답해설 | ③ 사진에서 피부가 더 환하게 보이도록 화장품을 사용하는 관행에 대해 설명하는 글이다. 글의 앞부분에서는 사진술에서 화장품으로 얼굴에 생기를 불어넣는 방식이 언급되었고, 이후에는 이런 효과를 낼 수 있는 피부 미백제 광고에 대해 언급하고 있으므로, 글의 주제로 가장 적절한 것은 ③이다.

어휘

associated with ~와 관련된
portraiture (그림 · 사진 등에 의한) 인물 묘사
enliven 활기 띠게 하다
reference 참조 사항을 달다, 참고 문헌을 싣다
heighten 강화하다, 높이다 aesthetic 미의, 미학의
valuation 평가, 감정

21 독해 > 밑줄 어휘 > 어휘 추론 답 ③

| 해석 | 'Play'의 저자이자 정신과 의사인 Stuart Brown은 '놀이는 그 자체를 위해 행해지는 것이다'라고 언급했다. 그는 '그것은 자발적이고, 즐거우며, 소속감을 제공하고, 시간으로부터 당신을 데려간다. 그리고 행위 그 자체는 결과보다 더 중요하다.'라고 쓴다. 이러한 정의를 염두하면, 놀이의 잠재적 장점들을 쉽게 인식할 수 있다. 놀이는 자신과 타인과의 관계를 키워준다. 그것은 스트레스를 완화하고 행복감을 높여 준다. 그것은 감정이입, 창의력, 협동심을 키워준다. 그것은 강건함과 배짱의 성장을 뒷받침한다. 아이들이 놀이의 기회를 박탈당할 때, 그들의 발달은 현저하게 ③ 향상될(→ 약화될) 수 있다. 놀이는 매우 중요하기 때문에 UN 인권고등판무관은 놀이는 모든 어린이의 기본 권리라고 선언했다. 놀이는 하찮은 것이 아니다. 그것은 '실제 일'이 끝나고 난 후에 하는 일이 아니다. 놀이는 유년기의 실제 일이다. 그것을 통해, 아이들은 온전하고 행복한 어른이 될 수 있는 가장 좋은 기회를 얻게 된다.

| 정답해설 | ③ 아이들에게 '놀이(play)'가 지니는 중요성에 대해 설명하는 글이다. 놀이에 대한 장점들을 서술하는 가운데 ③ 이전에 아이들이 놀이의 기회를 박탈당했을 경우가 언급되었고, ③이 포함된 문장에서는 이에 따른 결과를 유추해야 한다. 따라서, 아이들이 놀이의 기회를 박탈당한다면, 그들의 발달은 향상되는(enhanced) 것이 아니라 약화되거나(weakened) 혹은 손상될(damaged) 수 있음을 알 수 있다. 따라서 낱말의 쓰임이 적절하지 않은 것은 ③이다.

어휘

for one's own sake 자신을 위해서 psychiatrist 정신과 의사
voluntary 자발적인 pleasurable 즐거운, 유쾌한
relieve 완화하다 engagement 참여, 연대
empathy 감정이입, 공감 collaboration 협동, 협업
grit 배짱, 용기 deprive A of B A에게 B를 빼앗다

22 독해 > 빈칸의 내용 추론하기 > 빈칸 어휘 추론 답 ③

| 해석 | Lewis Pugh는 영국의 지구력 수영 선수로, 그는 차가운 바다에서 장거리 수영을 하는 것으로 가장 유명하다. 그는 기후 변화와 오염의 영향으로부터 세계의 바다와 수로를 보호해야 할 긴급한 필요성에 주의를 환기시키는 방법으로써 추운 곳에서 수영을 한다. 2019년에 Pugh는 에베레스트 산 근처의 네팔 Khumbu 지역에 위치한 Imja 호수에서 수영하기로 결정했다. 첫 번째 시도가 실패한 후, Lewis는 해발 5,300미터에서 수영하는 최고의 방법을 논의할 평가 회의를 열었다. 그는 수영을 빨리 끝내고 차가운 물에서 벗어나고 싶어서, 수영을 할 때 보통 매우 공격적이다. 하지만 이번에는 ③ 겸손을 보여주었고 천천히 수영했다.

① 슬픔 ② 분노
③ 겸손 ④ 자신감

| 정답해설 | ③ 기후 변화와 오염에 대해 환기시키는 방법으로 추운 바다에서 수영을 하는 Lewis Pugh에 대한 글이다. 네팔에 있는 한 호수에서 첫 번째 시도가 실패한 후 열린 평가 회의가 있었고, 이후 그가 한 행위가 빈칸을 포함한 문장에서 언급되었다. 수영할 때 차가운 물에서 빨리 나오고 싶어서 보통 수영할 때 매우 공격적이라고 언급했는데, But에 이어 빈칸이 이어졌으므로, 그가 보여준 모습은 공격적인 것과는 대조적인 말이 들어가야 한다. 따라서 그가 보여준 모습은 '겸손(humility)'임을 알 수 있다.

어휘

endurance 지구력 urgent 긴급한
get out of (장소에서) 나가다, 도망치다

23 독해 > 글의 일관성 파악하기 > 글의 흐름과 무관한 문장 답 ①

| 해석 | 패스트패션은 최신 패션 트렌드에 대응하기 위해 저렴한 의류를 빠른 속도로 생산하는 방식이다. 패스트패션 시대에 쇼핑이 오락의 한 형태로 진화함에 따라, 고객들은 지속 가능성 전문가들이 버리기 문화라고 부르는 것에 일조하고 있다. 이는 고객들이 제품을 재활용하거나 기부하기보다는 일단 쓸모없다고 판단되면 그냥 폐기한다는 것을 의미한다. ① 소비자들은 패스트패션 브랜드 의류의 품질에 대해 전반적으로 만족하고 있다. 결과적으로, 이러한 버려지는 품목들은 환경에 엄청난 부담을 더한다. 일회용(버리기) 문화와 패스트패션 위기를 해결하기 위해, 패션의 지속 가능성 개념이 주목을 받고 있다. 지속 가능한 패션은 사회 경제적 및 환경 문제를 고려하면서 가능한 한 지속 가능하게 생산, 유통 및 활용되는 의류, 신발 및 액세서리를 포함한다.

| 정답해설 | ① 패스트패션에 대해 정의를 내리고, 환경에 미치는 부정적인 영향을 설명하는 글이다. 글 전체적으로 부정적인 흐름으로 서술하는 가운데, ③ 이후에서 이에 대한 해결책을 제시하고 있다. ①에 이어진 문장에서 소비자들이 패스트패션 의류의 품질에 만족한다는 긍정적인 내용이 언급되었는데, ② 다음에 As a result에 이어진 문장의 주어 these discarded items는 ① 이전에 언급된 부분에 연결이 되고 있음을 알 수 있고, 또한 환경에 엄청난 부담을 더한다는 부정적인 내용이 이어졌으므로 흐름과 관계가 없는 문장은 ①이 가장 적절하다.

24   독해 > 대의 파악 > 요지 · 주장 찾기   답 ④

| 해석 | 주름은 노화의 확실한 신호이며, 뼈 건강이 감소하고 있다는 암시일 수도 있다. Yale 의과대학 연구진은 나이와 골량(骨量)에 영향을 주는 것으로 알려진 요인들과 무관하게, 피부 주름이 깊어지고 악화되는 일부 여성들도 낮은 골밀도를 지닌다는 것을 발견했다. 피부와 뼈는 나이가 들면서 소실되는 공통의 구성 단백질인 1형 콜라겐을 공유한다고 연구 저자 Lubna Pal 박사는 말한다. 눈썹 사이의 주름, 즉 콧등 위의 세로선은 잘 부러지는 뼈의 가장 강력한 표시로 보인다고 그녀는 말한다. 장기적인 연구가 필요하지만, 피부는 뼈의 수준에서 무슨 일이 일어나는지 반영하는 것으로 보인다고 Pal은 말한다.

| 정답해설 | ④ 핵심어는 주름(wrinkles)으로, 노화의 확실한 신호이자 뼈 건강을 알려준다는 취지의 글이다. 첫 번째 문장에 이어 Yale 의과대학에서 발견한 실험 결과를 인용해 주제문에 대한 구체적인 예시를 들고 있으므로 글의 요지로 가장 적절한 것은 ④이다.

25   독해 > 세부내용 찾기 > 내용 불일치 찾기   답 ③

| 해석 | 명상은 많은 심리적, 육체적 이점 덕분에 삶의 질을 향상시킬 수 있다. Clinical Psychology Review의 한 연구에 따르면, 명상과 같은 마음 챙김 기반의 개입은 특히 스트레스 영역에서 정신 건강을 향상시키는 것으로 나타났다. 어렵거나 스트레스를 받는 순간에 직면했을 때, 우리 몸은 스트레스를 조절하는 스테로이드 호르몬인 코르티솔과 우리의 자연적인 싸움과 도피 반응, 다른 많은 기능들을 만들어 낸다. 만성적인 스트레스는 지속적이고 높은 수준의 코르티솔을 유발할 수 있으며, 이는 심혈관 및 면역 체계와 장 건강을 포함한 여러분의 건강에 부정적인 영향을 미칠 수 있다. 마음을 진정시키고 감정을 조절하는 데 중점을 둔 명상은 신체의 만성적인 스트레스를 줄이고 부작용의 위험을 낮추는 데 도움을 줄 수 있다.
① 명상은 우리에게 정신적 그리고 신체적으로 모두 이익이 된다.
② 코르티솔은 스트레스를 받는 상황에서 배출된다.
③ 스트레스는 보통 우리의 심혈관계에 영향을 미치지 않는다.
④ 명상은 신체의 만성적인 스트레스를 낮추는 데 도움이 될 수 있다.

| 정답해설 | ③ Chronic stress can cause sustained and elevated levels of cortisol, which can lead to other negative effects on your health, including cardiovascular and immune systems~에서 만성적인 스트레스가 심혈관에 부정적인 영향을 미칠 수 있다고 했으므로 ③은 글의 내용과 일치하지 않는다.

합격예상 체크

〈법원직 연도별 합격선〉

2022 합격기준

2024	2023	2022	2021	2020

맞힌 개수	/25문항	점수	/100점

➡ □ 합격 □ 불합격

취약영역 체크

문항	정답	영역	문항	정답	영역
1	①	문법 > 명사와 일치	14	②	독해 > 글의 일관성 파악하기
2	①	독해 > 요약	15	④	문법 > 명사와 일치
3	①	독해 > 요약	16	②	독해 > 대의 파악
4	③	독해 > 글의 일관성 파악하기	17	③	독해 > 빈칸의 내용 추론하기
5	④	독해 > 세부내용 찾기	18	①	문법 > 동사의 형태
6	④	독해 > 빈칸의 내용 추론하기	19	①	문법 > 문장의 구조와 동사 유형
7	①	독해 > 세부내용 찾기	20	②	독해 > 빈칸의 내용 추론하기
8	③	독해 > 밑줄 어휘	21	③	독해 > 글의 일관성 파악하기
9	③	독해 > 요약	22	②	독해 > 대의 파악
10	④	독해 > 글의 일관성 파악하기	23	①	독해 > 대의 파악
11	①	문법 > 접속사, 시제, 분사	24	②	독해 > 세부내용 찾기
12	③	독해 > 빈칸의 내용 추론하기	25	③	독해 > 세부내용 찾기
13	①	독해 > 글의 일관성 파악하기			

⬇ 영역별 틀린 개수로 취약영역을 확인하세요!

어휘	/0	문법	/5	독해	/20	생활영어	/0

➡ 나의 취약영역: _____

※ [정답해설]과 [오답해설] 선지의 50% 표시는 〈1초 합격예측 서비스〉를 통해 수집된 선지 선택률을 나타냅니다.

1	문법 > 명사와 일치 > 일치	오답률 14%	답 ①

| 해석 | 어떤 작업이나 직무에 적합한 보호복을 선택하는 것은 일반적으로 주어진 위험에 대한 분석이나 평가에 의해 좌우된다. 노출의 빈도와 유형뿐만 아니라 착용자의 예상되는 활동이 이 결정에 투입되는 전형적인 변수들이다. 예를 들어, 소방관은 다양한 연소 물질에 노출된다. 따라서 특화된 다층 직물 계통이 주어진 열 관련 문제들에 대처하기 위해 사용된다. 이것은 일반적으로 상당히 무겁고 어떤 화재 상황에서도 본질적으로 최고 수준의 보호 기능을 제공하는 보호 장비가 된다. 이와는 대조적으로, 돌발성 화재가 존재할 가능성이 있는 지역에서 일해야 하는 산업 노동자는 매우 다른 세트의 위험과 요구 사항을 가지고 있다. 많은 경우, 면직물 위에 착용하는 방염 커버올 작업복은 위험을 적절히 해결한다.

| 정답해설 | ① 86% (A) 문장 전체의 주어는 the selection이므로 단수 동사 is로 수일치가 되어야 한다.

(B) 동사 are used에 이어지는데, be used to + R은 '~를 위해 사용되다'의 의미이고, be used to R-ing는 '~에 익숙하다'의 의미이다. 맥락상 주어인 직물 계통이 열 관련 문제들에 대처하기 위해 '사용되는' 것이므로 to meet이 올바르다.

(C) 선행사 areas에 이어진 관계사로 뒤에 1형식 문장의 완전한 절이 이어졌으므로, 관계부사 where가 적절하다.

어휘

appropriate 적절한, 적합한   dictate 좌우하다

---

analysis 분석   assessment 평가
hazard 위험   frequency 빈도
variable 변수   input 투입하다
determination 결심, 결정   specialized 특화된
flash fire 돌발성 화재   flame-resistant 내염성의
coverall 커버올, 옷 위에 입는 위아래가 붙은 작업복
adequately 적절히   address 해결하다, 처리하다

2	독해 > 요약	오답률 19%	답 ①

| 해석 | 인도에서는 인구의 3분의 1인 약 3억 6천만 명이 숲속에 혹은 숲과 매우 가까운 곳에 살고 있다. 이 사람들의 절반 이상이 공식적인 빈곤선 미만에 살고 있으며, 결과적으로 그들은 숲에서 얻는 자원에 결정적으로 의존한다. 인도 정부는 이제 숲의 상업적 관리에 그들을 참여함으로써 많은 것을 개선하려는 목적의 프로그램을 운영하고, 이런 방식으로 그들이 필요한 식량과 재료를 계속 얻을 수 있게 하면서, 동시에 숲 수확물을 판매할 수 있게 한다. 만약 이 프로그램이 성공한다면, 숲 거주자들은 더 부유해지겠지만, 그들은 전통적인 삶의 방식과 문화를 보존할 수 있을 것이며, 숲은 지속 가능하게 관리될 것이므로, 야생 생물은 고갈되지 않을 것이다.
⇒ 인도 정부는 숲을 (B) 파괴하지 않으면서 숲 근처에 사는 사람들의 삶을 (A) 개선하려고 노력중이다.

	(A)	(B)
①	개선하다	파괴하는
②	통제하다	보존하는

③ 개선하다　　　제한하는
④ 통제하다　　　확대하는

| 정답해설 | ① ⌈81%⌉ 인도에서 숲속의 혹은 숲 근처에 사는 가난한 사람들을 위해 인도 정부가 개선책으로 진행하는 활동을 서술하는 글이다. 프로그램이 성공하면 숲 거주자들은 부유해지면서 한편으로 전통적인 삶의 방식과 문화를 보존하고 숲을 지속 가능하게 관리할 것이라고 했으므로 (A)에는 improve가, (B)에는 without을 고려해 부정적인 표현인 ruining이 들어가는 것이 가장 적절하다.

[어휘]

approximately 대략, 약	poverty line 빈곤선
consequently 결과적으로	obtain 얻다, 획득하다
prosperous 부유한, 번창하는	preserve 보존하다
sustainably 지속 가능하게	wildlife 야생 생물
deplete 고갈하다	

3　　독해 > 요약　　　　오답률 31%　　답 ①

| 해석 | 유행병 동안에는 얼굴 표정의 신호나 접촉이 없으므로, 대화의 다른 측면들에 더 집중할 필요성이 있는데, 어조와 억양에 더 중점을 두고, 속도를 늦추며, 성가신 소리를 내지 않고 소리의 크기를 늘리는 등이다. 얼굴 표정이 없다면, 말의 많은 뉘앙스는 쉽게 놓칠 수 있으므로, 눈맞춤이 훨씬 더 중요성을 지니기 마련이다. 일부 병원 직원들은 이 문제를 해결하기 위해 혁신적인 방법을 개발했다. 간호 전문가들 중 한 명은 만성적으로 아픈 자신의 어린 환자들이 그녀의 얼굴을 볼 수 없다는 점에 깊이 우려하여, 다양한 얼굴 스티커를 인쇄하여 어린이들이 가리키도록 했다. 이제 어떤 병원들 역시 이제 환자에게 직원을 쉽게 식별할 수 있게 하는 '얼굴 시트'를 제공하며, 마스크를 쓰고 있을 때 환자들에게 자신과 동료들을 다시 소개하는 것이 항상 유용하다.

> 일부 병원과 직원들은 유행병 동안 환자들과의 대화를 (B) 보완하는 (A) 대체 방식들을 찾고 있다.

	(A)	(B)
①	대체의	보완하다
②	성가시게 하는	분석하다
③	효율적인	방해하다
④	혼란을 주는	개선하다

| 정답해설 | ① ⌈69%⌉ 유행병 시기 동안 마스크 착용으로 인해 병원에서 간호 전문가들과 환자들 사이에 얼굴 표정을 알 수가 없어서, 얼굴 스티커와 얼굴 시트를 이용해 식별이 가능하게 했고, 이는 매우 유용하다고 했으므로 (A)에는 alternative가, (B)에는 complement가 들어가는 것이 가장 적절하다.

[어휘]

in the absence of ~이 없어서	pandemic 전국[세계]적인 유행병
inflection 억양	chronically 만성적으로
provide A with B A에게 B를 제공하다	
identification 식별, 확인	

4　　독해 > 글의 일관성 파악하기 > 글의 순서　　오답률 19%　　답 ③

| 해석 | 일단 그들이 어미를 떠나면, 영장류들은 자신들이 마주치는 새로운 식량들이 안전하고 모을 가치가 있는지에 대해 계속해서 결정을 내려야 한다.
(C) 스스로를 실험 도구로 사용하는 것이 하나의 선택이지만, 사회적 영장

류들은 더 나은 방법을 찾아냈다. Kenneth Glander는 이것을 '샘플링'이라고 부른다. 짖는원숭이가 새로운 서식지로 이동할 때, 무리 중 한 마리의 원숭이가 나무로 가서, 잎을 몇 개 먹고, 하루를 기다린다.
(B) 만약 그 식물이 특별히 강한 독소를 가지고 있다면, 샘플러 시스템은 그것을 분해하려고 시도할 것이고, 보통 그 과정에서 원숭이를 아프게 할 것이다. "나는 이것이 발생하는 것을 본 적이 있습니다."라고 Glander는 말한다. "그 무리의 다른 원숭이들은 큰 관심을 갖고 지켜보고 있습니다. 만약 그 동물이 아프면, 다른 동물은 그 나무에 가지 않지요. 하나의 신호가 주어지는 것인데, 바로 사회적 신호입니다."
(A) 같은 이유로, 만약 그 샘플러가 괜찮다고 느끼면, 며칠 후에 그것은 그 나무에 다시 들어가 조금 더 먹은 다음, 다시 기다렸다가 천천히 많은 양을 늘린다. 마지막으로, 만약 그 원숭이가 건강을 유지한다면, 나머지 원숭이들은 이것이 괜찮다고 생각하고 그 새로운 식량을 받아들인다.

| 정답해설 | ③ ⌈81%⌉ 영장류들이 어미를 떠나 마주치게 되는 새로운 식량들이 안전한지에 대해 결정을 내리는 과정을 설명한 글이다. 주어진 문장에서 결정을 내려야 한다고 했고, 사회적 영장류들이 더 나은 방법을 찾아냈다고 언급하면서 '샘플링'에 대해 언급한 (C)가 먼저 오는 것이 자연스럽다. 글을 쓸 때 보통 성과 이름을 포함한 전체 이름을 먼저 언급한 후 성만 언급하므로 Kenneth Galnder가 포함된 (C)가 Glander만 언급된 (B)보다 먼저 오는 것이 적절하다. (C)의 마지막 부분에서 나뭇잎을 먹고 하루를 기다린다고 했으므로 이후의 내용을 서술하고 있는 (B)가 그 다음에 오는 것이 적절하고, 샘플링 과정을 통해 괜찮은 것을 확인하고 새로운 식량으로 받아들인다고 언급한 (A)가 마지막에 연결되어야 한다.

[어휘]

primate 영장류	encounter 만나다, 마주치다
experiment 실험	habitat 서식지
troop (사람·새·동물의) 떼, 무리	harbor (동물 등이) 거처가 되다
toxin 독소	
by the same token 같은 방식으로, 게다가	
dose 1회 복용량	adopt 채택하다, 선택하다

5　　독해 > 세부내용 찾기 > 내용 불일치 찾기　　오답률 11%　　답 ④

| 해석 | 일본이 제2차 세계대전에서 패망한 뒤, 대다수의 한민족들 (100~140만 명)이 일본을 떠났다. 1948년 즈음, 한민족의 인구는 약 60만 명에 달했다. 이 한민족들과 그들의 자손들은 흔히 자이니치(문자 그대로 '일본에 거주하는')라고 불렸는데, 이는 전후 직후에 등장한 용어이다. 일본에 남아 있는 조선인들은 다양한 이유로 남아 있었다. 식민지 시대에 기업, 제국 관료, 군대에서 성공적인 경력을 쌓았거나, 전쟁 직후 개방된 경제적 기회를 이용한 한국인들은 해방 후 가난하고 정치적으로 불안정한 한국으로 돌아갈 위험을 감수하기보다는 일본 사회에서 상대적으로 특권의 지위를 유지하는 것을 선택했다. 본국으로 송환된 일부 한국인들은 열악한 환경이 너무 지겨워서 일본으로 돌아가기로 결정했다. 일본에서 살고 있는 다른 한국인들은 출항 항구 중 한 곳으로 가는 기차 요금을 낼 여유가 없었으며, 일본인 배우자와 일본 태생의 일본어를 사용하는 자녀를 둔 사람들 중에는, 새로운 환경의 문화적, 언어적 어려움을 탐색하기보다는 일본에 머무르는 것이 더 이치에 맞았다.

| 정답해설 | ④ ⌈89%⌉ 한국으로 돌아갈 교통비를 마련하지 못한 사람들이 일본에서 살 수 밖에 없는 상황이 언급되었지만, 그렇다고 해서 일본인과 결혼했다는 내용은 없으므로 자이니치에 대한 내용과 일치하지 않는 것은 ④이다. 한국으로 오지 않고 일본에 사는 이유 중 하나로, 일본인 배우자가 언급되었다.

어휘

defeat 패배	ethnic Korean 한민족, 한국 교포
descendant 후손, 자손	
be referred to as ~로 언급되다, 불리다	
reside 거주하다, 살다	imperial 제국의
bureaucracy 관료제	opt 선택하다, 고르다
privileged 특권[특전]을 가진	impoverished 가난한
liberation 해방, 광복	repulse ~을 지겹게 하다
spouse 배우자	navigate 탐색하다, 찾다

---

6 독해 > 빈칸의 내용 추론하기 > 빈칸 어구 추론   오답률 8%   답 ④

| 해석 | 사람들이 ④ 자신들의 신호를 좀 더 충분히 발전시켜야 하는 몇 가지 직업이 있다. 우리는 주심과 심판이 자신들의 팔과 손을 사용하여 선수들에게 방향을 알리는 것을 보는데, 이는 손가락 하나를 위로 올리는 것이 타자는 아웃이고 삼주문에 떠나야 한다는 것을 의미하는 크리켓 경기에서 그러하다. 오케스트라 지휘자들은 자신들의 움직임을 통해 음악가들을 관리한다. 서로 멀리 떨어진 곳에서 일하는 사람들은 만약 그들이 의사소통하고 싶다면, 특별한 신호를 발명해야 한다. 기계가 매우 시끄러운 공장이나, 학교 아이들로 가득 찬 수영장 주변의 인명 구조원과 같이 시끄러운 환경에서 일하는 사람들도 마찬가지이다.
① 자신의 부모와 자녀들을 지원하다
② 완전히 새로운 업무 스타일에 적응하다
③ 기본 인권을 위해 법정에서 싸우다
④ 자신들의 신호를 좀 더 충분히 발전시키다

| 정답해설 | ④ 92% 빈칸이 포함된 첫 문장에 이어 말이 아닌 팔과 손, 신체의 움직임을 통해 소통할 수 밖에 없는 환경에 대해 다양한 예시를 들고 있는 글이다. 따라서 빈칸에 들어갈 것으로 가장 적절한 것은 ④이다.

어휘

referee 주심, 심판	umpire 심판
conductor 지휘자	

---

7 독해 > 세부내용 찾기 > 내용 불일치 찾기   오답률 11%   답 ①

| 해석 | 연구에서 동물 이용 반대자들은 약물이나 다른 화합물의 안전성을 테스트하기 위해 동물을 사용하는 것 또한 반대한다. 제약업계에서는, 복용될 때, 인간에게 암을 유발하는 것으로 알려진 19가지 화학물질 중, 단지 7가지가 생쥐와 쥐의 암을 유발했다는 점에 주목했는데, 이는 국립 암 연구소(Barnard and Koufman, 1997)가 정한 기준을 사용한 것이다. 예를 들어, 항우울제인 노미펜신은 쥐, 토끼, 개, 원숭이에게서 아주 적은 독성을 보였지만, 인간에게는 간 독성과 빈혈을 유발했다. 이것과 다른 경우에, 일부 화합물은 동물 실험에 의해 예측되지 않은 심각한 부작용이 인간에게는 있고, 치료받은 인간이 장애나 심지어 죽음에 이를 수도 있는 상태가 된다는 것을 보여 준다. 동물 연구의 종식을 요구하는 연구자들은 자신들이 인간의 임상 실험, 부검 실험실의 지원을 받는 관찰과 같은 이용 가능한 더 나은 방법이 있다고 분명히 말한다.

| 정답해설 | ① 89% 두 번째 문장 Within the pharmaceutical industry, it was noted that out of 19 chemicals known to cause cancer in humans when taken, only seven caused cancer in mice and rats에서 인간에게 암을 유발하는 19개의 화학물질 중 7개만이 쥐의 암을 유발했다고 했으므로, 7개가 인간에게 영향을 미쳤다고 한 ①은 글의 내용과 일치하지 않는다.

어휘

opponent 반대자	compound 화합물
pharmaceutical 약학의, 약제의	antidepressant 항우울제
toxicity 독성	adverse reaction 부작용
clinical trial 임상 실험	observation 관찰
autopsy 부검, 시체 해부	

---

8 독해 > 밑줄 어휘 > 어휘 추론   오답률 31%   답 ③

| 해석 | 찬물 샤워는 수온이 화씨 70도 미만으로 하는 모든 샤워이다. 그것은 건강상의 이점을 지닐 수 있다. 우울증이 있는 사람들에게, 찬물 샤워는 일종의 부드러운 전기충격 요법으로 작용할 수 있다. 찬물은 당신의 뇌에 많은 전기 자극을 보낸다. 그것들은 당신의 시스템을 자극하여, 경각심, 명료성, 그리고 에너지 레벨을 증가시킨다. 때때로 행복 호르몬이라고도 불리는 엔도르핀도 분비된다. 이 효과는 행복감과 낙관주의로 이어진다. 비만인 사람들에게는, 일주일에 2~3차례 찬물 샤워를 하면 신진대사가 증가할 수 있다. 그것은 시간이 지남에 따라 비만과 싸우는 데 도움이 될 수 있다. 찬물 샤워가 정확히 어떻게 사람들이 살을 빼는 데 도움을 주는지에 대한 연구는 ③ 분명하다(→ 불분명하다). 하지만, 그것은 찬물이 특정 호르몬 수치를 고르게 하고 위장계를 치료할 수 있다는 것을 보여 준다. 이러한 효과는 찬물 샤워의 체중 감량을 유도하는 기능을 추가할 수 있다. 게다가, 규칙적으로 할 때, 찬물 샤워는 우리의 순환계를 더 효율적으로 만들 수 있다. 어떤 사람들은 또한 아마도 더 나은 순환 때문에, 찬물 샤워의 결과로 피부가 더 좋아 보인다고 말한다. 운동선수들은 운동 부상 후 치유를 위한 찬물을 지지하는 데이터를 최근에야 보았음에도 불구하고, 수년 동안 이러한 이점을 알고 있었다.

| 정답해설 | ③ 69% 찬물 샤워가 살을 빼는 데 도움이 된다는 것에 대한 연구가 명확하다고 언급했고, 역접의 접속사 However 다음에 찬물이 특정 호르몬 수치를 고르게 하고, 위장계를 치료한다는 긍정적인 내용이 이어졌으므로, 연구는 불분명하지만 찬물이 좋다는 긍정적인 내용이 이어지는 것이 자연스럽다. 따라서 ③의 clear는 unclear로 바꿔야 맥락상 자연스럽다.

어휘

depression 우울증	impulse 자극
alertness 경각심	release 방출하다
obese 비만의	metabolism 신진대사
obesity 비만	circulatory 순환계의
circulation 순환	

---

9 독해 > 요약   오답률 19%   답 ③

| 해석 | 연구원들은 한 개인이 갈등이 발생했을 때 그것에 대처하는 습관적인 방법에 관심을 가져 왔다. 그들은 이 접근법을 갈등 스타일이라고 불렀다. 몇 가지 명백한 갈등 스타일이 있으며, 각각 장단점이 있다. 협력 스타일은 관련된 모든 사람들에게 최상의 결과가 제공될 가능성을 극대화하는 방식으로 문제를 해결하는 경향이 있다. 협력 스타일의 장점은 신뢰를 창출하고, 긍정적인 관계를 유지하며, 헌신을 구축하는 것이다. 그러나 시간이 많이 걸리고 갈등 중에 다른 사람과 협력하는 데 많은 에너지가 필요하다. 경쟁 스타일은 목표를 달성하지 못한 사람에게 적대감을 키울 수 있다. 그러나 경쟁 스타일은 갈등을 신속하게 해결하는 경향이 있다.

협력 스타일은 (A) 상호 이해에 큰 가치를 두는 사람에게 사용될 수 있고, 반면에 (B) 시간 효율성을 선호하는 사람은 경쟁 스타일을 선택할 수 있다.

	(A)	(B)
①	재정 능력	상호 작용
②	시간 절약	평화로움
③	상호 이해	시간 효율성
④	효율성	일관성

| **정답해설** | ③ 81% 한 개인에게 갈등이 발생했을 때 대처하는 접근법을 갈등 스타일이라고 하고, 이 중 협력 스타일과 경쟁 스타일의 특성에 대해 서술한 글이다. 협력 스타일은 관련된 사람들에게 최상의 결과가 제공될 가능성을 극대화한다고 했으므로 이와 관련된 표현으로 (A)에는 mutual understanding이 적절하다. 경쟁 스타일은 목표를 달성하지 못한 사람에게 적대감을 키운다는 단점도 있지만 갈등을 신속하게 해결한다고 했으므로 (B)에는 time efficiency가 적절하다는 것을 유추할 수 있다.

어휘

habitual 습관적인   cope with ~에 대처하다
conflict 갈등, 분쟁   pros and cons 장단점; 찬반양론
collaborate 협업하다   commitment 헌신
hostility 적대감

오답률 TOP1

10 독해 > 글의 일관성 파악하기 > 글의 순서   오답률 58%   답 ④

| **해석** | 분쟁 해결의 역사적 진화는 냉전의 정점이었던 1950년대와 1960년대에 추진력을 얻었는데, 그때 핵무기 개발과 초강대국 간의 갈등이 인간의 생존을 위협하는 것처럼 보였다.
(C) 다른 학문 분야의 선구자 집단이 국제 관계, 국내 정세, 산업 관계, 지역 사회 또는 개인 간에 발생하든 간에, 유사한 속성을 가진 일반적인 현상으로 갈등을 연구하는 가치를 보았다.
(B) 그러나 일부 사람들은 그것들을 진지하게 받아들이지 않았다. 국제 관계 전문직은 국제 분쟁에 대한 자체적인 이해를 가지고 있었고 새로운 접근법의 가치를 제안된 대로 보지 않았다.
(A) 새로운 아이디어에 내포된 분석과 실천의 결합은 전통적인 학술 기관 혹은 외교관 및 정치인과 같은 현역들의 전통과 조화를 이루기에 쉽지 않았다.

| **정답해설** | ④ 42% 분쟁 해결의 역사적 진화에 대해 설명하는 글이다. 주어진 문장에서 냉전의 정점의 시대에 분쟁 해결의 추진력을 얻었다고 한 데 이어, 다른 학문 분야의 선구자들이 갈등을 일반적인 현상으로 연구하는 가치를 보았다고 한 (C)가 그 다음에 이어지는 것이 자연스럽다. 이어서 역접의 연결사 However가 나오고 일부 사람들에게 (C)의 선구자들과는 달리 진지하게 받아들여지지 않았다고 한 (B)가 와야 하고, (B)와 비슷한 흐름의 내용이 이어진 (A)가 그 다음에 와야 자연스럽다.

어휘

evolution 진화   resolution 해결
at the height of ~의 절정에   nuclear weapon 핵무기
discipline 학문 분야   property 특성, 특징
domestic 국내의   combination 결합
implicit 함축적인   reconcile 조화시키다; 화해시키다
institution 기관   diplomat 외교관

11 문법 > 접속사, 시제, 분사   오답률 19%   답 ①

| **해석** | 경제학을 이해하는 해법은 항상 의도하지 않은 결과가 있다는 것을 받아들이는 것이다. 사람들이 자신만의 정당한 이유로 취하는 행동은 그들이 상상하거나 의도하지 않은 결과를 낳는다. 지정학에서도 마찬가지다. 기원전 7세기에 확장을 시작한 로마의 마을이 500년 후 지중해 세계를 정복하기 위한 마스터플랜을 가지고 있었는지는 의문이다. 그러나 주민들이 이웃 마을에 대해 취한 첫 번째 행위는 현실에 제약을 받고 의도하지 않은 결과로 가득 찬 과정을 시작했다. 로마는 계획대로 되지 않았고, 그렇게 그저 발생한 일도 아니었다.

| **정답해설** | ① 81% (A) accepting의 목적어인 명사절을 이끄는 연결사인데, 뒤에 유도부사 there가 이끄는 1형식 완전한 절이 이어졌으므로 접속사 that이 와야 한다. what은 불완전한 절을 이끌어야 하므로 적절하지 않다.
(B) 로마가 확장을 시작한 것이 과거(started)이므로, 지중해 세계를 제패하겠다고 마스터플랜을 가지고 있었던 것은 그 이전인 대과거가 되어야 하므로 had가 올바르다.
(C) 등위 상관접속사 both A and B로 병치된 구조로, 과거분사 constrained와 호응해 과거분사 filled가 와야 한다.

어휘

unintended 의도하지 않은   envision 상상하다, 마음에 그리다
set in motion ~을 움직이게 하다, 도화선에 불을 당기다
constrain 구속하다, 속박하다

12 독해 > 빈칸의 내용 추론하기 > 빈칸 어구 추론   오답률 8%   답 ③

| **해석** | 물과 문명은 떨어질 수 없는 관계이다. '수력학 문명'의 개념은 물이 역사를 통틀어 많은 대규모 문명에서 통합적인 배경이자 정당화라고 주장한다. 예를 들어, 다양한 여러 세기의 중국 제국들은 부분적으로 황하를 따라 홍수를 통제함으로써 살아남았다. 수력학 이론에 대한 한 가지 해석은 인구를 대도시로 모으는 것이 정당한 이유는 물을 관리한다는 것이다. 또 다른 해석은 대규모 물 프로젝트가 대도시의 부상을 가능하게 한다는 것을 시사한다. 로마인들은 물과 권력의 관계를 이해하고 있었는데, 로마 제국이 통제하는 땅 전체에 광대한 수로 네트워크를 구축했기 때문이며, 그 중 많은 부분이 온전하게 남아 있다. 예를 들어, 프랑스 남부의 퐁 뒤 가르드(Pont du Gard)는 오늘날 인류가 물 기반 시설에 투자한 증거로 남아있다. 로마 총독들은 ③ 자신들의 권위를 집중시키고 강화하는 방법으로 도로, 교량 및 수도 시스템을 건설했다.
① 젊은이들을 교육하는 데 집중하기
② 지역 시장에서 자유 무역을 금지하기
③ 자신들의 권위를 집중시키고 강화하기
④ 다른 나라에 자신들의 재산을 넘겨주기

| **정답해설** | ③ 92% 첫 문장에서 물과 문명은 떨어질 수 없는 관계라고 제시한 후 몇몇 문명들의 사례를 들어 구체적인 내용을 전개하는 글이다. 로마 제국의 사례에서, 로마인들이 물과 권력의 관계를 이해하고 있었다고 언급한 후 그 증거로 관대한 수로 네트워크를 건설한 것을 들고 있다. 따라서 빈칸에 들어갈 것으로 ③이 가장 적절하다.

어휘

go hand-in-hand 관련되다, 함께 가다
unifying 통합적인   context 배경

justification 정당화   interpretation 해석
intact 손상되지 않은, 온전한   infrastructure 기반 시설

오답률 TOP3

13 독해 > 글의 일관성 파악하기 > 글의 순서 [오답률 56%] 답 ①

| 해석 | 모호함은 너무 불편해서 심지어 좋은 소식을 나쁜 소식으로 바꿀 수도 있다. 당신은 지속적인 복통으로 병원에 간다. 의사는 이유를 알 수 없어서, 검사를 받으라고 당신을 검사실로 보낸다.

(B) 일주일 후, 결과를 듣기 위해 당신은 다시 호출된다. 당신이 마침내 그녀의 진료실에 들어갔을 때, 의사는 미소를 지으며 당신에게 검사가 모두 음성이었다고 말한다.

(A) 그리고 무슨 일이 일어나는가? 당신의 즉각적인 안도감이 이상한 불편함으로 대체될 수 있다. 당신은 아직도 그 고통이 무엇인지 모른다! 어딘가에 설명이 있어야만 한다.

(C) 그것은 암일 수도 있고 그냥 그들이 놓쳤을 수도 있다. 어쩌면 더 심각할 수도 있다. 분명히 그들은 원인을 찾을 수 있어야 한다. 당신은 명확한 답이 없어 좌절감을 느낀다.

| 정답해설 | ① [44%] 주어진 문장에서 모호함(ambiguity)이 주는 불편함에 대해 언급한 후 이에 대한 예시로 복통으로 병원에 진료를 받으러 가는 상황이 제시되었다. 검사를 한 후 이에 대한 결과 통보가 있어야 하므로 처음에 (B)가 오는 것이 적절하다. (B)에서 검사 결과가 음성이라는 소식을 들은 후 이후에 상황이 연결이 되어야 하는데, (A)에서 처음의 안도감이 불편함으로 대체되고, 여전히 설명이 필요한 상황이라는 내용이 이어졌다. 마지막으로 (C)에서 그 불편함으로 인해 진단 결과에 대한 의심이 심각해지는 상황이 전개되었다. 따라서 글의 순서로 가장 적절한 것은 ①이다.

| 어휘 |

ambiguity 모호함, 불확실함   persistent 지속적인
negative [생리] 음성의   figure out 알아내다
relief 안도, 안심 안도, 안심   weird 이상한, 기묘한
discomfort 불편함   frustrated 좌절하는
definitive 명확한; 최종적인

오답률 TOP2

14 독해 > 글의 일관성 파악하기 > 주어진 문장의 삽입
                                      [오답률 57%] 답 ②

| 해석 | 우리가 출근을 위해 옷을 입는 방식은 새로운 선택의 요소를 떠맡았고, 그것으로 새로운 걱정거리를 갖게 되었다. 10여 년 전부터 등장하기 시작한 '약식 복장의 날' 혹은 '캐주얼 데이'를 갖는 관행이 직원들의 생활을 더 편하게 하고, 돈을 절약하며, 사무실에서 좀 더 편안함을 느낄 수 있도록 의도된 것이었다. ② 그러나 그 효과는 정반대였다. 평범한 직장 의류 외에도 직원들은 '직장 캐주얼' 의류를 마련해야 했다. 그것은 사실 주말에 집에서 입었던 운동복과 티셔츠가 될 수는 없었다. 그것은 편안하면서 동시에 진중한 특정 이미지를 유지해 주는 의류 선택이어야 했다.

| 정답해설 | ② [43%] 출근 복장에 대해 새롭게 등장한 선택에 대해 서술하고 있는 글이다. '캐주얼 데이'를 도입해 직원들의 편안함을 유도했지만, 오히려 '캐주얼 데이'를 위한 의류를 마련해야 했다는 내용이 핵심이다. 주어진 문장에서 역접의 연결사 however에 이어 효과가 정반대였다고 했으므로, 출근 복장에 대한 대비를 이루는 부분을 찾아야 한다. ② 이전까지 '캐주얼 데이'를 소개하고 이에 대

한 긍정적인 의도가 제시되었는데, In addition to에 이어진 부분에서 직원들이 오히려 '캐주얼 데이' 복장에 대한 부담을 지게 되었다고 했으므로, 흐름이 달라졌음을 알 수 있다. 따라서 주어진 문장이 들어가기에 가장 적절한 곳은 ②이다.

| 어휘 |

take on (일 등을) 떠맡다; (양상·색채 등을) 나타내다. 띠다
anxiety 걱정, 불안   reverse 거꾸로 된, 반대의
sustain 유지하다, 지탱하다

---

15 문법 > 명사와 일치 > 일치 [오답률 33%] 답 ④

| 해석 | 당신은 당신이 원하는 결과에 가장 잘 맞는 연구 방법을 선택해야 한다. 당신은 많은 사람들에게 질문하고 보고서 형식으로 전체 분석을 제공할 수 있는 온라인 설문 조사를 실행하거나, 질문을 일대일로 하는 것이 더 적은 범위의 선택된 사람들로부터 필요한 답변을 얻는 더 좋은 방법이라고 생각할 수 있다. 당신이 어느 쪽을 선택하든 같은 방법으로 비교할 필요가 있을 것이다. 사람들에게 같은 질문을 하고 답변을 비교하라. 유사점과 차이점을 모두 찾아라. 패턴과 추세를 찾아라. 기록 방식과 데이터 분석 방법을 결정하는 것이 중요하다. 간단한 자체 제작 스프레드 시트는 기본 연구 데이터를 기록하기에 충분할 것이다.

| 정답해설 | ④ [67%] 문장 전체의 주어가 동명사 deciding이므로 단수로 수일치가 되어야 하며 is로 바꿔야 올바르다.

| 오답해설 | ① [11%] 앞에 명사 method가 있고 뒤에 부사와 주어 없이 동사 suits가 이어진 불완전한 절이므로 관계대명사 that이 올바르게 왔다.

② [11%] 밑줄 앞에 등위접속사 and가 있으므로 병치 구조임을 알 수 있다. 주절의 목적어이자 선행사인 online에 이어 관계대명사 that이 이끄는 형용사절이 이어졌다. 관계대명사절의 동사 enables와 병치되었으므로 단수 동사 provides는 올바르다. 관계대명사 that은 선행사인 online을 지칭하므로 단수로 수일치가 올바르게 이루어졌다.

③ [11%] 양보부사절을 이끄는 복합관계형용사로 선행사를 포함한다. whichever가 명사 way를 수식하고, 주어와 타동사는 있지만 목적어가 없는 불완전한 절이 이어진 올바른 구조이다.

| 어휘 |

suit 어울리다   similarity 유사성
spreadsheet 스프레드시트

---

16 독해 > 대의 파악 > 요지·주장 찾기 [오답률 8%] 답 ②

| 해석 | 일부 범죄자들은 범죄가 제공할 수 있는 흥분과 전율을 좋아하기 때문에 불법 행동을 할 수도 있다. 사회학자 Jack Katz는 '범죄의 유혹(Seductions of Crime)'이라는 매우 영향력 있는 저서에서 범죄 행위는 사람들을 범죄의 삶으로 '유혹'하는 즉각적인 이점이 있다고 주장한다. 어떤 사람들에게는, 좀도둑질과 기물파손이 매력적인데, 그 이유는 범죄로부터 무사히 빠져나가는 것이 개인의 능력을 보여주는 짜릿한 경험이기 때문이다. 흥분에 대한 욕구는 체포와 처벌의 두려움에 대응할 수 있다. 사실, 일부 범죄자들은 추가된 '전율' 때문에 특히 위험한 상황을 의도적으로 찾아내는 성향이 있다. 욕구나 흥분은 범죄 선택의 중요한 예측 변수이다.

| 정답해설 | ② [92%] 범죄자들이 범죄를 저지르는 원인에 대해 설명하는 글이다. 첫 번째 문장이 주제문으로 범죄가 제공하는 흥분과

전율을 경험하기 위해 범죄를 저지른다고 했고, 이어서 사회학자 저서를 통해 부연하고 있다. 흐름의 전환 없이 글을 전개했으므로 글의 요지로 가장 적절한 것은 ②이다.

어휘

criminal 범죄의; 형사상의	offender 범죄자
thrill 전율	seduction 유혹
criminality 범죄성, 범행	attractive 매력적인
demonstration 표출, 표명	counter 대응하다
apprehension 체포	deliberately 의도적으로
predictor 예측 변수	

---

17 독해 > 빈칸의 내용 추론하기 > 빈칸 어휘 추론
오답률 3%　답 ③

| 해석 | 애착의 중요성을 보여주는 한 전형적인 연구에서, 위스콘신 대학의 심리학자 Harry Harlow와 Margaret Harlow는 새끼 원숭이들의 반응을 조사했다. 새끼들은 생물학적 어미로부터 분리되었고, 두 가지의 대리모가 새끼들의 우리에 보내졌다. 하나는 철사 엄마였는데, 나무로 된 둥근 머리, 차가운 철사 뭉치, 새끼 원숭이가 빨 수 있는 젖병으로 구성되었다. 두 번째 엄마는 따뜻한 테리천 담요에 싸인 고무 스펀지 형태였다. 새끼 원숭이들은 음식을 먹기 위해 철사 엄마에게 갔지만, 그것들은 따뜻한 테리천 엄마를 압도적으로 선호했고 상당히 더 많은 시간을 함께 보냈다. 따뜻한 테리천 엄마는 음식을 제공하지 않았지만, ③ 편안함을 제공했다.
① 일자리　　　② 약
③ 편안함　　　④ 교육

| 정답해설 | ③ 97% 애착에 대한 연구 과정과 결과를 서술한 글이다. 새끼 원숭이들과 두 가지 유형의 대리모 실험을 통해, 음식보다는 따뜻한 느낌을 주는 대리모를 선호했다고 했으므로, 빈칸에 들어갈 것으로 ③이 가장 적절하다.

어휘

attachment 애착	investigate 조사하다
infant 유아	consist of ~로 구성되다
mesh 그물망, 철사	wrapped in ~에 싸인
terry-cloth 테리 직물	blanket 담요
overwhelmingly 압도적으로	

---

18 문법 > 동사의 형태 > 시제
오답률 39%　답 ①

| 해석 | 나의 친부모는 입양을 위해 (나를) 포기했고 나는 생애 첫 10년을 고아원에서 보냈다. 나는 내가 뭔가 잘못되었다고 생각하며 여러 해를 보냈다. 만약 내 부모님이 나를 원하지 않는다면, 누가 그럴 수 있겠는가? 나는 내가 무엇을 잘못했는지, 왜 그렇게 많은 사람들이 나를 멀리 보냈는지 알아내려고 애썼다. 이제 나는 그 누구에게도 가까이 가지 않는다. 왜냐하면 내가 그렇게 하면 그들이 나를 떠날지도 모르니까. 나는 어렸을 때 살아남기 위해 감정적으로 고립되어야 했고, 여전히 어렸을 때 내가 가졌던 가정들을 바탕으로 움직인다. 나는 버려지는 것이 너무 두려워서 모험을 하거나 최소한의 위험조차 감수하지 않을 것이다. 나는 이제 마흔 살이 되었지만, 여전히 어린아이처럼 느껴진다.

| 정답해설 | ① 61% 앞에 등위접속사가 있으므로 병치 구조가 되어야 한다. 구조와 맥락상 주어 I의 첫 번째 동사인 was released에 이어진 두 번째 동사이므로 시제를 반영해 과거동사 spent로 바꿔야 한다.

| 오답해설 | ② 22% 타동사구 figure out의 목적어인 명사절을 이끌고 있다. what에 이어 불완전한 절이 나왔으므로 올바르다.

③ 3% 타동사 isolate의 목적어로 주어와 일치하므로 재귀대명사로 올바르게 표현했다.

④ 14% 주절의 부사 so와 호응해 결과의 부사절을 이끄는 접속사 that에 이어 완전한 절이 올바르게 나왔다.

어휘

release (물건·사람을) 떼어놓다	orphanage 고아원
isolate 고립시키다	assumption 가정, 추측
deserted 버려진	
venture 위험을 무릅쓰고 하다, 과감히 하다	

---

19 문법 > 문장의 구조와 동사 유형 > 동사와 문장의 5형식
오답률 42%　답 ①

| 해석 | 음악은 일상생활로 옮길 수 있는 심리 치료 효과를 가질 수 있다. 많은 학자들은 사람들이 음악을 심리 치료 매개체로써 이용할 것을 제안했다. 음악 치료는 광범위하게 '개인의 심리적, 육체적, 인지적 또는 사회적 기능을 향상시키기 위한 치료 또는 재활의 보조 수단으로 음악을 사용하는 것'으로 정의될 수 있다. 음악으로부터의 긍정적인 정서적 경험은 치료 과정을 향상시켜, 전통적인 인지/행동 방법과 그것들의 일상적인 목표로의 전이를 강화할 수 있다. 이것은 부분적으로 음악과 일상 행동에 의해 유발된 감정적 경험이 긍정적인 감정과 동기 부여를 초래하는 중첩된 신경 경로를 공유하기 때문일 수 있다.

| 정답해설 | ① 58% suggest는 완전타동사로 목적어로 동명사 혹은 that절을 목적어로 취한다. 이 구조에서 suggest와 명사 people에 이어 to use가 오면서 5형식 문장처럼 보일 수 있지만 suggest는 불완전타동사가 아니다. 따라서 이 문제의 suggested는 주절의 동사로 보고 접속사 that이 생략된 후 종속절의 주어로 people이, 동사로 to use를 대체하는 것이 와야 함을 알 수 있다. 이 경우, suggested는 '제안'의 동사로 that절의 동사는 'should + 동사원형'이 와야 하고, 이때 should는 생략이 가능하므로 to use를 should use 혹은 use로 바꿔야 한다.

| 오답해설 | ② 28% 형용사 psychological, physical, cognitive and social의 수식을 받는 명사로 적절하다.

③ 6% 등위접속사 and가 있으므로 병치 구조가 되어야 한다. 구조와 맥락상 조동사 may의 첫 번째 동사원형 improve와 병치되어야 하므로 동사원형으로 올바르게 왔다.

④ 8% '이유'의 접속사 because의 주어인 emotional experiences의 동사가 되어야 하므로 복수형으로 수일치가 올바르게 이루어졌다. elicited by music and everyday behaviors는 분사구로 주어인 명사 emotional experiences를 수식하고 있다.

어휘

transfer 옮기다	adjunct 부속물; 조수, 협력자
rehabilitation 재활	cognitive 인지적인
partially 부분적으로	elicit 끌어내다
overlapping 중첩된	neurological 신경학의, 신경의
pathway 경로, 통로	
responsible for ~에 원인이 있는; ~에 책임이 있는	

20 독해 > 빈칸의 내용 추론하기 > 빈칸 어휘 추론

오답률 39% | 답 ②

| 해석 | 문화적 해석은 대개 측정 가능한 증거보다는 ② 편견에 근거하여 이루어진다. 주장은 순환하는 경향이 있다. 사람들은 게으르기 때문에 가난하다. 우리는 어떻게 그들이 게으르다는 것을 '아는' 걸까? 그들이 가난하기 때문이다. 이러한 해석의 주모자들은 낮은 생산성이 게으름과 노력 부족이 아니라 생산으로 이어지는 자본 투입 부족에서 온다는 것을 거의 이해하지 못한다. 아프리카 농부들은 게으르지는 않지만, 토양 영양분, 트랙터, 지선 도로, 관개 구획, 저장 시설 등이 정말로 부족하다. 아프리카인들이 거의 일을 하지 않고 따라서 가난하다는 고정관념은 남녀를 불문하고 몹시 힘든 노동인 일상적인 마을에서 하루를 보냄으로써 남자와 여자의 힘든 노동이 일반적인 마을에서 하루를 보내면서 잠문혀진다.

① 통계 ② 편견
③ 외모 ④ 환경

| 정답해설 | ② 61% 문화적 해석은 증거보다 '편견'에 근거하여 이루어진다는 내용의 글이다. 빈칸이 포함된 첫 번째 문장에 이어 게으른 사람들이 가난하다는 주장에 대해 언급하면서, 사실상 가난의 원인이 게으름이 아닌 자본 투입 부족 등의 다른 요인이 있다고 서술하고 있다. 구체적인 사례로 아프리카인들에 대한 고정관념 (stereotype)을 언급하고 있으므로 빈칸에 들어갈 것으로 가장 적절한 것은 stereotype과 비슷한 의미인 '편견(prejudice)'이다.

| 어휘 |

interpretation 해석 measurable 측정 가능한
circular 순환하는 productivity 생산성
input 투입, 입력 feeder road 지선 도로
irrigate 관개하다, 물을 대다 facility 시설
stereotype 고정관념 put ~ to rest 잠문우다
backbreaking 몹시 힘든 norm 전형, 평균; 규범

21 독해 > 글의 일관성 파악하기 > 주어진 문장의 삽입

오답률 34% | 답 ③

| 해석 | 자유시장은 농업에서 결코 효과를 본 적이 없었고 앞으로도 그럴 것이다. 가족 농장의 경제적 의미는 기업의 그것과 매우 다르다. 가격이 떨어지면, 기업은 직원들을 정리해고하고 공장을 돌리지 않을 수 있다. 결국 시장은 공급과 수요 사이의 새로운 균형을 찾는다. ③ 하지만 식품에 대한 수요는 탄력적이지 않은데, 사람들은 식품이 싸다고 해서 더 많이 먹지 않기 때문이다. 그리고 농부들을 해고하는 것이 공급을 줄이는 데 도움이 되지 않는다. 당신은 나를 해고할 수는 있지만, 내 땅을 해고할 수는 없는데, 돈이 더 필요하거나 자기가 나보다 더 유능하다고 생각하는 다른 농부가 와서 농사를 지으러 올 것이기 때문이다.

| 정답해설 | ③ 66% 농업이 자유시장 원리에 적용되지 않는다는 취지의 글이다. 가족 농장과 기업을 비교했을 때, 기업은 가격이 떨어지면 정리해고나 공장을 돌리지 않는 등의 조치를 취해 공급과 수요의 균형을 찾는다는 내용이 ③ 이전에 전개되었는데, ③ 뒤에 나온 등위접속사 And에 이어 농부들을 해고하는 것이 공급을 줄이는 데 도움이 되지 않는다면서, 농업에 대해 서술하고 있다. 따라서 역접의 접속사 But에 이어 음식에 대한 수요는 탄력적이지 않다고 하면서 농업과 관련된 내용이 나오는 것이 자연스우므로 주어진 문장이 들어가기에 가장 적절한 곳은 ③이다.

| 어휘 |

agriculture 농업
economics (한 나라의) 경제 상태, 경제적 의미
lay off 정리해고하다
idle (기계·엔진 등을) 공회전시키다, 헛돌게 하다

22 독해 > 대의 파악 > 주제 찾기

오답률 11% | 답 ②

| 해석 | 일일 훈련은 운동선수, 특히 몰입 훈련이 거의 전업인 엘리트 운동선수에게 특별한 영양적 요구 사항을 만든다. 그러나 레크리에이션 스포츠조차도 영양 문제를 일으키기 마련이다. 그리고 스포츠에 대한 당신의 참여 정도가 어느 정도이든, 만약 당신이 훈련에서 최대의 수확을 얻으려면, 이러한 문제들을 충족시켜야만 한다. 잘 먹지 않으면, 당신은 훈련의 목적 중 많은 부분을 잃을 수 있다. 최악의 경우, 식단 문제와 (영양) 부족은 훈련 성과를 직접적으로 해칠 수 있다. 다른 상황에서는, 당신은 나아질 수 있지만, 당신의 잠재성보다 낮은 비율로 혹은 경쟁자들보다 더 느린 정도로 나아질 것이다. 그러나 긍정적인 측면에서, 매일 올바른 식사 계획이 있다면, 당신이 훈련에 몰두하는 것은 충분히 보상받을 것이다.

① 신체 유연성을 증진시키는 방법
② 운동할 때 잘 먹는 것의 중요성
③ 과도한 다이어트로 인한 건강 문제들
④ 지속적인 훈련을 통해 기술을 발전시키기

| 정답해설 | ② 89% 운동선수를 비롯해 스포츠에 참여하는 사람들 모두 영양적으로 필요한 부분이 있다는 내용의 글이다. 흐름의 전환 없이, 여러 예시들을 들어 서술하고 있으므로 주제로 가장 적절한 것은 ②이다.

| 어휘 |

commitment 몰입, 헌신 involvement 참여, 몰입
deficiency 부족, 결핍 impair 선상시키다

23 독해 > 대의 파악 > 주제 찾기

오답률 6% | 답 ③

| 해석 | Ernst Gombrich라는 매우 존경받는 미술사학자는 '보는 사람의 몫'이라는 것에 대해 글을 썼다. Gombrich는 관람자가 작품을 '완성'한다고 믿었고, 작품의 의미 중 일부는 그 작품을 보는 사람에게서 나온다고 믿었다. 따라서 당신은 그것이 당신이기 때문에, 예술 작품을 완성하는 관람자로서, 정말로 틀린 대답은 없다. 만약 당신이 갤러리에서 미술 작품을 감상하고 있다면, 작품 옆에 있는 벽에 써 있는 글을 읽어라. 만약 직원이 있다면, 질문을 던져라. 함께 관람하는 사람들에게 그들이 어떻게 생각하는지 물어보라. 질문을 던지는 것은 더 많은 것을 이해하는 열쇠이며, 그것은 예술뿐만 아니라 삶의 모든 것에 적용된다. 하지만 무엇보다도, 예술 작품 앞에서 자신감을 가져라. 만약 당신이 한 예술 작품을 주의 깊게 보고 있다면, 당신은 의도된 관람자이고 당신이 생각하는 것이 중요하다. 당신이 중요한 유일한 비평가이다.

| 정답해설 | ③ 94% 미술사학자가 제시한 '보는 사람의 몫'이라는 표현을 언급하고, 이에 대해 설명하는 글이다. 글 전체적으로 예술 작품을 완성하는 관람자(viewer)라고 했고, 마지막 문장에서 우리가 한 작품을 주의 깊게 보는 경우 우리가 유일한 비평가라고 했으므로 글의 주제로 가장 적절한 것은 ③이다.

| 어휘 |

beholder 보는 사람, 관람자 complete 완성하다
contemplate 주의 깊게 관찰하다; 심사숙고하다
count 중요하다

24 독해 > 세부내용 찾기 > 내용 불일치 찾기 [오답률 11%] 답 ②

| 해석 | 아르헨티나는 남아메리카의 남부 지역의 거의 절반을 차지하는 세계에서 8번째로 큰 나라이다. 스페인에 의한 식민지화는 1500년대 초에 시작되었으나, 1816년 Jose de San Martin이 아르헨티나 독립을 위한 운동을 주도하였다. 아르헨티나의 문화는 19세기 후반에 대대적인 유럽인들의 이주와, 20세기 초에는 주로 스페인과 이탈리아로부터의 이주로 크게 영향받았다. 대다수의 사람들은 적어도 명목상 가톨릭 신자이며, 남아메리카에서 가장 큰 유대인 인구(약 300,000명)를 가지고 있다. 1880년부터 1930년까지, 농업 발전 덕분에, 아르헨티나는 세계에서 가장 부유한 10대 국가 중 하나였다.

| 정답해설 | ② [89%] 글 중간에서 유럽인들, 특히 스페인과 이탈리아에서 대규모 이주가 있었다고 서술했다. 북미 출신 이주민들은 글에서 언급되지 않았으므로 정답은 ②이다.

[어휘]

comprise 차지하다, 구성하다   independence 독립
migration 이주   nominally 명목상으로는

25 독해 > 세부내용 찾기 > 내용 불일치 찾기 [오답률 31%] 답 ③

| 해석 | Sonja Henie는 아이스링크와 스크린에서 세계에서 가장 유명한 피겨 스케이터 중 한 명으로, 한 분야에서 그녀의 기술로 유명하다. 3개의 올림픽 금메달 수상자이자, 노르웨이와 유럽 챔피언으로서, Henie는 스릴 넘치는 연극적이면서 운동다운 스타일의 피겨 스케이팅을 발명했다. 그녀는 짧은 치마, 하얀 스케이트, 그리고 매력적인 동작들을 소개했다. 그녀의 화려한 스핀과 점프는 모든 경쟁자들의 기준을 높였다. 1936년, 20세기 폭스사는 그녀를 'One in a Million'에 출연시키기로 계약했고, 그녀는 곧 할리우드의 주연 여배우들 중 한 명이 되었다. 그녀가 여배우로서 연기한 1941년 영화 'Sun Valley Serenade'는 3개의 아카데미상 후보에 올랐다. Henie의 나머지 영화는 찬사를 덜 받았지만, 그녀는 아이스 스케이팅에서 인기 급상승을 일으켰다. 1938년에, 그녀는 Hollywood Ice Revues라는 호화로운 투어 쇼를 시작했다. 그녀의 많은 사업은 그녀에게 부를 주었지만, 그녀의 가장 위대한 유산은 어린 소녀들에게 스케이트를 타도록 영감을 준 것이었다.

| 정답해설 | ③ [69%] the movie 'Sun Valley Serenade' received three Academy Award nominations which she played as an actress에서 출연한 영화는 수상한 것이 아니라 '후보에 오른(nomination)' 것이므로 ③은 글의 내용과 일치하지 않는다.

[어휘]

theatrical 연극의, 극장의   attractive 매력적인
spectacular 화려한, 멋진   raise the bar 기준을 높이다
nomination 지명, 후보에 오름   acclaim 열렬히 환호하다, 격찬하다
trigger 유발하다, 촉발하다
surge (감정·군중 등의) 큰 파동, 격동
launch 시작하다   extravagant 사치스러운
venture 투기적 사업   fortune 부, 재산
legacy 유산

합격예상 체크

〈법원직 연도별 합격선〉

2021 합격기준!

맞힌 개수	/25문항	점수	/100점

➡ □ 합격 □ 불합격

취약영역 체크

문항	정답	영역	문항	정답	영역
1	④	독해 > 요약	14	②	독해 > 대의 파악
2	④	독해 > 세부내용 찾기	15	①	독해 > 대의 파악
3	④	문법 > 준동사, 형용사와 부사, 대명사	16	①	독해 > 대의 파악
4	②	독해 > 글의 일관성 파악하기	17	④	독해 > 밑줄 어휘
5	②	문법 > 준동사	18	①	문법 > 접속사, 준동사, 조동사
6	④	독해 > 글의 일관성 파악하기	19	②	독해 > 글의 일관성 파악하기
7	①	독해 > 빈칸의 내용 추론하기	20	②	독해 > 글의 일관성 파악하기
8	②	독해 > 글의 일관성 파악하기	21	②	독해 > 글의 일관성 파악하기
9	①	독해 > 빈칸의 내용 추론하기	22	③	독해 > 글의 일관성 파악하기
10	③	독해 > 밑줄 어휘	23	②	독해 > 세부내용 찾기
11	③	독해 > 대의 파악	24	②	독해 > 대의 파악
12	④	독해 > 대의 파악	25	②	독해 > 세부내용 찾기
13	④	문법 > 준동사			

⬇ 영역별 틀린 개수로 취약영역을 확인하세요!

어휘	/0	문법	/4	독해	/21	생활영어	/0

➡ 나의 취약영역: _____

※ [정답해설]과 [오답해설] 선지의 50% 표시는 〈1초 합격예측 서비스〉를 통해 수집된 선지 선택률을 나타냅니다.

1	독해 > 요약	오답률 38%	답 ④

| 해석 | 미생물은 계산을 할 수 있는 존재가 아니다. 그것들은 당신이 비눗물로 수백만 개의 미생물을 학살할 때 당신이 어떤 고통을 야기하는지 신경 쓰지 않는 것처럼, 그것들은 자신들이 당신에게 무슨 짓을 하는지 신경쓰지 않는다. 병원체가 당신을 신경 쓸 때는 그것이 당신을 너무 잘 죽일 때 뿐이다. 만약 그것들이 이동하기 전에 당신을 제거한다면, 그것들은 스스로 죽어 사라질 것이다. 사실 이런 일이 가끔 일어난다. Jared Diamond가 지적하기를, 역사는 "한때 끔찍한 전염병을 야기했고, 그러고 나서 그것들이 왔던 것처럼 불가사의하게 사라진" 질병들로 가득하다. 그는 강력했지만 다행히 일시적인 영국의 속립열(military fever)을 인용했는데, 이 병은 1485년에서 1552년에 맹위를 떨쳤고, 사그라들기 전까지 수만 명을 사망하게 했다. 너무 지나친 효율성은 전염성이 있는 어떤 유기체에게도 좋은 것은 아니다.

⬇

> 병원균이 더욱 (A) 전염성이 있을수록, 그것은 더 빠르게 (B) 사라질 가능성이 있다.

	(A)	(B)
①	약한	사라지다
②	약한	퍼지다
③	전염성이 있는	퍼지다
④	전염성이 있는	사라지다

| 정답해설 | ④ 62% 첫 문장에서 미생물은 계산을 할 수 있는 존재

가 아니라고 했고, 이런 속성에 따라 일시적으로 격렬하게 발생했다가 사람들이 죽으면 함께 사라지는 전염병에 대해 서술했다. 따라서 병원균이 전염성이 강하면 그만큼 사람들이 빨리 사망하므로 병원균 또한 더 빠르게 사라질 것임을 유추할 수 있다. 따라서 빈칸에 들어갈 것으로 가장 적절한 것은 ④이다.

| 어휘 |

microorganism 미생물	calculate 계산하다
distress 괴롭히다	slaughter 도살하다
eliminate 제거하다, 없애다	die out 사멸하다, 죽어 없어지다
terrifying 무서운	epidemic 유행병
robust 강건한, 튼튼한	mercifully 다행히, 자비롭게
transient 일시적인, 순간적인	
rage (전쟁·돌림병 등이) 맹위를 떨치다	
efficiency 효율성	

오답률 TOP 2

2	독해 > 세부내용 찾기 > 지칭어 추론	오답률 54%	답 ④

| 해석 | 만약 글의 내용이 충실하고 훌륭하면, 결국 작가의 분위기와 기질이 드러나면서 작품을 희생하지 않을 것이다. 그러므로, (특유의) 문체를 얻기 위해서는, 우선 어느 것에도 영향을 주지 않는 것부터 시작하라. 즉, 독자가 글의 의미와 본질에 주의를 기울이도록 하라. 신중하고 솔직한 작가는 문체에 대해 걱정할 필요가 없다. 당신이 언어 사용에 능숙해질 때, 당신의 문체가 드러날 것인데, 이는 당신 자신이 등장하기 때문이고, 이런 일이 발

생할 때 당신을 다른 사람들과 분리시키는 장벽을 깨고 마침내 글의 중심이 당신이 서는 것이 점차 쉽다는 것을 알게 될 것이다. 다행히도, 창작이나 창조의 행위는 정신을 단련시킨다. 글쓰기는 생각에 잠기는 한 가지 방법이며, 글쓰기 연습과 습관은 <u>사고를 배출시킨다</u>.

① 마음을 치료하기
② 세심해지도록 돕기
③ 자신의 호기심을 충족시키기
④ 배경에 자신을 배치하기

| **정답해설** | ④ 46% 글의 내용이 충실하고 훌륭하면 작품을 희생하지 않고도 작가의 분위기와 기질을 드러내며, 이런 글을 쓰기 위해 작가에게 필요한 요소들을 서술하고 있는 글이다. 고유의 문체(style)를 얻기 위해 작가는 걱정하기보다 독자가 글의 의미와 본질에 주의를 기울이도록 하라고 했고, 창작의 행위는 정신을 단련시킨다고 했으므로, drains the mind는 주어진 선지 내에서 ④가 가장 적절함을 알 수 있다. drain은 '소모시키다'의 의미도 있지만 글의 맥락상 '배출시키다'의 의미로 보는 것이 적절하며, ④번 외의 나머지 선지들은 글쓰기와 관련해 언급된 것이 아니므로 정답으로 적절하지 않다.

어휘

solid (지식 · 학문 등이) 내용이 충실한; 단단한
temper 성격, 화
reveal 드러내다, 밝히다
at the expense of ~의 대가로, ~를 희생하여
proficient 숙달된, 능숙한
separate 분리하다; 개별적인   barrier 장벽, 장애물
composition 작문, 작곡
discipline ~을 훈련[단련]하다
drain 배출시키다; 배수하다; 소모시키다

---

3   문법 > 준동사, 형용사와 부사, 대명사   오답률 28%   답 ④

| **해석** | 인생에서 자기 자신과 우리의 많은 것에 대한 불만 중 일부는 실제 상황에 기반을 두고 있으며, 일부는 거짓이고 단순히 실제라고 (A) 인식되는 것이다. 그 인식된 것들은 분류되고 폐기되어야 한다. 현실은 바뀔 수 있거나 바뀔 수 없는 범주에 속하게 될 것이다. 만약 후자에 해당한다면, 우리는 그것을 받아들이기 위해 노력해야 한다. 만약 전자에 있다면, 우리는 오히려 그것을 제거, 교환 혹은 수정하기 위해 노력하는 대안을 가지게 된다. 우리 모두는 인생에서 독특한 목적을 가지고 있다. 그리고 우리 모두는 재능이 있는데, 단지 (B) 다르게 재능이 있을 뿐이다. 그것은 한 가지, 다섯 가지 혹은 열 가지의 재능이 주어진 것이 공평한지 아니면 불공평한지에 대한 논쟁은 아니다. 그것은 우리가 우리의 재능으로 무엇을 했는가에 대한 논쟁이다. 그것은 우리가 주어진 (C) 것들에 얼마나 잘 투자했는지에 관한 것이다. 만약 자신의 삶이 불공평하다는 관점을 고수한다면, 그것은 정말로 신에 대한 모욕을 하고 있는 것이다.

	(A)	(B)	(C)
①	인식하다	다른	그것들을
②	인식하다	다르게	~한 것들을
③	인식된	다른	그것들을
④	인식된	다르게	~한 것들을

| **정답해설** | ④ 72% (A) perceive는 타동사로 '~을 인식하다'의 의미이다. 등위접속사 and를 두고 형용사 false와 병치 구조를 이루고 있으므로 (A)는 형용사 혹은 형용사의 기능을 하는 준동사가 와야 한다. 따라서 동사원형 혹은 본동사인 perceive는 적절하지 않다. 의미상으로 some은 dissatisfactions로 불만족은 '인식되는' 것

이므로 수동의 의미가 되어야 한다.

(B) gifted는 형용사이므로 형용사를 수식할 수 있는 부사 differently가 올바르다.

(C) 타동사 have invested의 목적어에 해당하는 올바른 대명사를 찾는 문제로, 목적어에 이어 목적격 관계대명사가 생략된 수식어구인 (that) we have been given이 이어졌으므로, those가 적절하다. 앞에서 언급된 명사를 대명사로 받을 때 수식어구(of + 명사, 형용사구, 분사구, 관계사절 등)가 있으면 that 혹은 those로 받아야 한다.

어휘

be based on ~에 기반을 두다   circumstance 상황, 환경
false 거짓의, 허위의   perceived 인식되는
discard 버리다   classification 분류, 범주
strive to ~하고자 노력하다   remove 제거하다
modify 바꾸다, 수정하다   purpose 목적
gifted 타고난 재능이 있는, 천부적인   argument 주장; 논쟁, 말다툼
invest 투자하다   hold on to ~을 계속 유지하다
outlook 전망, 관점   offence 모욕; 위반, 범죄

---

4   독해 > 글의 일관성 파악하기 > 글의 순서   오답률 33%   답 ②

| **해석** | 사람들은 경쟁자보다 낮은 가격이나 더 낮은 가격을 부과함으로써, 자신들이 더 많은 고객을 확보할 것이라고 생각한다. 이것은 일반적인 오류이다.

(B) 그것은 당신이 경쟁 업체에 비해 인하된 가격을 부과할 때, 고객 시장의 하층을 유치하기 때문이다. 이 고객들은 적은 비용으로 더 많은 것을 원하고 종종 당신의 사업에서 더 많은 시간과 간접비를 차지한다. 그들은 또한 여러분이 상대하기에 가장 어렵고 계속 만족시키기에 어려울 수 있다.

(C) 또한 아이러니하게도, 더 괜찮은 고객들을 쫓아버리게 되는데, 그들은 더 높은 수준의 제품이나 서비스에 대해 더 높은 가격을 지불하기 마련이기 때문이다. 우리는 많은 경쟁자들이 시장에 진입해서 유지하기 어려운 일요 요금을 부과하는 것을 보아왔다. 그들은 종종 할당량을 채우기 위해 고군분투하기도 하고, 오래지 않아 포기하고 다른 일을 하는 것으로 넘어간다.

(A) 따라서, 당신이 시작할 때, 더 낮은 양, 더 높은 마진의 제품과 서비스를 제공하는 것이 훨씬 더 낫다. 만약 어쩔 수 없다면, 가격을 낮추기 위해 언제나 협상을 할 수 있다. 하지만 인상 협상을 하게 될 경우는 드물다.

| **정답해설** | ② 67% 경쟁을 위해 경쟁자보다 더 낮은 가격을 부과하는 것이 오류임을 설명하는 글이다. 주어진 문장에 이어, 오류임을 전제한 문장을 대명사 It으로 받아 이유를 설명하는 (B)가 처음에 와야 한다. (B)에서 인하된 가격으로 유인된 고객들에 대한 단점을 서술했고, 이에 따른 부정적인 결과로 높은 수준의 제품과 서비스에 대해 높은 가격을 지불하는 더 괜찮은 고객들을 쫓아버리게 된다는 내용의 (C)가 이어져야 한다. 이어서 연결사 therefore이 나오고 앞에서 언급된 내용의 결론으로 어떻게 해야 하는지 설명하면서 가격을 올리는 것이 낮추는 것보다 어렵다는 말로 끝맺음을 한 (A)가 오는 것이 적절하다. 따라서 정답은 ②이다.

어휘

charge (대금을) 청구하다   competitor 경쟁자
fallacy 오류   overhead 간접비

deal with ~에 대처하다, ~을 다루다
sustainable 유지[지속]할 수 있는   quota 할당[분담]량
give up 포기하다   move on to ~로 옮기다
negotiate 협상하다   rare 드문

| **5** | 문법 > 준동사 > 동명사 | 오답률 28% | 답 ② |

| 해석 | 글쓰기를 즐기는 아이들은 흔히 자신의 작품을 인쇄물로 보는 것에 관심이 있다. 한 가지 비공식적인 접근은 시를 타이핑하고, 인쇄해서 게시하는 것이다. 아니면 당신은 사진이 있는 많은 아동 도서 작가들의 시선집을 만들 수 있다. 그러나 진정으로 열심이고 야심찬 아이들에게는 출판을 위한 시를 제출하는 것이 가치 있는 목표이다. 그리고 아이들의 원본 시를 인쇄하는 여러 웹 및 인쇄 방법들이 있다. 어린이 시인들이 원고 제출 프로토콜(문체, 형식 등등)에 익숙해지도록 도와라. 그들이 가장 자랑스러워하는 시를 선택하고, 제출된 모든 것의 사본을 보관하고, 부모의 허락을 받아라. 그러고 나서 그들의 작품을 받아서 인쇄물로 나올 때 그들과 함께 축하하라. 그들을 축하하고, 그들의 성과를 공개적으로 보여 주고, 소문을 내라. 그리고, 물론, 그들의 작품이 거절된다면 지지와 격려를 해 주어라.

| 정답해설 | ② 72% 부사구(But for children~)에 이어지는 문장의 첫 단어이다. 명령문의 동사원형이 될 수도 있으나 뒤에 본동사인 is가 있으므로 submit은 주어가 되어야 한다. 따라서 명사의 기능을 할 수 있는 동명사 submitting 혹은 to부정사 to submuit으로 바뀌어야 한다.

| 오답해설 | ① 0% 구조와 맥락상 주절의 주어인 children을 지칭하고 뒤에 이어진 명사 work를 수식해야 하므로 복수형 소유격인 their가 올바르게 왔다.
③ 7% Let과 호응하는 목적보어인 원형부정사 choose의 목적어를 이끄는 연결사이다. 종속절 내의 주어는 they, 동사는 are로 which poems가 전치사 of의 목적어 역할을 해야 함을 알 수 있다. 명사절을 이끌고 있으므로 의문사로 왔으며 뒤에 이어진 명사 poems를 수식하는 의문형용사로 '어떤'의 의미로 올바르게 쓰였다.
④ 21% 동사 showcase를 수식해야 하므로 부사로 올바르게 왔다.

[어휘]

dedicated 열렬한, 헌신적인   ambitious 야심에 찬
submit 제출하다   publication 출판
manuscript 원고   worthy 훌륭한
permission 허락, 허가   celebrate 축하하다, 기념하다
showcase 소개하다; 진열[전시]하다

| **6** | 독해 > 글의 일관성 파악하기 > 주어진 문장의 삽입 | 오답률 33% | 답 ④ |

| 해석 | 푸에블로 인디언 문화에서, 옥수수는 사람들에게 생명의 상징이다. '태양과 빛의 할머니'인 Corn Maiden은 이 선물을 가져와서 사람들에게 생명의 힘을 불어 넣었다. 옥수수가 태양에 의해 생명을 얻었을 때, Corn Maiden은 태양의 불을 인간의 몸에 가져와, 인간에게 자연을 통해 그녀의 사랑과 힘의 여러 표상들을 보여 준다. 각각의 Maiden은 아이들에게 주는 것과 같은 사랑으로 길러진 하나의 옥수수 씨앗을 가져다 주고, 이 씨앗 하나는 전체 부족을 영원히 유지해 줄 것이다. ④ 부족의 사랑과 힘으로, 그 작은 씨앗은 충분히 성장해 크게 자라 사람들을 위한 작물이 된다. Corn Maiden은 영혼이 부족 사람들과 함께 영원히 존재한다.

| 정답해설 | ④ 67% 주어진 문장에서 the tribe와 the tiny seeds를 통해 이전에 부족과 씨앗에 대해 제시되어야 함을 알 수 있다. 또한 그 작은 씨앗이 성장해 크게 자라 작물이 된다는 세부 내용이 이어졌으므로, 그 이전에는 씨앗에 대한 언급이 있어야 함을 알 수 있다. 따라서 ③에 이어진 문장에서 처음으로 one seed of corn이 이어졌으므로 그 이전에는 주어진 문장이 들어갈 수 없고, ④에 이어 씨앗을 가져온 Corn Maiden의 영혼이 영원히 부족 사람들에게 존재한다는 내용이 나왔으므로 주어진 문장이 들어갈 곳으로 가장 적절한 것은 ④이다.

[어휘]

representation 표상, 표현   nurture 양육하다, 기르다
sustain 유지하다, 부양하다   tribe 부족
mature 성숙하다, 충분히 발달하다; 성숙한
crop (작물이) 되다; 작물   tribal 부족의, 종족의

| **7** | 독해 > 빈칸의 내용 추론하기 > 빈칸 어구 추론 | 오답률 50% | 답 ① |

| 해석 | 너도밤나무, 참나무, 가문비나무 및 소나무는 항상 새로운 생장을 하며, 오래된 것을 제거해야 한다. 가장 분명한 변화는 매년 가을에 일어난다. 잎들은 지신들의 역할을 해 왔다. 그것들은 이제 시들어서 충해(蟲害)로 가득하다. 나무들이 그들에게 작별을 고하기 전에, 나무들은 잎들에 노폐물을 붓는다. 당신은 나무들이 이 기회를 이용하여 배설을 하고 있다고 말할 수 있겠다. 그런 다음 그것들은 약한 조직층을 만들어 잎이 자라고 있는 잔가지에서 각각의 잎을 떼어내고, 다음 미풍이 불 때, 잎들은 땅으로 떨어진다. 이제 땅을 뒤덮고 있는, 그래서 당신이 나뭇잎 사이로 돌아다닐 때 그토록 만족스러운 바스락 소리를 만들어내는 그 나뭇잎들은 기본적으로 ① 나무의 화장실 휴지인 것이다.

① 나무의 화장실 휴지   ② 식물의 부엌
③ 나무의 폐   ④ 곤충의 부모

| 정답해설 | ① 50% 나무들이 새로운 생장을 하면서 오래된 것(잎)을 제거하는 과정에 대한 글이다. 지문 중간에 가을에 잎들을 떨어뜨리는 과정을 배설(relive themselves)에 비유했으므로, 결국 바닥을 덮고 있는 바스락거리는 소리를 내는 나뭇잎들은 나무에게 있어 화장실 휴지와 같다고 볼 수 있다. 따라서 빈칸에 들어갈 것으로 가장 적절한 것은 ①이다.

[어휘]

beech 너도밤나무   oak 참나무
spruce 가문비나무   pine 소나무
get rid of ~을 제거하다   obvious 분명한, 명백한
purpose 목적
be riddled with ~을 (좋지 않은 것으로) 채우다
bid adieu 이별을 고하다   pump A into B A를 B에게 주입시키다
relieve oneself 용변을 보다, 배설하다
twig 어린[작은] 가지   breeze 미풍, 산들바람
rustling 바삭바삭 소리 나는   scrunch (사람이 걸어서) 소리를 내다
scuffle 허둥지둥[소리를 내면서] 가다

| 해석 | 허구는 많은 쓰임이 있고 그 중 하나는 공감대를 형성하는 것이다. 당신이 TV를 시청하거나 영화를 볼 때, 당신은 다른 사람들에게 일어나는 일들을 보고 있다. 산문 소설은 26개의 글자와 몇 개의 구두점으로 당신이 만들어 내는 것이고, 당신과 당신만이 상상력을 사용하여 세상을 창조하고 그곳에 살면서 다른 눈을 통해 밖을 내다본다. 당신은 사물을 느끼고, 그렇지 않으면 결코 알 수 없을 장소와 세상을 방문하게 된다. ② 다행히도, 지난 10년 동안, 세계에서 가장 아름다우면서 알려지지 않은 많은 장소가 주목을 받아 왔다. 당신은 저 밖에 있는 다른 모든 사람들도 나라는 것을 알게 된다. 당신은 다른 누군가이고, 당신이 당신의 세상으로 돌아올 때, 당신은 약간 달라질 것이다.

| 정답해설 | ② 93% 전체적으로 허구가 하는 역할 중 공감대를 형성하는 것에 대해 서술한 글이다. 허구의 요소로 TV, 영화, 산문 소설들이 언급되었고, 상상력을 사용하며 다른 눈을 통해 세상을 알게 되고 결국 이런 과정을 통해 스스로가 약간은 달라진다고 언급했다. ②번 문장에서 주어는 물리적인 장소들(places)로, 지난 10년간 가장 아름다우면서 알려지지 않은 장소가 주목을 받아왔다고 했는데, 이는 공감대 형성과는 거리가 먼 내용이므로 흐름상 가장 어색한 문장은 ②이다.

어휘

fiction 허구, 소설, 픽션	empathy 공감, 감정이입
prose 산문	punctuation mark 구두점
in the spotlight 주목받아	slightly 약간, 조금

| 해석 | 버드나무와 백양나무의 씨앗은 너무 작아서 당신은 날아다니는 폭신폭신한 털에서 두 개의 작은 어두운 색깔의 점만을 알아낼 수 있을 뿐이다. 이 씨앗들 중 하나의 무게는 0.0001그램에 불과하다. 이렇게 에너지 비축량이 적기 때문에, 묘목은 원기가 다 고갈되기 전에 겨우 1~2밀리미터만 자랄 수 있고 어린 잎들을 이용해 스스로 만들어 내는 양분에 의존해야 한다. 하지만 그것은 작은 싹을 위협하는 경쟁이 없는 곳에서만 효과가 있을 뿐이다. 그 위에 그늘이 드리워지는 다른 식물들은 즉시 그 새 생명을 소멸시킬 것이다. 그래서 이런 폭신폭신한 작은 씨앗 꾸러미가 가문비나무 숲이나 너도밤나무 숲에 떨어지면, 씨앗의 생명은 시작도 하기 전에 끝난다. 그것이 바로 버드나무와 백양나무들이 ① 비어 있는 땅에 정착하는 것을 선호하는 이유이다.
① 비어 있는 땅에 정착하는 것을 선호하다
② 초식동물에게 식량으로 선택되어 왔다
③ 인간의 간섭을 피하도록 진화해 왔다
④ 죽은 잎들을 멀리 겨울까지 달고 있다

| 정답해설 | ① 55% 버드나무와 백양나무의 작은 씨앗들이 생존하는 방법에 대한 글이다. 씨앗들이 매우 작기 때문에 에너지 비축량도 적고, 원기가 고갈되기 전에 양분에 의존해 살아남을 수 있다고 서술하는데, 이는 경쟁이 없는 장소에서만 효과가 있다고 했다. 빈칸에는 버드나무와 백양나무가 경쟁 없이 살아남을 수 있는 내용과 관련된 표현이 와야 하므로, 가장 적절한 것은 ①이다.

어휘

willow 버드나무	poplar 백양나무, 포플러나무
fluffy 솜털 같은, 폭신폭신한	meagre 빈약한, 불충분한

reserve 비축, 저장	seedling 어린 나무, 묘목
run out of ~이 동나다	competition 경쟁
threaten 위협하다	sprout 새싹
shade 그늘, 응달	extinguish 소멸시키다
spruce 가문비나무	beech 너도밤나무

| 해석 | 좋은 워킹화는 중요하다 대부분의 주요 스포츠 브랜드는 워킹을 위해 특별히 고안된 신발을 제공한다. 스타일보다는 착화감과 편안함이 더 중요한데, 신발은 지탱이 되는 느낌을 주어야 하지만 너무 끼거나 단단히 죄는 느낌이 들어서는 안된다. 갑피(甲皮)는 가볍고, 통기성이 있으면서 유연해야 하며, 깔창 내에 습기가 없고 깔창은 충격을 흡수해야 한다. 뒤꿈치 굽은 ③ 낮추어져(→ 높여져)야 하고, 따라서 신발 뒤쪽의 밑창은 앞쪽보다 두 배 더 두껍다. 마지막으로, 앞심은 당신이 스포츠 양말을 신고 있을 때조차도 운동용 양말을 신었을 때도 공간이 여유 있어야 한다.

| 정답해설 | ③ 67% 좋은 워킹화에 대해 설명하는 글이다. ③에 이어진 내용에서 신발 뒤쪽의 밑창이 앞창보다 두 배 더 두껍다고 했으므로, 뒤꿈치 굽은 더 높여져야 함을 알 수 있다. 따라서 lowered를 raised로 바꾸는 것이 적절하다.

어휘

athletic 운동의, 체육의	fit (옷 등의) 맞음새
comfort 편안함	supportive 지지하는, 유지하는
constricting 단단히 죄는	upper (신발의) 갑피
flexible 유연한	insole 깔창
moisture-resistant 방습의	sole 밑창
shock-absorbent 충격을 흡수하는	
spacious (집·방·공간 등이) 널찍한, 넓은	

| 해석 | 만약 당신의 자녀들이 비디오 게임을 할 때마다 싸운다면, 당신은 그들이 게임을 하려고 앉을 때 그들의 말을 들을 수 있을 정도로 확실히 가까이 있어라. 그들이 공격적으로 사용하는 특정한 말이나 목소리 톤을 듣고, 그것이 발전하기 전에 개입하려고 노력하라. 일단 화가 가라앉으면, 아이들을 앉히고 꾸짖거나 비난하지 말고 그 문제에 대해 논의해라. 아이들 각자에게 방해받지 않으면서 말할 기회를 주고, 그들 스스로 문제에 대한 해결책을 생각해 내도록 하라. 아이들이 초등학생 나이가 될 때쯤, 그들은 그 해결책들 중 어느 것이 서로 좋은 것이고 어느 것이 효과가 있고 시간이 지남에 따라 서로에게 만족시킬 가능성이 가장 높은지를 평가할 수 있다. 그들은 또한 해결책이 더 이상 효과가 없을 때 문제들을 재검토하는 것을 배워야 한다.
① 당신의 자녀가 자신들의 테스트를 평가하도록 요구하라.
② 당신의 자녀가 서로 경쟁하도록 만들어라.
③ 당신의 자녀가 갈등을 해결하는 것을 배우도록 도우라.
④ 당신의 자녀에게 논쟁에서 이기는 방법을 가르쳐라.

| 정답해설 | ③ 95% 자녀들이 싸울 때, 부모로서 그 문제를 해결할 수 있는 방법을 제시하는 글이다. 해결 방식으로 그저 혼내는 것이 아닌 자녀들 스스로 문제에 대한 해결책을 찾도록 만들어 주라고 했으므로 글의 요지로 가장 적절한 것은 ③이다.

어휘

aggressive 공격적인	intervene 개입하다, 간섭하다
temper 화, 성격	accuse 비난하다

uninterrupted 방해받지 않는 / come up with (생각을) 떠올리다
solution 해결책 / evaluate 평가하다

12 독해 > 대의 파악 > 요지·주장 찾기　오답률 5%　답 ④

| 해석 | 무슨 수를 써서라도 세균을 피하려는 추세가 현재 있다. 우리는 욕실, 부엌, 공기를 소독한다. 우리는 손을 소독하고 세균을 죽이기 위해 구강 청결제로 가글을 한다. 어떤 사람들은 가능한 한 사람과의 접촉을 피하고 세균에 감염될까 봐 악수조차 하지 않는다. 내가 생각하기에 어떤 사람들은 자신들의 생각을 제외한 모든 것을 정화한다고 말해도 무방할 것 같다. '거품 속의 소년(the Boy in the Bubble)'의 이야기를 기억하는가? 그는 면역 체계 없이 태어나서 사람과의 접촉 없이, 완전한 무균실에서 살아야만 했다. 물론 모든 사람들이 청결과 개인 위생에 대한 합리적인 기준을 유지하기 위해 신중한 조치를 취해야 하지만, 많은 경우에, 우리는 극단적으로 가는 것은 아닐까? 우리가 대부분의 세균과 접촉하게 되면, 우리의 몸은 세균을 파괴하고, 그 세균은 다시 우리의 면역 체계와 질병을 퇴치할 수 있는 능력을 강화시킨다. 따라서, 이러한 '좋은 세균들'은 실제로 우리를 더 건강하게 만든다. 모든 세균을 피해 멸균 환경에서 살 수 있다고 해도, 그러면 우리는 '거품 속의 소년'처럼 되지 않을까?

| 정답해설 | ④ 95% 세균을 건강에 부정적인 요소로 보고 피하려는 현상에 대해 서술하다가 '거품 속의 소년'에 대한 이야기를 통해 너무 극단적으로 세균을 피하는 것에 대해 우려하는 내용이 이어졌다. 글의 뒷부분에서 '좋은 세균'에 대해 언급하면서 이것들은 우리를 더 건강하게 만든다고 했으므로 글의 요지로 ④가 가장 적절하다.

어휘
trend 추세, 경향 / disinfect 소독[살균]하다
sanitize (청소·살균 등으로) 위생적으로 만들다
germ 세균 / for fear of ~하지 않도록
purify 정화하다, 정제하다 / immune 면역의
prudent 신중한 / hygiene 위생
go overboard 극단에 흐르다, 지나치게 열중하다
destroy 파괴하다 / sterile 균이 없는, 살균한; 불모의

오답률 TOP3
13 문법 > 준동사 > 분사　오답률 51%　답 ④

| 해석 | 황금 도시로 알려진 Jaisalmer는 Khyber Pass로 가는 길에 있는 예전의 캐러밴(대상 행렬)의 중심지였고, 모래 바다 위에 솟아 있으며, 그곳의 30피트 높이의 성벽과 중세의 사암으로 된 요새는 사파이어 빛 하늘로 솟아오른 조각된 첨탑과 궁전을 보호한다. 좁고 구불구불한 길과 숨겨진 사원들이 있는 Jaisalmer는 '아라비안 나이트'에서 바로 나왔고, 이곳의 생활은 거의 변하지 않아서 13세기로 거슬러 올라가 있는 당신 자신을 상상하기 쉽다. 그곳은 인구의 4분의 1이 성벽 안에 살면서 여전히 제 기능을 하는 인도에서 유일한 요새 도시이기도 하고, 그곳은 다져진 길에서 벗어나 충분히 멀리 있어서 관광업으로 인한 최악의 파괴를 겪지 않았다. 그 도시의 부유함은 본래 지나가는 낙타 캐러밴들에게 부과한 상당한 통행료에서 비롯되었다.

| 정답해설 | ④ 49% 완전한 절에 이어진 'with + 분사구문'으로 'with + 명사 + 분사'의 구조이다. 이때 분사는 명사를 서술하는 기능을 하는데, 인구의 4분의 1이 성벽 안에 '살고 있는' 것이므로 현재분사 living으로 바꿔야 한다.

| 오답해설 | ① 2% 분사구문의 생략된 주어는 이어지는 문장의 주어인 Jaisalmer로 그 도시는 황금 도시로 '알려진' 것이므로 수동분

사구문을 이끄는 과거분사 Known으로 바꾸는 것이 적절하다.

② 40% 앞에 완전한 절이 이어졌고 접속사 없이 its 30-foot-high~ fort에 이어졌으므로 본동사도 명사도 올 수 없다. 구조상 its 30-foot-high~ fort를 주어로 하는 분사구문이 이어져야 하고, 밑줄 뒤에 목적어에 해당하는 명사 carved spires가 있으므로 능동의 현재분사인 sheltering으로 바꾸는 것이 적절하다. 주어가 다를 때 분사구문 앞에 주격의 형태로 의미상의 주어를 둔 독립분사구문이다.

③ 9% which에 이어 불완전한 절이 와야 하는데 가주어 it, 진주어 to imagine이 포함된 완전한 절이 왔다. 주절의 so와 호응해 '매우 ~해서 …하다'의 표현이 되어야 하므로 접속사 that으로 바꾸는 것이 적절하다.

어휘
caravan 대상(隊商); (짐마차·트럭으로 이동하는) 대열
on the route to ~으로 가는 도중에 / medieval 중세의
fort 요새 / shelter ~을 보호하다
spire 뾰족탑 / soar 높이 솟다
winding 굽이치는, 나선형의 / lane 차로, 통로
alter 바꾸다, 변경하다 / fortress 요새
spare ~에게 위해를 가하지 않다 / ravage 파괴, 약탈

14 독해 > 대의 파악 > 요지·주장 찾기　오답률 5%　답 ②

| 해석 | 학식 있는 사람들은 세상의 문제에 냉담하지도 무관심하지도 않다. 이러한 문제에 관한 책은 그 어느 때보다도 많이 출판되고 있지만, 일반 대중의 관심을 끄는 책은 거의 없다. 마찬가지로, 새로운 연구 발견은 대학에서 끊임없이 이루어지고 있으며, 전 세계 컨퍼런스에서 공유되고 있다. 안타깝게도, 이 활동의 대부분은 이기적인 것이다. 과학을 제외하고, 그리고 여기서도 선택적으로만, 새로운 식견들이 우리의 삶을 향상시키는 데 도움이 되는 방식으로 대중에게 흘러가지 않는다. 그러나, 이러한 발견들은 단순히 엘리트들의 소유물이 아니며, 선택된 소수의 전문가들에게만 남아서는 안 된다. 각각의 개인은 자신만의 삶의 결정을 내려야 하며, 우리가 누구인지 그리고 우리를 위해 좋은 것은 무엇인가에 대한 현재의 이해에 비추어 그러한 선택을 해야 한다. 그것에 관해서는, 우리는 어떻게든 모든 사람이 새로운 발견에 접근하게 하는 방법을 찾아야 한다.

| 정답해설 | ② 95% 글 앞부분에서 세상의 문제에 대한 책들이 많이 출간되고 새로운 연구 발견이 끊임없이 이루어지지만 이를 이기적인 것으로 여기고 있다고 했다. 중간에 역접의 접속사 yet에 이어 이러한 발견들이 엘리트나 전문가들의 소유물이 아니라고 언급하면서 모든 사람이 새로운 발견에 접근할 수 있는 방법을 찾아야 한다고 했으므로 필자의 주장으로 가장 적절한 것은 ②이다.

어휘
indifferent 무관심한 / self-serving 이기주의의, 이기적인
insight 통찰력, 식견 / property 소유물, 재산; 특성
possession 소유, 재산
in light of ~의 관점에서, ~에 비추어

| **해석** | 언어는 개인에게 정체성과 소속감을 준다. 아이들이 자랑스럽게 자신의 언어를 배우고 집과 이웃에서 말할 수 있게 되면, 아이들은 높은 자존감을 갖게 될 것이다. 더욱이, 모국어의 참된 가치를 아는 아이들은 외국어를 구사할 때 스스로 성취자라고 느끼지는 않을 것이다. 향상된 자아 정체성과 자존감으로, 아이의 수업 성과도 발전할 것인데, 이는 그러한 아이는 언어적 소외감에 대한 걱정을 덜고 학교에 다니기 때문이다.
① 아동 발달에 있어 모국어의 중요성
② 아이들의 외국어 학습에 미치는 영향
③ 아이들의 자존감을 향상시키는 방법
④ 언어 분석의 효율성

| **정답해설** | ① 60% 언어가 정체성과 소속감을 준다는 내용의 글로 아이들이 모국어를 배우고 그 가치를 알게 될 때 자존감도 올라가고 수업 성과도 발전할 것이라고 서술하였다. 따라서 글의 주제로 가장 적절한 것은 ①이다.

어휘

identity 정체성　　　　　　　　belonging 소유, 소속
self-esteem 자존감　　　　　　mother tongue 모국어
self-identity 자기 동일성, 개성

| **해석** | 많은 동물들이 혼자 생활하지는 않는다. 그들은 함께 살고 일함으로써 세상과 더 효과적으로 상호 작용할 수 있다는 것을 발견했거나, 어쩌면 자연이 그들을 위해 발견했을지도 모른다. 예를 들어, 만약 어떤 동물이 혼자서 먹이를 사냥한다면, 그것은 자신보다 훨씬 작은 동물을 잡아서 죽이고 먹을 수 있다. 그러나 만약 동물들이 집단으로 함께 모여 있다면, 그들은 자신보다 더 큰 동물을 잡아서 죽일 수 있다. 한 무리의 늑대가 말을 죽일 수 있는데, 이것은 그 집단을 아주 잘 먹여 살릴 수 있다. 따라서, 혼자 일하는 것보다는 함께 일한다면, 같은 숲에 있는 같은 동물들은 더 많은 음식을 이용할 수 있다. 협력에는 다른 장점이 있다. 동물들은 서로에게 위험을 경고하고, 더 많은 음식을 찾을 수 있고(만약 그들이 별도로 검색한 다음 음식을 찾는 데 성공한 동물들을 따라 가면), 아프고 부상당한 동물들에게 얼마간의 돌봄을 제공할 수도 있다. 짝짓기와 번식 또한 동물들이 멀리 떨어져 사는 것보다 하나의 집단에서 살면 더 쉽다.
① 동물들이 사회적이 되는 것의 장점들
② 협력 행위의 단점들
③ 동물과 인간의 공통적인 특징들
④ 짝짓기와 번식에 있어서의 경쟁들

| **정답해설** | ① 81% 첫 문장에서 많은 동물들이 혼자 생활하지 않는다고 했고, 이어지는 내용에서 집단으로 생활할 때 갖는 장점들을 여러 예시를 통해 설명하고 있다. 따라서 글의 주제로 가장 적절한 것은 ①이다.

어휘

loner 혼자 행동[생활]하는 사람　　band together 무리를 이루다
pack 무리, 떼　　　　　　　　　　　cooperation 협업, 협력
benefit 이점, 장점　　　　　　　　　alert 경고하다
separately 별도로, 각자　　　　　　succeed in ～에서 성공하다
reproduction 번식; 복제; 재생산

| **해석** | 대학에서의 철학 공부가 나의 호기심을 북돋아주었다. 그 수업은 우리가 공부해야 할 수많은 철학자들을 목록에 싣고 있었고, 나는 처음에 우리의 임무는 일종의 세속적인 성경으로서 그들의 작품을 배우고 흡수하는 것이라고 생각했다. 그러나 나는 나의 개인 교사가 내가 그들의 이론을 암송하는 것에 관심이 있는 것이 아니라 과거의 철학자들을 권위자가 아닌 자극제로 활용하면서, 나 자신의 발전을 돕는 것에만 관심이 있다는 것을 알게 되어 기뻤다. 그것이 나의 지적 자유의 핵심이었다. 이제 나는 나 자신을 위해 생각하고, 어떤 것에 그리고 모든 것에 의문을 제기하고, 내가 그것을 옳다고 생각했을 때에만 동의할 수 있는 공식적인 허가를 받았다. 훌륭한 교육을 받았더라면 훨씬 더 일찍 그 허가를 받았을 것이다. 아아, 어떤 사람들은 그것을 결코 받아 본 적이 없는 것 같고 마치 신성불가침인 것처럼 다른 사람들의 규칙을 계속 암송하고 있다. 결과적으로, 그들은 다른 사람들의 세계에 자신도 모르게 ④ 반대자(→ 추종자)가 되는 것이다. 이제 나는, 철학은 전문적인 철학자들에게 맡겨지기에는 너무 중요하다고 생각한다. 우리 모두는 초등학교부터 철학자처럼 생각하는 법을 배워야 한다.

| **정답해설** | ④ 51% 필자가 대학에서 철학을 공부하면서 철학이라는 학문이 오로지 전문가들의 영역이 아닌 자신의 발전에 도움이 되고 지적 자유의 핵심이라는 사실을 깨달았다는 글이다. 글의 중반부에서 더 일찍 훌륭한 교육을 받았다면 지적 자유에 대한 허가를 받았을 것이라고 언급하면서, 그렇지 않은 다른 사람들은 그저 다른 사람들의 세계에 자신도 모르게 '따르고 있다'는 내용이 전개되었다. 따라서 ④의 opponents는 '추종자'의 의미를 지닌 followers로 바꿔야 자연스럽다.

어휘

curiosity 호기심
be supposed to + 동사원형 ～해야만 한다
absorb 흡수하다　　　　　　　　secular 세속적인
tutor 개인 교사　　　　　　　　　recite 암송하다
stimulant 자극제, 각성제　　　　authority 권위자
permission 허가, 허락　　　　　　opponent 반대자

| **해석** | 돌이켜 보면, 과학자들은 마야의 지도자들이 수세기 동안 강우량에 대한 자신들의 불확실한 의존성에 대해 알고 있었다는 증거를 발견했다. 물 부족은 이해되고 있었을 뿐만 아니라 기록되고 이를 위해 계획되었다. 마야인들은 강우량이 적은 해 동안에 (물의) 보전을 시행하여, 재배된 작물의 유형, 공공 용수의 사용 및 식량 배급을 엄격히 규제했다. 3천년 통치의 전반부 동안, 마야인들은 몇 개월 간의 가뭄 동안 빗물을 저장하기 위해 더 큰 규모의 지하 인공 호수와 수조를 계속 건설했다. 공을 들여 장식된 그들의 사원들도 인상적이었지만, 물을 모아서 보관하기 위한 효율적인 시스템은 설계와 공법에 있어 걸작이었다.

| **정답해설** | ① 56% (A) 명사 evidence에 이어진 연결사이므로 명사절을 이끄는 what은 쓸 수 없다. 또한 (A)에 이어 완전한 절이 이어졌으므로 that은 접속사이며, 명사 evidence의 동격절을 이끌고 있다.
(B) 완전한 절의 마지막에 있는 명사 containers를 수식할 수 있는 준동사가 와야 하는데, (B)에 이어 명사 rainwater가 이어졌으므로 이를 목적어로 삼을 수 있는 능동 구조의 준동사인 to store가 와야 한다.

(C) 형용사 impressive가 문장의 맨 앞에 왔고 접속사 as가 이끄는 절이 이어졌으므로 '양보 부사절'임을 알 수 있다. 따라서 도치 이전의 문장에서 주어와 동사에 이어 보어로 impressive가 와 야 하므로 불완전자동사인 were가 올바르다.

어휘

uncover 발견하다	be aware of ~을 인지하다, 알다
dependence 의존	shortage 부족
enforce 시행하다, 집행하다	conservation 보존
regulate 규제하다	crop 작물
reign 통치	artificial 인공의
drought 가뭄	elaborately 공을 들여
warehouse 창고에 넣다[보관하다]; 창고	

오답률 TOP 1

19 독해 > 글의 일관성 파악하기 > 글의 순서 오답률 63% 답 ②

| 해석 | 종교는 확실히 사람에게서 최고를 이끌어 낼 수 있지만, 그것이 그러한 속성을 가진 유일한 현상은 아니다.

(B) 아이를 갖는 것은 종종 사람에게 놀랄 만큼 성숙해지는 효과가 있다. 잘 알려져 있듯이, 홍수나 허리케인과 같은 자연재해가 그렇듯이, 전시(戰時)는 사람들에게 일어날 수 있는 많은 기회를 준다.

(C) 그러나 하루하루 지속되는 평생의 준비를 위해서는, 아마도 종교만큼 효과적인 것은 없을 것이다. 그것은 힘 있고 재능 있는 사람들을 더 겸손하고 참을성 있게 만들고, 그것은 평범한 사람들이 자신의 경지를 초월하게 하며, 그것은 절실하게 술이나 마약 혹은 범죄로부터 멀리 떨어져 있도록 도움이 절실히 필요한 많은 사람들에게 든든한 지원을 제공한다.

(A) 그렇지 않은 경우 자기도취적이거나 천박한, 혹은 조잡하거나 단순히 그만두는 사람들은 우리 모두가 자랑스러워할 어려운 결정을 내리는 데 그들에게 도움을 주는 삶에 대한 관점을 부여받을 때, 자신들의 종교에 의해 종종 고귀해진다.

| 정답해설 | ② 37% 주어진 문장에서 종교가 확실히 최고를 이끌어 낼 수 있지만 그러한 속성을 가진 유일한 현상은 '아니라고' 했고, 따라서 종교 외의 다른 현상인 아이를 갖는 것, 전시의 기회 등을 언급한 (B)가 맨 처음에 나와야 한다. (A)에는 종교에 의해 사람들이 고귀해질 수 있다고 서술하고 있고, (C)에서는 역접의 접속사 But에 이어 다시 평생의 준비를 위해 종교가 가장 효과적이라고 하는 (B)와 대비를 이루는 내용이므로 (A)보다는 (B)가 먼저 온 후, (A)가 마지막에 와야 자연스럽다. 따라서 글의 순서로 가장 적절한 것은 ②이다.

어휘

religion 종교
bring out the best 좋은 점을 끌어내다

phenomenon 현상	property 속성, 특징
abundance of 많은, 풍부한	occasion 기회, 경우
disaster 재해, 재난	brace 대비하다; 떠받치다, 보강하다
sturdy 튼튼한, 견고한	desperately 필사적으로, 절실하게
shallow 천박한	crude 조잡한; 천연 그대로의
ennoble 고상[고귀]하게 하다	perspective 관점

20 독해 > 글의 일관성 파악하기 > 글의 순서 오답률 9% 답 ②

| 해석 | 더 많은 사람들이 더 많은 자원을 필요로 하는데, 이것은 인구가 증가함에 따라, 지구의 자원이 더 빨리 고갈된다는 것을 의미한다.

(B) 이 고갈의 결과는 인간이 지구에서 증가하는 인구 수를 수용하기 위해 지구로부터 자원을 빼앗아 감에 따른 삼림 벌채와 생물 다양성의 손실이다.

(A) 인구 증가는 또한 대부분 이산화탄소 배출로 인한 온실가스 증가를 초래한다. 시각화를 하면, 4배의 인구 증가를 목도한 그 동일한 20세기 동안, 이산화탄소 배출량은 12배 증가했다.

(C) 온실가스가 증가함에 따라, 기후 패턴도 증가하고, 이는 궁극적으로 기후 변화라는 장기적인 패턴을 초래한다.

| 정답해설 | ② 91% 주어진 문장에서 인구가 증가함에 따라 지구의 자원이 더 빠르게 고갈된다고 했고, 이 내용을 (B)의 this depletion으로 받아 고갈에 대한 결과로 삼림 벌채와 생물 다양성의 손실을 언급하는 것이 자연스럽다. 인구 증가에 따른 자원의 고갈에 이어 (A)에서 부연의 부사 also와 함께 인구 증가에 따른 온실가스의 증가를 언급하였고, 구체적인 수치를 들어 설명했으므로 (A)가 그 다음에 오는 것이 적절하다. 마지막으로 온실가스가 증가하면서 이는 결국 기후 변화를 초래한다고 서술한 (C)가 오는 것이 자연스럽다. 따라서 정답은 ②이다.

어휘

resource 자원	depletion 고갈
deforestation 삼림 벌채	biodiversity 생물 다양성
strip A of B A로부터 B를 제거하다	accommodate 수용하다
emission 배출	visualization 시각화

21 독해 > 글의 일관성 파악하기 > 글의 흐름과 무관한 문장 오답률 35% 답 ②

| 해석 | 인간 생물학 및 생리학에 대한 광범위한 교육을 받은 의학 인류학자들은 질병 전염 패턴과 특정 집단이 말라리아 및 수면병과 같은 질병의 존재에 어떻게 적응하는지 연구한다. 바이러스와 박테리아의 전염은 사람들의 식단, 위생 및 기타 행동에 크게 영향을 받기 때문에, 많은 의학 인류학자들은 전염병 학자와 팀을 이루어 질병 확산에 영향을 미치는 문화적 관행을 파악한다. ② 대부분의 학생들이 성공적인 의료 경력이 주는 재정적 보상보다는 인도주의적 이유로 의학에 입문한다는 것이 흔히 일반적으로 받아들여지는 믿음일지 모르지만, 선진국에서는 지위와 보상의 전망이 아마도 하나의 동기요인일 것이다. 다른 문화들은 질병의 원인과 증상, 질병을 치료하는 최선의 방법, 전통 치료사와 의사의 능력, 그리고 치료 과정에 있어 지역사회 참여의 중요성에 대해 서로 다른 생각을 가지고 있다. 인간 공동체가 그러한 것들을 어떻게 인식하는지 연구함으로써, 의학 인류학자들은 병원과 다른 기관들이 좀 더 효과적으로 의료 서비스를 제공하도록 돕는다.

| 정답해설 | ② 65% 의학 인류학자들이 연구하는 것이 무엇인지를 상세하게 서술한 글이다. ②의 내용은 학생들이 의학에 입문하는 동기 유인에 대해 설명하고 있으므로 전체 흐름과 관계 없는 문장이다.

어휘

anthropologist 인류학자	extensive 광범위한
physiology 생리학	transmission 전염
sanitation 위생	identify 식별하다, 확인하다
humanitaian 인도주의적인	prospect 전망
incentive 동기 요인	symptom 증상
involvement 참여	perceive 인식하다

| 해석 | Sequoya(1760?~1843)는 테네시 동부에서 체로키 부족의 전통과 종교에 대한 지식으로 높이 평가 받는 명문가에서 태어났다.

(C) 어렸을 때, Sequoya는 체로키어 구전 전통을 배웠다. 그리고 성인이 되었을 때, 그는 유럽계 미국인 문화를 처음으로 경험하게 되었다. 그의 편지에서, Sequoya는 유럽계 미국인이 의사소통하는 데 사용했던 글쓰기 방법에 어떻게 매료되었는지를 언급한다.

(A) 글쓰기가 자신의 부족 사람들에게 미칠 수 있는 가능성을 인식하여, Sequoya는 1821년에 체로키 문자를 발명했다. 이 문자 체계로, Sequoya는 고대 부족의 관습을 기록할 수 있었다.

(B) 더 중요한 것은, 그의 문자가 체로키족이 신문과 책을 인쇄할 수 있도록 출판 산업을 발전시키는 데 도움이 되었다는 점이다. 취학 연령의 어린이들은 자신의 언어로 체로키 문화와 전통에 대해 배울 수 있었다.

| 정답해설 | ③ 88% 체로키족의 Sequoya라는 인물이 유럽계 미국인 문화를 접하면서 문자의 중요성을 인식하고 체로키 문자를 발명한 내용의 글이다. 주어진 문장에서 Sequoya의 출생에 대해 언급을 했고, As a child로 보아 출생 후 어렸을 때를 서술한 (C)가 그 다음에 와야 한다. (C)의 뒷부분에서 편지를 통해 글쓰기 방법에 매료된 내용이 나왔으므로, 문자가 미칠 가능성을 인식해 체로키 문자를 발명했다는 (A)가 이어지는 것이 자연스럽다. 마지막으로 문자 발명 이후 출판 산업을 발전시켰고, 체로키어로 어린이들이 문화와 전통을 배울 수 있었다는 내용이 thus와 함께 이어진 (B)가 와야 한다. 따라서 글의 순서로 가장 적절한 것은 ③이다.

어휘

prestigious 명망 있는, 일류의   oral tradition 구전 전통
fascinated 매료된, 매혹된

| 해석 | 사랑을 전파하세요
땅콩버터 모금 운동에서 굶주림과 싸우세요
약간의 도움이 필요한 지역의 가정을 도와 우리 지역사회에 기여하세요. 우리는 루이지애나 북동부에서 기아에 직면한 어린이, 가족들, 노인들에게 혜택을 주기 위해 제4회 연례 전 지역 땅콩버터 모금운동을 시작합니다.
땅콩버터는 어린이와 어른들이 좋아하는 단백질로 가득 찬 음식이므로 푸드뱅크에서 많이 필요한 기본 식료품입니다. 3월 29일 금요일 오후 4시까지 플라스틱 병에 든 땅콩버터나 기금을 먼로 푸드뱅크에 기부해 주세요. 땅콩버터 기부는 월요일부터 금요일까지 오전 8시부터 오후 4시까지 먼로의 4600 Central Avenue에 위치한 푸드뱅크 유통 센터에 놓으시면 됩니다. 금전적 기부는 여기서 하시거나 427-418-4581로 전화하시면 됩니다.

다른 하차(기부) 장소는 저희 웹사이트 http://www.foodbanknela.org를 방문해주시기 바랍니다.

| 정답해설 | ② 93% 안내문의 뒷부분에서 기부가 가능한 요일은 월요일에서 금요일까지라고 했으므로 토요일과 일요일에는 기부를 할 수 없을 것이다. 따라서 글의 내용과 일치하지 않는 것은 ②이다.

어휘

drive (특히 자선 등을 위한) 모금 운동
contribution 기부, 기여   assistance 지원, 원조, 도움
kick off ~을 시작하다   benefit ~에 이익을 주다
staple 기본[필수] 식품; 주요 산물   donate 기부하다
distribution 유통; 배급   monetary 금전의

| 해석 | 우리 가족 전체가 가난에 시달렸다. Garoghlanian 집안의 모든 분파는 이 세상에서 가장 가족의 모든 지점은 세계에서 가장 기가 막히고 우스꽝스러운 빈곤 속에 살고 있었다. 아무도 우리가 음식으로 우리 배를 채울 수 있을 만큼 돈을 벌었는지 이해할 수 없었다. 하지만, 무엇보다도 중요한 것은, 우리는 정직하기로 유명했다. 우리는 대략 11세기 동안 정직하기로 유명했고, 심지어 우리가 세상이라고 생각하려 했던 곳에서 가장 부유한 집안이었을 때 조차도 말이다. 우리는 자부심을 우선시하고, 그 다음이 정직, 그리고 그 후에 옳고 그름을 믿는다. 우리 중 그 누구도 세상의 그 누구도 이용하지 않을 것이다.

① 평화롭고 침착한
② 만족스럽고 자랑스러운
③ 공포에 휩싸이고 두려워하는
④ 경탄하고 놀라는

| 정답해설 | ② 86% 글의 첫 문장에서 가족 전체가 가난에 시달렸다고 언급했지만, 접속사 though에 이어 가난에도 오랜 시간 동안 집안이 정직함으로 유명했다고 서술하면서 세상의 그 어느 누구도 이용하지 않겠다고 했으므로, 화자의 심경으로 가장 적절한 것은 ②이다. honesty, pride, believed in right and wrong과 같은 표현을 통해 화자의 심경을 유추할 수 있다.

어휘

poverty 가난, 빈곤   pride 자부심
take advantage of ~를 이용하다

| 해석 | 생식의 인기가 증가하고 있음에도 불구하고, 당신은 여전히 조리된 채소에서 영양분을 얻을 수 있다. 예를 들어, 우리 몸은 토마토가 조리되었을 때 리코펜을 더 효과적으로 흡수할 수 있다. (그러나 생토마토는 여전히 리코펜의 좋은 공급원이라는 것을 명심하라.) 그러나 조리된 토마토는 생토마토보다 더 낮은 수치의 비타민 C를 함유한다. 따라서 만약 여러분이 수치를 높이려고 한다면, 생토마토를 고수하는 것이 더 나을 것이다. 당신이 그것들을 조리된 상태로 혹은 생으로 먹기로 결정하든, 토마토의 건강상의 이점을 희석시키지 않는 것이 중요하다. 만약 당신이 토마토 소스나 페이스트를 살 때는, 소금이나 설탕이 첨가되지 않은 종류를 선택하라. 혹은 더 나은 것은 가정에서 당신만의 소스를 조리하는 것이다. 그리고 토마토를 생으로 먹는다면, 소금을 약간만 치고 조금만 치고 칼로리와 포화지방이 낮은 샐러드 드레싱을 선택하라.

| 정답해설 | ② 91% Cooked tomatoes, however, have lower levels of vitamin C than raw tomatoes에서 조리된 토마토가 생토마토보다 비타민 C 수치가 낮다고 했으므로 반대로 서술한 ②는 글의 내용과 일치하지 않는다.

어휘

consume raw foods 생식하다   effectively 효과적으로
be better off 더 좋은 상태이다   sparingly 절약하여; 결핍되어
saturated fat 포화지방

합격예상 체크

〈법원직 연도별 합격선〉

맞힌 개수	/25문항	점수	/100점

➡ ☐ 합격 ☐ 불합격

취약영역 체크

문항	정답	영역	문항	정답	영역
1	②	독해 > 밑줄 어휘	14	③	문법 > 연결사
2	①	독해 > 빈칸의 내용 추론하기	15	③	문법 > 명사와 일치
3	②	독해 > 밑줄 어휘	16	②	독해 > 빈칸의 내용 추론하기
4	④	독해 > 대의 파악	17	③	독해 > 대의 파악
5	①	독해 > 요약	18	④	독해 > 세부내용 찾기
6	①	독해 > 글의 일관성 파악하기	19	④	독해 > 세부내용 찾기
7	①	독해 > 글의 일관성 파악하기	20	④	독해 > 대의 파악
8	①	독해 > 빈칸의 내용 추론하기	21	④	독해 > 밑줄 어휘
9	③	문법 > 준동사	22	④	독해 > 글의 일관성 파악하기
10	①	문법 > 준동사	23	③	독해 > 어휘 선택
11	②	독해 > 밑줄 어휘	24	③	독해 > 요약
12	②	독해 > 빈칸의 내용 추론하기	25	④	독해 > 글의 일관성 파악하기
13	①	독해 > 요약			

⬇ 영역별 틀린 개수로 취약영역을 확인하세요!

어휘	/0	문법	/4	독해	/21	생활영어	/0

➡ 나의 취약영역: _____

※ [정답해설]과 [오답해설] 선지의 50% 표시는 〈1초 합격예측 서비스〉를 통해 수집된 선지 선택률을 나타냅니다.

---

1 | 독해 > 밑줄 어휘 > 어휘 추론 | 오답률 44% | 답 ②

| 해석 | 지식을 사실과 동일시하는 것은 매력적이지만, 모든 사실이 지식의 항목은 아니다. 동전 한 개가 들어 있는 밀봉된 종이 상자를 흔든다고 상상해 보라. 당신이 상자를 내려놓을 때, 상자 안의 동전은 동전의 앞면이나 뒷면 중 하나가 나오게 떨어진다. 그것이 사실이라고 치자. 그러나 아무도 그 상자를 들여다보지 않는 한, 이 사실은 미지로 남는다. 그것은 지식의 영역 안에 있지 않다. 사실은 단순히 기록되는 것만으로 (A) 지식이 되는 것도 아니다. 당신이 '동전이 앞면으로 떨어졌다.'라는 문장을 종이의 한 면에 쓰고 '동전이 뒷면으로 떨어졌다.'라는 문장을 다른 면에 쓰면, 당신은 한 면에 사실을 적을 것이지만, 당신은 여전히 동전 던지기 결과에 대한 지식을 얻지 못할 것이다. 지식은 어떤 존재하는 주제의 부분에 대한 하나의 사실에 대한 어떤 종류의 접근을 요구한다. 그것(사실)에 접근하겠다는 마음이 (B) 없다면, 도서관과 데이터베이스에 저장된 어느 것이든 지식이 아니라 잉크 자국과 전자 흔적일 뿐이다. 어떤 경우라도 지식이 있으면, 이 접근은 개인에게 고유할 수도 있고 그렇지 않을 수도 있다. 동일한 사실이 한 사람에 의해 알려질 수도 있고 다른 사람들에 의해 알려지지 않을 수도 있다. 상식은 많은 사람들이 공유할 수 있지만, 어떤 주제에도 (C) 떨어진 지식은 없다.

(A)	(B)	(C)
① 사실	있다면	떨어진
② 지식	없다면	떨어진
③ 지식	있다면	붙어 있는
④ 사실	없다면	붙어 있는

| 정답해설 | ② 56% (A) 이전 문장에서 '이 사실은 미지로 남는다'고 했으므로, 다시 말하면, 그것은 '지식'의 영역이 아님을 유추할 수 있다.

(B) 이전 문장에서 지식은 사실에 대한 '접근(access)'을 요구한다고 했고, 이어진 문장에서 도서관이나 데이터베이스에 저장된 것들이 지식이 '아니라고' 했으므로, 지식 접근에 대한 마음이 '없다면(Without)'이 가장 적절하다.

(C) (B)와 유사한 흐름으로 주제가 없는 지식은 없다고 하는 것이 적절하므로 '떨어진(unattached)'이 가장 적절하다.

어휘

tempting 매력적인, 유혹하는
identify A with B A와 B를 동일시하다
seal 밀봉하다
look into ~을 조사하다, 살펴보다
access 접근
unique 고유의, 독특한
attach 붙이다, 첨부하다
contain 담다, 함유하다
realm 영역, 범위
trace 흔적; 추적하다
dangle 대롱대롱 매달리다

2

독해 > 빈칸의 내용 추론하기 > 빈칸 어구 추론

오답률 57%　　답 ①

| 해석 | 감수성이 예민한 젊은이들이 ① 또래 압력에 영향을 받는 유일한 사람들은 아니다. 우리들 대부분은 아마도 판매원에게 압박을 받은 경험이 있을 것이다. 영업 사원이 당신의 경쟁 업체의 70%가 자신의 서비스를 사용하고 있는데, 왜 당신은 그렇지 않은지를 말하면서 '사무용 솔루션'을 판매하려고 시도한 적이 있는가? 하지만 경쟁자의 70%가 바보들이라면? 혹은 그 70퍼센트가 너무 많은 추가 대가를 제공받았거나 기회를 거부할 수 없을 정도로 낮은 가격을 제시받았다면? 그 관행은 오로지 한 가지 일을 행하기 위해 고안되었고, 그 한 가지 일은 바로 당신이 구매를 하도록 압박을 하는 것이다. 당신이 뭔가를 놓치고 있거나 당신을 제외한 다른 모든 사람들이 알고 있다고 느끼게 하기 위해서이다.

① 또래 압력　　　　　　　　② 충동 구매
③ 괴롭히기 전략　　　　　　④ 치열한 경쟁

| 정답해설 | ① 43% 빈칸에 이어진 내용에서 판매원에게 압박을 받는 경험에 대해 언급하면서 구체적인 예로 판매원의 제품을 당신의 경쟁사들의 70%가 사용하고 있다고 영업을 하는 행위를 예로 들고 있으므로 빈칸에 들어갈 것으로 ①이 가장 적절하다.

어휘

impressionable 감수성이 예민한, 민감한
subject to ~을 당하기 쉬운
competitor 경쟁자　　　　　　sales rep 외판원
resist 저항[반항]하다　　　　idiot 바보
miss out 놓치다　　　　　　opportunity 기회

3

독해 > 밑줄 어휘 > 어휘 추론

오답률 17%　　답 ②

| 해석 | 자존감이 높은 사람들은 자신의 기술과 능력에 자신감을 가지고 있으며 삶이 그들에게 제공하는 도전에 직면하는 것을 즐긴다. 그들은 스스로를 믿고 기여할 수 있는 기회를 얻는 것을 즐기기 때문에 (A) 기꺼이 팀으로 일을 한다. 그러나 자존감이 낮은 사람들은 어색하고, 수줍어하며, 자신을 표현하지 못하는 경향이 있다. 종종 그들은 회피 전략을 선택함으로써 문제를 복잡하게 만드는데, 왜냐하면 그들이 하는 일이 무엇이든 실패로 이어질 것이라는 믿음을 (B) 가지고 있기 때문이다. 반대로, 그들은 자신이 가치가 없다는 느낌을 감추기 위해 뽐내고 오만한 행동을 보여줌으로써 자존감의 결핍을 상쇄할지도 모른다. 게다가, 그러한 사람들은 자신의 외부에 있는 이유를 찾음으로써 성공을 설명하는 반면, 자존감이 높은 사람들은 자신의 성공을 내면의 특성의 (C) 결과로 본다.

	(A)	(B)	(C)
①	기꺼이	부정하다	시도하다
②	기꺼이	가지고 있다	~의 결과로 보다
③	마지못해	가지고 있다	시도하다
④	마지못해	부정하다	~의 결과로 보다

| 정답해설 | ② 83% 첫 문장에서 자존감이 높은 사람들은 자신감이 있고 도전에 직면하는 것을 즐긴다고 했고 (A)가 포함된 문장에서 스스로에 대해 자신이 있고 기여할 수 있는 기회를 즐긴다고 했으므로, 이를 바탕으로 '기꺼이' 팀으로 일한다고 하는 것이 적절하다. (B)에는 주절의 내용이 회피 전략을 통해 자신들의 문제를 복잡하게 만든다고 했고, (B)가 포함된 문장에서 이에 대한 이유가 언급되고 있다. 자신들이 하는 어떤 것이든 실패로 이어질 것이라는 믿음을 '가지고' 있으므로 부정적인 결과가 나오는 것이므로, 맥락상 hold가 가장 적절하다. (C)에는 접속사 while을 두고 대비가 되는

내용이 이어졌는데, 주절에서는 자존감의 결핍이 있는 사람이 성공의 요인을 외부에서 찾는 내용이 나왔으므로 부사절에서는 높은 자존감을 가진 사람은 성공을 내면의 특성의 결과로 본다고 봐야 하므로 맥락상 attribute가 적절하다.

어휘

self-esteem 자존감　　　　　　　confidence 자신감
willingly 기꺼이, 자진해서　　　　unwillingly 마지못해, 부득이
contribute 기여하다, 공헌하다　　awkward 어색한, 서투른
compound (문제 등을) 악화시키다; 혼합하다
opt for ~을 선택하다　　　　　　avoidance 회피
deny 부정[부인]하다　　　　　　hold (생각·마음·감정을) 품다
conversely 반대로　　　　　　　compensate 보충하다, 보상하다
boastful 뽐내는, 젠체하는　　　　arrogant 거만한
unworthiness 가치없음　　　　　account for ~을 설명하다
attempt 시도하다　　　　　　　attribute ~의 원인으로 여기다; 특성
characteristics 특성

4

독해 > 대의 파악 > 제목 찾기

오답률 16%　　답 ④

| 해석 | 확실히, 숭고한 것에서 완전히 터무니없는 것에 이르기까지, 어떤 다른 종도 새롭고 독창적인 것을 고안할 수 있는 우리의 능력에 대한 권리를 주장할 수 없다. 다른 동물들은 분명 무언가를 짓는다. 새들은 복잡한 둥지를 짓고, 비버는 댐을 만들며, 개미는 정교한 터널망을 판다. "하지만 비행기들, 이상하게 기울어진 고층 건물들, Chia Pets 등은 꽤나 이상적이다."라고 Fuentes는 말하면서 진화적인 관점에서 "창의성은 두 다리로 걷는 것, 큰 뇌와 사물을 조작하기 위한 정말로 훌륭한 손을 갖는 것을 덧붙인다. 육체적으로 매력적이지 않은 영장류는 커다란 송곳니나 발톱, 날개 등 뚜렷한 신체적 이점이 없지만, 창조성은 대단히 동등하게 하는 것이며, 게다가 적어도 지금 당장은, 호모 사피엔스의 생존을 보장하고 있다.

① 인간의 창조성은 어디에서 오는가?
② 영장류의 신체적 특징은 무엇인가?
③ 다른 종에 비해 호모 사피엔스가 가지는 신체적인 장점
④ 창조성: 생존을 위해 인간이 지니는 고유한 특성

| 정답해설 | ④ 84% 지문 전체적으로 호모 사피엔스가 창조성으로 인해 다른 종에 비해 송곳니, 발톱, 날개 등과 같은 뚜렷한 신체적인 매력이 없음에도 생존을 할 수 있다는 것을 서술하고 있다. 이에 상응하는 호모 사피엔스가 가지고 있는 신체적인 요소로 두 다리로 걷는 것, 큰 뇌와 훌륭한 손을 언급하고 있으므로 글의 주제로 가장 적절한 것은 ④이다.

어휘

lay claim to ~에 대한 권리를 주장하다
capacity 능력
assemble 조립하다　　　　　　ridiculous 터무니없는
elaborate 정교한, 공들인　　　intricate 복잡한
unprepossessing 인상적[매력적]이지 않은　evolutionary 진화의, 진화론적인
primate 영장류　　　　　　　fang 송곳니
claw 발톱　　　　　　　　　obvious 분명한, 명백한
equalizer 동등[평등, 균일]하게 하는 것; 평형 장치

5 독해 > 요약   오답률 20%   답 ①

| 해석 | "대부분의 조류 식별은 일종의 주관적인 인상을 기반으로 하는데, 새가 움직이는 방식과 각기 다른 각도로 순간적으로 나타나는 모습들과 연속적인 다양한 모습들, 그리고 새가 머리를 돌리고, 날고, 방향을 바꿀 때, 당신은 연속적인 다양한 모양과 각도를 보게 된다."라고 Sibley는 말한다. 이 모든 것들이 합쳐져서 새의 독특한 인상을 만들어 내는데, 이는 실제로 분리되어 말로 설명될 수 없다. 들판에서 새를 관찰하는 것에 대해서, 당신은 시간을 들여 분석하지 않고, 그것이 이것을 보여 준다고, 그리고 이것을 보여 준다고 말한다. 따라서 그것은 이 종임에 틀림없다. 그것은 더 자연스럽고 본능적이다. 많은 연습을 한 후에, 당신은 그 새를 보고, 그것은 당신의 뇌에 작은 스위치를 작동시킨다. 그것은 맞는 것처럼 보인다. 당신은 한눈에 그것이 무엇인지를 안다."

↓

Sibley에 따르면, 조류 식별은 (B) 별개의 분석이라기 보다는 (A) 본능적인 인상을 기반으로 한다.

	(A)	(B)
①	본능적인 인상	별개의 분석
②	객관적인 연구	주관적인 판단
③	신체적인 외형	행동 특성
④	면밀한 관찰	거리를 둔 관찰

| 정답해설 | ① 80% 첫 문장에서 조류 식별은 '주관적인 인상'을 기반으로 하며, 새를 관찰함으로써 보게 되는 다양한 모습이 합쳐져서 새에 대한 독특한 인상을 만들어 낸다고 하였다. 마지막에 조류 식별은 자연스럽고 본능적이라고 했으므로 (A)에는 instinctive impression이 적절하다. (B)에는 중간에 조류 식별을 위해 분석할 시간을 갖지는 않는다고 하였으므로 discrete analysis가 적절하다.

어휘
identification 식별, 확인
instantaneous 순간적인, 즉각적인
sequence 연속, 순서; 배열
take apart 분리하다, 분해하다
instinctive 본능적인
at a glance 한눈에
subjective 주관적인
appearance 외모, 외관, 외형
combine 결합시키다, 통합하다
analyze 분석하다
trigger 유발하다, 촉발시키다

6 독해 > 글의 일관성 파악하기 > 글의 순서   오답률 33%   답 ①

| 해석 | 자동차가 사람에 대한 의존도가 낮아짐에 따라, 소비자가 제품을 사용하는 수단과 환경도 자동차 공유 및 단기 임대 프로그램에 참여하는 비율이 높아짐에 따라, 상당한 변화를 겪을 수 있다.
(A) 멀지 않은 미래에, 자동차가 필요할 때 운전자가 없는 차가 당신에게 올 수 있고, 다 사용하고 나면 주차 공간이 필요 없이 그것은 운전해서 가버릴 수 있다. 자동차 공유 및 단기 임대의 증가는 또한 외부 자동차 설계의 중요성에 부수적인 감소와 관련이 있다.
(C) 자동차 외관은 개인화와 자기 정체성을 위한 매개체 역할을 하기보다는, Free Car Media가 제공하는 브랜드 홍보 프로그램을 포함한 광고 및 기타 홍보 활동을 위한 채널을 점점 더 대표하게 될 수 있다.
(B) 그 결과, 자동차에서 파생되는 상징적 의미와 소비자의 개성과 지위와의 관계는 결국 변화할 가능성이 높다.

| 정답해설 | ① 67% 주어진 문장에서 차가 사람에게 의존도가 낮아지면서 소비자가 제품을 사용하는 수단과 환경이 바뀔 것이라고 언급하고 있다. 따라서 이에 따른 가까운 미래의 변화를 이야기하고 있는 (A)가 오는 것이 적절하다. 제시문에서 차가 사람에게 의존도가 낮아진다는 점을 주어 a driveless car로 묘사하고, 구체적인 변화를 서술하고 있다. (A)의 마지막 문장에서 외부 자동차 설계에 대해 언급하였고, 이를 (C)의 첫 문장의 car exteriors가 받아서 자동차 외관이 하는 역할을 서술하고 있다. 이후에 (B)의 As a result에 이어 전체 내용을 정리하고 있으므로 순서로 가장 적절한 것은 ①이다.

어휘
dependent on ~에 의존하는
undergo 겪다
participation 참여
be associated with ~와 관련이 있다
corresponding ~에 상응하는, ~와 일치하는
personalization 개인화, 개인의 기호에 맞추기
self-identity 자기 동일성; 개성
ambassador 대사
circumstance 환경, 상황
significant 중요한; 상당한
lease 임대하다
represent 대표하다; 표현하다
status 지위, 신분

7 독해 > 글의 일관성 파악하기 > 글의 순서   오답률 26%   답 ①

| 해석 | 일본의 조립 라인을 보기 위해 일본으로 건너간 미국 자동차 회사 임원들의 기막힌 사연이 있다. 조립 라인 끝에, 문에 경첩이 달려 있었는데, 이는 미국에서도 마찬가지이다.
(A) 하지만 뭔가 빠진 것이 있었다. 미국에서는 조립 라인 근로자가 고무 망치를 가지고 문 가장자리를 두드려 문이 완벽하게 맞는지 확인하곤 했다. 일본에서는 그런 작업이 존재하지 않는 것 같았다.
(B) 당황한 미국 자동차 임원들은 어느 시점에 문이 완벽하게 맞는지 물었다. 그들의 일본인 가이드는 그들을 바라보며 수줍게 미소를 지었다. "우리는 그것을 디자인할 때 딱 맞도록 합니다."
(C) 일본 자동차 공장에서는 문제를 조사하지 않고 데이터를 축적하여 최상의 해결책을 찾았는데, 그들은 처음부터 원하는 결과를 만들어 냈다. 만약 그들이 원하는 결과를 얻지 못했다면, 그들은 그것이 과정의 시작에서 내린 결정 때문이라는 것을 이해했다.

| 정답해설 | ① 74% 일본의 조립 라인을 견학한 미국 자동차 회사 임원들에 대한 사연으로, 제시문 뒤에서 문에 달려 있는 경첩에 대해 언급했고, (A)의 But에 이어 미국에서 경첩과 관련해 일본과 다른 부분을 설명하는 것이 자연스럽게 이어진다. (A)에서 언급된 차이에 대해 당황한 미국 임원들에 대한 이야기로 시작한 (B)가 그 다음에 오는 것이 적절하며, (B)에서 임원들이 질문한 부분에 대해 일본인 가이드가 답변한 내용이 (C)까지 이어지고 있으므로 글의 순서로 가장 적절한 것은 ①이다.

어휘
executive 임원, 경영진
hinge (문 등의) 경첩
rubber mallet 고무 망치
confused 당황한, 혼란스러운
accumulate 축적하다, 모으다
assembly line 조립 라인
missing 실종된, 없어진
tap 가볍게 두드리다
sheepishly 겁먹은 듯이, 주뼛주뼛

8	독해 > 빈칸의 내용 추론하기 > 연결어 추론
	오답률 35% 답 ①

| **해석** | Ekman의 연구와 누출에 대한 그의 생각으로 거슬러 올라가는 속임수에 대한 비언어적 단서에 대한 많은 연구가 있었다. 사람들이 다른 사람의 비언어적 행동을 거짓말을 간파하는 방법으로 사용한다는 것은 잘 입증되어 있다. 나와 다른 많은 사람들의 연구는 정직을 평가할 때 사람들이 다른 사람의 비언어적 행동에 대한 관찰에 의존한다는 것을 강력하게 뒷받침해 왔다. (A) 그러나 다양한 비언어적 행동과 거짓말을 하는 행위 사이의 연관성에 대한 사회 과학적 연구는 그 연관성이 일반적으로 매우 강하지 않거나 일관성이 없다는 것을 시사한다. 나의 연구에서, 나는 한 거짓말쟁이임을 폭로하는 것처럼 보이는 비언어적 신호들이 두 번째 거짓말쟁이에 의해 제공된 신호와 다르다는 것을 관찰했다. (B) 더욱이, 비언어적 행동과 속임수를 연결하는 과학적 증거는 시간이 지남에 따라 약해졌다. 사람들은 다른 사람들이 비언어적으로 스스로를 어떻게 표현하는지에 따라 정직을 추론하지만, 그것은 매우 제한된 효용과 타당성을 가지고 있다.

	(A)	(B)
①	그러나	더욱이
②	그 결과	이와 반대로
③	그러나	그럼에도 불구하고
④	그 결과	예를 들어

| **정답해설** | ① 65% (A) 이전에 정직을 평가할 때 사람들이 비언어적 행동에 대한 관찰에 의존한다고 하였는데, 빈칸에 이어 비언어적 행동과 거짓말에 대한 연관성이 없다는 점을 언급했으므로 역접의 연결사 However가 적절하다.

(B) 그 이전에 필자의 연구에서 거짓말임을 드러내는 비언어적 신호들이 다른 거짓말쟁이가 제공한 신호와 다르다는 관찰 내용을 언급했고, 빈칸에 이어 비언어적 행동과 속임수를 연결하는 과학적 증거는 시간이 지남에 따라 약해졌다고 했으므로 비슷한 흐름의 내용이 이어졌음을 알 수 있다. 따라서 부연의 연결사인 What's more가 적절하다.

어휘

nonverbal 비언어적인; 말이 서투른 cue 단서; 신호
deception 기만, 속임수
date back to ~까지 거슬러 올라가다
document ~을 증거 서류로 입증하다
detect 발견하다, 간파하다   reliance 의존, 신뢰
assess 평가하다   consistent 일관된
give away (비밀 · 진의 등을) 누설하다
infer 추론하다   validity 타당성, 유효성

9	문법 > 준동사 > 분사
	오답률 26% 답 ③

| **해석** | 신생 기업이 설립되자마자 그것은 은행 계좌가 필요할 것이고, 급여 계좌의 필요성은 빠르게 뒤따를 것이다. 심지어 가장 작은 사업체들과의 서비스에서부터 시작하여, 은행들은 급여 지불과 그에 관련된 세금 부과 서비스에 매우 경쟁적이다. 이것들은 기업이 최고 품질의 서비스와 얻을 수 있는 최고의 '무료' 회계 지원을 원하는 영역이다. 급여 지불 세법 변경은 특히 50개의 많은 주에서 판매 부서를 운영하려고 할 때, 따라잡아야 할 골칫거리다. 그리고 요구되는 보고서들은 회사 관리 직원들의 부담이다. 이 영역에서 은행의 증빙서류는 ADP와 같은 급여 서비스 대체제와 비교되어야 하지만, 결정이 이루어질 때는 미래와 장기적 관계를 명심해야 한다.

| **정답해설** | ③ 74% 명사 reports를 수식하는 분사로, 보고서들은 '요구되는' 것이므로 수동의 과거분사인 required로 바꿔야 한다.

| **오답해설** | ① 13% 완전한 절에 이어진 분사구문을 이끄는 현재분사로, 생략된 주어는 맥락상 앞 문장의 주어 the banks와 일치하는 올바른 구조이다.

② 6% 선행사 areas를 수식하는 형용사절을 이끄는 관계부사로 where에 이어 완전한 절이 올바르게 이어졌다.

④ 7% made와 함께 수동 구조로 쓰였다. 결정은 '이루어지고 있는' 것이므로 수동태로 적절하게 표현했고 is와 함께 현재진행수동태로 쓰였다.

어휘

start-up 신생 기업
incorporate ~을 법인[단체 조직]으로 만들다
payroll account 급여 계좌   competitive 경쟁적인
bookkeeping 부기   legislation 입법, 법안
burden 부담, 짐   administrative 관리[경영, 행정]상의
reference 참조, 참고   alternative 대안, 대체
ADP 자동 데이터 처리(Automatic Data Processing)
keep ~ in mind ~을 명심하다

오답률 TOP 3

10	문법 > 준동사 > 분사
	오답률 51% 답 ①

| **해석** | 많은 사람들이 동물 보호소를 방문하는 것이 너무 슬프거나 우울하다고 생각하기 때문에 그곳을 방문하는 것을 거부한다. 그들은 그렇게 안 좋게 느끼지 않아도 되는데, 왜냐하면, 많은 운 좋은 동물들이 교통사고, 다른 동물이나 인간들의 공격, 그리고 여러 요인에 영향을 받는 길 위의 위험한 삶으로부터 구조되기 때문이다. 마찬가지로 길을 잃은 많은 애완동물들이 그저 동물 보호소로 데려와지는 것만으로 당황한 주인들에 의해 발견되고 되찾아진다. 가장 중요한 것은, 입양 가능한 애완 동물이 집을 찾고, 아프거나 위험한 동물들은 인도적으로 고통에서 벗어나게 된다.

| **정답해설** | ① 49% depressed는 목적어인 it을 서술하는 목적보어인데, 구조와 맥락상 it은 동물 보호소를 방문하는 것을 지칭한다. depressed는 '우울한'의 의미로 주체가 사람이 되어야 하는데, 동물 보호소를 방문하는 것은 '우울하게 하는' 것이므로 현재분사 depressing으로 바꿔야 한다.

| **오답해설** | ② 17% where는 선행사 the streets를 지칭하는 관계부사로, 뒤에 완전한 절이 올바르게 이어졌다. 계속적 용법이므로 'and there'의 의미이다.

③ 13% 타동사 find의 수동형 동사로 주어인 애완동물들은 '발견되는' 것이므로 구조와 맥락상 올바르다.

④ 21% 주어인 명사 pets를 수식하는 형용사로 '입양 가능한'의 의미이다. 구조와 맥락상 올바르다.

어휘

depressed 우울한   subject to ~을 당하기 쉬운
reclaim 되찾다; 재생하다   distraught (마음이) 심란해진, 당황한
adoptable 채용[채택]할 수 있는   humanely 인도적으로, 자비롭게
relieve 구제하다; 없애다   suffering 고통

11 독해 > 밑줄 어휘 > 어휘 추론   오답률 56%   답 ②

| 해석 | EQ 테스트는 신뢰할 수 있는 테스트 방법으로 수행될 때, 여러분 자신에 대한 매우 유용한 정보를 제공할 수 있다. 수천 명의 사람들을 시험해 본 결과, 나는 많은 사람들이 자신들의 결과에 약간 놀란다는 것을 발견했다. 예를 들어, 자신이 매우 사회적으로 책임감 있고 종종 다른 사람들에 대해 걱정한다고 믿는 한 사람은 그 분야에서 (A) 평균 점수를 받았다. 그녀는 자신의 점수에 상당히 실망했다. 그녀는 사회적 책임에 대한 매우 높은 기준을 가지고 있었기 때문에 평가를 수행할 때 자신에게 극도로 (B) 강경했던 것으로 드러났다. 실제로, 그녀는 대부분의 사람들보다 사회적으로 (C) 더 책임감이 있었지만, 자신이 그랬던 것보다 훨씬 더 나을 수 있다고 믿었다.

	(A)	(B)	(C)
①	평균의	쉬운	덜
②	평균의	강경한	더
③	놀라운	강경한	덜
④	놀라운	쉬운	더

| 정답해설 | ② 44% (A) 앞서 많은 사람들이 자신을 테스트한 결과에 놀랐다는 내용이 왔고, 이에 대한 예시로 사회적으로 책임감이 있고 다른 사람들에게 관심이 있다고 믿는 한 사람이 그 분야에서 탁월한 점수가 아닌 '평균' 점수가 나왔다는 것이 자연스러우므로 average가 적절하다.
(B) 실망스러운 점수를 받은 사람이 사회적 책임에 대해 매우 높은 기준을 가지고 있었고 평가 수행 시 자신에게 '강경했음'을 유추할 수 있으므로 hard가 적절하다.
(C) 앞에서 서술된 내용으로 보아 그녀는 대부분의 사람들보다 사회적으로 '더' 책임감이 있음을 알 수 있으므로 more가 적절하다.

어휘
provide A with B A에게 B를 제공하다
be concerned about ~에 대해 걱정하다
average 평균의; 보통의, 평범한   extraordinary 특별한, 뛰어난
disappointed 실망한   assessment 평가

12 독해 > 빈칸의 내용 추론하기 > 빈칸 어구 추론   오답률 19%   답 ②

| 해석 | 사람은 자신에게 유리하게 증거를 사용하여 ② 특정한 믿음을 초래하려고 할 수 있다. 한 어머니가 아들에게 "이번 학기에 영어는 어떠니?"라고 묻자, 그는 "아, 방금 시험에서 95점을 받았어요."라고 유쾌하게 대답한다. 이 진술은 그가 다른 모든 시험에서 낙제했다는 사실과 그의 실제 평균은 55점이라는 사실을 감춘다. 그러나, 만약 그녀가 그 문제를 더 이상 추궁하지 않는다면, 어머니는 그녀의 아들이 그렇게 잘하고 있다는 것에 기뻐할지도 모른다. Linda는 Susan에게 "디킨스 책을 많이 읽었니?"라고 묻는다. Susan은 "아, Pickwick Papers는 내가 가장 좋아하는 소설 중 하나야."라고 대답한다. 이 말은 Pickwick Paper가 그녀가 읽은 디킨스의 유일한 소설이라는 사실을 숨길 수 있고, Linda에게 Susan이 디킨스의 열렬한 팬이라는 인상을 줄 수도 있다.
① 여분의 돈을 벌다
② 특정한 믿음을 초래하다
③ 기억력 문제를 숨기다
④ 다른 사람들이 죄책감을 느끼게 하다

| 정답해설 | ② 81% 빈칸에 포함된 문장이 주제 문장으로 이어서 두 가지 사례를 제시하고 있다. 첫 번째 사례에서 아들이 잘 치른 한 번의 시험을 자신에게 유리하게 어머니에게 언급함으로써 시험에서 낙제했다는 사실과 평균 점수가 낮다는 사실을 숨길 수 있다고 하였다. 두 번째 사례에서 디킨스 책을 읽어본 적이 있냐는 질문에 대해 가장 좋아한다는 하나의 제목을 언급함으로써, 그 외의 다른 소설을 읽지 않았다는 사실을 숨길 수 있고, 디킨스의 팬이라는 인상을 줄 수도 있다고 했으므로 빈칸에 들어갈 것으로 ②가 가장 적절하다.

어휘
to one's advantage ~에게 유리하게
statement 말, 진술   conceal 숨기다, 감추다
delighted 기쁜, 즐거운
disguise 겉을 꾸며 속이다; 위장시키다
enthusiast 열심인 사람

13 독해 > 요약   오답률 11%   답 ①

| 해석 | 우리가 우리의 외모, 우리의 정원, 우리가 준비한 저녁 식사, 혹은 사무실에서의 업무에 대해 칭찬을 받든 받지 않든 간에, 잘 수행된 업무에 대한 인정을 받는 것은 항상 만족스럽다. 확실히, 강화 이론은 가끔의 칭찬은 새로운 기술을 배우는 데 도움이 된다고 본다. 그러나, 일부 증거는 성과 개선에 있어 칭찬을 이용하는 것에 관한 전반적인 일반화에 대해 경고한다. 칭찬은 특정 업무에 대한 성과를 향상시키지만, 다른 업무에 대한 칭찬은 오히려 해로울 수 있는 것으로 보인다. 승리를 기대하는 고향 팬들의 열광적인 응원이 자신들의 팀의 몰락을 가져오는 상황을 상상해 보라. 이런 상황에서, 칭찬은 선수들에게 압박감을 조성해 경기력에 지장을 주는 것으로 보인다.

↓

(A) 칭찬이 성과에 도움을 주는 해를 끼치는지는 (B) 업무 유형에 달려 있다.

	(A)	(B)
①	칭찬	업무 유형
②	경쟁	팀워크의 질
③	칭찬	팀워크의 질
④	경쟁	업무 유형

| 정답해설 | ① 89% 칭찬이 새로운 기술을 배우는 데 도움이 된다는 강화 이론에 대해 언급한 후, 역접의 접속사 However에 이어, 성과 개선에 칭찬을 이용하는 것이 그저 좋은 것은 아니라는 내용을 서술하고 있다. 칭찬이 특정 업무에 대한 성과를 향상시키지만, 다른 업무에 대해서는 해로울 수 있다고 했으므로 (A)에는 글의 핵심인 praise가, (B)에는 task types가 가장 적절하다.

어휘
compliment 칭찬[찬양]하다   appearance 외모, 외견
assignment 과제, 임무   reinforcement 강화, 보강
see A as B A를 B로 보다   occasional 때때로의, 이따금의
caution against ~에 대해 경고[주의]를 주다
generalization 일반[보편]화   harmful 해로운
bring about ~을 초래하다, 일으키다
downfall 몰락, 파멸   disrupt 방해하다; 붕괴시키다

14 | 문법 > 연결사 > 접속사 | 오답률 19% | 답 ③

| 해석 | 미디어 소비를 익명의 사회적 관계의 맥락에서 고려할 때, 우리는 술집과 같은 공공장소에서 텔레비전을 보거나, 콘서트나 댄스 클럽에 가거나, 버스 또는 지하철에서 신문을 읽는 것과 같은 낯선 사람들과 있는 것과 관련된 경우를 의미한다. 일반적으로, 우리가 우리 주변의 사람들과 그리고 미디어 제품과 어떻게 상호 작용하는지를 지배하는 사회적 규칙들이 있다. 예를 들어, 우리 문화에서는 다른 사람의 어깨 너머로 책을 읽거나, 공공장소에서 일어나서 TV 채널을 바꾸는 것은 무례하거나, 적어도 공격적으로 여겨진다. 음악 팬이라면 어느 누구나 특정 종류의 콘서트에서 무엇이 적절한지 안다. 다른 사람들의 존재는 환경과 그에 따른 미디어 소비의 활동을 정의하는 데 종종 결정적인데, 비록 그 관계가 완전히 개인과 관계없다는 사실에도 불구하고 그러하다.

| 정답해설 | ③ 81% it is considered에 이어졌으므로 동사원형이나 본동사가 아닌 다른 형태의 준동사가 되어야 한다. 뒤에 등위접속사 or에 이어 to get up이 왔으므로 가주어 it과 호응하는 진주어인 to read로 바꿔야 한다.

| 오답해설 | ① 1% such as에 이어진 동명사 viewing과 병치가 되어야 하므로 동명사 going으로 올바르게 왔다. 뒤에 등위접속사 or에 이어 동명사 reading이 이어진 것 역시 자연스럽다.

② 9% 선행사 social rules를 수식하는 관계대명사절의 동사로 주격 관계대명사 that에 이어졌으므로 선행사인 rules에 수일치시켜 복수 동사로 올바르게 왔다.

④ 9% 양보의 전치사로 뒤에 동격절을 수반한 명사 the fact가 목적어로 올바르게 왔다.

어휘

consumption 소비	in the context of ~의 맥락에서
anonymous 익명의	occasion (특정한) 때, 경우
interact with ~와 상호작용하다	aggressive 공격적인; 적극적인
appropriate 적절한	impersonal 비인간적인, 냉담한

15 | 문법 > 명사와 일치 > 일치 | 오답률 6% | 답 ③

| 해석 | 우리 중 많은 사람들은 기억 상실이나 갑작스런 기억 상실로 인해 이름과 정체성을 기억할 수 없다고 생각한다. 이 신념은 기억 상실증이 일반적으로 영화, TV 및 문학에서 묘사되는 방식을 반영할 수 있다. 예를 들어, 영화 〈본 아이덴티티〉에서 맷 데이먼의 캐릭터를 만났을 때, 우리는 그가 누구인지, 왜 그가 하는 기술을 가지고 있는지, 어디에서 왔는지에 대한 기억이 없다는 것을 알게 된다. 그는 이 질문들에 답하기 위해 영화에서 많은 시간을 보낸다. 하지만, 당신의 이름과 신분을 기억하지 못하는 것은 현실에서 매우 드물다. 기억 상실증은 대부분 뇌손상으로 인해 희생자가 새로운 기억을 형성할 수 없게 되지만, 지난 4년간의 대부분의 기억은 손상되지 않는다; 어떤 영화들은 이 더 흔한 신드롬을 정확하게 묘사한다; 우리가 가장 좋아하는 메멘토.

| 정답해설 | ③ 94% 주어가 the inability이므로 단수 동사 is로 바꿔야 한다. to remember 이하는 주어인 명사 the inability를 수식하는 to부정사의 형용사적 용법으로 동사의 수일치에 영향을 미치지 않는다.

| 오답해설 | ① 0% 동사 is와 함께 수동태를 이룬다. portray가 타동사이므로 뒤에 목적어가 없다는 점과, 의미상 amnesia는 '묘사되는' 것이므로 과거분사 portrayed는 올바르다.

② 2% 동사 spend와 호응하는 R-ing로 '(시간 · 돈을) ~에 소비하다'의 의미이다.

④ 4% 'with + 명사 + 분사' 구문으로 intact는 형용사이므로 intact 앞에 현재분사 being이 생략된 것으로 볼 수 있다.

어휘

amnesia 기억 상실증	inability 무능, 불능
identity 정체성	portray 묘사하다, 표현하다
literature 문학	injury 상해, 부상
intact 온전한, 손상되지 않은	accurately 정확히

16 | 독해 > 빈칸의 내용 추론하기 > 빈칸 어구 추론 | 오답률 27% | 답 ②

| 해석 | 자연재해와 그것이 사람들과 그들의 재산에 미치는 부정적인 영향에 대해 현재 많은 것이 알려져 있다. 논리적인 사람은 누구나 그러한 잠재적인 영향을 피하거나 적어도 그러한 영향을 최소화하기 위해 행동이나 재산을 바꾸려는 것은 분명해 보인다. 그러나, 인간이 항상 이성적인 것은 아니다. 누군가가 개인적인 경험을 하거나 그런 경험을 가진 사람을 알기 전까지는, 대부분의 사람들이 잠재의식적으로 '여기서 그런 일은 일어나지 않을 거야' 혹은 '나에게 그런 일은 일어나지 않을거야'라고 믿는다. 위험, 발생 확률, 사건의 대가를 알고 있는 지식 있는 과학자들조차도 ② 항상 적절하게 행동하지는 않는다.

① 침묵하기를 거부하다
② 항상 적절하게 행동하지 않다
③ 유전적 요인을 가장 중요시하다
④ 자연재해를 정의하는 어려움을 겪다

| 정답해설 | ② 73% 지문 앞부분에서 자연재해와 재해가 미치는 부정적인 영향에 대해 언급한 후 이상적인 사람이라면 그 영향을 피하거나 최소화하기 위해 노력한다고 서술했다. 역접의 However에 이어 인간이 항상 이성적인 것은 아니라고 하면서 이에 대한 예시를 들어 설명하고 있으므로 빈칸에 들어갈 것은, 과학자들조차도 항상 이성적이지 않다는 맥락의 내용이 들어가야 한다. 따라서 정답으로 ②가 가장 적절하다.

어휘

hazard 위험	property 재산, 부동산; 특성
obvious 분명한, 명백한	modify 변경하다, 수정하다
rational 합리적인, 이성적인	subconsciously 잠재의식적으로
odds 확률, 가능성	

17 | 독해 > 대의 파악 > 주제 찾기 | 오답률 30% | 답 ③

| 해석 | 도시와 왕국의 부상과 교통 인프라의 개선은 전문화를 위한 새로운 기회를 가져왔다. 인구 밀도가 높은 도시는 전문 제화공과 의사뿐만 아니라 목수, 사제, 군인 및 변호사에게도 상근직을 제공했다. 정말로 좋은 와인, 올리브 오일 또는 도자기를 생산하는 것으로 명성을 얻은 마을들은 거의 독점적으로 해당 제품을 전문으로 하고, 필요한 다른 모든 제품에 대해 다른 부락과 거래하는 것이 가치가 있음을 발견했다. 이것은 많은 의미가 있었다. 기후와 토양은 다르다. 따라서 만약 토양과 기후가 포도나무에 훨씬 더 적합한 곳에서 더 매끄러운 품종을 살 수 있다면, 왜 뒷마당에서 평범한 와인을 마시는가? 만약 당신의 뒷마당의 진흙이 더 강하고 예쁜 화분을 만든다면, 교환을 할 수 있다.

① 기후와 토양이 현지 생산품에 어떻게 영향을 미치는가
② 지역 특산물에 대한 좋은 평판을 얻는 방식들

③ 사람을 전문화와 거래에 참여하도록 만든 것
④ 도시와 상근직 전문가들의 부상

| 정답해설 | ③ [70%] 전문화를 통한 새로운 기회에 대한 글로, 지역 특산물로 명성을 얻은 곳은 독점적으로 해당 제품을 전문으로 한다고 했고, 기후와 토양은 다르기 마련이므로, 결국 독점하고 있는 특산품을 서로 교환할 수 있다고 했다. 따라서 이 글의 주제로 가장 적절한 것은 ③이다.

어휘
infrastructure 기반 시설　　　　bring about 초래하다, 일으키다
densely 밀집하여, 빽빽이　　　　professional 직업의; 전문[본업]의
carpenter 목수　　　　　　　　　priest 신부, 사제
reputation 평판, 명성　　　　　　settlement 촌락, 부락
make sense 이치에 맞다　　　　　mediocre 평범한, 보통의

18　독해 > 세부내용 찾기 > 지칭어 추론　오답률 21%　답 ④

| 해석 | 아홉 살의 Ryon Kyote는 캘리포니아 나파에 있는 집에서 아침을 먹고 있었는데, 그때 인디애나의 한 학교가 점심 급식 계좌에 충분한 돈이 없는 6살짜리 여자아이의 식사를 빼앗았다는 뉴스를 보았다. Kyote는 그의 친구들에게 그런 일이 일어날 수 있는지를 물었다. 그의 어머니가 학군에 연락하여 알아냈을 때, 그녀는 학군의 학교 학생들이 모두 2만 5천 달러의 점심 식사 빚을 지고 있음을 알게 되었다. 그 학군은 빚진 학생들에게 불이익을 주지 않는다고 말하지만, Kyote는 약 74달러의 빚을 갚기 위해 저축한 용돈을 쓰기로 결정했는데, 이는 점심 식사 빚을 끝내려는 운동의 얼굴이 되었다. 10월에 캘리포니아 주지사인 Gavin Newsom이 '점심 식사 수치심'과 빚이 있는 학생들에게 질이 더 안 좋은 음식을 주는 것을 금지하는 법안에 서명했을 때, 그는 <u>이 문제</u>에 대한 인식을 높이는 데 있어 Kyote의 '공감과 용기'에 감사했다. "영웅은 모든 연령에서 나와요."라고 Kyote는 지적한다.
① 주지사가 점심 식사 빚이 있는 학생들에게 급식 품목을 거부하는 법안에 서명했다.
② Kyote가 급식 계좌의 돈을 다 써버려서 점심 식사를 뺏겼다.
③ 재정 부담이 있는 학군은 예산을 삭감했고 양질의 식사를 제공할 수 없었다.
④ 점심을 살 여유가 없는 학군 내 많은 학생들이 점심 식사 빚에 시달렸다.

| 정답해설 | ④ [79%] 돈이 없어 점심 식사 시간에 식사를 빼앗기는 수치스러운 일을 겪은 한 어린이의 뉴스를 접한 후 Kyote라는 어린이가 자신이 저축한 용돈을 점심 식사 빚을 지고 있는 학생들을 위해 쓰는 운동을 전개했고, 캘리포니아 주지사가 이를 통해 관련 법안에 서명했다는 내용이다. 따라서 the issue는 맥락상 ④가 가장 적절하다.

어휘
school district 학군
penalize 페널티를 주다; 벌점을 부과하다
allowance 용돈　　　　　　　　　ban 금지하다
empathy 공감, 감정이입　　　　　point out 지적하다; 가리키다

19　독해 > 세부내용 찾기 > 내용 불일치 찾기　오답률 6%　답 ④

| 해석 | 세계에서 가장 큰 심장은 청고래 안에 있다. 그것은 무게가 7톤이 넘는다. 그것은 방 하나 크기이다. 이 동물은 태어날 때 길이는 20피트, 무게는 4톤이다. 그것은 당신의 차보다 훨씬 더 크다. 그것은 매일 어미로부터 100갤런의 젖을 마시고 하루에 200파운드씩 체중이 는다. 그리고 7-8년

정도 되면 그것은 상상할 수 없을 정도의 사춘기를 겪고 그러고 나서 본질적으로 인간의 시야에서 사라지는데, 왜냐하면 짝짓기 습성, 이동 패턴, 식단, 군거 생활, 언어, 사회 구조, 그리고 질병에 대해 알려진 것이 거의 없기 때문이다. 지구상의 모든 바다에는 아마도 10,000마리의 청 고래가 살고 있으며, 우리가 거의 알지 못하는 지금까지 살았던 중 가장 큰 동물이다. 그러나 우리는 이것을 알고 있는데, 세계에서 가장 큰 심장을 가진 이 동물들은 일반적으로 짝을 이루어 이동하며, 그들의 찢어지는 열망의 소리인 관통하는 신음 소리는 수 마일까지 들릴 수 있다.

| 정답해설 | ④ [94%] 청고래는 짝을 이루어(in pairs) 이동한다고 했으므로 '혼자서' 이동한다고 한 ④는 글의 내용과 일치하지 않는다. 청고래의 소리가 물속을 관통해 수 마일까지 전달될 수 있는 것은 일치하는 내용이다.

어휘
endure 참다, 견디다　　　　　　puberty 사춘기, 성숙기
penetrate 관통하다; 스며들다　　moan 신음 소리를 내다
pierce 꿰뚫다　　　　　　　　　yearning 갈망하는

20　독해 > 대의 파악 > 주제 찾기　오답률 12%　답 ④

| 해석 | 신선 농산물을 취급할 때, 온도를 조절하는 것 외에도 공기 조절이 중요하다. 저장 중 탈수를 방지하기 위해 공기 중에 어느 정도의 수분이 필요하지만, 너무 많은 수분은 곰팡이의 성장을 촉진시킬 수 있다. 일부 상업용 저장 장치는 이산화탄소와 수분의 정도를 신중하게 조절하여 공기를 제어한다. 때로는 에틸렌 가스와 같은 다른 가스가 바나나 및 기타 신선 농산물의 최적의 품질을 달성하는 데 도움이 되도록 제어되는 정도로 주입될 수 있다. 가스와 습기 제어와 관련하여 저장된 식품 중 공기의 일부 순환이 필요하다.
① 공기 중에 있는 해로운 가스 제어의 필요성
② 식물과 과일을 기를 때 수분의 정도를 제어하는 최고의 방법
③ 매년 전세계적으로 늘어나는 탄소 발자국의 심각성
④ 식품 저장 시 가스와 습도의 특정 상태 제어의 중요성

| 정답해설 | ④ [88%] 첫 문장에서 신선 농산물 취급 시 온도 조절 외에 공기 조절이 중요하다고 했고, 이산화탄소와 수분의 정도를 조절해 공기를 제어한다는 내용이 이어졌다. 따라서 정답으로 ④가 가장 적절하다.

어휘
atmosphere 공기; 대기　　　　　moisture 수분, 습기
dehydration 탈수　　　　　　　　storage 저장
mold 곰팡이　　　　　　　　　　carbon dioxide 이산화탄소
regulate 규제하다, 조절하다　　　ethylene 에틸렌
optimal 최선[최상]의　　　　　　quality 품질; 성질
related to ~와 관련된　　　　　　circulation 순환

21　독해 > 밑줄 어휘 > 어휘 추론　오답률 25%　답 ④

| 해석 | 거짓말이 특정한 경우에 해로운 영향을 미치지 않는다고 해도, 거짓말이 발견되면 거짓말은 인간의 의사소통이 어떤 것에 의존하는지 진실을 말하는 일반적인 관행을 약화시키기 때문에, 그것은 도덕적으로 여전히 잘못된 것이다. 예를 들어, 내가 허영심 때문에 내 나이에 대해 거짓말을 한다면, 그리고 거짓말이 탄로난다면, 심각한 해를 끼치지 않았을지라도, 나는 대체로 당신의 신뢰를 손상시켰을 것이다. 그런 경우, 당신은 내가 장래에 말할 수 있는 어떤 것도 믿을 가능성이 훨씬 적어질 것이다. 따라서 모든 거짓말은 발견되었을 때, 간접적인 해로운 영향을 미친다. 그러나, 아주 가끔,

거짓말로 인해 발생하는 장점이 이러한 해로운 영향보다 더 우세할지도 모른다. 예를 들어, 만약 누군가가 심각하게 아프다면, 그들의 기대수명에 대해 거짓말을 하는 것은 아마도 그들에게 더 오래 살 기회를 줄 것이다. 반면에, 그들에게 진실을 말하는 것은 아마도 그들의 신체적 쇠퇴를 가속화시킬 우울증을 ④ 예방할(→ 심화시킬) 수 있을 것이다.

| 정답해설 | ④ 75% 거짓말이 해로운 영향을 미치지 않더라도 결국은 잘못된 것이라는 내용의 글이다. 글의 후반부에 아주 가끔은 거짓말로 인한 장점이 있을 수 있다고 언급하며, 이에 대한 예시로 거짓으로 기대 수명을 들은 환자가 더 오래 살 기회를 얻는다고 했다. On the other hand에 이어진 내용은 반대의 경우가 되어야 하므로 진실을 말하는 것이 우울증을 예방하는 것이 아니라 심화시킨다는 내용이 되도록 prevent를 intensify로 바꾸는 것이 적절하다.

어휘

harmful 해로운 | morally 도덕적으로
weaken 약화시키다 | vanity 허영심
undermine 몰래 손상시키다, 서서히 쇠퇴시키다
outweigh ~보다 뛰어나다, 중대하다
life expectancy 기대 수명 | depression 우울증
accelerate 가속화하다

---

22 독해 > 글의 일관성 파악하기 > 주어진 문장의 삽입

오답률 38% 답 ②

| 해석 | 바닷물의 몇 가지 공통적인 특성은 해양 생물들의 생존과 행복에 결정적이다. 물은 대부분의 해양 유기체 부피의 80에서 90%를 차지한다. 그것은 수영하고 떠다니는 유기체에게 부력과 몸을 지탱하는 힘을 주어 무거운 골격 구조에 대한 필요를 줄인다. ② 물은 또한 생명을 유지하기 위해 필요한 대부분의 화학 반응을 위한 매개체이다. 해양 유기체의 생명 과정은 투명성과 화학적 구성을 포함한 바닷물의 많은 기본적인 물리적, 화학적 특성을 차례로 변화시켜 유기체를 전체 해양 환경의 필수적인 부분으로 만든다. 유기체와 그들의 해양 환경 사이의 상호 작용을 이해하려면 바닷물의 더 중요한 물리적, 화학적 속성 중 일부에 대한 간단한 조사가 필요하다. 담수와 바닷물의 특성은 어떤 면에서 서로 다르므로, 우리는 먼저 담수의 기본 특성을 고려한 다음 그러한 특성들이 바닷물에서는 어떻게 다른지 조사한다.

| 정답해설 | ② 62% 주어진 문장에서 also로 보아 이전에 물에 대한 내용이 있어야 함을 유추할 수 있다. 처음에 바닷물이 해양 생물들에게 중요하다고 서술한 후 ①에 이어진 문장의 주어 It은 맥락상 앞 문장의 주어인 water를 지칭하므로 주어진 문장은 ①에 들어갈 수 없다. ②에 이어 주어로 해양 유기체의 생명 과정이 왔고 이는 바닷물의 물리적, 화학적 특성을 바꾼다고 했으므로 주어진 문장에서 언급한 물이 화학 반응의 매개체라는 내용에 대한 구체적인 서술임을 알 수 있다. 따라서 주어진 문장은 ②에 들어가야 한다.

어휘

property 특징, 특성 | crucial 결정적인, 중요한
inhabitant 서식 동물; 주민 | account for ~을 차지하다
buoyancy 부력 | floating 떠다니는, 부유하는
skeletal 골격의, 해골의 | sustain 유지하다, 지탱하다
alter 바꾸다 | transparency 투명성
integral 완전한, 필수의 | attribute 특성, 속성

---

23 독해 > 어휘 선택 > 어휘 추론

오답률 12% 답 ③

| 해석 | 여기 훨씬 더 놀라운 부분이 있는데, AI의 출현이 순수히 인간 체스 선수의 성적을 (A) 감소시키지 않았다는 것이다. 정반대이다. 저렴하고 매우 똑똑한 체스 프로그램은 그 어느 때보다 더 많은 사람들이, 그 어느 때보다 많은 토너먼트에서 체스를 하도록 (B) 격려했고, 선수들은 그 어느 때보다도 더 나아졌다. 지금은 Deep Blue가 처음으로 Kasparov를 이겼을 때보다 지금은 두 배 더 많은 그랜드 마스터들이 있다. 오늘날 최고의 인간 체스 선수인 Magnus Carlsen은 AI로 훈련을 받았으며, 모든 인간 체스 선수 중 가장 컴퓨터 같은 존재로 여겨졌다. 그는 또한 역대 (C) 가장 높은 인간 그랜드 마스터 등급을 가지고 있다.

	(A)	(B)	(C)
①	감소시키다	단념시키다	가장 높은
②	증가시키다	단념시키다	가장 낮은
③	감소시키다	격려하다	가장 높은
④	증가시키다	격려하다	가장 낮은

| 정답해설 | ③ 88% AI의 출현이 인간 체스 선수의 성적을 오히려 향상시켰다는 내용의 글이다. (A)에는 긍정적인 의미를 나타내기 위해 didn't를 고려해 부정적인 의미의 diminish가 적절하다. 비슷한 흐름이 이어지는 문장에서 (B)에 적절한 것은 '격려하다'라는 긍정적인 의미의 동사 inspired가 적절하다. (C)에는 앞 문장에서 AI로 훈련받은 최고의 인간 체스 선수를 언급하고 있으므로 (C) 역시 맥락상 긍정적인 표현인 highest가 가장 적절하다.

어휘

diminish 줄이다, 감소시키다 | opposite 정반대의 것; 정반대의
discourage 단념시키다 | inspire 격려하다, 고무하다
deem 간주하다, 여기다

---

24 독해 > 요약

오답률 15% 답 ③

| 해석 | 패션 오브제의 미적 가치는 미술 오브제의 미적 가치와 마찬가지로 자기 지향적이다. 소비자들은 매료되고자 하는 욕구와 스스로를 매력적인 다른 사람들로 둘러싸려고 하는 욕구를 지닌다. 그러나, 미술에서의 미적 가치와는 달리, 패션에서의 미적 가치는 타자 지향적이기도 하다. 외모의 매력은 다른 사람들의 반응을 이끌어 내고 사회적 상호 작용을 용이하게 하는 방법이다.

↓

패션 오브제의 미적 가치는 ③ 자기 지향적이기도 하고 타자 지향적이기도 하다.

① 본질적으로 오로지 자기 지향적인
② 상대방과 달리 단지 타자 지향적인
③ 자기 지향적이고 타자 지향적인
④ 본성과 상관없이 정의 내리기 힘든

| 정답해설 | ③ 85% 첫 문장에서 패션 오브제가 미술 오브제처럼 자기 지향적이라고 언급했다. However에 이어진 문장에서 패션에서의 미적 가치가 타자 지향적이기도 하다고 했으므로 이 둘을 모두 언급한 ③이 빈칸에 들어갈 것으로 가장 적절하다.

어휘

aesthetic 미학적인 | self-oriented 자기 지향적인
surround 둘러[에워]싸다 | attractive 매력적인
elicit 이끌어 내다, 유도하다 | facilitate 용이하게 하다

25	독해 > 글의 일관성 파악하기 > 주어진 문장의 삽입		
		오답률 18%	답 ④

| 해석 | 어떤 사람들은 꿈에 어떤 가치도 없다고 믿지만, 이러한 밤의 드라마를 무관하다고 치부하는 것은 잘못된 것이다. 기억하는 것에서 얻어지는 것이 있다. 우리는 더 연결되어 있고, 더 완전하며, 더 순조롭게 진행되고 있다고 느낄 수 있다. 우리는 영감, 정보 그리고 위안을 얻을 수 있다. 알버트 아인슈타인은 자신의 상대성 이론이 꿈에서 영감을 받았다고 말했다. 사실, 그는 꿈이 그의 많은 발견의 원인이 되었다고 주장했다. 우리가 왜 꿈을 꾸는지 묻는 것은 우리가 왜 숨을 쉬는지 묻는 것만큼이나 이치에 맞다. 꿈꾸는 것은 건강한 삶의 필수적인 부분이다. ④ 좋은 소식은 우리가 꿈을 기억하든 말든 이것이 사실이라는 것이다. 많은 사람들이 특정한 꿈을 기억하지 못하더라도, 깨어나자마자 문제에 대한 새로운 접근법으로 영감을 받는다고 말한다.

| 정답해설 | ④ 82% 꿈을 기억하든 말든, 꿈은 건강한 삶의 필수적인 부분이라고 주장하는 글이다. 주어진 문장의 this가 지칭하는 바는 전체적인 흐름을 봤을 때 긍정적인 내용으로, whether or not we remember our dreams가 마지막 문장의 even though they don't remember the specific dream으로 연결되는 것을 알 수 있으므로 주어진 문장은 ④에 들어가는 것이 가장 적절하다.

어휘

dismiss 무시하다; 해고하다
irrelevant 관계[관련]가 없는
on track 순조롭게 나아가서
comfort 위안
integral 필수의, 완전한
specific 특정한; 구체적인

nocturnal 밤의
complete 완벽한
inspiration 영감
make sense 이치에 맞다, 말이 되다
upon R-ing ~하자마자

합격을 당기는 전략
기출회독 최종점검
문제풀이 집중훈련

2025

에듀윌 9급공무원
7개년 기출문제집 영어

고객의 꿈, 직원의 꿈, 지역사회의 꿈을 실현한다

에듀윌 도서몰
book.eduwill.net

• 부가학습자료 및 정오표: 에듀윌 도서몰 > 도서자료실
• 교재 문의: 에듀윌 도서몰 > 문의하기 > 교재(내용, 출간) / 주문 및 배송